BLUEPRINTS in

PEDIATRICS

Second Edition

Bradley S. Marino, MD, MPP

Fellow
Department of Pediatrics, Division of Cardiology
Department of Anesthesia and Critical Care,
  Division of Critical Care
The Children's Hospital of Philadelphia
Philadelphia, Pennsylvania

Katie L. Snead, MD

Private Pediatrician in Group Practice
Raleigh, North Carolina

Julia A. McMillan, MD

Associate Professor
Department of Pediatrics
Johns Hopkins University School of Medicine
Baltimore, Maryland

**Blackwell
Science**

©2001 by Blackwell Science, Inc.

Editorial Offices:
350 Main Street, Malden, Massachusetts 02148, USA
Osney Mead, Oxford OX2 0E1, England
25 John Street, London WC1N 2BS, England
23 Ainslie Place, Edinburgh EH3 6AJ, Scotland
54 University Street, Carlton, Victoria 3053, Australia

Other Editorial Offices:
Blackwell Wissenschafts-Verlag GmbH, Kurfürstendamm 57, 10707 Berlin, Germany
Blackwell Science KK, MG Kodenmacho Building, 7–10 Kodenmacho Nihombashi, Chuo-ku, Tokyo 104, Japan

Distributors:

The Americas
Blackwell Publishing
c/o AIDC
P.O. Box 20
50 Winter Sport Lane
Williston, VT 05495-0020
(Telephone orders: 800-216-2522;
fax orders: 802-864-7626)

Australia
Blackwell Science Pty., Ltd.
54 University Street
Carlton, Victoria 3053
(Telephone orders: 03-9347-0300;
fax orders: 03-9349-3016)

Outside The Americas and Australia
Blackwell Science, Ltd.
c/o Marston Book Services, Ltd.
P.O. Box 269, Abingdon
Oxon OX14 4YN, England
(Telephone orders: 44-01235-465500;
fax orders: 44-01235-465555)

Acquisitions: Laura DeYoung
Development: Jessica Carlisle
Production: Maggie Dana, Pageworks
Manufacturing: Lisa Flanagan
Marketing Manager: Toni Fournier

Director of Marketing: Lisa Larsen
Cover Design by Hannus Design
Typeset by Pageworks
Printed and bound by Capital City Press

Printed in the United States of America

01 02 03 5 4 3 2

The Blackwell Science logo is a trade mark of Blackwell Science Ltd.,
registered at the United Kingdom Trade Marks Registry

Library of Congress Cataloging-in-Publication Data

Marino, Bradley S.
    Blueprints in Pediatrics / Bradley Marino, Katie Snead; faculty advisor, Julia A. McMillan.—2nd ed.
        p. ; cm. — (Blueprints, USMLE series steps 2 & 3 review series)
    Includes bibliographical references and index.
    ISBN 0-632-04486-1
    1. Pediatrics—Outlines, syllabi, etc. I. Snead, Katie. II. Title. III. Series.
    [DNLM: 1. Pediatrics—Outlines. WS 18.2 M339b 2001]
RJ48.3 .M37 2001
618.92'00076—dc21
                                                                            00-044416

Visit Blackwell Science on the Internet: http://blackwellscience.com

BLUEPRINTS IN PEDIATRICS
Second Edition

Blueprints USMLE Steps 2 and 3 Review Series

Current Books in the Series:

Blueprints in Medicine
Blueprints in Obstetrics and Gynecology
Blueprints in Psychiatry
Blueprints in Surgery

Forthcoming:

Blueprints in Emergency Medicine
Bluerints in Neurology
Blueprints Questions and Answers

For information on these titles and others, visit us on the Internet at
http://www.blackwellscience.com

Contents

Preface

Medical students, interns, and residents need high-yield, accurate clinical core content. The *Blueprints* series was developed to meet these needs and enable the reader to review the core material quickly and efficiently.

Although this series was designed for the medical student or resident reviewing for the USMLE, many students have stated that the books in the series have been helpful to them during their clerkship rotations and subinternships. Residents studying for the USMLE Step 3 often use the books for reviewing the areas that were not their specialty. For instance, surgical residents will use the peds book for review since they have not had a peds rotation in over two years.

This book is not meant to be comprehensive, but rather it is composed of the high-yield topics that consistently appear on the boards. The topics in each book were chosen after analyzing over 2000 review questions, which we believed to be representative of the questions on the USMLE Step 2 & 3 exams. By concentrating on these high-yield topics the user will be reviewing the material most likely to be covered in each discipline on the boards.

This revised edition includes USMLE style clinical questions to test your strengths in each core area. These questions help prepare medical students and residents for questions likely encountered on the wards and as a review before the Step 2 & 3 exams.

We hope that you find *Blueprints in Pediatrics* informative and useful. We welcome feedback and suggestions you may have about this book or any in the *Blueprints* series. Send to blue@blacksci.com.

The Publisher
Blackwell Science, Inc.

Watch for *Blueprints Questions & Answers*—coming in 2001!

Acknowledgments

This book is a tribute to our patients. Each day we are reminded how truly precious children are and what an honor it is to care for them. We are forever grateful to our colleagues, both resident and faculty, whose limitless understanding and support allow us to pursue projects such as this. We owe special thanks to Brian Stidham, MD, for his erudite chapter on pediatric ophthalmology. Finally, we would like to thank our families and friends, without whose support, patience, and encouragement none of this would be possible.

B.M.
K.S.
J.M.

Introduction

This book is an attempt to help the nonpediatrician understand that infants, children, and adolescents are not simply small adults. Congenital defects, the underdeveloped immune system, and conditions reflecting abnormalities in organ development all play an important role in the care of pediatric patients. In some cases, the diseases of children are different from those seen in adults; often, the differences lie in the mode of presentation.

The physicians who wrote this book attempted to organize their knowledge into a form that is concise, complete, and clear. They relied on the most current sources in the pediatric literature to provide the reader with both important facts and an understanding of the context in which pediatric medical care is delivered. Although they learned from the literature, it is their patients who taught them the importance of what they learned.

Julia A. McMillan, MD

Abbreviations

ABGs	arterial blood gases
ACTH	adrenocorticotropic hormone
ADA	adenosine deaminase
AIDS	acquired immunodeficiency syndrome
ALL	acute lymphocytic leukemia
ALT	alanine transaminase
AMP	adenosine monophosphate
ANA	antinuclear antibody
Angio	angiography
AP	anteroposterior
ARDS	adult respiratory distress syndrome
ASD	atrial septal defect
ASO	anti-streptolysin O
AST	aspartate transaminase
AZT	zidovudine
BCG	bacille Calmette-Guérin
BP	blood pressure
BUN	blood urea nitrogen
CALLA	common acute lymphocytic leukemia antigen
CBC	complete blood count
CDC	Centers for Disease Control
CF	cystic fibrosis
CFTR	cystic fibrosis transmembrane conductance regulator
CHF	congestive heart failure

CK	creatine kinase
CNS	central nervous system
COPD	chronic obstructive pulmonary disease
CRP	C-reactive protein
CSF	cerebrospinal fluid
CT	computed tomography
CXR	chest x-ray
DIC	disseminated intravascular coagulation
DMD	Duchenne's muscular dystrophy
DTP	diphtheria/tetanus/pertussis
DTRs	deep tendon reflexes
DVT	deep venous thrombosis
EBV	Epstein-Barr virus
ECG	electrocardiography
Echo	echocardiography
ECMO	extracorporeal membrane oxygenation
EEG	electroencephalography
ELISA	enzyme-linked immunosorbent assay
EMG	electromyography
ESR	erythrocyte sedimentation rate
FEV	forced expiratory volume
FTA-ABS	fluorescent treponemal antibody absorption
FVC	forced vital capacity
GA	gestational age
G6PD	glucose-6-phosphate dehydrogenase
GI	gastrointestinal
Hb	hemoglobin
HGPRT	hypoxanthine-guanine phosphoribosyl transferase
HIV	human immunodeficiency virus
HLA	human leukocyte antigen
HPI	history of present illness
HR	heart rate
ID/CC	identification and chief complaint
IFA	immunofluorescent antibody
Ig	immunoglobulin
IM	intramuscular
INH	isoniazid
IVC	inferior vena cava
JRA	juvenile rheumatoid arthritis

JVP	jugular venous pressure
KUB	kidneys/ureter/bladder
LDH	lactate dehydrogenase
LFTs	liver function tests
LP	lumbar puncture
L/S	lecithin-to-sphingomyelin (ratio)
LV	left ventricular
LVH	left ventricular hypertrophy
Lytes	electrolytes
MI	myocardial infarction
MMR	measles/mumps/rubella
MR(I)	magnetic resonance (imaging)
NG	nasogastric
NPO	nil per os (nothing by mouth)
NSAID	nonsteroidal anti-inflammatory drug
Nuc	nuclear medicine
PBS	peripheral blood smear
PCR	polymerase chain reaction
PDA	patent ductus arteriosus
PE	physical exam
PFTs	pulmonary function tests
PMI	point of maximal intensity
PPD	purified protein derivative
PT	prothrombin time
PTT	partial thromboplastin time
RBC	red blood cell
RF	rheumatoid factor
RPR	rapid plasma reagin
RR	respiratory rate
RSV	respiratory syncytial virus
RV	right ventricular
RVH	right ventricular hypertrophy
SBFT	small bowel follow-through
SIDS	sudden infant death syndrome
TMP-SMX	trimethoprim-sulfamethoxazole
TSH	thyroid-stimulating hormone
UA	urinalysis
UGI	upper GI
URI	upper respiratory infection

US	ultrasound
VMA	vanillylmandelic acid
VS	vital signs
VSD	ventricular septal defect
vWF	von Willebrand factor
WBC	white blood cell
XR	x-ray

Notice: The indications and dosages of all drugs in this book have been recommended in the medical literature and conform to the practices of the general medical community. The medications described do not necessarily have specific approval by the Food and Drug Administration for use in the diseases and dosages for which they are recommended. The package insert for each drug should be consulted for use and dosage as approved by the FDA. Because standards of usage change, it is advisable to keep abreast of revised recommendations, particularly those concerning new drugs.

For list of figure credits, please refer to page 339.

Emergency Management:
Evaluation of the Critically Ill or Injured Child

The critically ill or injured child must be evaluated rapidly to minimize morbidity and mortality. Whether the critically ill or injured child presents to the physician's office, local clinic, community hospital, or tertiary care center, the patient is stabilized by administering the basic life-support and advanced cardiac life-support measures recommended by the American Heart Association. Once the patient is clinically stable, a problem list can be generated and, if not already apparent, the cause of the child's symptomatology can be determined.

DIFFERENTIAL DIAGNOSIS

Of the causes of cardiorespiratory arrest, respiratory etiologies (45%), cardiac etiologies (25%), and primary central nervous system disorders (20%) account for 90% of all cases. The diagnoses of children, excluding neonates, requiring life support by body system are as follows:

Respiratory
- **Upper airway obstruction**—croup, epiglottitis, foreign body, laryngospasm, congenital anomalies, aspiration, bacterial tracheitis, neck trauma, thermal or chemical burns, retropharyngeal abscess, peritonsillar abscess;
- **Lower airway obstruction**—foreign body, pneumonia, reactive airway disease, bronchiolitis, congenital anomalies;
- **Restrictive lung disease**—pneumothorax, hemothorax, tension pneumothorax, pulmonary edema, polio, botulism, congenital anomalies;
- **Insufficient gas transfer**—chronic lung disease, pulmonary edema, adult respiratory distress syndrome, primary apnea, depression of the respiratory center in the brainstem.

Cardiac
- congenital heart disease
- primary dysrhythmia
- myocarditis
- dehydration
- pericarditis
- cardiac tamponade
- congestive heart failure

Central Nervous System
- meningitis
- encephalitis
- acute hydrocephalus
- head trauma
- seizure
- tumor
- hypoxic-ischemic injury

Gastrointestinal
- abdominal trauma
- bowel perforation or obstruction
- peritonitis

Metabolic
- diabetic ketoacidosis
- Addison's disease
- hyperthyroidism
- hypoglycemia
- hyperkalemia
- hypocalcemia
- hyponatremia

Multisystem
- sudden infant death syndrome
- drug intoxication (narcotics, tricyclic antidepressants, barbiturates, benzodiazepines)
- non–central nervous system tumors
- multiple trauma
- anaphylaxis
- hypothermia
- septic shock

Renal
- acute and chronic renal failure

CLINICAL MANIFESTATIONS AND TREATMENT

Primary Survey

The primary survey is the initial evaluation of the critically ill or injured child when life-threatening problems are identified and prioritized. The primary survey, as shown in Figure 1–1, involves assessment of **A**irway, **B**reathing, **C**irculation, **D**isability, and **E**xposure. The goals of **airway** management are to recognize and relieve obstruction, prevent aspiration of gastric contents, and promote adequate gas exchange. The airway is assessed to rule out foreign body or anatomic obstruction as follows:

- Immobilize cervical spine if spinal cord injury is a possibility.
- Clear the oropharynx with a Yankauer suction cath-

eter. Avoid blind finger sweep, because a foreign body may be forced further down the oropharynx.
- Use the jaw-thrust or chin-lift maneuver to open the airway, and remove any obstruction caused by the tongue or soft tissues of the neck.
- Place the head in the midline "sniffing position" by placing a rolled-up towel beneath the occiput. Hyperextension of the neck may result in obstruction of the airway.
- If indicated, place an oral airway or a nasopharyngeal airway.
- Start 100% oxygen via face mask.

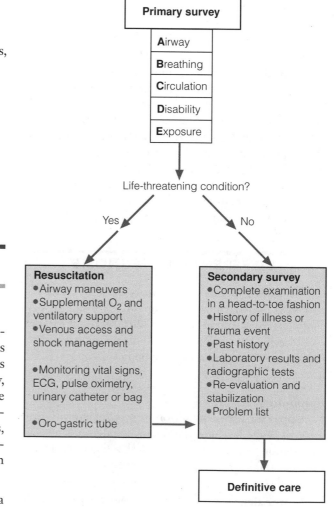

Figure 1–1 Algorithm of the initial assessment of the pediatric patient.

Once an airway is established, air exchange, or **breathing**, should be evaluated. Assess the presence and effectiveness of spontaneous respirations by examining chest wall excursion. Check blood oxygenation via pulse oximetry or arterial blood gas and blood CO_2 level by arterial or venous blood gas. Management is as follows:

- If there are effective spontaneous respirations and severe hypoxia and hypercarbia do not exist, move on to circulation. If chest wall excursion is not adequate, endotracheal tube placement is indicated.

- If the child is less than 8 years old, an uncuffed tube should be used to reduce the risk of subglottic edema and stenosis. In children less than 8 years old, the cricoid ring is narrow and provides the seal for the uncuffed tube. The size of the endotracheal tube = 4 + (age in years ÷ 4).

- Neonatal intubation is traditionally performed without premedication, but intubation of the infant or child is done with premedication in rapid sequence fashion in the following order:

  1. Preoxygenate with 100% oxygen.
  2. Administer a vagolytic drug (e.g., atropine).
  3. Apply cricoid pressure.
  4. Administer a sedative, hypnotic, and/or opioid drug (e.g., thiopental, versed, fentanyl).
  5. Administer a paralyzing dose of a neuromuscular blocking agent (e.g., vecuronium, pancuronium, succinylcholine). If succinylcholine is used, a defasciculating dose of a neuromuscular blocking agent should be given before administration of succinylcholine (e.g., vecuronium).

- In the hypotensive, hemodynamically unstable, or unconscious patient, rapid-sequence intubation is not indicated. Cricoid pressure should be applied, and the patient should be intubated.

- Rarely, a patient cannot be ventilated with a bag and mask or intubated, and an emergency needle cricothyrotomy is required to establish an airway.

For **circulation**, absence of a pulse in the large arteries of an unconscious patient who is not breathing defines a cardiac arrest. Using a cardiorespiratory monitor, the electrical activity of the heart should be assessed, followed by evaluation of pulse (central and peripheral), capillary refill, and blood pressure. In children, heart rate is the most sensitive measure of intravascular volume status, and capillary refill is the most sensitive measure of adequate circulation. Blood pressure fluctuations are an insensitive indicator, because hypotension is a late finding in hypovolemia. Children are more likely to present with asystole than with an arrhythmia, unless they have an underlying cardiac electrical abnormality.

If examination of the brachial pulse in the infant or the carotid pulse in the child indicates pulselessness, chest compressions should be conducted as described in Figure 1–2. Vascular access management during cardiopulmonary resuscitation is shown in Figure 1–3. Once access has been established, initial fluid resuscitation via intravenous or intraosseus line with lactated Ringer's solution or normal saline should be given as a 10–20 mL/kg bolus as quickly as possible. Fluid resuscitation is contraindicated if cardiorespiratory arrest is due to myocarditis or hypoplastic left heart syndrome. If there is no response or the patient has suffered acute blood loss, consider a 10-mL/kg infusion of plasmanate, albumin,

Infant	Older Child
Airway	
Determine unresponsiveness	
Call for help	
Position patient supine	
Support head and neck	
Head-tilt/chin lift or Jaw thrust	
No blind finger sweeps	
Breathing	
2 initial breaths	
Then: 20 breaths/min	Then: 15 breaths/min
Circulation	
Check brachial pulse	Check carotid pulse
Activate EMS System	
Compression location: 1 finger breadth below intermammary line on sternum	Compression location: lower 1/3 of sternum
Compression method: Hands encircle chest or 2 fingers on sternum	Compression method: 1 or 2 hands on sternum
Compression depth: 0.5–1"	Compression depth: 1–1.5"
Compression rate: >100/min	Compression rate: 80–100/min
Compression:ventilation ratio = 5:1	
Reassessment: Palpate pulse every 10 cycles	

Figure 1–2 Basic CPR in infants and children.

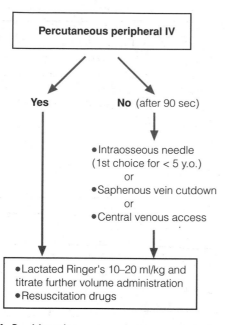

Figure 1–3 Vascular access management during cardiopulmonary resuscitation.

crystalloid, or type O-negative whole blood. When vascular access is obtained, a full set of screening tests should be obtained, including complete blood count, venous blood gas, electrolyte and chemistry panel, and blood glucose. If ingestion is a possibility, serum and urine toxicology and an acetaminophen and salicylate level may be obtained. If hypotension due to hemorrhage is suspected, gaining proximal control of the hemorrhage is critical. Military anti-shock trousers (MAST) suit application may be appropriate.

For a full discussion of drug physiology, indications, dosage, route of administration, effects, and side effects of the pharmaceuticals listed below, see *The Harriet Lane Handbook* or *Golden Hour: The Handbook of Advanced Pediatric Life Support.* Below are the indications and effects of each drug:

- **Atropine**
  Indication: bradycardia and atrioventricular block
  Effect: increases heart rate and conduction through the atrioventricular node by decreasing vagal tone

- **Bicarbonate**
  Indication: severe refractory metabolic acidosis and/or hyperkalemia
  Effect: increases blood pH

- **Elemental calcium** (calcium gluconate or calcium chloride)
  Indication: hypocalcemia, hyperkalemia, hypermagnesemia, and calcium channel blocker overdose
  Effect: increases ionized calcium and stabilizes myocardium when hyperkalemia or hypermagnesemia is causing electrocardiographic changes

- **Dextrose**
  Indication: hypoglycemia
  Effect: increases blood glucose level

- **Epinephrine** (1:10,000)
  Indication: given intravenously for asystole, bradycardia, ventricular fibrillation
  Effect: increases systemic vascular resistance, chronotropy and inotropy, thereby increasing cardiac output and blood pressure. By increasing systolic blood pressure, cerebral blood flow increases, and by increasing diastolic blood pressure, coronary perfusion increases.

- **Epinephrine** (1:1000)
  Indication: given for pulseless arrest after first dose of epinephrine (1:10,000) or as first dose down the endotracheal tube if vascular access is not obtained
  Effect: same as above

- **Lidocaine**
  Indication: ventricular ectopy
  Effect: helps make refractory ventricular tachycardia and ventricular fibrillation more susceptible to cardioversion and decreases the likelihood of recurrence of ventricular ectopy

- **Narcan (Naloxone)**
  Indication: presumed or known opiate intoxication
  Effect: rapid reversal of opiate effect

- Drugs that can be given by endotracheal tube include **L**idocaine, **A**tropine, **N**arcan, and **E**pinephrine (high dose).

In the hemodynamically unstable patient with tachydysrhythmias (ventricular tachycardia, ventricular fibrillation, or supraventricular tachycardia), defibrillation is indicated:

- Supraventricular tachycardia (SVT)—synchronized cardioversion 0.25–0.50 J/kg; double the dose if unsuccessful.

- Ventricular tachycardia—if hemodynamically stable, use intravenous lidocaine; if hemodynamically unstable, use synchronized cardioversion 1–2 J/kg.

Double the dose if unsuccessful and treat with lidocaine.

- Ventricular fibrillation—nonsynchronized defibrillation 2–6 J/kg. Repeat at twice the dose if unsuccessful, give epinephrine, and continue cardiopulmonary resuscitation. Precede subsequent defibrillation attempts with intravenous lidocaine or bretylium. Maximum dose is 360 J.

For **disability**, a rapid screening neurologic examination is performed to note pupillary response, level of consciousness, and localizing findings.

In preparation for the secondary survey, the patient should be undressed. Because of their large surface to body mass ratio, children cool rapidly, and passive heat loss can be problematic. Hypothermia and hyperthermia, or **exposure**, must be detected and dealt with promptly.

Secondary Survey

The secondary survey includes a detailed physical examination, a history of the illness or traumatic event, a past medical history, and indicated laboratory and radiographic studies. Once the patient has been stabilized during the primary survey, the secondary survey further defines the list of specific problems and prioritizes their treatment.

◆ KEY POINTS ◆

1. No matter what the cause of cardiorespiratory arrest, the algorithm outlined for pediatric basic and advanced cardiac life support should be followed. Remember to do the primary survey (**A**irway, **B**reathing, **C**irculation, **D**isability, **E**xposure) and then the secondary survey.

2. Approximately half of the causes of cardiorespiratory arrest are due to respiratory arrest, which can be brought about by upper airway obstruction, lower airway obstruction, restrictive lung disease, or an etiology that results in inadequate gas exchange.

3. The CPR algorithm is summarized in Figure 1–4.

---

4. If resuscitation does not establish cardiac output, the following mechanical or metabolic causes should be investigated: hypothermia, tension pneumothorax, hemothorax, cardiac tamponade, profound hypovolemia, profound metabolic imbalance, toxin ingestion, and closed head injury.

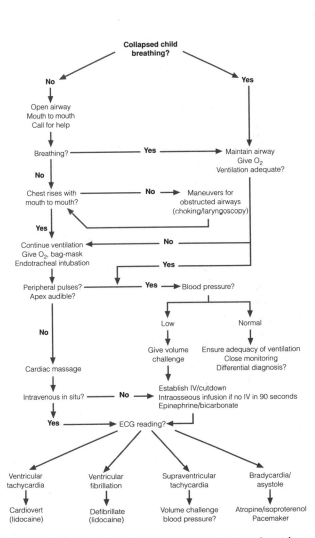

Figure 1–4 Cardiopulmonary resuscitation algorithm.

Poisoning, Burns, and Injury Prevention

Nowhere does the old adage "an ounce of prevention is worth a pound of cure" resonate truer than in pediatrics. Together, accidents and injuries are the largest cause of morbidity and mortality in children. When an untoward event occurs, timely evaluation and treatment may limit disability and preserve quality of life.

ACUTE POISONING

Poisoning is one of the more common pediatric medical emergencies, resulting in over 2 million emergency visits a year. About **80–85%** of poisonings occur in **children younger than 5 years** of age. These tend to involve only one substance and may denote either **accidental** ingestion or (more rarely) abuse by caretakers. **Adolescents** account for the remaining 15–20%; such ingestions are usually **intentional**, represent a suicide attempt or gesture, and may involve multiple substances. Recreational drug use in this older population can result in unintentional but fatal overdoses.

Clinical Manifestations

History and Physical Examination
The history should include the **substance ingested, when, how much**, and **subsequent behavior**. The characteristic clinical manifestations and treatment of the most common poisonings in children and adolescents are discussed in Table 2–1.

Differential Diagnosis
The possibility of toxicologic ingestion should be considered in any patient presenting with:

- altered mental status
- acute behavior changes
- seizures
- arrhythmias
- coma

Diagnostic Evaluation
Screening studies should include a pulse oxygenation check, D-stick, electrocardiogram, serum electrolytes and osmolarity, and a venous blood gas to determine pH. Toxicology screens are variably helpful; the clinician should inquire which substances in particular are screened for.

Treatment
Treatment should be based on the estimated **maximal potential dose** ingested. Children with significant ingestions and patients who are medically unstable require diligent observation and management of their airway, breathing, and circulation. Induction of **emesis** with syrup of ipecac is appropriate in some cases if the substance was recently ingested. **Gastric lavage** both removes and dilutes stomach contents. Pill fragments recovered by either method may aid in diagnosis. **Activated**

TABLE 2–1

Signs, Symptoms, and Treatment of Specific Pediatric Poisonings

Substance	Clinical Manifestations	Antidote/Treatment
Acetaminophen	Nausea/vomiting, anorexia, pallor, diaphoresis; may progress over days to jaundice, abdominal pain, liver failure	**A:** N-acetylcysteine **T:** gastric emptying if <2 hr since ingestion; activated charcoal if <4 hr since ingestion. Draw blood level at 4 hr and use available nomogram to assess risk of hepatotoxicity. If toxic, start oral N-acetylcysteine and continue for 72 hr
Anticholinergics (atropine, tricyclic antidepressants, antihistamines, phenothiazines)	Fever, mydriasis, flushing, dry skin, tachycardia, hypertension, cardiac arrhythmias, delirium, psychosis, convulsions, coma	**A:** physostigmine for atropine and antihistamines **A:** $NaHCO_3$, $MgSO_4$ for tricyclic antidepressants
Aspirin	Fever, hyperpnea, vomiting, tinnitus, lethargy, coma	**T:** gastric emptying if <6 hr since ingestion, activated charcoal, cathartics; fluid and electrolyte management
Cholinergics (organophosphates and other pesticides)	Nausea/vomiting, sweating, miosis, salivation, lacrimation, bronchorrhea, urination, defecation, weakness, muscle fasciculations, paralysis, confusion, coma	**A:** pralidoxime chloride **T:** gastric lavage, activated charcoal; prophylactic atropine
Hydrocarbons	Fever, nausea/vomiting, gastrointestinal bleeding, confusion, coma	**T: Prevent aspiration** (Aspiration results in chemical pneumonitis and significant lung tissue damage!) No gastric emptying techniques are necessary.
Iron	Vomiting, diarrhea, gastrointestinal bleeding, cyanosis, seizures, coma, metabolic acidosis	**A:** deferoxamine chelation **T:** emesis induction, gastric lavage, cathartics
Opiates	Pinpoint pupils, bradypnea, hypotension, hypothermia, stupor, coma	**A:** naloxone **T:** evaluate and secure airway as needed; gastrointestinal decontamination if appropriate; naloxone
Sedatives/hypnotics	Nystagmus, miosis or mydriasis, hypothermia, hypotension, bradypnea, confusion, ataxia, coma	**A:** flumazenil for benzodiazepines **T:** evaluate and secure airway if needed; maintain hemodynamic stability; activated charcoal with cathartic; supportive care
Sympathomimetics (amphetamines, cocaine, theophylline)	Fever, mydriasis, tachycardia, hypertension, sweating, delirium, psychosis, tremor, myoclonus, convulsions	**T:** gastric emptying, activated charcoal, cathartics; sedatives for severe agitation; control of hypertension; ample fluids

charcoal by mouth or nasogastric tube minimizes absorption by binding the substance and hastening its elimination; however, activated charcoal is ineffective in ingestions with alcohol, hydrocarbon, iron, and lithium.

Specific antidotes exist for several more commonly ingested drugs (see Table 2–1).

Prevention

Pediatricians have played a major role in decreasing the number and severity of poisonings, including lobbying for child-resistant medicine bottle caps and incorporating anticipatory guidance into well-child care visits, including "childproofing" the home, keeping medicines in a lock box, removing cleaning products from children's reach, and the judicious use of syrup of ipecac.

LEAD POISONING

Lead poisoning is one of the most important preventive health issues in primary care pediatrics. The elimination of lead in house paint (in 1977) and gasoline (in 1988) has decreased the average blood level of lead by 75%. The primary source of lead today is **lead-containing paint** present in buildings constructed before 1950. Children breathe in lead dust, ingest paint chips, and play in lead-contaminated soil. Although there is no direct correlation between blood levels and morbidity, levels of 10–19 μg/dL are considered mild, and the term "**lead poisoning**" is reserved for levels of **20 μg/dL** or greater.

Clinical Manifestations

Early symptoms of lead poisoning include irritability, hyperactivity, apathy, decreased play, anorexia, abdominal pain, constipation, and intermittent vomiting. Children with chronically elevated lead levels may manifest:

- developmental delay
- behavioral problems
- attention disorders
- poor school performance

Acute encephalopathy is the most serious complication of lead poisoning and is characterized by increased intracranial pressure, vomiting, ataxia, confusion, seizures, and coma.

Treatment

The most effective therapy involves **removing the poison from the child's environment**. Leaded paint should be stripped and surfaces cleaned with high-phosphate detergent and a special high-efficiency particle accumulator vacuum. Such overhaul invariably increases the amount of lead dust in the air, so the inhabitants must be temporarily housed elsewhere.

Symptomatic children should be immediately removed to a lead-free environment and treated with intravenous **dimercaprol** (BAL) followed by **edetate calcium-disodium** (EDTA). **Oral succimer** (DMSA) is an alternative in asymptomatic children with levels below 60 μg/dL.

Prevention

The Centers for Disease Control and Prevention recommends universal screening at approximately 12 months and 2 years.

MOTOR VEHICLE ACCIDENTS

Motor vehicle injuries remain the leading cause of accidental death in all age groups. Most infants and adolescents sustain trauma as vehicle occupants, whereas school-age children tend to be injured as pedestrians. Factors associated with an increased risk of automobile injury and death include:

- male gender
- age 15–19 years
- warm or inclement weather
- night or weekend driving
- alcohol intoxication

The routine use of **seat belts** and **child car seats** has been shown to be highly effective in reducing the incidence of severe injury and death. All states require car seat restraint of passengers under 40 pounds; children 20 pounds or heavier and 1 year of age or older may ride facing forward, whereas lighter infants must face the rear. Older children should remain belted with lap and shoulder straps at all times. Because air bags are designed primarily for adults, children should ride belted in the back seat whenever possible. **Bike helmets** decrease the risk of significant closed head trauma due to traffic accidents. Children younger than 10 years of age should be supervised while walking or playing near streets. **There is no evidence that driver education programs are an effective deterrent to accidents involving teenage drivers.**

DROWNINGS

Drowning is a frequent cause of morbidity and mortality in the pediatric population. Incidence peaks between 1 and 5 years and again in adolescence. Rates are twice as high in blacks and three times higher in boys. **Bathtubs** are the most common site of drowning in the first year of life. Large **buckets** and residential **pools** are particularly dangerous for toddlers, whereas **natural water sources** account for most adolescent injuries. Reliable predictors of outcome include:

- water temperature
- time of submersion
- degree of pulmonary damage
- effectiveness of early resuscitation efforts

Submersion for more than 5 minutes in warm water associated with significant aspiration and minimal response to initial cardiopulmonary resuscitation (CPR) virtually always results in major disability or death.

Toddlers and young children must be supervised at all times while in the bathtub or around pools or other bodies of water. Residential and commercial swimming pools should be fenced in and have locked gates. CPR training is available to parents through the American Heart Association and many area hospitals. Learning to swim is an important preventive measure but does not take the place of close supervision.

FOREIGN BODY ASPIRATION

The natural curiosity of children coupled with the toddler's tendency to put everything in the mouth make **foreign body aspiration** a frequent occurrence in the pediatric population. Most objects and food stuffs are immediately expelled from the trachea by coughing. Unfortunately, foreign bodies that lodge in the upper or lower respiratory tract are more problematic.

Epidemiology

The highest incidence is noted in children **6–36 months old**. Aspiration into the lower airways is much more common than tracheal obstruction. Inadequate supervision and inappropriate food choices for age place children at additional risk. **Nuts** account for over 50% of foreign body aspirations.

Differential Diagnosis

Patients who do not acutely obstruct their airways may present up to a week after the initial event with no witnessed episode of choking. Wheezing and respiratory distress may be mistaken for asthma; pneumonia is a consideration when breath sounds are decreased. Of note, findings on auscultation in cases of foreign body aspiration are **localized** to one side of the chest only.

Clinical Manifestations

Presentation varies depending on where the foreign body lodges in the respiratory tree (Table 2–2). If the obstruction is **complete**, the chest radiograph demonstrates significant one-sided atelectasis and the heart is drawn toward the affected lung throughout the entire respiratory cycle. However, a **partial** obstruction allows air to enter during inspiration, and it becomes trapped (ball-

TABLE 2–2

Signs and Symptoms Related to Specific Location of Aspiration

Location of Foreign Body	Common Signs and Symptoms
Trachea	
Total obstruction	Acute asphyxia, marked retractions
High partial obstruction	Decreased air entry, inspiratory and expiratory stridor, retractions
Low partial obstruction	Expiratory wheezing, inspiratory stridor
Main stem bronchus	Cough, expiratory wheezing
	Blood-tinged sputum*
Lobar/segmental bronchus	Decreased breath sounds†; wheezing, rhonchi

*Usually a later finding

†Localized to area of lung related to affected bronchus

Adapted from Cotton E and Yasuda K. Foreign body aspiration. Pediatr Clin North Am 1984;31:937.

valve obstruction). In these cases, the inspiratory film may appear normal, but the x-ray after expiration will show a hyperinflated obstructed lung with mediastinal shift **away** from the blockage (Fig. 2–1).

Treatment

Foreign bodies must be removed from the airway to alleviate symptoms. **Rigid bronchoscopy** is the treatment of choice. Thereafter, prognosis depends on the degree of lung damage, which is directly related to time interval to diagnosis. Most patients recover quickly with minimal sequelae.

Prevention

Infants are not developmentally prepared to protect their airways from small morsels of food, including hard candy, nuts, and popcorn. Small toys, coins, buttons, and balloons should be kept out of the toddler's reach. Choking is covered in basic CPR classes; however, the effective-

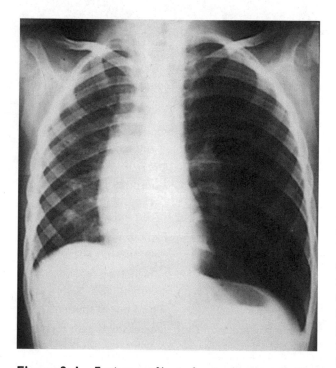

Figure 2–1 Expiratory film in foreign body aspiration with partial obstruction: the obstructed left lung is hyperinflated, whereas the heart (and mediastinum) are shifted to the right.

ness of the Heimlich maneuver or back blows is limited in instances of lower tract aspiration.

BURNS

Burns are the third leading cause of injury in children behind motor vehicle accidents and drownings and the second most frequent cause of accidental death. An estimated 15% of burns are the result of **abuse**. Fortunately, the great majority of burns are not life-threatening. Patients who survive severe burns are often left with significant scarring and disability.

Epidemiology

A full 85% of burns are **scald** injuries. **Flame** burns, usually accompanied by smoke inhalation, are less frequent but account for most deaths. A typical scenario for an **electric** burn involves a young child putting conductive material into a wall socket or an infant sucking on the connected end of an extension cord. **Contact** burns result from direct contact with a hot surface.

Risk Factors

Boys and children younger than 5 years of age are at the greatest risk for burn injury.

Clinical Manifestations

The evaluation of severity is based on **body surface area** and **depth**. **First-degree** burns involve only the epidermis; the skin is red and tender but does not *blister.* First-degree burns usually heal within a week with no residual scarring. **Second-degree** burns may be superficial (less than half the depth of the dermis) or deep (involving most of the dermis but leaving appendages such as sweat glands and hair follicles intact). Superficial partial-thickness burns resolve in a few weeks with little scarring; deep second-degree injuries result in significant scarring and may require skin grafting. Burns that extend into the subcutaneous tissue are classified as **third-degree**; **fourth-degree** burns involve fascia, muscle, bone, or joint tissue. Both are nontender due to sensory nervous tissue loss. Specific injury sites and patterns are characteristic of abuse (Fig. 2–2).

Treatment

Burned areas should be placed immediately in lukewarm water or covered with wet gauze or cloth. Minor burns

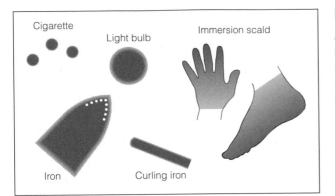

Figure 2–2 Burn injury patterns consistent with abuse.

respond to gentle cleansing, silver sulfadiazine (Silvadene), and dressing changes twice a day until re-epithelialization occurs. Burns that are **severe, circumferential, extensive** (more than 10–15% of the body) or that involve the face, hands, perineum, and feet require more specialized care. Treatment includes appropriate management of airway, breathing, and circulation issues; effective electrolyte and fluid therapy to account for increased fluid loss; prevention of infection; pain management; optimization of cosmetic recovery; and early mobility and rehabilitation.

Prevention

Installing and maintaining **smoke detectors** and decreasing **water heater thermostat** settings are the two most successful preventive measures for avoiding burn injury. All sleepwear for children should be constructed of flame-retardant material. Smoking cessation decreases the likelihood that matches or lighters will be left where children can readily experiment with them. Parents should be counseled to practice escape routes and reinforce the "stop, drop, and roll" technique for extinguishing fire.

CHILD ABUSE AND NEGLECT

Injuries intentionally perpetrated by a caretaker that result in morbidity or mortality constitute **physical abuse.** **Sexual abuse** is defined as the involvement of a child in any activity meant to provide sexual gratification to an adult. Failure to provide a child with appropriate food, clothing, medical care, schooling, and a safe environment establish **neglect.**

Epidemiology

Almost half the children who are brought for medical attention as a result of physical abuse are under 1 year of age; the great majority are preschoolers. It is estimated that 10% of emergency room visits involving children younger than 5 years of age result from abuse. Parents, the mother's boyfriend, and stepparents are the most frequent perpetrators.

Reports of sexual abuse have skyrocketed over the past few decades. The abuse may occur at any age. **Relatives and family acquaintances** account for most cases; molestation by strangers is uncommon. In 80% of reports, the victims are **girls**; most are abused by stepfathers, fathers, or other male family members. Male sexual abuse is probably underrecognized.

Neglect results in more deaths than physical and sexual abuse combined. It is the most common cause of **failure to thrive** in childhood.

Continued abuse occurs in a fourth of children returned to their homes. The **mortality** rate is 5%.

Risk Factors

Abuse and neglect occur at all socioeconomic levels but are more prevalent in the poor. Children with special needs (mental retardation, cerebral palsy, prematurity, chronic illness) are at particular risk. Caretakers who have themselves suffered abuse, who are alcohol or substance abusers, or who are under extreme stress are more likely to abuse or neglect.

Differential Diagnosis

Most cases of suspected abuse are subsequently substantiated by child protective services. Cuts and bruises are more likely to represent abuse if found in **low trauma areas**, such as the buttocks or back. Care should be taken to differentiate bruises from Mongolian spots, which commonly occur in these areas. Fractures that occur **before** ambulation are usually inflicted. Occasionally, osteogenesis imperfecta has been mistaken for abuse. Skin conditions such as bullous impetigo may mimic cigarette burns or other forms of abuse.

Clinical Manifestations

History

An injury that is **inconsistent with the stated history** coupled with **delay in obtaining appropriate medical care** strongly suggests abuse. Age-inappropriate sexual behavior and knowledge are consistent with sexual abuse.

Victims of physical or sexual abuse may act out by abusing others, attempting suicide, running away, or engaging in high-risk behaviors. Abuse places children at an increased risk for poor school performance, low self-esteem, and depression.

Physical Examination

As with burns, the location and pattern of injury may strongly suggest abuse (Fig. 2–3). Bruises, fractures, or lacerations in different stages of healing occur in chronic or repeated abuse. **Spiral fractures** in young children are virtually diagnostic; rib and skull fractures frequently result from abuse as well. Vigorous **shaking** results in retinal hemorrhages in infants.

Diagnostic Evaluation

A skeletal survey and bone scan reveal areas of past injury that may not be evident on physical examination. Children with extensive bruising should undergo coagulation studies to rule out hematologic abnormalities. When sexual abuse is suspected, rectal, oral, vaginal, and urethral specimens should be examined for *Neisseria gonorrhoeae*, *Chlamydia trachomatis*, and other sexually

transmitted diseases. Other studies include blood tests for syphilis and human immunodeficiency virus.

Treatment

Health care workers are **required by law** to report any suspicion of child abuse or neglect to state protection agencies. Victims should be immediately removed from their homes and placed in protective custody at a hospital or a state facility. Many family intervention programs that focus on social support and parenting skills are being evaluated across the country in an attempt to provide children with safer home environments.

SUDDEN INFANT DEATH SYNDROME

By definition, **sudden infant death syndrome** (SIDS) consists of the unexpected death of an infant for which the etiology remains unclear despite a thorough history, physical examination, and postmortem evaluation. The cause of SIDS remains unknown but is thought to be related to delayed maturation of brainstem respiratory control.

Risk Factors

Although multiple risk factors have been identified, none has proven prognostic value (Table 2–3).

Differential Diagnosis

Cases that initially appear to be SIDS may in fact result from infection, congenital heart disease, metabolic disorders, accidental trauma, or abuse.

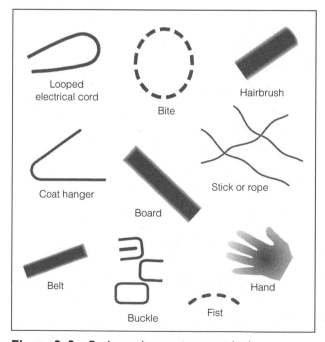

Figure 2–3 Body marks consistent with abuse.

TABLE 2–3	
SIDS: Risk Factors	
Prone sleeping position	Intrauterine drug exposure
Prematurity	Deficient prenatal care
Apnea	Low socioeconomic status
Maternal smoking	Perinatal asphyxia
Age 2–4 mo	

Prevention

Infants should be placed on their **backs** while sleeping. Contrary to popular belief, home apnea monitors do **not** decrease the likelihood of SIDS.

◆ KEY POINTS ◆

1. Together, accidents and injuries are the most common cause of pediatric morbidity and mortality.

2. Poisoning is usually accidental in toddlers and intentional in adolescents.

3. Lead poisoning places a child at high risk for developmental delay and behavior problems.

4. The routine use of seat belts and car seats is highly effective in reducing the incidence of severe injury and death.

5. Certain patterns of injury or burns suggest abuse.

6. Babies should be put to bed on their backs.

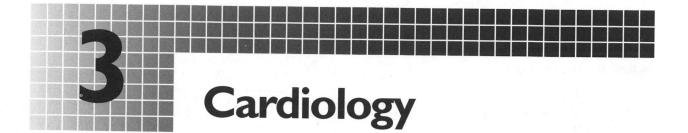

3 Cardiology

EVALUATION OF THE CYANOTIC NEONATE

Cyanosis is the physical sign characterized by blue mucous membranes, nail beds, and skin. Cyanosis results from an absolute concentration of deoxygenated hemoglobin of at least 3.0 g/dL. The absolute concentration, and not the ratio of oxygenated to deoxygenated hemoglobin, determines the presence of cyanosis. Factors that influence whether cyanosis will appear include the hematocrit, which reflects the absolute concentration of hemoglobin, and the factors that affect the O_2 dissociation curve (pH, P_{CO_2}, temperature, level of 2,3-diphosphoglycerate, and ratio of adult to fetal hemoglobin). Cyanosis should not be confused with acrocyanosis, which is blueness of the extremities due to peripheral vasoconstriction noted in the first 24–48 hours of life. Neonates with acrocyanosis have pink mucosal membranes.

Differential Diagnosis

The causes of cyanosis in the newborn are of cardiac, pulmonary, neurologic, or hematologic origin. The incidence of structural heart disease is about 8 in 1000 live births, and severe congenital heart disease occurs in approximately 1 in 400 live births. Pulmonary disorders may lead to cyanosis as a result of primary lung disease, airway obstruction, or extrinsic compression of the lung. Neurologic causes of cyanosis include central nervous system dysfunction and respiratory neuromuscular dysfunction. Table 3–1 delineates the causes of cyanosis.

Clinical Manifestations

History and Physical Examination

A complete birth history including maternal history, prenatal/perinatal/postnatal complications, history of labor and delivery, and neonatal course should be obtained. Exactly when the child developed cyanosis is critical, because certain congenital lesions present at birth and others may take as long as 1 month to reveal themselves. Table 3–2 lists the most common congenital heart defects presenting at different points during the neonatal period.

The initial physical examination should focus on the vital signs and cardiac and respiratory examinations, looking for evidence of right, left, or biventricular congestive heart failure and respiratory distress. Blue or dusky mucous membranes are consistent with cyanosis. If the neonate is stable from a cardiorespiratory standpoint, then a more complete examination can be performed, evaluating for rales, stridor, grunting, flaring, retractions, and evidence of consolidation or effusion on pulmonary examination. On cardiovascular examination, the precordial impulse is palpated, and the clinician should evaluate for systolic or diastolic murmurs, the intensity of S1, S2 splitting abnormalities, the presence of an S3 or S4, ejection click, opening snap, or rub. Examination of the extremities should focus on the strength and symmetry

TABLE 3–1

Differential Diagnosis of Cyanosis in the Neonate

Cardiac

Ductal-Independent Mixing Lesions
  Truncus arteriosus
  Total anomalous pulmonary venous return without
    obstruction
  D-transposition of the great arteries*

Lesions with Ductal-Dependent Pulmonary Blood Flow
  Tetralogy of Fallot
  Ebstein's anomaly
  Tetralogy of Fallot with pulmonary atresia**
  Critical pulmonic stenosis
  Tricuspid valve atresia with normally related great
    arteries**
  Pulmonic valve atresia with intact ventricular septum
  Heterotaxy**

Lesions with Ductal-Dependent Systemic Blood Flow
  Hypoplastic left heart syndrome
  Interrupted aortic arch
  Critical coarctation of the aorta
  Critical aortic stenosis
  Tricuspid atresia with transposed great arteries**

Pulmonary

Primary Lung Disease
  Respiratory distress syndrome
  Persistent pulmonary hypertension of the newborn
    (PPHN)
  Transient tachypnea of the newborn
  Meconium aspiration
  Pneumonia
  Pulmonary hemorrhage
  Cystic adenomatoid malformation
  Pulmonary hypoplasia
  Pulmonary arteriovenous malformation

Airway Obstruction
  Choanal stenosis or atresia
  Macroglossia

  Thyroid goiter
  Cystic hygroma
  Vocal cord paralysis
  Laryngotracheomalacia
  Laryngeal web
  Vascular ring or pulmonary sling
  Tracheoesophageal fistula
  Tracheal or bronchial stenosis
  Mediastinal mass (teratoma, thymoma)
  Absent pulmonary valve syndrome
  Pierre-Robin syndrome

Extrinsic Compression of the Lungs
  Pneumothorax
  Chylothorax
  Hemothorax

Neurological

CNS Dysfunction
  Drug-induced depression of respiratory drive
  Postasphyxial cerebral dysfunction
  Intraventricular hemorrhage
  Subarachnoid hemorrhage
  Subdural hematoma
  Meningitis
  Encephalitis
  Sepsis
  Shock
  Seizures
  Hypoglycemia

Respiratory Neuromuscular Dysfunction
  Neonatal myasthenia gravis
  Botulism
  Werdnig-Hoffman disease
  Phrenic nerve paralysis

Hematologic

  Methemoglobinemia
  Polycythemia

*A patent ductus arteriosus may improve mixing, especially with an intact ventricular septum.

**Most forms

TABLE 3–2

Common Congenital Heart Defects Presenting During the Neonatal Period

Age on admission: 0–6 days (n = 1603)

d-TGA	15%
HLHS	12%
TOF	8%
Coarctation	7%
VSD	6%
Other	52%

Age on admission: 7–13 days (n = 311)

Coarctation	20%
VSD	14%
HLH	9%
d-TGA	8%
TOF	7%
Other	42%

Age on admission: 14–28 days (n = 306)

VSD	18%
TOF	17%
Coarctation	12%
d-TGA	10%
PDA	5%
Other	38%

HLHS, hypoplastic left heart syndrome; TOF, tetralogy of Fallot; VSD, ventricular septal defect; PDA, patent ductus arteriosus.

Reprinted with permission from Graef JW, ed. Manual of pediatric therapeutics, 5th ed. Boston: Little, Brown, 1994.

of the pulses in the upper and lower extremities, evidence of edema, and cyanosis of the nail beds. If the cyanosis is limited to the extremities only, acrocyanosis is likely. Hepatosplenomegaly may be consistent with right ventricular or biventricular heart failure.

Diagnostic Evaluation

The goal of the initial evaluation of the cyanotic neonate is to determine whether the cyanosis is cardiac or noncardiac in origin. An electrocardiogram (ECG), chest radiograph, and hyperoxia tests should be performed. In addition, preductal and postductal oxygen saturation should be documented.

A hyperoxia test should be carried out in neonates with a resting pulse oximetry reading less than 95%, visible cyanosis, or circulatory collapse. The hyperoxia test consists of obtaining a baseline right radial (preductal) arterial blood gas measurement with the child breathing room air, $FiO_2=0.21$, and then repeating the measurement with the child inspiring 100% oxygen, $FiO_2=1.00$. Interpretation of the hyperoxia test is delineated in Table 3–3. A PaO_2 greater than 200 mm Hg on 100% oxygen excludes congenital heart disease from the differential. A PaO_2 less than 150 mm Hg on 100% oxygen suggests a cardiac lesion characterized by complete mixing without restricted pulmonary blood flow. A PaO_2 less than 50 mm Hg on 100% oxygen indicates a cardiac lesion with parallel circulation, a mixing lesion with restricted pulmonary blood flow.

The arterial partial pressure of oxygen (pO_2) should be measured directly via arterial puncture, though properly acquired transcutaneous oxygen monitor (TCOM) values for pO_2 are also acceptable. *Pulse oximetry should not be used for interpretation of the hyperoxia test*, because a neonate given 100% inspired oxygen may have an arterial pO_2 of 80 mm Hg with a pulse oximeter reading of 100% (abnormal), or an arterial pO_2 greater than 300 mm Hg with a pulse oximeter reading of 100% (normal). The workup of cyanotic congenital heart disease presenting with PaO_2 less than 50 mm Hg is shown in Table 3–4. Early performance of the hyperoxia test in a child with developing pulmonary disease can be helpful when cyanotic congenital heart disease is being considered later in the infant's course. Many infants with hyaline membrane disease may have a PaO_2 greater than 100 mm Hg in 100% oxygen early in their disease but not by the second or third day of life, when, because of severe hypoxia, a cardiac etiology may be considered. If a cardiac cause is deemed likely, obtain an echocardiogram and a cardiology consultation.

Pulse oximetry should be documented at preductal and postductal sites to assess for differential or reverse differential cyanosis. If the preductal saturation is higher than the postductal saturation, "differential cyanosis" exists, which results when there are normally related great arteries and deoxygenated blood from the pulmonary circulation enters the descending aorta through a patent ductus arteriosus. Differential cyanosis is seen in persistent pulmonary hypertension of the newborn (PPHN) and in lesions with left ventricular outflow tract obstruction (aortic arch hypoplasia, interrupted aortic arch, critical coarctation, and critical aortic stenosis aortic atresia).

In rare cases of "reverse differential cyanosis," the postductal saturation is higher than the preductal satu-

TABLE 3–3

Interpretation of the Hyperoxia Test

	$Fio_2 = 0.21$ Pao_2 (% saturation)		$Fio_2 = 1.00$ Pao_2 (% saturation)	$Paco_2$
Normal	70 (95)		>300 (100)	35
Pulmonary disease	50 (85)		>150 (100)	50
Neurologic disease	50 (85)		>150 (100)	50
Methemoglobinemia	70 (95)		>200 (100)	35
Cardiac disease				
Parallel circulation*	<40 (<75)		<50 (<85)	35
Mixing with restricted PBF†	<40 (<75)		<50 (<85)	35
Mixing without restricted PBF‡	40–60 (75–93)		<150 (<100)	35
	Preductal	*Postductal*		
Differential cyanosis§	70 (95)	<40 (<75)	Variable	35–50
Reverse differential cyanosis¶	<40 (<75)	>50 (>90)	Variable	35–50

Key: PBF = pulmonary blood flow.

*D-transposition of the great arteries with intact ventricular septum, D-transposition of the great arteries with ventricular septal defect.

†Tricuspid atresia with pulmonary stenosis or atresia, pulmonary atresia or critical pulmonary stenosis with intact ventricular septum, tetralogy of Fallot, or Ebstein's anomaly.

‡Truncus arteriosus, total anomalous pulmonary venous return, single ventricle, hypoplastic left heart syndrome.

§Persistent pulmonary hypertension of the newborn (PPHN), left ventricular outflow tract obstruction (aortic arch hypoplasia, interrupted aortic arch, critical coarctation, and critical aortic stenosis).

¶D-transposition of the great arteries with coarctation of the aorta or interrupted aortic arch, D-transposition of the great arteries and pulmonary hypertension.

Adapted from Barone MA, Ed. The Harriet Lane handbook, 14th ed. St. Louis: Mosby-Yearbook, 1996, p. 155.

ration. This *occurs only in children with transposition of the great arteries* when oxygenated blood from the pulmonary circulation enters the descending aorta through a patent ductus arteriosus.

Reverse differential cyanosis is seen in transposition of the great arteries with coarctation of the aorta or interrupted aortic arch and in transposition of the great arteries and pulmonary hypertension. In this circumstance, the descending aorta is filled with oxygenated blood from the pulmonary system and the lower extremities have a higher oxygen saturation than the upper extremities.

When the hyperoxia test and/or preductal/postductal oxygen saturation measurement indicates cardiac disease, the chest radiograph and ECG may be used to delineate which of the cardiac structural defects is most likely. The chest radiograph is obtained to determine the size of the heart and whether the pulmonary vascularity is increased or decreased. The ECG evaluates the heart rate, rhythm, axis, intervals, R-wave progression, and P-wave and ST/T wave morphology and helps determine if ischemia, atrial dilatation, or ventricular hypertrophy is present.

To differentiate among cyanotic congenital heart defects that present with a Pao_2 less than 50 mm Hg on

TABLE 3–4

Cyanotic Congenital Heart Disease Presenting with Pao$_2$ Less Than 50 mm Hg

Diagnosis	Heart Murmur	ECG Findings	CXR Findings
d-TGA with IVS	None	RVH normal for age	No CE with ↑ PBF
TAPVR with PV obstruction	None	RVH	PV congestion
Ebstein's anomaly	±TR murmur	RAE, RBBB, WPW	Massive CE; normal or ↓ PBF
Tricuspid atresia with PS or PA	±PS murmur	Superior axis, LVH	No CE with ↓ PBF
PA with IVS	±TR murmur, ±continuous murmur	LVH, QRS axis 0–90 degrees	±CE with ↓ PBF
Severe PS	PS murmur	RVH, QRS axis 0–90 degrees	±CE with ↓ PBF
Severe TOF	PS murmur	RVH	No CE with ↓ PBF
TOF with PA	±Continuous murmur	RVH	No CE with ↓ PBF

CXR, chest x-ray; IVS, intact ventricular septum; RVH, right ventricular hypertrophy; CE, cardiac enlargement; PBF, pulmonary blood flow; PV, pulmonary venous; TR, tricuspid regurgitation; LVH, left ventricular hypertrophy; RAE, right atrial enlargement; RBBB, right bundle branch block; PS, pulmonary stenosis; PA, pulmonary atresia; LVH, left ventricular hypertrophy; TOF, tetralogy of Fallot; ↑, increased; ↓, decreased; ±, present or absent.

Reprinted with permission from Graef JW, ed. Manual of pediatric therapeutics, 5th ed. Boston: Little, Brown, 1994.

the hyperoxia test, the clinician should first examine the chest radiograph. If massive cardiac enlargement is noted, Ebstein's anomaly is the most likely diagnosis. Once massive cardiac enlargement has been ruled out, the pulmonary vascularity becomes the focus. Increased pulmonary blood flow suggests the presence of d-TGA with intact ventricular septum, whereas pulmonary edema is a manifestation of total anomalous pulmonary venous return with obstruction.

The remaining diagnoses (tricuspid atresia with pulmonary atresia or pulmonary stenosis, pulmonic atresia with intact ventricular septum, critical pulmonic stenosis, tetralogy of Fallot, and tetralogy of Fallot with pulmonic atresia) all produce decreased pulmonary vascularity and normal or only slightly enlarged heart size. These defects are differentiated by their axis and the presence or absence of a murmur. Tricuspid atresia with pulmonic stenosis or pulmonic atresia is noted for its superior axis, lying in the 270- to 0-degree quadrant. Critical pulmonic stenosis and pulmonary atresia with an intact ventricular septum both have axes in the 0- to 90-degree quadrant. They are differentiated by the presence of the loud pulmonary ejection murmur heard in critical pulmonic stenosis. Similarly, tetralogy of Fallot and tetralogy of Fallot with pulmonic atresia both have

axes in the 90- to 180-degree quadrant, and they are distinguished from each other by the pulmonic stenosis murmur noted in tetralogy of Fallot.

Treatment

Newborns with mixing lesions without adequate mixing (d-TGA with intact ventricular septum) or defects that have ductal-dependent pulmonary blood flow or ductal-dependent systemic blood flow may require prostaglandin E$_1$ (PGE$_1$) infusion to maintain patency of the ductus arteriosus until definitive surgical treatment can be accomplished. Rarely, the patient with congenital heart disease may become progressively more unstable after the institution of PGE$_1$ therapy. This clinical deterioration after institution of PGE$_1$ is an important diagnostic finding that identifies the congenital heart defect as one that has obstructed blood flow out of the pulmonary veins or left atrium. Lesions that have impaired blood flow from the left atrium include hypoplastic left heart syndrome with restrictive or intact foramen ovale, other variants of mitral atresia with restrictive foramen ovale, transposition of the great arteries with an intact ventricular septum and restrictive foramen ovale, and total anomalous pulmonary venous return with obstruction.

CYANOTIC CONGENITAL HEART DISEASE, PART I: DUCTAL-INDEPENDENT MIXING LESIONS

Truncus Arteriosus

Truncus arteriosus (Fig. 3–1) is a rare form of cyanotic congenital heart disease that consists of a single arterial vessel arising from the base of the heart from which arise the coronary, systemic, and pulmonary arteries. A large ventricular septal defect is almost always present, and 30% have a right-sided aortic arch. In this disorder, there is complete mixing of systemic and pulmonary venous blood in the truncus arteriosus and the O$_2$ saturation in the aorta and pulmonary arteries is identical. This lesion along with other conotruncal anomalies (tetralogy of Fallot, interrupted aortic arch, VSO, isolated arch anomalies, and vascular ring) are associated with microdeletion of the twenty-second chromosome (22q11 deletion).

Clinical Manifestations

Moderate cyanosis is present at birth, and congestive heart failure develops in a matter of weeks as the pulmonary vascular resistance falls and shunting across the ventricular septal defect begins. On examination, a harsh holosystolic murmur is heard at the left sternal border, a widened pulse pressure is present, and bounding arterial pulses are palpated. There is a single loud second

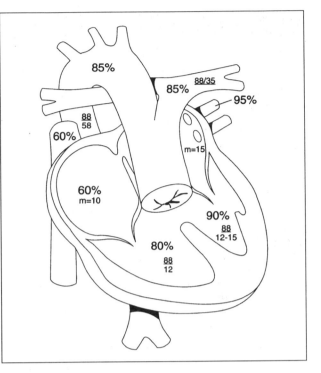

Figure 3–1 Truncus arteriosus (with right aortic arch). Typical anatomic and hemodynamic findings include: (a) a single artery arises from the conotruncus giving rise to coronary arteries (not shown), pulmonary arteries, and brachiocephalic vessels; (b) abnormal truncal valve (quadricuspid shown) with stenosis and/or regurgitation common; (c) right-sided aortic arch (occurs in approximately 30% of cases); (d) large conoventricular ventricular septal defect; (e) pulmonary artery hypertension with a large left-to-right shunt (note superior vena caval oxygen saturation of 60% and pulmonary artery oxygen saturation of 85%); (f) complete mixing (of the systemic and pulmonary venous return) occurs at the great vessel level.

heart sound on cardiovascular exam. Seventy percent of children with truncus arteriosus have biventricular hypertrophy on ECG. On chest radiograph, marked cardiomegaly, increased pulmonary vascularity, and right aortic arch may be seen. DiGeorge syndrome related to the 22q11 microdeletion may result in hypocalcemia.

Treatment

Initial management includes an anticongestive regimen of digoxin and diuretics. Surgical repair involves closing the ventricular septal defect so the trunk is baffled to the left ventricle and by interposing a conduit between the right ventricle and pulmonary arteries, which are disconnected from the trunk.

d-Transposition of the Great Arteries

d-Transposition of the great arteries (Fig. 3–2) accounts for 5% of congenital heart defects and is the most common form of cyanotic congenital heart disease presenting in the neonatal period. In this defect, the aorta arises anteriorly from the right ventricle and the pulmonary artery posteriorly from the left ventricle. There are three basic variants: d-TGA with intact ventricular septum (60%), d-TGA with ventricular septal defect (10%), and d-TGA with ventricular septal defect and pulmonic stenosis (30%).

In this defect, the pulmonary and systemic circuits are parallel rather than in series. The systemic circuit (deoxygenated blood) is recirculated through the body, whereas the pulmonary circuit (oxygenated blood) recirculates through the lungs. A mixing lesion such as an atrial septal defect, ventricular septal defect, or patent ductus arteriosus that allows mixing of the systemic and pulmonary circulations is necessary for survival.

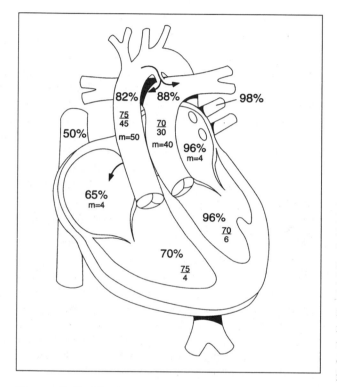

Figure 3–2 Transposition of the great arteries with an intact ventricular septum, a large patent ductus arteriosus (on PGE₁) and atrial septal defect (status post balloon atrial septostomy). Note the following: (a) The aorta arises from the anatomic right ventricle, and the pulmonary artery from the anatomic left ventricle; (b) "transposition physiology," with a higher oxygen saturation in the pulmonary artery than in the aorta; (c) "mixing" between the parallel circulations (see text) at the atrial (after balloon atrial septostomy) and ductal levels; (d) shunting from the left atrium to the right atrium via the atrial septal defect (not shown) with equalization of atrial pressures; (e) shunting from the aorta to the pulmonary artery via the ductus arteriosus; (f) pulmonary hypertension due to a large ductus arteriosus.

Clinical Manifestations

Cyanosis is present from birth, the degree varying with the associated mixing lesions. In the absence of mixing lesions, there is pronounced cyanosis, right ventricular heave, and a single loud S2 on examination. In d-transposition with intact ventricular septum, there is no murmur. In d-transposition with ventricular septal defect, there is a harsh holosystolic murmur at the left lower sternal border, whereas in d-transposition with ventricular septal defect and pulmonic stenosis, there is a harsh holosystolic murmur and systolic ejection murmur at the right upper sternal border. The ECG is normal in the newborn; however, right-axis deviation and right ventricular hypertrophy are eventually seen. The chest radiograph reveals increased pulmonary vascular markings in d-transposition with and without ventricular septal defect, but if pulmonic stenosis is critical, decreased pulmonary vascular markings could be present. Cardiomegaly with "egg-shaped silhouette" is often seen on chest radiograph.

Treatment

Initial management includes PGE₁ to keep the patent ductus arteriosus open and increase aorta (deoxygenated) to pulmonary artery (oxygenated) shunting. If needed, the Rashkind balloon atrial septostomy can be utilized to improve atrial mixing and relieve severe hypoxia. Surgical repair, utilizing the arterial switch procedure, is generally performed during the first week of life.

Total Anomalous Pulmonary Venous Connection Without Obstruction

Total anomalous pulmonary venous connection (TAPVC) (Fig. 3–3) is a rare lesion in which the pulmonary venous return is directed to the right atrium either directly or indirectly through venous channels. There are four variants:

- **Supracardiac** (50% of cases) blood drains into the innominate vein or into the superior vena cava;
- **Cardiac** (20% of cases) blood drains into the coronary sinus or directly into the right atrium;
- **Infradiaphragmatic** (20% of cases) blood drains into the portal or hepatic veins;
- **Mixed** (10% of cases) blood returns to the heart via a combination of the above routes.

TAPVC can occur with or without obstruction. Obstruction occurs when the anomalous vein enters a vessel at an acute angle. The presence or absence of obstruction determines whether there is pulmonary venous hypertension and cyanosis or increased pulmonary blood flow and cyanosis. In TAPVC without obstruction, there is a mixture of deoxygenated and oxygenated blood in the supracardiac/infracardiac vein, coronary sinus, or right atrium and the left atrium is filled by a right-to-left atrial shunt. As a result, there is increased pulmonary blood flow, mild pulmonary arteriolar hypertension, and moderate cyanosis.

Clinical Manifestations

Without obstruction, clinical findings are similar to those of an atrial septal defect. There is an active precordium with a right ventricular heave, a wide and fixed split S2 with a loud pulmonary component, and a systolic ejection murmur at the left upper sternal border. On chest radiograph, cardiomegaly is noted with increased pulmonary vascularity. On ECG, right-axis deviation and right ventricular hypertrophy are seen.

Treatment

Treatment of congestive heart failure is needed initially, and surgical redirection of aberrant vessels into the left atrium is necessary in the first month of life.

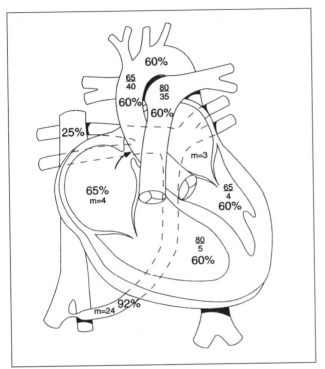

Figure 3–3   Infradiaphragmatic total anomalous pulmonary venous connection. Note the following: (a) pulmonary venous confluence does not connect with the left atrium, but descends to connect with the portal circulation below the diaphragm. This connection is frequently severely obstructed as shown; (b) obstruction to pulmonary venous return results in significantly elevated pulmonary venous pressures, decreased pulmonary blood flow, pulmonary edema and pulmonary venous desaturation (92%); (c) systemic to suprasystemic pressure in the pulmonary artery (in the absence of a patent ductus arteriosus, pulmonary artery pressures may exceed systemic pressures when severe pulmonary venous obstruction is present); (d) all systemic blood flow must be derived via a right-to-left shunt at the foramen ovale; (e) nearly equal oxygen saturations in all chambers of the heart (i.e., complete mixing at right atrial level), with severe hypoxemia (systemic oxygen saturation 60%) and low cardiac output (mixed venous oxygen saturation 25%).

CYANOTIC CONGENITAL HEART DISEASE, PART II: LESIONS WITH DUCTAL-DEPENDENT PULMONARY BLOOD FLOW

Tricuspid Atresia

Tricuspid atresia (Fig. 3–4) is a rare defect that consists of complete absence of right atrioventricular connection, and that absence leads to severe hypoplasia or absence

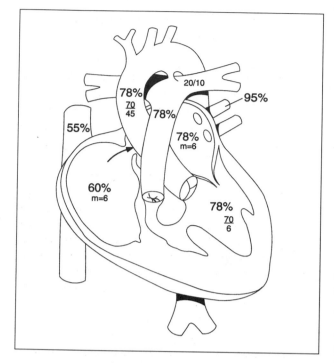

Figure 3–4   Tricuspid atresia with normally related great arteries and a small patent ductus arteriosus. Typical anatomic and hemodynamic findings include: (a) atresia of the tricuspid valve; (b) hypoplasia of the right ventricle; (c) restriction to pulmonary blood flow at two levels: a (usually) small ventricular septal defect and a stenotic pulmonary valve; (d) all systemic venous return must pass through the patent foramen ovale to reach the left ventricle; (e) complete mixing at the left atrial level, with systemic oxygen saturation of 78% (in FiO_2 of 0:21), suggesting balanced systemic and pulmonary blood flow.

men ovale or an atrial septal defect, and the left atrium and left ventricle handle both systemic and pulmonary venous return. Oxygenated and deoxygenated blood is mixed in the left atrium. Cyanosis is severe in the neonatal period and is proportionally related to the amount of pulmonary blood flow.

Clinical Manifestations

Neonates with tricuspid artresia with normally related great arteries present with progressive cyanosis, poor feeding, and tachypnea over the first 2 weeks of life. On cardiac examination, the harsh holosystolic murmur of the ventricular septal defect at the left lower sternal border and the continuous murmur of the patent ductus arteriosus are heard, if they are present. On ECG, there is a superior axis and left ventricular hypertrophy. Findings on chest radiograph include normal heart size and decreased pulmonary vascular markings.

Treatment

A child with tricuspid artresia with normally related great arteries should have PGE_1 started to maintain pulmonary flow, and a balloon atrial septostomy should be performed if the atrial defect is not adequate. Surgical management for tricuspid atresia with normally related great arteries involves placing a modified Blalock-Taussig shunt to maintain pulmonary blood flow. The modified Blalock-Taussig shunt is a Gor-Tex conduit placed between the subclavian artery and the pulmonary artery. Ultimately, a cavopulmonary anastamosis (hemi-Fontan or bidirectional Glenn) is performed to provide stable pulmonary blood flow. In some centers, a modified Fontan is performed to redirect the inferior vena cava and hepatic vein flow into the pulmonary circulation.

Pulmonic Atresia with Intact Ventricular Septum

Pulmonic atresia with intact ventricular septum (Fig. 3–5) is a rare defect consisting of pulmonary valvular and infundibular atresia and varying degrees of right ventricular and tricuspid valve hypoplasia. In this disorder, there is an obligate atrial shunt from right to left and pulmonary blood flow is dependent on a patent ductus arteriosus. Since there is no pulmonary outflow, the right ventricle is hypertensive and there is often moderate to severe tricuspid regurgitation. Pulmonary atresia with intact ventricular septum may also be associated with coronary artery–myocardial sinusoid communications. The coronary arteries may be quite abnormal, with areas of stenosis or complete atresia. In some cases, coronary perfusion

of the right ventricle. Of patients with tricuspid atresia, 70% have normally related great arteries and 30% have transposition of the great arteries. Ninety percent of the cases of tricuspid atresia have an associated ventricular septal defect. In children with tricuspid artresia with normally related great arteries, the ventricular septal defect allows blood to pass from the left ventricle to the right ventricular outflow and pulmonary arteries. The vast majority of patients with tricuspid artresia with normally related great arteries also have pulmonary stenosis. In tricuspid artresia with normally related great arteries the systemic venous return is shunted from the right atrium to the left atrium through the patent fora-

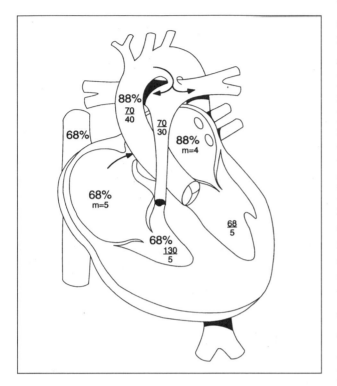

Figure 3–5 Pulmonary atresia with intact ventricular septum (PA/IVS) in a neonate with a nonrestrictive patent ductus arteriosus while receiving PGE₁. Typical anatomic and hemodynamic findings include: (a) hypertrophied, hypoplastic right ventricle; (b) hypoplastic tricuspid valve and pulmonary annulus; (c) atresia of the pulmonary valve with no antegrade flow; (d) suprasystemic right ventricular pressure; (e) pulmonary blood flow via the patent ductus; (f) right-to-left shunt at the atrial level with systemic desaturation. Many patients have significant coronary abnormalities with sinusoidal or fistulous connections to the hypertensive right ventricle or significant coronary stenosis (not shown).

may be dependent on the hypertensive right ventricle. If the coronaries are right ventricle (RV) dependent, any palliative procedure that decompresses the right ventricle may lead to myocardial infarction and death.

Clinical Manifestations

Neonates present at birth extremely cyanotic and tachypneic. Cardiac examination reveals a tricuspid regurgitation murmur in the left lower sternal border and the continuous murmur of a patent ductus arteriosus. On ECG, left ventricular hypertrophy and a leftward axis are

seen. On chest radiograph, decreased pulmonary markings and left ventricular hypertrophy are seen.

Treatment

PGE₁ should be started to ensure pulmonary blood flow initially. Prior to any surgery to provide more stable pulmonary flow, a cardiac catheterization must be performed to assess the coronary arteries. If the coronary circulation is not RV dependent, then a right ventricle to pulmonary artery conduit or pulmonary valvotomy is performed to provide pulmonary outflow. A modified Blalock-Taussig shunt is also typically performed to augment pulmonary blood flow further. If the coronary circulation is RV dependent, the RV is not decompressed and a modified Blalock-Taussig shunt is performed. In cases in which right ventricular development is minimal, a cavopulmonary anastomosis (hemi-Fontan or bidirectional Glenn) and modified Fontan are performed.

Tetralogy of Fallot

Tetralogy of Fallot (Fig. 3–6) is the third most prevalent cyanotic congenital heart lesion during the neonatal period and after the third week of life becomes the leading cause of cyanosis due to congenital heart disease in childhood. The four defects Fallot noted include an anterior malalignment ventricular septal defect, right ventricular outflow tract obstruction (50% infundibular stenosis, 10% pulmonary valve stenosis, and 30% infundibular stenosis and pulmonary valve stenosis), right ventricular hypertrophy, and an "overriding" large ascending aorta.

Clinical Manifestations

Neonates with tetralogy of Fallot are cyanotic because of right-to-left shunting across the ventricular septal defect and decreased pulmonary flow. Shunting occurs when the combination of the pulmonary vascular resistance and the resistance created by the right ventricular outflow tract obstruction exceed the peripheral vascular resistance. The degree of cyanosis is proportional to the severity of the right ventricular outflow tract obstruction. Blood shunted from the aorta to the pulmonary artery through the patent ductus arteriosus provides additional pulmonary blood flow. Neonates present with cyanosis of varying severity and characteristic periodic episodic cyanosis and agitation. These episodes of cyanosis are known as "tet spells." Tet spells are caused by an increase in right ventricular outflow tract resistance, leading to an increase in the right-left shunt. Such spells may last minutes to hours, may resolve spontaneously,

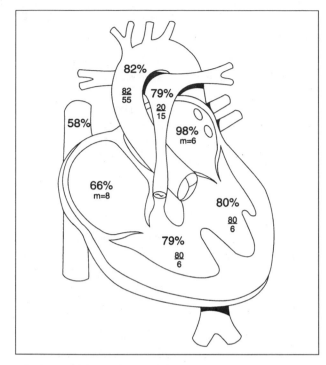

Figure 3–6   Tetralogy of Fallot. Typical anatomic and hemodynamic findings include: (a) an anteriorly displaced infundibular septum, resulting in subpulmonary stenosis, a large ventricular septal defect and overriding of the aorta over the muscular septum; (b) hypoplasia of the pulmonary valve, main and brain pulmonary arteries; (c) equal right and left ventricular pressures; (d) a right-to-left shunt at ventricular level, with a systemic oxygen saturation of 82%.

or may lead to progressive hypoxia, acidosis, and death. On cardiac examination, a right ventricular heave is often felt and a loud systolic ejection murmur is heard in the left upper sternal border due to right ventricular outflow tract obstruction. Also heard is the continuous murmur representing the patent ductus arteriosus shunt and the holosystolic murmur of the ventricular septal defect at the left lower sternal border. The ECG reveals right atrial dilation and right ventricular hypertrophy, whereas the chest radiograph shows normal heart size with decreased pulmonary vascular markings. Twenty-five percent of children with tetralogy of Fallot have a right-sided aortic arch.

Treatment

The treatment of "tet spells" is aimed at diminishing right-to-left shunting by increasing systemic vascular re-

sistance and decreasing pulmonary vascular resistance. "Tet spells" may be treated with supplemental oxygen, vagal maneuvers, morphine sulfate, vasoconstrictors, beta-blockers, and volume administration. Holding the infant over the shoulder and placing the child in a knee-chest position decreases preload and increases systemic vascular resistance. Morphine sulfate suppresses the respiratory center, stops hyperpnea, and dilates the pulmonary arteries. Vasoconstrictors raise the systemic vascular resistance, whereas beta-blockers minimize infundibular spasm. Volume is added to increase the systemic blood pressure, which minimizes right-to-left shunting. Metabolic acidosis must be corrected, because it increases pulmonary vascular resistance and thereby promotes right-to-left shunting across the ventricular septal defect. In most institutions, surgical repair is performed during the first 3–6 months of life.

Ebstein's Anomaly

Ebstein's anomaly (Fig. 3–7) is an extremely rare anomaly in which the leaflets of the tricuspid valve are displaced into the right ventricular cavity and a portion of the right ventricle is incorporated into the right atrium. Functional hypoplasia of the right ventricle results, as well as tricuspid regurgitation and/or stenosis. A patent foramen ovale is present in 80% of neonates with the anomaly, and there is a right-to-left shunt at the atrial level. The right atrium is massively dilated, which may result in supraventricular tachycardia. Wolff-Parkinson-White (WPW) syndrome is associated with Ebstein's anomaly. In severe cases of Ebstein's anomaly, the majority of the pulmonary blood flow comes from the patent ductus arteriosus and not the right ventricle.

Clinical Manifestations

Neonates present with cyanosis and congestive heart failure in the first few days of life. The cardiac examination reveals a widely fixed split S2, and a tricuspid regurgitant murmur is heard at the left lower sternal border. The ECG reveals a right bundle branch block with right atrial enlargement. Delta waves due to WPW syndrome and supraventricular tachycardia may manifest themselves. Chest radiograph reveals extreme cardiomegaly with notable right atrial enlargement and decreased pulmonary vascular markings.

Treatment

PGE$_1$ may help increase pulmonary blood flow, and congestive heart failure therapy with digoxin and diuretics is often useful. Propranolol may be used to suppress

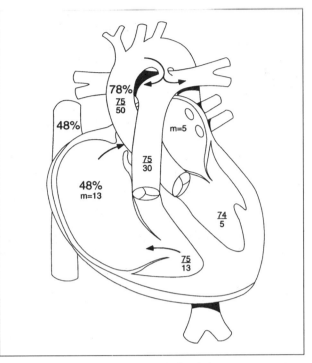

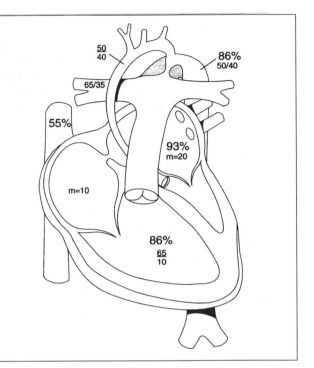

Figure 3–7 Ebstein's anomaly (with large nonrestrictive ductus arteriosus). Typical anatomic and hemodynamic findings include: (a) inferior displacement of the tricuspid valve into the right ventricle, which may also cause subpulmonary obstruction; (b) diminutive muscular right ventricle; (c) marked enlargement of the right atrium due to "atrialized" portion of right ventricle as well as tricuspid regurgitation; (d) right-to-left shunting at the atrial level (note arterial oxygen saturation of 78%); (e) a left-to-right shunt and pulmonary hypertension secondary to a large patent ductus arteriosus supplying the pulmonary blood flow; (f) low cardiac output (note low mixed venous oxygen saturation in the superior vena cava).

Figure 3–8 Hypoplastic left heart syndrome in a 24-hour-old patient with falling pulmonary vascular resistance and a nonrestrictive ductus arteriosus. Typical anatomic and hemodynamic findings include: (a) atresia or hypoplasia of the left ventricle, mitral and aortic valves; (b) a diminutive ascending aorta and transverse aortic arch, usually with an associated coarctation; (c) coronary blood flow is usually retrograde from the ductus arteriosus through the tiny ascending aorta; (d) systemic arterial oxygen saturation (in FiO_2 of 0.21) of 80%, reflecting relatively balanced systemic and pulmonary blood flows—the pulmonary artery and aortic saturations are equal (see text); (e) pulmonary hypertension secondary to the nonrestrictive ductus arteriosus; (f) minimal left atrial hypertension; (g) normal systemic cardiac output (note superior vena cava oxygen saturation of 65% and blood pressure (65/45).

supraventricular tachycardia if present. Surgical therapy to repair the abnormal tricuspid valve has had poor results.

CYANOTIC CONGENITAL HEART DISEASE, PART III: LESIONS WITH DUCTAL-DEPENDENT SYSTEMIC BLOOD FLOW

Hypoplastic Left Heart Syndrome

Hypoplastic left heart syndrome (HLHS) (Figs. 3–8 and 3–9) is the second most common congenital cardiac

lesion presenting in the first week of life and the most common cause of death from congenital heart disease in the first month of life. The syndrome is a continuum of anomalies that produce similar hemodynamic abnormalities. In this syndrome, there is hypoplasia of the left ventricle, aortic valve stenosis or atresia, mitral valve stenosis or atresia and hypoplasia of the ascending aortic with discrete coarctation of the aorta. These lesions reduce or eliminate blood flow through the left side of the

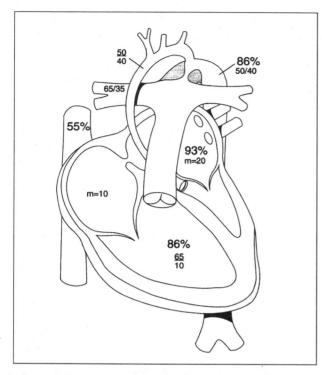

Figure 3–9 Acute circulatory collapse following constriction of the ductus arteriosus in hypoplastic left heart syndrome. These neonates are typically in shock with poor perfusion, tachycardia, acidosis and in respiratory distress. Note (a) the low cardiac output (as evidenced by the low mixed venous oxygen saturation in the superior vena cava of 55%); (b) narrow pulse pressure; (c) elevated atrial and ventricular end-diastolic pressure—elevated left atrial pressure may cause pulmonary edema (note left atrial saturation of 93%); (d) significantly increased pulmonary blood flow, as reflected in an arterial oxygen saturation (in Fio$_2$ of 0.21) of 86%.

heart, causing an obligatory left-to-right shunt at the atrial level and a right-to-left shunt at the ductus arteriosus. Systemic flow is completely ductal dependent, and coronary perfusion is retrograde.

Clinical Manifestations

As the ductus closes, neonates with HLHS become critically ill with congestive heart failure, moderate cyanosis, tachycardia, tachypnea, pulmonary rales (from pulmonary edema), and hepatomegaly. Poor or absent peripheral pulses and vasoconstricted extremities are charac-

teristic. The cardiac examination reveals an S3 and a loud single S2. The ECG is often normal for age. The chest radiograph reveals pulmonary edema.

Treatment

When the diagnosis is made, PGE$_1$ should be started to maintain ductal dependent systemic blood flow. No corrective surgery is available. The Norwood palliation, which is performed in the first week of life, allows the majority of neonates to survive infancy. The Norwood procedure involves amalgamation of the pulmonary artery and aorta to provide unobstructed systemic blood flow, artrial septectomy, and modified Blalock-Taussig shunt to provide adequate pulmonary blood flow. Those infants who survive the Norwood palliation have a cavopulmonary anastomosis performed at 4–6 months of age and a modified Fontan performed at 2 years of age. Some centers do not perform the Norwood palliation and proceed directly to heart transplant.

Interrupted Aortic Arch

There are three types of interrupted aortic arch (Fig. 3–10): type A is interruption beyond the left subclavian artery, type B is interruption between the left subclavian and left common carotid arteries, and type C is interruption between the left common carotid and the brachiocephalic arteries. In this anomaly, systemic blood flow is dependent on patency of the ductus arteriosus, which shunts blood from the pulmonary artery to the aorta. Interrupted aortic arch is often associated with DiGeorge syndrome, due to the 22q11 microdeletion.

Clinical Manifestations

Pulmonary edema occurs almost immediately. The clinical presentation is similar to that of critical coarctation of the aorta.

Treatment

PGE$_1$ therapy should begin immediately to maintain systemic blood flow via the right-to-left shunt through the patent ductus arteriosus. Emergent surgery is necessary to reanastomose the aortic segments.

Total Anomalous Pulmonary Venous Connection with Obstruction

The different types of TAPVC and the clinical manifestations and management of TAPVC without venous obstruction were described earlier. TAPVC with venous obstruction may occur with all variants but is more likely with the infradiaphragmatic type. In both obstructed and

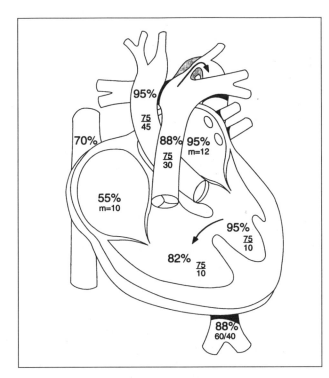

Figure 3–10 Interrupted aortic arch with restrictive patent ductus arteriosus. Typical anatomic and hemodynamic findings include: (a) atresia of a segment of the aortic arch between the left subclavian artery and the left common carotid (the most common type of interrupted aortic arch—"type B"); (b) a posterior malalignment of the conal septum resulting in a large ventricular septal defect and a narrow subaortic area; (c) a bicuspid aortic valve occurs in 60% of patients; (d) systemic pressure in the right ventricle and pulmonary artery (due to the large, nonrestrictive ventricular septal defect); (e) increased oxygen saturation in the pulmonary artery due to left-to-right shunting at the ventricular level; (f) "differential cyanosis" with a lower oxygen saturation in the descending aorta due to a right-to-left shunt at the patent ductus. Note the lower blood pressure in the descending aorta due to constriction of the ductus; opening the ductus with PGE_1 results in equal upper and lower extremity blood pressures, but continued "differential cyanosis."

nonobstructed defects, there is a mixture of deoxygenated and oxygenated blood in the supracardiac/infradiaphragmatic vein, coronary sinus, or right atrium and the left atrium is filled by a right-to-left atrial shunt. The presence of severe pulmonary edema differentiates obstructed from nonobstructed TAPVC. Obstruction of the pulmonary veins results in backup of oxygenated blood into the lungs, pulmonary edema, and severe cyanosis. The amount of oxygenated blood reaching the right atrium is small and the blood that goes from right-to-left across the foramen ovale is mostly deoxygenated.

Clinical Manifestations
A neonate with TAPVC with obstruction presents extremely cyanotic, tachypneic, and dyspneic. Examination reveals a right ventricular heave, a narrowly split S2, and a ventricular gallop (S3). The ECG in the neonate with obstructed veins may reveal right-axis deviation, right atrial dilatation, and right ventricular hypertrophy. The chest radiograph generally reveals normal heart size with pulmonary edema that may be hard to distinguish from hyaline membrane disease.

Treatment
In the initial treatment of TAPVC with obstruction, PGE_1 should not be given because the patent ductus arteriosus adds more blood volume to an already flooded pulmonary circuit. Management of congestive heart failure is needed initially, and if pulmonary edema is present, mechanical ventilation may be necessary. Surgical redirection of aberrant vessels into the left atrium should be performed emergently if obstruction is present.

ACYANOTIC CONGENITAL HEART DISEASE

Acyanotic cardiac defects that result in increased pulmonary blood flow include atrial septal defect, ventricular septal defect, patent ductus arteriosus, and common atrioventricular canal. Acyanotic lesions that result in pulmonary venous hypertension include coarctation of the aorta and aortic valve stenosis. The acyanotic structural anomaly that results in relatively normal pulmonary blood flow is pulmonary valve stenosis.

Atrial Septal Defects
Atrial septal defects account for 8% of congenital heart disease. There are three types of atrial septal defects:

- the ostium secundum defect seen in the midportion of the atrial septum;
- the ostium primum defect located in the low atrial septum;
- the sinus venosus defect found at the junction of the right atrium and the superior or inferior vena cava.

The degree of atrial shunting is dependent on the size of the ASD and the relative compliance of the ventricles in diastole. Since right ventricular diastolic compliance is usually less than left ventricular diastolic compliance, left-to-right shunting occurs at the atrial level, thus increasing flow across the tricuspid and pulmonary valves and increasing pulmonary blood flow.

Clinical Manifestations

Atrial septal defects are usually not associated with symptoms, although there may be a history of slow weight gain and frequent lower respiratory infections. On physical examination, the precordium is hyperdynamic, and a right ventricular heave is often present. A systolic ejection murmur in the pulmonic area and a mid-diastolic rumble in the lower right sternal border reflect the increased flow across the pulmonary and tricuspid valves. S2 is widely and constantly split. On chest radiograph, the heart and main pulmonary artery are enlarged and pulmonary vascularity is increased. The ECG often shows right ventricular hypertrophy or right ventricular conduction delay. Right-axis deviation is often seen in secundum defects, whereas primum defects have characteristic extreme left-axis deviation. On echocardiogram, the right ventricle is often enlarged, and Doppler flow mapping reveals the direction of flow across the defect and atrioventricular valve competence.

Treatment

Spontaneous closure of small secundum ASDs is likely to occur in the majority of cases in the first year of life. Ostium primum and sinus venosus ASDs do not close spontaneously and must be addressed surgically. The symptomatic child with an ASD has the defect closed as soon as possible. The timing of ASD repair in the asymptomatic infant or child is more controversial. In general, the defect should be repaired when circulatory arrest is not needed and when the likelihood of needing a blood transfusion is low. After 6 months of age, both of these criteria are generally met. Subacute bacterial endocarditis prophylaxis is not needed for secundum defects but is indicated in primum defects. The secundum defect is a low-flow nonturbulent lesion. Lesions that have high flow or are turbulent need subacute bacterial prophylaxis. Bacterial endocarditis and prophylaxis for subacute bacterial endocarditis is discussed in detail later in this chapter.

Ventricular Septal Defects

The ventricular septal defects (VSDs) are the most common congenital heart defect, accounting for 26% of all congenital cardiac lesions. The five types of ventricular septal defects are:

- conoventricular
- muscular
- inlet
- conoseptal hypoplasia
- malalignment

Muscular ventricular septal defects occur in the muscular portion of the septum and may be single or multiple and located in the posterior, apical, or anterior portion of the septum. The inlet VSD is an endocardial cushion defect and occurs in the inlet portion of the septum beneath the septal leaflet of the tricuspid valve. Conoseptal hypoplasia VSDs are positioned in the outflow tract of the right ventricle beneath the pulmonary valve. The conoventricular VSD occurs in the membranous portion of the ventricular septum. Malalignment VSDs result from malalignment of the infundibular septum. As long as pulmonary vascular resistance is lower than systemic vascular resistance, the shunt is left to right. Large defects eventually result in pulmonary hypertension, whereas small defects do not change pulmonary vascular hemodynamics. The amount of left ventricular and left atrial dilatation is directly proportional to the size of the left-to-right shunt. Right ventricular enlargement occurs when pulmonary vascular resistance increases. Over time, elevated pulmonary arterial pressures lead to pulmonary obstructive vascular disease (Eisenmenger syndrome) and the ventricular shunt reverses right to left. Clinical symptoms are related to the size of the shunt.

Clinical Manifestations

A small shunt produces no symptoms, whereas a large shunt without elevated pulmonary arterial pressures gives rise to growth failure, congestive heart failure, and chronic lower respiratory infections. The patient with a large VSD with Eisenmenger physiology presents with shortness of breath, dyspnea on exertion, chest pain, and cyanosis. The smaller the defect, the louder is the holosystolic murmur. As pulmonary vascular resistance increases, the holosystolic murmur shortens and the pulmonary component of S2 increases in intensity. In the presence of pulmonary vascular obstructive disease, a right ventricular heave, ejection click, short systolic ejection murmur, diastolic murmur of pulmonary valve insufficiency, and loud S2 are heard. Chest radiograph for small defects may be normal or show mild cardiomegaly and a slight increase in pulmonary vascularity, whereas in large left-to-right shunts cardiomegaly, increased pulmonary vascularity, and enlargement of the left atrium and left ventricle are seen. In small defects the ECG is normal, whereas with a large VSD, left atrial, left ventricular, or biventricular hypertrophy is seen. Right ventricular hypertrophy predominates when pulmonary vascular resistance is high. On echocardiogram, the defect can be visualized and Doppler flow mapping demonstrates the direction of flow.

Treatment

Most small VSDs close without intervention (40% by 3 years, 75% by 10 years), whereas the treatment for large VSDs is surgical closure before pulmonary vascular changes become irreversible. Congestive heart failure is treated with digoxin and lasix.

Common Atrioventricular Canal

The common atrioventricular canal defect (Fig. 3–11), which is an endocardial cushion defect, is caused by deficiencies of both atrial and ventricular septa and of the mitral and tricuspid valves. In an **incomplete atrioventricular canal** defect, the atrioventricular valves attach directly to the top of the muscular portion of the ventricular septum. As a result, there is no communication beneath the atrioventricular valves between the right and left ventricles. The communication at the atrial level is an ostium primum ASD. The mitral valve is cleft, and there may be some degree of mitral regurgitation. In **complete common atrioventricular canal**, there is a common atrioventricular valve whose leaflets are not attached to the muscular ventricular septum. As a result, there is a large defect located between the top of the muscular ventricular septum and the common atrioventricular valve. In this defect, there is a left-to-right shunt at the atrial (ostium primum ASD) and ventricular level. Because of the increase in pulmonary blood flow, pulmonary hypertension and vascular disease may develop.

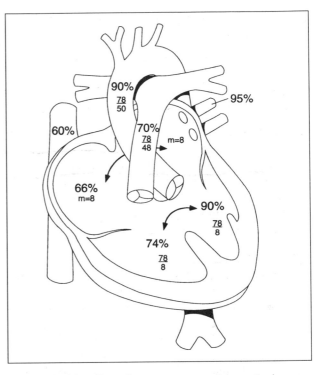

Figure 3–11 Complete common atrioventricular canal. Typical anatomic and hemodynamic findings include: (a) large atrial and ventricular septal defects of the endocardial cushion type; (b) single, atrioventricular valve; (c) pulmonary artery hypertension (due to large ventricular septal defect); (d) bidirectional shunting (with mild hypoxemia) at atrial and ventricular level when pulmonary vascular resistance is elevated in the initial neonatal period. With subsequent fall in pulmonary vascular resistance, the shunt becomes predominantly left-to-right with symptoms of congestive heart failure.

Clinical Manifestations

Incomplete common atrioventricular canal congestive heart failure is seen early in infancy with tachypnea, dyspnea, and poor feeding. On examination, a blowing holosystolic murmur is heard at the left lower sternal border due to the VSD, and an S2 with a widely fixed split is heard due to the atrial septal defect. The ECG reveals left-axis deviation, right atrial dilation, and left atrial dilation. The clinical manifestations of the incomplete common atrioventricular canal are the same as those described for an ostium primum ASD.

Treatment

Surgical repair for complete common atrioventricular canal is usually done within the first year of life. Complete heart block occurs in 5% of patients undergoing repair, and residual mitral insufficiency is often seen.

Patent Ductus Arteriosus

Patency of the ductus arteriosus accounts for 10% of congenital heart disease. There is a high incidence in premature neonates and a 2:1 female predominance. The ductus arteriosus connects the aorta and the left pulmonary artery just distal to the takeoff of the left subclavian artery from the aorta. The direction of flow through a large patent ductus arteriosus depends on the relative resistances in the pulmonary and systemic circuits. As long as the systemic vascular resistance is greater than the pulmonary vascular resistance, a left-to-right shunt is present. If pulmonary resistance rises above systemic resistance, a right-to-left shunt develops.

Clinical Manifestations

Symptoms are related to the size of the defect and the direction of flow. A small patent ductus arteriosus causes no symptoms. A large one with a left-to-right shunt may result in congestive heart failure, slowed growth, and repeated lower respiratory tract infections. Reversal of flow as a result of high pulmonary vascular resistance causes shortness of breath, dyspnea on exertion, and cyanosis. In a large shunt, bounding pulses, representing an aortic diastolic runoff, are palpable. The murmur, often referred to as a "machinery murmur," is continuous beginning after S1, peaks at S2, and trails off during diastole. If pulmonary vascular resistance rises, the diastolic and systolic murmurs become softer and shorter and S2 increases in intensity. The chest radiograph of a small patent ductus arteriosus is often normal, whereas the chest radiograph of the large patent ductus arteriosus will show cardiomegaly, increased pulmonary vascularity, and left atrial and left ventricular enlargement. The neonate with a small patent ductus arteriosus has a normal ECG, whereas the neonate with a large patent ductus arteriosus and a generous left-to-right shunt shows left or biventricular hypertrophy. Right ventricular hypertrophy predominates on ECG in the presence of increased pulmonary vascular resistance. The patent ductus arteriosus is best seen on echocardiogram using Doppler flow mapping.

Treatment

Indomethacin is often effective in closing the patent ductus arteriosus in the premature neonate by decreasing PGE_1 levels. A patent ductus arteriosus usually closes in the first month of life, but for those that do not, surgical ligation by thoracotomy or video-assisted thoracoscopic surgery or coil embolization by catheterization is curative.

Coarctation of the Aorta

Coarctation of the aorta (Fig. 3–12) accounts for 8% of congenital heart defects and has a male-to-female pre-

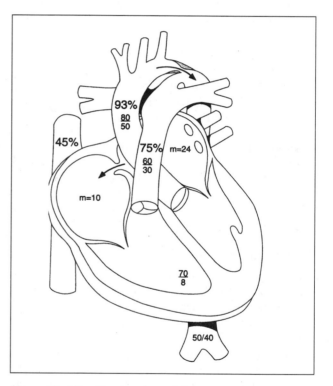

Figure 3–12 Coarctation of the aorta in a critically ill neonate with a nearly closed ductus arteriosus. Typical anatomic and hemodynamic findings include: (a) "juxtaductal" site of the coarctation; (b) a bicommissural aortic valve (see in 80% of patients with coarctation); (c) narrow pulse pressure in the descending aorta and lower body; (d) a bidirectional shunt at the ductus arteriosus. As in critical aortic stenosis (see Fig. 3–13) there is an elevated left atrial pressure, pulmonary edema, a left-to-right shunt at the atrial level, pulmonary artery hypertension and only a moderate (30-mm Hg) gradient across the arch obstruction. The low measured gradient (despite severe anatomic obstruction) across the aortic arch is due to low cardiac output.

dominance of 2:1. When coarctation of the aorta occurs in a female, Turner's syndrome must be considered. The obstruction is usually located in the descending aorta, at the insertion site of the ductus arteriosus. It may coexist with tubular hypoplasia of the aortic arch. The aortic valve is bicuspid in 80% of cases, and mitral valve anomalies may also be present. The coarctation results in mechanical obstruction between the proximal and distal aorta and in increased left ventricular afterload. Congestive heart failure develops in 10% of cases in infancy.

Clinical Manifestations
On examination, the femoral pulses are often weak and delayed relative to upper extremities—or are absent—and there is often upper extremity hypertension. Neonates with critical coarctation have ductal-dependent systemic blood flow and may present with circulatory collapse. Flow across the coarctation may produce a systolic ejection murmur heard at the apex. On chest radiograph, the aortic knob is enlarged; on ECG, right ventricular hypertrophy is seen in the neonate, and left ventricular hypertrophy is seen in the older child. The echocardiogram is used to visualize the defect and to check left ventricular performance.

Treatment
Repair is accomplished via balloon angioplasty or by surgical end-to-end anastomosis, subclavian flap repair, patch repair, or graft placement.

Aortic Stenosis
In aortic stenosis (Fig. 3–13), the valvular tissue is thickened and often rigid. Most commonly, the valve is bicuspid, with a single fused commissure and an eccentric orifice. The stenotic valve produces a pressure gradient between the left ventricle and the aorta that results in left ventricular hypertrophy and, over time, decreased compliance and ventricular performance.

Clinical Manifestations
The neonate with aortic stenosis may present with cardiovascular collapse or with a soft murmur. The level of symptomatology is related to the severity of the stenosis. The neonate with critical aortic stenosis has ductal-dependent systemic blood flow and may present with circulatory collapse after the ductus closes. A harsh systolic ejection murmur is heard at the right upper sternal border and is preceded by an ejection click heard best at the left lower sternal border. On chest radiograph,

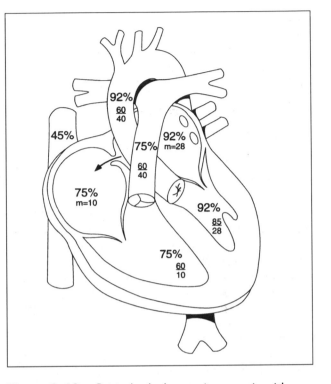

Figure 3–13 Critical valvular aortic stenosis with a closed ductus arteriosus. Typical anatomic and hemodynamic findings include: (a) a morphologically abnormal, stenotic valve; (b) poststenotic dilatation of the ascending aorta; (c) elevated left ventricular end diastolic pressure and left atrial pressures contributing to pulmonary edema (mild pulmonary venous and arterial desaturation); (d) a left-to-right shunt at the atrial level (note increase in oxygen saturation from superior vena cava to right atrium); (e) pulmonary artery hypertension (also secondary to the elevated left atrial pressure); (f) only a modest (25-mm Hg) gradient across valve. The low measured gradient (despite severe anatomic obstruction) across the aortic valve is due to a severely limited cardiac output, as evidenced by the low mixed venous oxygen saturation (45%) in the superior vena cava.

poststenotic dilatation of the ascending aorta is present, and in severe cases, pulmonary edema can be seen. The ECG may show left ventricular hypertrophy, and a strain pattern of ST depressions and inverted T waves may be seen. The valvular lesion, the degree of stenosis, and left ventricular function are all seen on echocardiogram.

Treatment

If intervention is required, relief of the aortic valve gradient may be accomplished by open surgical valvotomy or by balloon valvuloplasty. Both surgical valvotomy and balloon valvuloplasty may result in progressive aortic regurgitation that may require aortic valve replacement with a mechanical, homograft, or autograft valve (Ross procedure).

Pulmonic Stenosis

Pulmonic valve stenosis accounts for 5–8% of congenital heart defects. The pulmonary commissures are fused, the valve is domed and has a small central opening, and there is poststenotic dilatation of the main pulmonary artery. The valve is bicuspid or dysplastic in 10% of cases. Right ventricular hypertrophy occurs over time as the ventricle attempts to maintain cardiac output. In critical pulmonic stenosis, a decrease in the compliance of the right ventricle will increase right atrial pressure and may open the foramen ovale, producing a small right-to-left shunt.

Clinical Manifestations

Most patients are asymptomatic. Severe to critical pulmonary stenosis may cause dyspnea on exertion and angina. Right-sided congestive heart failure is rare, except in infants with critical pulmonic stenosis who may have ductal-dependent pulmonary blood flow. Characteristically, the ejection click of pulmonic stenosis varies with inspiration, and a harsh systolic ejection murmur is heard at the left upper sternal border. In severe stenosis, a thrill and right ventricular heave are palpable. On chest radiograph, heart size and pulmonary vascularity are normal, but the pulmonary artery segment is enlarged. On ECG, the degree of right ventricular hypertrophy and right-axis deviation correlates with the degree of stenosis. The transvalvular gradient and the degree of right ventricular hypertrophy can be measured by echocardiogram.

Treatment

Definitive treatment is accomplished by balloon valvuloplasty of the stenotic valve. Indications for pulmonary valvotomy include right ventricular pressure greater than 80% of left ventricular pressure or symptoms of right-sided congestive heart failure.

Thus far, this chapter has focused on the evaluation of the cyanotic neonate and the most common cyanotic and acyanotic congenital heart defects. Before moving to acquired structural heart disease, functional heart disease, arrhythmias, and shock, please see Table 3–5, which lists the classic findings for the 10 most common congenital heart lesions.

TABLE 3–5

Classic Findings for the 10 Most Common Congenital Heart Lesions

Lesion	Presentation	Physical Examination	ECG	X-ray
Ventricular septal defect	Murmur, CHF	Pansystolic murmur	LVH, RVH	+CE, ↑ PBF
Pulmonic stenosis	Murmur, ±cyanosis	Click, SEM	RVH	±CE, NL, or ↓ PBF
Tetralogy of Fallot	Murmur, cyanosis	SEM	RVH	±CE, ↓ PBF
Aortic stenosis	Murmur, ±CHF	Click, SEM	LVH	±CE, NL, PBF
Atrial septal defect	Murmur	Fixed split S$_2$	Mild RVH	±CE, ↑ PBF
Patent ductus	Murmur, ±CHF	Continuous murmur	LVH, ±RVH	±CE, ↑ PBF
Coarctation of aorta	Hypertension	↓Femoral pulses	LVH	±CE, NL, PBF
Transposition	Cyanosis	Marked cyanosis	RVH	±CE, NL, or ↑ PBF
AV canal defect	Murmur, ±CHF	Pansystolic murmur	"Superior" axis	±CE, ↑ PBF
Single ventricle	(Variable)	(Variable)	(Variable)	(Variable)

CE, cardiac enlargement; CHF, congestive heart failure; LVH, left ventricular hypertrophy; NL, normal; PBF, pulmonary blood flow; RVH, right ventricular hypertrophy; SEM, systolic ejection murmur.

Reprinted with permission from Graef JW, ed. Manual of pediatric therapeutics, 5th ed. Boston: Little, Brown, 1994.

ACQUIRED STRUCTURAL HEART DISEASE

Rheumatic Heart Disease

Rheumatic heart disease results from single or multiple episodes of acute rheumatic fever. Mitral regurgitation is the most common lesion found. Aortic insufficiency is also commonly found with or without mitral regurgitation. Mitral stenosis is less common and usually is the end result of multiple attacks of acute rheumatic fever. Least common is aortic stenosis. The tricuspid and pulmonary valves are almost never affected. Symptoms are proportional to the degree of valvular damage. Rheumatic fever is discussed in Chapter 12.

Kawasaki's Disease

Cardiac effects may include pericarditis, myocarditis, and transient rhythm disturbances. However, it is the development of coronary artery aneurysms, with their potential for occlusion or rupture, that makes the disease life-threatening. Coronary artery aneurysms develop during the subacute phase (11th to 25th day) in about 30% of cases but regress in most patients. Early therapy with intravenous immunoglobulin decreases the incidence of coronary artery aneurysms. High-dose aspirin therapy and intravenous immunoglobulin lessens the likelihood of late aneurysms. The echocardiogram is used to assess ventricular function and visualize pericardial fluid and coronary artery aneurysms. A thorough discussion of Kawasaki's disease is found in Chapter 11.

Endocarditis

Pathogenesis

Bacterial endocarditis, a microbial infection of the endocardium, is one of the most dreaded complications of structural heart disease. Although it may occur on normal valves, bacterial endocarditis is much more likely to occur on congenitally abnormal valves, valves damaged by rheumatic fever, acquired valvular lesions (mitral valve prolapse), prosthetic replacement valves, and as a consequence of jet streams of turbulent blood flow. Endocarditis is usually found on the low-pressure side of a turbulent lesion, because this is the easiest place for the bacteria to attach to the endocardial tissue.

In children, alpha hemolytic streptococci (*Streptococcus viridans*) and *Staphylococcus aureus* are the most common etiologic agents. *S. viridans* accounts for approximately 67% of the cases, whereas *S. aureus* is present in about 20% of cases. In vitro studies have shown these bacteria to have a propensity to adhere to human valves. When infection complicates cardiac surgery, *Staphylococcus epidermidis*, gram-negative bacilli, and fungi should be considered. Gram-negative organisms cause about 5% of cases of endocarditis in children. Neonates, immunocompromised patients, and intravenous drug abusers are at an increased risk for gram-negative bacterial endocarditis. Among the HACEK (*Haemophilus, Actinobacillus, Cardiobacterium, Eikenella, Kingella*) organisms, which are a rare cause of endocarditis, *H. influenzae* is the most common, frequently affecting previously damaged valves.

Risk Factors

Factors that may precipitate bacterial endocarditis include a previous episode of endocarditis, dental manipulation or infection, instrumentation of the gastrointestinal or genitourinary tract, intravenous drug abuse, an indwelling central venous catheter, and prior cardiac surgery. Cardiac surgery involving implantation of a prosthetic valve or creation of an aortopulmonary shunt places a child at an increased risk for bacterial endocarditis. Predisposing lesions with a moderate risk for bacterial endocarditis include uncorrected patent ductus arteriosus, VDS, uncorrected nonsecundum atrial septal defects, bicuspid aortic valve, mitral valve prolapse with regurgitation, rheumatic mitral or aortic valve disease, tetralogy of Fallot, aortic stenosis, and hypertrophic cardiomyopathy.

Clinical Manifestations

Fever is the most common finding in children with bacterial endocarditis. Often, a new or changing murmur is auscultated. Children with endocarditis usually display nonspecific symptoms such as chest pain, dyspnea, arthralgia, myalgia, headache, and malaise. Embolic phenomena such as hematuria with red cell casts and transient ischemic attack or stroke may be present. Other embolic phenomena such as Roth spots, splinter hemorrhages, petechiae, Osler nodes, and Janeway lesions are relatively rare in children with bacterial endocarditis. Splenomegaly is seen when the child has had the infection for several weeks or more. If the patient is an adolescent, inspect the skin for evidence of intravenous drug abuse. Bacterial endocarditis in the intravenous drug abuser usually involves the tricuspid valve.

Diagnostic Evaluation

Laboratory studies include a complete blood count, erythrocyte sedimentation rate (ESR), and urinalysis.

Four sets of blood cultures are obtained over 48 hours from different sites before antibiotic administration. In the seriously ill child, two sets of cultures may be obtained and then antibiotics may be started. Because bacteremia is continuous in endocarditis, there is no advantage to culturing only with temperature spikes. Positive blood cultures, an elevated ESR, hematuria, and anemia are most often found. An elevated white blood cell count with a left shift may or may not be present. The echocardiogram is used to define vegetations or thrombi in the heart. In most reported series, about 5% of cases of endocarditis are recorded as culture negative. When the blood cultures are negative, the presumptive diagnosis is based on the clinical syndrome.

Treatment

Treatment of culture-negative patients requires knowledge of the epidemiology and historic risk factors for that patient. Treatment of culture-positive patients is directed against the particular bacteria cultured. *S. viridans* is treated with penicillin G, and if a resistant species is present, gentamicin is added for synergy. Methicillin-susceptible staphylococcal species are treated with oxacillin, and methicillin-resistant staphylococcal species are eradicated with vancomycin. Therapy is continued for 4–8 weeks. Surgery is indicated for endocarditis when medical treatment is unsuccessful, refractory congestive heart failure exists, or there are serious embolic complications, myocardial abscess formation, or refractory prosthetic valve disease.

Prevention of endocarditis is necessary for all patients with structural congenital heart disease, rheumatic valve lesions, prosthetic heart valves, mitral valve prolapse with valve regurgitation, hypertrophic cardiomyopathy, transvenous pacemaker leads, and surgical systemic-to-pulmonary shunts and for patients with previous endocarditis. Antimicrobial prophylaxis is not indicated for an isolated secundum atrial septal defect, a repaired secundum atrial septal defect 6 months after patch placement, or a ligated patent ductus arteriosus 6 months after repair. Antibiotic regimens to prevent endocarditis during dental or respiratory procedures include oral amoxicillin or parenteral ampicillin and gentamicin. The latter recommendation is for high-risk patients, who are defined as children with prosthetic heart valves, systemic-to-pulmonary shunts, or previous endocarditis. Preventive treatment for gastrointestinal or genitourinary manipulation includes parenteral ampicillin and gentamicin or oral amoxicillin. Vancomycin can be added to gentamicin in penicillin-allergic patients.

◆ KEY POINTS ◆

1. Although bacterial endocarditis may occur on normal valves, it is much more likely to occur on congenitally abnormal valves, valves damaged by rheumatic fever, acquired valvular lesions (mitral valve prolapse), prosthetic replacement valves, and as a consequence of jet streams of turbulent blood flow.

2. Alpha hemolytic streptococci (*S. viridans*) and *S. aureus* are the most common etiologic agents.

Coronary Artery Disease

Coronary artery disease is rare in childhood, but the atherosclerotic process appears to begin early in life. There is evidence that progression of atherosclerotic lesions is influenced by genetic factors (familial hypercholesterolemia) and lifestyle (cigarette smoking; high-cholesterol, high-saturated-fat diet). Because many lifetime habits are formed during childhood, the opportunity exists to influence young people to adopt healthy ones.

FUNCTIONAL HEART DISEASE

Myocarditis

Most cases of myocarditis in North America result from enterovirus infection of the myocardium, predominantly coxsackie B virus and echovirus. It is unclear whether myocardial damage from viral myocarditis results from direct viral invasion or an autoimmune antibody response.

Clinical Manifestations

Depending on the degree of damage to the myocardium, patients may be asymptomatic, and the diagnosis is made only by finding ST and T wave changes on an ECG done for an unrelated reason, whereas others may present with fulminant congestive heart failure. Common symptoms include fever, dyspnea, palpitations, and chest pain (usually due to a secondary pericarditis). Signs include tachycardia, evidence of congestive heart failure, and S3 ventricular gallop. The ECG often reveals ST segment depression and T wave inversion, as well as arrhythmias and conduction defects. The chest radiograph varies from mild to marked cardiomegaly. Echocardiogram denotes dilated and/or hypocontractile ventricles. Pericardial effusion may be present. Endomyocardial biopsy may be indicated in select cases to confirm diagnosis. Viral etiology should be evaluated by obtaining viral cultures from the throat, stool, blood, and pericardial fluid if present.

Treatment

Therapy for patients with viral myocarditis is supportive to maintain perfusion and oxygenation. Treat arrhythmias, conduction abnormalities, and congestive heart failure as needed. Corticosteroids are contraindicated in the acute phase of viral myocarditis. The prognosis for patients with myocarditis depends on the extent of myocardial damage.

Dilated Cardiomyopathy

Dilated or congestive cardiomyopathy is characterized by myocardial dysfunction and ventricular dilatation. Although usually an idiopathic disorder, it can be caused by neuromuscular disease (Duchenne muscular dystrophy) or drug toxicity (doxorubicin or adriamycin). Dilation of the left ventricle results in congestive heart failure. An increase in left atrial pressure, pulmonary venous pressure, and pulmonary capillary wedge pressure results in pulmonary edema.

Clinical Manifestations

Symptoms include dyspnea, orthopnea, and paroxysmal nocturnal dyspnea. Eventually, right heart failure with dependent edema occurs, and a pulsus alternans may be noted. On cardiac examination, a right ventricular heave and a ventricular gallop are found. The ECG reveals rhythm disturbances, left ventricular hypertrophy, and nonspecific ST and T wave ischemic changes. Left ventricular function is evaluated by echocardiogram.

Treatment

Medical therapy includes inotropic agents to improve left ventricular function and vasodilators to decrease afterload. Diuretics decrease preload, and antiarrhythmic medications are used to control potentially fatal rhythm disturbances. If medical therapy fails, a heart transplant is performed.

Hypertrophic Cardiomyopathy

Also known as idiopathic hypertrophic subaortic stenosis, hypertrophic cardiomyopathy is an autosomal dominant genetic disorder in which the ventricular septum is thickened, resulting in left ventricular outflow tract obstruction. In the thickened stiff left ventricle, diastolic function is well preserved, but systolic function is compromised. Abnormal motion of the mitral valve results in mitral insufficiency.

Clinical Manifestations

Symptoms include dyspnea on exertion, chest pain, and syncope. There is often a bisferious pulse (double peaked) because ejection is hindered by septal obstruction, a ventricular gallop (S3), and murmurs indicative of mitral regurgitation and left ventricular outflow tract obstruction. ECG illustrates left-axis deviation, left ventricular hypertrophy, and possible ST- and T-wave changes consistent with ischemia or strain. Echocardiogram is diagnostic.

Treatment

Therapy is centered around preventing fatal arrhythmias and decreasing the stiffness of the left ventricle with negative inotropic medications, such as calcium channel blockers, and beta-adrenergic blocking agents. The avoidance of competitive sports is essential because sudden death during exertion is a significant risk.

◆ KEY POINTS ◆

1. Most cases of myocarditis in North America result from enterovirus infection of the myocardium.

2. Patients most typically present with fever, dyspnea, palpitations, chest pain, tachycardia, congestive heart failure, and ST-segment depression and T-wave inversion.

3. Dilated or congestive cardiomyopathy is characterized by myocardial dysfunction and ventricular dilatation; it is usually idiopathic.

4. Medical therapy for dilated cardiomyopathy includes inotropic agents to improve left ventricular function and vasodilators to decrease afterload. Diuretics decrease preload, and antiarrhythmic medications are used to control potentially fatal rhythm disturbances.

5. In hypertrophic cardiomyopathy, the ventricular septum is thickened, resulting in left ventricular outflow tract obstruction. An echocardiogram is diagnostic.

6. Therapy for hypertrophic cardiomyopathy is centered around preventing fatal arrhythmias and decreasing the stiffness of the left ventricle with negative inotropic medications.

ARRHYTHMIAS

Arrhythmias in children are much less common than in adults but can be just as life threatening. Arrhythmias result from disorders of impulse formation, impulse conduction, or both and are generally classified as follows:

Bradyarrhythmias

- Depressed pacemaker activity
- Conduction block

Tachyarrhythmias

- Narrow QRS complex supraventricular tachycardia
- Wide QRS complex ventricular or complex supraventricular tachycardia

Premature beats

- Atrial
- Ventricular

Bradyarrhythmias are the result of either depressed automaticity or block of an impulse, whereas tachyarrhythmias or premature beats arise from abnormal impulse formation caused by enhanced automaticity, reentry, or triggered activity. Arrhythmias may result from congenital, functional, or acquired structural heart disease; electrolyte disturbances (potassium, calcium, and magnesium); drug toxicity; poisoning; or an acquired systemic disorder. A list of etiologies predisposing children to arrhythmias is listed in Table 3–6.

Bradyarrhythmias

As already stated, bradyarrhythmias result from depressed pacemaker activity or conduction block. Bradycardias due to a depressed pacemaker include sinus bradycardia and sick sinus syndrome, and bradycardias due to conduction block include first-degree heart block, second-degree heart block, and third-degree (complete) heart block. Second-degree heart block is further divided into Mobitz type I block (Wenckebach), Mobitz type II block, and fixed-ratio arteriovenous (AV) block.

Differential Diagnosis

Figure 3–14 shows the rhythm strips of various bradycardias. **Sinus bradycardia** is associated with increased vagal tone, hypoxia, central nervous system disorders with increased intracranial pressure, hypothyroidism, hyperkalemia, hypothermia, drug intoxication (digitalis, beta-blockers, calcium channel blockers) and prior atrial surgery. It is also a normal finding in healthy athletic teenagers. The ECG reveals a normal P wave with nor-

---

TABLE 3–6

Factors Predisposing to Dysrhythmias

Congenital heart disease
    Supraventricular dysrhythmias: Ebstein anomaly (may also present with WPW syndrome), atrial septal defects, atrial surgery, L-transposition of the great arteries (may also present with heart block), after Fontan operation
    Ventricular dysrhythmias: aortic valve disease, pulmonary valve disease, after tetralogy of Fallot repair, anomalous left coronary artery (may also present with heart block)
    Heart block (varying degrees): after open-heart surgery, atrial septal defect, total anomalous pulmonary venous return, Ebstein's anomaly
Isolated conduction system disorders
    WPW syndrome
    Prolonged QT interval syndromes
    Maternal history of collagen vascular disease (systemic lupus erythematosus)
Associated with systemic illness
    Infectious myocarditis
    Kawasaki disease (mucocutaneous lymph node syndrome)
    Idiopathic dilated or hypertrophic cardiomyopathy
    Friedreich's ataxia (atrial tachycardia or fibrillation)
    Muscular dystrophies (Duchenne, periodic paralysis)
    Glycogen storage diseases (Pompe disease)
    Collagen vascular diseases (rheumatic carditis, rheumatic arthritis, lupus, periarteritis nodosa, dermatomyositis)
    Endocrine disorders (hyperthyroidism, adrenal dysfunction)
    Metabolic and electrolyte disturbances (hyperkalemia, hypocalcemia, hypoxia, beriberi)
Drug toxicity
    Chemotherapeutic agents (adriamycin)
    Tricyclic antidepressants
    Cocaine
    Digitalis, beta-adrenergic blockers
    Asthma medications (sympathomimetics, aminophylline)
Other causes
    Blunt chest trauma (myocardial contusion)
    Increased intracranial pressure

Reprinted with permission from Nichols DG, et al. Golden hour: the handbook of advanced pediatric life support, 2nd ed. St. Louis: Mosby Yearbook, 1996.

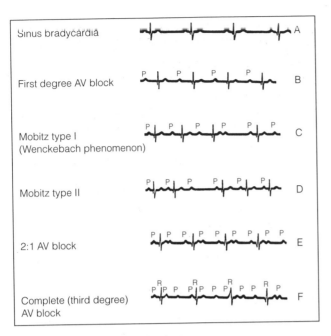

Figure 3–14 Bradyarrhythmias.

mal AV conduction at rates less than 100 bpm in the neonate and 60 bpm in the older child. Escape rhythms of atrial, junctional, or ventricular origin may be seen.

Sick sinus syndrome refers to severe sinus node dysfunction that manifests itself as acute pauses and bradycardia with bursts of supraventricular tachycardia (SVT). If SVT bursts are present, the phenomenon is called tachy-brady syndrome. It usually occurs several years after open-heart surgery that involves suture lines in the atrium. The ECG shows slow atrial or junctional rhythms. Episodic SVT (atrial fibrillation or atrial flutter) is seen on ECG accompanying the bradycardia in tachy-brady syndrome.

First-degree heart block is associated with increased vagal tone, digitalis and beta-blocker administration, congenital heart disease (atrial septal defect, atrioventricular canal defect, Ebstein's anomaly, and corrected transposition), rheumatic fever, and cardiomyopathy. On ECG, the PR interval is prolonged for age (more than 0.14 second for infants, more than 0.16 second for children, and more than 0.18 second for adolescents). The rhythm is regular, originates in the sinus node, and has a normal QRS morphology.

Second-degree heart block refers to episodic interruption of AV nodal conduction:

- **Mobitz type I (Wenckebach)** denotes progressive prolongation of the PR interval over several beats until a QRS is dropped. This cycle repeats itself often, although the number of beats in a cycle may not be constant. The QRS configuration is normal. Etiologies for this rhythm are the same as those for first-degree heart block.

- **Mobitz type II** is caused by a problem in the bundle of His–Purkinje fiber system. Unlike first- or second-degree heartblock, Mobitz type II results from AV nodal dysfunction. It is a more serious bradycardia than first-degree heart block or Wenckebach because it can progress to complete heart block. On ECG, there is sudden AV conduction failure with a dropped QRS after a normal P wave. No preceding PR interval prolongation is seen in normal conducted impulses.

- **Fixed-ratio AV block** is an arrhythmia in which the QRS complex follows only after every second (third or fourth) P wave, causing 2:1 (3:1 or 4:1) AV block. There is a normal PR interval in conducted beats. There is usually a normal or slightly prolonged QRS. Fixed-ratio block results from either AV node or His bundle injury, and intracardiac recordings are required to distinguish the site of injury. Patients may progress to complete heart block.

Third-degree heart block occurs when no atrial impulses are conducted to the ventricles. The atrial rhythm and rate are normal for the patient's age, and the ventricular rate is slowed markedly (40–55 bpm). If an escape rhythm arises from the AV node (junctional rhythm), the QRS interval (idioventricular rhythm) is of normal duration, but if an escape rhythm arises from the distal His bundle or Purkinje fibers, the QRS interval is prolonged. Congenital complete AV block can be an isolated abnormality or can be associated with corrected transposition of the great arteries, atrioventricular canal defect, or maternal collagen vascular disease. Other causes include open-heart surgery (especially after large ventricular septal defect closure), cardiomyopathy, or Lyme disease. Newborns with congenital complete heart block may present with hydrops fetalis. They suffer an increased risk of dying during the first year of life, especially if the ventricular rate is less than 55 bpm and/or the QRS is widened. Complete heart block in the postoperative period is usually transient and lasts for up to 2 weeks.

Treatment

No intervention is necessary for sinus bradycardia if cardiac output is maintained. A management algorithm for sinus bradycardia is shown in Figure 3–15. Symptomatic bradycardia resulting from sick sinus syndrome is treated the same as sinus bradycardia. Long-term management for sick sinus syndrome involves pacemaker implantation.

No treatment is necessary for first- or second-degree heart block (Mobitz type I). Mobitz type II, fixed-ratio AV block, and third-degree heart block all require pacemaker placement. In Mobitz type II and fixed-ratio AV block, prophylactic pacemaker insertion is essential to avert complete long-term heart block.

By definition, complete heart block requires transcu-

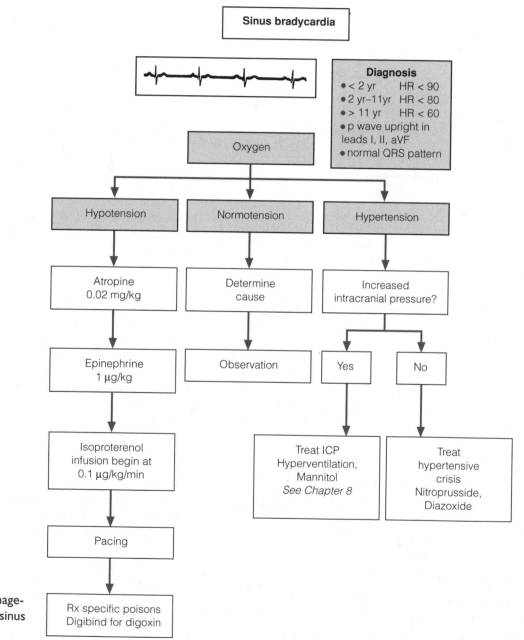

Figure 3–15 Management algorithm for sinus bradycardia.

taneous or transvenous pacing acutely as well as long-term pacemaker placement. Third-degree heart block is managed with either ventricular demand pacing or AV sequential pacing. Figure 3–16 is a management algorithm for AV block.

Tachyarrhythmias

Narrow-complex tachycardias have a QRS morphology similar or identical to that of normal sinus rhythm. They include most, but not all, SVTs (some complex SVTs have a widened QRS). Narrow-complex tachycardias include sinus tachycardia, paroxysmal SVT (AV node re-entry tachycardia, automatic ectopic atrial tachycardia, "orthodromic" WPW syndrome), atrial fibrillation, and atrial flutter. Narrow-complex tachycardias are relatively well tolerated acutely.

Conversely, wide-complex tachycardias, with a QRS more than 0.12 second, are a medical emergency. They include ventricular tachycardia, ventricular fibrillation, and complex SVT (Wolff-Parkinson-White (WPW)

syndrome with antidromic conduction and SVT with aberrancy).

Differential Diagnosis

Figure 3–17 shows the rhythm strips of the various tachycardias, and Table 3–7 shows the rates and characteristics of common tachyarrhythmias. Causes of each tachyarrhythmia are as follows:

Narrow complex tachycardias

- Sinus tachycardia—fever, stress, dehydration, and anemia;

- SVT—most cases are idiopathic, WPW syndrome, Ebstein's anomaly, L-transposition of the great arteries;

- Atrial flutter—atrial surgery, myocarditis, structural heart disease with dilated atria (Ebstein's anomaly, TA, rheumatic heart disease of the mitral valve);

- Atrial fibrillation—most often seen with left atrial enlargement (rheumatic heart disease of the mitral

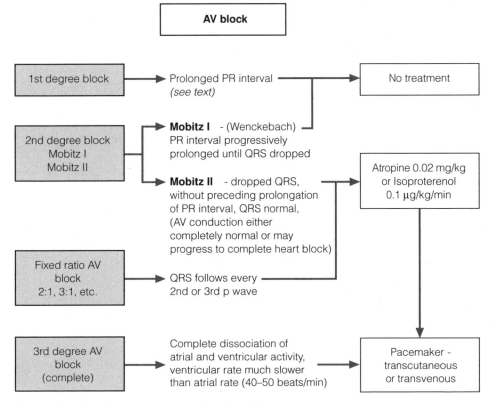

Figure 3–16 Management algorithm for AV block.

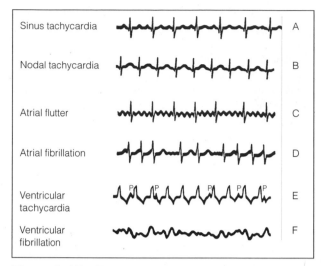

Figure 3–17 Tachydysrhythmias.

valve, VSD, systemic or pulmonary palliative shunt placement); other causes that result in right atrial or biatrial enlargement include atrial septal defect, Ebstein's anomaly, WPW syndrome, and myocarditis.

Wide-complex tachycardia

- Ventricular tachycardia—severe congenital or acquired heart disease, drug ingestion, or WPW;
- Ventricular fibrillation—terminal rhythm that develops after hypoxia, ischemia, or high-voltage electrical injury; predisposing factors include WPW syndrome and long QT syndrome.

Treatment
Narrow-Complex Tachycardia

Treatment of sinus tachycardia involves correcting the underlying cause of the tachycardia. Figure 3–18 outlines a management algorithm for supraventricular tachycardia. Treatment for stable SVT progresses from vagal

TABLE 3–7

The Rates of Characteristics of Common Tachydysrhythmias

	Rate		Characteristics		
Rhythm	Atrial	Ventricular	Atrial Activity	Ventricular Activity	AV Conduction
Supraventricular tachycardia	150–350, regular	150–350, regular	Often not seen, or P wave may be in QRS or T	Normal or right bundle	1:1
Atrial flutter	250–350, regular	125–350, regular	Saw-tooth flutter waves in II, III, AVF	Normal	1:1, 2:1, or 3:1
Atrial fibrillation	300–600, irregular	100–350, irregular	Irregular fibrillation waves	Normal, bundle branch block, or bizarre	Varying
Ventricular tachycardia	Equals ventricular rate or less, regular	150–300, regular	Can be retrograde and inverted or normal	Bizarre, regular	1:1 retrograde or no relation
Ventricular fibrillation	—	100–300 irregular	—	Bizarre, irregular	—

Reprinted with permission from Nichols DG, et al. Golden hour: the handbook of advanced pediatric life support. St. Louis: Mosby Yearbook, 1991.

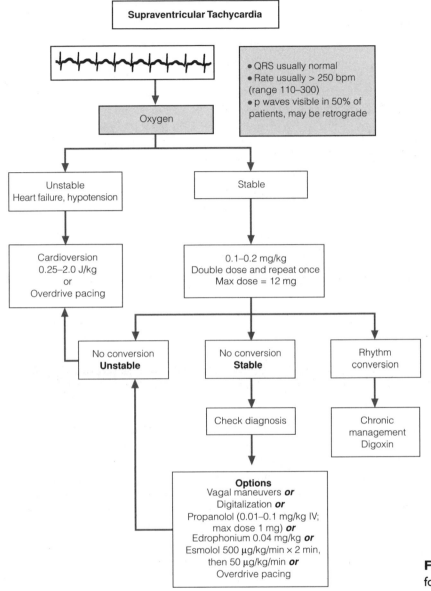

Figure 3–18 Management algorithm for supraventricular tachycardia.

maneuvers to pharmacotherapy to cardioversion. Vagal maneuvers enhance vagal tone to slow conduction in the AV node and often result in termination of the arrhythmia. Vagal tone is increased by applying ice to the face in infants and through carotid massage in older children. Ocular compression should be avoided because it can result in permanent eye damage. If vagal maneuvers are ineffective in stable SVT, adenosine is given to break the arrhythmia. If adenosine returns the child to normal si-

nus rhythm, the child is started on digoxin to reduce the risk of future events. If adenosine reveals WPW syndrome, use a beta-blocker, because the use of digoxin can speed up conduction over the accessory pathway and result in a ventricular arrhythmia. For this reason, digoxin should be avoided in WPW syndrome, and propranolol or cardioversion should be used to break the tachy-arrhythmia. When unstable SVT is present and the patient has congestive heart failure or hypotension, cardioversion or transesophageal overdrive pacing is indicated. Synchronized cardioversion is required to avoid the inadvertent development of ventricular fibrillation.

In unstable atrial flutter, synchronized cardioversion or overdrive pacing is used when rapid intervention is necessary because of congestive heart failure. Once cardioversion has occurred, digoxin, beta-blockers, or a quinidine/digoxin combination is given to help prevent recurrence. If the child is hemodynamically stable, he or she should be loaded with digoxin and then given quinidine and procainamide to attempt to convert the arrhythmia. It is critical to load with digoxin before giving quinidine or procainamide, because these drugs have vagolytic activity that could inadvertently increase the ventricular rate and cause acute hemodynamic deterioration.

If atrial fibrillation presents for more than a few days, anticoagulation is needed before converting the rhythm to decrease the risk of embolization of atrial clots. Digoxin decreases AV conduction, slows the rate, and occasionally converts the rhythm. Quinidine or procainamide is often effective in converting atrial fibrillation, and both are good long-term maintenance drugs. Synchronized cardioversion converts most cases to sinus rhythm.

Wide-Complex Tachycardia

Treat wide-complex ventricular tachycardia due to complex SVT (WPW syndrome with antidromic conduction or SVT with aberrancy) as though the patient has ventricular tachycardia. Hypotensive or unresponsive patients should be treated immediately with cardiopulmonary resuscitation (CPR) and synchronized cardioversion. After cardioversion, sinus rhythm can be maintained with intravenous lidocaine. Normotensive patients with acute onset ventricular tachycardia can be treated with intravenous lidocaine, procainamide, and/ or bretylium in an attempt to break the arrhythmia without cardioversion.

Children with ventricular fibrillation should receive CPR and must be defibrillated with nonsynchronized cardioversion. Giving epinephrine may turn fine fibrillation into coarse fibrillation and allow successful defibrillation. The management algorithms for both ventricular tachycardia and ventricular fibrillation/pulseless ventricular tachycardia are outlined in Figure 3–19 and Figure 3–20, respectively.

◆ KEY POINTS ◆

1. Bradyarrhythmias with widened QRS complexes are likely escape rhythms from the His bundle or Purkinje system and are at high risk for progression to complete heart block.

2. Symptomatic sick sinus syndrome, second-degree heart block (Mobitz type II and fixed-ratio AV block), and third-degree heart block all need pacing.

3. Narrow-complex tachycardias tend to be well-tolerated acutely, whereas wide-complex tachycardias are considered a medical emergency.

4. Treat wide-complex tachycardia due to complex SVT (WPW or SVT with aberrancy) as though the patient has ventricular tachycardia.

5. When treating SVT, rule out WPW, because the treatment for WPW is different from that for simple SVT.

SHOCK

Shock is a syndrome of acute hemostatic derangement involving multiple organ systems, which results in failure of cellular metabolism. The final common pathway to all the etiologies of shock is hypotension, which leads to cellular hypoperfusion, metabolic acidosis, and cellular death. Three relationships explain hypotension in shock:

- **Blood pressure** = cardiac output × systemic vascular resistance;
- **Cardiac output** = stroke volume × heart rate;
- **Stroke volume** is determined by preload (ventricular end diastolic volume), afterload (systemic vascular resistance), and myocardial contractility.

The three stages in shock are: compensated, uncompensated, and irreversible. In the compensated stage, homeostatic mechanisms maintain essential organ perfusion. Blood pressure, urine output, and cardiac function all seem to be normal. In the uncompensated stage, homeostatic mechanisms fail because of ischemia, endothelial injury, and the elaboration of toxic materials. Eventually,

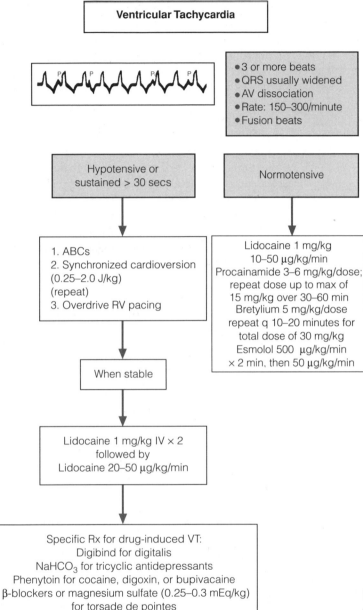

Figure 3–19 Management algorithm for ventricular tachycardia.

cellular function deteriorates and widespread abnormalities occur in all organ systems. When this process has caused irreparable functional loss in essential organs and death is inevitable, the terminal or irreversible stage of shock is reached.

The types of shock include hypovolemic, cardiogenic, distributive, and septic. Hypovolemic shock results from decreased intravascular volume, which results in decreased venous return and myocardial preload. Because of the reduction in myocardial preload, there is a resultant decrease in stroke volume, cardiac output, and blood pressure. This is the most common etiology of shock in children. Cardiogenic shock is the result of "pump failure." Inadequate stroke volume results in diminished cardiac output and hypotension. Distributive shock results from an abnormality in vasomotor tone that leads

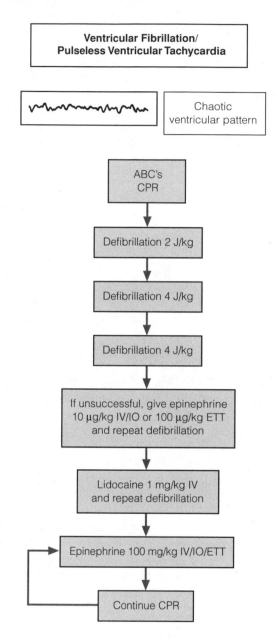

Figure 3–20 Management algorithm for ventricular fibrillation.

to maldistribution of a normal circulatory volume and a state of relative hypovolemia, which, if severe enough, may cause shock. Because of peripheral pooling, preload is reduced, causing a decreased stroke volume and cardiac output. Systemic vascular resistance is also decreased due to vasomotor dysfunction. Because both systemic vascular resistance and cardiac output are reduced, severe hypotension results. Septic shock results when certain pathogens infect the blood. All three mechanisms just mentioned play a role in septic shock. The early compensated stage of septic shock is characterized by decreased vascular resistance (distributive shock), whereas in the late uncompensated phase, hypovolemia from third spacing and pump failure due to myocardial depression become more apparent. Compensated septic shock is called "warm" sepsis, and uncompensated septic shock is referred to "cold" sepsis.

Differential Diagnosis

The etiologies of each type of shock are listed below:

Hypovolemic

- Water and electrolyte losses—vomiting, diarrhea, diabetes insipidus, renal losses, heat stroke, intestinal obstruction, burns;
- Hemorrhage—trauma, surgery, gastrointestinal bleeding;
- Plasma losses (third spacing)—burns, nephrotic syndrome, sepsis, intestinal obstruction, peritonitis, pancreatitis.

Cardiogenic

- Congenital heart disease—HLHS, interrupted aortic arch, critical coarctation of the aorta, critical aortic stenosis, cortical mitral stenosis, critical pulmonic stenosis;
- Ischemic heart disease—anomalous coronary artery, Kawasaki's disease;
- Cardiomyopathies—dilated hypertrophic, infectious, radiation, chemotherapy;
- Arrhythmias—SVT, junctional ectopic tachycardia;
- Infectious—myocarditis, sepsis;
- Other causes—trauma, asphyxia, hypothermia, drug toxicity, tamponade, hypoglycemia.

Distributive

- Anaphylaxis;
- Neurologic injury (head injury, spinal cord injury);
- Drug toxicity (barbiturates, phenothiazines, antihypertensives, benzodiazepines);
- Sepsis.

Septic

- Infection (see Table 3–8 for list of pathogens that cause septic shock).

Miscellaneous

- Pulmonary embolism (blood, air, fat);
- Adrenal insufficiency.

TABLE 3–8

Common Pathogens That Can Cause Septic Shock

Neonates
    Group B β-hemolytic streptococci
    Enterobacteriaceae
    Listeria monocytogenes
    Staphylococcus aureus
    Herpes simplex
Infants
    Haemophilus influenzae
    Streptococcus pneumoniae
    Staphylococcus aureus
Children
    Streptococcus pneumoniae
    Neisseria meningitidis
    Staphylococcus aureus
    Enterobacteriaceae
    Haemophilus influenzae
Immunocompromised
    Enterobacteriaceae
    Staphylococcus aureus
    Pseudomonadaceae
    Candida albicans

Reprinted with permission from Rogers MC, Herfaer MA, eds. Handbook of pediatric intensive care, 2nd ed. Baltimore: Williams & Wilkins, 1995.

Clinical Manifestations

History and Physical Examination

The history focuses on potential causes. Consider hypovolemic shock if there is a history of vomiting, diarrhea, polyuria, burns, trauma, surgery, gastrointestinal bleeding, intestinal obstruction, long periods in the sun, or pancreatitis. A history of congenital heart disease, arrhythmias, or chemotherapy (adriamycin) administration may indicate cardiogenic shock. Distributive shock should be contemplated when there is a history of toxic ingestion, anaphylaxis, or head or spinal cord injury.

Serial vital signs are critical in the diagnosis and management of children with shock. Symptoms of hypovolemic, cardiogenic, and late "cold" uncompensated septic shock include vasoconstriction, tachycardia, cold extremities, poor peripheral pulses, altered consciousness, pallor, sweating, ileus, and oliguria. This is contrasted by distributive and early "warm" compensated septic shock in which vasodilation, warm extremities, tachycardia, a widened pulse pressure, and adequate urine output are seen.

Diagnostic Evaluation

During the stabilization period, the clinician must determine into which category of shock the patient's illness falls. Any patient with shock should be placed on a cardiac monitor. The level of tachycardia is the best determinant of the level of intravascular depletion or vasomotor abnormality. Hypotension is a late finding and occurs only after 40% of the intravascular volume has been depleted. Diagnostic tests are determined on the basis of the specific causes suspected. Echocardiograms are helpful to rule out cardiogenic shock. If an infectious etiology is suspected, the appropriate cultures should be obtained. For hypovolemic shock resulting from vomiting or diarrhea, obtaining an electrolyte panel is necessary to determine the appropriate rehydration fluid.

Treatment

The treatment of shock is aimed at ensuring perfusion of critical vascular beds (coronary, cerebral, renal) and preventing or correcting metabolic abnormalities arising from cellular hypoperfusion. Hypoxemia is treated to limit or reduce the level of metabolic acidosis. Correcting metabolic acidosis results in better cellular function, myocardial performance, and decreased systemic and pulmonary vascular resistance.

Hypovolemic shock is treated with normal saline or lactated Ringer's solution (see Chapter 7 for details). If hemorrhage is the cause of the hypovolemia, type O or crossmatched whole blood or packed red cells may be given in addition to fluid. In cardiogenic shock from congenital heart defect surgery, balloon angioplasty or valvotomy may be indicated. Children with severe ischemic injury to the heart and myocarditis may need a heart transplant. In distributive shock due to anaphylaxis intravenous steroids, benadryl, subcutaneous epinephrine, and albuterol nebulizers are needed. Sometimes intubation for laryngospasm and vasopressors for intractable hypotension are needed. Septic shock is treated with vasopressors, fluids, and antibiotics. Antibiotics are considered a resuscitation medication for septic shock.

◆ KEY POINTS ◆

1. Determine the category of shock and whether the patient has early or late manifestations.

2. Hypovolemic shock accounts for most cases of shock.

3. In hypovolemic shock, blood pressure depression is a late finding, and the level of tachycardia is the most sensitive measure of intravascular fluid status.

4. In septic shock, antibiotics are a resuscitation medication and their administration should not be delayed.

4 Development

DEVELOPMENTAL MILESTONES

Neurologic, intellectual, and physical development in infants and children occurs in an orderly and sequential manner. Table 4–1 lists the normal progression of developmental milestones. The information is subdivided into gross motor, visual motor (same as fine motor–adaptive), language, and social milestones.

The two developmental screens most commonly used by pediatricians include the Denver II developmental screening test and the Clinical Adaptive Test (CAT)/ Clinical Linguistic and Auditory Milestone Scale (CLAMS). The Denver II divides streams of development into gross motor, fine motor–adaptive, language, and personal-social. The CAT rates problem-solving and visual motor ability, and the CLAMS assesses language development from birth to 36 months of age.

Sometimes the developmental process does not progress appropriately, and developmental disabilities may be suspected. Abnormal development can be subdivided into the phenomena of developmental delay, dissociation, and deviancy. **Developmental delay** refers to a performance significantly below average in a given skill area. A **developmental quotient** (DQ) below 70 constitutes developmental delay. **Developmental dissociation** refers to a substantial difference in the rate of development between two skill areas. An example of a developmental discrepancy between gross motor and language development is the child with isolated mental retardation whose gross motor development is normal. **Developmental deviancy** refers to nonsequential development within a given area of skill. For example, the development of hand preference at 12 months is a departure from normal sequence and may be related to an abnormality of the other extremity. The DQ reflects the child's rate of development: DQ = (developmental age ÷ chronological age) × 100.

Language is the best indicator of future intellectual achievement. Language development is divided into two streams, receptive and expressive, each assigned a separate DQ. Table 4–2 lists some rules of thumb in language screening.

THEORIES OF DEVELOPMENT

There are many different theories on development, yet the work of Erikson, Freud, and Piaget is deemed the most important and influential (Table 4–3). Erikson's ideas revolve around psychosocial development, whereas Freud's ideology centers on psychosexual development. Cognitive development is the thrust of Piaget's work (Table 4–4).

SEXUAL DEVELOPMENT

Adolescence refers to the passage from childhood to adulthood, whereas puberty refers to those biologic

TABLE 4–1

Developmental Milestones

Age	Gross Motor	Visual Motor	Language	Social
1 mo	Raises head slightly from prone, makes crawling movements, lifts chin up	Has tight grasp, follows to midline	Alerts to sound (e.g., by blinking, moving, startling)	Regards face
2 mo	Holds head in midline, lifts chest off table	No longer clenches fist tightly, follows object past midline	Smiles after being stroked or talked to	Recognizes parent
3 mo	Supports on forearms in prone, holds head up steadily	Holds hands open at rest, follows in circular fashion	Coos (produces long vowel sounds in musical fashion)	Reaches for familiar people or objects, anticipates feeding
4–5 mo	Rolls front to back and back to front, sits well when propped, supports on wrists and shifts weight	Moves arms in unison to grasp, touches cube placed on table	4 mo: orients to voice 5 mo: orients to bell (localizes laterally), says "ah-goo," razzes	Enjoys looking around environment
6 mo	Sits well unsupported, puts feet in mouth in supine position	Reaches with either hand, transfers, uses raking grasp	6 mo: babbles 7 mo: orients to bell (localized indirectly) 8 mo: "dada/mama" indiscriminately	Recognizes strangers
9 mo	Creeps, crawls, cruises, pulls to stand, pivots when sitting	Uses pincer grasp, probes with forefinger, holds bottle, fingerfeeds	9 mo: Understands "no," waves bye-bye 10 mo: "dada/mama" discriminately; orients to bell (directly) 11 mo: one word other than "dada/mama"; follows one-step command with gesture	Starts to explore environment; plays pat-a-cake
12 mo	Walks alone	Throws objects, lets go of toys, hand release, uses mature pincer grasp	12 mo: uses two words other than "dada/mama," immature jargoning (runs several unintelligible words together). 13 mo: uses three words 14 mo: follows one-step command without gesture	Imitates actions, comes when called, cooperates with dressing
15 mo	Creeps upstairs, walks backward	Builds tower of two blocks in imitation with examiner, scribbles in imitation	15 mo: uses 4–6 words 17 mo: knows 7–20 words, points to five body parts, uses mature jargoning (includes intelligible words in jargoning)	
18 mo	Runs, throws toy from standing without falling	Turns two to three pages at a time, fills spoon and feeds himself	19 mo: knows eight body parts	Copies parent in tasks (sweeping, dusting); plays in company of other children

TABLE 4–1 (continued)

Developmental Milestones

Age	Gross Motor	Visual Motor	Language	Social
21 mo	Squats in play, goes up steps	Builds tower of five blocks, drinks well from cup	Uses two-word combinations, uses 50 words, and two-word sentences	Asks to have food and to go to toilet
24 mo	Walks up and down steps without help	Turns pages one at a time, removes shoes, pants, etc.; imitates stroke with a pencil	Uses pronouns (I, you, me) inappropriately, understands two-step commands	Parallel play
30 mo	Jumps with both feet off floor, throws ball overhand	Unbuttons, holds pencil in adult fashion, differentiates horizontal and vertical line	Uses pronouns appropriately, understands concept of "I," repeats two digits forward	Tells first and last names when asked; gets self drink without help
3 yr	Pedals tricycle, can alternate feet when going up steps	Dresses and undresses partially, dries hands if reminded, draws a circle	Uses three-word sentences, uses plurals and past tense; knows all pronouns; minimum 250 words; understands concept of "2"	Group play, shares toys, takes turns, plays well with others, knows full name, age, sex
4 yr	Hops, skips, alternates feet going downstairs	Buttons clothing fully, catches ball	Knows colors, says song or poem from memory, asks questions	Tells "tall tales," plays cooperatively with a group of children
5 yr	Skips alternating feet, jumps over low obstacles	Ties shoes, spreads with knife	Prints first name, asks what a word means	Plays competitive games, abides by rules, likes to help in household tasks

Reprinted with permission from Johnson KB, ed. The Harriet Lane handbook, 13th ed. St. Louis, Mosby Year Book, 1993:136–138.

TABLE 4–2

Rules of Thumb for Language Screening

Age (yr)	Speech Production	Articulation (Amount of Speech Understood by a Stranger)	Following Commands
1	1–3 words		1-step commands
2	2- to 3-word phrases	$1/2$	2-step commands
3	Routine use of sentences	$3/4$	
4	Routine use of sentence sequences; conversational give-and-take	Almost all	
5	Complex sentences; extensive use of modifiers, pronouns, and prepositions	Almost all	

Reprinted with permission from Behrman RE, Kliegman RM, eds. Essentials of pediatrics, 2nd ed. Philadelphia: WB Saunders, 1994:24.

TABLE 4–3

Stage Theories of Socioemotional Development

	Birth–18 mo	18 mo–3 yr	3–6 yr	6–12 yr	Adult
Erikson (Psychosocial development)	**Trust vs Mistrust** Infants learn to trust, or mistrust, that their needs will be met by the world, especially by the mother.	**Autonomy vs Shame, Doubt** Children learn to exercise will, to make choices, to control themselves, or they become uncertain and doubt that they can do things by themselves.	**Initiative vs. Guilt** Children learn to initiate activities and enjoy their accomplishments, acquiring direction and purpose. If they are not allowed initiative, they feel guilty for their attempts at independence.	**Industry vs. Inferiority** Children develop a sense of industry and curiosity and are eager to learn, or they feel inferior and lose interest in the tasks before them.	**Identity vs. Role Confusion** Adolescents come to see themselves as unique and integrated persons with an ideology, or they become confused about what they want out of life.
Freud (Psychosexual development)	**Oral Stage** Infants obtain gratification through stimulation of the mouth, as they suck and bite.	**Anal Stage** Children obtain gratification through exercise of the anal musculature during elimination or retention.	**Phallic Stage (Oedipal)** Children develop sexual curiosity and obtain gratification through masturbation. They have sexual fantasies about the parent of the opposite sex and guilt about their fantasies.	**Latency Stage** Children's sexual urges are submerged, they put their energies into acquiring cultural skills.	**Genital Stage** Adolescents have adult heterosexual desires and seek to satisfy them.
Piaget (see Table 4–4)	Sensorimotor	Preoperational		Concrete operations	Formal operations

Reprinted with permission from Behrman RE, Kliegman RM, eds. Essentials of pediatrics, 2nd ed. Philadelphia: WB Saunders, 1994:24.

changes that lead to reproductive capability. The events of puberty occur in a predictable sequence, but the timing of the initiation and the velocity of the changes are highly variable among individuals. The integration of the pubertal changes into the adolescent's self-concept is crucial to normal adolescence.

In males, the initiation sequence of sexual development is testicular enlargement, followed by penile enlargement, height growth spurt, and pubic hair. This progression is shown in Figure 4–1.

In females, the order of pubertal events in sexual development is thelarche (breast buds), followed by height growth spurt, pubic hair, and menarche. Figure 4–2 illustrates these changes.

The Tanner staging system is used to determine where a child is in the pubertal process. Tanner stages for the male genitalia, female breasts, and male and female pubic hair are shown in Table 4–5. Pubertal abnormalities are addressed in Chapter 6.

TABLE 4–4

Jean Piaget's Stages of Cognitive Development

Stage	Description	Major Developments
Sensorimotor Birth to 2 yr	Learning occurs through activity, exploration, and manipulation of the environment. Motor and sensory impressions form the foundation of later learning.	Learns to differentiate self from world—beginning sense of self-identity. Formation and integration of schemes—as in learning that sucking on a nipple produces milk or that shaking a rattle produces a noise. Achieves object permanence—that things exist even when not visible. Simple tool use.
Preoperational 2–6 or 7 yr	Child capable of symbolic representations of world, as in use of language, play, and deferred imitation. Still not capable of sustained, systematic thought.	Engages in symbolic play—can represent something with something else. Some decline in egocentricity—can take greater account of others' points of view. Develops language and drawing as modes of representing experience.
Concrete operations 6 or 7–11 yr	Child becomes capable of limited logical thought processes, as in seeing relationships and classifying, as long as manipulable, concrete materials are available.	Becomes aware that some aspects of things remain the same despite changes in appearance (conservation). Can mentally reverse a process or action (reversibility). Can focus on more than one aspect of a situation at a time (decentration). Can deduce new relationships from sets of earlier ones (transitivity). Can order things in sequence (seriation). Can group objects on the basis of common features (classification).
Formal operations 12 yr through adulthood	Can reason logically and abstractly. Can formulate and test hypotheses. Thought no longer depends on concrete reality. Can consider possibilities.	Can deal with abstract ideas. Can manipulate variables in a scientific situation. Can deal with analogies and metaphors. Can reflect on own thinking. Can work out combinations and permutations.

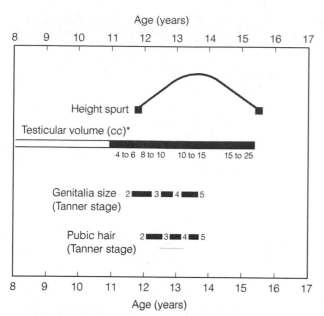

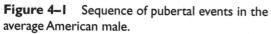

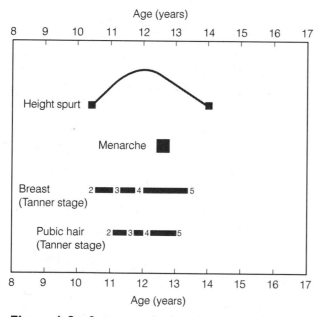

Figure 4–1 Sequence of pubertal events in the average American male.

Figure 4–2 Sequence of pubertal events in the average American female.

<table>
<tr><td colspan="2">TABLE 4–5</td></tr>
</table>

Secondary Sex Characteristics: Tanner

Breast development

Stage I	Preadolescent; elevation of papilla only.
Stage II	Breast bud; elevation of breast and papilla as small mound; enlargement of areolar diameter (11.15 ± 1.10).
Stage III	Further enlargement and elevation of breast and areola; no separation of their contours (12.15 ± 1.09).
Stage IV	Projection of areola and papilla to form secondary mound above level of breast (13.11 ± 1.15).
Stage V	Mature stage; projection of papilla only due to recession of areola to general contour of breast (15.33 ± 1.74).

Note: Stages IV and V may not be distinct in some patients.

Genital development (male)

Stage I	Preadolescent; testes, scrotum, and penis about same size and proportion as in early childhood.
Stage II	Enlargement of scrotum and testes, skin of scrotum reddens and changes in texture; little or no enlargement of penis (11.64 ± 1.07).
Stage III	Enlargement of penis, first mainly in length; further growth of testes and scrotum (12.85 ± 1.04).
Stage IV	Increased size of penis with growth in breadth and development of glans; further enlargement of testes and scrotum and increased darkening of scrotal skin (13.77 ± 1.02).
Stage V	Genitalia adult in size and shape (14.92 ± 1.10).

Pubic hair (male and female)

Stage I	Preadolescent; vellus over pubes no further developed than that over abdominal wall (i.e., no pubic hair).
Stage II	Sparse growth of long, slightly pigmented downy hair, straight or only slightly curled, chiefly at base of penis or along labia. (Male: 13.44 ± 1.09. Female: 11.69 ± 1.21)
Stage III	Considerably darker, coarser and more curled; hair spreads sparsely over junction of pubes. (Male: 13.9 ± 1.04. Female: 12.36 ± 1.10)
Stage IV	Hair resembles adult in type; distribution still considerably smaller than in adult. No spread to medial surface of thighs. (Male: 14.36 ± 1.08. Female: 12.95 ± 1.06)
Stage V	Adult in quantity and type with distribution of the horizontal pattern. (Male: 15.18 ± 1.07. Female: 14.41 ± 1.12)
Stage VI	Spread up linea alba: "male escutcheon."

◆ KEY POINTS ◆

1. Two separate developmental assessments are more predictive than a single assessment, and testing should be performed in all areas of development to assess for delay, dissociation, or deviancy.

2. The reader does not need to learn all the developmental milestones. Simply identify a few critical ages and learn developmentally what is expected, or, alternatively, take each category of development (gross motor, visual motor, language, and social) and note the important milestones and the age at which they should be seen.

3. The events of puberty occur in a predictable sequence, but the timing of the initiation and the velocity of the changes are highly variable among individuals.

4. The initiation sequence of sexual development for males is testicular enlargement, penile enlargement, height growth spurt, and pubic hair, whereas the sequence for females is thelarche (breast buds), height growth spurt, pubic hair, and menarche.

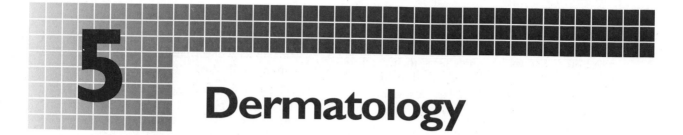

5 Dermatology

VIRAL RASHES

Clinical Manifestations

Exanthems are rashes that arise as cutaneous manifestations of infectious diseases. Some common viral exanthems include measles (rubeola), rubella (German measles), roseola infantum (exanthem subitum), erythema infectiosum (Fifth disease), hand-foot-mouth disease, varicella (chickenpox), and herpes zoster.

Although **measles** is becoming uncommon in developed countries where vaccines are used, it continues to be a major health problem worldwide. Sporadic epidemics of measles continue in the United States despite efforts to eradicate the disease. Measles is caused by a paramyxovirus, and its clinical course has three stages. The incubation period is 8–12 days after initial exposure to the virus; there are no signs and symptoms during this stage. A prodrome follows, consisting of malaise, fever (sometimes as high as 105°), cough, coryza, and conjunctivitis. Within 2–3 days after the onset of symptoms, Koplik's spots (small irregular red spots with central gray or bluish white specks) appear on the buccal mucosa. About 5 days after the onset of symptoms, an erythematous maculopapular rash erupts on the head and spreads toward the feet, lasting about 4–5 days. Diagnosis is made by the distinctive history and characteristic clinical findings. A fourfold or greater increase in hemagglutination inhibition antibodies over 2 weeks confirms the diagnosis. Measles prevention is discussed in Chapter 12.

Rubella is generally innocuous when acquired postnatally, but when a fetus is infected during gestation, the results can be devastating. For details on congenital rubella see Chapter 13. Rubella is caused by rubella virus, an RNA togavirus. Clinical manifestations in postnatally acquired rubella are absent in many cases. In children, there is no prodrome during the incubation period of 14–21 days. When symptoms do occur, rubella is characterized by an erythematous, maculopapular, discrete rash, with generalized lymphadenopathy and slight fever. The posterior auricular, cervical, and suboccipital nodes are the lymph nodes most commonly enlarged. Transient polyarthralgia and polyarthritis are common in adolescents. Encephalitis and thrombocytopenia are rare complications. The rash rarely lasts longer than 5 days. Fever may accompany the onset of rash. Postnatally acquired rubella is confirmed by a fourfold or greater rise in hemagglutination inhibition or complement fixing antibodies. The diagnosis of rubella is often difficult because the symptoms are mild and may be confused with those of enteroviral infection, roseola, toxoplasmosis, infectious mononucleosis, mild measles, and scarlet fever. Rubella prevention is discussed in Chapter 12.

Roseola infantum is a common, acute disease of infants and young children caused by herpes virus 6. The illness begins with an abrupt fever characterized by temperatures of 103–106° that persists for 1–5 days. During the fever, the child appears well and has no physical findings to explain the fever. Around the third or fourth day of fever, a maculopapular rash appears on the trunk and spreads peripherally. The fever typically resolves as the rash appears. Initially, leukocytosis up to 20,000 with a left shift may exist, but by the second day of illness, leukopenia and neutropenia may be noted. Complications are uncommon, although febrile seizures may occur due to the rapid increase in temperature during the onset of infection.

Erythema infectiosum (Fifth disease) is a mild, self-limited, systemic illness caused by the DNA-containing parvovirus B-19. It primarily occurs in epidemics. Usually, there is no prodrome, and fever may be absent or low grade. The rash progresses through three stages. It begins as a marked erythema of the cheeks, which gives a "slapped cheek" appearance. An erythematous, pruritic, maculopapular rash then starts on the arms and spreads to the trunk and legs. The third stage is characterized by fluctuations in the severity of the maculopapular rash and usually lasts 2–3 weeks. Fluctuations occur with temperature changes and exposure to sunlight. Complications include arthritis, hemolytic anemia, and encephalopathy. Parvovirus B-19 infection during pregnancy is associated with fetal hydrops and death.

Hand-foot-mouth disease is a common acute disease of young children during the spring and summer caused by coxsackie A viruses. There is usually a prodrome of fever, anorexia, and oral pain, followed by crops of ulcers on the tongue and oral mucosa and a maculopapular vesicular rash on the hands, feet, and occasionally the buttocks. Diagnosis is made by the history and the constellation of symptoms.

Varicella (chickenpox) is a highly contagious disease caused by primary infection with varicella-zoster virus. It is usually a mild, self-limited disease in normal children. Its severity can range from a few lesions and a low-grade fever, to hundreds of lesions and a temperature up to 105° to fatal disseminated disease in immunocompromised children. After an incubation period of 10–21 days, there is a prodrome consisting of mild fever, malaise, anorexia, and occasionally a scarlatiniform or morbilliform rash. The characteristic pruritic rash occurs the following day, appearing first on the trunk and then spreading peripherally. The rash begins as red papules and develops rapidly into clear "teardrop" vesicles that are about 1–2 mm in diameter. The vesicles then become cloudy, break, and form scabs. The lesions occur in widely scattered "crops" so there are usually several stages of lesions present at the same time. Vesicles often occur on mucous membranes. Patients are infectious from 24 hours before the appearance of the rash until all the lesions are crusted, which usually occurs 1 week after the onset of the rash.

Chickenpox is a clinical diagnosis. In unclear cases, a Tzanck prep, looking for multinucleated giant cells, can be performed on a vesicle, or a pharyngeal swab or swab of vesicular fluid can be sent for viral culture. Alternatively, acute and convalescent sera can be tested for a fourfold increase in antibody titer. Progressive varicella with meningoencephalitis and hepatitis occurs in immunocompromised children and is associated with a 20% mortality rate. See Chapter 12 for information on the new varicella vaccine.

Herpes zoster (shingles) represents a reactivation of varicella-zoster virus infection and occurs predominantly in adults who previously have had varicella and have circulating antibodies. After chickenpox, varicella-zoster virus retreats to the dorsal root ganglion, and, as a result, when it reactivates it follows a dermatomal distribution. Although it occurs in children, it is uncommon in those younger than 10 years old. An attack of herpes zoster begins with pain along the affected sensory nerve and is accompanied by fever and malaise. A vesicular eruption then appears in crops confined to the dermatomal distribution and clears in 7–14 days. The rash may last as long as 4 weeks, however, with pain persisting for weeks or months. Similar to chickenpox, diagnosis is made by clinical presentation, and unclear cases are diagnosed via Tzanck prep.

Other complications from herpes zoster include encephalopathy, aseptic meningitis, Guillan-Barre syndrome, pneumonitis, thrombocytopenia purpura, cellulitis, and arthritis.

Treatment

In uncomplicated cases, treatment is mainly supportive. Fever is treated with acetaminophen and/or ibuprofen and fluids. Aspirin should be avoided, because aspirin therapy for fever in the setting of a viral infection is associated with Reye's syndrome. The itching associated with Fifth disease, varicella, and herpes zoster is treated with an antihistamine medication. During chickenpox, daily bathing in lukewarm water reduces the risk of secondary bacterial infection. Herpes zoster can be quite painful, and narcotics are sometimes needed. Immunocompromised children who are exposed to someone with varicella-zoster virus infection are given varicella-zoster immune globulin within 96 hours of the exposure and

TABLE 5-1

Superficial Fungal Infections

Name	Etiology	Manifestations	Diagnosis	Therapy
Tinea capitis (ringworm)	*Microsporum audouinii, Trichophyton tonsurans, M. canis*	Prepubertal infection of scalp, hairshafts; "black dot" alopecia; *T. tonsurans* common in blacks	*M. audouinii* fluorescence —blue-green with Wood's lamp*; +KOH, culture	Griseofulvin; selenium sulfide shampoo
Kerion	Inflammatory reaction to tinea capitis	Swollen, boggy, crusted, purulent, tender mass with lymphadenopathy; secondary distal "id" reaction common	As above	As above, plus steroids for "id" reactions
Tinea corporis (ringworm)	*M. canis, T. rubrum,* others	Slightly pruritic ringlike, erythematous papules, plaques with scaling and slow outward expansion of the border; check cat or dog for *M. canis*	+KOH, culture; *M. canis* fluorescence—blue-green with Wood's lamp; *differential diagnosis: granuloma annulare, pityriasis rosea, nummular eczema, psoriasis*	Local miconazole or clotrimazole
Tinea cruris (jock itch)	*Epidermophyton floccosum, T. mentagrophytes, T. rubrum*	Symmetric, pruritic, scrotal sparing, scaling plaques	+KOH, culture; *differential diagnosis: erythrasma (Corynebacterium minutissimum)*	Local miconazole, clotrimazole, undecylenic acid, or tolnaftate; wear loose cotton underwear
Tinea pedis (athlete's foot)	*T. rubrum, T. mentagrophytes*	Moccasin or interdigital distribution, dry scales, interdigital maceration with secondary bacterial infection	+KOH, culture; *differential diagnosis: C. minutissimum erythrasma*	Medications as above; wear cotton socks
Tinea unguium (onychomycosis)	*T. mentagrophytes, T. rubrum, Candida albicans*	Uncommon before puberty; peeling of distal nailplate; thickening, splitting of nails	+KOH, culture	Oral ketoconazole or griseofulvin
Tinea versicolor	*Malassezia furfur*	Tropical climates, steroids or immunosuppressive drugs; uncommon before puberty; chest, back, arms; oval hypo- or hyperpigmentation in blacks, red-brown in whites; scaling patches	+KOH; orange-gold fluorescence with Wood's lamp; *differential diagnosis: pityriasis alba*	Selenium sulfide shampoo, topical sodium hyposulfite, oral ketoconazole
Candidiasis	*C. albicans*	Diaper area, intense erythematous plaques or pustules, isolated or confluent	+KOH, culture	Topical nystatin; oral nystatin treats concomitant oral thrush

*Wood's lamp examination uses an ultraviolet source in a completely darkened room. Trichophyton usually has no fluorescence.

Reprinted with permission from Behrman RE, Kliegman RM, eds. Essentials of pediatrics, 2nd ed. Philadelphia: WB Saunders, 1994:385.

observed closely. Acyclovir is reserved for immunocompromised patients with disseminated varicella.

◆ KEY POINTS ◆

1. Viral exanthems are generally benign and treated symptomatically.
2. The exanthems are differentiated by history and rash appearance. Diagnostic tests can be confirmatory after resolution but add little to the treatment plan.
3. Children with chickenpox are contagious from 24 hours before the onset of rash until all lesions have crusted over.

BACTERIAL RASHES

Bacterial rashes of the skin are common and are in most cases the result of group A beta-hemolytic streptococcus and/or *Staphylococcus aureus* infection. Depending on the particular isolate, a variety of different rashes can result. *S. aureus* infection causes bullous and nonbullous impetigo, scalded skin syndrome, folliculitis, and cellulitis, whereas skin infection with group A beta-hemolytic streptococcus can result in nonbullous impetigo and cellulitis.

Clinical Manifestations

Bullous impetigo, which is caused by *S. aureus*, begins as red macules that progress to bullous (fluid-filled) eruptions on an erythematous base. These lesions range from a few millimeters to a few centimeters in diameter. After the bullae rupture, a clear, thin, varnish-like coating forms over the denuded area. *S. aureus* can be cultured from the vesicular fluid. Bullous impetigo lesions can be mistaken for cigarette burns, raising the suspicion of abuse.

Nonbullous impetigo, which is caused by both group A beta-hemolytic streptococcus and *S. aureus*, begins as papules that progress to vesicles and then to painless pustules measuring about 5 mm in diameter with a thin erythematous rim. The pustules rupture, revealing a honey-colored thin exudate that then forms a crust over a shallow ulcerated base. Local lymphadenopathy is common with streptococcal impetigo. Fever is uncommon with both bullous and nonbullous impetigo. The caus-

ative organism can usually be isolated from the lesions.

Staphylococcal scalded skin, which is caused by exfoliative isolates of *S. aureus*, is most common in infancy and rarely occurs beyond age 5. Onset is abrupt with diffuse erythema, marked skin tenderness, and fever. Within 12–24 hours of onset, superficial flaccid bullae develop and then rupture almost immediately, leaving a beefy, red, weeping surface. Exfoliation may affect most of the body, and there is usually a positive Nikolsky's sign (separation of the epidermis on light rubbing). The initial focus of staphylococcal infection may be minor or not apparent. Unruptured bullae contain sterile fluid.

Folliculitis is a *S. aureus* infection of the shaft of the hair follicle. Superficial folliculitis is common and easily treated. Deep forms of this infection include sties, furuncles (boils), and carbuncles. Sties are created by the infection of eyelid cilia. Furuncles begin as superficial folliculitis and are most frequently found in areas of hair-bearing skin that are subject to friction and maceration, especially the scalp, buttocks, and axillae. Carbuncles are an accumulation of furuncles.

Cellulitis is a localized, acute inflammation of the skin characterized by erythema and warmth. Cellulitis in children is most often caused by group A beta-hemolytic streptococcus or *S. aureus* infection. These bacteria are normal flora of the skin, and a break in the integument allows entry into the dermis and epidermis. This is why trauma-related cellulitis is usually caused by group A beta-hemolytic streptococcus or *S. aureus* infection. The location of the infection is important, because in rare cases the cellulitis may arise from an underlying osteomyelitis, septic arthritis, sinusitis, or deep wound infection. Before the use of *Haemophilus influenzae* type b vaccine began, *H. influenzae* type b was a significant pathogen resulting in many cases of cellulitis by hematogenous spread. *H. influenzae* type b cellulitis is now rarely seen. Currently, *Streptococcus pneumoniae* is the most common cause of hematogenously spread cellulitis. Hematogenously spread *S. pneumoniae* often penetrates the face and periorbital area. Cellulitis of the face, depending on whether it resulted from trauma or hematogenous spread, can result from all the pathogens mentioned: group A beta-hemolytic streptococcus, *S. aureus*, *S. pneumoniae*, or *H. influenzae* type b.

Treatment

Limited nonbullous impetigo can be treated topically with mupirocin ointment. Bullous impetigo and nonbullous impetigo, if the lesions are numerous, are treated with a first-generation cephalosporin such as cephalexin, which is an oral drug that is effective against both staphylococcus and group A streptococcus. The caretaker can remove any honey-colored crusts with twice daily cool compresses.

Mild to moderate cases of staphylococcal scalded skin are treated with an oral anti-staphylococcal medication. Children with severe cases should be treated as though they have a second-degree burn with meticulous fluid management and intravenous oxacillin.

Superficial folliculitis responds to aggressive hygiene and topical mupirocin, whereas folliculitis of the male beard is unusually recalcitrant and needs an oral antistaphylococcal drug. Simple furunculosis is treated with moist heat, and sties are treated with a local ophthalmic antibiotic. Larger and deeper furuncles may need to be incised and drained. After drainage, they need only topical mupirocin treatment.

Children with mild cellulitis can be treated with an antistaphylococcal/streptococcal antibiotic by mouth, such as cephalexin or amoxicillin-clavulanic acid. Those with severe infection who have lymphangitic streaking or lymphadenopathy may be hospitalized and given a parenteral antibiotic, such as oxacillin. Facial or periorbital cellulitis is usually treated with intravenous cefuroxime and admission to the hospital for observation. The cefuroxime provides streptococcal, staphylococcal, and *H. influenzae* coverage. When orbital or periorbital cellulitis is present or a peripheral skin cellulitis results in lymphadenopathy or lymphangitic streaking, a blood culture should be sent to determine whether bacteremia is present.

◆ KEY POINTS ◆

1. *S. aureus* and group A beta-hemolytic streptococcus cause most bacterial skin infections.

2. Because of the Hib vaccine, *S. pneumoniae* has replaced *H. influenzae* as the most common pathogen in hematogenously spread cellulitis.

3. The child with peripheral cellulitis with lymphadenopathy and/or lymphangitic streaking and the child with orbital or periorbital cellulitis should have a blood culture sent to determine whether bacteremia is present.

SUPERFICIAL FUNGAL RASHES

Essentially three fungal organisms cause superficial tinea infections: **Trichophyton**, **Microsporum**, and **Epidermophyton**. Tinea infections can be divided into the following types:

- Tinea capitis (scalp)
- Tinea corporis (body, "ringworm")
- Tinea cruris (genitocrural, "jock-itch")
- Tinea pedis (foot, "athlete's foot")
- Tinea unguis (nails)

Tinea versicolor, another type of yeast infection caused by *Malassezia furfur*, is characterized by superficial tan or hypopigmented oval scaly lesions on the neck, upper part of the back, chest, and proximal arms in a Christmas tree distribution. Dark-skinned individuals tend to have hypopigmented lesions during the summer when uninfected skin darkens from sunlight exposure.

Diaper rash may result from atopic dermatitis, primary irritant dermatitis, or primary or secondary *Candida albicans* infection. Eighty percent of diaper rashes lasting greater than 4 days are colonized with *Candida*. Fiery red, papular lesions with peripheral scales in the skin folds and satellite lesions are typical for candidal diaper rash.

Table 5–1 outlines the etiology, manifestations, diagnosis, and therapy of the most common superficial fungal infections.

INFESTATIONS

Scabies

Scabies is caused by the mite *Sarcoptes scabiei*. The characteristic linear burrows and arcuate intraepidermal tunnels are dug by the female mite. Transmission is usually person to person, but mites may be transferred from bedding, clothes, or other fomites.

Clinical Manifestations
History and Physical Examination
There is usually acute onset of an extremely pruritic rash characterized by pruritic linear burrows; the distinctive burrows are pathognomonic. Secondary bacterial infection is uncommon. Severe pruritus, especially at night,

may precede skin lesions. In older children and adults, areas of involvement include the webs of fingers and toes, axillae, flexures of arms and wrists, belt line, and areas around the umbilicus, nipples, genitals, and lower buttocks. In infants, palms, soles, head, and neck are involved.

Differential Diagnosis

The differential diagnosis includes atopic dermatitis, contact dermatitis, drug reaction, insect bites, and papular urticaria.

Diagnostic Evaluation

Burrows are usually apparent to the naked eye. If scabies is suspected and burrows are not readily apparent, applying topical tetracycline and examining the skin with a Wood's lamp may be helpful. Lesions should be scraped with a mineral oil–coated scalpel blade and the debris placed on a slide and covered. Under low power, look for mites, ova, or fecal pellets. Yield with this procedure is good if done correctly; diagnosis is usually based on clinical appearance and response to treatment.

Treatment

The condition is treated with 5% permethrin cream (Elimite) or 1% lindane lotion (Kwell). Oral antihistamines may be given for pruritus. Family members must be treated, even if asymptomatic. Clothing and bed linen should be machine-washed in hot water (more than 120°). Parents must be warned that pruritus can persist for 1–2 weeks after infestation has resolved.

Pediculosis

Pathogenesis

The three forms of pediculosis are pediculosis capitis (head lice), caused by *Pediculus humanus capitis*; pediculosis pubis (pubic lice or crabs), caused by *Phthirus pubis*; and pediculosis corpora (body lice), caused by *Pediculus humanus corpora*. Ova hatch in 6–10 days. Both nymphs and adult lice live off human blood.

Epidemiology

Head lice are common in school-aged children and children who attend daycare centers. All socioeconomic groups are infected.

Hair length does not influence infestation, and the presence of infestation does not indicate uncleanliness. Transmission occurs by direct contact with an infected individual or by indirect contact via brushes, combs, and hats.

The pubis variety of lice is common in adolescents and young adults, is transmitted through sexual contact, and is considered a sexually transmitted disease. The pubic louse can also be transmitted by towels. If found in the eyelids of children, it should be considered a marker for child sexual abuse.

Body lice are very uncommon in the United States and are not discussed further.

Clinical Manifestations
History and Physical Examination

Head lice result in extreme scalp pruritus at the hairline, accompanied by scalp erythema, excoriations, and crusts. Secondary bacterial infection is uncommon. The clinician may see live lice or nits on hair shafts.

The symptoms associated with pediculosis pubis infection mirror those found with head lice but are most often found in the pubic or perianal area. Pubic lice may also be found on the thighs, axillae, beard, mustache, or eyelids in children. A characteristic sign of heavy pubic lice infestation is the presence of bluish or slate-colored macules on the chest, abdomen, or thighs.

Differential Diagnosis

Head lice must be differentiated from tinea capitis, folliculitis, and impetigo.

Diagnostic Evaluation

Identification of nits, nymphs, and lice may be made by the naked eye. Nits fluoresce a pearly color under a Wood's lamp.

Treatment

To treat head lice, apply 1% permethrin cream rinse (NIX) or pyrethrin (RID, A-200), repeat in 1 week, and then reexamine for visible lice or viable nits. Soak combs and hair accessories in alcohol for 1 hour after removing any visible nits. Other family members should be examined and treated, and the child's school must be notified.

For the pubic variety, application of 1% lindane shampoo for 5 minutes or pyrethrin lotion (RID, A-200) for 10–20 minutes is generally adequate therapy. All sexual partners must be treated, and a full sexually transmitted disease workup is recommended.

For eyelid infestation, apply petrolatum to asphyxiate the lice and nits.

ACNE

Pathogenesis

Acne vulgaris is due to enlargement of sebaceous glands, increased sebum production, proliferation of *Proprionibacterium acnes*, and secondary inflammatory changes. There is a predilection for face, chest, and back. Lesions progress from comedones (whiteheads), to open comedones (blackheads), to pustules, to papules, to nodules (cysts), and finally to atrophic and hypertrophic scars. Androgens are the stimulus to sebaceous gland development and secretion. At puberty, hormonal stimuli lead to increased growth and development of sebaceous follicles. Female patients with severe acne or virilization often have high levels of circulating androgens.

Epidemiology

Acne is a very common, self-limited, multifactorial disorder of the sebaceous follicles, noted during the teenage years. Lesions may begin as early as 8–10 years of age. Prevalence increases steadily throughout adolescence and then decreases in adulthood. Although girls often develop acne at a younger age than boys do, severe disease affects boys 10 times more frequently because of higher androgen levels. In fact, 15% of all teenage boys have severe acne.

Risk Factors

Risk factors include male gender, puberty, oral contraceptive pill use, oily complexion, Cushing's syndrome, or any other process that results in increased androgens.

Clinical Manifestations

History

Determine when the acne started and whether there is a family history of acne. A full menstrual history should be taken to determine whether there is a correlation between the onset of menses and the patient's acne exacerbations. Find out if the patient is chronically exposed to heavy oils or greases and what cosmetics, hair care products, and skin cleansers the patient uses. Obtain a thorough medication history, because many drugs cause acne. Define how the patient's acne has been treated in the past. Finally, ask if there is any effect from stress or emotional upset on acne activity.

Physical Examination

Assess distribution, morphology, and severity of lesions. It is important to differentiate common acne from nodulocystic acne. The patient's response to therapy can be monitored by using a grading system or taking serial photographs.

Differential Diagnosis

The acneiform rashes include acne vulgaris, drug-induced acne, Cushing's syndrome or other pathologies that increase endogenous steroid secretion, and perioral dermatitis. Rosacea, an acneiform eruption of the central face and neck, is sometimes confused with acne.

Corticosteroids, androgens, danazol, iodides, and bromides most commonly exacerbate acne. Other possible stimuli include isoniazid, lithium, halothane, vitamin B_{12}, and hyperalimentation. These drugs are not directly comedogenic but "prime" the follicular epithelium to the comedogenic effects of sebum.

Treatment

Treatment should be individualized depending on gender and severity, type, and distribution of lesions. In mild acne, there are a few comedones, and it is treated with benzoyl peroxide and topical antibiotics, both of which are bacteriostatic. Mild acne responds to therapy without scarring.

Many comedones and some papules and pustules are characteristic of moderate acne. Therapy uses benzoyl peroxide, tretinoin, and topical antibiotics. There is a variable response to treatment, and scarring is a possibility with this severity of acne.

Severe acne is characterized by inflammatory papules,

pustules, cysts, abscesses, and scarring. Modes of treatment include topical therapy, as for moderate acne and systemic antibiotics, and sebaceous gland suppressive agents. Systemic antibiotics used include tetracycline, erythromycin, clindamycin, and minocycline. Tetracycline is contraindicated in pregnant or nursing women because of its teratogenicity and in children less than 12 years old because it stains their teeth. Sebaceous gland suppressors include estrogens, steroids, and retinoic acid (Accutane). Because of its teratogenicity, a negative pregnancy test must be obtained within 2 weeks of initiating retinoic acid (Accutane) therapy, and contraception must be used from 1 month before to 1 month after therapy. Accutane therapy usually lasts 4–5 months.

◆ KEY POINTS ◆

1. There is no one way to treat acne; use what works.
2. Before using Accutane or tetracycline in females, a negative pregnancy test must be obtained to avoid teratogenicity.

PSORIASIS

Pathogenesis

The pathogenesis of psoriasis is unknown. A multifactorial inheritance pattern has been proposed. Children with HLA type C6 are clearly more likely to develop the disease. Histologically, there is hyperproliferation of the epidermis, and epidermal turnover time is noted to be distinctly accelerated in those affected. The rash usually appears at sites of physical, thermal, or mechanical trauma. This is known as the Kobner phenomenon, a valuable diagnostic feature of the disease.

Epidemiology

Psoriasis is considered by some to be an adult disease, but 10% of the cases of psoriasis begin before the age of 10 and 35% begin before the age of 20. Fifty percent of children with psoriasis have a positive family history for the disease. If psoriasis is present during adolescence, it is likely a lifelong disease.

Risk Factors

HLA inheritance is part of the mode of transmission; therefore, a positive family history is a significant risk factor.

Clinical Manifestations

History and Physical Examination

The rash consists of erythematous papules that coalesce to form plaques with sharply demarcated borders and a silvery or yellow-white scale. The scales tend to build up into layers, and their removal may result in pinpoint bleeding (Auspitz sign). The distribution of the rash, which is nonpruritic, is usually symmetric, with plaques appearing over the knees, elbows, scalp, and genital area. These are sites of repeated trauma. The scalp frequently has a thick, adherent scale with alopecia at sites of involvement. The nails often demonstrate punctate stippling or pitting, detachment of the nail plate (onycholysis), and accumulation of subungual debris. Examination of the palms and soles reveals scaling and fissuring.

Differential Diagnosis

The differential diagnosis for a psoriatic rash in children includes uncommon disorders such as Reiter's syndrome, pityriasis rubra pilaris, and lichen planus. Reiter's syndrome, in contrast to simple psoriasis, has a psoriatic-like rash that involves the mucous membranes. In some severe cases in which the rash is also accompanied by arthritis, the lesions of the mucous membrane are the main differentiating point between psoriasis and Reiter's syndrome. Occasionally, atopic dermatitis may be confused with psoriasis. The two are differentiated by the fact that eczema is pruritic and psoriasis is not. Scalp lesions may be confused with seborrheic dermatitis or tinea capitis.

Diagnostic Evaluation

The diagnosis is a clinical one. Skin biopsy reveals a hyperplastic epidermis.

Treatment

Psoriasis, like eczema, is characterized by remissions and exacerbations. The most important aspect of treating psoriasis is to educate the patient and family that the disease is a recurrent one that cannot be cured but can be controlled with conscientious therapy. No matter where the rash is or its severity, the goal of psoriasis therapy is to keep the skin well hydrated. Tar preparations may be added to the daily bath or used as an ointment to be placed on the rash. For more severe cases, natural sunlight or ultraviolet B light may be used in conjunction with the tar lubricant. For small areas of involvement, fluorinated steroids may be successful; the least potent but effective dose should be used, because adrenal suppression can occur.

◆ KEY POINTS ◆

1. Psoriasis, like eczema, cannot be cured and is characterized by remissions and exacerbations that can be controlled with conscientious therapy.
2. Psoriasis occurs at skin points of repeated trauma, and the rash is nonpruritic.
3. Treatment consists of keeping the skin well hydrated with tar preparations that help hold moisture in the skin.

ALLERGIC RASHES

Atopic Dermatitis (Eczema)

Atopic dermatitis (eczema) is a common skin disorder of infancy and childhood and affects 5% of children before the age of 5. Seventy percent of affected children have first-degree relatives exhibiting some form of allergic disease, and 30–50% of children with atopic dermatitis go on to develop allergic rhinitis or asthma. Approximately 60% of affected children develop atopic dermatitis within the first year of life and 90% within the first 5 years of life.

Clinical Manifestations
History and Physical Examination
The rash is characterized by erythema, edema, papules, and weeping in the active phase. Scales and lichenification may develop later. Paroxysmal and severe pruritus is the hallmark of eczema. The itching is a constant feature that creates an "itch-scratch-itch cycle." If there is no pruritus, it is unlikely that the rash is atopic dermatitis. Cellulitis can often be superimposed on a base of eczema. *S. aureus and S. pyogenes* are the usual bacterial agents.

The three clinical phases are:

- Phase I—infantile eczema (2 months–2 years): Rash appears on the face, neck, scalp, trunk, and extensor surfaces of extremities and progresses to phase II in one-third of patients.
- Phase II—childhood eczema (2–10 years): Rash is present on flexor surfaces predominantly (antecubital, popliteal, neck, wrists, sometimes hands and feet), and one-third progress to adolescent eczema.
- Phase III—adolescent eczema: Hands (mostly), eyelids, neck, feet, and flexor areas have rash.

Atopic dermatitis tends to remit and exacerbate. Typically, the eruptions become milder with age, and longer remissions occur. Triggers include excessive bathing and hand washing, occlusive clothing (especially wool), sweating, stress, and possibly food allergy (eggs, milk, seafood, nuts, wheat, and/or soy).

Differential Diagnosis
Some of the more common rashes that must be differentiated from eczema include seborrheic dermatitis, diaper dermatitis, contact dermatitis, scabies, psoriasis, drug reactions, fungal infections, and ichthyosis vulgaris.

Eczematous lesions are not exclusively due to atopic dermatitis, as a variety of immunodeficiencies can cause similar rashes. These include Wiskott-Aldrich syndrome, agammaglobulinemia, Leiner disease (C5 deficiency), and histiocytosis X.

Diagnostic Evaluation
The eosinophil count and serum IgE level are often elevated. IgE levels wax and wane with the activity of the disease. A more detailed immunologic evaluation may be necessary in the presence of failure to thrive or recurrent systemic infections.

Treatment
The most important aspect of treating eczema is to educate the patient and the family that the disease is a recurrent one that cannot be cured but can be controlled with conscientious therapy. Therapy is directed at controlling dryness, inflammation, and pruritus. General measures include avoiding extremes of temperature and humidity, chemicals, strong soaps, certain allergy-triggered foods, wool, and synthetic materials.

Severe atopic dermatitis is treated with wet compresses soaked in aluminum acetate solution (Burrow's solution), oatmeal baths (Aveeno bath), antipruritics (hydroxyzine), emollients (Eucerin cream), and topical steroids (1% hydrocortisone cream).

Treatment of chronic atopic dermatitis is directed at rehydration of the skin and frequent bathing with a moisturizing soap followed by emollients. Emollients are applied frequently during the day to reduce dryness and avoid the "itch-scratch-itch" cycle. Topical steroids should be applied for frequent flare-ups.

Urticaria

Urticaria (hives) is the most common type of hypersensitivity reaction in the skin and affects up to 20% of children at some time. It is IgE mediated and results from reintroduction of an agent to which the immune system has been previously sensitized. Common causes of immune mediated urticaria include drugs (penicillin), food (fish, eggs, peanuts, chocolate), physical factors (cold, light, heat), blood and blood products, and infections (Epstein-Barr virus, hepatitis, streptococcal pharyngitis). Nonimmunologic urticaria can occur after first exposure to such agents as aspirin, opiates, or contrast media.

Clinical Manifestations

An urticarial rash consists of wheals, which are raised, pale, pink pruritic areas of edema of the upper dermis. The rash evolves over several hours or perhaps in a single day. The diagnosis is clinical and based on characteristic appearance and, when possible, a history of exposure. The presence of concurrent arthritis and fever suggests the diagnosis of serum sickness.

Treatment

Avoiding the precipitating cause is the key to prevention. Cold compresses can be applied to pruritic areas, and the child may be given antihistamines by mouth. Antipruritic medication may be used to relieve itching, and arthralgias or arthritis can be treated with ibuprofen.

Erythema Multiforme

Erythema multiforme is an acute self-limited hypersensitivity reaction that is uncommon in children. Common etiologic agents include viral infection (herpesvirus, adenovirus, Epstein-Barr virus), mycoplasma pneumoniae infection, drug ingestion (sulfa drugs especially), immunizations, and food reactions.

Clinical Manifestations

In **erythema multiforme**, there is a symmetric distribution of lesions evolving through multiple morphological stages: erythematous macules, papules, plaques, vesicles, and target lesions. The lesions change over days, not hours. Urticaria (hives) evolves over hours, not days, and is not symmetric in distribution. Erythema multiforme tends to occur over the dorsum of the hands and feet, palms and soles, and extensor surfaces of extremities, but may spread to the trunk. Burning and itching are common. Systemic manifestations include fever, malaise, and myalgias.

Stevens-Johnson syndrome is the most severe form of erythema multiforme. There is a prodrome for 1–14 days of fever, malaise, myalgias, arthralgias, arthritis, headache, emesis, and diarrhea. This is followed by sudden onset of high fever, erythema multiforme skin lesions, and inflammatory bullae of two or more mucous membranes (oral mucosa, lips, bulbar conjunctiva, and anogenital area). In the most severe cases, involvement of most of the gastrointestinal, respiratory, or genitourinary tracts may be seen. Untreated, this syndrome has a mortality rate of approximately 10%.

Toxic epidermal necrolysis is the most severe form of cutaneous hypersensitivity, considered by some to be a variant of Stevens-Johnson syndrome. Although the occurrence in children is rare, a 30% mortality rate is associated with it. The pathogenesis is not well understood, but most cases are secondary to medications, especially sulfa drugs, anticonvulsants, and nonsteroidal anti-inflammatory agents. Onset is acute with high fever, a burning sensation of the mucous membranes, and/or oral and conjunctival erythema and erosions. The presentation of the skin resembles that of staphylococcal scalded skin with widespread erythema, tenderness, blister formation, and detachment of the epidermis causing denudation (positive Nikolsky's sign). Mucous membrane involvement is severe and the nails may be shed. Systemic complications include elevated liver enzymes, renal failure, and fluid and electrolyte imbalance. Sepsis and shock are frequent causes of death.

Treatment

For uncomplicated erythema multiforme, symptomatic treatment and reassurance are all that is necessary. Oral antihistamines, moist compresses, and oatmeal baths are helpful. The lesions resolve over a 1–3-week period with some hyperpigmentation. The use of corticosteroids is controversial.

Treatment of the patient with Stevens-Johnson syndrome includes hospitalization with barrier isolation, fluid and electrolyte support, the treatment of common secondary infection of the skin, moist compresses to bullae, and colloidal baths. For oral mucosal lesions, mouthwashes with viscous lidocaine, diphenhydramine, and Maalox (aluminum hydroxide, magnesium hydroxide) are comforting. Because corneal ulceration, keratitis, uveitis, and panophthalmitis are possible, an ophthalmology consultation is recommended.

Children with toxic epidermal necrolysis are treated as though they have a full-body second-degree burn. Fluid therapy and reverse barrier isolation are critical to survival.

◆ **KEY POINTS** ◆

1. Think of allergic rashes as a spectrum of hypersensitivity reactions worsening in severity from urticaria to erythema multiforme to Stevens-Johnson syndrome to toxic epidermal necrolysis.

2. Eczema is a chronic disease that cannot be cured but in which remissions and exacerbations can be controlled with conscientious therapy.

3. Urticaria is the most common type of hypersensitivity reaction in the skin and affects one in five children.

4. Stevens-Johnson syndrome is erythema multiforme with oral mucosal bullae, whereas toxic epidermal necrolysis is similar to staphylococcal scalded skin in that both result in sloughing of the epidermal layer.

Endocrinology

DIABETES MELLITUS

Pathogenesis

Diabetes mellitus is a chronic metabolic disorder characterized by hyperglycemia and abnormal energy metabolism due to absent or diminished insulin secretion or action at the cellular level. **Insulin-dependent diabetes mellitus** (IDDM) type 1 results from lack of insulin production in the B cells of the pancreas. Although the precise etiology of IDDM is unknown, genetic, autoimmune, and environmental factors have all been implicated in causation. The presence of DR3 and DR4 major histocompatibility antigens increases the lifetime risk for an individual developing IDDM, as does having a first-degree relative with IDDM. Approximately 5% of the siblings and offspring of IDDM sufferers develop IDDM, and there is a 50% concordance among identical twins. The presence of anti–islet cell antibodies in 85% of individuals with recent onset IDDM and the increased appearance of other autoimmune diseases in children with IDDM make the case for an autoimmune etiology. The environmental role in disease pathogenesis remains unclear, but it is suspected that a normal immunologic response to a viral infection in the genetically predisposed individual results in autoimmune destruction of B cells in the islets of Langerhans. No particular virus has been determined to be directly responsible.

It is only after 90% of B-cell function has been destroyed that loss of insulin secretion becomes clinically significant. With the loss of insulin, the major anabolic hormone, a catabolic state develops, that is characterized by decreased glucose utilization and increased glucose production by gluconeogenesis and glycogenolysis. Because insulin is lacking in the bloodstream, glucose is unable to enter the cells of the periphery and hyperglycemia results. The body, unable to obtain glucose as an energy source, begins to make keto acids. The production of keto acids is brought about by an increase in the catabolic mediators glucagon, epinephrine, growth hormone (GH), and cortisol. These messengers trigger lipolysis, fatty acid release, and keto-acid synthesis. When the blood glucose concentration exceeds 180 mg/dL, the resultant glycosuria causes an osmotic diuresis with increased urine output (polyuria). If insulin deficiency is severe, ketones are produced in significant quantities, the blood's native buffering capacity is overwhelmed, and **diabetic ketoacidosis** (DKA) results.

DKA is characterized by hyperglycemia, metabolic acidosis (ketoacidosis), dehydration, and lethargy. This condition is a medical emergency and may progress to coma and, in severe cases, death. The most common cause of DKA in the known diabetic is inadequate insulin dosing. The condition may also be triggered by insulin resistance, brought about by intercurrent illness or some other extreme physiologic stress. Frequently, new onset diabetics present in DKA. Complications of DKA management include hypoglycemia, hypokalemia, and cerebral edema. In addition to DKA, the other major complication seen in IDDM is hypoglycemia from insulin overdose, decreased caloric intake, or increased exercise without a concomitant increase in calories.

Noninsulin-dependent diabetes mellitus (NIDDM) results from insulin resistance. Insulin secretion is normal or increased and insulin receptors are decreased. NIDDM is extremely rare in childhood, and its discussion is therefore limited.

Epidemiology and Risk Factors

IDDM is the most common endocrine-metabolic disease in childhood, occurring in 1 in 500 children and adolescents. NIDDM also occurs in childhood, but is much rarer than IDDM. Most cases occur during early adolescence. The main risk factor for IDDM is a family history, whereas the main risk factor for NIDDM is morbid obesity in isolation or from a genetic disorder such as Prader-Willi syndrome.

Clinical Manifestations

History and Physical Examination

A history of new onset weight loss, polydipsia, polyphagia, and polyuria is consistent with type I diabetes mellitus. Unless there has been significant weight loss (IDDM) or there is marked obesity (NIDDM), the physical examination is generally normal in diabetes mellitus.

When DKA is suspected in a child with known IDDM, important historic information includes the usual insulin dose, the last insulin dose, the child's diet over the previous day, and whether the child has been ill or emotionally or physically stressed recently. The child with DKA appears acutely ill and suffers from moderate to profound dehydration. He or she reports polyuria, polydipsia, fatigue, headache, nausea, emesis, and abdominal pain. The child's mental status may vary from confused to comatose. On physical examination, tachycardia and hyperpnea (Kussmaul's respirations) are generally noted. There may be a fruity odor to the breath due to the ketosis. Intravascular volume depletion may be so marked that hypotension is detected. Although cerebral edema is rare, it is often fatal. Changing mental status, unequal pupils, decorticate or decerebrate posturing, and/or seizures indicate cerebral edema. Early identification and aggressive management of increased intracranial pressure are pivotal to improve outcome.

Symptoms of hypoglycemia are due to catecholamine release (trembling, diaphoresis, flushing, and tachycardia) and to cerebral glucopenia (sleepiness, confusion, mood changes, seizures, and coma).

Differential Diagnosis

Secondary diabetes may occur when there is insulin antagonism from excess glucocorticoids (Cushing's syndrome), hyperthyroidism, pheochromocytoma, GH excess, or with thiazide diuretics.

Diagnostic Evaluation

A random blood glucose level greater than 200 mg/dL, which is verified on a repeat test, is consistent with a diagnosis of IDDM. If early IDDM is suspected, obtain a fasting blood glucose concentration (no caloric intake for at least 8 hours) and perform an oral glucose tolerance test and obtain a 2-hour postload blood glucose concentration. A fasting blood glucose concentration greater than 126 mg/dL and a 2-hour postload blood glucose concentration greater than 200 mg/dL are suggestive of IDDM. If an elevated glucose concentration is discovered during a well-child or acute-illness visit, a glucose tolerance test should be performed. Islet cell antibodies in the serum may be found in the new onset insulin-dependent diabetic; poorly controlled diabetics have high levels of glycosylated hemoglobin.

In children with suspected DKA, the serum glucose concentration is grossly elevated, and the venous pH and serum P_{CO_2} is low. Metabolic acidosis from ketosis results in diminished pH, and the response to metabolic acidosis is a compensatory respiratory alkalosis and a drop in serum P_{CO_2}. Because of the osmotic diuresis, blood urea nitrogen is elevated and there is loss of phosphate, calcium, and potassium. Although there is a total body loss of potassium, serum potassium may be low, normal, or even high depending on the level of acidosis. When acidosis is present, protons move from the extracellular space to the intracellular space and potassium moves from the intracellular space to the extracellular space to maintain electroneutrality. Until the catabolic state is reversed with insulin, the urine is positive for ketones, and until the serum concentration of glucose falls below 180 mg/dL, the urine is positive for glucose.

Treatment

The immediate goals in treatment of new onset IDDM and DKA are to restore fluid and electrolyte losses and to reverse the catabolic state through exogenous insulin therapy.

The child with IDDM is treated through insulin replacement, diet, exercise, education, psychological support, and regular medical follow-up. The newly diagnosed diabetic requires 0.5 to 1.0 unit/kg/day of insulin. It is customary to give two-thirds of the total daily dose before breakfast and one-third before dinner, and the human insulin is divided between short-acting regular insulin and intermediate-acting NPH insulin. The proportion of intermediate-acting to short-acting insulin is approximately 2:1 in the A.M. and 1:1 in the P.M. If hyperglycemia is present between breakfast and lunch, the amount of regular insulin should be increased, and if hyperglycemia is noted later in the day, the amount of intermediate insulin should be increased. Blood glucose concentrations are assessed before meals and at bedtime. At times of medical, surgical, or emotional stress, additional insulin may be needed. The diabetic diet is structured to provide adequate calories and nutrients to minimize hyperglycemia, to minimize the catabolic state, and to promote adequate growth. Decreasing the number and duration of hyperglycemic episodes has been shown to minimize long-term complications.

If hypoglycemia occurs, a child may ingest a carbohydrate snack to increase the serum glucose concentration. If the child is vomiting, Monogel instant glucose or cake icing may be applied to the buccal mucosa to provide glucose, and if the child is stuporous or having a seizure, intravenous glucose or intramuscular glucagon may be given.

DKA is a medical emergency and must be dealt with promptly. Initial fluid resuscitation is accomplished by giving a normal saline or lactated Ringer's solution 20 mL/kg intravenous bolus. While the fluid bolus is running in, the total fluid deficit is calculated based on the amount of dehydration. Half the fluid deficit plus maintenance should be given over the first 8 hours and the remainder of the deficit plus maintenance over the next 16 hours. The level of hyperglycemia is assessed, an intravenous insulin bolus of 0.1 unit/kg is given, and an insulin drip is started at 0.1 unit/kg/hr to reverse the catabolic state. The goal is to decrease the serum glucose 100 mg/dL/hr. A glucose level that falls too quickly could precipitate cerebral edema. If the glucose falls less than 50 mg/dL/hr, increase the rate of the insulin drip, and if the glucose concentration falls more than 100 mg/dL/hr, continue the insulin drip and add D5W to the intravenous fluids. When serum glucose approaches 250 to 300 mg/dL, D5W should be added to ensure that the insulin drip will not cause hypoglycemia. Acidosis usually corrects with rehydration and insulin therapy. Serum glucose can be checked every 4 hours, but dextrose sticks are needed each hour. Bicarbonate is administered only if the pH is less than 7.10 or the serum bicarbonate is less than 5 mEq/L. Venous blood gases should be followed every 2–4 hours. Serum electrolytes are measured every 4 hours. As the acidosis is corrected, potassium moves intracellularly, thereby dropping the initial serum potassium concentration, so potassium should be added to the replacement fluids.

Prognosis

Complications from IDDM include microvascular disease of the eye (retinopathy), kidney (nephropathy), and nerves (neuropathy). Microvascular disease is generally not seen until the child has been insulin dependent for a minimum of 10 years. Accelerated large vessel atherosclerotic disease can lead to myocardial infarction and/or stroke. New research has shown that both types of vascular complications are minimized by tight glucose control.

◆ KEY POINTS ◆

1. Diabetes mellitus is a chronic metabolic disorder characterized by hyperglycemia and abnormal energy metabolism due to absent or diminished insulin secretion or action at the cellular level.

2. Insulin-dependent diabetes mellitus (IDDM) type 1 results from lack of insulin production in the B cells of the pancreas.

3. A history of new onset weight loss, polydipsia, polyphagia, and polyuria is consistent with type 1 diabetes mellitus.

4. Long-term complications from IDDM include microvascular disease (retinopathy, nephropathy, and neuropathy) and accelerated large vessel atherosclerotic disease.

DIABETES INSIPIDUS

In diabetes insipidus, there is loss of antidiuretic hormone secretion from the posterior pituitary gland and an inability to concentrate the urine. Diabetes insipidus can occur after head trauma or with a brain tumor or central nervous system infection. Surgical interruption of the pituitary stalk during craniopharyngioma removal often results in diabetes insipidus. Only rarely is diabetes insipidus an isolated idiopathic disorder.

Clinical Manifestations

The child with diabetes insipidus has abrupt onset polydipsia and polyuria. If the cause of the diabetes insipidus is a brain tumor impinging on the pituitary gland, focal neurologic signs and visual abnormalities may be noted.

The increased urine output may reach 5–10 L/day, with a urine specific gravity and urine osmolality that are quite low. Over time, serum sodium and serum osmolality increase, as hemoconcentration occurs from free water loss. In unclear cases, the water deprivation test is used to document diabetes insipidus. Remonstrating antidiuretic hormone (ADH) secretion is critical to differentiate ADH deficient diabetes insipidus from nephrogenic diabetes insipidus. Nephrogenic diabetes insipidus is a rare X-linked recessive disease in which the collecting ducts do not respond to ADH.

Treatment

DDAVP, an ADH analogue, is given intranasally to stimulate the kidneys to retain water and reverse the polyuria, polydipsia, and hypernatremia.

◆ KEY POINTS ◆

1. In diabetes insipidus, there is loss of ADH secretion and an inability to concentrate the urine.

2. Diabetes insipidus can occur after head trauma or with a brain tumor or central nervous system infection.

SHORT STATURE

Short stature is a common concern of parents, and its presence may be normal or pathologic. Normal causes include familial (genetic) short stature and constitutional delay. Eighty percent of cases of short stature are attributable to these two causes. Pathologic causes may result in either disproportionate or proportionate short stature. Etiologies that result in proportionate short stature are much more prevalent than those of disproportionate short stature.

Disorders that result in disproportionate short stature affect the long bones predominantly and include rickets, which is caused by activated vitamin D deficiency, and achondroplasia, an autosomal dominant disorder.

Diseases that cause proportionate short stature may result from either a prenatal or postnatal insult to the growth process. Prenatal etiologies include intrauterine growth retardation, placental dysfunction, intrauterine infections, teratogens, and chromosomal abnormalities. The most common chromosomal abnormalities that result in short stature are trisomy 21 and Turner's syndrome. Postnatal causes include malnutrition, chronic systemic diseases, psychosocial deprivation, drugs, and endocrine disorders. Common endocrine defects that result in short stature include hypothyroidism, growth hormone (GH) deficiency, glucocorticoid excess, and precocious puberty. The following discussion focuses on the most common causes of short stature, which include familial (genetic) short stature, constitutional delay, GH deficiency, primary hypothyroidism, Cushing's disease, chronic systemic diseases, psychosocial deprivation, Turner's syndrome, and medications.

Differential Diagnosis

Children with **familial short stature** establish growth curves at or below the fifth percentile by the age of 2. They are otherwise completely healthy, with a normal physical examination. Unlike children with constitutional delay, who have a delayed pubertal onset and bone age, these children have a normal bone age and puberty occurs at the expected time. Short stature is usually found in at least one parent, but height inheritance is complex and the diminutive ancestor may be more distant.

Children with **constitutional delay** grow and develop at or below the fifth percentile at normal growth velocities. This results in a curve parallel to the fifth percentile. Puberty is significantly delayed, which results in a delay in skeletal maturation. Because these children fail to enter puberty at the usual age, their short stature and sexual immaturity are accentuated when their peers enter puberty. Family members are usually of average height, but there is often a history of short stature in childhood and delayed puberty in other family members. The parents of children with constitutional delay should be counseled that their child's growth is a normal variant and that the child will likely mature to the height expected for their family.

GH deficiency accounts for approximately 5% of cases of short stature referred to endocrinologists. Children with classic GH deficiency grow at a diminished growth velocity, less than 5 cm/yr, and have delayed skeletal maturation. A history of birth asphyxia or neonatal hypoglycemia or physical findings of microphallus of midline defects are suggestive of idiopathic GH deficiency. GH deficiency secondary to hypothalamic or pituitary tumor usually is associated with other neurologic or visual impairments. In an older child with more recent onset of subnormal growth, the index of suspicion for tumor should be high.

Primary hypothyroidism causes marked growth failure because of a diminished growth velocity and skeletal maturation. Because primary hypothyroidism is easily treated with Synthroid, a thyroxine T_4, T_3RU, and thyrotropin (TSH) level should be measured, even in the absence of symptoms, to rule out any degree of hypothyroidism when evaluating short stature.

Cushing's disease is a rare cause of short stature. Hypercortisolism, from either exogenous steroid therapy or endogenous oversecretion, may have a profound growth-suppressing effect. Usually, other stigmata of Cushing's syndrome are present if growth suppression has occurred.

Chronic systemic diseases can result in short stature either from lack of caloric absorption or from caloric depletion from increased metabolic demands. Cyanotic heart disease, cystic fibrosis, poorly controlled diabetes mellitus, chronic renal failure, and severe rheumatoid arthritis are disorders that increase metabolic demands and diminish growth. Alternatively, inflammatory bowel disease, celiac sprue, and cystic fibrosis reduce caloric absorption and produce short stature.

Some children who live in emotionally or physically abusive or neglectful environments develop functional GH deficiency. Children with **psychosocial deprivation** have bizarre behaviors that include food hoarding, drinking from puddles and toilet bowls, as well as immature speech, disturbed sleep-wake cycles, and an increased pain tolerance. Clinically, they resemble children with GH deficiency, with marked retardation of bone age and pubertal delay. If GH testing is done while the child remains in the hostile environment, there is a blunted GH response, and when the child is removed from the deprived environment, GH testing reverts to normal and catch-up growth is noted.

One of the manifestations of **Turner's syndrome**, which is discussed in detail in Chapter 9, is short stature. The clinical manifestations of Turner's syndrome can sometimes be subtle. Therefore, testing for gonadotropins and a karyotype is indicated in the female adolescent with short stature and delayed puberty. Elevated gonadotropins indicate primary ovarian failure, and a 45, XO karyotype is diagnostic.

Chronic administration of certain **medications** may result in poor growth. Such drugs include steroids, Dexedrine, and Ritalin. Supplemental steroids cause hypercortisolism, whereas the etiology of stimulant suppression of growth is unknown.

Clinical Manifestations

History

Important historical information includes the child's prenatal and birth history, the pattern of growth, the presence of chronic disease, long-term medication use, the achievement of developmental milestones, and the growth and pubertal patterns of the patient's parents and siblings. Obtaining and evaluating the child's growth charts are vitally important. The child who has followed the fifth percentile for height since infancy and the child who has fallen from the 50th percentile for height to the fifth percentile have two different processes at work. The first child likely has either constitutional delay or genetic short stature, whereas the second child may have a chronic systemic disease that is resulting in lack of height growth.

Physical Examination

Since the most common causes of short stature are constitutional delay and familial short stature, the majority of physical examinations done on children with short stature are normal. It is critical to plot the child's height and weight on the appropriate growth curve for age. In addition to height, arm span and upper- to lower-body segment ratio is measured to check for pathologic disproportionate causes of short stature. In young children, the head circumference should also be evaluated to check for failure to thrive. In children with failure to thrive, weight and height are diminished and the head circumference is often spared, because the brain is the last organ of the body to be calorically deprived. When examining the child with short stature, the physician may find dysmorphic features in a pattern suggestive of a particular syndrome. The integument should be examined for cyanosis indicating potential congenital heart disease, abnormal pigmentation noted in Cushing's syndrome, and the stigmata of hypothyroidism. The thyroid is palpated to determine its size, its consistency, and the presence of thyroid nodules. The lungs and heart are examined to identify chronic cardiopulmonary disease. Abdominal tenderness or bloating may indicate inflammatory bowel disease or celiac sprue. Tanner staging for both boys and girls must be documented to help differentiate among familial short stature, constitutional delay, and precocious puberty. A thorough neurologic and fundoscopic examination may reveal underlying central nervous system disease that may result in GH deficiency.

Diagnostic Evaluation

Because most cases of short stature result from either familial short stature or constitutional delay, diagnostic studies are generally not necessary unless abnormalities are found on exam. A bone age assessment helps to delincate familial short stature from constitutional delay; an advanced bone age likely indicates precocious puberty; a normal bone age, familial short stature; and a delayed bone age, constitutional delay or Turner's syndrome.

Thyroid function tests may be done to rule out hypothyroidism, and a urinalysis and set of renal function tests are needed to rule out chronic renal disease. A complete blood count with differential and an erythrocyte sedimentation rate may be performed to reveal evidence of chronic systemic infection or an anemia of chronic disease. The child's nutritional status can be examined through the serum albumin and total protein counts. An insulin-like growth factor-1 and a postexercise GH level may be procured to look for GH deficiency. If a chromosomal anomaly is considered, obtaining a karyotype may be helpful. If an intracranial process is suspected, obtaining a magnetic resonance image of the head may identify a hypothalamic or pituitary process that is resulting in decreased GH secretion from the pituitary.

The child with familial short stature has few therapeutic options. Only in the most severe cases has GH been given with good results to minimize the negative psychological effects of extremely short stature. Because puberty in these children occurs at the expected time, the social and emotional problems seen with children with constitutional delay are reduced greatly. Unfortunately, the potential ultimate height of the child with genetic short stature is still low.

For most children with constitutional delay, reassuring of the family and patient that the child's short stature is a normal variant suffices. In some select patients with no signs of puberty by age 14 years, a 4- to 6-month treatment with the appropriate sex hormone may help to modestly increase stature and pubertal development for psychological support until true pubertal development begins.

Children with GH deficiency are managed with biosynthetic human GH by subcutaneous injection every day. Accelerated growth velocity on GH treatment results in catch-up growth in most children. If puberty is delayed beyond age 14 years, the addition of sex steroids may be considered, both to augment the growth response to GH and to stimulate secondary sexual development.

Primary hypothyroidism is treated with Synthroid. After several weeks of therapy, the growth velocity generally returns to normal and over time there may be some catch-up growth. Unlike GH therapy, Synthroid therapy does not promote catch-up growth.

To manage the short stature associated with Cushing's disease, the physician must identify and treat the etiology. Girls with short stature due to Turner's syndrome may receive GH to increase their final adult height. Short stature due to psychosocial deprivation is treated by removing the child from the poor environment, and short stature due to medications is reversed by discontinuing the offending medication.

◆ KEY POINTS ◆

1. Eighty percent of cases of short stature result from normal growth and development and are due to either familial (genetic) short stature or constitutional delay.

2. Pathologic causes may result in either disproportionate or proportionate short stature; proportionate short stature is more prevalent than disproportionate short stature.

3. The most common pathologic etiologies of proportionate short stature include GH deficiency, primary hypothyroidism, Cushing's disease, chronic systemic diseases, psychosocial deprivation, Turner's syndrome, and medications.

THYROID DYSFUNCTION

Hyperthyroidism

Most cases of hyperthyroidism in children are caused by Grave's disease. Other causes include a hyperfunctioning "hot" thyroid nodule or acute suppurative thyroiditis. Grave's disease results from autoimmune-induced thyroid hyperplasia. Thyrotoxicosis is caused by circulating thyroid-stimulating immunoglobulins binding to thyrotropin receptors on thyroid cells, resulting in diffuse hyperplasia and increased levels of free T_4. Neonatal Grave's disease results from transplacental passage of maternal thyroid-stimulating immunoglobulins. In congenital Grave's disease, males and females are affected equally, whereas in the acquired variant, the female to male ratio is 5:1.

Clinical Manifestations

Symptoms include a voracious appetite without weight gain or with weight loss, heat intolerance, emotional lability, restlessness, excessive sweating, frequent loose stools, and poor sleep. Exophthalmos is uncommon in children, but older children may complain of palpitations. There is often a deterioration in school performance and a change in behavior. On physical examination, the child may be flushed, fidgety, and warm with proptosis, a hyperactive precordium, resting tachycardia, and a widened pulse pressure. The thyroid gland is generally enlarged, smooth, firm (but not hard), and nontender. Often a fine tremor is noted and proximal muscle weakness is present. Acute onset tachycardia, hyperthermia, diaphoresis, fever, nausea, and vomiting indicate thyroid storm, which can be life threatening. Thyroid storm, also known as malignant hyperthyroidism, is rare in children.

Infants with neonatal Grave's disease tend to stare, are jittery and hyperactive, and have an increased appetite and poor weight gain. Tachycardia is usually present, and thyromegaly may be palpable.

In hyperthyroidism, T_4 levels are elevated, triiodothyronine resin uptake (T_3RU) is elevated, and TSH is suppressed. Long-acting thyroid stimulator is found in 50% of patients with Grave's disease.

Treatment

Medical therapy for congenital hyperthyroidism is the administration of propylthiouracil (PTU). Neonatal Grave's disease generally resolves over the first several months of life. In the infant who is hemodynamically compromised by hyperthyroidism, parenteral fluids, digoxin, and propranolol may be necessary.

PTU administration is also used to treat Grave's disease and must be titrated carefully, because an overdose can result in hypothyroidism. Fifty percent of children with Grave's disease have a spontaneous remission and may be taken off antithyroid medication after 12–24 months of treatment.

Surgery is reserved for hyperfunctioning "hot" thyroid nodules that do not respond to PTU therapy or for children with long-standing Grave's disease that has not responded to antithyroid medication.

Hypothyroidism

Congenital hypothyroidism is discussed in Chapter 13. Acquired hypothyroidism during childhood or adolescence is known as juvenile hypothyroidism. The most common cause of juvenile hypothyroidism is Hashimoto's thyroiditis, which is a chronic lymphocytic thyroiditis that results in autoimmune destruction of the thyroid gland. Other causes of hypothyroidism include panhypopituitarism, ectopic thyroid dysgenesis, administration of antithyroid medications, and surgical or radioactive iodine ablation for treatment of hyperthyroidism. The incidence of hypothyroidism in girls is four times greater than in boys. There is often a family history of Grave's disease or Hashimoto's thyroiditis. Most children present at adolescence; it is unusual to develop thyroiditis before 5 years of age.

Panhypopituitarism is caused by damage to the hypothalamic-pituitary axis resulting from either primary pituitary dysfunction or secondary hypothalamic failure. Loss of thyrotropin-releasing hormone from the hypothalamus or TSH from the pituitary results in hypothyroidism. Craniopharyngioma is a common cause of panhypopituitarism and hypothyroidism.

Clinical Manifestations

Symptoms generally appear after the first year of life and include cold intolerance, diminished appetite, lethargy, and constipation. Physical findings include slow linear growth, delayed puberty, immature body proportions, paucity of speech, motor retardation, coarse puffy facies, dry thin hair, dry skin, and deep tendon reflexes with a delayed relaxation time.

Thyroid function tests reveal a depressed total T_4 serum concentration and a depressed T_3RU level. If primary hypothyroidism is present, an elevated serum TSH concentration is noted. If secondary hypothyroidism is present, the TSH level may be depressed, normal, or elevated. The detection of thyroid autoantibodies indicates an autoimmune basis of disease, whereas palpation of a thyroid nodule should be evaluated with a thyroid scan.

Treatment

Thyroid replacement with synthetic L-thyroxine is dosed and adjusted to maintain normal serum T_4 levels. Follow-up is frequent to monitor T_4 levels, growth, and development.

◆ KEY POINTS ◆

1. Most cases of hyperthyroidism in children are caused by Grave's disease, which is an autoimmune-induced thyroid hyperplasia.

2. Neonatal Grave's disease results from transplacental passage of maternal thyroid-stimulating immunoglobulins.

3. In primary hyperthyroidism, T_4 levels are elevated, T_3RU is elevated, and TSH is suppressed.

4. Medical therapy for Graves' disease consists of propylthiouracil (PTU) administration.

5. The most common cause of juvenile hypothyroidism is Hashimoto's thyroiditis, which is a chronic lymphocytic thyroiditis that results in autoimmune destruction of the thyroid gland.

6. Thyroid function tests reveal a decreased T_4 serum concentration, decreased T_3RU, and elevated serum TSH concentration.

7. Hypothyroidism is treated with synthetic L-thyroxine.

ADRENAL DYSFUNCTION

Congenital Adrenal Hyperplasia

The clinical characteristics of congenital adrenal hyperplasia depend on which enzyme in the pathway of steroidogenesis is deficient. The two most common defects are 21-hydroxylase deficiency and 11-hydroxylase deficiency.

21-Hydroxylase deficiency accounts for 90% of the cases of congenital adrenal hyperplasia. The disease is inherited as an autosomal recessive trait and tends to occur as either classic salt wasting 21-hydroxylase deficiency or as virilizing 21-hydroxylase deficiency. A schematic for steroidogenesis in the adrenal cortex is shown in Figure 6–1. 21-Hydroxylase is needed to produce aldosterone and cortisol. 21-Hydroxylase deficiency results in a build up of the precursors of aldosterone and cortisol synthesis, which are then metabolized to androgens. Specifically, 17-hydroxyprogesterone levels increase, which are then metabolized to dihydroepiandrosterone and androstenedione. Both forms of 21-hydroxylase deficiency result in decreased cortisol and aldosterone

secretion, increased corticotropin (ACTH), and increased 17-hydroxyprogesterone.

11-Hydroxylase deficiency accounts for 5% of the cases of congenital adrenal hyperplasia and is also inherited as an autosomal recessive trait. Similar to 21-hydroxylase deficiency, 11-hydroxylase deficiency impairs the production of aldosterone and cortisol. 11-Hydroxylase converts 11-deoxycortisol to cortisol and deoxycorticosterone to corticosterone in the aldosterone pathway. With reduction or absence of 11-hydroxylase, cortisol and aldosterone precursors build up and are shunted to androgen synthesis.

Clinical Manifestations

In congenital 21-hydroxylase deficiency, female infants are born with ambiguous genitalia. Clitoromegaly and labioscrotal fusion may result in erroneous male sex assignment. There is normal ovarian development, and internal genital structures are female. Male infants born with the defect have no genital abnormalities. Symptoms of emesis, salt wasting, dehydration, and shock develop in the first 2–4 weeks of life. Hyponatremia and hyperkalemia result from lack of aldosterone and hypoglycemia from decreased levels of cortisol. Worsening hyponatremic dehydration culminates in shock and acidosis in severe cases. The diagnosis of 21-hydroxylase deficiency is made by documenting elevated serum levels of 17-hydroxyprogesterone. Prenatal diagnosis can be made in the siblings of affected children by measurement of elevated 17-hydroxyprogesterone in the amniotic fluid and HLA typing, because siblings who share the defect have the same HLA type.

In 11-hydroxylase deficiency, there is overproduction of deoxycorticosterone, which has mineralocorticoid activity and results in hypernatremia, hypokalemia, and hypertension. Diagnosis is based on the measurement of increased levels of 11-deoxycortisol and deoxycorticosterone in the serum or their tetrahydrometabolites in the urine. Serum androstenedione and testosterone are also elevated, and renin and aldosterone levels are depressed.

Treatment

Therapy for 21-hydroxylase deficiency includes cortisol and mineralocorticoid therapy. Cortisol therapy reduces ACTH secretion and overproduction of androgens, and mineralocorticoid administration is adjusted to normalize serum renin levels. Surgical correction of female genital abnormalities is accomplished early. The linear growth and sexual development of children with 21-

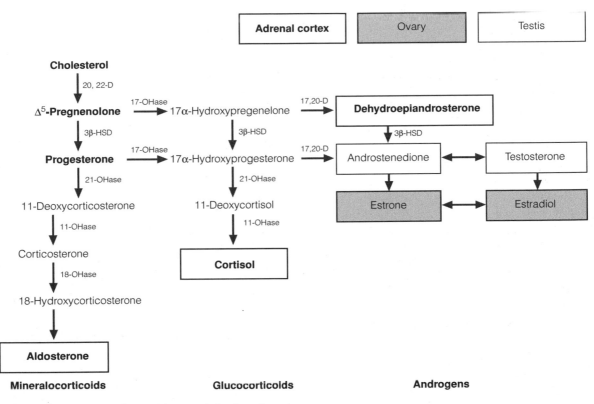

Figure 6–1 A schematic of steroidogenesis in the adrenal cortex.

hydroxylase deficiency must be monitored closely. Undertreatment, as indicated by elevated 17-hydroxyprogesterone, androstenedione, and renin levels and by accelerated advancement of skeletal maturity, leads to excessive growth, premature sexual hair growth, and virilization of the child. Ultimately, undertreatment may lead to premature epiphyseal fusion and adult short stature. Overtreatment with cortisol suppresses growth and may cause symptoms of hypercortisolism.

◆ KEY POINTS ◆

1. 21-Hydroxylase deficiency accounts for 90% of the cases of congenital adrenal hyperplasia. The disease is inherited as an autosomal recessive trait and tends to occur as either classic salt wasting 21-hydroxylase deficiency or as virilizing 21-hydroxylase deficiency.

2. In congenital 21-hydroxylase deficiency, female infants are born with ambiguous genitalia, whereas male infants born with the defect have no genital abnormalities.

3. In salt wasting 21-hydroxylase deficiency, symptoms of emesis, salt wasting, dehydration, and shock develop in the first 2–4 weeks of life.

4. The diagnosis of congenital adrenal hyperplasia is made by documenting elevated levels of 17-hydroxyprogesterone in the serum.

5. Therapy for 21-hydroxylase deficiency includes cortisol and mineralocorticoid therapy.

Precocious Puberty

Precocious thelarche refers to isolated early breast development. The usual age of onset is 12 to 24 months. Premature thelarche is likely due to small transient bursts of estrogen from the prepubertal ovary or from increased sensitivity to low levels of estrogen in the prepubertal female. Premature adrenarche refers to the early appearance of sexual hair before the age of 8 in girls and the age 9 in boys. This benign condition is due to early maturation of adrenal androgen secretion.

True precocious puberty is defined as secondary sex characteristics presenting in girls before the age of 7.5 years and in boys before the age of 9 years and may be either gonadotropin dependent or gonadotropin independent. True central (gonadotropin-dependent) precocious puberty is more common in girls than in boys. Precocious puberty in girls is usually idiopathic, whereas in boys it is often due to tumors of the central nervous system. Tumors causing gonadotropin-dependent precocious puberty (GDPP) include gliomas, pinealomas, and hamartomas. Other causes of GDPP include hydrocephalus, head injury, central nervous system congenital malformation, and central nervous system infection.

Gonadotropin-independent precocious puberty (GIPP) is extremely rare and is seen in McCune-Albright syndrome (polyostotic fibrous dysplasia of bone), familial precocious puberty in boys (testitoxicosis), and Leydig cell tumors.

Clinical Manifestations

In precocious thelarche, gonadotropin and serum estrogen levels are in the prepubertal range, and linear growth acceleration and advancing skeletal maturation are not present. This nonprogressive, benign condition is distinguished from true precocious puberty by the normal growth rate and bone age noted with premature thelarche.

In premature adrenarche, the levels of adrenal androgens are normal for pubertal stage but elevated for chronologic age. The child's bone age is usually slightly advanced. Children with premature adrenarche must be evaluated for other causes of increased androgen production, such as congenital adrenal hyperplasia or adrenal tumor. In children with evidence of significant androgen effect (advanced bone age, growth acceleration, and acne), measurement of adrenal steroids and androgens before and after ACTH administration is used to identify children with congenital adrenal hyperplasia.

The clinical manifestations of GDPP include premature development of secondary sexual characteristics and an accompanying growth spurt. If the GDPP is secondary to pathology of the central nervous system, then focal neurologic signs are often present. Diagnosis is based on advanced bone age and pubertal levels of gonadotropins and estrogen or testosterone. A pubertal pattern of elevated gonadotropins after infusion of gonadotropin-releasing hormone (GnRH) is indicative of GDPP. In GIPP, gonadotropins are low and GnRH has no effect on gonadotropin levels.

Treatment

Premature thelarche is a benign condition that resolves spontaneously and does not require any treatment. Premature adrenarche that is not caused by congenital adrenal hyperplasia is also a benign condition that resolves without therapy.

GDPP is treated with injections of long-acting preparations of GnRH. GnRH analogues suppress gonadotropin release and thereby decrease secondary sex characteristics, slow skeletal growth, and prevent the fusion of long bone epiphyseal plates.

◆ KEY POINTS ◆

1. True precocious puberty is defined as secondary sex characteristics presenting in girls before the age of 7.5 years and in boys before the age of 9 years and may be either gonadotropin dependent or gonadotropin independent.

2. True central (gonadotropin-dependent) precocious puberty is more common in girls than in boys. Precocious puberty in girls is usually idiopathic, whereas precocious puberty in boys is often due to tumors of the central nervous system.

3. The clinical manifestations of gonadotropin-dependent precocious puberty (GDPP) include premature development of secondary sexual characteristics and an accompanying growth spurt.

4. GDPP is treated with injections of long-acting preparations of gonadotropin-releasing hormone.

Cushing's Syndrome

Cushing's syndrome is a constellation of symptoms and signs that result from high cortisol levels and is due to either endogenous overproduction of cortisol or excessive exogenous treatment with pharmacologic doses of cortisol. Endogenous causes include Cushing's disease and adrenal tumors. Cushing's disease, also known as bilateral adrenal hyperplasia, is the most common etiology of Cushing's syndrome in children older than 7 years. In most instances, it is caused by a microadenoma of the pituitary gland resulting in ACTH oversecretion. Rarely, in the young child or infant, a malignant carcinoma of the adrenal gland is seen. Most adrenal tumors that cause Cushing's syndrome are adenomas.

Clinical Manifestations
The classic signs and symptoms of Cushing's syndrome include "moon" facies, buffalo hump, truncal obesity, abdominal striae, acne, slow growth, hypertension, and muscle weakness. Most adrenal tumors are virilizing.

Initial laboratory studies include documentation of an elevated serum cortisol level and an increased 24-hour urine free cortisol test. If hypercortisolism is demonstrated, the dexamethasone suppression test is performed to document the presence of Cushing's syndrome. Dexamethasone is given in the late evening, and a cortisol level is measured the next morning. Failure of the dexamethasone to suppress the morning cortisol level is consistent with Cushing's syndrome. A prolonged dexamethasone suppression test is used to differentiate Cushing's disease from an adrenal tumor. Low-dose dexamethasone is given over a 2-day period, followed by high-dose dexamethasone over a 2-day period. If serum and urine cortisol levels are suppressed to less than 50% of baseline, Cushing's disease is unlikely. If low-dose dexamethasone fails to suppress cortisol levels and high-dose dexamethasone does, then hypercortisolism is likely due to bilateral adrenal hyperplasia from a pituitary adenoma. If high dose dexamethasone fails to diminish cortisol levels, then an adrenal tumor is suspected. When evaluating a child with Cushing's syndrome, obtaining computed tomography scans of the pituitary and the adrenal glands is helpful to determine if pathology exists.

Treatment
Adrenal tumors are treated with surgical removal. Similarly, bilateral adrenal hyperplasia is treated with surgical excision of the pituitary adenoma. Trans-sphenoidal microsurgery is the most effective method of microadenoma removal. Perioperative stress dosing of glucocorticoids is needed to avoid adrenal insufficiency.

◆ KEY POINTS ◆

1. Cushing's syndrome is a constellation of symptoms and signs that result from high cortisol levels and is due to either endogenous overproduction of cortisol or excessive exogenous treatment with pharmacologic doses of cortisol. Cushing's disease is the most common non-iatrogenic cause of Cushing's syndrome.

2. The classic signs and symptoms of Cushing's syndrome include "moon" facies, buffalo hump, truncal obesity, abdominal striae, acne, slow growth, hypertension, and muscle weakness.

Addison's Disease

Addison's disease, or primary adrenal insufficiency, may be congenital or acquired and results in decreased cortisol secretion. Depending on the disease process, there may be a concomitant decrease in aldosterone release. In the newborn, primary adrenal insufficiency may be due to adrenal hypoplasia, ACTH unresponsiveness, adrenal hemorrhage, or ischemic infarction with sepsis (Waterhouse-Friderichsen syndrome). In older children and adolescents, autoimmune adrenal insufficiency is most common. It may occur alone or in association with another autoimmune endocrinopathy such as thyroiditis or IDDM. Adrenoleukodystrophy is an X-linked recessive disorder of long-chain fatty acid metabolism that results in adrenal insufficiency and progressive neurologic dysfunction.

In contrast to primary adrenal insufficiency, secondary adrenal insufficiency is due to ACTH deficiency. The most common cause of ACTH deficiency is chronic steroid therapy that results in suppression of pituitary ACTH. Pituitary tumors and craniopharyngiomas also result in depressed pituitary ACTH secretion from either destruction of the pituitary or pituitary compression.

Clinical Manifestations
Symptoms from primary adrenal insufficiency include weakness, nausea, vomiting, weight loss, and salt craving. Physical findings include postural hypotension and increased pigmentation over joints and on scar tissue, lips, nipples, and the buccal mucosa. The postural hypoten-

sion and salt craving are due to lack of aldosterone, whereas the increased pigmentation is due to increased ACTH secretion to increase poor adrenal performance. Melanocyte-stimulating hormone is a by-product of the ACTH biosynthetic pathway. Adrenal crisis is characterized by fever, vomiting, dehydration, and shock. It may be precipitated by intercurrent illness, trauma, or surgery.

Electrolyte abnormalities include hyponatremia, hyperkalemia, and mild metabolic acidosis from dehydration. The serum cortisol level by definition is low and is unresponsive to injection of ACTH (corticotropin stimulation test). If the corticotropin stimulation test is abnormal, a prolonged ACTH stimulation test is necessary to rule out secondary adrenal insufficiency.

Treatment

Adrenal crisis, also known as Addisonian crisis, is a life-threatening condition that should be treated without delay. Correction of electrolyte abnormalities and dehydration is required immediately with 5% dextrose in normal saline and stress dose intravenous glucocorticoids. Treatment with dexamethasone instead of hydrocortisone permits ACTH testing to be carried out while treatment is initiated, because dexamethasone does not interfere with cortisol testing after ACTH stimulation.

Long-term management consists of maintenance doses of oral glucocorticoids and mineralocorticoids. The glucocorticoid dosage is increased during times of acute metabolic stress to avoid adrenal insufficiency.

◆ KEY POINTS ◆

1. Primary adrenal insufficiency may be congenital or acquired and results in decreased cortisol secretion, whereas secondary adrenal insufficiency is due to ACTH deficiency.

2. Symptoms from primary adrenal insufficiency include weakness, nausea, vomiting, weight loss, salt craving, postural hypotension, and increased pigmentation.

3. Adrenal crisis is characterized by fever, vomiting, dehydration, and shock. It may be precipitated by intercurrent illness, trauma, or surgery.

4. Electrolyte abnormalities found in adrenal crisis include hyponatremia, hyperkalemia, and metabolic acidosis from dehydration.

Fluid, Electrolyte, and pH Management

The human body is designed to function optimally at a certain set environmental equilibrium. In reality, body systems are constantly adjusting to both internal and external challenges. The younger the patient, the relatively more intolerant he or she is to changes in **fluid volume, distribution, composition**, and **pH**.

DEHYDRATION

Dehydration in the pediatric patient is usually secondary to **vomiting** or **diarrhea**. Infants and toddlers are particularly susceptible because of the limited ability of the immature kidney to conserve water, a relatively high percentage of total body water, and dependence on caretakers to meet their needs. Regardless of etiology, the cornerstone of dehydration management is the **judicious replacement of fluid and electrolytes**.

Clinical Manifestations

History
A careful **history** clarifies the differential and provides information concerning the acuity, source, and quantity of fluid lost. Recent **weight loss** and **decreased urine output** are important indicators of the degree of deficiency. Data concerning the color, consistency, frequency, and volume of stool and/or emesis influence initial diagnostic and therapeutic measures.

Many chronic medical illnesses may present acutely with dehydration, including diabetes, metabolic disorders, cystic fibrosis, and congenital adrenal hyperplasia. Renal conditions such as diabetes insipidus and renal tubular acidosis are associated with polyuria. Children who are neglected or refuse to drink because of severe oropharyngeal pain may also develop significant dehydration.

Physical Examination
The most important objective of the physical examination is assessing the **degree of dehydration** (Table 7–1). **Tachycardia** is the earliest manifestation in children; unfortunately, it is notoriously nonspecific. The respiratory rate remains normal early on but increases as metabolic acidosis intervenes. **Hypotension** is a late and ominous development. Skin, eye, and central nervous system findings also assist in the evaluation.

Diagnostic Evaluation
Serum electrolyte levels should be determined for any significantly dehydrated child. The results influence the composition and rate of replacement fluid chosen. Dehydration may be isotonic, hypotonic (hyponatremic), or hypertonic (hypernatremic), depending on the nature of the fluid lost and replacement fluids provided by the caretaker (Table 7–2).

Isotonic dehydration is the most common form and suggests that either compensation has occurred or water losses roughly equal sodium losses. **Hypotonic dehydration** is diagnosed when the serum sodium is less than 130 mEq/L. Children who lose electrolytes in their stool

TABLE 7–1

Clinical Estimation of Degree of Dehydration

	Mild	Moderate	Severe
Body fluid lost (mL/kg)	<50	50–100	>100
Weight loss (%)	<5	5–10	>10
Stage of shock	Impending*	Compensated	Uncompensated
Vital signs			
Heart rate	Slight ↑	↑ (orthostasis)	↑↑
Respiratory	Normal	Normal	↑ (Hyperpnea)
Blood pressure	Normal	Normal (orthostasis)	↓
Skin			
Capillary refill (finger)	<2 sec	2–3 sec	>3 sec
Elasticity (<2 yr)	Normal	↓	↓↓ (tenting)
Anterior fontanel	Normal	Depressed	Depressed
Mucous membranes	Normal/dry	Dry	Dry
CNS			
Mental status	Normal	Altered	Depressed
Eyes			
Tearing	Normal/absent	Absent	Absent
Appearance	Normal	Sunken	Sunken
Laboratory tests			
Urine			
Volume	Small	Oliguria	Oliguria-anuria
Osmolarity (mOsm/L)	600	800	Maximal
Specific gravity	1.020	1.025	Maximal
Blood			
Blood urea nitrogen	Upper normal	Elevated	High
pH	7.40–7.22	7.30–6.92	7.10–6.80

*Signs of dehydration may be less evident or appear later in hypernatremic dehydration; conversely, they may be more pronounced or appear sooner in hyponatremic dehydration.

Reprinted with permission from Fleisher GR, Ludwig S, eds. Textbook of pediatric emergency medicine. Baltimore, MD: Williams & Wilkins, 1993:148.

TABLE 7–2

Probable Deficits of Water and Electrolytes in Severe Dehydration

Condition*	H₂O (mL/kg)	Sodium (mEq/kg)	Potassium (mEq/kg)	Chloride (mEq/kg)
Diarrheal dehydration				
Hypotonic [Na] <130 mEq/L	20–100	10–15	8–15	10–12
Isotonic [Na] = 130–150 mEq/L	100–120	8–10	8–10	8–10
Hypertonic [Na] >150 mEq/L	100–120	2–4	0–6	0–3
Hypertonic pyloric stenosis	100–120	8–10	10–12	10–12
Diabetic ketoacidosis	100	8	6–10	6

*[Na] refers to the serum or plasma sodium concentration.

Reprinted with permission from Hellerstein S. Fluid and electrolytes: clinical aspects. Pediatr Rev 1993;14:109.

and are supplemented with free water or dilute juices often present in this manner. **Hypertonic dehydration** indicates a serum sodium greater than 150 mEq/L and is uncommon in children.

Usually, the serum bicarbonate concentration is decreased secondary to metabolic acidosis; however, protracted vomiting may result in alkalosis. The difference between the sum of the measured cations and anions, termed the **anion gap**, is normally 12 ± 4; Table 7–3 lists conditions associated with changes in the measurement. Blood urea nitrogen (BUN) and serum creatinine (Cr) increase over several days as the glomerular filtration rate falls; a BUN/Cr ratio of greater than 20 is consistent with prerenal failure.

Treatment

Oral rehydration therapy (ORT) is the preferable treatment for mild to moderate dehydration. The World Health Organization recommends that solutions contain 90 mEq/L sodium, 20 mEq/L potassium, and 20 g/L glucose. The administration of free water or diluted juices may precipitate severe hyponatremia and is contraindicated. ORT is particularly labor intensive; a caretaker provides the child with small amounts of fluids at regular intervals. When administered correctly, ORT is an extremely effective method of rehydration.

TABLE 7–3

Changes in the Anion Gap

Increased Anion Gap	Normal Anion Gap	Decreased Anion Gap
Hypokalemia	Hypernatremic dehydration	Hyperkalemia
Hypocalcemia		Hypercalcemia
Hypomagnesemia	Renal tubular acidosis	Hypermagnesemia
Hyperphosphatemia		Hypoalbuminemia
Diarrheal dehydration	Hyperalimentation	Lithium poisoning
Lactic acidosis		
Diabetic ketoacidosis		
Salicylate poisoning		
Renal failure		
Methanol poisoning		
Uremia		

Severe dehydration leads to life-threatening **hypovolemic shock**. These children should receive 20 mL/kg intravenous boluses of isotonic fluid (normal saline or Ringer's lactate) until their condition stabilizes (see Chapter 1). Clinical estimation of the degree of dehydration and the results of electrolyte studies define subsequent therapy. The goal is to achieve normal fluid status over 24 hours by meeting **maintenance** needs, replacing the deficit, and keeping up with **ongoing losses**.

Maintenance therapy is based on the child's weight and is computed using the Holliday-Seger method: 100 mL/kg/day for the first 10 kg in weight plus 50 mL/kg/day for the next 10 kg plus 25 mL/kg/day for each kg thereafter. In general, one-fourth to one-half normal saline with 5% dextrose and 20 mEq KCl/L meets maintenance glucose and electrolyte needs.

Most deficits are replaced over 24 hours, with half given in the first 8 hours and the rest over the next 16 hours. One important exception occurs in the child with hypertonic dehydration; in these cases, the deficit should be replaced over 48–72 hours to prevent excessive fluid shifts and brain edema. Ongoing losses (usually in stool) are replaced milliliter for milliliter with intravenous fluid compared in electrolyte content with that being lost. For example, an 18-kg infant with a normal serum sodium judged to be 10% dehydrated has lost an estimated 2000 mL of fluid (1000 mL weighs approximately 1 kg). Half the deficit is replaced over the first 8 hours, with the balance given over the next 16 hours. Maintenance therapy must be included. The child received a 20-mL/kg bolus initially.

1. 2000 mL ÷ 2 = 1000 mL (one-half the total deficit); 360 mL (20 mL/kg) have already been replaced. Therefore, 640 mL is given over the first 8 hours at 80 mL/hr. This should be added to the 60 mL/hr the child requires to meet maintenance needs. Rate = 80 mL/hr + 60 mL/hr = 140 mL/hr.

2. The second half (1000 mL) is replaced over the next 16 hours (63 mL/hr) along with the maintenance rate (60 mL/hr). Rate = 63 mL/hr + 60 mL/hr = 123 mL/hr.

The composition of the replacement fluid varies depending on the initial laboratory values. Replacement fluid should be potassium-free until the patient demonstrates an ability to excrete the electrolyte by urinating. Bicarbonate or acetate therapy may be appropriate when the pH and serum levels are still dangerously low after the initial boluses.

Patients with profound hyperglycemia or electrolyte disturbances due to an underlying pathologic process (i.e., diabetic ketoacidosis) may require the more specialized management discussed elsewhere in this review.

◆ KEY POINTS ◆

1. Children are more susceptible to severe dehydration than are adults.

2. The history and physical examination are the best determinants of the degree of dehydration.

3. Dehydration may be isotonic, hypotonic, or hypertonic.

4. When calculating fluid needs, remember to replace previous losses, keep up with ongoing output, and provide maintenance therapy.

EDEMA

Edema is the accumulation of fluid in the interstitial space. This collection results from the retention of sodium and water, diminished intravascular oncotic pressure, or abnormal vascular permeability. Inflammation, trauma, allergic reactions, and occluded lymphatics produce focal edema.

Differential Diagnosis

Generalized edema in children is usually **nephrotic, cardiac, gastrointestinal,** or **hepatic** in origin (Fig. 7–1).

Clinical Manifestations

History

Generalized edema is often insidious in onset. **Pregnancy** should be considered in the sexually active female. Certain **medications**, such as oral contraceptive pills, are associated with edema formation in some people. Sweating with feeding, shortness of breath, and cyanosis sug-

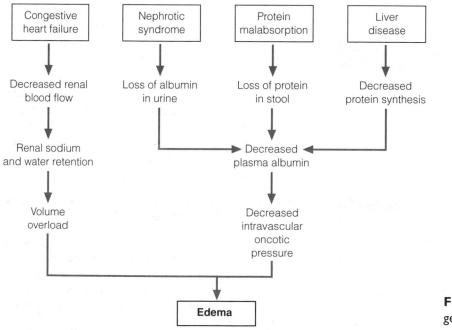

Figure 7–1 Mechanisms of generalized edema.

gest a **cardiac** origin. Chronic diarrhea is present in most **malabsorptive disorders**.

Children who have had a recent skin or throat infection or hematuria may have **glomerulonephritis**. Jaundice and pruritus accompany **liver disease**. Henoch-Schönlein purpura (HSP) presents with lower extremity edema, joint pain, and a purpuric rash. Rapid development of edema occurs during an **allergic** reaction.

Physical Examination

Children with **nephrotic syndrome**, the most common cause of generalized edema in childhood, appear well. Periorbital swelling, ascites, and a drop off in growth are variably present. Crackles on lung examination, tachypnea, and hepatomegaly are consistent with congestive heart failure. Patients with pericardial effusion may manifest a cardiac rub and jugular venous distention. Edema of the scalp, hands, and feet accompanied by an erythematous macular rash spreading up the lower extremities is classic during the onset of HSP. In infants, sickle cell anemia may present with acute painful swelling of the distal extremities (hand-foot syndrome). Fever and nonblanching skin lesions are characteristic of **vasculitis**.

Diagnostic Evaluation

Screening laboratory tests include serum electrolytes, liver function tests, protein and albumin levels, urine dip for protein, a complete blood count, and an erythrocyte sedimentation rate. A chest radiograph revealing a large heart and pulmonary edema is consistent with heart failure. Proteinuria is virtually diagnostic for nephrotic syndrome in the case of generalized edema.

Treatment

Correcting the underlying disorder is the most effective treatment.

◆ KEY POINTS ◆

1. Edema is the accumulation of fluid in the interstitial space.
2. Generalized edema in children may be nephrotic, cardiac, gastrointestinal, or hepatic in origin.

HYPONATREMIA

Hyponatremia (serum sodium less than 130 mEq/L) may occur in the face of decreased, normal, or increased total body sodium content. In children, the most common setting is **dehydration** associated with vomiting and diarrhea, discussed earlier.

Clinical Manifestations

History and Physical Examination

The severity of clinical manifestations depends on both the **level of sodium** in the extracellular space and the **rate of change** from normal. Falling levels that occur over several days are tolerated better than rapid losses. Anorexia and nausea are early, nonspecific complaints. Neurologic findings include confusion, lethargy, and decreased tendon reflexes. **Seizures** and **respiratory arrest** are life-threatening complications.

Diagnostic Evaluation

The laboratory workup of hyponatremia includes serum electrolytes, glucose, blood urea nitrogen and creatinine, serum osmolality, liver function tests, protein, and lipid levels. (The true serum Na is 1.6 mEq higher than the measured Na for every 100 mg/dL rise in glucose, and 0.002 mEq higher for every mg/dL rise in serum lipid levels.) Urine sodium (U_{Na}) and specific gravity (USG) also assist in diagnosis (Fig. 7–2).

Treatment

Dehydration is treated with fluid resuscitation as discussed earlier. Hyponatremia due to other causes requires fluid restriction and treatment of the underlying disorder. The cautious use of 3% hypertonic saline is limited to life-threatening situations (i.e., intractable seizures).

HYPERNATREMIA

Hypernatremia is uncommon in children in the absence of dehydration (discussed earlier). Signs and symptoms include muscle weakness, irritability, and lethargy. Seizures and coma are the major complications.

Dehydration is the most common setting for hypernatremia in children.

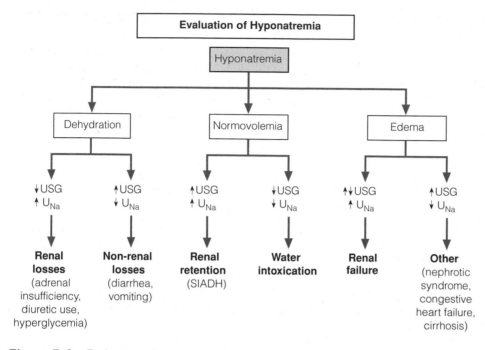

Figure 7–2 Evaluation of hyponatremia.

HYPERKALEMIA

Normal serum potassium values range from 3.5 to 5.0 mEq/L; a measurement of 5.5 mEq/L or greater is considered **hyperkalemia**. In children, the most common cause of an abnormally high potassium level is artifactual, due to the hemolysis of red cells during sample collection. Transcellular shifts in acidosis increase serum potassium without changing total body content; for every unit reduction in arterial pH, plasma potassium increases 0.2–0.4 mEq/L. Disorders and medications that interfere with renal excretion of the electrolyte precipitate true hyperkalemia.

Differential Diagnosis

Common causes of hyperkalemia include:

- acidosis
- severe dehydration
- potassium-sparing diuretics
- excessive parenteral infusion

Other less common but important conditions to consider include:

- adrenal corticoid deficiency (i.e., Addison's disease)
- renal tubular acidosis
- massive crush injury
- beta-blocker or theophylline intoxication

Clinical Manifestations

Paresthesias and weakness are the earliest symptoms; flaccid paralysis and tetany occur late. Cardiac involvement correlates with specific progressive electrocardiogram (ECG) changes; T-wave elevation is followed by loss of P waves, widening QRS complexes, and S-T depression. Ventricular fibrillation and cardiac arrest occur at serum levels of at least 10 mEq/L.

Treatment

The treatment of hyperkalemia is threefold. **Calcium gluconate** protects the heart by stabilizing the cardiac cell membrane. Infusion of sodium bicarbonate or insulin (and glucose) drives potassium into the cells. Cation exchange resins (i.e., Kayexalate) and hemodialysis are the only measures that actually remove potassium from the body.

HYPOKALEMIA

Hypokalemia in the pediatric population is usually encountered in cases of alkalosis secondary to vomiting, administration of loop diuretics, or diabetic ketoacidosis. Signs and symptoms include weakness, tetany, constipation, polyuria, and polydipsia. Muscle breakdown leading to myoglobinuria may compromise renal function. ECG changes are noted at levels of no more than 2.5 mEq/L; cardiac arrhythmias can occur and are more likely when digitalis is present. Blood pressure changes and urine electrolyte results assist in diagnosis (Table 7–4). Treatment consists of correcting pH (when increased) and replenishing potassium stores.

METABOLIC ACIDOSIS

Metabolic acidosis results from the loss of HCO_3^- or the addition of H^+ in the extracellular fluid. It is the most common acid–base disorder encountered in the pediatric population. Primary metabolic acidosis can be differentiated from compensated respiratory alkalosis by the following equation: $Paco_2 = 1.5 \times HCO_3^- + 8 \pm 2$. An actual $Paco_2$ lower than the computed value indicates metabolic acidosis secondary to a primary respiratory disorder.

Clinical Manifestations

Hyperpnea is the most consistent clinical finding in metabolic acidosis; other signs and symptoms are related to the underlying disorder. Important laboratory studies include serum electrolytes, blood urea nitrogen, creatinine, glucose, venous or arterial blood gas, and urine dipstick for pH and glucose. The calculated anion gap assists in diagnosis (see Table 7–3).

Treatment

The intravenous administration of sodium bicarbonate should be reserved for cases in which the serum pH is no more than 7.0 and the cause is unknown or difficult to reverse. Patients receiving alkali therapy require fre-

TABLE 7–4

Hypokalemia: Diagnosis

| | Decreased Stores | | | |
| | Hypertension | Normal BP | | Normal Stores |
		Renal	Extrarenal	
Causes	Renovascular disease	R.T.A.	Skin losses	Alkalosis
	Excess renin	Fanconi syndrome	GI losses	↑ Insulin
	Congenital adrenal hyperplasia	Bartter syndrome	High CHO diet	Leukemia
		Antibiotics	Enema abuse	
	Excess mineralocorticoid	Diuretics	Laxative abuse	
	Cushing's syndrome		Anorexia nervosa	
Laboratory data	↑ Urine potassium	↑ Urine potassium	↓ Urine potassium	↑ Urine potassium
Management		Replace potassium in all cases. Treat causes.		

Reprinted with permission from Johnson KB, ed. The Harriet Lane handbook. St. Louis, MO: Mosby, 1993:171.

quent pH, sodium, potassium, and calcium monitoring; complications include alkalosis, hypokalemia, hypernatremia, and hypocalcemia.

of mineralocorticoid excess (i.e., renal artery stenosis); potassium supplements are necessary in these cases.

METABOLIC ALKALOSIS

Metabolic alkalosis is much less common than acidosis in children. "Contraction" alkalosis results from the loss of fluid high in H^+ or Cl^-, as may occur with protracted gastric vomiting or chronic thiazide or loop diuretic administration. Patients with cystic fibrosis may develop metabolic alkalosis due to excessive electrolyte losses in the sweat. Volume expansion and chloride replacement correct the alkalosis unless it is associated with disorders

◆ KEY POINTS ◆

1. Metabolic acidosis is a relatively common disorder in pediatric patients.

2. The equation $Pa_{CO_2} = 1.5 \times HCO_3^- + 8 (\pm 2)$ can help distinguish between primary and secondary metabolic acidosis.

3. $NaHCO_3$ (sodium bicarbonate) should be used only when acidosis is severe or difficult to correct.

8

Gastroenterology

ABDOMINAL PAIN

Abdominal pain is one of the most common symptoms the pediatrician sees, and it has a complex differential diagnosis. Abdominal pain may be acute or chronic/recurrent (at least three episodes within 3 months), and it may represent a surgical, medical, or emotional condition. Chronic/recurrent abdominal pain occurs in approximately 10% of children 5–15 years old, and less than 10% of these cases result from an organic cause.

Differential Diagnosis

The causes of abdominal pain are listed in Table 8–1 and are classified as common, uncommon, and rare. Common etiologies in aggregate account for 90% of cases of abdominal pain, and uncommon causes result in 1–10% of cases. The designation of rare indicates that the disease process is found in less than 1% of patients with abdominal pain. Surgical diseases are defined as those etiologies that may require surgery.

Clinical Manifestations

History

The history should localize the pain and determine its quality and temporal characteristics and its exacerbating and alleviating factors. With "inflammatory" pain, the child tends to lie still, whereas with "colicky" pain, the child cannot remain still. Colicky pain usually results from obstruction, whereas inflammatory pain is caused

by an infected or perforated organ or viscus. Determine what the child's usual diet is, what he or she has eaten recently, and whether there has been a change in diet. Dietary indiscretion is a common cause of abdominal pain. Always ascertain whether the child has any drug or food allergies or has had previous abdominal surgeries. After laparotomy, small bowel obstruction becomes more likely. Establish whether the pain is accompanied by anorexia, nausea, emesis, diarrhea, or constipation. Determine if the emesis is bloody or bilious and if the diarrhea is bloody or mucosal. Bilious emesis indicates ileus or obstruction, whereas bloody emesis points to esophagitis, gastritis, or duodenitis. Bloody or mucosal diarrhea suggests bacterial enterocolitis. Anorexia, fever, and right lower quadrant abdominal pain is probably appendicitis.

Discuss the stooling habits of the child, because constipation is a common etiology of chronic abdominal pain. Dysuria and abdominal pain are indicative of a urinary tract infection, whereas sore throat and abdominal pain implicates pharyngitis. Find out if there is a history of trauma. Obtaining a good sexual history in the adolescent is critical. If there is a history of vaginal discharge and fever, pelvic inflammatory disease (PID) should be considered. Inquiring about ill contacts can give helpful clues to the diagnosis, because viral gastroenteritis is quite contagious and very common. A family history of lactose intolerance, Crohn's disease, ulcerative colitis, or irritable bowel syndrome increases the likeli-

TABLE 8–1

Differential Diagnosis of Abdominal Pain

		Acute Abdominal Pain		
Infectious Disease	Noninfectious Medical Disease	Surgical Disease	Trauma	Emotional
Common	**Common**	**Common**	**Common**	**Common**
Viral gastroenteritis (Rotavirus)	Dietary indiscretion	Appendicitis	None	None
Bacterial enterocolitis (Salmonella, Shigella, Yersinia, Campylobacter)				
Food poisoning (*S. aureus*, salmonella)				
Mesenteric lymphadenitis,				
Group A streptococcal pharyngitis				
Urinary tract infection				
Uncommon	**Uncommon**	**Uncommon**	**Uncommon**	**Uncommon**
Pelvic inflammatory disease	Cholecystitis/ cholelithiasis	Small or large bowel obstruction (adhesions)	Bowel perforation	Conversion reaction/ hysteria
Lower lobe pneumonia	Diabetes mellitus	Incarcerated hernia	Intramural hematoma	
Viral hepatitis	Pregnancy with or without ectopic location	Intussusception	Intraperitoneal blood	
Herpes zoster		Meckel's diverticulum	Musculocutaneous injury	
Peritonitis (post-trauma, instrumentation, spontaneous)	Testicular torsion	Malrotation and/or volvulus		
Infectious mononucleosis	HSP	Cholecystitis/cholelithiasis		
	Rare	**Rare**	**Rare**	
	Malignancy (leukemia/lymphoma)	Solid tumors (rupture or hemorrhage)	Pancreatic rupture	
	Nephrolithiasis	Testicular torsion	Retroperitoneal hematoma	
	Obstructive nephropathy		Liver/spleen laceration or hematoma	
	Pancreatitis			
	Kawasaki's disease			
	Polyarteritis nodosa			
	SLE			

	Recurrent Chronic Abdominal Pain		
Infectious Disease	Noninfectious Medical Disease	Surgical Disease	Emotional
Common	**Common**	**Common**	**Common**
Urinary tract infection	Gastroesophageal reflux	None	Anxiety reaction
	Constipation		Task-induced phobia (school or sports)
	Lactase deficiency		Secondary gain
	Mittelschmerz syndrome		"Psychophysiologic" (depression, idiopathic recurrent pain)
	Dysmenorrhea		

TABLE 8–1 *(continued)*

Differential Diagnosis of Abdominal Pain

Infectious Disease	Noninfectious Medical Disease	Surgical Disease	Emotional
Uncommon	**Uncommon**	**Uncommon**	**Uncommon**
Parasitic infection (ascariasis, giardiasis, strongyloidiasis, trichinelliasis)	Medication use (erythromycin, aspirin, anticonvulsants, bronchodilators) Sickle cell crisis (abdominal crisis) Ulcerative colitis Crohn's disease Peptic ulcer disease Food allergy Hiatal hernia Hepatomegaly Aerophagia	Crohn's disease (ileal stenosis) Ulcerative colitis	Irritable bowel syndrome
	Rare		
	Hirschsprung's disease Abdominal migraine Acute intermittent porphyria Abdominal epilepsy Abdominal masses/malignancies (lymphoma, neuroblastoma, ovarian lesions, Wilms' tumor) Collagen vascular disease Cystic fibrosis (intestinal obstruction) Endometriosis Hematocolpos Chronic pancreatitis		

Acute Lower Abdominal Pain in the Sexually Active Adolescent Female

	Urinary Tract	Reproductive Tract
	Cystitis Pyelonephritis Urethritis	Pelvic inflammatory disease Cervicitis Dysmenorrhea (primary/secondary) Pregnancy (intrauterine/ectopic) Endometriosis Mittelschmerz Ovarian cyst (torsion/rupture) Ruptured follicle Septic abortion Threatened abortion Torsion of the adnexa Tubo-ovarian abscess

Key: HSP, Henoch-Schönlein purpura; SLE, Systemic lupus erythematosis

Adapted from Markel H, Oski JA, Oski FA, et al. The portable pediatrician. Philadelphia: Hanley and Belfus, 1992:2.

hood of these diagnoses because they are genetically based. Changes in the child's environment (home, friends, school) or behavior (poor school performance, increasingly argumentative) may suggest that the abdominal pain is not the result of organic disease.

Physical Examination

The goal of the abdominal examination is to ascertain whether the child has an abdominal process that requires surgical intervention. Before formally examining the child's abdomen, watch the child walk, climb onto the examination table, and interact with both parents and staff to gain an appreciation for the degree of incapacitation or emotional overlay that may be present. Inspect, auscultate, and palpate the abdomen. Try to elicit peritoneal signs: rebound tenderness, guarding, psoas or obturator signs, rigidity of the abdominal wall. Unless the diagnosis is thought to be uncomplicated viral gastroenteritis, a rectal examination should be performed to detect tenderness or hard stool and to do a stool guaiac examination. If the patient is an adolescent female, a pelvic examination should be performed. Unless there is cervical motion tenderness, PID is unlikely.

Diagnostic Evaluation

The diagnostic test strategy is dictated by the history and findings of the physical examination. If the cause of the pain is thought to be a surgical one, then a surgical consultation should be obtained. Of the common causes of acute or chronic/recurrent abdominal pain, surgical causes are the most likely to require immediate intervention.

A complete blood count with manual differential, serum electrolytes and chemistries, amylase, stool guaiac examination, urinalysis, and radiographic studies should be performed if there has been abdominal trauma or an acute surgical condition is suspected. Blood should also be typed for possible transfusion. A barium swallow with upper gastrointestinal examination, pH probe, and an endoscopic examination may be used to evaluate for reflux. When uncomplicated viral gastroenteritis is the most likely cause, no studies need be performed, but if bacterial enterocolitis is being considered, stool should be obtained for culture and Wright stain to look for PMNs. Group A streptoccocal pharyngitis and PID require appropriate cultures. If constipation is suspected, the clinician should do a rectal examination to check the rectal vault, and in some severe cases, abdominal radiographs

may be indicated. To diagnose a urinary tract infection, a urine dip looking for nitrites and leukocyte esterase, formal urinalysis, and urine culture should be performed.

Treatment

Treatment is directed at the underlying cause of the pain. Surgical problems are treated accordingly. Group A streptococcal pharyngitis, urinary tract infections, and PID require appropriate antibiotics. Individuals with lactase deficiency benefit from a lactose-free diet or exogenous lactase replacement. Patients with reflux esophagitis benefit from small, frequent meals (rather than infrequent large ones), sitting upright for 30 minutes after a meal or sleeping at a 45-degree angle after eating, avoidance of late evening meals, a prokinetic agent, and an H2-blocker. Children with emotional-related abdominal pain require patience, reassurance, and in some cases professional psychiatric assistance. Constipation can be treated with prune juice, mineral oil, or Colace. In some cases, disimpaction, cathartics, or enemas may be required.

Below are short discussions about disorders that present with abdominal pain that are frequently tested on the national boards.

◆ KEY POINTS ◆

1. Determine whether the pain is acute or chronic/recurrent and whether a medical, surgical, or emotional disorder is most likely.

2. If the patient is an adolescent female, a pelvic examination must be done, and genitourinary pathology must be considered.

Appendicitis

Appendicitis is the most common indication for abdominal surgery in childhood. Appendicitis results from bacterial invasion of the appendix, which is more likely when the lumen is obstructed by a fecalith, parasite, or lymph node. Appendicitis occurs most frequently in children between 10 and 15 years of age. Less than 10% of patients are younger than 5 years of age.

Clinical Manifestations

Classically, fever, emesis, anorexia, and diffuse periumbilical pain develop. Subsequently, pain and abdominal tenderness localize to the right lower quadrant as the parietal peritoneum becomes inflamed. Guarding, rebound tenderness, and obturator and psoas signs are commonly found. The appendix tends to perforate 36 hours after pain begins. The incidence of perforation and diffuse peritonitis is high, especially in children under 2 years, when diagnosis may be delayed. Atypical presentations are common in childhood, especially with retrocecal appendicitis. The retrocecal appendix usually does not induce right lower quadrant pain until after perforation. Diarrhea is also a common symptom of retrocecal appendicitis. Bacterial enterocolitis caused by Campylobacter and Yersinia may mimic appendicitis because both can result in right lower quadrant abdominal pain and tenderness. Diagnosis of appendicitis is established clinically by history and by physical examination, which should include a rectal examination to detect tenderness or a mass. A moderately elevated white blood cell count with a left shift, usually not elevating above 20,000, is often seen in appendicitis. A plain film of the abdomen may demonstrate a fecalith. Abdominal ultrasound is used to identify the inflamed appendix.

Treatment

Laparotomy and appendectomy are performed, before perforation it is hoped. When appendicitis results in perforation, the patient should be given ampicillin, gentamicin, and flagyl to treat peritonitis from intestinal flora. The mortality rate rises significantly with perforation.

◆ KEY POINTS ◆

1. Appendicitis is the most common indication for abdominal surgery in childhood.

2. Fever, emesis, anorexia, and diffuse periumbilical pain develop initially and then the pain and abdominal tenderness localize to the right lower quadrant when the parietal peritoneum becomes inflamed. Guarding, rebound tenderness, and obturator and psoas signs are commonly found.

Intussusception

Intussusception results from telescoping of one part of the intestine into another. Intussusception causes impaired venous return, bowel edema and ischemia, necrosis, and perforation. It is one of the most common causes of intestinal obstruction in infancy. Most intussusceptions are ileocolic, where the ileum invaginates into the colon at the ileocecal valve. In patients beyond the neonatal period but under the age of 2 years (the period of peak incidence), no lead point of the intussusception is typically found. A previous viral infection may cause hypertrophy of the Peyer's patches or mesenteric nodes, which are hypothesized to act as the lead point in intussusception. A specific lead point is identified in only about 5% of cases but should be sought in neonates or in children over the age of 5 years. Recognizable lead points in intussusception include Meckel's diverticulum, an intestinal polyp, lymphoma, or a foreign body. Meckel's diverticulum usually presents as melena unassociated with abdominal pain or intussusception. Intussusception has also been associated with Henoch-Schönlein purpura.

Clinical Manifestations

Violent episodes of irritability, colicky pain, and emesis are interspersed with relatively normal periods. Rectal bleeding occurs in 80% of patients but only rarely in the form of the classic "currant jelly" stools (stools containing bright red blood and mucus). The degree of lethargy demonstrated by the child may be striking. A tubular mass is palpable in about 80% of patients. A plain abdominal film may show a paucity of gas in the right lower quadrant or evidence of obstruction with air-fluid levels. A barium enema or air enema demonstrates a coiled-spring appearance to the bowel, which is diagnostic. Stool should be tested for occult blood.

Treatment

Fluid resuscitation with normal saline or lactated Ringer's solution is usually necessary. Hydrostatic reduction with barium enema or pneumatic reduction with air enema is successful in 75% of cases. Peritoneal signs are an absolute contraindication to this procedure. Laparotomy and direct reduction is indicated when reduction by enema is either unsuccessful or contraindicated. The immediate recurrence rate is about 15%. When a specific lead point is identified, the recurrence rate is higher.

◆ KEY POINTS ◆

1. Most intussusceptions are ileocolic, in which the ileum invaginates into the colon at the ileocecal valve.

2. In patients beyond the neonatal period but under the age of 2 years (the period of peak incidence), no lead point of the intussusception is typically found.

3. Recognizable lead points of intussusception include Meckel's diverticulum, an intestinal polyp, lymphoma, or a foreign body.

4. Violent episodes of irritability, colicky pain, and emesis are interspersed with relatively normal periods. Rectal bleeding may occur but only rarely in the form of the classic "currant jelly" stools.

5. Hydrostatic reduction with barium enema or pneumatic reduction with air enema is successful in 75% of cases.

EMESIS

Vomiting is one of the most common presenting symptoms in pediatrics and can be caused by both gastrointestinal and nongastrointestinal pathologies. Complications of severe, persistent emesis include dehydration and hypochloremic, hypokalemic, metabolic alkalosis. Forceful emesis can result in a Mallory-Weiss tear of the esophagus at the gastroesophageal junction or erosion of the gastric cardia, whereas chronic emesis can result in distal esophagitis.

Differential Diagnosis

- Infectious: viral gastroenteritis (especially rotavirus and Norwalk virus), bacterial enterocolitis sepsis, hepatitis, food poisoning (*Staphylococcus aureus*, *Clostridium perfringens*, Salmonella), PID, peritonitis, pharyngitis, pneumonia, otitis media, tonsillitis, urinary tract infection.

- Metabolic: DKA, inborn errors of metabolism, adrenal crisis, renal or hepatic failure.

- Central nervous system: increased intracranial pressure, ventricular-peritoneal shunt malfunction, meningitis, encephalitis, labyrinthitis, migraine, Reye's syndrome, seizure, tumor.

- Gastrointestinal:

  Infant—gastroesophageal reflux, cow or soy milk protein intolerance, bowel obstruction (duodenal atresia, pyloric stenosis, malrotation with or without volvulus, incarcerated hernia, intussusception, Meckel's diverticulum with torsion, Hirschsprung's disease).

  Child—appendicitis, bowel obstruction (malrotation with or without volvulus much less likely than in the infant, incarcerated hernia, intussusception, Meckel's diverticulum with torsion, adhesions, post-traumatic obstruction from duodenal hematoma, ruptured viscus, or superior mesenteric artery syndrome).

- Respiratory: reactive airway disease.

- Oncology: chemotherapeutic agents.

- Toxic ingestion: salicylates, theophylline, caustic agents, digoxin, lead.

- Emotional: "psychogenic," bulemia.

- Gynecologic: pregnancy.

Clinical Manifestations

History

The history should differentiate between true vomiting and "spitting up" (gastroesophageal reflux) and whether the emesis is acute or chronic. Establish the frequency, appearance (bloody or bilious), amount, and timing of the emesis. Emesis shortly after feeding in the infant is probably gastroesophageal reflux. If the emesis is projectile and the child is 1–3 months old, pyloric stenosis must be considered. Define the child's usual diet and whether it has changed recently. Determine whether there has been weight loss or lack of weight gain since the emesis began. Poor weight gain and emesis may indicate pyloric stenosis or metabolic disorder. Find out if the child is on any medications. Macrolide antibiotics are known to cause emesis and diarrhea. Chemotherapeutic agents commonly cause emesis. Ascertain the possibility of toxic ingestion. Establish if the child has a history of intraventricular hemorrhage or hydrocephalus. If the child has a ventricular-peritoneal shunt, learn how many shunt revisions the child has had and the typical symptom pattern when the child obstructs. Define associated symptoms such as fever, diarrhea, abdominal pain, headache, sore throat, seizure, dysuria, and syncope. Emesis and seizure or emesis and headache may indicate an intracranial process. Diarrhea, emesis, and fever are seen with gastroenteritis. Fever, abdominal pain, and emesis are typical for appendicitis, whereas bilious emesis and abdominal pain are seen with intestinal obstruction. Emesis and syncope may result from pregnancy.

Physical Examination

On physical examination, the initial assessment should focus on the child's vital signs, weight, and hydration status. Signs and symptoms of dehydration include tachycardia, tachypnea, weight loss, dry mucous membranes, and sunken eyes. A sunken anterior fontanelle indicates dehydration, whereas a bulging fontanelle intimates increased intracranial pressure as the cause of the emesis. Papilledema also indicates increased intracranial pressure. Otitis media may result in emesis, so checking tympanic membranes is useful. Examine the throat, because pharyngitis and lymphadenopathy can cause emesis. Pneumonia can result in emesis, so the lung fields should be auscultated for crackles or an asymmetric examination. Emesis and vaginal discharge in the female adolescent warrant a pelvic examination to evaluate for PID. The abdominal examination should focus on bowel sounds and the presence of distention, tenderness, or masses. Hypoactive bowel sounds may indicate ileus or obstruction, whereas hyperactive bowel sounds suggest gastroenteritis or obstruction. Abdominal mass with emesis may indicate intussusception or malignancy, whereas tenderness and emesis may indicate appendicitis, peritonitis, or PID.

Diagnostic Evaluation

Specific laboratory studies depend on the suspected cause. Appropriate cultures and a complete blood count with manual differential should be sent if an infectious cause is deemed likely. Obtain a chest radiograph when pneumonia is suspected. If a surgical process within the abdomen is considered, obtain an upright and plain abdominal film, a complete blood count, and an electrolyte and chemistry panel. An ammonia level, serum amino acids, and urine organic acids are taken if metabolic disease is suspected. If a urinary tract infection is suspected, a urinalysis and urine culture should be requested.

Treatment

If the cause appears to be a self-limited nonsurgical infectious process (viral gastroenteritis or bacterial enterocolitis) and the patient is not significantly dehydrated and can be hydrated effectively, outpatient therapy is indicated. Oral rehydration therapy, which is discussed in Chapter 7, is recommended for dehydrated infants. For older children, encourage fluids and advance a soft, bland diet as tolerated. Children who are severely dehydrated or unable to effectively orally hydrate themselves should be admitted to the hospital.

When a surgical etiology is suspected, seek a surgical consultation, and if ventricular-peritoneal shunt malfunction is believed to be causing emesis, obtain a computed tomography of the head, a shunt series, and a neurosurgical consultation. Gastroesophageal reflux and its treatment are discussed extensively later.

Following are short discussions on disorders that present with emesis that are frequently tested on the national boards.

◆ KEY POINTS ◆

1. Most cases of emesis are caused by gastroesophageal reflux, acute gastroenteritis, or systemic disorders such as tonsillitis, otitis media, or urinary tract infection (UTI).

2. Most children with uncomplicated viral gastroenteritis and mild dehydration can be treated as outpatients with oral rehydration therapy.

Pyloric Stenosis

Pyloric stenosis is an important cause of gastric outlet obstruction and vomiting in the first 2 months of life, with a peak incidence at 2–4 weeks of life, and occurs in 1 in 500 infants. Male infants are affected 4:1 over female infants, and it occurs more frequently in infants with a family history of the condition.

Clinical Manifestations

Projectile nonbilious vomiting is the cardinal feature seen in virtually all patients. Physical findings vary with the severity of the obstruction. Dehydration and poor weight gain are common when the diagnosis is delayed. The classic finding of an olive-sized, muscular, mobile, nontender mass in the epigastric area occurs in most cases. Visible gastric peristaltic waves may be seen. Ultrasonography reveals the hypertrophic pylorus. Hypokalemic, hypochloremic, metabolic alkalosis with dehydration is seen secondary to persistent emesis in the most severe cases.

Treatment

Initial treatment involves nasogastric tube placement and correction of dehydration, alkalosis, and electrolyte abnormalities. Pyloromyotomy should take place as soon as the metabolic anomalies have been satisfactorily corrected.

◆ **KEY POINTS** ◆

1. Pyloric stenosis is an important cause of gastric outlet obstruction and emesis in the first 2 months of life, with a peak incidence at 2–4 weeks of life.

2. Projectile nonbilious vomiting is the cardinal feature seen in most patients.

3. Pyloromyotomy should take place as soon as the metabolic anomalies have been satisfactorily corrected.

Malrotation and Volvulus

Malrotation occurs when the small intestines abnormally rotate in utero, resulting in malposition in the abdomen and abnormal posterior fixation of the mesentery. When the intestine attaches improperly to the mesentery, it is at risk for twisting on its vascular supply; the twisting phenomenon is called volvulus. The most common age of presentation is under 1 month.

Clinical Manifestations

The history almost always includes bilious emesis. In older children, a past history of attacks, termed "cyclic vomiting," may be elicited. Physical examination may reveal abdominal distention, blood-stained emesis or stool, and shock. Abdominal radiographs reveal gas in the stomach with a paucity of air in the intestine. An upper gastrointestinal series with small bowel follow-through confirms the diagnosis by illustrating the abnormal position of the ligament of Treitz and the cecum. A positive stool guaiac examination is a poor prognostic sign, indicating significant bowel ischemia.

Treatment

Operative correction of the malrotation and the volvulus should be undertaken as soon as possible, because bowel ischemia, metabolic acidosis, and sepsis can progress quickly to death.

◆ **KEY POINTS** ◆

1. Malrotation occurs when the intestines abnormally rotate in utero, resulting in malposition in the abdomen and abnormal posterior fixation of the mesentery. When the intestine attaches improperly, it is at risk for volvulus.

2. An upper gastrointestinal series with small bowel follow-through confirms the diagnosis by confirming the abnormal position of the ligament of Treitz and the cecum.

GASTROESOPHAGEAL REFLUX

Gastroesophageal reflux (GER) is the regurgitation of stomach contents into the esophagus due to an incompetent lower esophageal sphincter. A small degree of reflux is common in all infants, and it is only infants who have moderate to severe chronic reflux that tend to come to the pediatrician's attention. In this group, complications include failure to thrive, aspiration pneumonia, esophagitis, choking or apneic episodes, hematemesis, anemia, and chronic fussiness.

Differential Diagnosis

Incompetence of the lower esophageal sphincter may be the result of prematurity, esophageal disease, obstructive lung disease, overdistention of the stomach caused by overeating, or medication (theophylline). If the infant is having forceful emesis or projectile vomiting, reflux is not the most likely cause, and the differential for emesis just discussed should be considered.

The differential diagnosis for GER in the adolescent may include pneumonia, costochondritis, pericarditis, pulmonary embolism, arrhythmias, ischemia due to an anomalous coronary artery, pancreatitis, cholecystitis, peptic ulcer disease, and anxiety.

Clinical Manifestations

History

When GER is suspected in an infant, determine if the infant is "spitting up" or having projectile emesis and if the emesis is bloody or bilious. Establish what formula the infant eats and how it is mixed. Ascertain how much the infant eats during each feeding and how often the child is fed, because one of the most common causes of GER is overfeeding. Find out if the infant is fed sitting up or lying down and in what position the infant is placed after feeding. Any reflux a child might have will worsen if he or she is lying down or if after the meal the child is not held in an upright position for a period of time. If the emesis is independent of meals, it is probably not reflux. A history of coughing, gagging, and arching of the back with extensor posturing during feeding may result from direct aspiration, whereas the presence of these symptoms soon after feeding may suggest GER. In severe reflux, the infant may have poor weight gain.

In the older child, GER is often manifested as epigastric abdominal or chest pain. Define the pain's location and severity and whether it radiates and is constant or intermittent. Burning epigastric or chest pain is probably reflux in the adolescent, especially if it occurs after meals when the patient lies down.

Physical Examination
In most cases, the physical examination of the child with gastroesophageal reflux is normal. In severe cases, some infants will present with failure to thrive. Discussion of the diagnosis, workup, and treatment of failure to thrive is found in Chapter 16.

Diagnostic Evaluation

The diagnosis of mild reflux is made by the characteristic history. In moderate or severe reflux, the diagnosis of GER may be confirmed by barium swallow with upper gastrointestinal examination, pH probe placement in the esophagus, or upper gastrointestinal endoscopy. If severe reflux or projectile emesis is present in the small infant, forms of gastric (pyloric stenosis) or intestinal obstruction (duodenal stenosis or atresia, malrotation with volvulus) should be considered. An abdominal ultrasound and barium swallow are useful to confirm normal anatomy and normal gastric emptying.

The child with mild to moderate reflux generally has an unremarkable complete blood count and electrolyte panel, but in severe reflux, a hypochloremic, hypokalemic, metabolic alkalosis may exist. These children fail to thrive and may have pyloric stenosis.

If the chest examination is abnormal in the presence of reflux, obtain a chest radiograph to look for aspiration pneumonia or chronic changes due to recurrent aspiration.

Treatment

Infants with GER should receive small, frequent feedings in the upright position and thickened feeds with rice cereal and be maintained in the prone head-up position for at least 20 minutes after a feed. If these measures fail, Reglan or Cisapride may be used to improve gastric motility and increase the rate of gastric emptying. If esophagitis is documented, antacids may be useful.

In cases where medical management fails, the Nissen fundoplication may be necessary. In this procedure, the fundus of the stomach is wrapped around the distal esophagus to increase baseline lower esophageal sphincter pressure.

Older children or adolescents with reflux should also have small, frequent meals, eat slowly, and maintain the upright position after meals. Meals after 7 P.M. should be discouraged, and intermittent doses of Maalox may be helpful. In refractory cases, cimetidine or ranitidine is useful.

◆ KEY POINTS ◆

1. Most cases of gastroesophageal reflux occur in the infant and adolescent populations and will not require medical attention.

2. Most infants with moderate GER respond to small, frequent feedings in the upright position, thickened feeds with rice cereal, and maintenance of the prone head-up position for at least 20 minutes after feeding.

3. The most common symptoms of GER in the adolescent are burning epigastric pain and chest pain.

DIARRHEA

Diarrhea is defined as an increase in the frequency and the water content of stools. Viral gastroenteritis accounts for 70–80% of acute diarrhea in North America. The complications of acute diarrhea include dehydration, electrolyte and acid–base disturbance, bacteremia and sepsis, and malnutrition in chronic diarrheal cases. Enteritis refers to small bowel inflammation, whereas colitis refers to large bowel inflammation.

Differential Diagnosis

Acute diarrhea:
- Intraintestinal infections:

    Viral gastroenteritis—rotavirus, enterovirus, adenovirus, Norwalk agent.

Bacterial enterocolitis—Shigella, Salmonella, Yersinia, Campylobacter, *E. coli* (enteroinvasive/enteropathogenic), *C. difficile* after long-term/multiple-antibiotic therapy, *N. gonorrhoeae, C. trachomatis.*

- Extraintestinal infections: otitis media, urinary tract infection.

- Gastrointestinal: intussusception, appendicitis, hyperconcentrated infant formula.

- Toxic ingestion: iron, mercury, lead, fluoride ingestion.

- Antibiotic induced: any antibiotic.

- Renal: hemolytic uremic syndrome.

- Vasculitis: Henoch-Schönlein purpura.

Chronic recurrent diarrhea:

- Infectious: parasites (amoebiasis, giardiasis, cryptosporidium).

- Gastrointestinal: cow/soy milk intolerance, overfeeding, ulcerative colitis, Crohn's disease, Hirschsprung's disease, lactase deficiency, irritable bowel disease, encopresis, excessive fructose intake, cystic fibrosis, celiac sprue.

- Allergy: food allergies.

Clinical Manifestations

History

Define whether the diarrhea is acute or chronic/recurrent, and establish the frequency, appearance (bloody/mucosal/currant-jelly), amount, consistency, and color of the diarrhea. Find out the child's usual diet and whether it has changed recently, because dietary indiscretions and manipulations may result in diarrhea. Small infants will have diarrhea when they are fed hyperconcentrated formula. If the child has traveled out of the country, consider a parasitic or bacterial enterocolitis. To determine the severity of the diarrhea, establish if there has been weight loss or lack of weight gain since the diarrhea began. Learn what medications the child is taking, because certain medications, especially antibiotics and chemotherapeutic agents, may cause diarrhea. Find out if the patient has had any ill contacts recently, as viral gastroenteritis is highly contagious. If a close contact of the child is a food handler, salmonella should be considered. Foul-smelling diarrhea that floats in the toilet is likely steattorhea from cystic fibrosis.

Physical Examination

On physical examination, the initial assessment should focus on the child's vital signs, weight, and hydration status. Signs and symptoms of dehydration include tachycardia, tachypnea, weight loss, and dry mucous membranes. A sunken anterior fontanelle and sunken eyes also indicate dehydration. Occasionally, otitis media is associated with diarrhea. The abdominal examination focuses on bowel sounds and the presence of distention, tenderness, or masses. Hypoactive bowel sounds may indicate ileus or obstruction, whereas hyperactive bowel sounds suggest gastroenteritis or obstruction. Abdominal mass with diarrhea could indicate intussusception or malignancy.

The difference in the child's baseline weight and present weight is a very accurate measure of dehydration in an acute diarrheal situation. Unfortunately, the baseline weight is not always available. In such cases, the percent dehydration can be estimated using the clinical appearance and vital signs. This is discussed in Chapter 7.

Diagnostic Evaluation

When evaluating a child with diarrhea, inspecting the stool is critical to evaluation and the treatment plan. If there is a history of bloody and/or mucous stool noted on inspection, a bacterial pathogen should be considered. To investigate a possible bacterial enterocolitis, a bacterial and viral stool culture can be done, and stool should be stained for fecal leukocytes.

If a bacterial pathogen is being considered and the child is less than 3 months old, a blood culture should be performed because the incidence of secondary bacteremia from salmonella enterocolitis is much higher in this age group. If viral gastroenteritis is the likely cause and the child is being admitted for dehydration, obtaining a rotazyme assay is helpful to confirm rotavirus as the causative agent. Rotavirus causes 65% of infant diarrhea during the winter months. When there is a history of long-term/multiple-antibiotic use, get a *C. difficile*toxin assay. Stool ova and parasites should be tested for on the child with chronic diarrhea, on the child with a history of foreign travel or recent camping, and on the immuno compromised child with diarrhea. If the child appears toxic or moderate to severe dehydration is noted, a complete blood count with manual differential, electrolyte panel, and urine analysis is indicated. Urinary tract infection is evaluated by urine dipstick, urine micro, and urine culture.

Treatment

For uncomplicated viral gastroenteritis without significant dehydration, the current recommendations are to feed through the diarrhea. The continuation of normal feedings results in less intestinal denudement, improved nutritional absorption, and a faster return to a normal stooling pattern. If the infant is also vomiting, replace one feed with Ricelyte or Pedialyte to calm the stomach and then return to normal feeds. Often, the parents need to give smaller feedings more frequently to accommodate the intestinal irritation from the gastroenteritis and to minimize emesis. Infants who do not tolerate their regular formula and are not significantly dehydrated or toxic appearing may be orally rehydrated at home. See Chapter 7 for details on oral rehydration therapy.

For the infant 0–12 months old with diarrhea for more than 5 days, with suspected enterocolitis (fecal leukocytes), or with exposure to Salmonella, a stool culture should be done. In addition to the stool culture, a blood culture should be performed if the infant is less than 3 months and has fecal leukocytes. If the stool culture is positive and the infant is afebrile and nontoxic appearing, the infant is re-examined and observed at home. If the stool culture is positive and the infant is febrile, the infant's age determines therapy. The infant younger than 3 months is admitted to the hospital, a blood culture is done, and intravenous antibiotics are started. The infant older than 3 months is admitted to the hospital and a blood culture is done, but antibiotics are withheld pending the results of the blood culture. Any infant with a positive stool culture who looks toxic or has a positive blood culture is admitted for intravenous antibiotics and evaluation for pyelonephritis, meningitis, and osteomyelitis.

Older children with viral gastroenteritis should be encouraged to drink isotonic fluids like soup or apple juice with saltine crackers. The apple juice must be diluted 1:1 with water, because the high glucose content will actually worsen the diarrhea. Admission is indicated for the child who is more than 5% dehydrated and cannot effectively orally rehydrate himself. See Chapter 7 for details on intravenous rehydration.

Viral gastroenteritis requires no pharmacologic therapy. Antidiarrheal medications are contraindicated, because they may cause toxic megacolon. In general, antibiotics are not indicated for bacterial enterocolitis.

Exceptions include colitis caused by *Salmonella typhi*, Shigella, enteroinvasive *E. coli*, and *C. difficile*. A summary of the bacterial pathogens and their treatment is given in Chapter 12. Parasitic gastrointestinal infections should be treated with the appropriate antimicrobial. Treat otitis media and urinary tract infection with appropriate antibiotics. Antibiotic-related diarrhea remits when the offending antibiotic is discontinued. Intussusception is treated by hydrostatic reduction with barium enema, air enema, and/or surgery.

◆ KEY POINTS ◆

1. The most common cause of diarrhea in children is viral gastroenteritis.

2. Bacteremia is more likely in infants under 3 months of age with bacterial enterocolitis.

3. Most children with uncomplicated viral gastroenteritis or bacterial enterocolitis can be orally rehydrated.

4. Do not use antidiarrheal medications in children with acute diarrhea.

5. Feed through diarrhea in infants. Recovery is faster, because there is less sloughing of the intestinal mucosa.

CONSTIPATION

Constipation is defined as infrequent passage of hard, dry stools. Constipated infants fail to completely empty the colon with bowel movements and over time stretch the smooth muscle of the colon, resulting in a functional ileus. In contrast to constipation, obstipation is the absence of bowel movements. Beyond the neonatal period, the most common cause (90–95%) of constipation is due to voluntary withholding or functional constipation. Intentional withholding is often noted from the very beginning of toilet training. A family history of similar problems is often obtained. Stool retention may be due to conflicts in toilet training but is usually caused by pain on defecation, which creates a fear of defecation and further retention. Voluntary withholding of stool increases distention of the rectum, which decreases rectal sensation, necessitating an even greater fecal mass to initiate the urge to defecate. Complications of stool retention include impaction, abdominal pain, overflow diarrhea resulting from leakage around the fecal mass, anal fissure, rectal bleeding, and urinary tract infection caused by extrinsic pressure on the urethra.

Encopresis, which is daytime or nighttime soiling by formed stools in children beyond the age of expected toilet training (4–5 years), is another complication of constipation. In older children, it is important to ask specifically about soiling, because such information may not be expressed due to embarrassment. These children are unable to sense the need to defecate because of stretching of the internal sphincter by the retained fecal mass.

Organic causes of failure to defecate include decreased peristalsis, decreased expulsion, and anatomic malformation. Organic etiologies are delineated below.

Differential Diagnosis

*   **Nonorganic**: functional constipation (intentional withholding), dysfunctional toilet training.

*   **Organic**:

    Dietary—low-fiber diet, inadequate fluid intake;

    Gastrointestinal—functional ileus, Hirschsprung's disease, anal stenosis, rectal abscess or fissure, stricture postnecrotizing enterocolitis (NEC), collagen vascular diseases;

    Drugs or toxins—lead, narcotics, phenothiazines, vincristine, anticholinergics;

    Neuromuscular—meningomyelocele, tethered spinal cord, infant botulism, absent abdominal muscles;

    Metabolic—cystic fibrosis, hypothyroidism, hypokalemia, hypercalcemia.

Clinical Manifestations

History and Physical Examination

Abdominal pain due to constipation is often diffuse and constant. The pain may be accompanied by nausea, but vomiting is unusual. Stools are hard, difficult to pass, and infrequent. Ascertain the content of the child's diet and whether it has changed recently, because particular foods can exacerbate constipation. Discuss the psychological state of the child with the parents and determine whether voluntary withholding is the most likely diagnosis. Document what medications the child is taking, because certain drugs induce constipation. If a history of diarrhea

or fecal spotting alternating with periods of constipation exists, a diagnosis of Hirschsprung's disease or encopresis should be entertained.

On examination, the abdomen is diffusely uncomfortable rather than tender and the left colon may be easily palpable and full of feces. Rectal examination usually reveals a rectal vault full of stool. Be sure to look for anal fissure or any other rectal process that would make defecation painful.

Diagnostic Evaluation

If the diagnosis is unclear, a plain abdominal film can be helpful, as a colon full of stool makes the diagnosis of constipation. If hypothyroidism is considered, free T_4, TSH, and T_3RU levels are indicated. If hypokalemia or hypocalcemia is a potential cause, an electrolyte and chemistry panel may be obtained. When Hirschsprung's disease is suspected, a rectal mucosal biopsy is required to make the diagnosis. A lead level assists in diagnosing plumbism as the cause of constipation. Genetic testing or a sweat test can confirm suspected cystic fibrosis.

Treatment

Most children with functional constipation can be treated through dietary changes. The child's fluid intake should be increased, the amount of simple carbohydrates (junk food) decreased, the amount of fiber and bulk in the diet (leafy vegetables, cereals) increased, and the child should begin daily ingestion of undiluted prune juice or apple juice. Senekot or Colace should be reserved for children in whom dietary measures are insufficient. The routine use of laxatives or enemas is discouraged.

The constipated child with impaction may be manually disimpacted or may receive a pediatric Fleet enema with a stool softener (Colace), osmotic agent (mineral oil), or peristalsis inducer (Senekot). Treat an anal fissure by softening the stools, avoiding the insertion of objects in the anus (thermometer), keeping the rectum as clean as possible, and applying petroleum jelly locally with each diaper change. Hirschsprung's disease should be managed in consultation with a pediatric surgeon and/or gastroenterologist. A short discussion on Hirschsprung's disease appears below.

In children with cystic fibrosis and those who have received vincristine, constipation can be so persistent and intractable that Go-lytely cleanouts are needed. Go-lytely is a powerful osmotic cathartic. In some severe cases, constipation due to psychologic causes requires counseling or psychotherapy.

HIRSCHSPRUNG'S DISEASE

Hirschsprung's disease, or congenital aganglionic megacolon, which occurs in 1:5000 children, results from the failure of the ganglion cells of the myenteric plexuses to migrate down the developing colon. As a result, the abnormally innervated distal colon remains tonically contracted and obstructs the flow of feces. Hirschsprung's disease is three times more common among boys and accounts for 20% of neonatal intestinal obstruction. In 75% of cases, the aganglionic segment is limited to the rectosigmoid colon, whereas 15% extend beyond the splenic flexure.

Clinical Manifestations

The diagnosis should be suspected in any infant who fails to pass meconium within the first 24 hours of life and who requires repeated rectal simulation to induce bowel movements. In the first month of life, the neonate develops evidence of obstruction with poor feeding, bilious vomiting, and abdominal distention. In some cases, particularly those with short segment (less than 5 cm) involvement, the diagnosis goes undetected into childhood. In the older child, failure to thrive may be seen, as well as intermittent bouts of intestinal obstruction, enterocolitis with bloody diarrhea, and, occasionally, bowel perforation, sepsis, and shock.

Stool that is palpable throughout the abdomen and an empty rectum on digital examination are most suggestive of the disease. Abdominal radiograph shows distention of the proximal bowel and no gas or feces in the rectum. Barium enema may demonstrate a transition zone between the narrowed abnormal distal segment and the dilated normal proximal bowel. Anal manometry demonstrates failure of the internal sphincter to relax with balloon distention of the rectum. Rectal biopsy revealing no ganglion cells and hypertrophied nerve trunks is necessary for the diagnosis.

Treatment

Hirschsprung's disease is treated surgically in two stages. The first stage involves the creation of a diverting colostomy with the bowel that contains ganglion cells, thus permitting decompression of the ganglion-containing bowel segment. In the second stage, the aganglionic segment is removed by pulling the ganglionic segment through the rectum. This procedure is postponed until the infant is 12 months old or delayed for 3–6 months when the disease has been diagnosed in an older child. The mortality rate for this disorder is low in the absence of enterocolitis, and the major complications include anal stenosis (5–10%) and incontinence (1–3%).

GASTROINTESTINAL BLEEDING

There are a plethora of disorders in childhood that cause gastrointestinal bleeding. Gastrointestinal bleeding may be acute or chronic, gross or microscopic, and may manifest itself as hematemesis, hematochezia, or melena.

Hematemesis refers to the emesis of fresh or old blood from the gastrointestinal tract. Fresh blood becomes chemically altered to a "ground coffee" appearance within 5 minutes of exposure to gastric acid. Hematochezia is the passage of fresh (bright red) or dark maroon blood from the rectum. The source is usually the colon, although upper gastrointestinal tract bleeding that has a rapid transit time can also result in hematochezia. Melena is shiny, jet black, tarry stools that are guaiac positive and usually results from upper gastrointestinal bleeds. The blood has been chemically altered during passage through the gut.

Differential Diagnosis

The differential diagnosis for gastrointestinal bleeding is generally divided into upper and lower gastrointestinal tract etiologies. Upper gastrointestinal bleeding occurs at a site proximal to the ligament of Treitz, whereas lower gastrointestinal bleeding occurs distally. Although hematemesis from upper gastrointestinal bleeding can be seen in critically ill children from esophagitis and/or gastritis or in children with portal hypertension from esophageal varices, most gastrointestinal bleeding in children is from the lower tract and manifests itself as rectal bleeding. Table 8–2 lists the most common causes of rectal bleeding by age. Minor bleeding presents as stool streaked with blood after stool is passed and is usually due to an anal fissure or polyp. Inflammatory diseases, such as inflammatory bowel disease or infectious enterocolitis, result in diarrheal stool mixed with blood. Causes of hematochezia include inflammatory bowel disease, Meckel's diverticulum, hemolytic uremic syndrome, Henoch-Schönlein purpura, and infectious enterocolitis. Table 8–3 lists the associated signs and symptoms of the major causes of gastrointestinal bleeding.

Clinical Manifestations

History

Define the onset and duration of bleeding, color (bright red versus dark maroon versus tarry black), rate (brisk versus gradual), and type of bleeding (hematochezia, hematemesis, melena, blood-streaked stool). Establish if the child has a chronic medical condition that could result in gastrointestinal bleed, any previous gastrointestinal surgery, or a hematologic problem.

For upper gastrointestinal bleeding, ask specifically about forceful vomiting, ingestion of ulcerogenic drugs (salicylates, nonsteroidal anti-inflammatory drugs, steroids), and a family history of liver disease or peptic ulcer disease. For lower gastrointestinal tract bleeding, inquire about diarrhea, infectious contacts, foreign travel, antibiotic use, and constipation with large or hard stools and difficult or painful defecation.

Always obtain a 24- to 48-hour food history, because multiple episodes of "red" vomitus or diarrhea could result from the ingestion of red fluids or foods (Kool-Aid, beets, red Jello, Tylenol elixir). Melena can occur in children who have ingested iron, bismuth, blackberries, or spinach.

Physical Examination

The immediate priority when examining a child with gastrointestinal bleeding is to determine if hypovolemia exists from an acute bleed. Vital signs should be examined for orthostatic changes or for evidence of shock (tachycardia, tachypnea, hypotension). The earliest sign of significant gastrointestinal bleeding is a raised resting heart rate. A drop in blood pressure is not seen until at least 40% of the intravascular volume is depleted. Dermatologic abnormalities such as petechiae and purpura indicate coagulopathy, whereas cool/clammy skin with pallor is suggestive of shock or anemia. On abdominal examination, evaluate for evidence of masses (a right lower quadrant mass may be due to Crohn's disease or intussusception), tenderness (epigastric tenderness suggests peptic ulcer disease, right lower quadrant tenderness may be due to Crohn's disease or infectious enterocolitis), and hepatosplenomegaly and caput of medusa (evidence of portal hypertension and risk or varices). Evaluate capillary refill (thenar eminence in neonates and infants) by extremity examination. On rectal examination, look for anal fissure, which is best seen by spreading the buttocks and everting the anal canal (most fissures are located at 6 and 12 o'clock), perform a stool guaiac examination, feel for hard stool, and look for a dilated rectum in children with chronic constipation and/or anal fissure.

Diagnostic Evaluation

Unless the source of bleeding is clearly from the nasopharynx, an anal fissure, or hemorrhoids, a complete blood count with manual differential, coagulation studies, and a type and cross should be sent.

TABLE 8–2

Causes of Rectal Bleeding by Age of Patient

Newborn	Infant to 2 Yr	2 Yr to Preschool	Preschool to Adolescence
Vitamin K$_1$ deficiency	Anal fissure	Infectious diarrhea	IBD
Ingested maternal blood	Milk colitis	Polyp	Infectious diarrhea
Cow/soy milk enterocolitis	Infectious diarrhea	Anal fissure	Peptic ulcer
Infectious diarrhea	Intussusception	Meckel's diverticulum	Esophageal varices
Necrotizing enterocolitis	Polyp	Intussusception	Polyp
Hirschsprung's disease	Meckel's diverticulum	HUS	
		HSP	

Less frequent causes

Volvulus	Esophagitis	PUD	Anal fissure
	HUS		
Duplication cyst	Duplication cyst	Esophageal varices	HUS
Vascular malformation	PUD	IBD	HSP
Stress ulcer	Vascular malformation	Esophagitis	Esophagitis

HUS, hemolytic uremic syndrome; HSP, Henoch-Schönlein purpura; PUD, peptic ulcer disease.

Adapted from Hillemeier C. Rectal bleeding in childhood. Pediatr Rev 1983;5:34 by permission.

TABLE 8–3

Diagnosis of Gastrointestinal Bleeding

Site	Cause	Associated Signs and Symptoms
Upper	Medications	Ingestion of ASA, other NSAIDs
	Varices	Splenomegaly or evidence of liver disease
	Esophagitis	Dysphagia, vomiting, dyspepsia, irritability in infants
	Peptic ulcer	Epigastric pain, meal-related, may be increased at night. Family history
Lower	Fissure	Bright red blood on surface of stool; pain, constipation; fissure often visible on anal eversion
	Polyp	Bright red blood on surface of stool; painless; very rarely palpable on rectal examination
	Milk colitis	Blood mixed with stool, diarrhea; patient may have hypoproteinemia, edema
	Meckel's	May be blood mixed with stool, clots; usually a lot of blood; drop in hemoglobin
	IBD	Diarrhea, fever, abdominal pain, poor growth, associated signs and symptoms (joint pain, rash, iritis, etc.)
	Bacterial colitis	Abdominal pain, diarrhea, fever, antibiotics, infectious contact, ingestion of contaminated food, foreign travel
	HSP	Joint pain, purpura, abdominal pain, nephritis (casts, RBCs in urine)
	HUS	Diarrhea, renal failure, thrombocytopenia, microangiopathic hemolytic anemia
	Intussusception	Infant, young child; intermittent abdominal pain, vomiting, pallor, red currant jelly stool, right-sided mass

HSP, Henoch-Schönlein purpura; HUS, hemolytic uremic syndrome; ASA, acetylsalicylic acid; NSAID, nonsteroidal anti-inflammatory drug.

If the bleeding source is unclear and the patient is unstable, the clinician should use gastric lavage to determine whether the bleeding is from the upper or lower gastrointestinal tract. A well-lubricated nasogastric or orogastric tube of the largest bore possible should be placed and the stomach lavaged with room temperature normal saline until lavage fluid is clear. Do not use iced saline because it may cause hypothermia. Esophageal varices are not a contraindication to the placement of a nasogastric or orogastric tube. Return of clear lavage fluid makes the diagnosis of upper gastrointestinal bleeding unlikely, although occasionally duodenal ulcers may bleed only distally. Return of guaiac-positive bright red blood or "coffee grounds" that eventually clear indicates upper gastrointestinal bleeding that has remitted. Persistent return of bright red blood indicates active bleeding and mandates aggressive intravenous fluid management.

In the stable patient, a thorough history and physical examination with consideration of the age-related causes will usually lead to diagnosis. Gastric lavage is unnecessary in children with minor or nonacute gastrointestinal bleeding. The precise diagnosis is usually made by upper or lower endoscopy.

If there is bloody diarrhea, obtain stool for methylene blue staining and stool culture. In the neonate with bloody stool, necrotizing enterocolitis must be considered and an abdominal film and sepsis workup should be performed. Where swallowed maternal blood is suspected as the cause of gastrointestinal bleeding, the Apt test is performed on the child's stool to differentiate maternal blood from the blood of the neonate. If oral blood is noted and there is a worsening pulmonary examination, obtain a chest radiograph to look for pulmonary hemorrhage. When Meckel's diverticulum is suspected, a Meckel's scan can be performed.

Treatment

In the unstable child with severe bleeding or hypovolemia, follow the primary and secondary survey as outlined in Chapter 1. Remember, a normal hemoglobin or hematocrit does not rule out severe acute bleeding; full hemodilution takes up to 12 hours in the acutely bleeding patient. Intravenous normal saline or Ringer's lactate at 10 mL/kg boluses should be given until the patient is stable. Type O whole blood should be reserved for the unstable patient with acute bleeding that cannot quickly be brought under control. The most common error in management of the child with severe gastrointestinal bleeding is inadequate volume replacement. Hy-

potension is a late finding and fluid resuscitation should be governed by the level of tachycardia.

The stable child without heavy bleeding or signs of hypovolemia should be evaluated and treated according to the particular diagnosis.

Figure 8–1 illustrates a useful algorithm for the evaluation and management of gastrointestinal bleeding. Three common causes of gastrointestinal bleeding—Meckel's diverticulum, ulcerative colitis, and Crohn's disease—are discussed below.

◆ KEY POINTS ◆

1. Upper gastrointestinal bleeding occurs at a site proximal to the ligament of Treitz, whereas lower gastrointestinal bleeding occurs distally.

2. Most gastrointestinal bleeding in children is from the lower tract and manifests itself as rectal bleeding.

3. The earliest sign of significant gastrointestinal bleeding is a raised resting heart rate. A drop in blood pressure is not seen until at least 40% of the intravascular volume is depleted.

Meckel's Diverticulum

Meckel's diverticulum, the vestigial remnant of the omphalomesenteric duct, is the most common anomaly of the gastrointestinal tract. It is present in 2–3% of the population and is located within 100 cm of the ileocecal valve in the small intestine. The peak incidence of bleeding from the diverticulum is 2 years of age. Heterotopic tissue, usually gastric, is 10 times more common in symptomatic cases because of acid secretion and ulceration.

Clinical Manifestations

The most common presentation of Meckel's diverticulum is painless rectal bleeding. Eighty-five percent of patients with Meckel's diverticulum have melena, 10% will develop intestinal obstruction from intussusception or volvulus, and 5% suffer from painful diverticulitis mimicking appendicitis. Diagnosis is made by performing a Meckel's scan. The technetium-99 pertechnetate scan, preceded by prepentagastrin stimulation or a histamine H2 receptor antagonist (cimetidine), identifies the ectopic acid-secreting cells creating the hemorrhage in the diverticulum.

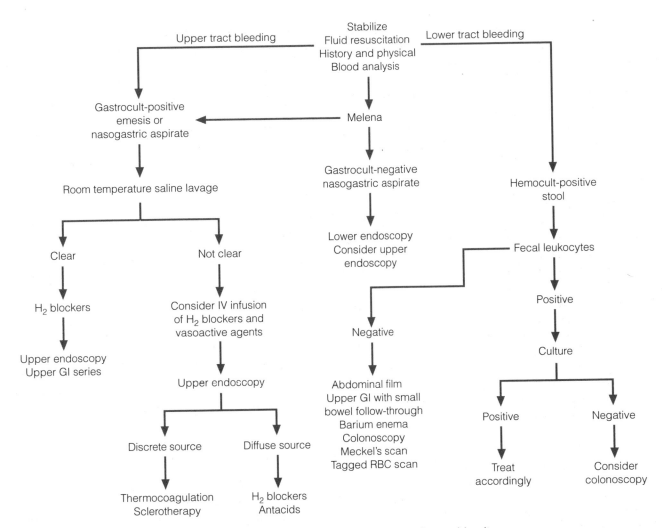

Figure 8–1 Algorithm for evaluation and management of gastrointestinal tract bleeding.

Treatment

Definitive treatment is surgical resection.

Inflammatory Bowel Disease

Inflammatory bowel disease (IBD) is a generic term for Crohn's disease and ulcerative colitis, which are chronic inflammatory disorders of the intestines.

Ulcerative colitis produces diffuse superficial colonic ulceration and crypt abscesses. It involves the rectum in 95% of patients, with or without contiguous extension higher in the colon. Ulcerative colitis does not affect the small intestine.

The pathology of Crohn's disease involves transmural inflammation in a discontinuous pattern, which results in skip lesions. Crohn's disease may involve any part of the gastrointestinal tract (mouth to anus). The process is ileocolic in 60% of cases, involves the small intestine in 30% of cases, and impairs the colon in only 10% of cases. Fibrosis is transmural, and strictures are common. Granulomas are observed in up to 30% of patients. Internal and/or external fistula formation occurs in up to 40% of patients.

Although the exact etiology of these disorders is not known, a combination of genetic, environmental, psychological, infectious, and immunologic mechanisms have been implicated. IBD is most common in whites and Jews and occurs equally in males and females. Most pediatric patients are adolescents, but both diseases have been reported in infancy.

Clinical Manifestations

Crampy abdominal pain, recurrent fever, weight loss, and diarrhea are common manifestations in Crohn's disease. Although diarrhea is common, it is not universal in Crohn's disease. Rectal bleeding is noted in only 35% of cases of Crohn's disease. Abdominal pain tends to be more severe in Crohn's disease than in ulcerative colitis, may be diffuse, and is frequently worse in the right lower quadrant. Perianal disease may produce skin tags, fissures, fistulas, or abscesses. Anorexia, poor weight gain, and delayed growth occur in 40% of patients.

Most children with ulcerative colitis exhibit bloody mucinous diarrheal stool (100%), abdominal pain (95%), and tenesmus (75%). Ninety percent of patients exhibit mild to moderate disease. Mild disease is defined as less than six stools per day, no fever, no anemia, and no hypoalbuminemia, whereas moderate disease has greater than six stools per day, fever, anemia, and hypoalbuminemia. Severe disease may be fulminant with high fever, abdominal tenderness, distention, tachycardia, leukocytosis, hemorrhage, severe anemia, and more than eight stools per day. Toxic megacolon and intestinal perforation are rare complications. Carcinoma of the colon is a severe complication of chronic disease. After 10 years of disease, there is a cumulative risk of 1–2% per year for the development of carcinoma. Table 8–4 compares Crohn's disease and ulcerative colitis.

Extraintestinal sequelae, similar in both diseases, may precede or accompany gastrointestinal symptoms and include polyarticular arthritis, ankylosing spondylitis, primary sclerosing cholangitis, chronic active hepatitis, sacroiliitis, pyoderma gangrenosum, erythema nodosum, nephrolithiasis, aphthous stomatitis, episcleritis, recurrent iritis, and uveitis.

Because ulcerative colitis involves the rectum in 90% of patients, proctosigmoidoscopy and biopsy are indicated. Visualization of the mucosa in ulcerative colitis reveals diffuse superficial ulceration and easy bleeding. In Crohn's disease, direct visualization and biopsy of the ileocecal area is not always possible.

Roentgenographic examination with a double air-contrast barium enema demonstrates diffuse colonic lesions

TABLE 8–4

Comparison of Crohn's Disease and Ulcerative Colitis

Feature	Crohn's Disease	Ulcerative Colitis
Malaise, fever, weight loss	Common	Common
Rectal bleeding	Sometimes	Usual
Abdominal mass	Common	Rare
Abdominal pain	Common	Common
Perianal disease	Common	Rare
Ileal involvement	Common	None (backwash ileitis)
Strictures	Common	Unusual
Fistula	Common	Unusual
Skip lesions	Common	Not present
Transmural involvement	Usual	Not present
Crypt abscesses	Unusual	Usual
Granulomas	Common	Not present
Risk of cancer	Slightly increased	Greatly increased

Modified from Andreoli TE, Carpenter CJ, Plum F, et al. Cecil essentials of medicine. Philadelphia: WB Saunders, 1986:746.

and pseudopolyp formation in ulcerative colitis. This examination should be delayed in patients with severely active disease to avoid precipitating toxic megacolon. Crohn's disease often reveals ileal and/or colonic involvement with skip lesions, rectal sparing, segmental narrowing of the ileum (string sign), and longitudinal ulcers.

Anemia is common and usually is associated with iron deficiency. Megaloblastic anemia secondary to folate and vitamin B_{12} deficiency may also be present. An elevation of the erythrocyte sedimentation rate is seen in about 50% of cases of ulcerative colitis and in 80% of Crohn's disease cases. Hypoalbuminemia, due to poor protein intake, is common in individuals with severe symptoms. Serum aminotransferase levels are increased if hepatic inflammation is a complicating feature. Stool examination reveals blood and fecal leukocytes with a negative stool culture.

Differential Diagnosis

The differential diagnosis of IBD includes chronic bacterial or parasitic causes of diarrhea, appendicitis, hemolytic uremic syndrome, Henoch-Schönlein purpura, and radiation enterocolitis. Enteric infections include *C. difficile*, *Campylobacter jejuni*, *Yersinia enterocolitica*, amebiasis, and giardiasis.   .

Treatment

Sulfasalazine is the mainstay of treatment for mild and moderate ulcerative colitis and Crohn's disease of the colon. It has no efficacy in Crohn's disease involving the small bowel. Corticosteroids remain the most effective therapy for Crohn's disease of the small bowel and are added to sulfasalazine therapy in moderate ulcerative colitis. Severe ulcerative colitis is treated with intravenous alimentation, high-dose corticosteroids, sulfasalazine, and cyclosporine.

Because daily corticosteroid therapy can inhibit growth, attempts should be made to use alternative day therapy when possible. Metronidazole is used to treat severe perirectal fistulae in patients with Crohn's disease. Azathioprine and 6-mercaptopurine are steroid-sparing drugs used in patients with severe Crohn's disease who are dependent on high-dose corticosteroids.

Because anorexia and increased nutrient losses in the stool are common in children with IBD, adequate calories and protein are essential. Oral supplements, nasogastric tube feedings, and, in some severe cases, central venous hyperalimentation are necessary. Vitamin and mineral supplementation, especially iron, may be required.

Patients with ulcerative colitis for more than 10 years need annual colonoscopy and rectal biopsy due to the high risk of colon cancer development.

Surgery is eventually needed in 25% of patients with ulcerative colitis and 70% of children with Crohn's disease. Surgery is indicated in ulcerative colitis when there is fulminant colitis with severe blood loss or toxic megacolon, intractable disease with a high-dose steroid requirement, steroid toxicity, growth failure, or colonic dysplasia. Ileoanal pull-through after colectomy is the procedure of choice. Surgery is performed in Crohn's disease when there is hemorrhage, obstruction, perforation, severe fistula formation, or ureteral obstruction. In general, conservatism is warranted because removal of the diseased bowel is not curative in Crohn's disease. Recurrence rates of about 50% after segmental resection have been reported.

◆ KEY POINTS ◆

1. Ulcerative colitis produces diffuse superficial colonic ulceration and crypt abscesses. It involves the rectum in 95% of patients, with or without contiguous extension higher in the colon.

2. Ulcerative colitis does not affect the small intestine.

3. Most children with ulcerative colitis exhibit bloody mucosal diarrheal stool, abdominal pain, and tenesmus.

4. Roentgenographic examination with a double air-contrast barium enema demonstrates diffuse colonic lesions and pseudopolyp formation in ulcerative colitis.

5. Sulfasalazine is the mainstay of treatment in mild and moderate ulcerative colitis.

6. Ulcerative colitis places the child at high risk for the development of colon cancer.

7. The pathology of Crohn's disease involves transmural inflammation in a discontinuous pattern, which results in skip lesions. Crohn's disease may involve any part of the gastrointestinal tract (mouth to anus).

8. Crampy abdominal pain, recurrent fever, weight loss, and diarrhea are common manifestations in Crohn's disease.

9. Roentgenographic examination with a double air-contrast barium enema in Crohn's disease demonstrates ileal and/or colonic involvement with skip lesions, rectal sparing, segmental narrowing of the ileum (string sign), and longitudinal ulcers.

10. Sulfasalazine is the mainstay of treatment in mild and moderate Crohn's disease of the colon. It has no efficacy in Crohn's disease involving the small bowel.

11. Corticosteroids remain the most effective therapy for Crohn's disease of the small bowel and are added to sulfasalazine therapy in moderate ulcerative colitis.

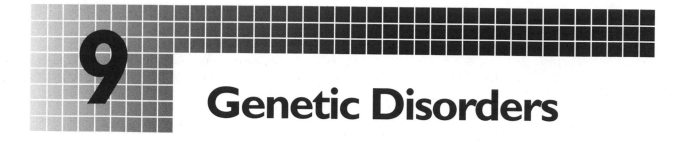

Genetic Disorders

The population risk for medically significant birth defects is approximately 3% of all liveborn infants, and congenital anomalies result in 10% of neonatal deaths. However, not all birth defects are detected at birth; examples include some forms of congenital heart disease and certain metabolic defects. The entire spectrum of human development is guided by the interaction of genetics and environment. Most birth defects are caused by environmental factors, genetic alterations, or a combination of both. In some cases, birth defects are caused by unknown factors and are called sporadic disorders. Genetic disorders may be divided into single gene disorders and chromosomal disorders.

ENVIRONMENTAL FACTORS

Environmental factors are known to cause at least 10% of all birth defects. Teratogens are environmental agents that cause congenital anomalies by interfering with embryonic or fetal organogenesis, growth, or cellular physiology or by disrupting previously normal tissue. A teratogenic exposure before implantation (days 7–10 postconception) results in loss of the embryo or will have no effect. To disrupt organogenesis, a teratogen must be present before 12 weeks' gestation, and any teratogenic exposure after 12 weeks' gestation will predominantly affect growth and central nervous system development.

Teratogens include infectious agents, high-dose radiation, maternal metabolic disorders, mechanical forces, and drugs. Infectious teratogens include toxoplasmosis, syphilis, rubella, varicella-zoster virus, cytomegalovirus, and herpesvirus. These congenital infections are discussed in detail in Chapter 13. The most common maternal metabolic disorder that has teratogenic potential is diabetes mellitus; 10% of infants of diabetic mothers have a birth defect. The types of anomalies seen involve the central nervous system (anencephaly, myelomeningocele, holoprosencephaly), heart, vertebral column, and renal system. Situs inversus and caudal regression syndrome (sacral agenesis) can also occur. The teratogen is believed to be persistent hyperglycemia, and the congenital anomalies seen in infants of diabetic mothers account for 50% of the mortality found in these children. Another prominent maternal metabolic disorder that may produce teratogens is phenylketonuria (PKU), which is discussed in detail later in this chapter.

High-dose radiation is another teratogen that can cause fetal malformations by interfering with cell division and organogenesis. Generally, the dose received by the fetus from diagnostic x-ray studies falls well below the threshold for teratogenic effect.

Abnormal intrauterine mechanical forces can also result in deformities. Intrauterine tumors, fibroids, or abnormal uterine anatomy may result in a fetus that is constrained, thereby causing a breech presentation, facial distortions, dislocations of the hips, and/or club feet. Oligohydramnios, which is discussed in Chapter 13, may also result in severe fetal constraint and structural anomalies such as compressed facies, club foot, low-set ears, scaphoid abdomen, and diminished chest wall size resulting in pulmonary hypoplasia. Amniotic band syndrome is attributed to entanglement of fetal parts with the amnion and results in limb hypoplasia and transverse amputations. Table 9–1 lists the most common teratogenic drugs and their effects.

◆ KEY POINTS ◆

1. Environmental factors cause 10% of birth defects.

2. Infectious agents, high-dose radiation, maternal metabolic disorders, mechanical forces, and drugs can all serve as teratogens.

3. A teratogenic exposure before 12 weeks' gestation affects organogenesis and tissue morphogenesis, whereas an exposure thereafter retards fetal growth and central nervous system development.

SINGLE-GENE DISORDERS

Each human has between 30,000 and 50,000 genes that are packaged into 46 chromosomes (22 pairs of autosomes and 1 pair of sex chromosomes). More than 3000 different single-gene disorders have been described, which are classified by their mode of inheritance (autosomal dominant, autosomal recessive, or X-linked).

Autosomal Dominant Disorders

Autosomal dominant disorders result from a mutation of one gene of a pair coding for a structural protein. Any individual with an autosomal dominant disorder has a 50% chance of passing on the mutant gene to their offspring. Thus, each child of an affected individual has a 50% chance of being affected. A mutant gene usually is inherited from one parent with the same condition. Sometimes an individual is the first person in a family to display an autosomal trait due to spontaneous mutation. The recurrence risk in another child for the parents of a child with a spontaneous mutation is the same as the chance of the spontaneous mutation occurring de novo. It is common for autosomal dominant genes to cause conditions that manifest themselves with varying degrees of severity among affected individuals. This phenomenon is known as variable expressivity or variable penetrance.

TABLE 9–1

Common Teratogenic Drugs

Drug	Results
Alcohol	Fetal alcohol syndrome, microcephaly, congenital heart disease
Aminopterin	Mesomelia, cranial dysplasia
Coumadin	Hypoplastic nasal bridge, chondrodysplasia punctata
Isotretinoin (Accutane)	Facial and ear anomalies, congenital heart disease
Lithium	Ebstein's anomaly
Methyl mercury	Microcephaly, blindness, deafness, retardation
Penicillamine	Cutis laxa syndrome
Phenytoin (Dilantin)	Hypoplastic nails, intrauterine growth retardation, typical facies
Radioactive iodine	Fetal hypothyroidism
Stilbestrol (DES)	Vaginal adenocarcinoma during adolescence
Streptomycin	Deafness
Testosterone-like drugs	Virilization of female
Tetracycline	Enamel hypoplasia
Thalidomide	Phocomelia
Trimethadione	Congenital anomalies, typical facies
Valproate	Spina bifida

Table 9–2 lists some of the most important autosomal dominant diseases. A detailed discussion on von Willebrand's disease, the most common autosomal dominant disorder, is found in Chapter 10.

Autosomal Recessive Disorders

Autosomal recessive disorders occur when both maternal and paternal genes of a gene pair have a mutation. Many autosomal recessive disorders are due to mutations in genes coding for enzymes. Since half of the normal enzyme activity is adequate under most circumstances, a person with only one mutant gene is not affected. Therefore, individuals who are homozygous for a defective gene are clinically affected and heterozygotes are not. Both

TABLE 9–2

Autosomal Dominant Diseases

	Frequency	Comments
Peutz-Jeghers syndrome		Mucocutaneous pigment, GI hamartoma
Huntington disease	1:2500	Chromosome 4 (short arm)
Adult polycystic kidney disease	1:1200	Chromosome 16 (short arm)
Neurofibromatosis	1:3000	Chromosome 17, 50% new mutations
Bilateral acoustic neuroma (neurofibromatosis II)	$1:1 \times 10^6$	Chromosome 22 (long arm)
Protein C deficiency	1:15,000	Gene cloned; chromosome 2 (short arm) spontaneous thrombosis

Hereditary angioedema (HANE)
    Type I (decreased protein)
    Type II (dysfunctional protein)
	1:10,000	Deficiency of C1 esterase inhibitor, chromosome 11, idiomorphic variants

Hereditary hemorrhagic telangiectasia (Osler-Weber-Rendu disease)	1–2:100,000	Angiodysplasia
Myotonic dystrophy	1:25,000	Chromosome 19 (long arm)
Familial retinoblastoma	1:20,000	Multifocal tumor, chromosome 13, gene cloned
von Willebrand disease	1:100	Chromosome 12, male = female incidence
Tuberous sclerosis	1:29,900	Chromosome 19; adenoma sebaceum, seizures, retardation
Gilbert disease		Indirect hyperbilirubinemia
Hereditary spherocytosis	1:5000	Spectrin deficiency, some variants autosomal recessive
Marfan syndrome	1:20,000	Variable penetrance
Achondroplasia	0.5–1.5:10,000	90% new mutations
Alpha-1-antitrypsin deficiency	1:3000	Gene cloned: chromosome 14 cirrhosis, emphysema
Hyperlipidemia	1:500	Possible prevention of heart disease

GI, gastrointestinal.

parents of a child with an autosomal recessive disorder, if they are unaffected, are heterozygous for that gene, and each child of such a couple has a 25% risk of inheriting the disorder. Cystic fibrosis is the most common autosomal recessive disorder in whites of European descent and affects 1 in 2000 newborns in this population. A thorough discussion of cystic fibrosis is presented in Chapter 20. Sickle cell anemia is the most common autosomal recessive disorder in blacks in the United States and affects 1 in 625 individuals in this population. Chapter 10 discusses sickle cell anemia in detail. Table 9–3 delineates the most notable autosomal recessive disorders.

Most inborn errors of metabolism, with the exception of ornithine transcarbamylase deficiency (OTCD), are autosomal recessive disorders. Although individual metabolic disorders are rare, collectively they are responsible for significant morbidity and mortality. Metabolic disorders are caused by specific defects in enzyme structure or function or by abnormalities in the proteins that transport metabolites to cells or across cell membranes. Inborn metabolic errors result in accumulation of excess precursors, toxic metabolites of excess precursors, and/or deficiency of the products needed for normal metabolism. Certain ethnic groups are at increased risk for specific metabolic errors.

TABLE 9–3

Autosomal Recessive Diseases

	Frequency	Comments
Congenital adrenal hyperplasia (21-hydroxylase)	1:5000–15,000; 1:700 in Yupik Eskimo	Chromosome 6, linked to HLA groups
Phenylketonuria	1:14,000	Gene cloned; chromosome 12
Sickle cell anemia	1:625 in African Americans	Gene cloned; chromosome 11
Cystic fibrosis	1:2000 in whites	Gene cloned; chromosome 7
Gaucher disease	1:2500 in Ashkenazi Jews	Gene cloned; chromosome 1 (long arm)
Tay-Sachs disease	1:3000 in Ashkenazi Jews	Gene cloned; chromosome 15 (long arm)
Galactosemia	1:60,000	Gene cloned; chromosome 9 (short arm)
Infantile polycystic renal failure	1–2:14,000	Renal and hepatic cysts
Wilson disease	1:200,000	Gene cloned; chromosome 13 (long arm)
Fanconi anemia	?	Absent thumb, chromosomal breaks

HLA, human leukocyte antigen.

Reproduced from Behrman RE, Kliegman RM, eds. Essentials of pediatrics, 2nd ed. Philadelphia: WB Saunders, 1994.

Common manifestations of inborn errors include emesis and acidosis after initiation of feeding with breast milk or formula, unusual odor of urine or sweat, hepatosplenomegaly, mental retardation, severe acidosis, hyperammonemia, early infant death, growth retardation, and seizures.

Metabolic defects are generally divided into disorders of amino acid and organic acid metabolism, ammonia metabolism, carbohydrate metabolism, the lipidoses, and the mucopolysaccharidoses. Examples of amino acid metabolic defects include PKU, homocystinuria, and tyrosine deficiency. The most prevalent urea cycle defect is OTCD, which is one of the few metabolic defects that are X-linked. The most common disorders of carbohydrate metabolism include galactosemia and the glycogen storage diseases. Tay-Sachs, Gaucher, and Niemann-Pick diseases are examples of lipidoses, whereas Hurler's syndrome is an example of the mucopolysaccharidoses. Although lipidoses and mucopolysaccharidoses are extremely rare in the general population, Tay-Sachs and Gaucher diseases have a much higher incidence in Ashkenazi Jews.

Phenylketonuria
PKU is the most common of these disorders, occurring in 1 in 14,000 live births, and is the best studied of the amino acid disorders. PKU results from a deficiency in the enzyme phenylalanine hydroxylase, which converts phenylalanine to tyrosine. The lack of phenylalanine hydroxylase results in high serum concentrations of the toxic metabolites phenylacetic acid and phenyllactic acid.

Clinical Manifestations
Unlike most amino acid disorders, symptoms of PKU are not seen in early infancy but rather in childhood if the disorder is untreated. Neurologic manifestations include moderate to severe mental retardation, hypertonicity, tremors, and behavioral problems. Tyrosine is needed for the production of melanin, so the block in the conversion of phenylalanine to tyrosine results in hypopigmentation in most cases.

Treatment
Prevention of mental retardation in PKU is achieved by early detection and dietary restriction of phenylalanine. Most states include PKU detection on their mandatory neonatal screens. To maintain intellectual capabilities, a lifelong dietary restriction of phenylalanine is recommended. Pregnant women with PKU who do not adhere to the dietary restriction dramatically increase the risk of their child having microcephaly, mental retardation, and congenital heart disease.

Homocystinuria
Homocystinuria is caused by a defect in the amino acid metabolic pathway that converts methionine to cysteine

and serine. The incidence of the cystathionine synthetase deficiency is 1 in 100,000 live births. The neonatal screen used by most states measures increased methionine levels in the blood.

Clinical Manifestations

There are no symptoms in infancy. Clinical manifestations observed during childhood include a Marfan's body habitus (long thin limbs and digits, scoliosis, sternal deformities, and osteoporosis), dislocated eye lenses, mild to moderate mental retardation, and vascular thromboses that result in childhood stroke or myocardial infarction.

Treatment

Dietary management is extremely difficult because restriction of sulfhydryl groups leads to a very low-protein, foul-tasting diet.

Galactosemia

Occurring with an incidence of 1 in 60,000, galactosemia is the most common error of carbohydrate metabolism. It is caused by a deficiency of the enzyme galactose-1-phosphate uridyl transferase, resulting in impaired conversion of galactose-1-phosphate to glucose-1-phosphate that can then undergo glycolysis.

Clinical Manifestations

Unlike PKU and homocystinuria, clinical manifestations are noted within a few days to weeks after initiation of feedings with formula or breast milk. Initial symptoms include evidence of liver failure (hepatomegaly, direct hyperbilirubinemia, disorders of coagulation), abnormal renal function (acidosis, glycosuria, aminoaciduria), emesis, anorexia, and poor growth. Cataracts may develop eventually. Liver sequelae, renal problems, and cataracts are limited to the first few years of life. Galactosemic infants have an increased risk of *Escherichia coli* sepsis. Older children tend to have severe learning disabilities, whether or not they were treated in infancy. Affected females have a high incidence of ovarian hypofunction and premature ovarian failure. Neonatal screening tests are of limited use for severely affected infants, who may die before the result is available. Diagnosis is made by demonstrating an extreme reduction in the level of erythrocyte galactose-1-phosphate uridyl transferase. Laboratory findings include a direct hyperbilirubinemia, elevated alanine aminotransferase and aspartate aminotransferase, prolonged prothrombin time and partial thromboplastin time, hypoglycemia, and albuminuria. Galactose in the urine is detected by a positive reaction for reducing substances and no reaction with glucose oxidase on urine strip tests.

Treatment

Treatment centers around eliminating all formulas and foods containing galactose.

Glycogen Storage Diseases

Glycogen storage diseases (GSDs) are a group of conditions that result from deficiency in one of the several enzymes involved in glycogen synthesis or breakdown. Glycogen is the storage form of glucose and is found most abundantly in the liver, where it serves to modulate blood glucose, and in muscles, where it facilitates anaerobic work. Because of the number of different enzymes involved in glycogen metabolism and their locations, the clinical manifestations of the GSDs are variable. See Table 9–4 for a synopsis of GSDs. The most common GSDs are type I, von Gierke's disease; type II, Pompe's disease; and type V, McArdle's disease; all are autosomal recessive disorders.

X-Linked Disorders

X-linked disorders occur when a male inherits a mutant gene on the X chromosome from his mother. The affected male is termed hemizygous for the gene, because he has only a single X chromosome and a single set of X-linked genes. The mother of the affected individual is heterozygous for that gene, because she has a normal X chromosome and a mutant one. She may demonstrate partial manifestation of the disorder due to lionization in which only one X chromosome is transcriptionally active in each cell. Recurrence risk for X-linked disorders differs depending on whether the mother or the father has the abnormal gene. If the father has the defective X chromosome and is therefore affected, he will pass the defective X chromosome on to his daughters, creating carriers for the disorder. If the mother has the abnormal X chromosome and she is a carrier, there is a 50% chance she will pass the chromosome to her progeny. If her daughters receive the damaged X chromosome, they will be carriers for the disease, and her sons who receive the chromosome will be affected with the disease. Common X-linked disorders include hemophilia A and B, glucose-6-phosphate dehydrogenase deficiency (G6PD), Duchenne muscular dystrophy, OTCD, and fragile X syndrome. Discussions on G6PD and hemophilia A and B are found in Chapter 10. Table 9–5 lists the most common X-linked disorders and their respective incidence.

TABLE 9–4

Glycogen Storage Diseases*

Disease	Affected Enzyme	Organs Affected	Clinical Syndrome	Neonatal Manifestations	Prognosis
Type I von Gierke	Glucose-6-phosphatase	Liver, kidney, GI tract, platelets	Hypoglycemia, lactic acidosis, hepatomegaly, hypotonia, slow growth, diarrhea, bleeding disorder, gout, hypertriglyceridemia, xanthomas	Hypoglycemia, lactic acidemia, liver may not be enlarged	Early death from hypoglycemia, lactic acidosis; may do well with supportive management; hepatomas occur in late childhood
Type II Pompe	Lysosomal α-glucosidase	All, notably striated muscle, nerve cells	Symmetric profound muscle weakness, cardiomegaly, heart failure, shortened PR interval	May have muscle weakness and/or cardiomegaly	Very poor; death in the 1st year of life is usual; variants exist
Type III Forbes	Debranching enzyme	Liver, muscles	Early in course hypoglycemia, ketonuria, hepatomegaly that resolves with age; may show muscle fatigue	Usually none	Very good for hepatic disorder; if myopathy present, it tends to be like that of type V
Type IV Andersen	Branching enzyme	Liver, ? nerves	Hepatic cirrhosis beginning at several months of age; early liver failure	None	Very poor; death from hepatic failure before age 4 yr
Type V McArdle	Muscle phosphorylase	Muscle	Muscle fatigue beginning in adolescence	None	Good, with sedentary lifestyle
Type VI Hers	Liver phosphorylase	Liver	Mild hypoglycemia with hepatomegaly, ketonuria	Usually none	Probably good
Type VII Tarui	Muscle phosphofructokinase	Muscle	Clinical findings similar to type V	None	Similar to that of type V
Type VIII	Phosphorylase kinase	Liver	Clinical findings similar to type III, without myopathy	None	Good

*Except for hepatic phosphorylase kinase and muscle phosphoglycerate kinase, which are X-linked, the remaining disorders are autosomal recessive.

GI, gastrointestinal.

Reproduced from Behrman RE, Kliegman RM, eds. Essentials of pediatrics, 2nd ed. Philadelphia: WB Saunders, 1994.

Ornithine Transcarbamylase Deficiency

OTCD is a urea cycle defect and is one of the few inborn errors of metabolism that is inherited in an X-linked manner. In the urea cycle, ornithine joins with carbamylphosphate through the action of ornithine transcarbamylase (OTC) to form citrulline within the mitochondria. When OTC is not present or exists at levels less than 20% of normal, ornithine and carbamylphosphate build up. Because of OTC deficiency, the nitrogen-containing moiety in ornithine cannot be converted to urea and excreted and, instead, ammonia is formed, which results in severe hyperammonemia when a protein challenge is given. Although males are primarily affected, up to one-third of female carriers manifest symptoms due to lionization. Genetic heterogeneity exists, so that some affected males have a less severe clinical course.

TABLE 9–5

X-Linked Recessive Disease

	Frequency	Comments
Lesch-Nyhan syndrome	1:100,000	Hypoxanthine-phosphoribosyl transferase
Ornithine transcarbamylase deficiency	?	Gene cloned—milder disease in females
Duchenne muscular dystrophy	1:5000	Gene cloned—high spontaneous mutation rate
Hemophilia A + B	1:10,000	Gene cloned; factor replacement needed
Fragile X syndrome	1:2000	25% of mentally retarded males—macrocephaly, macro-orchidism, demonstrates anticipation
Bruton agammaglobulinemia	$1:1 \times 10^5$	Recurrent infections
Chronic granulomatous disease	$1:1 \times 10^6$	Recurrent infections, some variants autosomal recessive
Glucose-6-phosphate dehydrogenase deficiency	10% of American blacks	Oxidant-induced hemolysis
Color blindness	$1:1 \times 10^5$	

Reproduced from Behrman RE, Kliegman RM, eds. Essentials of pediatrics, 2nd ed. Philadelphia: WB Saunders, 1994:127.

Clinical Manifestations

Within 24–48 hours after the initiation of protein-containing feedings, the newborn becomes progressively lethargic and may develop seizures as the serum ammonia becomes greater than 500 μg/dL. Female carriers may develop headaches and emesis after protein meals and manifest mental retardation and learning disabilities. Diagnosis is made by measuring the level of orotic acid in the urine, which is the by-product of carbamylphosphate metabolism.

Treatment

Treatment centers on an extremely-low-protein diet and the exploitation of alternative pathways for nitrogen excretion using benzoic acid and phenylacetate. Early intervention may minimize deleterious affects from the defect, but management is complex and extremely difficult for parents to maintain.

Fragile X Syndrome

Fragile X is an X-linked form of mental retardation that occurs in 1 in 1000 males. Diagnosis is made by detection of a fragile site on the distal end of the long arm of the X chromosome. Clinical manifestations may include macrosomia at birth with a head circumference greater than the 95th percentile, macro-orchidism seen at puberty, dysmorphic facial features (large jaw and large ears), and moderate mental retardation with a disproportionately severe delay in expressive language develop-

ment. Some males with fragile X syndrome have no clinical features other than mental retardation. Female carriers of the fragile X chromosome may have an IQ below normal. Autism occurs in children with the fragile X chromosome at a frequency greater than that found in the general population. There is no treatment for the syndrome.

◆ KEY POINTS ◆

1. Single-gene defects are classified by their mode of inheritance into autosomal dominant, autosomal recessive, and X-linked disorders.

2. In autosomal dominant disorders, the phenomenon of incomplete penetrance results in variable expression of the defective gene.

3. Genes defective in autosomal dominant disorders typically code for structural proteins, whereas those in autosomal recessive disorders code for enzymes.

4. Most inborn errors of metabolism, with the noted exception of ornithine transcarbamylase deficiency, are autosomal recessive disorders.

5. Because PKU and homocystinuria do not manifest themselves until damage to the central

nervous system has been done, following up on neonatal screens is extremely important.

6. In the child with progressive developmental delay and/or mental retardation without a known etiology, inborn errors in metabolism and fragile X syndrome should be considered.

CHROMOSOME DISORDERS

Chromosomal disorders occur in 5 in 1000 live births, or approximately 0.6%. Most chromosomal defects arise de novo during gametogenesis, so that an infant can be conceived with a chromosomal abnormality without any prior family history. Chromosomal anomalies can also be present in a parent and passed to an offspring. Sometimes this is associated with a family history of multiple spontaneous abortions or a higher than chance frequency of giving birth to children with chromosomal problems. Chromosomal abnormalities present at conception often lead to spontaneous abortion; approximately 50% of first-trimester spontaneous abortions have chromosomal defects. Even the chromosomal anomalies that are observed at term, such as trisomy 21 and Turner's syndrome, represent only a fraction of the individuals conceived with these chromosomal problems. Chromosomal disorders are divided into abnormalities of number or structure and content and may involve the autosomes or the sex chromosomes. Birth defects due to autosomal anomalies are generally more severe than those due to sex chromosome abnormalities. Numeric defects of the autosomes include trisomy 13, trisomy 18, and trisomy 21. Examples of sex chromosome numerical abnormalities are Klinefelter's syndrome and Turner's syndrome. Structural anomalies result from chromosomal breakage, unbalanced translocation, deletion, duplication, inversion, isochromosome formation, and centromeric fragmentation. Examples of structural chromosome problems include Prader-Willi syndrome, cri-du-chat syndrome, retinoblastoma, and Wilm's tumor.

Indications for obtaining chromosomal studies include confirmation of a suspected chromosomal syndrome, multiple organ system malformations, significant developmental delay or mental retardation not otherwise explained, short stature or extremely delayed menarche in girls, infertility or a history of multiple spontaneous abortions, ambiguous genitalia, and/or advanced maternal age. Karyotyping of fetuses of mothers of advanced age may be accomplished through amniocentesis or chorionic villus sampling.

Autosomal Trisomies

Trisomy 21

Trisomy 21, or Down syndrome, is the most common autosomal chromosomal abnormality in humans, with an incidence of 1 in 700 live births. Of children with Down syndrome, 95% have 47 chromosomes with three number 21 chromosomes, which results from chromosomal nondisjunction during maternal meiosis. The risk of having a child with an extra chromosome 21 increases with advancing maternal age. This risk rises dramatically after the age of 35. The reason for this increase is unknown. Of children with Down syndrome, 4% have 46 chromosomes with a translocation of the third number 21 chromosome to another chromosome. Three-fourths of all cases of translocation are not familial but occur de novo. One-fourth of translocation cases are familial, meaning that one of the parents has a balanced translocation involving one number 21 chromosome and another chromosome. One percent of children with Down syndrome have chromosome mosaicism, with some cells having 46 chromosomes and two number 21 chromosomes and some cells having 47 chromosomes with three number 21 chromosomes. The mosaicism results from a mitotic division error that occurred during embryonic development.

Clinical Manifestations

Common dysmorphic facial features include flat facial profile, upslanted palpebral fissures, a flat nasal bridge with epicanthal folds, a small mouth with a protruding tongue, micrognathia, and short ears with downfolding ear lobes. Other dysmorphic features are excess skin on the back of the neck, microcephaly, a flat occiput (brachycephaly), short stature, a short sternum, small genitalia, and a gap between the first and second toes ("sandal gap toe"). Anomalies of the hand include single palmar creases (simian creases) and short, broad hands (brachydactyly) with fingers marked by an incurved fifth finger and a hypoplastic middle phalanx (clinodactyly). Functional and structural abnormalities include generalized hypotonia (obstructive sleep apnea), cardiac defects (endocardial cushion defects and septal defects are seen in 50% of cases), gastrointestinal anomalies (duodenal atresia and Hirschsprung's disease), atlanto-axial instability, developmental delay and moderate mental retardation, and hypothyroidism. There is a higher frequency of leukemia in children with trisomy 21 than in the general population. During the third and fourth decades, an Alzheimer-like dementia develops.

Treatment
With improved medical, educational, and vocational management, life expectancy for patients with Down syndrome now extends well into adulthood.

Trisomy 13
Trisomy 13 occurs in 1 in 10,000 live births. Of children with trisomy 13, 75% have 47 chromosomes with three number 13 chromosomes, which results from chromosomal nondisjunction during meiosis. The risk of having a child with an extra chromosome 13 increases with advancing maternal age, although it is not as dramatic as with trisomy 21. Twenty percent of children with trisomy 13 have 46 chromosomes with a translocation of the third number 13 chromosome to another chromosome. Three-fourths of all cases of translocation are not familial but occur de novo. One-fourth of translocation cases are familial, meaning that one of the parents has a balanced

translocation involving one number 13 chromosome and another chromosome. Five percent of children with trisomy 13 have mosaicism, with some cells having 46 chromosomes and two number 13 chromosomes and some cells having 47 chromosomes with three number 13 chromosomes. The mosaicism results from a mitotic division error that occurred during embryonic development. The clinical manifestations of trisomy 13 are shown in Table 9–6. Prognosis for patients with trisomy 13 is extremely poor; 50% die before reaching 1 month of age, and 90% die by 1 year of age.

Trisomy 18
Trisomy 18 occurs in 1 in 8000 live births. Ninety percent of the cases of trisomy 18 are the result of meiotic nondisjunction, and 10% of the cases are mosaics caused by mitotic nondisjunction in the zygote. Chromosome translocation as the cause of trisomy 18 is extremely rare. Advanced maternal age increases the risk of trisomy 18 but not as much as is seen with trisomy 21 and trisomy 13. The clinical manifestations of trisomy 18 are shown in Table 9–6. The prognosis for patients with trisomy

---

TABLE 9–6

Findings That May Be Present in Trisomy 13 and Trisomy 18

	Trisomy 13	Trisomy 18
Head and face	Scalp defects (cutis aplasia)	Small and premature appearance
	Micro-ophthalmia, corneal abnormalities	Tight palpebral fissures
	Cleft lip and palate (60–80%)	Narrow nose and hypoplastic nasal alae
	Microcephaly	Narrow bifrontal diameter
	Sloping forehead	Prominent occiput
	Holoprosencephaly (arhinencephaly)	Micrognathia
	Capillary hemangiomas	Cleft lip and/or palate
Chest	Congenital heart disease (VSD, PDA, ASD) 80%	Congenital heart disease (VSD, PDA, ASD)
		Short sternum
Extremities	Overlapping of fingers and toes (clinodactyly)	Limited hip abduction
	Polydactyly	Clinodactyly and overlapping of fingers: index over 3rd, 5th over 4th
	Hypoplastic nails	Rocker-bottom feet
		Hypoplastic nails
General	Developmental delays and prenatal and postnatal growth retardation	Developmental delays and prenatal and postnatal growth retardation
	Renal abnormalities	
	Nuclear projections in neutrophils	

ASD, atrial septal defect; PDA, patent ductus arteriosus; VSD, ventricular septal defect.

Reproduced from Behrman RE, Kliegman RM, eds. Essentials of pediatrics, 2nd ed. Philadelphia: WB Saunders, 1994:132.

13 is extremely poor; 30% die before reaching 1 month of age, and 90% die by 1 year of age.

Sex Chromosome Abnormalities

Sex chromosome anomalies involve abnormalities in the number or structure of the X and/or Y chromosomes.

Turner's Syndrome

Turner's syndrome occurs in 1 in 5000 live births but may occur in up to 1% of fetuses. Of fetuses with Turner's syndrome, 98% expire in utero from cystic hygroma or hydrops fetalis. In this syndrome, only one X chromosome exists or is normal (monosomy X). To avoid the Turner phenotype, a female must have two complete and active p arms (short arms) on two separate X chromosomes. Because advancing maternal age does not increase the risk for Turner's syndrome, the presumption is that the syndrome results not from an abnormal gamete but from defective embryonic cell division after fertilization.

Several genotypes can result in the Turner's phenotype. In 60% of cases, the karyotype is 45,XO, in which the female is simply missing an X chromosome. In 25% of cases, there are two X chromosomes but there is deletion of the short arm (p arm) of one of the X chromosomes or a long arm isochromosome is created. The isochromosome results from duplication of the long arm (q arm) and loss of the short arm (p arm) on that particular X chromosome, so that there is a centromere and two long arms (q arms). Mosaicism occurs in 15% of cases, usually affecting two or more cell lines. If two cell lines are affected, then the genotype is generally 45,XO and either 46,XX or 46,XY. If three cell lines are affected, the karyotype is usually 45,XO, 46,XX, and 47,XXX. Because the syndrome does not result from errors in gametogenesis, recurrence risk for parents who have a child with Turner's syndrome does not increase compared with that of the general population.

Clinical Manifestations

Dysmorphic features include lymphedema of the hands and feet at birth, a shield-shaped chest, widely spaced hypoplastic nipples, a webbed neck, a low hairline, cubitus valgus (increased carrying angle), short stature, and multiple pigmented nevi. Functional and structural abnormalities include gonadal dysgenesis, gonadoblastoma, renal anomalies, congenital heart disease, autoimmune thyroiditis, and learning disabilities. Gonadal dysgenesis is present in 100% of patients and is associated with primary amenorrhea and a lack of pubertal development due to loss of ovarian hormones. The gonads are appropriately infantile at birth but regress during childhood and become "streak" ovaries by puberty. In mosaics with a Y chromosome in one of their cell lines, gonadoblastoma is common. Therefore, prophylactic gonadectomy is necessary in these patients. Renal anomalies occur in 40% of those afflicted with Turner's syndrome. Duplication of the collecting system and horseshoe kidney are two of the more common defects seen. Congenital heart disease occurs in 20% of patients, and common defects include coarctation of the aorta, aortic stenosis, and bicuspid aortic valve. As a consequence of having only one functional X chromosome, females with Turner's syndrome display the same frequency of sex-linked disorders as males. The diagnosis is made by karyotype. Because of their mosaicism, some girls suspected of having Turner's syndrome have a 46,XX karyotype in the peripheral blood, and a skin biopsy will be necessary to make the diagnosis.

Treatment

Short stature has been successfully treated using parenteral human growth hormone and oral anabolic steroids. Secondary sexual characteristics can be developed with estrogen and progesterone. As mentioned earlier, gonadectomy is indicated in mosaics with a Y chromosome cell line. With the rare exception of a few mosaics, women with Turner's cannot become pregnant.

Klinefelter's Syndrome

Klinefelter's syndrome affects 1 in 1000 newborn males and is due to an extra X chromosome. Of males with the syndrome, 80% have a 47,XXY karyotype, and 20% are a mosaic with one normal 46,XY cell line and one abnormal 47,XXY cell line. Recurrence risk is the same as the initial risk in the general population.

Clinical Manifestations

Infants and prepubertal males are not identified because of the absence of recognizable features. At puberty, males are incompletely masculinized and usually have a female body habitus with decreased body hair, gynecomastia, small phallus, and small and soft testes. Infertility results from hypospermia or aspermia. Often, affected males are taller than average relative to their families and their arm span is generally greater than their height. There may be mild mental retardation. Gonadotropin levels are usually elevated as a result of inadequate testosterone levels.

Treatment

Testosterone therapy may be helpful at adolescence to improve secondary sexual characteristics.

Structural Chromosome Deletions

Partial deletions are caused by the loss of chromosomal material from the ends of chromosomes (terminal chromosomal deletion) or by the loss of material from the middle or inner portion of a chromosome (interstitial deletion). Although most chromosomal deletions arise de novo, terminal deletions may result from a child inheriting an unbalanced chromosome translocation from a parent who has a balanced translocation. Wilm's tumor and retinoblastoma result from interstitial deletions and are discussed in depth in Chapters 17 and 18, respectively.

Cri-du-chat Syndrome

Cri-du-chat syndrome occurs in 1 in 50,000 newborns. The syndrome results from a terminal deletion from the short arm of chromosome 5 (5_p^-). Affected children have a characteristic cat-like cry. Central nervous system manifestations include microcephaly and profound mental retardation, whereas ocular malformations include cataracts and optic atrophy. Many patients survive into adulthood.

Prader-Willi Syndrome

Prader-Willi syndrome occurs in 1 in 15,000 newborns and is associated with an interstitial deletion of the long arm of chromosome 15 (deletion of 15q11–13). Approximately 70% of those affected have a chromosome deletion in the paternally derived chromosome 15, whereas 5% have a translocation involving 15q. The remaining 25% have a normal-appearing chromosome complement with two copies of maternal chromosome 15. This is known as maternal disomy, and the syndrome results from the lack of a paternal copy of chromosome 15. The existence of maternal disomy as a cause of Prader-Willi syndrome is an example of genetic imprinting, a newly recognized phenomenon in which some genes are expressed differently depending on whether they were inherited from the mother or the father. Recurrence risk is 1 in 100, unless the chromosome 15 deletion results from a parental translocation, which is extremely rare.

Clinical Manifestations

Dysmorphisms include narrow bifrontal diameter, almond-shaped palpebral fissures, a down-turned mouth, and small hands and feet. Short stature and hypogonadotropic hypogonadism with small genitalia and incomplete puberty are seen. These children suffer from severe infantile hypotonia associated with feeding difficulties and failure to thrive in infancy. Severe central obesity develops during childhood due to appetite dysregulation. Obstructive sleep apnea and Pickwickian syndrome may develop due to the morbid obesity. These children eat constantly unless food is locked away. There is severe developmental delay and mild mental retardation, with characteristic impulse control problems.

Treatment

For the average family, strict dietary control is attempted but difficult to enforce. Those affected can live normal life spans with medical, vocational, and living situation assistance. The complications of the obesity, obstructive sleep apnea, and diabetes mellitus tend to shorten the individual's life span.

◆ KEY POINTS ◆

1. Approximately 50% of first trimester spontaneous abortions have chromosomal abnormalities.

2. Chromosomal disorders are divided into abnormalities of number or of structure and content and may involve the autosomes or the sex chromosomes.

3. Birth defects due to autosomal anomalies are generally more severe than those due to sex chromosome abnormalities.

4. Indications for obtaining chromosomal studies include confirmation of a suspected chromosomal syndrome, multiple organ system malformations, significant developmental delay or mental retardation not otherwise explained, short stature or extremely delayed menarche in girls, infertility or a history of multiple spontaneous abortions, ambiguous genitalia, and/or advanced maternal age.

10 Hematology

ANEMIA

Anemia is defined as a hemoglobin concentration or hematocrit that is greater than 2 standard deviations below the mean value for age and sex. It is important to recognize that anemia is not a disease but rather a symptom of another disorder. The hemoglobin concentration and hematocrit are relatively high in the newborn but then decline, reaching a nadir at approximately 6 weeks in the premature infant and 2–3 months in the term infant. This reduction is known as the "physiologic anemia" of infancy. Thereafter, the hemoglobin concentration and hematocrit rise gradually during childhood, reaching adult values after puberty.

Differential Diagnosis

Anemia results from decreased red cell production, increased red cell destruction, or blood loss. Decreased red cell production is due to either deficiency of hematopoietic precursors or bone marrow failure, and increased red cell destruction results from hemolytic disease, which may be due to extracorpuscular or intracorpuscular defects. Extracorpuscular abnormalities include isoimmune, autoimmune, and nonimmune hemolytic anemia. Intracorpuscular disorders such as intrinsic membrane defects, hemoglobinopathies, and enzymopathies also cause hemolytic anemia. Acute blood loss from the gastrointestinal tract or from trauma or chronic blood loss from gastrointestinal or menstrual bleeding can result in

anemia. Table 10–1 delineates the most common causes of anemia.

The adjusted reticulocyte count (ARC) is used to determine whether there has been an adequate erythropoietic response to the given anemia. The ARC is calculated as follows:

$$ARC = \frac{hematocrit\ (measured)}{hematocrit\ (expected)} \times reticulocyte\ count.$$

An ARC less than 2 suggests ineffective erythropoiesis, whereas an ARC greater than 2 signifies effective erythropoiesis. Anemia caused by a lack of production of red blood cells, therefore, has an ARC less than 2, whereas anemias resulting from hemolysis or chronic blood loss have an ARC more than 2.

Clinical Manifestations

History

Exploring the dietary history is critical to evaluate for iron, B_{12}, or folate deficiency anemia. The presence of pica is suggestive of both iron-deficiency anemia and lead poisoning. Signs of overt or occult bleeding, such as melena, hematochezia, hematuria, hematemesis, abnormal menses, or epistaxis, are important clues to determining the type and cause of the anemia. The perinatal history should be discussed to rule out twin-twin transfusion or fetomaternal transfusion. If there is a family history of splenectomy or cholecystectomy, a hemolytic anemia may be present, and the clinician may want to

TABLE 10–1

Differential Diagnosis of Anemias Defined by Adjusted Reticulocyte Count and Mean Corpuscular Volume

Decreased Red Cell Production: Adjusted Reticulocyte Count < 2 (inadequate reticulocytosis)				
Deficiency of Hematopoietic Inputs			Bone Marrow Failure	
Microcytic Anemias		Macrocytic Anemias	Normocytic Anemias	Macrocytic Anemias
Defective Heme Synthesis	Defective Globin Synthesis	Defective DNA Synthesis		
Iron deficiency	Alpha thalassemia	Folate deficiency	TEC	Congenital red cell aplasia
Anemia of chronic disease	Beta thalassemia	Vitamin B$_{12}$ deficiency	Anemia of chronic disease	Diamond-Blackfan syndrome
Lead poisoning		Drugs that interfere with folate metabolism (phenytoin, methotrexate, trimethoprim)	Parvovirus B-19– induced aplastic crisis	Fanconi's anemia
Pyridoxine (vitamin B$_6$ deficiency)			Marrow infiltration from malignancy	Idiopathic aplastic anemia
Copper deficiency		Metabolic disorders (orotic aciduria, methylmalonic aciduria, Lesch-Nyhan syndrome)	Chronic renal disease	Preleukemia/leukemia
Vitamin E deficiency			Acute blood loss— trauma	Irradiation
			Drug toxicity— myelosuppressive agents	Chronic liver disease
				Hypothyroidism
				Drug toxicity (azidothymidine, valporic acid, carbamazepine)

consider enzymopathies, hemoglobinopathies, and red blood cell membrane defects in the differential. Determining the ethnic/racial history of a family is helpful when hemoglobinopathies are considered. Always ascertain whether the patient is taking any medications that may depress bone marrow or cause hemolysis.

Physical Examination

In general, examine the patient for pallor, evidence of congestive heart failure (hepatosplenomegaly, lower extremity edema, tachycardia), pancytopenia (petechiae, purpura), bleeding (positive stool guaiac or gastrocult, gross hematuria), hemolytic disease (scleral icterus, jaundice, urobilinogen in the urine), or an infiltrative disorder (lymphadenopathy, hepatosplenomegaly). If the child has failure to thrive, consider anemia of chronic disease.

Specific physical findings in the evaluation of anemia are found in Table 10–2.

Diagnostic Evaluation

The goal of testing is to determine whether the anemia results from a decrease in production, an increase in destruction, or blood loss. The mean corpuscular volume and adjusted reticulocyte count categorize the disorder into a microcytic, normocytic, or macrocytic anemia, with an adequate or inadequate reticulocytosis.

Laboratory tests needed to evaluate anemia include, at minimum, a complete blood count with manual differential and red blood cell indices, reticulocyte count, and blood smear. Peripheral blood smear is critical to assess the red cell morphology, the white cell number and morphology, and the platelet number and size. If

TABLE 10–1 (*continued*)

Differential Diagnosis of Anemias Defined by Adjusted Reticulocyte Count and Mean Corpuscular Volume

	Increased Red Cell Production: *Adjusted Reticulocyte Count >2 (adequate reticulocytosis)*					
		Hemolytic Anemias— *Normocytic*		*Chronic Blood Loss—Normocytic* *Gastrointestinal Bleeding* *Menstrual Bleeding*		
	Extracorpuscular Defects			*Intracorpuscular Defects*		
Isoimmune *Hemolytic Anemia*	*Autoimmune* *Hemolytic Anemia*	*Nonimmune* *Hemolytic Anemia*	*Intrinsic* *Membrane Defects*	*Hemo-* *globinopathies*	*Enzymopathies*
ABO or minor antigen incompatibility	Idiopathic Postinfectious (mycoplasma, Epstein-Barr virus) Chronic autoimmune disease (SLE) Drugs (penicillin, quinidine, alphamethyldopa) Non-Hodgkin's lymphoma	Microangiopathic (DIC, HUS, TTP, malignant hypertension, preeclampsia, renal graft rejection) Damage from nonendothelialized surfaces (artificial heart valve— "Waring blender" syndrome, AVM, Kasabach-Merritt syndrome) Hypersplenism Abetalipoproteinemia Toxins (snake venom, copper, arsenic) Malaria Burns	Hereditary spherocytosis Hereditary elliptocytosis Hereditary stomatocytosis PNH	Hemoglobin SS Hemoglobin S-C Hemoglobin S-Bthal	G6PD deficiency Pyruvate kinase deficiency

TEC, transient erythroblastopenia of childhood; AVM, arteriovenous malformation; DIC, disseminated intravascular coagulation; G6PD, glucose-6-phosphate dehydrogenase; HUS, hemolytic uremic syndrome; PNH, paroxysmal nocturnal hemoglobinuria; SEL, systemic lupus erythematosis; TTP, thrombotic thrombocytopenic purpura.

hemolysis is suspected, a chemistry and electrolyte panel, Coomb's test (indirect and direct), haptoglobin, hemopexin, and a urinalysis looking for urobilinogen may be performed. If a hemoglobinopathy is considered, a hemoglobin electrophoresis may be of assistance. If an enzymopathy is suspected, performing a glucose-6-phosphate dehydrogenase deficiency (G6PD) test may be helpful. If iron-deficiency anemia is high on the differential, a serum iron level, total iron binding capacity, and serum ferritin level are needed for analysis. A lead level is indicated if lead poisoning is contemplated. An erythrocyte sedimentation rate is helpful if anemia of chronic disease is considered likely. To identify chronic or acute gastrointestinal bleeding, a stool guaiac or gastrocult test of gastric contents is useful. If a macrocytic anemia is found, both folate and vitamin B_{12} levels are needed.

Treatment

Treatment varies depending on the cause of the anemia. Following this section are short discussions on the anemias that appear most often on USMLE exams.

TABLE 10–2

Physical Findings in the Evaluation of Anemia

System	Observation	Significance
Skin	Hyperpigmentation	Fanconi, dyskeratosis congenita
	Café-au-lait spots	Fanconi anemia
	Vitiligo	Vitamin B_{12} deficiency
	Partial oculocutaneous albinism	Chédiak-Higashi syndrome
	Jaundice	Hemolysis
	Petechiae, purpura	Bone marrow infiltration, autoimmune hemolysis with autoimmune thrombocytopenia, hemolytic uremic syndrome
	Erythematous rash	Parvovirus, Epstein-Barr virus
	Butterfly rash	SLE autoantibodies
Head	Frontal bossing	Thalassemia major, severe iron deficiency, chronic subdural hematoma
	Microcephaly	Fanconi anemia
Eyes	Microphthalmia	Fanconi anemia
	Retinopathy	SS, SC disease
	Optic atrophy	Osteopetrosis
	Blocked lacrimal gland	Dyskeratosis congenita
	Kayser-Fleisher ring	Wilson's disease
	Blue sclera	Iron deficiency
Ears	Deafness	Osteopetrosis
Mouth	Glossitis	B_{12} deficiency, iron deficiency
	Angular stomatitis	Iron deficiency
	Cleft lip	Diamond-Blackfan syndrome
	Pigmentation	Peutz-Jeghers syndrome (intestinal blood loss)
	Telangiectasia	Osler-Weber-Rendu syndrome (blood loss)
	Leukoplakia	Dyskeratosis congenita
Chest	Shield chest or widespread nipples	Diamond-Blackfan syndrome
	Murmur	Endocarditis: prosthetic valve hemolysis
Abdomen	Hepatomegaly	Hemolysis, infiltrative tumor, chronic disease, hemangioma, cholecystitis
	Splenomegaly	Hemolysis, sickle cell disease, (early) thalassemia, malaria, lymphoma, Epstein-Barr virus, portal hypertension
	Nephromegaly	Fanconi anemia
	Absent kidney	Fanconi anemia
Extremities	Absent thumbs	Fanconi anemia
	Triphalangeal thumb	Diamond-Blackfan syndrome
	Spoon nails	Iron deficiency
	Beau line (nails)	Heavy metal intoxication, severe illness
	Mees line (nails)	Heavy metals, severe illness, sickle cell anemia
	Dystrophic nails	Dyskeratosis congenita
Rectal	Hemorrhoids	Portal hypertension
	Heme positive stool	Intestinal hemorrhage
Nerves	Irritable, apathy	Iron deficiency
	Peripheral neuropathy	Deficiency of vitamins B_1, B_{12}, and E, lead poisoning
	Dementia	Deficiency of vitamins B_{12} and E
	Ataxia, posterior column signs	Vitamin B_{12} deficiency
	Stroke	Sickle cell anemia, paroxysmal nocturnal hemoglobinuria

SLE, systemic lupus erythematosus.

Reprinted with permission from Behrman RE, Kliegman RM, eds. Essentials of pediatrics, 2nd ed. Philadelphia: WB Saunders, 1994.

Microcytic Anemias with Deficiency of Hematopoietic Inputs

Hypochromic microcytic red blood cells indicate impaired synthesis of the heme or globin components of hemoglobin. Defective heme synthesis may be the result of iron deficiency, lead poisoning, chronic inflammatory disease, pyridoxine deficiency, or copper deficiency. Defective globin synthesis is characteristic of the thalassemia syndromes. Iron-deficiency anemia, the thalassemia syndromes, and anemia of chronic disease are the most common causes of hypochromic, microcytic anemias. Lead poisoning, which may cause a mild hypochromic, microcytic anemia, is discussed in detail in Chapter 2.

Iron-Deficiency Anemia

Iron deficiency is by far the most common cause of anemia during childhood and is most often seen between 6 and 24 months of age. It can be seen as early as 3 months of age in the premature infant who had inadequate iron stores at birth. Nutritional iron deficiency usually develops when rapid growth and an expanding blood volume put excessive demands on iron stores. This can occur during infancy, when iron stores are inadequate, at birth due to low birth weight, or when an infant or toddler receives a diet exclusively comprising milk or low-iron formula. Children who receive whole cow's milk are at risk for microscopic intestinal hemorrhage, which results in chronic blood loss and iron deficiency. Nutritional iron deficiency can also occur during adolescence when a rapid growth spurt coincides with a diet with suboptimal iron content. This is a particular problem in adolescent females because of iron loss during menses.

Dietary risk factors include limited breast feeding (less than 6 months) or extended exclusive breast feeding (more than 1 year), early institution of solids, excessive whole milk or low-iron-containing formula intake, tea, and the absence of iron supplements. Although the concentration of iron in breast milk is less than that found in cow's milk, the iron that is present in breast milk is much more bioavailable.

Iron deficiency resulting from blood loss can occur in the prenatal, perinatal, or postnatal period. Prenatal iron loss can occur from fetomaternal transfusion or from twin-to-twin transfusion. Perinatal bleeding may result from obstetric complications such as placental abruption or placenta previa. Postnatal blood loss may occur from obvious sources such as surgery or from trauma or may be occult, as occurs with idiopathic pulmonary hemosiderosis, parasitic infestations, or inflammatory bowel disease.

Clinical Manifestations

Mild iron deficiency is relatively asymptomatic. As iron deficiency becomes increasingly severe, the infant develops anorexia, irritability, apathy, and easy fatigability. On physical examination, the milk-fed anemic infant is pale and sallow and has glossitis, angular stomatitis, and/or spoon nails. With moderate to severe anemia, the child is tachycardic and has a systolic ejection murmur at the left upper sternal border. If the anemia is very severe (hemoglobin less than 3 g/dL), the infant may show signs of congestive heart failure, which include tachycardia, an S3, cardiomegaly, hepatomegaly, distended neck veins, and rales on lung examination.

The laboratory findings typical for iron-deficiency anemia, the thalassemias, lead poisoning, and anemia of chronic disease are found in Table 10–3. Bone marrow examination is not clinically indicated to confirm the diagnosis. When performed, it demonstrates micronormoblastic hyperplasia of the erythroid line.

Treatment

Mild to moderate iron-deficiency anemia, without evidence of congestive heart failure, is treated with 3–6 mg/kg/day of iron. Therapy is continued for 3 months to allow hematocrit normalization and the replenishment of tissue stores. If the hematocrit has not normalized by the end of the first month of therapy and compliance has been established, other causes of hypochromic microcytic anemia should be considered. Although infants can tolerate remarkable degrees of anemia, especially if the decline in hemoglobin is gradual, infants with extremely severe anemia who have cardiac decompensation must be transfused very slowly with 3–5 mL/kg of packed

TABLE 10–3

Laboratory Findings for the Common Microcytic Anemias

	Iron Deficiency	Thalassemia Trait	Thalassemia Major	Plumbism	Chronic Disease
RDW	↑	NL	↑	↑	NL
MCV	↓	↓	↓	↓	NL↓
RBC no.	↓	NL	↓	↓	↓
FEP	↑	NL	NL	↑↑	↑
Hgb A$_2$	↓	β-↑ α-NL	β-↑ α-NL	NL	NL
Iron	↓	NL	↑	NL	↓
TIBC	NL↑	NL	NL ↑	NL	NL ↓
% saturation	↓	NL	↑	NL	↓
Ferritin	↓	NL	↑	NL	NL ↑

FEP, free erythrocyte protoporphyrin; hgb, hemoglobin; TIBC, total iron-binding capacity; ↑, increased; ↓, decreased; NL, normal.

Reprinted with permission from Graef JW, ed. Manual of pediatric therapeutics, 5th ed. Boston: Little, Brown, 1994.

red blood cells every 4 hours, until the patient's condition has stabilized.

◆ KEY POINTS ◆

1. Iron-deficiency anemia, the thalassemia syndromes, and anemia of chronic disease are the most common causes of hypochromic, microcytic anemias.

2. Iron deficiency is by far the most common cause of anemia during childhood and is most often seen between 6 and 24 months of age.

3. Mild to moderate iron-deficiency anemia, without evidence of congestive heart failure, is treated with 3–6 mg/kg/day of elemental iron. Therapy is continued for 3 months to allow hematocrit normalization and the replenishment of tissue stores. If the hematocrit does not normalize by the end of the first month of therapy and compliance has been established, other causes of hypochromic microcytic anemia should be considered.

Alpha and Beta Thalassemia
Pathogenesis and Clinical Manifestations

The thalassemias are hereditary hemolytic anemias characterized by decreased or absent synthesis of one or more globin subunits of the hemoglobin molecule. Alpha thalassemia results from reduced synthesis of alpha globin chains, whereas beta thalassemia results from reduced synthesis of beta globin chains. Mechanisms responsible for the thalassemias include gene deletion or abnormalities in the transcription or translation of messenger RNA. Alpha thalassemia results from deletion of one or more of the four alpha genes normally present, whereas beta thalassemia most often is caused by errors in the transcription or translation of mRNA. A comparison of the thalassemia syndromes is delineated in Table 10–4.

The hematologic consequences of the different types of alpha thalassemia are determined by the number of gene deletions present. These deletions can be cis or trans. Cis deletions occur when the two genes missing are on one chromosome, whereas trans deletions signify a single alpha globin gene deletion on each of the two chromosomes. Different races and ethnicities have varying rates of both cis and trans deletions of alpha globin genes in their population. This factor is discussed later.

TABLE 10–4

Comparison of the Thalassemia Syndromes

Genetic Abnormality	Percent Hemoglobin			Other	Clinical Syndrome
	Hb A	Hb A$_2$	Hb F		
Normal αβ	90–98	2–3	2–3	—	None
Beta-thalassemias					
Thalassemia major					
β-thal⁰ β-thal⁰	0	2–5	95	—	Severe anemia, abnormal growth, iron overload, needs transfusion, Cooley anemia
β-thal⁺ β-thal⁺	Very low	2–5	20–80	—	Severe hypo/micro anemia with Hb 7–9 g/dL, hepatosplenomegaly, bone changes, iron overload, less need for transfusion
Thalassemia intermedia (varied genetic globin abnormalities)	Overlaps with thalassemia major				
Thalassemia minor					
β β-thal⁰ or β β-thal⁺	90–95	5–7	2–10	RBC	Hypo/micro-blood smear, mild to no anemia
Alpha-thalassemias					
Homozygous α-thalassemia	—	—	—	Hb H (β4) Hb Bart (γ4)	Hydrops fetalis, stillborn
— — / — —					
Hemoglobin H disease	60–70	2–5	2–5	Hb H 30–40	Hypo/micro anemia, Hb 7–10 g/dL, Heinz bodies
— — / — α					
Alpha-thalassemia trait	90–98	2–3	2–3		Hypo/micro smear, no anemia
— α/ — α					
α α/ — —					
Silent carrier	90–98	2–3	2–3		Normal
— α/α α					

Reprinted with permission from Behrman RE, Kliegman RM, eds. Essentials of pediatrics, 2nd ed. Philadelphia: WB Saunders, 1994.

Those afflicted with a one-gene deletion are considered silent carriers for alpha thalassemia, as they have a normal hemoglobin concentration, hematocrit, and normal red blood cell indices. The condition can be measured only by quantitative measurement of globin chain synthesis or by gene analysis. A carrier can produce offspring with alpha thalassemia minor (two-gene deletion) or hemoglobin H disease (three-gene deletion).

The two-gene deletion is known as alpha thalassemia minor. This defect manifests itself as a mild hypochromia, microcytosis on smear with or without a very mild anemia. Alpha thalassemia minor can be confused with mild iron deficiency. The hemoglobin electrophoresis is normal in these children, and the diagnosis is one of exclusion confirmed by documenting parental microcytosis.

Hemoglobin H disease results from three-gene deletion defect. Although sufficient alpha globin is produced to allow the fetus to come to term, these neonates have significant anemia and elevated levels of hemoglobin Bart's. Hemoglobin Bart's is a gamma globin tetramer. In utero, gamma globin chains are the analogue of the beta globin chain and cease expression soon after birth, when beta globin synthesis commences. Fetal hemoglobin, which consists of two alpha globin chains and two gamma globin chains, predominates at birth. It is the dearth of alpha globin chains and the resultant free gamma globin chains that result in hemoglobin Bart's. At birth, hemoglobin Bart's accounts for 10–40% of the total hemoglobin in children with hemoglobin H disease. With the loss of gamma globin synthesis and the onset of beta globin predominance after birth, hemoglobin Bart's diminishes and hemoglobin H predominates. Hemoglobin H, which consists of a beta globin tetramer, accounts for 30–40% of the total hemoglobin, and normal hemoglobin A accounts for approximately 60–70% of the hemoglobin total. This diagnosis is most common in children with Southeast Asian ancestry in whom the cis deletion is most common.

Homozygous alpha thalassemia, or hemoglobin Bart's disease, occurs when there is a four-gene deletion. Failure to produce any alpha globin chains results in gamma globin tetramers (hemoglobin Bart's). Hemoglobin Bart's has a high affinity for oxygen and does not release it to the tissue. The result is severe anemia, heart failure, hepatosplenomegaly, generalized edema, and death in utero due to hydrops fetalis. As with the three-gene deletion, the hydrops fetalis is most common in Southeast Asians in whom the cis deletion is seen most often.

Beta thalassemia can be subdivided into homozygous (beta thalassemia major) and heterozygous forms (beta thalassemia minor). Beta thalassemia major results either from complete absence of beta globin synthesis (B0/B0 genotype) due to defective transcription of mRNA or from partial reduction of gene product (B+/B+ genotype) due to translational errors. The child with beta thalassemia minor, the heterozygous form, has one normal beta globin gene and one abnormal beta globin gene.

Beta thalassemia major manifests itself as a severe hemolytic anemia with marked splenomegaly during the first year of life. If untreated, the child will develop bone marrow hyperplasia and extramedullary hematopoiesis that produces characteristic features such as tower skull, frontal bossing, maxillary hypertrophy with prominent cheekbones, and an overbite. Failure to thrive is prominent. Death occurs within the first few years of life due to progressive congestive heart failure if the patient is not supported with blood transfusions. Despite the severity of the anemia, there is reticulocytopenia, reflecting ineffective hematopoiesis. Peripheral blood smear reveals marked hypochromia, microcytosis, anisocytosis, and poikilocytosis. On hemoglobin electrophoresis, hemoglobin A is either markedly decreased or totally absent. On quantitative hemoglobin electrophoresis, hemoglobin F accounts for 95% in the B0/B0 genotype and 20–80% in the B+/B+ genotype. If the diagnosis is in question or the hemoglobin electrophoresis is equivocal, checking the parental smears and indices for thalassemia is advised.

A mild hemolytic anemia is the only symptom of beta thalassemia minor. On blood smear, the hypochromia, microcytosis, and anisocytosis are disproportionately severe given the degree of anemia. Hemoglobin electrophoresis shows elevation of the hemoglobin A2 level and sometimes a mild elevation of hemoglobin F.

Epidemiology
Beta thalassemia is most often found in populations originating from the Mediterranean, Middle East, and India. Alpha thalassemia is most common in African, Southeast Asian, Mediterranean, and Middle Eastern populations. Alpha thalassemia occurs in 1.5% of African Americans. The most severe forms of alpha thalassemia, three- and four-gene deletions, are seen in the Southeast Asian population due to the prevalence of the cis deletion.

Treatment
Therapy for children with beta thalassemia major consists of frequent transfusions with packed red blood cells to ameliorate the anemia and to prevent congestive heart failure. Usually, 10–20 mL/kg of leukodepleted red blood cells every 3–5 weeks is needed to maintain the hematocrit above 30%. This regimen eliminates an increased erythropoietic drive, allowing normal linear growth and bone development. Suppression of erythropoiesis limits the stimulus for increased iron absorption, which helps to minimize iron overload. Splenectomy is considered when transfusional requirements exceed 250 mL/kg/yr. Iron overload develops in children with beta thalassemia whether they are transfused or not, due to hyperabsorption of dietary iron. When the bone marrow storage capacity for iron is exceeded, iron accumulates in the liver, heart, pancreas, gonads, and skin, producing the symptoms of hemochromatosis. As a result, many transfusion-dependent thalassemics succumb to congestive heart failure in their late teens. To minimize the mor-

bidity associated with iron overload, patients are treated with chelating agents such as desferoxamine. Due to the constant state of increased erythropoiesis, folic acid supplementation is recommended for patients not maintained on chronic transfusion therapy, to prevent folate deficiency and megaloblastic anemia. Bone marrow transplantation is curative, but because of its associated morbidity and mortality, this procedure is performed in only a few centers using HLA-matched sibling donors.

Principles of therapy for hemoglobin H disease are the same as those for beta thalassemia major. The need for transfusion and chelation therapy depends on the severity of the anemia.

No treatment is necessary for alpha or beta thalassemia minor. Genetic counseling is recommended. Because the smear of iron-deficiency anemia and alpha and beta thalassemia minor are quite similar, the child with presumed iron-deficiency anemia who does not respond to oral iron therapy and is believed to be compliant should have a hemoglobin electrophoresis to rule out alpha or beta thalassemia minor. The child with alpha thalassemia has a normal hemoglobin electrophoresis, whereas the electrophoresis of the child with beta thalassemia minor may show an elevated hemoglobin A2 and hemoglobin F.

◆ KEY POINTS ◆

1. Alpha thalassemia results from reduced synthesis of alpha globin chains, whereas beta thalassemia results from reduced synthesis of beta globin chains.

2. Alpha thalassemia results from deletion of one or more of the four alpha genes normally present, whereas beta thalassemia most often is caused by errors in the transcription or translation of mRNA.

Anemia of Chronic Disease

Anemia of chronic disease can result from chronic inflammatory diseases such as inflammatory bowel disease and juvenile rheumatoid arthritis; chronic infections, such as tuberculosis; and malignancy. Typically, anemia of chronic disease is normocytic; 25% of cases of anemia of chronic disease have microcytosis. Anemia of chronic disease results from an inability to mobilize iron from its storage sites in macrophages. The chronic inflammatory

state triggers cytokines that result in reticuloendothelial blockade within the marrow. A modest decrease in the survival time of red blood cells and a relatively limited erythropoietin response also contributes to the anemia.

Clinical Manifestations

The anemia is mild in degree (hemoglobin concentration is 7–10 g/dL). The laboratory findings typical for anemia of chronic disease are noted in Table 10–3. As in iron-deficiency anemia, the serum iron level is reduced, whereas in contrast to iron-deficiency anemia, the total iron-binding capacity is low and the serum ferritin level is normal or increased. Bone marrow examination shows micronormoblastic hyperplasia and an increase in storage iron, but a decrease in the number of iron-containing erythroblasts.

Treatment

The anemia resolves when the underlying condition is treated adequately. Therapy with medicinal iron is unnecessary unless true iron deficiency is also present.

◆ KEY POINTS ◆

1. Anemia of chronic disease can result from chronic inflammatory diseases, chronic infections, and malignancy.

2. Typically, anemia of chronic disease is normocytic; 25% of cases of anemia of chronic disease have microcytosis.

3. Anemia of chronic disease results from an inability to mobilize iron from its storage sites in macrophages.

Normocytic Anemias with Decreased Red Cell Production

Normocytic anemias result from the failure of the bone marrow to produce adequate numbers of red blood cells due to systemic illness. Bone marrow function can be impaired by fibrosis, malignant infiltration, transient marrow failure, or failure to synthesize erythropoietin (chronic renal disease). Transient marrow failure states include transient erythroblastopenia of childhood, parvovirus B-19 induced aplastic crisis, and drug toxicity from myelosuppressive agents. A normocytic anemia also occurs with acute blood loss. Re-equilibration of the total blood volume, before erythropoiesis, results in the anemia. Chronic inflammatory states result in anemia of chronic disease, which was discussed above in microcytic anemias. Of anemias associated with chronic disease, 75% result in normocytic anemias, whereas 25% result in microcytic anemias.

Transient Erythroblastopenia of Childhood

Transient erythroblastopenia of childhood (TEC) is an acquired pure red cell aplasia that occurs between the ages of 6 months and 5 years of age. Peak incidence is 2 years of age. In contrast to Diamond-Blackfan syndrome, which is a macrocytic pure red cell aplasia, 85% of cases of TEC occur after 1 year of age, there are no other associated anomalies, and fetal hemoglobin and i antigen is not present. TEC is a normocytic anemia caused by bone marrow suppression. Viral infection is thought to be the major cause of TEC, but no specific etiology has been identified.

Clinical Manifestations

The history and physical examination are unremarkable except for gradual onset of pallor over the course of weeks. Peripheral smear is normal other than reticulocytopenia. Bone marrow examination reveals reticulocytopenia, few erythroid precursors, and normal myeloid and platelet precursors.

Treatment

The hematocrit is usually at its nadir at the time of diagnosis. Recovery is spontaneous, and transfusions are necessary only if the patient has symptoms of congestive heart failure.

◆ KEY POINTS ◆

1. TEC, a normocytic anemia caused by bone marrow suppression, is an acquired pure red cell aplasia with a peak incidence at 2 years of age.

2. Viral infection is thought to be the major cause of TEC, but no specific etiology has been identified.

3. Recovery from TEC is spontaneous.

Normocytic Anemias with Increased Red Cell Production

Hemolytic Anemia

Normocytic anemias with increased red cell production are most commonly caused by hemolytic anemias.

Hemolytic disorders produce red cell destruction and anemia, which is sensed by the kidneys, resulting in erythropoietin release and bone marrow erythropoiesis. Hemolytic anemias are caused by factors extrinsic to the red cell or by defects intrinsic to the red cell. In general, extracorpuscular defects are acquired and intracorpuscular defects are hereditary.

Extracorpuscular anomalies are divided into isoimmune, autoimmune, and nonimmune hemolytic anemias. Isoimmune hemolytic anemia results from antibodies produced by one individual against the red blood cells of another individual of the same species. ABO or minor antigen incompatibility is an example of isoimmune hemolytic anemia and is discussed in Chapter 13. Autoimmune hemolytic anemia results from antibodies generated by an individual's immune system against his or her own red blood cells. Autoimmune hemolytic anemias can be idiopathic, postinfectious (mycoplasma, Epstein-Barr virus), or drug induced (penicillin, quinidine, alpha-methyldopa) or may result from a chronic autoimmune disease (systemic lupus erythematosis) or malignancy (non-Hodgkin's lymphoma). Therapy for autoimmune hemolytic anemia varies depending on the etiology of the hemolysis and the clinical condition of the patient. In general, treatment is supportive with the careful use of packed red blood cell transfusions and corticosteroids. Transfusion is often difficult, as autoantibodies react with virtually all red blood cells, making crossmatching challenging. In some severe chronic cases, intravenous immunoglobulin, immunosuppressive pharmacotherapy, and or splenectomy may be indicated.

The antibodies that cause isoimmune and autoimmune hemolytic anemias may be of the IgG or IgM classes. Antibodies of the IgG class tend to be warm reactive (maximal activity at 37°) and are considered incomplete antibodies. They coat the surface of the red blood cells and fix early complement components but cannot agglutinate red blood cells or activate the complement cascade through the entire hemolytic sequence. Hemolysis occurs extravascularly due to trapping of the opsonized red blood cells by macrophages in the reticuloendothelial system. IgG antibodies are associated with autoimmune diseases, lymphomas, and viral infections. These antibodies are identified by the direct Coombs' test. Antibodies of the IgM class are usually cold reactive (maximal activity at low temperatures) and are deemed complete antibodies. They agglutinate red blood cells and activate the complement sequence through C9, causing lysis of red blood cells. Hemolysis occurs intravascularly. IgM antibodies are associated with mycoplasma pneumonia, Epstein-Barr virus, and transfusion reactions.

Nonimmune hemolytic anemias can be microangiopathic (disseminated intravascular coagulation, thrombotic thrombocytopenic purpura, hemolytic uremic syndrome, malignant hypertension, giant hemangioma, preeclampsia, renal graft rejection) or can be due to damage from nonendothelialized surfaces (artificial heart valve, "Waring blender" syndrome, arteriovenous malformation, Kasabach-Merritt syndrome), hypersplenism, abetalipoproteinemia, toxins (snake venom, copper, arsenic), malaria, or burns.

Intracorpuscular defects include intrinsic membrane defects such as hereditary spherocytosis, hereditary elliptocytosis, hereditary stomatocytosis, and paroxysmal nocturnal hemoglobinuria (PNH). PNH is the only intracorpuscular disorder that is not inherited. Hemoglobinopathies (hemoglobin SS, S-C, S-Bthal) and enzymopathies (G6PD deficiency, pyruvate kinase deficiency) are also intracorpuscular disorders. Following are discussions about hereditary spherocytosis, sickle cell anemia, and G6PD deficiency, three of the most common intracorpuscular defects.

◆ KEY POINTS ◆

1. Normocytic anemias with increased red cell production are most commonly caused by hemolytic anemias.

2. Hemolytic anemias are caused by factors extrinsic to the red cell or by defects intrinsic to the red cell. In general, extracorpuscular defects are acquired and intracorpuscular defects are hereditary.

3. Extracorpuscular anomalies are divided into isoimmune, autoimmune, and nonimmune hemolytic anemias.

4. Intracorpuscular defects include intrinsic membrane defects, hemoglobinopathies, and enzymopathies.

Hereditary Spherocytosis

Hereditary spherocytosis is an autosomal dominant hemolytic anemia caused by a defect in spectrin, the major supporting protein of the red blood cell membrane. The defect leads to a loss of membrane fragments and

the formation of microspherocytes (small spherical red blood cells with a high volume-to-surface ratio). Microspherocytes have less deformability than normal red blood cells, and as a result the malformed red cells find it difficult traversing the sinusoids of the spleen. The rigid microspherocytes become trapped in the microvasculature of the spleen and are hemolyzed.

Clinical Manifestations

Hereditary spherocytosis varies greatly in clinical severity, ranging from a severe hemolytic anemia with growth failure, splenomegaly, and chronic transfusion requirements in infancy necessitating early splenectomy to an asymptomatic, well-compensated, mild hemolytic anemia that may be discovered incidentally. The newborn with this disorder may present with jaundice severe enough that exchange transfusion is required. Infants and children may present with pallor and splenomegaly. Occasionally, patients may present with aplastic crisis, after parvovirus B-19 infection. Because of chronic hemolysis, teenagers may develop gallstones and present with symptoms of cholecystitis. The physical examination reveals pallor, scleral icterus, and mild to moderate splenomegaly. Laboratory studies reveal a mild normocytic anemia, reticulocytosis, and indirect hyperbilirubinemia. During aplastic crisis, the mild anemia becomes severe and reticulocytopenia occurs. Diagnosis is confirmed by a positive osmotic fragility test.

Treatment

Treatment includes folic acid supplementation to meet the needs of increased red blood cell turnover and red blood cell transfusions during aplastic crisis. Definitive therapy is splenectomy, which alleviates anemia, reticulocytosis, and scleral icterus, although microspherocytes persist. Splenectomy should be put off until the age of 6 to allow for full development of the immune system. The earlier splenectomy is performed, the more at risk the child is for sepsis from encapsulated organisms.

◆ KEY POINTS ◆

1. Hereditary spherocytosis is caused by a defect in the major supporting protein of the red blood cell membrane.

2. The defect leads to a loss of membrane fragments and the formation of microspherocytes,

which are less deformable than normal red blood cells.

3. Diagnosis is confirmed by a positive osmotic fragility test.

Sickle Cell Anemia
Pathogenesis

Sickle cell anemia is an autosomal recessive disorder that results from a valine for glutamine substitution in the sixth amino acid position of the beta globin chain. This substitution results in an alteration of the quaternary structure of the hemoglobin molecule, which, under conditions of deoxygenation, promotes aggregation of hemoglobin into long polymers that align themselves into rigid paracrystalline gels and distorts the red blood cell into a sickle shape. Sickling shortens red blood cell survival time and results in a chronic hemolytic anemia. Sickled cells also cause microvascular obstruction, which leads to tissue ischemia and infarction. The sickling phenomenon is accentuated by hypoxia, acidosis, increased or decreased temperature, and dehydration. If only one of the two beta globin genes is affected, the individual has sickle cell trait, which is the heterozygous state. If both beta globin genes have the genetic substitution, the patient is homozygous for hemoglobin S and has sickle cell anemia.

Epidemiology

Sickle cell anemia is the most common cause of hemolytic anemia in the African American population, as well as the most common autosomal recessive disorder in African Americans, affecting 1 in 625 individuals. It is also found in Greeks, Italians, and Saudi Arabians.

Clinical Manifestations and Management

Sickle cell trait is generally asymptomatic. Rarely, an individual will exhibit painless hematuria and/or inability to properly concentrate the urine. On rare occasion, patients with sickle cell trait have sickle cells on peripheral blood smear. Sickle cell trait is diagnosed by hemoglobin electrophoresis. Typically, the hemoglobin electrophoresis reveals 55–60% hemoglobin A, 2–3% hemoglobin A2, and 40–45% hemoglobin S. It is important to detect the trait for genetic counseling.

Unlike sickle cell trait, sickle cell anemia causes severe morbidity and mortality. Quantitative hemoglobin electrophoresis shows 0% hemoglobin A, 85–95% hemoglobin S, 2–3% hemoglobin A2, and 5–15% hemo-

globin F. In most cases, diagnosis is made from newborn screening tests. Diagnosis can also be made by a positive Sickledex prep demonstrating the patient's red cells sickle at low oxygen tension. The clinical manifestations of sickle cell anemia are highly variable, result from anemia, infection, and/or vasoocclusion and are shown in Table 10–5.

At approximately 4 months of age, after the percent of hemoglobin F diminishes and the percent of hemoglobin S rises, the child develops a progressive hemolytic anemia. The anemia of sickle cell disease is a chronic, well-compensated, severe anemia that is rarely transfusion dependent. Common manifestations of the anemia include pallor, jaundice, splenomegaly in infancy, a systolic ejection murmur in the pulmonic region, and delayed sexual development and growth. Splenic sequestration, aplastic crisis, and hyperhemolytic crisis all superimpose life-threatening acute declines in hemoglobin concentration on the chronic compensated anemia of sickle cell disease. In splenic sequestration, the spleen suddenly becomes engorged with red blood cells, trapping a significant portion of the blood volume, and may lead to hypovolemic shock. Peak incidence of sequestration is 6 months–2 years. Aplastic crisis is due to viral suppression of red blood cell precursors in the bone marrow, most often by parvovirus B-19. A hyperhemolytic crisis occurs when a sickle cell patient with G6PD deficiency is exposed to an oxidative stress, resulting in acute hemolysis superimposed on a chronic hemolytic anemia. Medications or infection usually cause the acute hemolysis. Splenic sequestration, aplastic crisis, and hyperhemolytic crisis are treated by transfusion if the patient is hemodynamically compromised. Due to the presence of chronic hemolytic anemia, gallstone formation and cholecystitis is common during adolescence.

As the sickled cells traverse the spleen, they cause microvascular obstruction, infarction, and fibrosis of the spleen. This process, known as autoinfarction, causes the spleen to gradually regress in size; by the age of 4, the spleen is no longer palpable. More important, autoinfarction diminishes the capability of the spleen to filter encapsulated bacterial organisms and places the infant at great risk for overwhelming sepsis, meningitis, and pneumonia from *Streptococcus pneumoniae* or *Haemophilus influenzae*. Any infant or child who has sickle cell disease and fever, a temperature greater than 38.5°C, must be evaluated immediately. Although the child likely has a benign viral infection, sepsis must be ruled out. Along with bacterial sepsis, children with sickle cell disease are

TABLE 10–5

Clinical Manifestations of Sickle Cell Anemia*

Manifestation	Comments
Anemia	Chronic, onset 3–4 mo of age; may require folate therapy for chronic hemolysis. Hematocrit usually 18–26%
Aplastic crisis	Parvovirus infection, reticulocytopenia; acute and reversible
Sequestration crisis	Massive splenomegaly, shock; treat with transfusion
Hemolytic crisis	May be associated with G6PD deficiency
Dactylitis	Hand-foot swelling in early infancy
Pain crisis	Microvascular painful vasoocclusive infarcts of muscle, bone, bone marrow, lung, intestines
Cerebral vascular accidents	Large and small-vessel sickling and thrombosis (stroke); requires chronic transfusion
Acute chest syndrome	Infection and/or infarction, severe hypoxemia, infiltrate, dyspnea, rales
Chronic lung disease	Pulmonary fibrosis, restrictive lung disease, cor pulmonale
Priapism	Causes eventual impotence; treat with transfusion, oxygen, or corpora cavernosa-to-spongiosa shunt
Ocular	Retinopathy
Gall bladder disease	Bilirubin stones; cholecystitis
Renal	Hematuria, papillary necrosis, renal-concentrating deficit; nephropathy
Cardiomyopathy	Heart failure (fibrosis)
Leg ulceration	Seen in older patients
Infections	Functional asplenia, defects in properdin system; pneumococcal bacteremia, meningitis, and arthritis; deafness from meningitis in 35%; *H. influenzae* sepsis, Salmonella, and *Staphylococcus aureus* osteomyelitis; severe Mycoplasma pneumonia; transfusion-acquired HIV, hepatitis A, B, C, D, and E, EBV, CMV
Growth failure, delayed puberty	May respond to nutritional supplements
Psychological problems	Narcotic addiction, dependence unusual; chronic illness

*Clinical manifestations with sickle cell trait are unusual but include renal papillary necrosis (hematuria), sudden death on exertion, intraocular hyphema extension, and sickling in unpressurized airplanes.

CMV, cytomegalovirus; EBV, Epstein-Barr virus; G6PD, glucose-6-phosphate dehydrogenase.

Reprinted with permission from Behrman RE, Kliegman RM, eds. Essentials of pediatrics, 2nd ed. Philadelphia: WB Saunders, 1994.

at risk for septic joints and osteomyelitis due to splenic malfunction. Osteomyelitis is often caused by Salmonella, which translocates across the intestinal mucosa into the bloodstream. To minimize life-threatening infection, penicillin prophylaxis is started at approximately 4 months, and vaccinations are given against *S. pneumoniae*, and *H. influenzae* type b. *H. influenzae* type b (Hib) vaccine is given at the 2-month, 4-month, and 6-month visits and then again between 12 months and 15 months of age. Pneumococcal vaccine is given at age 2 years and then again at 4–6 years of age. Penicillin prophylaxis is continued to at least 5 years of age.

Vasoocclusive crises result from microvascular infarcts, may occur in any organ or tissue of the body, and are commonly precipitated by infection, cold exposure, dehydration, venous stasis, or acidosis. In most cases, a trigger is not identified. Pain crisis of the bones is the most common type of vasoocclusive crisis. Pain usually localizes to the long bones of the arms, legs, vertebral column, and/or sternum. Pain crises usually last from

2 to 7 days and are treated with nonsteroidal anti-inflammatory drugs and/or narcotics. Hand-foot syndrome, or dactylitis, occurs at 4–6 months of age and is the earliest clinical manifestation of vasoocclusive disease in the sickle cell patient. Dactylitis is a symmetrical painful swelling of the dorsal surface of the hands and feet and is caused by a vascular necrosis of the metacarpal and metatarsal bones. Avascular necrosis of the femoral heads is another vasoocclusive manifestation in bone, but it typically occurs in the adolescent population.

Microvascular obstructive disease can also occur in the lungs, central nervous system, penis, myocardium, and intestine. Acute chest syndrome is a vasoocclusive crisis within the lungs and is often associated with infection and/or infarction. Patients present with hypoxia, respiratory distress, and progressive pulmonary infiltrates. Oxygen, analgesia, antibiotics, and exchange transfusion are used to maximize respiratory status and minimize further pulmonary damage. Similarly, occlusion of the large cerebral vessels results in cerebrovascular accident. Patients present with mental status changes, seizures, and/or focal paralysis. Because of the high risk of recurrence, children who have had a stroke are placed on chronic transfusion protocols to minimize the risk of future cerebrovascular accident by keeping the hemoglobin S percentage below 30%. Priapism occurs most typically in boys between 6 and 20 years of age. The child develops sudden painful engorgement of the penis that will not subside. Acute chest syndrome, stroke, and priapism are treated by exchange transfusion to decrease the percent hemoglobin S to below 30% in an attempt to minimize vaso-occlusive disease.

By adolescence, the effects of chronic myocardial microvascular obstruction and infarction are evident by an enlarged hypertrophic heart. Many adults eventually succumb to congestive heart failure from progressive myocardial damage. Abdominal crisis results from microvascular obstruction of the intestinal circulation. Patients present with ileus and rebound tenderness, mimicking the acute abdomen. The pain may be familiar to the patient and readily recognized as "crisis pain." If the abdominal pain is consistent with the child's normal pain constellation during crisis, a period of observation during hydration and analgesia administration is warranted. If the abdominal pain is not typical for the patient during vaso-occlusive crisis, a consultation from a surgeon should be sought.

◆ KEY POINTS ◆

1. Sickle cell anemia is an autosomal recessive disorder that results from an amino acid substitution on the beta globin chain. This substitution results in an alteration of the structure of the hemoglobin molecule, which, under conditions of deoxygenation, promotes aggregation of hemoglobin into long polymers that distort the red blood cell into a sickle shape.
2. Sickling shortens red blood cell survival time and results in a chronic hemolytic anemia.
3. The clinical manifestations of sickle cell anemia result from anemia, infection, and/or vaso-occlusion.

Glucose-6-Phosphate Dehydrogenase Deficiency

G6PD deficiency is the most common red blood cell enzymopathy and is transmitted as an X-linked recessive trait. The lack of this enzyme in the hexose monophosphate shunt pathway results in a depletion of NADPH and the inability to regenerate reduced glutathione, which is needed to protect the red blood cell from oxidative stress.

The two prototypic variants are the A- variant and the Mediterranean variant. The A- variant is found in approximately 10% of African Americans in the United States and is associated with an isoenzyme that deteriorates rapidly, with a half-life of 13 days. The Mediterranean variant occurs predominantly in persons of Greek and Italian descent and its isoenzyme is extremely unstable, with a half-life of several hours.

When there is an oxidative stress on the red blood cell, exposed sulfhydryl groups on the hemoglobin are oxidized, leading to dissociation of heme and globin moieties, with the globin precipitating as Heinz bodies. The damaged red cells are then removed from the circulation by the reticuloendothelial system; severely damaged cells may lyse intravascularly. Known oxidants include sulfonamides, nitrofurantoin, primaquine, and dimercaprol. Hemolysis may also be precipitated by fava beans and infection, especially in young children.

Clinical Manifestations

The classic course of G6PD deficiency is episodic hemolytic anemia that is usually drug induced. Patients with the A- variant have a limited hemolysis confined to the older red blood cell population. Recovery occurs as young red blood cells with enzyme activity sufficient to resist oxidative stress emerge from the bone marrow. Hemolysis is most common in males, who possess a single abnormal X chromosome. Heterozygous females who have randomly inactivated a higher percentage of the normal gene may become symptomatic, as may homozygous females with the A- variant. One percent of African American females are A- variant homozygous. Patients with the Mediterranean variant have hemolysis that destroys most of their red cells and may require transfusions until the drug is eliminated from their bodies. Patients with the most severe degrees of G6PD deficiency not only have chronic hemolysis, but also their neutrophils demonstrate defective oxidative killing because of the depletion of NADPH, which serves as an electron donor to the membrane-bound oxidase that produces bactericidal oxygen species.

On peripheral blood smear, the red cells appear to have "bites" taken out of them; these cells are known as blister cells. The bitten areas result from phagocytosis of Heinz bodies by splenic macrophages. During hemolytic episodes, physical examination reveals jaundice and dark urine. The dark urine results from high levels of urobilinogen and hemoglobinuria. Hemoglobinuria results from intravascular hemolysis. Laboratory tests reveal an indirect hyperbilirubinemia and a low haptoglobin and hemopexin. Initially, the hemolysis exceeds the ability of the bone marrow to compensate, so the reticulocyte count may be low for the first 3–4 days.

The diagnosis of G6PD deficiency is made by finding deficient NADPH formation on G6PD assay. G6PD levels may be normal in the setting of acute, severe hemolysis because the most deficient cells have been destroyed. Repeating the test at a later time when the patient is in a steady-state condition, testing the mother of males with suspected G6PD deficiency, and/or performing electrophoresis to identify the precise variant facilitates diagnosis.

Treatment

Patients with variants of G6PD deficiency that are associated with acute acquired hemolysis need to avoid drugs that initiate hemolysis. Treatment is supportive, including packed red blood cell transfusion when significant cardiovascular compromise is present and protecting the kidneys against damage from precipitated free hemoglobin by maintaining hydration and urine alkalinization.

◆ KEY POINTS ◆

1. Glucose-6-phosphate dehydrogenase deficiency is the most common red blood cell enzymopathy and is transmitted as an X-linked recessive trait.

2. The lack of this enzyme in the hexose monophosphate shunt pathway results in a depletion of NADPH and an inability to regenerate reduced glutathione, which is needed to protect the red blood cell from oxidative stress.

Macrocytic Anemias with Decreased Red Cell Production

Macrocytic anemias are subdivided according to the presence or absence of megaloblastosis. Megaloblastic anemia results from deficiency of hematopoietic inputs. Causes include vitamin B_{12} and folate deficiency, drugs that interfere with folate metabolism (phenytoin, methotrexate, trimethoprim), and metabolic disorders (orotic aciduria, methylmalonic aciduria, Lesch-Nyhan syndrome). Macrocytic anemias without megaloblastosis result from bone marrow failure and include bone marrow failure syndromes (Diamond-Blackfan syndrome, Fanconi's anemia, idiopathic aplastic anemia, preleukemia), drugs (azidothymidine, valproic acid, carbamazepine), chronic liver disease, and hypothyroidism.

Megaloblastic Macrocytic Anemias Due to Deficiency of Hematopoietic Inputs
Vitamin B_{12} Deficiency

Vitamin B_{12} is a coenzyme for 5-methyl-tetrahydrofolate formation that is needed for DNA synthesis. It is found in meat, fish, cheese, and eggs. Dietary vitamin B_{12} deficiency is rare in developed countries, because vitamin B_{12} stores are large. The sole exception is the infant who is exclusively breast fed by a mother who is a strict vegetarian. The usual cause of vitamin B_{12} deficiency is a selective or generalized absorptive problem. Vitamin B_{12} is absorbed in the terminal ileum after combination with intrinsic factor, which is produced by the gastric parietal cells. Once absorbed into the bloodstream, vitamin B_{12} is transported by transcobalamin II to the liver, where it is stored. Any condition that alters intrinsic factor production interferes with intestinal absorption in the ileum or that reduces transcobalamin II levels reduces the availability of vitamin B_{12}. Disorders such as congenital pernicious anemia (absent intrinsic factors), juvenile pernicious anemia (autoimmune destruction of intrinsic factor), and transcobalamin II deficiency result in vitamin B_{12} deficiency. Other causes include ileal resection, small bowel bacterial overgrowth, and presence of the fish tapeworm *Diphyllobothrium latum*.

Clinical Manifestations

The effects of vitamin B_{12} deficiency on the gastrointestinal mucosa include glossitis, diarrhea, and weight loss. Neurologic sequelae include paresthesias, peripheral neuropathies, and, in the most severe cases, dementia, ataxia, and/or posterior column spinal degeneration. Vitiligo is the main dermatologic manifestation.

Megaloblastic changes on peripheral blood smear include ovalocytosis, neutrophils with hypersegmented nuclei (more than four per cell), nucleated red blood cells, basophilic stippling, and Howell-Jolly bodies. The mean corpuscular volume usually elevates above 100 fL. Intramarrow hemolysis, also known as ineffective erythropoiesis, results in an elevated serum lactate dehydrogenase, indirect hyperbilirubinemia, and serum iron level. In severe cases, megaloblastic anemia may be accompanied by leukopenia and thrombocytopenia.

Diagnosis is confirmed by a subnormal serum level of vitamin B_{12}. In nondietary deficiency, the Schilling test helps delineate pernicious anemia from bacterial overgrowth. In this test, an oral dose of radiolabeled vitamin B_{12} is given, and its absorption is checked by urinary excretion. If urinary excretion is minimal, an oral dose of intrinsic factor is given. Normal urinary excretion after intrinsic factor confirms the diagnosis of pernicious anemia. Inadequate urinary excretion after intrinsic factor indicates possible bacterial overgrowth. Antibiotics are given, and if vitamin B_{12} urinary excretion then increases, the diagnosis of bacterial overgrowth is made.

Treatment

Treatment for all forms of vitamin B_{12}, with the exception of bacterial overgrowth and fish tapeworm, is a 50–100 µg intramuscular loading dose injection. Maintenance therapy is a 100-µg injection once a month to prevent recurrence. The erythropoietic response is rapid, with marrow megaloblastosis improving within hours, reticulocytosis appearing by day 3 of therapy, and anemia resolving within 1–2 months.

Folate Deficiency

Folate is found in liver, green vegetables, cereals, and cheese and is converted to tetrahydrofolate, which is required for DNA synthesis. Because folate stores are relatively small, deficiency may develop within 1 month and anemia within 4 months of deprivation. Etiologies include inadequate dietary intake, impaired absorption of folate, increased demand for folate, and abnormal folate metabolism. Dietary deficiency of folic acid is unusual in developed countries. Children at risk are infants fed goat's milk, evaporated milk, or heat-sterilized milk or formula; each has inadequate folate content. Malabsorptive states of the jejunum, such as ulcerative colitis, Crohn's disease, and celiac sprue, can cause folate deficiency. Increased demand for folate occurs with conditions characterized by an increased rate of red blood cell turnover (hyperthyroidism, pregnancy, chronic hemolysis, malignancy). Relative folate deficiency may develop if the diet does not provide adequate folate to meet these needs. Certain anticonvulsant drugs (phenytoin, phenobarbital) interfere with folate metabolism.

Clinical Manifestations

Specific symptoms are often absent, although pallor, glossitis, malaise, anorexia, poor growth, and recurrent infection may be seen. Unlike vitamin B_{12} deficiency, neurologic disease is not associated with folate deficiency. Laboratory findings include low folate and normal vitamin B_{12} serum levels. Megaloblastic changes on peripheral blood smear and bone marrow aspirate are the same as those noted with vitamin B_{12} deficiency.

Treatment

It is imperative to not misdiagnose B_{12} deficiency as folate deficiency, because treatment with folate may result in hematologic improvement and allow for progressive neurologic deterioration. Treatment with 1 mg of folate given orally each day for 1–2 months will treat the anemia and replenish body stores. Clinical response is rapid, following a time course similar to that of vitamin B_{12} replacement therapy. In the event that maintenance therapy is required, usually with chronic hemolytic conditions, 1 mg orally per day is sufficient.

◆ KEY POINTS ◆

1. Megaloblastic macrocytic anemias due to deficiency of hematopoietic inputs can result from vitamin B_{12} and folate deficiency, drugs that interfere with folate metabolism, and some rare metabolic disorders.

2. Vitamin B_{12} is a coenzyme for 5-methyltetrahydrofolate formation, which is needed for DNA synthesis. Dietary vitamin B_{12} deficiency is rare in developed countries, because vitamin B_{12} stores are large. The usual cause of vitamin B_{12} deficiency is a selective or generalized absorptive problem.

3. Folate is converted to tetrahydrofolate, which is required for DNA synthesis. Because folate stores are relatively small, deficiency may develop within 1 month and anemia within 4 months of deprivation.

4. Neurologic sequelae of vitamin B_{12} deficiency include paresthesias, peripheral neuropathies, and, in the most severe cases, dementia, ataxia, and/or posterior column spinal degeneration.

5. It is imperative to not misdiagnose B_{12} deficiency as folate deficiency, because treatment with folate may result in hematologic improvement while allowing progressive neurologic deterioration.

Nonmegaloblastic Macrocytic Anemias Due to Bone Marrow Failure

Diamond-Blackfan

Diamond-Blackfan syndrome is an autosomal recessive, pure red cell aplasia of unknown etiology.

Clinical Manifestations

Onset of anemia occurs soon after birth in the first few months of life; 90% of cases are observed within the first year of life. Infants present with mild macrocytosis and reticulocytopenia. On hemoglobin electrophoresis, there is an elevated hemoglobin F, and fetal i antigen is present on the red cells. Twenty-five percent of patients have associated congenital anomalies that include short stature, web neck, cleft lip, shield chest, and triphalangeal thumb. These children are at high risk for leukemia later in life.

Treatment

Seventy-five percent of patients respond to high-dose corticosteroid therapy but must receive therapy indefinitely. Those who do not respond to steroid treatment are transfusion dependent and are at risk for the complications of iron overload.

Idiopathic Aplastic Anemia

Idiopathic aplastic anemia is an acquired failure of the hematopoietic stem cells that results in pancytopenia. The disorder may result from exposure to chemicals (benzene, phenylbutazone), drugs (chloramphenicol, sulfonamides), infectious agents (hepatitis virus), or ionizing radiation. In many circumstances, no clear-cut etiologic agent is identified, and the case is classified as idiopathic.

Clinical Manifestations

These patients suffer from pancytopenia on complete blood count, and bone marrow aspirate reveals a hypocellular marrow.

Treatment

Antithymocyte or antilymphocyte globulin is often temporarily effective, but serum sickness is a nearly universal side effect and relapse is common. High-dose corticosteroids are often used in combination with antithymocyte globulin. Cyclosporin A has been effective in some cases, but hepatic dysfunction, renal insufficiency, and immunosuppression limit its utility. Bone marrow transplantation is the sole effective treatment; without transplantation, 80% of patients die within 3 months of diagnosis. It is important to avoid transfusions if transplantation is being considered to decrease the number of sensitizing products the patient might come in contact with before transplantation. If the patient is neutropenic, antibiotics will probably be needed.

Fanconi's Anemia

Fanconi's anemia is an autosomal recessive disorder that results in pancytopenia and is commonly associated with pigmentary, skeletal, renal, and developmental abnormalities. The disorder results from defective DNA repair mechanisms that lead to excessive chromosomal breaks and recombinations. These chromosomal anomalies, not limited to the hematopoietic stem cells, are found in all cells of the body. Onset of pancytopenia is usually before age 10; mean age is 8 years.

Clinical Manifestations

Common signs include hyperpigmentation and cafe-au-lait spots, microcephaly, microphthalmia, short stature, horseshoe or absent kidney, and absent thumbs. Hematologic manifestations are characterized by progressive pancytopenia. Macrocytosis is universal even before the onset of anemia, and hemoglobin F is seen on hemoglobin electrophoresis. Of children with Fanconi's anemia, 10% will develop leukemia during adolescence due to faulty DNA repair.

Diagnosis is confirmed by demonstrating increased chromosomal breakage with exposure to diepoxybutane or other agents that damage DNA.

Treatment

Supportive care with transfusions and antibiotics is the basis of therapy. Some patients respond to androgens, but the effect is transient. Corticosteroids are often given with the androgens to counterbalance androgen-induced growth acceleration. Bone marrow transplantation is the treatment of choice, if an HLA-matched donor can be found. Because of chromosomal sensitivity, the preparative radiation and chemotherapeutic regimen must be modified because normal protocols result in severe morbidity and mortality.

◆ KEY POINTS ◆

1. Macrocytic anemias without megaloblastosis result from bone marrow failure and include bone marrow failure syndromes (Diamond-Blackfan syndrome, Fanconi's anemia, idiopathic aplastic anemia, preleukemia), drugs, chronic liver disease, and hypothyroidism.

2. Diamond-Blackfan syndrome is an autosomal recessive pure red cell aplasia and is associated with short stature, web neck, cleft lip, shield chest, and triphalangeal thumb.

3. Idiopathic aplastic anemia is an acquired failure of the hematopoietic stem cells that results in pancytopenia.

4. Fanconi's anemia is an autosomal recessive disorder that results in pancytopenia and is commonly associated with pigmentary, skeletal, renal, and developmental abnormalities.

DISORDERS OF HEMOSTASIS

Normal hemostasis requires the integrity of the blood vessels, platelets, and soluble clotting factors. Bleeding derangements can result from abnormal hemostatic plug formation, which occurs in platelet disorders; aberrant clot formation, which is noted in defects of the coagulation cascade; or with vascular abnormalities.

Examples of vascular anomalies that result in bleeding include Ehlers-Danlos syndrome, vitamin C deficiency (scurvy), and Henoch-Schönlein purpura (HSP). Ehlers-Danlos syndrome is a hereditary defect of collagen synthesis, whereas scurvy is an acquired disorder of collagen production. HSP is a vasculitis that is associated with abdominal pain, arthritis, nephritis, and a characteristic purpuric rash over the buttocks and lower extremities.

Platelet Disorders

Platelet disorders can be either quantitative or qualitative. Quantitative abnormalities are detected by the platelet count or platelet estimate on peripheral blood smear, whereas qualitative disorders are detected by the bleeding time or platelet aggregation studies. Platelet production is evaluated by assessing the number of megakaryocytes in the bone marrow aspirate. Thrombocytopenia is the most common cause of abnormal bleeding; a platelet count below 150,000/mm[u;3] constitutes thrombocytopenia. A low platelet count can result from inadequate production or increased destruction of platelets.

Decreased platelet production can result from failure of the bone marrow or bone marrow suppression. Bone marrow failure states resulting in thrombocytopenia include disorders causing pancytopenia (Fanconi's anemia, idiopathic aplastic anemia, preleukemia/leukemia), thrombocytopenia-absent radius (TAR) syndrome, and Wiskott-Aldrich syndrome. TAR syndrome, also known as congenital megakaryocytic hypoplasia, is an inherited autosomal recessive trait in which thrombocytopenia develops in the first few months of life and then resolves spontaneously after 1 year of age. Transient leukocytosis is common and often raises the suspicion of leukemia. Deformity of the radii is pathognomonic. In contrast to Fanconi's anemia, in which the thumb is absent, the thumb is present in TAR syndrome. Wiskott-Aldrich syndrome is an X-linked disorder characterized by hypogammaglobulinemia, eczema, and thrombocytopenia. Bone marrow transplantation results in cure of the immunodeficiency and thrombocytopenia and resolution of the eczema. Etiologies of thrombocytopenia caused by bone marrow suppression include chemotherapeutic agents, acquired viral infections (human immunodeficiency virus [HIV], Epstein-Barr virus, measles), as well as congenital TORCH (toxoplasmosis, syphilis, rubella, cytomegalovirus, herpes virus, HN) infections, and certain drugs (anticonvulsants, sulfonamides, quinidine, quinine, thiazide diuretics). Acquired postnatal infections, with the exception of HIV, and drug reactions usually cause transient thrombocytopenia, whereas congenital infections may produce prolonged suppression of bone marrow function.

Thrombocytopenia due to shortened platelet survival is much more common than thrombocytopenia due to inadequate production. Immune mediated mechanisms are the most common cause of platelet destruction. Thrombocytopenia in the newborn can result from isoimmune or autoimmune antibodies. Isoimmune IgG antibodies are produced against the fetal platelets when the fetal platelet crosses the placenta and presents itself to the maternal immune system. If there is an antigen on the fetal platelet that does not exist on the maternal platelet, it will be recognized as foreign and isoimmune antibodies will be created against the antigen. Maternal antiplatelet antibodies then cross the placenta and attack the fetal platelet, which is then destroyed in the fetal spleen. This disorder is known as neonatal isoimmune thrombocytopenic purpura. The maternal antiplatelet antibody does not produce maternal thrombocytopenia. Autoimmune IgG antibodies are transferred to the fetus through the placenta when there is maternal idiopathic thrombocytopenic purpura, maternal systemic lupus erythematosis, or maternal drug-induced thrombocytopenia. In all three cases, maternal autoantibodies cross the placenta and attack the fetal platelets. In contrast to isoimmune antibodies, autoimmune antibodies result in maternal thrombocytopenia. Because of the high risk of intracranial hemorrhage during vaginal delivery, it is recommended that fetuses with autoimmune or isoimmune thrombocytopenia be delivered by cesarean section. After birth, fetuses with severe isoimmune or autoimmune thrombocytopenia may be treated with corticosteroids and/or intravenous immunoglobulin until the maternal antiplatelet antibodies dissipate. During childhood, autoantibodies from idiopathic thrombocytopenic purpura (ITP) and systemic lupus erythematosis can also cause thrombocytopenia. Below is a detailed discussion of childhood ITP.

Microangiopathic hemolytic anemias also cause thrombocytopenia by decreasing platelet survival. These diseases result in anemias secondary to intravascular red cell destruction and depletion of platelets and clotting factors. Microangiopathic disorders include disseminated intravascular coagulation (DIC), hemolytic-uremic syndrome (HUS), and thrombotic thrombocytopenic purpura (TTP). DIC is presented below. HUS is characterized by a microangiopathic hemolytic anemia, renal cortical injury, and thrombocytopenia and is a major cause of acute renal failure in children. It is caused by the verotoxin-producing gram-negative organisms, such as *Escherichia coli* species 0157:H7, that bind to endothelial cells producing endothelial edema and damage. Because of the endothelial cell injury, there is localized clotting and platelet activation. Microangiopathic hemolytic anemia results from mechanical injury to red cells as they pass through the injured vascular endothelium, and thrombocytopenia results from platelet adhesion to the damaged endothelium. Sixty to 80% of patients with HUS require early intervention with dialysis. Most children survive the acute phase and recover normal renal function. In TTP, platelet consumption precipitated by a plasma factor or the lack of an inhibitory factor appears to be the primary process. There is moderate deposition of fibrin and, as a result, red cell destruction.

Diminished platelet survival can also result from trapping as seen with giant hemangioma and hypersplenism. Hypersplenism, which has many causes, occurs when elements of the blood pool in the spleen. It most commonly occurs secondary to sickle cell anemia, the thalassemia syndromes, Gaucher disease, and portal hypertension. Table 10–6 lists the common causes of thrombocytopenia during the neonatal, infant, and childhood periods.

◆ KEY POINTS ◆

1. Abnormal hemostatic plug formation occurs in platelet disorders.

2. Platelet disorders can be either quantitative or qualitative, and thrombocytopenia is the most common cause of abnormal bleeding.

3. Thrombocytopenia due to shortened platelet survival is much more common than thrombocytopenia due to inadequate production and is caused by isoimmune antibodies, autoimmune antibodies, and microangiopathic hemolytic anemias.

TABLE 10–6

Causes of Thrombocytopenia

Neonate

Maternal ITP,* SLE, drugs, preeclampsia
Isoimmune*
Congenital megakaryocytic hypoplasia
(thrombocytopenia absent radius)
Giant hemangioma
Sepsis*
DIC
TORCH infections

Infant

Wiskott-Aldrich syndrome
Viral infections* ± hemophagocytic syndrome
Drugs
Neuroblastoma
Leukemia*
Hemolytic-uremic syndrome
Sepsis ITP*

Childhood

ITP*
Drugs*
Aplastic anemia
Leukemia*
Hypersplenism (thalassemia, Gaucher, portal
hypertension)
Sepsis
SLE
Virus-induced hemophagocytic syndrome
ITP with autoimmune hemolytic anemia (Evan's
syndrome)
AIDS

*Common.

ITP, idiopathic thrombocytopenic purpura; SEL, systemic lupus erythematosus; DIC, disseminated intravascular coagulation; TORCH, toxoplasmosis, rubella, cytomegalovirus, and herpes simplex; AIDS, acquired immunodeficiency syndrome.

Reprinted with permission from Behrman RE, Kliegman RM, eds. Essentials of pediatrics, 2nd ed. Philadelphia: WB Saunders, 1994.

Idiopathic Thrombocytopenic Purpura (ITP)

ITP refers to a thrombocytopenia for which a cause is not apparent. ITP results from the development of antiplatelet antibodies that bind to the platelet membrane. These antibody-coated platelets are then destroyed in the reticuloendothelial system. Rarely, ITP may be the presenting symptom of an autoimmune disease such as systemic lupus erythematosis or HIV infection.

Clinical Manifestations

Children typically present 1–4 weeks after a viral illness or immunization, with abrupt onset of petechiae and ecchymoses on the skin and bleeding of the mucous membranes. Bleeding is severe after trauma. Severe internal hemorrhage is rare, although stroke has been noted with platelet counts below 10,000.

Other than thrombocytopenia, the complete blood count is normal. Large platelets are commonly seen on peripheral blood smear, and serology reveals antiplatelet antibodies. Diagnosis of ITP does not require a bone marrow aspirate. However, if there are atypical findings on the peripheral blood smear, marrow examination is indicated to determine if leukemia or idiopathic aplastic anemia is present. In ITP, bone marrow aspiration reveals normal myeloid and erythroid elements and an increased number of megakaryocytes.

Treatment

Approximately 80% of the cases of acute ITP resolve spontaneously within 6 months. Some cases, however, become relapsing or chronic.

Clinically significant bleeding or severe thrombocytopenia (platelet count less than 20,000), is treated with high-dose steroids, intravenous immunoglobulins (IVIG), and platelet transfusion. Corticosteroids and IVIG decrease the duration of severe thrombocytopenia but do not affect the long-term outcome of ITP. Both measures decrease the rate of clearance of antibody-coated platelets in the reticuloendothelial system but do not diminish the production of antiplatelet antibodies.

Chronic ITP, which is defined as 6–12 months of persistent thrombocytopenia, is treated with IVIG and/ or splenectomy. Repeated treatments with IVIG have been effective in delaying splenectomy, whereas splenectomy induces remission in 70–80% of the cases of chronic ITP. In refractory cases in which steroids, IVIG, and splenectomy have failed, immunosuppression with chemotherapeutic agents and plasmapheresis may be indicated. Amicar, a drug that inhibits fibrinolysis, is used in the most refractory cases when uncontrolled epistaxis or oral bleeding is occurring.

◆ KEY POINTS ◆

1. ITP results from autoimmune antibody formation against host platelets.

2. Approximately 80% of the cases of acute ITP resolve spontaneously within 6 months. Some cases, however, become relapsing or chronic.

3. Clinically significant bleeding or severe thrombocytopenia (platelet count less than 20,000) is treated with high-dose steroids, intravenous immunoglobulins, and platelet transfusion.

4. Chronic ITP is treated with intravenous immunoglobulins and/or splenectomy. Splenectomy induces remission in 70–80% of the cases of chronic ITP.

Disseminated Intravascular Coagulation (DIC)

Normal homeostasis is a balance between hemorrhage and thrombosis. In DIC, this balance is altered by severe illness so that the patient has activation of both coagulation (thrombin) and fibrinolysis (plasmin). Coagulation elements, especially platelets; fibrinogen; and clotting factors II, V, and VIII, are consumed, as are the anticoagulant proteins, especially antithrombin III, protein C, and plasminogen. Endothelial injury, release of thromboplastic procoagulant factors into the circulation, and impairment of clearance of activated clotting factors directly activate the consumptive coagulopathy. Acute and chronic conditions associated with DIC are listed in Table 10–7. Intravascular activation of the coagulation cascade leads to fibrin deposition in the small blood vessels, tissue ischemia, release of tissue thromboplastin, consumption of clotting factors, and activation of the fibrinolytic system.

Clinical Manifestations

The bleeding diathesis is diffuse. There is bleeding from venipuncture sites and around indwelling catheters. Gastrointestinal and pulmonary bleeding can be severe, and hematuria is common. Traumatized sites bleed

TABLE 10–7

Conditions Associated with DIC

Acute	Chronic
Sepsis	Polycythemia
Congenital infection	Hemangioma
Asphyxia-hypoxia	Arteriovenous malformation
Trauma	Retained dead fetus
Shock	Malignancy
Burns	Pre-eclampsia
Heat stroke	Malignant hypertension
Snake bites	Cirrhosis
Transfusion reactions	Renal vein thrombosis
Promyelocytic leukemia	
Respiratory distress syndrome	
Adult respiratory distress syndrome	
Hepatitis/hepatic failure	

Reprinted with permission from Behrman RE, Kliegman RM, eds. Essentials of pediatrics, 2nd ed. Philadelphia: WB Saunders, 1994.

briskly. Thrombotic lesions affect extremities, skin, kidneys, and brain. Both ischemic and hemorrhagic stroke can occur.

The diagnosis of DIC is a clinical one bolstered by laboratory evidence. Thrombocytopenia is evident along with a prolonged prothrombin time (PT), partial thromboplastin time (PTT), and thrombin time. The fibrinogen and factor V and VIII levels are low, and elevated fibrin split products and d-dimers are noted. The peripheral blood smear reveals schistocytes, which are classically seen with microangiopathic disease.

Treatment

The treatment of DIC is supportive. The disorder that caused DIC must be treated and hypoxia, acidosis, or perfusion abnormalities need to be corrected. If bleeding persists, fresh frozen plasma, which replaces depleted clotting factors, and platelets should be given. Heparin may be useful in the presence of significant arterial or venous thrombotic disease unless sites of life-threatening bleeding coexist.

Defects of the Coagulation Cascade

Coagulation disorders can be inherited or acquired. The most common congenital defects are hemophilia A and B and von Willebrand's disease, whereas vitamin K deficiency is an important acquired coagulation defect.

Hemophilia A and B

Hemophilia A is caused by deficiency of factor VIII and occurs in 1:5000 males, whereas hemophilia B results from factor IX deficiency and is found in 1:25,000 males. Both are X-linked recessive disorders. With the exception of the genes for factors VIII and IX, virtually all other clotting factors are coded on autosomal chromosomes and are thereby inherited in an autosomal fashion. The lack of factor VIII or IX causes a delay in the production of thrombin, which catalyzes the formation of the primary fibrin clot by the conversion of fibrinogen to fibrin and stabilizes the fibrin by activating factor XIII.

Clinical Manifestations

Other than their factor replacement regimens, hemophilia A and B are indistinguishable clinically, and the severity of each disorder is determined by the degree of factor deficiency. Severe hemophiliacs, children with less than 1% of normal factor, may have spontaneous bleeding and will bleed with very minor trauma. Patients with moderate hemophilia, 1–5% of normal factor, require moderate trauma to induce bleeding episodes. In mild hemophilia, in which greater than 5% of normal factor is present, significant trauma is necessary to induce bleeding, and spontaneous bleeding does not occur. Mild hemophilia may go undiagnosed for many years, whereas severe hemophilia manifests itself during infancy. Hemophilia is characterized by spontaneous or traumatic hemorrhages, which can be subcutaneous, intramuscular, or within joints (hemarthroses). Life-threatening internal hemorrhage may follow trauma or surgery. In newborns with hemophilia, there may be intracranial bleeding secondary to traumatic delivery or after circumcision; otherwise, bleeding complications are uncommon in the first year of life. With a positive family history, circumcision should be avoided.

In both forms of hemophilia, the PTT is prolonged. In hemophilia A, factor VIII coagulant activity (VIII:C) is low, whereas in hemophilia B, factor IX activity is low. Table 10–8 compares hemophilia A, hemophilia B, and von Willebrand's disease.

Treatment

The goal of therapy is to prevent long-term crippling orthopedic injuries due to hemarthroses. For life-threatening bleeding, levels of 80–100% of normal factors VIII and IX are necessary. For mild to moderate bleeding episodes, an example of which is hemarthroses, a 40% factor level is appropriate. Desmopressin acetate (DDAVP) is a synthetic vasopressin analogue that releases factor VIII from tissue stores. When it is administered, it triples or quadruples the initial factor VIII level of a patient with hemophilia A but has no effect on factor IX levels. If adequate hemostatic levels of factor VIII can be achieved with DDAVP, it is the treatment of choice for those afflicted with mild to moderate hemophilia A. DDAVP is an antidiuretic hormone analogue, and hemophiliacs who frequently use DDAVP should be monitored for hyponatremia due to water retention. Acute bleeding episodes are best treated in the home once the patient has attained the appropriate age and the parents have learned home treatment. Bleeding associated with surgery, trauma, or dental extraction often can be anticipated and excessive bleeding can be prevented with appropriate replacement therapy. Aminocaproic acid (Amicar), an inhibitor of fibrinolysis, may help treat oral bleeding after a dental procedure. It is generally given before and after the procedure.

Patients treated with older factor VIII or IX preparations were at high risk for hepatitis B, C, or D and HIV. HIV and hepatitis C testing of the blood did not begin until the mid-1980s, and as a result, many hemophiliacs contracted the viruses. Of hemophiliacs who received plasma-derived factor products between 1979 and 1984, 90% became HIV seropositive. Acquired immunodeficiency syndrome is the most common cause of death in older patients with hemophilia. Newer pooled concentrates are safer, and all recombinant preparations should be completely safe from viral agents.

TABLE 10–8

Comparison of Hemophilia A, Hemophilia B, and von Willebrand's Disease

	Hemophilia A	Hemophilia B	von Willebrand's Disease
Inheritance	X-linked	X-linked	Autosomal dominant
Factor deficiency	Factor VIII	Factor IX	von Willebrand factor and VIIIC
Bleeding site(s)	Muscle, joint, surgical	Muscle, joint, surgical	Mucous membranes, skin, surgical, menstrual
PT	Normal	Normal	Normal
APTT	Prolonged	Prolonged	Prolonged or normal
Bleeding time	Normal	Normal	Prolonged or normal
Factor VIII coagulant activity (VIIIC)	Low	Normal	Low or normal
vWF:Ag	Normal	Normal	Low
vWF:Act	Normal	Normal	Low
Factor IX	Normal	Low	Normal
Ristocetin-induced platelet agglutination	Normal	Normal	Normal or low
Platelet aggregation	Normal	Normal	Normal

Reprinted with permission from Behrman RE, Kliegman RM, eds. Essentials of pediatrics, 2nd ed. Philadelphia: WB Saunders, 1994.

Another significant complication of therapy is the formation of inhibitor antibodies. Inhibitor antibodies are IgG immunoglobulins directed against transfusion factors VIII and IX in congenitally deficient patients. Inhibitors arise in 15% of those patients with factor VIII deficiency and in 1% of those with factor IX deficiency. The treatment of bleeding patients with an inhibitor is difficult. For low-titer inhibitors, options include continuous factor VIII infusions or administration of porcine factor VIII. For high-titer inhibitors, it usually is necessary to administer a product that bypasses the inhibitor, such as activated prothrombin complex concentrates or recombinant factor VIIa. The use of frequent high doses of PT complex concentrates, and especially of the activated products, paradoxically increases the risks of thrombosis, which has resulted in fatal myocardial infarction and stroke. Induction of immune tolerance with continuous antigen exposure plus immunosuppression may be beneficial.

◆ KEY POINTS ◆

1. Hemophilia A results from a deficiency of factor VIII and hemophilia B from a lack of factor IX. Both disorders are inherited in an X-linked recessive fashion.

2. Other than their factor replacement regimens, hemophilia A and B are indistinguishable clinically, and the severity of each disorder is determined by the degree of factor deficiency.

3. Hemophilia is characterized by spontaneous or traumatic hemorrhages, which can be subcutaneous, intramuscular, or within joints (hemarthroses). Life-threatening internal hemorrhage may follow trauma or surgery.

4. The goal of therapy is to prevent long-term crippling orthopedic injuries due to hemarthroses.

von Willebrand's Disease

von Willebrand's disease is caused by deficiency of von Willebrand factor (vWF), an adhesive protein that connects subendothelial collagen and platelets when platelets are activated and binds to circulating factor VIII protecting it from rapid clearance. von Willebrand's disease is inherited as an autosomal dominant trait. vWF is either quantitatively deficient (partial or complete) or qualitatively abnormal (dysproteinemia).

Clinical Manifestations

The clinical manifestations of von Willebrand's disease are similar to those of thrombocytopenia and include mucocutaneous bleeding, epistaxis, gingival bleeding, cutaneous bruising, and menorrhagia. In severe von Willebrand's disease, factor VIII deficiency may be profound and the patient may also have manifestations similar to those of hemophilia A. If there is little or no vWF in the blood to bind factor VIII, factor VIII is cleared quickly from the circulation, resulting in factor VIII deficiency. Approximately 80% of patients with von Willebrand's disease have classic type I disease, which results in mild to moderate deficiency of vWF.

Laboratory testing includes measurement of the amount of protein, usually accomplished by immunologic detection of vWF antigen (vWF:Ag), and vWF activity (vWF:Act). vWF activity is measured functionally by the ristocetin cofactor assay (vWF:RCo), which uses the antibiotic ristocetin to induce vWF to bind to platelets. The patient typically has a prolonged bleeding time, due to the effect of vWF deficiency on platelet activity, and a prolonged PTT, which results from the effect of vWF deficiency on factor VIII activity. In Table 10–8, the findings in classic von Willebrand's disease are compared with those in hemophilia A and B.

Treatment

The treatment of von Willebrand's disease depends on the severity of bleeding. DDAVP is the treatment of choice for most bleeding episodes in patients. When high levels of vWF are needed and the patient cannot be satisfactorily treated with DDAVP, treatment with a virally attenuated vWF-containing concentrate (Humate P) may be appropriate. The dosage can be calculated using the same formula used for factor VIII replacement in hemophilia A. Cryoprecipitate may also be used, but it cannot be virally attenuated. Hepatitis B vaccine should be given before exposure to plasma-derived products. As in all bleeding disorders, aspirin should be avoided.

◆ KEY POINTS ◆

1. von Willebrand's disease is caused by deficiency of von Willebrand factor, an adhesive protein that connects subendothelial collagen and platelets when platelets are activated and binds to circulating factor VIII, protecting it from rapid clearance.

2. The clinical manifestations of mild to moderate von Willebrand's disease are similar to those of thrombocytopenia and include mucocutaneous bleeding, epistaxis, gingival bleeding, cutaneous bruising, and menorrhagia.

3. In severe von Willebrand's disease, factor VIII deficiency may be profound and the patient may also have manifestations similar to hemophilia A.

4. DDAVP is the treatment of choice for the majority of bleeding episodes in patients.

Vitamin K Deficiency

Coagulation factors II, VII, IX, and X and antithrombotic factors protein C and protein S are synthesized in the liver and are dependent on vitamin K for their activity. When vitamin K is deficient, normal coagulation does not occur. Vitamin K deficiency occurs in malabsorptive states, especially with cystic fibrosis or with antibiotic suppression of bacteria that produces vitamin K. Overdose of coumadin, a drug that interferes with vitamin K metabolism, causes deficiency of vitamin K factors. Similarly, maternal use of coumadin or anticonvulsant therapy (phenobarbital, phenytoin) may also result in vitamin K deficiency in the newborn. The most common disorder resulting from vitamin K deficiency is hemorrhagic disease of the newborn, which occurs in neonates who do not receive administration of vitamin K at birth.

Clinical Manifestations

Although most newborn infants are born with reduced levels of vitamin K-dependent factors, only a few develop hemorrhagic complications. Because breast milk is a poor source of vitamin K, breast-fed infants who do not receive prophylactic vitamin K on the first day of life are at the highest risk for hemorrhagic disease of the infant. Peak incidence is at 2–10 days of life. The recommended preventive dose of vitamin K is 1.0 mg given intramuscularly. The disorder is marked by generalized ecchymoses, gastrointestinal hemorrhage, and/or bleeding from the circumcision site and umbilical stump. Affected neonates are at risk for intracranial hemorrhage.

Both the PTT and PT are prolonged in vitamin K deficiency, because factors of both extrinsic and intrinsic pathways are affected. Prolongation of the PT is a more sensitive test for vitamin K deficiency because most infants have transient prolongation of the PTT at birth. The coagulopathy seen with hemorrhagic disease may be confused with liver disease or DIC, both of which have a prolonged PT and decreased factor VII level. Table 10–9 differentiates vitamin K deficiency, liver disease, and DIC by laboratory data.

TABLE 10–9

Differentiation of Vitamin K Deficiency, Liver Disease, and DIC

Laboratory Test	Vitamin K Deficiency	Liver Disease	DIC
PT	↑	↑	↑
Platelets	nl	↓ to nl	↓
Fibrinogen	nl	↓	↓
Factor VIII	nl	nl to ↑	↓
Fibrinogen degradation products	nl	nl to ↑	↑
Factor VII	↓	↓	↓ to nl

nl, normal.

Reprinted with permission from Barone MA. The Harriet Lane handbook, 14th ed. St. Louis: Mosby-Yearbook, 1996.

Treatment

Nutritional disorders and malabsorptive states respond to parenteral administration of vitamin K. Fresh frozen plasma or prothrombin complex concentrate, which is a mixture of coagulation factors II, VII, IX, and X, is indicated for severe bleeding.

◆ KEY POINTS ◆

1. Coagulation factors II, VII, IX, and X and antithrombotic factors protein C and protein S are synthesized in the liver and are dependent on vitamin K for their activity.

2. The most common disorder resulting from vitamin K deficiency is hemorrhagic disease of the newborn, which occurs in neonates who are exclusively breast fed and do not receive administration of vitamin K at birth.

3. The coagulopathy seen with hemorrhagic disease may be confused with liver disease or DIC, both of which have a prolonged PT and decreased factor VII level.

Immunology, Allergy, and Rheumatology

IMMUNOLOGY

The immune system, composed of specialized cells and molecules, is responsible for recognizing and neutralizing foreign antigens. Specific complex interactions produce adaptive inflammatory responses and defend against infection. Immunodeficiency syndromes increase susceptibility to infection, malignancy, and autoimmune disorders. Unfortunately, even a "normal" immune reaction may result in undesirable consequences, such as tissue-damaging inflammation, life-threatening anaphylaxis, or graft rejection (Table 11–1).

Disorders of Humoral Immunity

B cells produce antibodies, the primary effectors of humoral immunity. Antibodies are a vital component of the immune system, particularly in defense against extracellular pathogens such as encapsulated bacteria. A variety of antibodies activate complement, serve as opsonins, inhibit microbial adherence to mucous membranes, and neutralize various toxins and viruses. As a group, B-cell immunodeficiency syndromes are the most common encountered in pediatric practice.

Clinical Manifestations

History and Physical Examination

A history of recurrent infections with **encapsulated** organisms such as *Haemophilus influenzae* and *Streptococcus pneumoniae* and failure to respond to appropriate antibiotic therapy is suspicious for a primary B-cell deficiency.

Differential Diagnosis

X-linked (Bruton's) agammaglobulinemia occurs in males and appears early in infancy as maternally derived antibody levels fall. These patients do not produce antibodies and have virtually no B cells. In addition to their susceptibility to encapsulated organisms, individuals with this disorder are prone to severe, often life-threatening enterovirus infections.

Common variable immunodeficiency is an inherited disorder of hypogammaglobulinemia with equal distribution between the genders. Infections are usually less severe; however, the incidences of lymphoma and autoimmune disease are increased in these patients.

Selective IgA deficiency is the mildest and most common immunodeficiency syndrome. Serum levels of the other antibody classes are usually normal. Patients react normally to viral infections but are more susceptible to bacterial infections of the respiratory, gastrointestinal, and urinary tracts.

Diagnostic Evaluation

Quantitative measurement of total and fractionated serum immunoglobulin levels is an important screening test for specific deficiencies and for panhypogammaglobulinemia. Antibody titers generated against tetanus, diphtheria, and pneumococci after immunization assess antibody function.

TABLE 11–1

Clinical Characteristics of Immune Component Deficiencies

Disorders of Humoral Immunity

Frequent, recurrent, pyogenic infections with extracellular encapsulated organisms (*S. pneumo, H. flu*)

Frequent bacterial otitis, sinusitis, bronchiectasis, and pneumonia

Specific labs: quantitative immunoglobulin levels with subclasses; specific antibody responses

Phagocytic disorders:

Recurrent skin infections, abscesses with catalase (+) bacteria (*S. aureus, E. coli*), *Pseudomonas,* and fungi

Abscess formation associated with bacterial infections in lung, liver, and lymph nodes

Difficult to clear bone, joint infections

Specific labs: absolute neutrophil count; nitroblue tetrazolium test; adhesion, chemotaxic, phagocytic, bactericidal assays

Disorders of Cell-Mediated Immunity

Frequent, recurrent infections with opportunistic or low grade organisms (*Candida,* mycobacteria, protozoa [PCP]), and viruses

Increased incidence of autoimmune disorders, malignancies

Anergy

Specific labs: absolute lymphocyte count; mitogen stimulation response; delayed hypersensitivity skin testing

Complement deficiencies:

Recurrent bacterial infections with pyogenic extracellular, encapsulated organisms (*S. pneumo, H. flu*), often involving skin, respiratory tract

Increased susceptibility to recurrent meningococcal disease and disseminated *N. gonorrhoeae*

Increased incidence of autoimmune disease

Specific labs: total hemolytic complement (CH50); classical, alternative component assays

---

Treatment

The mainstays of therapy are appropriate antibiotic use and periodic gammaglobulin administration. **Intravenous gammaglobulin** (IVIG) provides antibody replace-ment and has revolutionized the treatment of humoral immunodeficiency syndromes. Early recognition and aggressive treatment of bacterial infections decrease morbidity and mortality and improve quality of life.

◆ KEY POINTS ◆

1. Most immunodeficiency syndromes encountered in pediatrics are humoral.

2. Humoral immunodeficiency predisposes patients to infection with encapsulated organisms.

3. Quantitative immunoglobulin studies and antibody titers against vaccine toxins are abnormal in patients with humoral immune dysfunction.

4. IVIG provides antibodies to patients with humoral immunodeficiency.

Disorders of Cell-Mediated Immunity

T-cells modulate most immune responses, primarily through the secretion of interleukins. In addition, they are major effectors of cell-mediated immunity, important in the defense against intracellular and opportunistic infections. Certain subclasses are capable of killing tumor and viral-infected cells. Patients with dysfunctional T cells are at increased risk for autoimmune disorders. T-cell diseases generally impart significantly greater morbidity and mortality to their victims than humoral disorders alone; survival beyond childhood is rare. DiGeorge syndrome, a congenital disorder, and human immunodeficiency virus, an acquired one, both represent T-cell immunodeficiencies. Patients with near-total thymic hypoplasia are highly susceptible to opportunistic infections such as fungi and *Pneumocystis carinii*.

Clinical Manifestations
History and Physical Examination

Most patients with **DiGeorge syndrome** present early in infancy with disease unrelated to the immune system (e.g., congenital heart disease, hypocalcemic tetany from thymic hypoplasia). Other structures and organs derived from the branchial pouches during embryogenesis may be malformed as well, including the ears and face. The severity of the immunodeficiency is extremely variable.

Diagnostic Evaluation

Absolute lymphocyte counts are normal or moderately decreased. T-cell function, measured by in vitro mitogen stimulation and intradermal delayed hypersensitivity testing, is absent or significantly compromised. No thymic shadow is seen on chest x-ray.

Treatment

The immunodeficiency of DiGeorge syndrome has been successfully treated with both thymic and bone marrow transplantation. Initial therapy should be aimed at repairing associated congenital heart defects and maintaining normocalcemia.

◆ KEY POINTS ◆

1. Patients with cell-mediated immune dysfunction are susceptible to opportunistic infections such as *Pneumocystis carinii* and autoimmune disorders.

2. Persistent hypocalcemic tetany and/or aortic arch anomalies suggest DiGeorge syndrome.

Combined Immunodeficiency Syndromes

Combined humoral and cell-mediated immunodeficiencies tend to be inherited and manifest a wide range of clinical severity. Affected patients display increased susceptibility to both traditionally virulent and opportunistic infections.

Ataxia-telangiectasia is a rare autosomal-recessive disorder characterized by variable humoral and cell-mediated immune deficits, cerebellar ataxia, and oculocutaneous telangiectasia (small dilated vessels easily visible along the bulbar conjunctiva and skin surface). The incidence of malignancy, especially non-Hodgkin's lymphoma and gastric carcinoma, is increased. No specific therapy is available; most patients are wheelchair-bound by puberty and die prematurely.

Wiskott-Aldrich syndrome is an X-linked recessive disorder of B- and T-cell immunity, atopic dermatitis, and thrombocytopenia. Survival to adulthood is rare because of bleeding, infections, and associated malignancies.

Severe combined immunodeficiency disease is a particularly devastating disorder characterized by substantial deficits in both humoral and cell-mediated immunity. Patients are susceptible to a wide range of infections and usually present with multiple illnesses in the first few months of life. Bone marrow transplantation has been curative; gene therapy is now being studied as a possible alternative treatment.

Disorders of Phagocytic Immunity

Phagocytes are responsible for removing particulate matter from the blood and tissues by ingesting and destroying microorganisms. These cells must be able to adhere to the endothelium, move through the tissues to their site of action, engulf the harmful matter, and kill it intracellularly. **Chronic granulomatous disease** (CGD) is the most common inherited disorder of phagocytic immunity.

Clinical Manifestations
History and Physical Examination

CGD is characterized by chronic or recurrent pyogenic infections caused by bacterial and fungal pathogens that produce catalase. Although the most common form of this disorder is inherited as an X-linked trait, autosomal inheritance has also been reported. Abscesses and granuloma formation occur in the lymph nodes, liver, spleen, lungs, skin, and gastrointestinal tract. Failure to thrive, chronic diarrhea, and persistent candidiasis of the mouth and diaper area are common. Affected individuals are also at increased risk for opportunistic infections and disseminated viral disease.

Diagnostic Evaluation

White blood count typically ranges between 10,000 and 20,000/μl with 60–80% polymorphonuclear cells. Leukocyte chemotaxis is normal. The hallmark laboratory abnormality is the inability of affected cells to reduce nitroblue tetrazolium to formazan.

Treatment

All patients with CGD should receive daily prophylactic trimethoprim-sulfamethoxazole. Judicious antibiotic therapy during infections is critical. **Gamma interferon therapy** has been shown to reduce the incidence of serious infection. Bone marrow transplantation is not as successful as in other immunodeficiency syndromes.

◆ KEY POINTS ◆

1. Chronic granulomatous disease is characterized by chronic or recurrent infections due to catalase-producing bacteria or fungi.

2. Gamma interferon reduces the incidence of serious infection.

Disorders of Complement Immunity

Although quantitative deficiencies of virtually all complement components have been described, they are less common than the classes of disease mentioned earlier. Patients with complement disorders have increased susceptibility to bacterial infections and a higher incidence of rheumatologic disease. In particular, deficiencies of the terminal complement components C5–C8 increase the likelihood of *Neisseria meningitidis* infections.

Transient Hypogammaglobulinemia of Infancy

Although maternal IgG is actively transported across the placenta and is protective throughout the first few months of life, neonates are considered relatively immunocompromised hosts. All serum immunoglobulin classes are present at birth, but most do not reach adult levels until early to middle childhood. Over the first 6–8 weeks of life, maternally derived immunoglobulins decrease and are replaced by the child's growing production. Thus, infants are particularly susceptible to infection at 6–12 weeks, their immunologic nadir.

Transient hypogammaglobulinemia of infancy is a recognized disorder in which acquisition of normal infant immunoglobulin levels is delayed. Although some of these patients are subsequently diagnosed with other primary immunodeficiencies, most eventually develop normal immunity.

ALLERGY

An allergic reaction is an undesirable immune-mediated response to an environmental stimulus. Allergies have been implicated as a contributing factor in anaphylaxis, reactive airway disease, allergic rhinitis, and atopic dermatitis. Allergic reactions range from mild to life-threatening and are *never* considered adaptive.

Allergic Rhinitis

Pathogenesis

Allergic rhinitis is a type 1 hypersensitivity immune response to environmental allergens, including airborne pollens, animal dander, mold, house mites, and cigarette smoke. The offending allergen binds to IgE on mast cells in the upper respiratory tract with subsequent release of inflammatory mediators. Allergic rhinitis is the most frequent cause of chronic or recurrent clear rhinorrhea in the pediatric population.

Epidemiology

Seasonal allergic rhinitis, or **hay fever**, is limited to months of pollination (Table 11–2) and is uncommon before 5 years of age. Perennial disease persists year round, usually in response to household allergens.

Risk Factors

Atopy and genetic predisposition are the major risk factors. Early heavy allergen exposure also increases the likelihood of subsequent disease.

Clinical Manifestations
History

Patients with allergic rhinitis are plagued with nasal congestion, profuse watery rhinorrhea, and sneezing. Associated allergic conjunctivitis is common. Unrelenting postnasal drip produces frequent coughing or throat-clearing.

Physical Examination

On examination, the nasal mucosa appears boggy and bluish. Two characteristic features of allergic rhinitis are "allergic shiners" (dark circles that develop under the eyes secondary to venous congestion) and the "allergic salute" (a horizontal crease across the middle of the nose due to a constant upward wiping motion with the hand).

Differential Diagnosis

Infectious rhinitis is much more common than allergic rhinitis in infants and toddlers and often mucopurulent. Sinusitis causes chronic rhinorrhea and postnasal drip associated with facial tenderness, cough, or headache. When a nasal foreign body is present, the discharge is usually thick and foul-smelling.

TABLE 11–2

Seasonal Pollination Patterns

Allergen	Typical Season
Tree pollens	Early spring
Grass pollens	Late spring/early summer
Ragweed	Late summer to first frost

Diagnostic Evaluation

Usually, a careful history confirms the diagnosis. Elevated serum and nasopharyngeal eosinophil levels, positive skin tests, and intranasal allergen challenges support the diagnosis if additional studies are needed.

Treatment

The most effective treatment for any allergic condition is **allergen avoidance**. Switching to air conditioning in the summer (rather than keeping the windows open) affords some protection to patients with pollen allergies. Eliminating animal dander and limiting exposure to cigarette smoke are also helpful.

Pharmacotherapy is an important adjunct if avoidance is not possible. Histamine blockers are the mainstay of treatment. Topical and inhaled sympathomimetics (the most popular being pseudoephedrine) are useful for short-term therapy only and, if taken improperly, may result in severe rebound congestion. Intranasal cromolyn controls sneezing and itching but does not affect nasal congestion. The most effective therapy to date is nasal topical steroids; most patients improve dramatically with very few side effects. Allergy shots are painful, time-consuming, risky, and expensive; they are indicated only for severe symptoms not controlled with conventional pharmacotherapy.

Occasionally, congestion is so severe that children become exclusively "mouth-breathers," which leads to dental malocclusion. If the tonsils and adenoids become involved, obstructive sleep apnea may ensue.

◆ KEY POINTS ◆

1. Allergic rhinitis may be seasonal or perennial.
2. Allergic rhinitis should be considered in any child with chronic or recurrent rhinorrhea and upper respiratory tract symptoms.
3. "Allergic shiners" and the "allergic salute" are characteristic features of allergic rhinitis.
4. Nasal topical steroids are the most effective therapy to date.

Reactive Airway Disease

Reactive airway disease (RAD; also termed asthma) is discussed in detail in Chapter 20. A significant proportion of RAD is thought to be "extrinsic," or allergic, in nature. Allergens frequently associated with RAD attacks include molds, dust mites, pet dander, cigarette smoke, pollens, foods, and cockroaches. The most effective treatment is allergen avoidance; further therapy is discussed in Chapter 20.

Atopic Dermatitis

The "**allergic triad**" consists of allergic rhinitis, reactive airway disease, and atopic dermatitis (eczema). Atopic dermatitis is a chronic relapsing and remitting inflammatory skin reaction to specific allergens. Eczema usually appears in infancy and affects upward of 10% of the pediatric population. Genetic predilection is the highest risk factor.

Clinical Manifestations

The typical rash consists of a pruritic, erythematous, weeping papulovesicular reaction that progresses to scaling, hypertrophy, and lichenification. In infants younger than 2, the eruption involves the extensor surfaces of the arms and legs, the wrists, the face, and the scalp; the diaper area is invariably spared. Flexor areas predominate in older age groups, as well as the neck, wrists, and ankles. The diagnosis of atopic dermatitis is primarily clinical, based on history, physical examination, and response to treatment. The differential diagnosis includes contact dermatitis and psoriasis, a chronic nonallergic skin disorder (see Chapter 5).

Treatment

Patients should avoid hot water and strong soaps. Lotions should be administered routinely to combat dryness. Tight clothing and heat may precipitate exacerbations. Topical corticosteroids are the mainstay of treatment. Severe chronic eczema may be complicated by bacterial superinfection.

Urticaria and Angioedema

Urticaria describes the typical raised edematous hives on the skin or mucous membranes resulting from vascular dilation and increased permeability. The lesions itch, blanch, and generally resolve within a few hours to days. Angioedema is a similar process confined to the lower dermis and subcutaneous areas; the depth results in a well-demarcated area of swelling devoid of pruritus, erythema, or warmth. Although acute urticaria and angioedema occur frequently in the pediatric population, chronic forms are rare.

Clinical Manifestations

The diagnosis is based on a detailed history of recent exposures or changes in the patient's environment. The multiple allergens and conditions associated with urticaria and angioedema include foods, medications, infections, and some systemic illnesses. Clinical manifestations may be delayed as long as 48 hours after the initial encounter. Hereditary forms exist; patients with hereditary angioedema have an inherited C1 esterase inhibitor deficiency. Often the etiology remains a mystery.

Treatment

Treatment depends on severity, which ranges from mild to life-threatening (i.e., swelling around the airway). Subcutaneous epinephrine is the treatment of choice in emergency situations, followed by intravenous diphenhydramine and steroids. Oral antihistamines, sympathomimetics, and occasionally oral steroids are appropriate in milder cases.

Food Allergies

Pathogenesis

Steady advances have been made in food allergy research over the past decade. It is important to distinguish between food intolerance (an undesirable nonimmunologic reaction) and true food allergy, which is mediated by immune mechanisms.

Epidemiology

Food allergies typically present in infancy and often disappear in early childhood. Relatively few foods are represented; **peanuts, eggs, milk proteins, soy, wheat,** and **fish** account for over 90% of reported cases. Exclusive breast feeding may delay presentation unless the mother is ingesting the offending proteins regularly.

Clinical Manifestations

History and Physical Examination

A detailed history, including daily records of intake and symptoms, is essential for the diagnosis. Clinical manifestations include irritability, colic, diarrhea, malabsorption, gastrointestinal bleeding, and failure to thrive. Symptoms that develop during weaning are particularly suspicious.

Diagnostic Evaluation

Although skin testing may be helpful in some cases, the double-blind, placebo challenge–food challenge is the current gold standard. Several foods are eliminated from the patient's diet for a period before testing. Then the foods are disguised and tested, alternating with placebos, over several days. A challenge is considered positive if signs and symptoms recur after ingestion.

Treatment

Treatment entails eliminating the offending food from the diet. In children with severe, widespread allergies, elemental hypoallergenic formulas are available. Exposure to specific food allergens has been associated with atopic dermatitis, urticaria, and reactive airway disease attacks.

◆ KEY POINTS ◆

1. Peanuts, eggs, milk, soy, wheat, and fish account for the overwhelming majority of food allergies.
2. Signs and symptoms include colic, diarrhea, and failure to thrive.
3. The double-blind, placebo challenge–food challenge is the gold standard of diagnosis.

RHEUMATOLOGY

Rheumatology involves the diagnosis and treatment of a variety of loosely related chronic, recurrent arthritic, and connective tissue disorders. Most are thought to result from misdirected host defense mechanisms; the immune system fails to recognize "self" antigens and initiates an inappropriate inflammatory response against the host. Usually, autoantibodies are produced and may be recovered from plasma or tissue samples, assisting with diagnosis. Arthritis, the most common rheumatologic complaint, is the primary manifestation of juvenile rheumatoid arthritis. In systemic lupus erythematosus, antigen-antibody complexes are deposited in arteriole walls throughout the body. The skin, skeletal muscle, and gastrointestinal tract are the major disease sites in dermatomyositis.

Juvenile Rheumatoid Arthritis

Pathogenesis

Juvenile rheumatoid arthritis (JRA) consists of a group of immunologic disorders characterized by chronic synovitis. The arthritis is accompanied by villous hypertrophy, hyperplasia of the synovial lining layer, edema, hyperemia, vascular endothelial hyperplasia, and infiltration of lymphocytes and plasma cells. Diagnosis is based on fulfilling specific clinical criteria (Table 11–3).

Epidemiology

JRA, as is true of most rheumatologic conditions, occurs more commonly in girls. Many patients are afflicted between 1 and 3 years of age, although the disease may also present in late childhood and adolescence. Onset may be polyarticular, oligoarthritic (pauciarticular), or systemic (Table 11–4).

Risk Factors

Many patients have a positive family history for other rheumatologic disorders. Certain HLA types also have been associated with increased risk of disease (i.e., **HLA-B27** and pauciarticular JRA).

Clinical Manifestations

History and Physical Examination

Noteworthy clinical specific and systemic manifestations are listed in Table 11–5.

Differential Diagnosis

Virtually any rheumatologic disorder can present initially with isolated arthritis. Other conditions to consider include septic arthritis, toxic synovitis, Lyme disease, and reactive arthritis. Noninflammatory causes of limb and joint pain are discussed in detail in Chapter 19.

Diagnostic Evaluation

Anemia and leukocytosis are common, especially in systemic disease. The erythrocyte sedimentation rate is

---

TABLE 11–3

Diagnostic Criteria for the Classification of JRA

Age of onset <16 years
Arthritis in ≥1 joints defined as *swelling* or *effusion* or the presence of two or more of the following signs: *limitation of range of motion, tenderness* or *pain* on motion, or **increased heat**
Duration of disease ≥ 6 weeks
Type of onset of disease during the first 6 months
  Polyarthritis: ≥ 5 joints
  Oligoarthritis or pauciarticular disease: ≤ 4 joints
  Systemic disease: arthritis with intermittent fever
Exclusion of other forms of juvenile arthritis

Cassidy JT, Levenson JE, Bass JC, et al. A study of classification criteria for a diagnosis of juvenile rheumatoid arthtritis. *Arthritis Rheum* 1986;29:274.

TABLE 11–4

Classification of JRA

	Polyarthritis	Oligoarthritis	Systemic
Total cases (%)	40–50	40–50	10–20
Number, pattern of joints involved	≥5; symmetric	≤4; may be only a single joint	Variable
Type of joints involved	Large (knees, elbows, ankles, wrists) and cervical joints	Knees and/or ankles	Any joint
Severity of systemic involvement	Moderate	Rare	Severe*
Development of chronic uveitis (%)	5	20	Rare
Rh factor (+) (%)	10	Rare	Rare
ANA factor (+) (%)	50	80	10

*Including a high, spiking fever one to two times a day and a characteristic rheumatoid rash (erythematous macules on trunk, extremities) lasting <1 hr.

Modified from Cassidy JT. Connective tissue diseases and amyloidosis. In: Oski FA, DeAngelis CD, Feigin FD, et al.,eds. Principles and practice of pediatrics, 2nd ed. Philadelphia: J.B. Lippincott Company, 1994:246.

TABLE 11–5

Signs and Symptoms in JRA

Specific	Systemic
Morning stiffness	Fatigue
Night pain	Anorexia
Rheumatoid nodules	Failure to thrive
Guarding	Low-grade fever
Refusal to bear weight	Rash
Deformity	Irritability
	Lymphadenopathy
	Hepatosplenomegaly

---

variably elevated. Rheumatoid factor and antinuclear antibodies may or may not be present, depending on the classification. Synovial fluid analysis typically reveals a white blood cell count of 10,000–20,000/µL and high protein with decreased glucose and complement levels. Radiographs reveal soft tissue swelling early; later, bony erosion and narrowing of the joint spaces occur.

Treatment

Treatment consists of medical management with inflammatory-suppression drugs (nonsteroidal anti-inflammatory drugs, immunosuppressive drugs, steroids, etc.) and physical therapy. Functional or cosmetic surgery is generally delayed until growth is complete.

Most patients with JRA experience little permanent disability and remain in remission for long periods. Severe involvement often leads to joint destruction and deformity. Children with pauciarticular disease may develop iridocyclitis and vision loss. Systemic JRA is associated with pulmonary, hepatic, central nervous system, and cardiac disorders.

◆ KEY POINTS ◆

1. Juvenile rheumatoid arthritis is characterized by chronic synovitis and is classified according to degree of involvement (polyarticular, oligoarticular, systemic).

2. Anti-inflammatory drugs and physical therapy are the mainstays of treatment.

Systemic Lupus Erythematosus

Pathogenesis

Systemic lupus erythematosus (SLE) is a classic example of the immune system gone awry. Characterized by widespread connective tissue inflammation and arteriolar vasculitis, SLE produces significant, often disfiguring disease. SLE develops when the immune system somehow begins to recognize "self" nuclear proteins, cytoplasmic contents, and connective tissue as "foreign" and attempts to neutralize or remove them. Antigen-antibody immune complexes become deposited in the walls of small arteries, resulting in inflammation and necrosis. This immune complex vasculitis is the basic pathologic lesion responsible for the extensive clinical manifestations.

Epidemiology

SLE usually appears in late childhood or adolescence and is far more common in females.

Risk Factors

There is little question that increased susceptibility to SLE is inherited; in fact, most patients with connective tissue disease have a positive family history for some sort of rheumatic disorder.

Clinical Manifestations

History and Physical Examination

The diagnosis of SLE is based on clinical criteria (Table 11–6). The onset may be precipitous and rapidly progressive or insidious with a slow steady course. Fever, malaise, and weight loss are frequent constitutional complaints. Arthritis of the hands, wrists, elbows, shoulders, knees, and ankles produces pain out of proportion to the physical signs; in fact, the arthritis of SLE is neither erosive nor deforming. Central nervous system involvement may present at any time over the course of the disease.

Lupus nephritis is the most common clinical manifestation and is often present at diagnosis. The World Health Organization classifies renal involvement as normal (type I, 6%, renal failure extremely rare), mesangial (type II, 20%, renal failure rare), focal proliferative (type III, 23%, renal failure uncommon), diffuse proliferative (type IV, 40%, progressive renal failure common, high mortality), and membranous disease (type V, renal failure uncommon).

TABLE 11–6

Criteria for the Classification of SLE

Malar (butterfly) rash
Discoid-lupus rash
Photosensitivity
Oral or nasal mucocutaneous ulcerations
Nonerosive arthritis
Nephritis
    Proteinuria >0.5 g/day
    Cellular casts
Encephalopathy
    Seizures
    Psychosis
Pleuritis or pericarditis
Cytopenia
Positive immunoserology
    Antibodies to nDNA
    Antibodies to Sm nuclear antigen
    Positive LE preparation
    Biologic false test for syphillis
Positive antinuclear antibody test

Four of 11 criteria provide a sensitivity of 96% and a specificity of 96%. Any one item satisfies that criterion.

Reprinted from Cassidy JT, Petty RE. Textbook of pediatric rheumatology, 2nd ed. New York: Churchill Livingstone, 1990.

Diagnostic Evaluation

Anemia, leukopenia (with a predominance of neutrophils), and thrombocytopenia are characteristic. Complement levels, including **C3, C4,** and **CH50,** are generally depressed or falling, especially during active disease. A positive antinuclear antibody test is very sensitive but not necessarily specific. Elevation in double-stranded DNA antibodies parallels disease severity. All patients with SLE eventually demonstrate LE cells (tissue cells with lupus erythematosus bodies in their cytoplasm); however, this test may be negative early in the course.

Treatment

Treatment is long term and multifactorial. Careful attention must be paid to nutritional status and fluid balance. Limiting sun exposure improves skin problems. Aggressive characterization and treatment of renal disease, including renal biopsy and frequent imaging, are invaluable in minimizing morbidity. Hypertension is a relatively common complication that is usually well controlled with conventional therapy. Because certain forms of SLE appear to be drug-induced, drug exposure, particularly anticonvulsant and hydralazine administration, should be carefully monitored and avoided when possible.

Anti-inflammatory therapy remains the mainstay of pharmacologic treatment. Oral prednisone is prescribed as needed for maintenance therapy; high-dose oral or intravenous pulse therapy is preferable during acute exacerbations. For patients who do not respond, other immunosuppressants such as cyclophosphamide can be tried.

Overall, prognosis and quality of life are improving. Renal disease produces the most significant morbidity; renal failure is the leading cause of death after infection. **Libman-Sacks endocarditis** is a serious cardiac complication. Most patients with SLE do not achieve normal life expectancy.

◆ KEY POINTS ◆

1. SLE consists of widespread connective tissue inflammation and vasculitis.

2. The diagnosis of SLE is clinical.

3. Lupus nephritis is the most common clinical manifestation, resulting in significant morbidity.

4. Typical laboratory findings include falling complement levels, positive antinuclear antibody and double-stranded DNA antibody titers, and LE cells.

5. The disease usually responds to immunosuppressant therapy.

Dermatomyositis

Pathogenesis

Dermatomyositis is an inflammatory disease involving the small vessels of the skin, striated muscle, and occasionally the gastrointestinal tract. Immune complexes are deposited in the walls of arterioles, capillaries, and venules, leading to inflammation, ulceration, bleeding, and fibrinous repair. Polymyositis, a similar inflammatory muscular condition without skin findings, occurs less frequently in the pediatric population.

Epidemiology

Onset usually occurs in the later childhood years. Like most rheumatologic conditions, dermatomyositis is more common in females.

Risk Factors

Predisposition is heritable, and the condition seems to be associated with viral illnesses in some cases.

Clinical Manifestations
History and Physical Examination

Patients report a history of malaise, fatigue, weight loss, and intermittent fevers. Progressive muscle weakness of the pelvic and shoulder girdle muscle groups accompanied by the characteristic violaceous dermatitis of the eyelids, hands, elbows, knees, and ankles virtually clinches the diagnosis. The weakness may advance to involve the anterior neck, trunk, and muscle groups used for swallowing, phonation, and respiration. Long-standing inflammation eventually results in calcium deposits in the skin (calcinosis cutis), cutaneous striation, scarring, and significant muscle atrophy.

Diagnostic Evaluation

The most striking laboratory abnormality is marked elevation of **serum creatinine kinase**, an enzyme released during muscle breakdown. Specific electromyography and histologic results are characteristic of the disorder. Serum acute-phase reactant levels (erythrocyte sedimentation rate, C-reactive protein) correlate with disease severity.

Treatment

Treatment consists of rest, appropriate physical therapy, and immunosuppressants. As long as muscle enzyme levels remain high, activity is limited and the primary aim of therapy is to prevent contractures with positioning and splints. High-dose prednisone is prescribed in an attempt to control the inflammatory response. Once evidence of muscle destruction begins to abate, steroid doses are tapered and strengthening exercises are gradually added. Patients whose disease does not respond to oral steroids may require intravenous pulse steroids or methotrexate.

Oropharyngeal, chest wall, and respiratory muscle weakness predisposes patients to aspiration. Respiratory failure necessitating mechanical ventilation is rare. Most children diagnosed with dermatomyositis recover with no permanent disability within a few years. About 10% progress to wheelchair dependence and premature death.

◆ KEY POINTS ◆

1. Dermatomyositis is an inflammatory disease of the small vessels of the skin, striated muscle, and gastrointestinal tract.
2. The weakness begins in the proximal extremity muscle groups and is accompanied by a characteristic violaceous dermatitis.
3. Serum creatinine kinase levels are markedly elevated.
4. The weakness may progress to involve the respiratory and oropharyngeal muscles.

Vasculitides

A number of other connective tissue diseases, including polyarteritis nodosa and Henoch-Schönlein purpura, present with vasculitis as the primary manifestation. **Kawasaki disease**, a vasculitis postulated to be infectious in origin, is limited to the pediatric population.

Clinical Manifestations and Treatment
Polyarteritis Nodosa

Insidious in onset, variable in symptomatology, waxing and waning, polyarteritis nodosa often proves difficult to diagnose. Signs and symptoms may include any of the following: vague systemic complaints, painful erythematous skin nodules, purpura, hypertension, hematuria, abdominal pain, encephalopathy, and neuropathy. The fingers and toes become gangrenous in extreme disease. The erythrocyte sedimentation rate is invariably elevated during active disease. Diagnosis rests on signature vascular lesions on biopsy. Corticosteroids and immune suppressants are the mainstays of therapy. Prognosis is fair; mortality is related to renal or cardiac complications.

Henoch-Schönlein Purpura

Henoch-Schönlein purpura is an immunologically mediated vasculitis involving the gastrointestinal tract, skin, joints, and kidneys. It occurs in young children, peaks in the winter months, and may be preceded by a viral or group A streptococcal upper respiratory infection. Gastrointestinal involvement is usually significant, including abdominal pain, vomiting, ileus, and upper and lower tract bleeding. Glomerulonephritis may progress to acute renal failure. The characteristic nonthrombocytopenic purpuric or maculopapular rash over the buttocks and lower extremities is almost always observed. Treatment is supportive; corticosteroids have not been found to be particularly helpful. The prognosis for full recovery within 4–6 weeks is excellent. Long-term complications parallel the severity of renal sequelae.

Kawasaki Disease

Kawasaki disease, first described in 1961 in Japan, is a systemic vasculitis characterized by high fever, lymphadenopathy, and mucocutaneous lesions. It occurs almost exclusively in infants and young children and is more common in males. An infectious etiology has been suggested but never confirmed. Current criteria for diagnosis are noted in Table 11–7.

The most serious complications are cardiac, including **coronary vasculitis** and **aneurysm formation**. Prognosis is tied to severity of cardiac involvement; cardiac instability can produce arrhythmias, infarction, or congestive heart failure within days of presentation. Aneurysms and coronary artery disease persist and may result in death months to years later.

Corticosteroids are **contraindicated** in Kawasaki disease; increased aneurysm formation has been tied to their use. Aspirin is prescribed during the acute course as an antiplatelet agent. IVIG therapy administered over 2–3 days results in profound improvement. Both high-dose aspirin therapy and IVIG therapy significantly reduce the risk of coronary artery aneurysms.

TABLE 11–7

Criteria for Diagnosis of Kawasaki Disease

1. Fever lasting ≥ 5 days
2. Bilateral conjunctivitis
3. Changes of lips and oral cavity
   Dry, red, fissured lips
   Strawberry tongue
   Diffuse erythema of mucous membranes
4. Changes of peripheral extremities
   Erythema of palms and soles
   Indurative edema of hands and feet
   Membranous desquamation from fingertips
5. Polymorphous rash (primarily on the trunk)
6. Acute nonpurulent swelling of cervical lymph node to >1.5 cm in diameter

Five criteria are required for diagnosis. One of the signs listed under 3 and 4 is sufficient to establish these criteria.

Modified recommendations of the Japan MCLS Research Committee, 1974.

◆ KEY POINTS ◆

1. Henoch-Schönlein purpura is characterized by abdominal pain, vomiting, gastrointestinal bleeding, and nonthrombocytopenic purpura over the buttocks and lower extremities.

2. Kawasaki disease presents with high fever, lymphadenopathy, and mucocutaneous lesions.

3. Corticosteroids are contraindicated in Kawasaki disease.

4. High-dose aspirin therapy and IVIG reduce the risk of coronary artery aneurysms in Kawasaki disease.

12 Infectious Disease

Infections result in more morbidity and mortality in children worldwide than all other causes combined. At the turn of the twentieth century, 18% of children in the United States did not survive to age 5 years, and 56% of those deaths attributed to infectious illnesses. Even today, poor sanitation, overcrowding, and limited access to health care contribute to the high incidence of disease in poverty-stricken areas both here and abroad. New pathogens continue to appear; for example, human immunodeficiency virus (HIV) was unheard of 20 years ago. Equally disconcerting is the rapid emergence of resistance to known antibiotics. Some organisms cause specific clinical syndromes in children not often found in adults. Other infections may be more severe or treated differently in the pediatric setting.

VACCINATIONS

Routine Immunizations

Active immunization involves stimulating an individual's immune system to develop a rapid protective response during future infectious exposures. A vaccine contains all or part of either a weakened form of the organism or one of its products. Table 12–1 contains a simplified version of the current vaccination guidelines recommended by the American Academy of Pediatrics Committee on Infectious Diseases.

Despite their long history of safe use and impressive cost-to-benefit ratio, vaccines should be held or delayed

in certain circumstances. Table 12–2 lists absolute and relative contraindications to vaccine administration and some common misconceptions.

Additional Vaccinations

Children with **congenital, iatrogenic,** or **functional** (i.e., sickle cell disease) **asplenia** should receive both **pneumococcal** and **meningococcal** vaccines. A yearly **influenza** vaccine is recommended for patients with chronic pulmonary disease (including reactive airway disease), cardiac disease, or sickle cell disease and patients receiving immunosuppressive therapy.

FEVER OF UNKNOWN ORIGIN

Temperature elevation can result from natural variation, exercise, infection, inflammation, malignancy, or hypothalamic dysfunction. The most frequent cause of fever in children is infection. Constant or recurrent fevers with no clear etiology despite evaluation represent a diagnostic challenge termed "fever of unknown origin" (FUO).

Differential Diagnosis

FUO in the pediatric population is usually a common disorder presenting in an uncommon manner, rather than a "zebra." Diagnostic considerations include:

- **infection**: hepatitis, cytomegalovirus (CMV), Epstein-Barr virus (EBV); parasites; fungi in the immunocompromised child; brucellosis, leptospiro-

TABLE 12–1

Vaccination Schedules

Recommended (number in parentheses indicates the number in the sequence of immunizations)

Birth–2 mo	HBV (1)
1–4 mo	HBV (2)
2 mo	DTP (1), IPV (1), Hib (1), Prevnar (1)
4 mo	DTP (2), IPV (2), Hib (2), Prevnar (2)
6 mo	DTP (3), Hib (3), Prevnar (3)
6–18 mo	HBV (3), OPV (3)
12–15 mo	Hib (4), MMR (1)
12–18 mo	varicella (1), Prevnar (4)
15–18 mo	DTaP (4)
4–6 yr	DTaP (5), OPV (4), MMR (2)
11–16	Td (and every 10 yr thereafter)

sis, tularemia; endocarditis; septic arthritis, osteomyelitis; intra-abdominal and liver abscesses

- **connective tissue disease**: juvenile rheumatoid arthritis, systemic lupus erythematosus
- **malignancy**: leukemia, lymphoma, neuroblastoma
- inflammatory bowel disease
- Kawasaki syndrome

- drug fevers
- thyrotoxicosis
- sarcoidosis
- familial dysautonomia (Riley-Day syndrome)

Clinical Manifestations

History

The age and gender of the patient narrow the differential. Inflammatory bowel disease and connective tissue disorders are uncommon in younger children. Autoimmune disorders occur more frequently in females. Sexual history, travel history, fever curve, current medications, exposure to animals, tick bites, family history, and complete review of systems are other important subjects to address.

Physical Examination

As the phrase "fever of unknown origin" implies, the physical examination is often inconclusive. Conjunctivitis, the absence of tears, rashes, lymphadenopathy, point tenderness, oral ulcers, thrush, heart murmurs, organomegaly, masses, abdominal tenderness, and mental status changes are important to note and may guide laboratory investigation.

Diagnostic Evaluation

The initial workup can be done as an outpatient procedure in older well-appearing patients. Neonates and

TABLE 12–2

Contraindications to Vaccination

Absolute Contraindications	Relative Contraindications	Not Contraindications
Severe anaphylactic or allergic reaction upon previous administration of vaccine	Immunosuppressive therapy (all live vaccines)	Mild illness with or without low-grade fever
Moderate to severe illness with or without fever	Egg allergy (MMR)	Current antibiotic therapy
Encephalopathy within 7 days of administration (pertussis)	Seizure within 3 days of last dose (pertussis)	Recent infectious disease exposure
Immunodeficiency in patient or household contact (OPV)	Shock within 48 hr of last dose (pertussis)	Positive PPD
Pregnancy (MMR; OPV/IPV)	Fever ≥ 40.5 within 48 hr of last dose (pertussis)	Prematurity*
Congenital disorders of immune function (all live vaccines)		

*Premature infants should be vaccinated according to chronologic age except if infant is still hospitalized at 2 mo, OPV should be delayed until discharge or if mother is HBsAg(–), Hep B vaccine should be delayed until child ≥ 2000 g.

toxic-appearing children should be hospitalized. Screening tests may identify the organ system involved and degree of disruption.

Screening laboratory tests include complete blood count and differential, serum electrolytes, blood urea nitrogen (BUN) and creatinine, urinalysis, liver function tests and alkaline phosphatase, chest x-ray, blood, urine, and possibly cerebrospinal fluid (CSF) cultures, stool for cultures and parasite studies, erythrocyte sedimentation rate (ESR), skin testing for tuberculosis, rheumatoid factor, and antinuclear antibodies. More expensive and invasive studies may be warranted based on screening results. In about 25% of cases, no etiology is determined, and the patients recover.

◆ KEY POINTS ◆

1. A persistent fever of unclear etiology despite appropriate studies is termed "fever of unknown origin."

2. Abnormalities in any organ system may produce an FUO.

3. The age and gender may help limit the differential.

4. Screening laboratory tests help isolate the organ system involved.

BACTEREMIA AND SEPSIS

Bacteremia is the presence of bacteria in the blood. Bacteremia is further described as occult if the occurrence is transient and self-limited without any obvious source of infection. Bacteremia should be suspected in the child between 6 and 36 months with a fever greater than 102.2°F and leukocytosis. The majority of episodes are due to *Streptococcus pneumoniae* and resolve spontaneously in 24–48 hours.

In contrast, **sepsis** is bacterial invasion of the intravascular compartment and may be life-threatening. Sepsis is uncommon in immunocompetent children older than 3 months. Affected patients present appearing quite ill (toxic) and may develop shock. The workup of suspected sepsis includes cultures from the blood, urine, and occasionally CSF. Usually, a chest x-ray is obtained as well. These tests should be completed in short order because of the rapidly progressive nature of the disease. Empiric treatment with a third-generation cephalosporin

is coupled with supportive or resuscitative measures as needed.

OTITIS MEDIA

Pathogenesis

Acute infection of the middle ear accounts for more physician visits than any other pediatric illness. The middle ear is normally sterile; a patent but collapsible eustachian tube allows fluid drainage from the middle ear into the nasopharynx but prevents the retrograde entry of normal upper respiratory flora. In children, the angle of entry, short length, and decreased tone of the tube increase susceptibility to infection. Chronic, untreated, or recurrent ear infections lead to **conductive hearing loss**, predisposing children to delayed or impaired speech development.

Epidemiology

Otitis media (OM) is more common in children 6–36 months. About 30% of cases are caused by viruses and heal without specific therapy. The other 70% represent bacterial infections, most commonly *S. pneumoniae* (33%), nontypable *Haemophilus influenzae* (20%), and *Moraxella catarrhalis* (6–10%). Chronic suppurative OM is more likely to be caused by *Staphylococcus aureus*, *Pseudomonas aeruginosa*, or mixed pathogens and is often difficult to eradicate.

Risk Factors

Caretaker smoking, bottle feeding, day-care attendance, allergic disease, craniofacial anomalies, immunodeficiency, and chronic middle ear effusion all predispose children to OM.

Clinical Manifestations

History and Physical Examination

Ear pain, fever, and fussiness are the most common complaints; however, younger patients may have just one or none. Usually, OM is preceded by cold symptoms (cough, rhinorrhea, congestion). On physical examination, the affected tympanic membrane appears opaque and erythematous and may be bulging or retracted, obscuring the typical landmarks.

Differential Diagnosis

Otitis externa (inflammation of the external ear canal) also accompanies ear pain; however, the tympanic membranes should appear normal on physical examination. The pain of otitis externa is exacerbated by manipulation of the external ear. A tympanic membrane that is erythematous without any other signs of disease may be caused by vigorous crying and should not be considered OM.

Diagnostic Evaluation

Decreased mobility by pneumatic otoscopy is a consistent finding of otitis media.

Treatment

The pathogens responsible for OM generally respond to oral amoxicillin; resistant organisms may require ampicillin-clavulanic acid or a second- or third-generation cephalosporin. Tympanocentesis to determine the responsible pathogen is indicated in cases of treatment failure or persistent effusion. When more than four infections have occurred within a year (or three in 6 months), daily prophylactic therapy with sulfisoxazole is initiated. Thereafter, recurrences warrant consideration of tympanostomy tube placement.

In addition to hearing loss, possible complications include perforation of the tympanic membrane, excessive scarring (tympanosclerosis), cholesteatoma formation, and chronic suppurative OM. Most spontaneous perforations due to OM resolve without specific treatment or sequelae. Labyrinthitis and mastoiditis may result from direct spread of organisms into the inner ear and mastoid air cells, respectively.

◆ KEY POINTS ◆

1. The three most common bacteria implicated in OM are *S. pneumoniae*, nontypable *H. influenzae*, and *Moraxella catarrhalis*.

2. OM typically presents with ear pain and fever, although it may present with neither.

3. Prophylactic antibiotic therapy or tympanostomy tubes should be considered in patients with multiple ear infections.

4. Chronic or repeated infection predisposes to permanent conductive hearing loss.

SINUSITIS

The maxillary and ethmoid sinuses are present at birth; the sphenoid and frontal sinuses develop later in childhood. The spectrum of pathogens responsible for sinusitis is virtually identical to that for OM. Sinusitis is often difficult to diagnose in a young child; the classic symptoms of headache, facial pain, and sinus tenderness may be absent or difficult to articulate, and sinus plain films are much less sensitive than in the adult. The differential diagnosis includes viral upper respiratory tract infections and nasal foreign body. A history of fever and chronic purulent nasal drainage coupled with tenderness on examination satisfy clinical diagnostic criteria. If the presence or extent of infection are in question, computed tomography (CT) is quite reliable at detecting mucosal thickening, air-fluid levels, and opacification. Antibiotic coverage is similar to that for OM, although treatment should continue for 14–21 days. Persistent infections may require surgical drainage. Complications are uncommon but include osteitis, bony erosion, optic neuritis, orbital cellulitis, and intracranial extension.

HERPANGINA

Herpangina is a symptom complex caused by enteroviruses, most notably coxsackie A. It is typically diagnosed during the spring and summer in younger children. Initially, the patient develops a high fever and very sore throat. Occasionally, the pain will be so severe that the child refuses to swallow, necessitating hospital admission for intravenous hydration. On examination, characteristic vesicular lesions that progress to ulcers are seen scattered over the soft palate, tonsils, and pharynx. Primary herpetic gingivostomatitis infections may present in a similar manner, although the lesions are generally more widespread over the gums, lips, and mucosa. Herpangina is self-limited (5–7 days) and requires no specific therapy. When similar lesions are noted on the palms and soles (and occasionally on the buttocks), the more inclusive name **hand, foot, and mouth disease** is used.

STREPTOCOCCAL PHARYNGITIS

Pathogenesis

Group A beta-hemolytic streptococci (*Streptococcus pyogenes*) comprise the most important source of bacterial pharyngitis. Other sources of pharyngitis do not require specific therapy. However, antimicrobial therapy for streptococcal disease is imperative because of the frequency of **suppurative** (peritonsillar abscess, retropharyngeal abscess) and **nonsuppurative** (rheumatic fever, poststreptococcal glomerulonephritis) sequelae.

Epidemiology

"Strep throat" afflicts older children and adolescents; it is rare before age 3. The organism is spread person-to-person through infected oral secretions.

Clinical Manifestations

History and Physical Examination

Classic symptoms include sore throat, fever, headache, malaise, nausea, and occasionally abdominal pain; enlarged, erythematous, exudative tonsils and tender cervical lymphadenopathy are noted on examination. Petechiae may be present on the soft palate as well. Rhinorrhea and coughing, the hallmarks of viral upper tract infections, are notably absent. The diagnosis of scarlet fever is made when a characteristic erythematous, "sandpaper-like" rash accompanies the fever and pharyngitis. The rash appears on the neck or trunk, spreads to the extremities, and may desquamate on resolution of respiratory symptoms.

Differential Diagnosis

Differentiating viral pharyngitis and infectious mononucleosis from streptococcal pharyngitis may be impossible based on clinical symptoms; a throat culture or antigen detection test for group A streptococcus is definitive.

Diagnostic Evaluation

A definitive diagnosis is critical when streptococcal pharyngitis is suspected. Any pharyngitis associated with a positive rapid antigen test for group A streptococcus must be treated. False-negative antigen tests are frequent with some types of assays, so treatment is based on culture results when the antigen test is negative.

Treatment

Patients with documented group A streptococcal pharyngitis should receive a 10-day course of penicillin to prevent rheumatic heart disease. Erythromycin is an acceptable alternative for individuals who are allergic to penicillin. The treatment of scarlet fever is identical to that for streptococcal pharyngitis.

Acute rheumatic fever (ARF) occurs 3–4 weeks after streptococcal pharyngitis in a small percentage of untreated patients. ARF is an inflammatory condition involving the connective tissues of the heart (carditis, valvular destruction), joints (transient migratory polyarthritis), and CNS (late-developing but transient chorea). Diagnosis rests on fulfilling the Jones criteria (Table 12–3). Initially, fever, dyspnea, chest pain, cardiac murmur, and arthritis predominate; most long-term morbidity comes from valvular destruction and scarring, resulting in mitral or aortic valve insufficiency or stenosis. Acute episodes respond favorably to antibiotics, anti-inflammatory drugs, and cardiac management. ARF has a high recurrence rate after subsequent pharyngitic infections; affected individuals should receive prophylactic penicillin therapy.

Acute poststreptococcal glomerulonephritis may follow either group A streptococcal pharyngitis or streptococcal skin infections and is not prevented by antibiotic therapy. It is common in younger patients, rarely

TABLE 12–3

Revised Jones Criteria for the Diagnosis of Acute Rheumatic Fever (Requires 2 Major, or 1 Major and 2 Minor Criteria)

Major manifestations
    Carditis
    Polyarthritis
    Chorea
    Erythema marginatum
    Subcutaneous nodules
Minor manifestations
    Clinical
        Fever
        Arthralgia
        Previous rheumatic fever/rheumatic heart disease
    Laboratory
        Acute-phase reaction*
        Prolonged PR interval
Additional criteria
    Supporting evidence of preceding streptococcal
        infection (increased ASO or other streptococcal
        antibodies), or
    Positive throat culture for group A streptococci, or
    Recent scarlet fever

*Elevated serum erythrocyte sedimentation rate, C-reactive protein; leukocytosis.

results in chronic renal disease (as it may in adults), and does not recur. Clinical manifestations follow infection by about 10 days and include hematuria, edema, proteinuria, and decreased urination. Hypertension may complicate the course. Treatment consists of penicillin therapy and diuretics and antihypertensives as needed; steroids are rarely indicated.

◆ KEY POINTS ◆

1. Although a positive group A streptococcal antigen test is quite accurate, a negative antigen test is insufficiently sensitive, so culture results should guide therapy.

2. Acute rheumatic fever involves the heart (valvular destruction), joints, and brain.

3. Acute poststreptococcal glomerulonephritis may follow either skin or pharyngeal infection; most children recover without significant morbidity.

MONONUCLEOSIS

Pathogenesis

Mononucleosis is a clinical syndrome of pharyngitis, systemic lymphadenopathy, fatigue, and atypical lymphocytosis. Infectious mononucleosis is most commonly caused by Epstein-Barr virus (EBV) or cytomegalovirus (CMV).

Epidemiology

Both EBV and CMV are spread through infected saliva and are usually encountered in early childhood, resulting in minor illness. Thereafter, the organism remains essentially dormant in a small percentage of B cells. The mononucleosis syndrome occurs more frequently among individuals infected in late childhood or adolescence; a significant minority escape infection until adolescence or early adulthood (hence the term "kissing disease").

Clinical Manifestations

History and Physical Examination

The pharyngitis associated with mononucleosis is often severe and exudative. Fever, profound fatigue, and systemic lymphadenopathy are the rule. Involvement of the liver and spleen may produce tenderness and/or enlarge-

ment. Although the pharyngitis usually resolves within a week, the malaise typically lasts much longer.

Differential Diagnosis

Classic mononucleosis is caused by EBV and accounts for about four of five cases. CMV produces a similar syndrome. Other infections that may present with mono-like symptomatology include toxoplasmosis, human herpes virus 6, and HIV; atypical lymphocytosis is generally absent in these diseases. Pharyngitis due to group A streptococci or adenovirus is difficult to distinguish from that of mononucleosis. When pharyngitis is not the predominant symptom, acute leukemia becomes a consideration.

Diagnostic Evaluation

The most striking laboratory result is significant **lymphocytosis** with up to 20% **atypical** cells. Liver transaminases may be moderately elevated. A heterophile antibody test for EBV using a few drops of blood allows simple, rapid detection in the physician's office or emergency room; however, it has limited sensitivity, especially in young children. Serologic antibody testing is available for EBV and CMV (Fig. 12–1).

Treatment

The disorder is self-limited, and treatment is supportive. Activity restrictions (i.e., no contact sports) are advised when splenomegaly is present because of the possibility of splenic rupture.

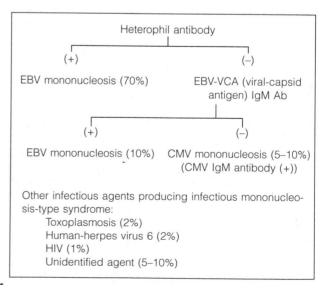

Figure 12–1 Serologic workup of mononucleosis syndrome and possible etiologies.

Complications are relatively common. Neutropenia, hemolytic anemia, and thrombocytopenia may occur but are reversible and result in little morbidity. Serious but rare sequelae include airway obstruction and splenic rupture. Concurrent treatment with ampicillin precipitates a characteristic (but harmless) rash. Immunocompromised individuals are at risk for severe disseminated disease and lymphoproliferative disorders.

◆ KEY POINTS ◆

1. Classic mononucleosis is caused by Epstein-Barr virus.

2. Typical mononucleosis is characterized by profound fatigue, systemic lymphadenopathy, fever, and atypical lymphocytosis.

3. Therapy is supportive. Contact sports should be avoided during the acute phase.

CROUP

Croup is an upper respiratory syndrome usually caused by parainfluenza and consisting of hoarseness, a barky cough, and inspiratory stridor. It is most pronounced in young children but also afflicts adolescents and adults. Incidence increases during the spring and fall and is occasionally epidemic. At its most severe, the disease progresses to partial or total airway obstruction.

Clinical Manifestations

History and Physical Examination
The onset of croup is variable. Some children with no previous symptoms wake up with stridor in the middle of the night, whereas others develop fever, congestion, sore throat, and a cough over a few days. The **barky cough** is unmistakable and virtually diagnostic, sounding somewhat like a seal. Respiratory compromise varies from minimal stridor with agitation to severe distress with tachypnea, flaring, retractions, and impending airway obstruction.

Differential Diagnosis

The differential diagnosis varies depending on the most prominent manifestation. Cough and hoarseness may result from allergies, bronchitis, vocal cord abnormalities, and, less commonly, epiglottitis. When airway ob-

struction is present, epiglottitis and noninfectious conditions (foreign body aspiration, severe food allergy, angioneurotic edema) must be considered.

Diagnostic Evaluation

A chest radiograph can sometimes distinguish croup from epiglottitis when the diagnosis is uncertain (Figs. 12–2 and 12–3), but direct laryngoscopy in the operating room is recommended in these cases.

Treatment

Most children with croup never become symptomatic enough to prompt a visit to the doctor. Those who do are usually treated at home; cough and stridor respond well to cool night air or humidity. In the emergency

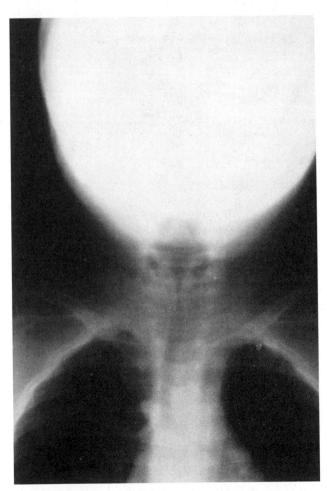

Figure 12–2 Croup in a 3 year old. Note the "steeple sign" indicative of subglottic narrowing.

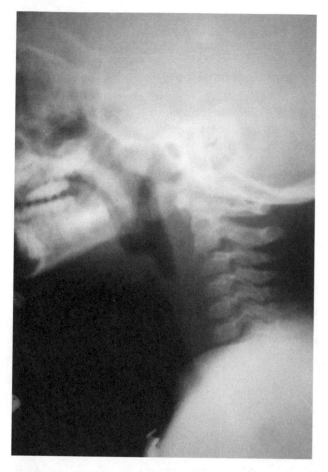

Figure 12–3   Epiglottitis in a 4 year old with massive edema of the epiglottis, thickened aryepiglottic folds, and effacement of the valleculae.

room, stridorous infants receive nebulized racemic epinephrine and steroids. Impending respiratory failure and airway obstruction constitute medical emergencies and are addressed accordingly (see Chapter 1).

◆ KEY POINTS ◆

1. Croup presents with tachypnea, stridor, and a "barky" cough.

2. Infants with severe stridor due to croup are treated with nebulized racemic epinephrine and steroids.

EPIGLOTTITIS

Pathogenesis

Epiglottitis consists of inflammation and edema of the epiglottis and aryepiglottic folds. It is considered a life-threatening emergency because of the propensity of the swollen tissues to suddenly and irreversibly occlude the airway.

Epidemiology

Epiglottitis is uncommon before age 24 months and after age 7 years. Most cases occur during the winter months in children 3–5 years old. Because of routine administration of the **Hib vaccine**, the incidence of epiglottitis has significantly decreased over the past 5 years. Organisms other than *H. influenzae* known to cause epiglottitis include *S. pneumoniae* and group A streptococci.

Risk Factors

Failure to keep the Hib vaccination up to date is the greatest risk factor for epiglottitis.

Clinical Manifestations

History and Physical Examination

Fever, sore throat, hoarseness, and stridor develop over 1–2 days. On examination, the patient appears toxic, is occasionally tachypneic, and may be leaning forward with the neck slightly extended. Drooling is common.

Differential Diagnosis

The differential diagnosis is similar to that for croup.

Diagnostic Evaluation

Lateral airway films aid in the diagnosis but are not recommended given the delay in appropriate care.

Treatment

If epiglottitis is strongly suspected, timely transportation to the operating room for intubation under anesthesia is paramount. Emergency cricothyrotomy may be performed if an endotracheal airway cannot be secured in the face of rapidly progressive obstruction. Intravenous (IV) cefuroxime offers empiric coverage until blood and throat cultures taken in the operating room provide identification and antibiotic sensitivity profile of the infecting organism.

RESPIRATORY SYNCYTIAL VIRUS BRONCHIOLITIS (RSV)

Pathogenesis

In older children and adults, RSV causes no more than the common cold. In infants, the virus infects the bronchioles, which become hyperreactive and filled with cellular debris. Progression to respiratory failure is a serious and potentially fatal complication. RSV is highly contagious, with spread via infective respiratory secretions and contaminated fomites.

Epidemiology

This infection is responsible for more hospitalizations than any single other infectious agent, with more than 100,000 inpatient stays annually in the United States. RSV bronchiolitis occurs in yearly epidemics during the winter and early spring. Most children have been infected at least once by the age of 3 years, and recurrent infections are common. The disease is most severe in infants 2–6 months of age, former premature infants, and children with underlying heart or lung disease.

Risk Factors

Children with congenital or acquired immunodeficiencies are more susceptible to severe disease.

Clinical Manifestations

History

Older infants present with fever, copious rhinorrhea, mouth breathing, and tachypnea. Often, household contacts have upper respiratory symptoms as well. In neonates, **apnea** is a frequent presentation of RSV infection.

Physical Examination

Fever and tachypnea may be the only signs on physical examination. Alternatively, the child may be in severe respiratory distress with retractions, nasal flaring, and tracheal tugging. Wheezing, nasal congestion, and profuse clear rhinorrhea are invariably present. Hypoxia is not uncommon in severely affected patients.

Differential Diagnosis

Other respiratory viruses, including influenza, parainfluenza, and rhinovirus, may also cause bronchiolitis; however, RSV is by far the most frequent pathogen during epidemic months. The wheezing associated with bronchiolitis may be difficult to distinguish from reactive airway disease in many cases.

Diagnostic Evaluation

The virus may be cultured from nasal secretions; however, rapid antigen testing is an acceptable and practical alternative.

Treatment

Hypoxic or severely distressed patients should be admitted for observation and oxygen therapy as needed. Children with oxygen saturation greater than 94%, minimal respiratory distress, good fluid intake, reliable caretakers, and good follow-up may be managed as outpatients.

The benefit of bronchodilators and corticosteroids (based on principles similar to those for reactive airway disease) is controversial to say the least. Ribavirin, an antiviral agent, may shorten the course of symptoms and viral shedding; it is occasionally administered in an aerosol form to patients with underlying heart or lung pathology. RespiGam, an intravenous RSV polyclonal antibody, and Synagis, an injectable RSV monoclonal antibody, provide passive prophylaxis and are recommended during the winter months for patients at risk for severe disease.

The mortality rate for hospitalized patients is about 1%. Children with congenital heart defects, chronic lung disease, and immunodeficiency fare particularly poorly. Patients previously hospitalized with documented RSV have more airway hyperresponsiveness as a group later in life than does the general population; cause versus effect has not been elucidated.

◆ **KEY POINTS** ◆

1. RSV bronchiolitis is a potentially severe infection in infants.

2. The condition presents with wheezing, upper respiratory tract infection (notably copious rhinorrhea), and, occasionally, low oxygen saturation.

3. Apnea is a frequent presentation in neonates.

4. In most cases, oxygen and supportive care are appropriate.

5. Children with underlying heart or lung disease may benefit from ribavirin.

PERTUSSIS

Infection with *Bordetella pertussis* causes a "common cold" in adults but may result in life-threatening lower respiratory disease in neonates and infants.

Clinical Manifestations

History and Physical Examination

The classic presentation in young children is "whooping cough." The **catarrhal phase** consists of 1–2 weeks of low-grade fever, cough, and coryza. Then comes a 3- to 8-week **paroxysmal phase** characterized by paroxysms of cough followed by inspiratory stridor (the "whoop"). Post-tussive emesis is common. The cough may drag on for 3–12 months during the **convalescent phase**, although other symptoms usually remit. Newborns with severe disease may present with the typical paroxysmal cough followed by choking and progressive cyanosis.

Diagnostic Evaluation

Leukocytosis (>30,000 white blood cells/μL) with a predominance of atypical lymphocytes is highly suggestive of pertussis in a child with respiratory symptoms. Nasopharyngeal secretions contain the organism, which may be detected by fluorescent antibody staining or culture.

Treatment

Young infants with severe disease (episodic hypoxia, decreased oral intake, mucous aspiration) should be hospitalized for observation and supportive care. Erythromycin may shorten the duration of illness if given early in the catarrhal phase; unfortunately, the diagnosis is usu-

ally missed until the characteristic cough appears. Erythromycin is still recommended for patients beyond the catarrhal stage to decrease the period of infectivity; a 14-day course completely eradicates the organism from the nasopharynx and respiratory tract.

Immunization against pertussis should take place at 2, 4, 6, and 12 months and again at 4–6 years. Mild side effects are quite common and include swelling and redness around the injection site, decreased appetite, and low-grade fever. The vaccine is 95% effective against severe illness, although at least one-third of immunized individuals experience mild infections.

◆ **KEY POINTS** ◆

1. The "whoop" in pertussis is the long, stridorous inspiration after the paroxysmal cough.

2. Leukocytosis with a predominance of atypical lymphocytes is typical of pertussis.

3. The drug of choice is erythromycin.

PNEUMONIA

Pathogenesis

Although the lower airways communicate with the outside environment, the lungs normally remain sterile. Pneumonia in children may result from the same viruses that cause upper tract infection: RSV, adenovirus, parainfluenza, influenza, and enteroviruses. *S. pneumoniae* is the predominant cause of bacterial pneumonia in normally healthy patients. *Mycoplasma pneumoniae* is an important source of lower tract infection in both children and adults. Up to 50% of patients with bacterial pneumonia show concurrent viral disease, suggesting a facilitative role.

Epidemiology

In immunocompetent individuals, the **age of the child** alone suggests an etiologic organism. Mycoplasma infections are uncommon in children under 5 years. *S. pneumoniae* should be considered a source in any community-acquired lower tract infection. Other bacterial causes are rare but include *H. influenzae* type b, *S. aureus*, and group A streptococci. In the neonatal period, group B streptococci and *Listeria monocytogenes* top the list; Chlamydia often surfaces 2–3months after birth in infants born to women with untreated genital *C. trachomatis*.

Risk Factors

Conditions associated with an increased risk of bacterial pneumonia include:

- bronchopulmonary dysplasia
- cystic fibrosis
- neurologic devastation with decreased level of consciousness
- gastroesophageal reflux/aspiration
- upper airway anatomic defects (tracheoesophageal fistula, cleft palate)
- hemoglobinopathies (including sickle cell disease)
- immunodeficiency/immunosuppressive therapy

Clinical Manifestations

History

Viral pneumonia is usually preceded by typical upper respiratory symptoms (dry cough, rhinorrhea, postnasal drip, coryza, low-grade fever). Infants and young children with bacterial pneumonia may present with nonspecific constitutional complaints, including fever, irritability, poor feeding, vomiting, and lethargy. Fever, chills, dyspnea, chest pain, and productive cough are more common in older patients. Mycoplasma pneumonia is generally milder; fever is low grade or absent, with persistent dry cough and malaise.

Physical Examination

Any indication of respiratory distress can signal pneumonia, although tachypnea and chest discomfort are the most common. Profuse crackles, wheezing, and widespread rales suggest diffuse involvement more characteristic of viral or mycoplasma pneumonia. Focal findings such as decreased breath sounds, dullness to percussion, and asymmetric crackles favor a bacterial origin. Cyanosis is uncommon except in severe disease.

Differential Diagnosis

Children often have difficulty localizing and articulating their symptoms. In addition, sputum for culture and Gram stain may be impossible to obtain. The patient's past medical history, physical examination, and chest radiograph usually clarify the diagnosis. Pneumonia is much more common in the pediatric population than are other conditions with similar presentations, including congestive heart failure, chemical pneumonitis, pulmonary embolism, some connective tissue disorders, and primary or metastatic malignancy.

Diagnostic Evaluation

The physical examination is the best test for diagnosing pneumonia; early infections may be symptomatic without radiographic changes. However, the chest radiograph remains an excellent test for defining the extent and pattern of involvement and ruling out other possible diagnoses (i.e., pleural effusions). Bacterial pneumonia causes lung consolidation; bronchopneumonia, often with a small pleural effusion, is characteristic of mycoplasma. Aspiration pneumonia is typically located in the right middle or right upper lobes. Viral pneumonia appears as streaky interstitial disease without alveolar compromise. These patterns offer guidelines; although the chest x-ray may assist with the most likely diagnosis, it is hardly definitive.

Treatment

Therapy depends on the most likely etiologic pathogen once the patient has been evaluated. Any child with persistent hypoxia or respiratory distress should be admitted to the hospital for observation and oxygen therapy as needed.

Cefuroxime or penicillin is appropriate IV therapy when bacterial disease is suspected. Most viral infections are self-limited and require supportive care only. In the outpatient setting, amoxicillin is sufficient for most cases of bacterial pneumonia, although amoxicillin-clavulanic acid or a second- or third-generation cephalosporin may be necessary when *H. influenzae* or *S. aureus* are present. None of these agents covers mycoplasma; erythromycin is recommended for "walking pneumonia" due to mycoplasma and suspected Chlamydia pneumonia in the neonate.

The most frequent complication is development of a pleural effusion large enough to compromise respiratory effort. Pleurocentesis with possible chest tube placement provides rapid relief. Empyema results when purulent fluid from an adjacent lung infection drains into the pleural space. Lung abscesses may complicate anaerobic infections and those due to the more common gram-positive organisms.

MENINGITIS

Pathogenesis

Almost any pathogen can infect the leptomeninges and cerebrospinal fluid (CSF). Viral meningitis is typically a benign, acute, self-limited illness; bacterial meningitis is a life-threatening condition associated with substantial morbidity and mortality. The term aseptic meningitis refers to meningeal inflammation of nonbacterial origin and includes viral, mycoplasma, rickettsial, parasitic, and even noninfectious etiologies.

Epidemiology

Most meningitis is viral or bacterial in origin. Viral meningitis is rarely encountered in patients over 30 years. Enteroviruses constitute the largest source, occurring primarily in the late summer and early fall. Bacterial meningitis is most common in infants aged 6–12 months, with *S. pneumoniae* being the primary pathogen followed by *H. influenzae* and *Neisseria meningitidis*. Neonatal meningitis is a separate entity; group B streptococci and *Escherichia coli* are the top isolates in the newborn period. Herpes meningitis can result from perinatal and sexually acquired infections.

Risk Factors

Risk factors for bacterial meningitis are the same as those for sepsis, because most cases follow hematogenous seeding. Direct spread can occur secondary to trauma, mastoiditis, sinusitis, and anatomic defects in the scalp or skull. In the neonate, low birth weight, prolonged rupture of membranes, maternal fever, chorioamnionitis, and invasive prolonged supportive care predispose to septicemia and a resulting meningitis; myelomeningocele also increases the risk.

Clinical Manifestations

History

Viral meningitis is preceded by a nonspecific prodromal phase of fever, malaise, sore throat, and myalgias. The development of a stiff neck and severe headache is accompanied by nausea, vomiting, irritability, lethargy, and photophobia. A herpangitic or herpetic rash may suggest the etiology. Unless complicated by encephalitis, symptoms generally resolve over 2–4 days and may improve after lumbar puncture.

In bacterial meningitis, the prodromal phase is absent and the fever is generally quite high. Mental status changes, focal neurologic signs, ataxia, seizures, and shock are not uncommon.

Physical Examination

A bulging fontanelle (in infants), cranial nerve palsies, and papilledema on examination indicate increased intracranial pressure. Nuchal rigidity and positive **Kernig's** (flexion of the leg at the hip with subsequent pain on extension) and **Brudzinski's** (involuntary leg flexion on passive neck flexion) signs are markers for meningeal irritation. Sepsis due to *N. meningitidis* may be obvious when widespread purpuric skin lesions are present.

Differential Diagnosis

The differential diagnosis for infectious meningitis includes encephalitis, which may develop concurrently or subsequently (see Chapter 15). Other conditions that may present with a similar clinical picture include drug intoxication or side effects, recent sustained anoxia or hypoxia, primary or metastatic central nervous system (CNS) malignancy, bacterial endocarditis with embolism, intracranial hemorrhage/hematoma, malignant hypertension, and developmental or demyelination disorders.

Diagnostic Evaluation

Lumbar puncture is by far the most specific and sensitive laboratory test for determining the presence and etiologic agent of meningitis. Color and viscosity, cell counts and differential, Gram stain, glucose, and protein levels should be determined. Blood and CSF cultures increase the chances of culturing the responsible pathogen. Rapid latex antigen tests for the most likely organisms are available in many laboratories. The presence of CSF leukocytes in patients over 1 month of age, particularly if polymorphonuclear cells, suggests meningitis.

Many red blood cells on a "clean" (nontraumatic) tap are consistent with herpes meningitis or subdural hemorrhaging. Lumbar puncture in a child with increased intracranial pressure should not be attempted until an expanding mass lesion is excluded by CT or magnetic resonance imaging because of the potential for brainstem herniation. Other contraindications include cardiopulmonary instability and skin infection overlying the site for tap.

Treatment

When the diagnosis of uncomplicated viral meningitis is unequivocal, hospitalization is generally not necessary. If bacterial meningitis cannot be ruled out, the patient should be hospitalized urgently for observation and IV antibiotic therapy.

Third-generation cephalosporins cefotaxime and ceftriaxone achieve therapeutic levels in the CSF and provide broad-spectrum coverage of the most likely pathogens in the infant and child; ampicillin and chloramphenicol together are an acceptable alternative. Neonates receive ampicillin for group B streptococci and Listeria; gentamycin is added to address gram-negative pathogens. Once an organism and its sensitivities have been documented, more specific treatment can be used. The course of therapy for bacterial meningitis is 10 days, except in the neonatal period, when 2–3 weeks is recommended. A repeat lumbar puncture to document sterile CSF may be performed 48 hours after the initiation of therapy.

The current mortality rate for bacterial meningitis outside the neonatal period is less than 5%. However, 15–30% of patients experience some persistent neurologic deficit, most commonly hearing loss, developmental delay, behavior problems, motor incoordination, and seizures.

Almost one-third of neonates who develop bacterial meningitis die from the disease. A significant minority of the survivors exhibit long-term sequelae, such as hearing loss, developmental delay, profound mental retardation, hydrocephalus requiring shunting, seizures, and spasticity. Morbidity and mortality are higher after gram-negative infections.

◆ KEY POINTS ◆

1. Bacterial meningitis is a life-threatening condition.

2. It is most common between ages 6 and 12 months.

3. Lumbar puncture is invaluable in the diagnosis and treatment strategy of meningitis.

4. An expanding mass lesion must be ruled out in patients before lumbar puncture because of potential herniation.

5. The neurologic morbidity from bacterial meningitis in neonates is relatively high.

INFECTIOUS DIARRHEA

Pathogens cause diarrhea by a variety of mechanisms. For example, some bacteria invade intestinal tissue directly, whereas others secrete injurious toxins before or after ingestion. Viruses, parasites, and protozoa are also capable of inflicting disease. Excessive stooling causes dehydration, inadequate nutrition, and electrolyte abnormalities, all of which are poorly tolerated in infants and small children.

Clinical Manifestations

History

The history should include information about symptoms in other family members, recent travel, medication use, immune status, day-care center attendance, source of drinking water, duration of symptoms, fever curve, and number, color, and character of stools.

In bacterial diarrhea, Salmonella, Shigella, *E. coli*, *Yersinia enterocolitica*, and *Campylobacter jejuni* are the most frequent causes; *Vibrio cholerae* may be acquired during travel to India, Africa, or the Middle East and from eating undercooked Gulf Coast shellfish. Patients with bacterial diarrhea present with fever, significant abdominal cramping, malaise, and tenesmus; vomiting is less common. The stools contain mucous and may be guaiac (+) or mixed with blood. Occasionally, particularly in patients with Yersinia, severe pain localizes to the right lower quadrant, creating a "pseudo-appendicitis" picture.

In cholera, the stools quickly become colorless and flecked with mucus, termed "rice-water" stools. Severe diarrhea leading to hypovolemic shock may develop in hours to a few days.

Rotavirus is the major cause of nonbacterial gastroenteritis in infants and toddlers. Infections peak between November and April. Complaints include runny diarrhea, vomiting, and low-grade fever; upper respiratory symptoms are not uncommon. The diarrhea may be voluminous and unrelenting, leading to severe dehydration, acidosis, and electrolyte disturbances.

Giardiasis is the most commonly reported parasitic disease in the United States. More water-related outbreaks of diarrhea are due to *Giardia lamblia* than any other organism. The illness presents with frequent, foul-smelling, watery stools that rarely contain blood or mucus; abdominal pain, nausea, vomiting, anorexia, and flatulence often accompany the diarrhea. Symptoms generally resolve within 5–7 days, although some cases linger for more than a month, and the stool is infective for significantly longer.

Physical Examination

The main goals of the physical examination are estimating the degree of dehydration and ruling out a surgical abdomen.

Differential Diagnosis

The most common cause of acute diarrhea in the pediatric population is infection. Other conditions associated with diarrhea include malabsorption, antibiotic use, cystic fibrosis, and inflammatory bowel disease.

Diagnostic Evaluation

Electrolyte and renal function studies (Na^+, K^+, Cl^-, HCO_3^-, BUN, creatinine) tailor replacement therapy in significantly dehydrated children. Abdominal radiographs are generally normal or nonspecific. Blood, mucus, and fecal leukocytes suggest a bacterial origin for the illness, such as Salmonella, Shigella, invasive and enterohemorrhagic *E. coli*, and *Y. enterocolitica*. Bacterial stool culture results take several days but are helpful in determining the need for antibiotics. If there is a history of antibiotic use, stool should be tested for *Clostridium difficile* toxin detection. Rapid antigen testing is available for rotavirus. If *G. lamblia* infection is suspected, multiple stool samples from different times should be examined for cysts. Endoscopic biopsy may be indicated if the diarrhea becomes chronic and no etiology has been discovered.

Treatment

Fluid and electrolyte management is the cornerstone of therapy aimed at infectious diarrhea (see Chapter 7). Treatment incorporates oral rehydration whenever possible; aggressive parenteral therapy may be required in severe cases. Antidiarrheal agents should be avoided.

If the child has significant systemic symptoms (ill-appearing, high fever, malaise), bloody stools, or fecal leukocytes, empiric trimethoprim-sulfamethoxazole is reasonable until culture results become available. Unfortunately, antibiotic therapy prolongs Salmonella shedding and should be reserved for systemic infections. Erythromycin is the treatment of choice for *C. jejuni*. Patients positive for *C. difficile* toxin receive oral metronidazole. Although quinacrine is the most effective therapy against Giardia, furazolidone liquid suspension is usually prescribed due to taste considerations; metronidazole is another alternative.

Salmonella is capable of invading the bloodstream and causing extraintestinal disease, including meningitis, arthritis, and (particularly in sickle cell patients) osteomyelitis. Occasionally, children with shigellosis present with **neurologic** manifestations (lethargy, seizures, mental status changes), possibly due to a neurotoxin elaborated by the organism. *Shigella dysenteriae* and *E. coli* 0157:H7 produce an enterotoxin ("Shiga" or Shiga-like toxin) associated with **hemolytic uremic syndrome**, a serious complication consisting of microangiopathic hemolytic anemia, nephropathy, and thrombocytopenia. Almost 25% of individuals infected with *Y. enterocolitica* develop subsequent **erythema nodosum**. Patients with chronic giardiasis are at risk for failure to thrive resulting from ongoing malabsorption.

As long as the patient does not develop hypovolemic shock, prognosis for full recovery is excellent. Even in life-threatening cases, appropriate management may prevent permanent sequelae.

◆ KEY POINTS ◆

1. The most common cause of acute diarrhea in the pediatric population is infection.

2. Infectious diarrhea may be bacterial, viral, or parasitic.

3. Careful fluid and electrolyte management is the most important treatment in infectious diarrhea.

4. Children with shigellosis may present with mental status changes.

5. *S. dysenteriae* and *E. coli* 0157:H7 have been associated with hemolytic uremic syndrome.

HEPATITIS

Pathogenesis

Viral hepatitis is the collective term for a group of viral infections in which the liver is the primary target organ. Five distinct species are now known to cause disease: hepatitis A virus (HAV), hepatitis B virus (HBV), delta virus, hepatitis C virus (HCV), and hepatitis E virus (HEV). Table 12–4 provides a comparison and summary of the agents known to cause viral hepatitis.

Epidemiology

HAV is a hardy picornavirus acquired via fecal-oral transmission. The variable incubation time is followed by a brief period of viremia and excretion in the stool. Infection with HAV is often asymptomatic, especially in children. HBV is the most serious etiology known to cause viral hepatitis and a human **carcinogen** second only to tobacco in prominence. It is transmitted through contact with infected bodily fluids. In 1990, over a billion people were estimated to have been infected worldwide. HDV, made up of single-stranded RNA, HBsAg, and the delta antigen, is a "defective" virus in that it requires the presence of an active HBV infection to replicate. HCV and HEV, among those viruses known to cause non-A, non-B hepatitis (NANB), occur much less commonly than do HAV and HBV.

Risk Factors

Male homosexuality and unprotected sex with multiple partners increase the risk of contracting HBV and HCV. Risk factors for HAV and HEV include foreign travel, poor sanitation, and contact with children in day care.

Clinical Manifestations

History

Patients with hepatitis present with headache, nausea, vomiting, abdominal pain, diarrhea, anorexia, and fever, generally lasting 3–7 days. However, a wide range of severity exists, from asymptomatic to severe discomfort.

TABLE 12–4

Viruses Responsible for Hepatitis: Comparison and Summary

Family	HAV Picornavirus (RNA)	HBV Hepadnavirus (DNA)	Delta "Defective" RNA virus	HCV RNA	HEV RNA
Transmission	Fecal-oral	Parenteral	Parenteral	Parenteral	Fecal-oral
Period of incubation (days)	15–50	45–180	28–180	60–180	14–56
Period of infectivity	Late incubation to early symptomatic state	When HBsAg seropositive	When anti-HDV seropositive	?	?
Fulminant hepatitis	<1%	Uncommon	Common when coinfective with HBV	Uncommon	Uncommon except during third trimester of pregnancy
Chronic hepatitis	No	5–10% of adults; up to 90% of infected newborns	Common	Common	No
Carrier state	No	5–10%	Common	Common	No
Vaccine	Yes	Yes	Indirect through HBV	No	No

Physical Examination

Scleral icterus and jaundice are the most consistent findings on physical examination but are absent in most affected children. The liver is enlarged and tender in many patients with acute hepatitis. A benign-appearing rash may be present early in the course.

Differential Diagnosis

EBV, CMV, enterovirus, and other viral infections can also cause hepatitis. Isolated liver disease is uncommon; usually, other organ systems are prominently involved as well.

Diagnostic Evaluation

Liver enzymes are uniformly elevated in hepatitis. Because the clinical manifestations are so similar, specific serologic tests are indispensable for securing an accurate diagnosis (Figs. 12–4 and 12–5). The presence of IgM-specific anti-HAV confirms HAV infection. Tests are also available to detect antibodies to the delta antigen. NANB hepatitis is a diagnosis of exclusion.

Three different particles are found in the serum of patients infected with HBV. The Dane particle is the largest one, made up of a core antigen (HBcAg) and envelope antigen (HBeAg) surrounded by a spherical shell of HBsAg ("surface") particles. Note the presence of anti-HBc antibodies after HBsAg disappears and be-

fore the development of anti-HBs antibodies (the "core window") in Figure 12–5. Table 12–5 presents the clinical course and serologic markers important in diagnosing disease stage. Anti-HBs heralds resolution of the illness and confers lifelong immunity; a few of these patients, however, develop fulminant disease with overwhelming hepatocellular destruction and a high mortality.

Treatment

Both active and passive forms of immunization are available, depending on the source of infection. An HAV vaccine exists but is not widely used, mostly because the disease is usually benign and self-limited. Immune globulin will prevent clinical disease when administered within 14 days of exposure. The HBV vaccine series is now recommended for all infants in the United States; although the risk of infection at this age is very low (excluding vertical transmission), vaccinating early in childhood when well child care is more consistent should result in population immunity. Infants of infected mothers should receive both the vaccine and the immunoglobulin to prevent the disease. Alpha-interferon has shown promise in treating adult patients with chronic HBV hepatitis; studies in children are less encouraging. There is no specific treatment for HDV. Alpha-interferon has been weakly effective in cases of chronic HCV infection;

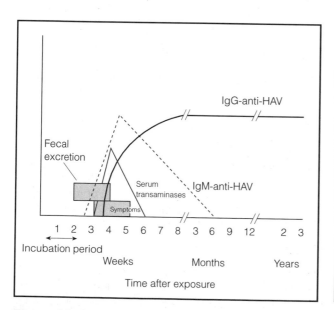

Figure 12–4 The course of acute hepatitis A.

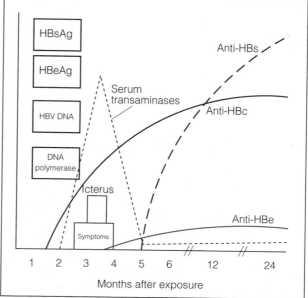

Figure 12–5 The course of acute hepatitis B.

TABLE 12–5

Comparison of Disease States in HBV

	Symptomatic HBV	Resolved HBV	Chronic HBV	Carrier State
HBsAg	+	–	+	+
Anti-HBs	–	+	–	–
Anti-HBc	+	+	+	+
HBeAg	–	–	±	±
Anti-HBe	–	+	±	±

only supportive care is available to HEV-infected individuals.

The prognosis for patients with hepatitis depends on the virus responsible:

* HAV: Very few patients develop fulminate hepatitis, but the mortality rate among those who do is almost 50%.

* HBV: HBV persists as chronic hepatitis in 5–10% of infected adults and may be relatively benign or more severe. Chronic persistent hepatitis B is characterized by little cellular inflammation and usually resolves within a year. Chronic active hepatitis is more aggressive, progressing to cirrhosis and increasing the risk of hepatocellular carcinoma. Finally, certain individuals become "carriers," that is, they have little or no symptomatology during their course, but remain HBsAg positive and therefore capable of infecting others. Chronic infection and active carriage are more likely among infected children than adults. Among newborns infected via vertical transmission, the carrier rate may be as high as 90%.

* HDV: When HDV and HBV are acquired simultaneously, the recipient is at greater risk for more severe chronic hepatitis B and fulminate hepatitis associated with a higher mortality rate. When an individual is infected with HDV on top of pre-existing HBV, acute exacerbation and an accelerated course result. The risk of progressing to cirrhotic liver disease is increased when HDV is present.

* NANB: Half of those infected with HCV develop chronic hepatitis with an increased risk for cirrhosis. HEV does not appear to result in chronic hepatitis; however, it carries a high relative mortality (10–20%

in women infected in the third trimester; 1–2% in the normal population).

◆ KEY POINTS ◆

1. HAV and HEV are spread via fecal-oral transmission; HBV and HCV are transmitted through infected bodily fluids.

2. Children may not present with jaundice or scleral icterus.

3. Anti-HBc antibodies are present in the serum after HBsAg has been cleared but before anti-HBs appears.

4. Children are more likely than adults to develop chronic HBV infection and active carriage.

5. The HBV vaccine series is recommended for all children at birth, 1–2 months, and 6–18 months. Newborns born to HBsAg-positive mothers receive a high initial vaccine dose and immunoglobulin.

SYPHILIS

Pathogenesis

Syphilis is primarily a sexually transmitted disease in humans resulting from infection with the spirochete *Treponema pallidum.*

Epidemiology

Syphilis in the pediatric population may be acquired in utero (congenital syphilis) or transmitted sexually. The incidence of syphilis has increased sharply over the last several years. Coinfection with other sexually transmitted diseases is common.

Risk Factors

Risk factors for syphilis include being born to a woman with syphilis and unprotected sex with an infected partner.

Clinical Manifestations
History and Physical Examination
About 50% of infants born to untreated infected mothers show symptoms of congenital syphilis, including hepatomegaly, splenomegaly, mucocutaneous lesions,

jaundice, lymphadenopathy, and the characteristic "**snuffles.**"

After a variable incubation period (usually 2–4 weeks), infected individuals enter the **primary** stage of syphilis, characterized by the classic chancre at the inoculation site: a well-demarcated, firm, strangely painless genital ulcer with an indurated base. Because the lesion heals spontaneously within 2 weeks, patients with primary syphilis often do not seek medical attention.

Secondary syphilis is frequently manifested by widespread dermatologic involvement coinciding with dissemination of the spirochete throughout the body. Onset follows the primary stage directly, often while the chancre is still present. Although the typical rash is generalized (including the soles and palms), erythematous, and maculopapular, syphilis may appear with virtually any dermatologic condition imaginable. Some patients also develop systemic symptoms including fever, sore throat, mucosal ulcerations, malaise, and generalized lymphadenopathy; patchy alopecia and thinning of the lateral third of the eyebrow have also been associated with secondary syphilis.

Differential Diagnosis

Syphilis is one of the great masqueraders, a disease with a wide spectrum of presentation. The presence of the rash, if characteristic, greatly aids in diagnosis.

Diagnostic Evaluation

Chancre scrapings (and mucosal secretions in infected neonates) demonstrate rapid mobile organisms moving in a corkscrew-like motion under dark-field microscopy. Aspiration of enlarged lymph nodes may also yield the organism. Both the VDRL (developed by the Venereal Disease Research Laboratory of the U.S. Public Health Service) and the rapid plasma reagin (RPR) are excellent blood screening tests for high-risk populations, providing rapid, inexpensive, quantitative results. Both are nontreponemal tests for antibodies to a lipodal molecule rather than the organism itself. Both are considered highly sensitive when titers are high or when the test is complemented by historical or physical evidence of the disease. However, infectious mononucleosis, connective tissue disease, endocarditis, tuberculosis, and IV drug use may all result in false-positive VDRL and RPR results. By contrast, treponemal tests, such as the fluorescent treponemal antibody absorption (FTA-ABS) and microhemagglutination test, are much less likely to produce

false positives, unless Lyme disease is present. Although neither test is definitive, a positive screening VDRL or RPR coupled with a positive FTA-ABS in a newborn or sexually active adolescent is virtually diagnostic of untreated syphilis. Nontreponemal tests may become negative after treatment, whereas treponemal studies remain positive for life.

Treatment

Parenteral penicillin G remains the treatment of choice for any stage of infection and fully eradicates the organism from the body. Benzathine penicillin has been recommended when CNS infection is ruled out by the absence of nontreponemal antibody in the CSF.

Because **tertiary syphilis** develops several years after the primary exposure, it is rare in the pediatric population. Granulomatous lesions called gummas destroy surrounding tissues, especially in the skin, bone, heart, and CNS. Unfortunately, tertiary syphilis may occur without any previous primary or secondary manifestations.

◆ KEY POINTS ◆

1. Syphilis may be transmitted sexually or vertically.

2. Most patients are diagnosed in the secondary stage of syphilis, when widespread dermatologic manifestations are present.

3. Neonates present with "snuffles," hepatosplenomegaly, mucocutaneous lesions, jaundice, and lymphadenopathy.

4. The VDRL and RPR are excellent screening tests but may produce false positives.

5. Parenteral penicillin G is the treatment of choice unless CSF infection can be ruled out.

HERPES

Genital herpes usually results from infection with herpes simplex virus (HSV) type 2. Small mucosal tears or skin cracks are inoculated with the virus, usually during sexual activity. Genital herpes is one of the most common sexually acquired diseases, and the incidence has been rising for the last three decades.

Clinical Manifestations

History and Physical Examination

After a variable incubation period (5–14 days), genital burning and itching progress to vesicular, often pustular, lesions that burst to form painful, shallow ulcers that heal without scarring. Fever, pharyngitis, headache, and malaise may accompany the primary episode. After acquisition, the virus ascends peripheral nerves to dorsal root ganglia, where it may lie latent or spark periodic recurrences, which are generally milder. Asymptomatic shedding does occur.

Diagnostic Evaluation

Giant multinucleated cells with intranuclear inclusions are found in scrapings from the ulcerous base. HSV may be cultured from the active lesions or asymptomatic infected individuals in 1–4 days; rapid antigen testing is also available.

Treatment

Acyclovir (topical or parenteral) diminishes the length of both symptoms and shedding but does not eradicate the organism. It has limited efficacy in recurrent episodes. Continued prophylactic use of oral acyclovir has been shown to prevent or reduce the frequency of recurrences.

PELVIC INFLAMMATORY DISEASE

Pathogenesis

Pelvic inflammatory disease (PID) is a constellation of signs and symptoms related to the ascending spread of pathogenic organisms from the lower female genital tract to the cervix, endometrium, and fallopian tubes.

Epidemiology

Over 1 million cases of PID occur annually in the United States. The etiology is generally polymicrobial, with *Chlamydia trachomatis* and *Neisseria gonorrhoeae* being by far the most common isolates. Barrier contraceptive methods are protective. Any *N. gonorrhoeae* or genital Chlamydia infection in a prepubertal child is conclusive evidence of sexual abuse.

Risk Factors

Risk factors include age (adolescence), sexual intercourse with multiple partners, unprotected intercourse, and pre-existing mucosal sexually transmitted disease.

Clinical Manifestations

History, Physical Examination, and Diagnostic Evaluation

The clinical diagnosis of PID is based on the presence of three **required** and one of several **supporting** symptoms:

- Required: abdominal pain and tenderness, cervical motion tenderness, adnexal tenderness;

- Supporting: temperature greater than 38°C, leukocytosis, elevated ESR, greater than 20 white blood cells/hpf or intracellular gram-negative diplococci on endocervical smear, white blood cell count and/or bacteria on culdocentesis, inflammatory mass by ultrasound.

Differential Diagnosis

Other gynecologic conditions and intra-abdominal pathology are included in the differential diagnosis:

- Gynecologic: ectopic pregnancy, ruptured ovarian cyst, septic abortion;

- Nongynecologic: appendicitis, pyelonephritis, inflammatory bowel disease.

Treatment

Patients with PID should be treated for both *N. gonorrhoeae* and *C. trachomatis*. A single dose of a long-acting third-generation cephalosporin, such as ceftriaxone or cefixime, is sufficient to eradicate *N. gonorrhoeae*; ciprofloxacin, oflaxacin, or spectinomycin may be used as well. Azithromycin eradicates *C. trachomatis* in one large dose; alternatively, a 7-day course of doxycycline is appropriate. Significant infections require more extensive courses of therapy. Patients who are admitted to the hospital for severe vomiting or blood pressure instability should receive therapy with an IV antibiotic treatment, including both a third-generation cephalosporin and doxycycline, and preventive education.

Twenty percent of infected women will become infertile after a single episode of PID. Other gynecologic complications include increased risks for ectopic pregnancy, dyspareunia, chronic pelvic pain, and adhesions.

N. gonorrhoeae is capable of invading the bloodstream and thus any organ system. Joint involvement is most common. The **arthritis** may affect only one joint or may be polyarticular and migratory with associated tenosynovitis and skin lesions. Although *C. trachomatis* seldom causes systemic illness, untreated individuals may go on to develop **Reiter's syndrome** (a constellation of urethritis, conjunctivitis, and arthritis). **Fitz-Hugh-Curtis syndrome**, a form of perihepatitis, is a known complication of infection with either organism.

◆ KEY POINTS ◆

1. *C. trachomatis* and *N. gonorrhoeae* are the most common isolates in pelvic inflammatory disease.

2. The diagnosis of PID is clinical, based on history, physical examination, and supporting laboratory results.

3. A long-acting third-generation cephalosporin (for *N. gonorrhoeae*) and azithromycin (for *C. trachomatis*) constitute appropriate outpatient therapy in mild infections.

HUMAN PAPILLOMAVIRUS

Anogenital warts are caused by specific strains of human papillomavirus (HPV) distinct from those that produce the ordinary skin wart. HPV is the most common viral sexually transmitted disease, with triple the prevalence of herpes. Inoculation occurs wherever there is direct physical contact with infected mucosa, followed by a 2- to 3-month incubation period.

Clinical Manifestations

The recipient may remain asymptomatic (i.e., a carrier); more likely, he or she will develop several small flat or exophytic (condylomata acuminata) growths clustered in the anogenital area. In males, the warts may appear anywhere on the external genitalia and perianal areas. Women typically present with condylomata along the labia and vulva and subsequent spread to the perineum and rectum. Subclinical cervical involvement does occur and significantly increases a woman's risk of cervical cancer when HPV strains 16 or 18 are involved.

Treatment

No treatment fully eradicates the infection. Initial management consists of local chemical ablation therapy with podophyllin or 5-fluorouracil. Persistent cases may require electrocautery, laser therapy, or surgical excision. Relapses are the rule.

Yearly Pap smear screening for atypical or neoplastic epithelial cells has produced a substantial decline in the severity of cervical cancer at diagnosis. All sexually active women should receive gynecologic and Pap smear evaluations yearly.

VULVOVAGINAL INFECTIONS

Trichomoniasis, bacterial vaginosis, and candida vaginitis are all bothersome but relatively benign vaginal infections collectively manifested by changes in the amount and character of vaginal secretions.

Clinical Manifestations and Treatment

Trichomonas Vaginalis

Trichomoniasis results from sexually transmitted *T. vaginalis*, a mobile flagellated protozoan. Most infected individuals remain asymptomatic, although urethritis is not uncommon in men. Typical symptoms in women include a malodorous, frothy gray discharge and vaginal discomfort. Some patients also develop dysuria and vague lower abdominal pain. The cervix and vaginal mucosa may be either normal or visibly irritated and inflamed. A fresh wet prep of the vaginal fluid reveals polymorphonuclear leukocytes and the characteristic motile trichomonads. Metronidazole, in a single 2-gram oral dose, is the treatment of choice for patients and their partners.

Bacterial Vaginosis

Bacterial vaginosis, long thought to be harmless, is now known to increase the risks of PID, chorioamnionitis, and premature birth. Formerly known as Gardnerella vaginitis, this symptom complex is also caused by *Mycoplasma hominis* and certain anaerobes. The epidemiology of the disease suggests sexual transmission, although the data remain unclear. Infection is usually asymptomatic except for a thin, white, foul-smelling discharge that turns "fishy" in odor upon mixing with potassium hydroxide. The clinical diagnosis is based on patient history (much more common in sexually active females), the appearance and odor of discharge, a vaginal pH greater than 4.5, and characteristic "clue" cells on the wet prep (squamous epithelial cells with "smudged" borders due to adherent bacteria). Once again, a single dose of metronidazole effectively cures the infection. Concurrent antibiotic treatment of male partners seems to have no effect on recurrence rates.

Vaginal Candidiasis

Vulvovaginal candidiasis is not a sexually transmitted disease. All women are colonized with Candida; however, factors such as antibiotic use, pregnancy, diabetes, immunosuppression, and oral contraceptive use predispose women to candidal overgrowth (moniliasis). Signs and symptoms include a thick white vaginal discharge with vaginal itching and burning. Yeast and pseudohyphae are apparent on wet prep treated with potassium hydroxide. Over-the-counter local antifungal creams are safe and generally effective.

◆ KEY POINTS ◆

1. Trichomoniasis is diagnosed by demonstrating motile trichomonads on fresh wet prep and treated with metronidazole.

2. Bacterial vaginosis, often caused by *M. hominis*, should be suspected when the vaginal pH is greater than 4.5 and clue cells are seen on wet prep. Metronidazole is effective.

HIV AND ACQUIRED IMMUNODEFICIENCY SYNDROME

Pathogenesis

HIV is a retrovirus that infects and kills CD4 T-cells, resulting in progressive immunodeficiency. Pediatric cases account for 1–2% of the total in the United States. Most infections in children are acquired in utero or perinatally (80%); smaller numbers result from transfusions and sexual transmission. HIV causes a wide range of clinical manifestations in children, the most severe of which is acquired immunodeficiency syndrome (AIDS).

Epidemiology

About 30% of HIV(+) pregnant women pass the disease to their infants, regardless of the route of delivery. Many of these women are asymptomatic and may not realize that they are infected. Treatment of infected pregnant women with AZT during the third trimester, followed by treatment of the infant for the first 6 weeks of life, has been shown to reduce the vertical transmission rate to about 8%. IV drug abuse is reported in approximately 70% of infected women. The disease is more common in urban populations, lower socioeconomic classes, and racial minorities.

Risk Factors

Risk factors include birth to an HIV(+) mother, birth to a woman who uses IV drugs and shares needles, and birth to a woman with multiple sexual partners who does not practice safe sex. Other groups at risk include patients who received multiple units of blood products (i.e., hemophiliacs) before March 1985, victims of sexual abuse, and adolescents who engage in high-risk behavior.

Clinical Manifestations

History and Physical Examination

HIV may present in infants and children with any one or several of the following signs and symptoms: generalized lymphadenopathy, hepatomegaly, splenomegaly, failure to thrive, recurrent or chronic diarrhea, oral candidiasis, parotitis, and developmental delay. Respiratory manifestations include lymphoid interstitial pneumonia and *Pneumocystis carinii* pneumonia (PCP). Regression in developmental milestones, progressive encephalopathy, and CNS lymphoma are unfortunate neurologic complications. The heart and kidney may show signs of involvement as well. Recurrent, often severe bacterial and opportunistic (fungal, disseminated herpes or CMV, and *Mycobacterium avium*) infections are the hallmark of the acquired helper T-cell immunodeficiency.

PCP, CNS lymphoma, and lymphocytic interstitial pneumonitis (LIP) are considered AIDS-defining illness in the pediatric population; when any of these conditions occurs, the child is considered to have AIDS regardless of the absolute CD4 count.

Differential Diagnosis

HIV has become a "great masquerader" because of its variable presentation; the virus can affect any organ system and symptoms are often nonspecific.

Diagnostic Evaluation

Infants born to HIV(+) mothers are always seropositive for maternally derived IgG antibodies to the virus; thus, the enzyme immunoassays used for screening older populations are not helpful in children before 18 months of age. In these cases, direct testing for the virus, such as polymerase chain reaction p24 antigen detection, or viral culture should be used. Infants should be tested by age 1 month and again between age 4–6 months if initially negative. Children who are persistently negative for both viral and antibody at age 2 can be safely assumed to be disease free.

The most striking and consistent finding in children with HIV and AIDS is a falling or low CD4 cell count; this, coupled with a normal CD8-cell number, results in the characteristic decreased CD4/CD8 ratio. The CD4 count is age specific, so normal ranges must be checked. An absolute CD4 cell count of less than 200 (or ratio less than 20%) changes the diagnosis from HIV to AIDS.

Treatment

The standard of care consists of antiretroviral drugs such as AZT (zidovudine) and ddI (didanosine), protease inhibitors, and prophylaxis against PCP, the most common and serious opportunistic infection. Trimetho-prim-sulfa-methoxazole 3 consecutive days a week in twice-daily dosing is the treatment of choice. New pharmacologic therapies have drastically improved the chances of living longer with HIV.

◆ KEY POINTS ◆

1. Without treatment with AZT, about a third of infants born to HIV(+) mothers will themselves remain HIV(+). Treatment of both the mother and newborn with AZT has been shown to decrease this risk.

2. PCP, CNS lymphoma, and LIP are AIDS-defining illnesses in the pediatric population.

3. Following the CD4 count over time gives some indication of the progression of immunodeficiency.

VIRAL INFECTIONS OF CHILDHOOD

Viral infections are quite common in the infant and young child but decrease with age because of acquired immunity. Several viral illnesses that are frequently encountered in the pediatric population are not usually seen in adults. Most of these present with characteristic rashes that permit reliable clinical diagnosis. Live attenuated vaccines are routinely administered for measles, mumps, rubella, and chickenpox. Roseola and erythema infectiosum are generally benign in children. Table 12-6 describes the typical presentations and complications of these viral illnesses in children, which are discussed further in Chapter 5.

ROCKY MOUNTAIN SPOTTED FEVER

Pathogenesis

Rocky Mountain spotted fever (RMSF) is caused by *Rickettsia rickettsii*, the prototypic rickettsial infection. Rickettsia are neither viruses nor bacteria. They resemble bacteria in that they have a cell wall and divide by binary fission; however, they require intracellular cofactors for reproduction. Most rickettsia are tick-borne pathogens.

Epidemiology

RMSF occurs most often during the summer and fall months in tick-infested areas of the southeastern states and the Ohio River Valley.

Risk Factors

The most significant risk factor is residence in or travel to an endemic area.

Clinical Manifestations

History and Physical Examination

The tick bite is followed in 5–10 days by fever, headache, myalgias, and a characteristic rash that begins on the wrists and ankles and spreads proximally over several hours. Typically, the palms and soles are involved as well. The maculopapular lesions progress to form petechiae, corresponding to a widespread vasculitis of the small blood vessels.

Differential Diagnosis

Meningococcemia and measles (especially atypical measles) may be confused with RMSF. History of vaccination with a killed (rather than attenuated) measles vaccine points to atypical measles. Occasionally, differentiation between meningococcemia and RMSF requires culture; until the true diagnosis is known, the patient should be treated for both disorders. Ehrlichia is a rickettsial infection associated with neutropenia; however, no rash is present.

Diagnostic Evaluation

Although immunofluorescent staining of skin biopsies taken from rash sites may demonstrate the organism, there is no reliable diagnostic test that becomes positive

TABLE 12–6

Presentations and Complications of Childhood Viral Illnesses

Virus	Exanthem	Other Presenting Features	Known Complications
Measles (paramyxovirus)	Confluent, erythematous maculopapular rash that starts on the head and progresses caudally*	Coryza, cough, conjunctivitis, Koplik's spots (small red spots with bluish centers on the buccal mucosa early in disease)	Pneumonia, myocarditis/ pericarditis, thrombo-cytopenic purpura, encephali-tis; rare: subacute sclerosing panencephalitis (progressive degenerative CNS disease), death
Mumps (paramyxovirus)	Typically none	Swollen salivary, especially parotid, glands	Orchitis in pubescent males, hearing loss; rare: meningitis, encephalitis, death
Rubella (togavirus)	Similar to measles but does not coalesce	Cervical, suboccipital, posterior auricular lymphadenopathy	Rare: arthritis in older patients, aplastic crisis in patients with hemoglobinopathies, encephalitis, hydrops fetalis
Roseola (human herpes virus 6)	Similar to measles but starts on trunk and spreads toward extremities	Acute-onset high fever in a well-appearing child before the development of rash	Febrile seizures (no more common than with other febrile illnesses)
Erythema infectiosum (fifth disease; parvovirus)	"Slapped cheeks," followed by reticular erythematous maculopapular rash beginning on the arms and spreading to the trunk and legs	Virtually asymptomatic	Rare: arthritis in older patients, hemolytic anemia, encephalopathy
Chickenpox (varicella; herpes virus)	Pruritic teardrop-shaped vesicles that break and crust over, beginning on face or trunk and spreading to extremities	Scattered crops of lesions appear over several days, so lesions in different stages of development and resolution are observed simultaneously	Rare: pneumonia, secondary bacterial infection, meningoencephalitis, hepatitis, Reye syndrome

*Atypical measles, where the rash starts in the distal extremities and moves cephalad, was seen in individuals vaccinated with a killed virus during 1963–1967.

early enough in the course of the disease to guide therapy. Thus, the clinician must maintain a high suspicion for the disease.

Treatment

Treatment with tetracycline or chloramphenicol is beneficial when instituted within the first 5 days of symptoms but not thereafter. Untreated RMSF may lead to thrombocytopenia, coagulopathy, heart, lung, gastrointestinal, renal, and particularly devastating CNS complications.

LYME DISEASE

Pathogenesis

Lyme disease is a tick-borne illness resulting from infection with the spirochete *Borrelia burgdorferi*. The disease was first described 20 years ago in Lyme, Connecticut; isolation of the causative organism occurred several years later.

Epidemiology

Although cases have been reported across the country, most are clustered around the Northeast, Midwest, and West Coast, corresponding to the population distribution of the two known tick vectors, *Ixodes scapularis* and *pacificus*. The incidence of Lyme disease peaks during the summer and early fall. The typical patient is a child or adolescent who lives or plays in wooded areas; infants rarely contract the disease because they are less mobile.

Risk Factors

The most significant risk factor is living or vacationing in an endemic area.

Clinical Manifestations

History

Most patients do not recall a tick bite, which typically occurs 7–10 days before the onset of symptoms. A characteristic rash called **erythema migrans** (large erythematous macules progressing to annular lesions with central clearing) develops at the site of inoculation, often followed by multiple secondary lesions. The primary lesion may be quite large, averaging 16 cm in diameter. The rash lasts about 3 weeks, accompanied intermittently by fever, headache, stiff neck, malaise, and arthralgia.

Physical Examination

On resolution of the rash, about 50% of patients develop recurrent attacks of asymmetric mono- or oligoarthritis of the large joints, particularly the knee. Related neurologic conditions typically occur within 4 weeks of the tick bite; aseptic meningitis, cranial nerve palsies (especially CN VII), and peripheral radiculoneuropathy are the most common.

Differential Diagnosis

The differential diagnosis depends on the presentation. When the rash is atypical, it may be confused with erythema multiforme or erythema marginatum (seen in rheumatic fever). The differential of arthritis also includes JRA, reactive arthritis, and Reiter's syndrome. Conditions to consider when neurologic manifestations are present are those listed for aseptic meningitis earlier.

Diagnostic Evaluation

For the most part, Lyme disease is a clinical diagnosis, based on suggestive history and the characteristic rash on physical examination. The organism can be cultured from the skin lesions, blood, and other body fluids, but growth is slow and the yield is low. Antibody titers often remain negative for the first few weeks of the disease; in addition, antibodies to *B. burgdorferi* cross-react with other spirochetes, including syphilis, although VDRL and RPR remain negative in patients with Lyme disease.

Treatment

Treatment initiated early while the rash is present prevents later manifestations of the disease, including arthritis and neurologic sequelae.

Children older than 8 years should receive oral doxycycline for 14 days or until asymptomatic, whichever is longer. Younger children are treated with amoxicillin. Severe or persistent arthritis, cardiac, or CNS disease warrant parenteral therapy with high-dose penicillin G or ceftriaxone. Symptoms that do not remit within 30 days of therapy are unlikely to be due to residual infection.

Cardiac involvement, in the form of myocarditis or conduction abnormalities, is an uncommon but potentially serious complication. About 10% of patients with arthritis progress to severe erosive disease. Additional neurologic complications include encephalitis and Guillian-Barré syndrome.

◆ KEY POINTS ◆

1. The Northeast, Midwest, and West Coast have the highest incidence of Lyme disease.

2. Most patients do not recall a tick bite.

3. The typical rash, erythema migrans, may be accompanied by fever, headache, and arthralgia.

4. Fifty percent of patients experience recurrent bouts of arthritis.

5. Lyme disease is treated with amoxicillin in children younger than 8 years, and with doxycycline in older children.

THE IMMUNOCOMPROMISED HOST

The specific congenital immunodeficiency syndromes are discussed in detail in Chapter 11. Immunocompromise also may be an acquired state, either because of specific immunosuppression therapy for another condition or as a result of AIDS. The spectrum of pathogens capable of causing significant disease is much greater in these children, and progression is potentially accelerated. Regardless of the etiology, the presence of fever or other signs of infection in the immunocompromised patient constitutes a medical emergency.

Any organism known to cause serious illness in the normal host is a potential pathogen in deficient hosts as well. Diseases that may be benign and self-limited in the immunocompetent patient may be poorly tolerated by a less prepared immune system. Finally, some infections that occur in immunocompromised individuals are not known to cause disease in intact hosts (Table 12–7).

Clinical Manifestations

Diagnosis of a source of infection in immunocompromised patients is often hampered by their inability to produce a normal defensive response, such as inflammation. The history should be probed for recent exposures, previous pathogens, and known colonization. A meticulous physical examination is essential. Even if a source is found, pan-cultures should be obtained to define the extent of invasion, including blood, urine, throat, and occasionally CSF and bronchoalveolar lavage aspirate cultures in addition to a chest x-ray. Further imaging may be required to rule out abscess formation.

Treatment

Aggressive antimicrobial therapy is the mainstay of treatment. Febrile but well-appearing patients should be treated with a broad-spectrum antibiotic with antipseudomonal efficacy such as ceftazidime. An aminoglycoside should be added in patients who seem ill. Any indication of indwelling line infections warrants coverage with vancomycin. Vesicular lesions resembling herpes or varicella are treated with parenteral antiviral agents such as acyclovir. In the patient who does not improve after a week of broad-spectrum therapy or who has known or suspected invasive fungal disease, an antifungal agent such as amphotericin should be considered.

TABLE 12–7

Infective Organisms Associated with Host Immunodeficiency Syndromes

Immunodeficiency	Associated Pathogens
Neutropenia (acute leukemia, chemotherapy, bone marrow suppression)	Bacterial sepsis, pneumonia, sinusitis, cellulitis, urinary tract infection, *Candida, Aspergillus, Listeria, Cryptococcus*
Cellular immune deficiency (Hodgkin's disease, irradiation, steroids, cyclosporine, HIV)	PCP, *Toxoplasma/Cryptosporidium*, disseminated herpes/ CMV, invasive *Candida*
Humoral immune deficiency (splenectomy, chronic lymphocytic leukemia)	Encapsulated bacterial sepsis, pneumonia, meningitis, osteomyelitis (*S. pneumoniae* and *H. influenzae*)

13 Neonatology

PRENATAL TERATOGENS

Drugs

Fetal Alcohol Syndrome

Alcohol is the most common teratogen to which fetuses are exposed. Maternal alcohol ingestion results in a spectrum of effects in the neonate, ranging from mild reduction in cerebral function to classic fetal alcohol syndrome. The amount of alcohol consumed by the mother appears to correlate with the degree to which the fetus is affected. With the exception of the Native American population, fetal alcohol syndrome occurs in 1:1000 newborns. The incidence is much higher in the Native American population because of a higher incidence of alcoholism. The syndrome affects 40% of the offspring of women who drink more than four to six drinks per day while pregnant.

Clinical Manifestations

Features of fetal alcohol syndrome include microcephaly and mental retardation, intrauterine growth retardation, facial dysmorphisms, and renal and cardiac defects. Facial anomalies include midfacial hypoplasia, micrognathia, a flattened philtrum, short palpebral fissures, and a thin vermillion border.

Treatment

Treatment is aimed at minimizing morbidity and mortality from renal and cardiac defects and assisting the child with mental retardation with activities of daily living.

Cocaine

Cocaine causes maternal hypertension and placental vasoconstriction with diminished uterine blood flow and fetal hypoxia. These effects are associated with an increased rate of spontaneous abortion, placental abruption, fetal distress, meconium staining, preterm birth, intrauterine growth retardation, and low Apgar scores at birth.

Clinical Manifestations

Maternal cocaine use is associated with congenital anomalies, intracranial hemorrhage, and necrotizing enterocolitis. Congenital anomalies include cardiac defects, skull abnormalities, and genitourinary malformations. Cocaine-exposed infants have demonstrated abnormalities in respiratory control and have an increased risk of sudden infant death syndrome (SIDS). Long-term defects include attention and concentration deficits and an increased incidence of learning disabilities.

Infants may undergo withdrawal with irritability, increased tremulousness, state lability, inability to console, and poor feeding in the first few days of life. These symptoms are thought to be caused by cocaine blocking the reuptake of neurotransmitters at presynaptic terminals in the central nervous system.

Treatment

During the perinatal period, therapy is supportive. At school age, many of these children have special learning needs.

◆ KEY POINTS ◆

1. Cocaine causes placental insufficiency and fetal hypoxia, which is associated with an increased rate of spontaneous abortion, placental abruption, fetal distress, meconium staining, preterm birth, intrauterine growth retardation, and low Apgar scores at birth.

2. Infants may undergo withdrawal with irritability, increased tremulousness, state lability, inability to console, and poor feeding in the first few days of life.

3. Long-term defects include attention and concentration deficits and an increased incidence of learning disabilities.

Heroin and Methadone

Heroin and methadone are the two narcotics to which fetuses are most commonly exposed. About 10,000 heroin-dependent babies are born in the United States each year, and 5000 narcotic-addicted pregnant women are in methadone treatment programs. Methadone maintenance is prescribed for pregnant women to decrease the stress that unreliable heroin dosing and uncontrolled withdrawal in utero places on the fetus.

Clinical Manifestations

Heroin is not associated with congenital anomalies, but maternal use causes intrauterine growth retardation, an increased risk of SIDS, and infant narcotic withdrawal syndrome. It is unclear whether the abnormalities of fetal growth seen with narcotic abuse are due to the direct effect of the drug or to other environmental factors, such as the poor maternal nutrition that is often associated with maternal narcotic use.

Methadone is also not linked to congenital defects, but maternal use results in microcephaly, an increased risk of SIDS, and narcotic withdrawal syndrome. Other sequelae include abnormal interactive behavior, hyperactivity, emotional lability, and poor motor control.

Narcotic withdrawal syndrome, which generally occurs within the first 4 days of life, is characterized by irritability, poor sleeping, a high-pitched cry, diarrhea, sweating, sneezing, seizures, poor feeding, and poor weight gain. The risk of neonatal withdrawal is higher with methadone (75%) than with heroine (50%). Methadone withdrawal tends to be later in onset and more protracted, sometimes lasting as long as 1 month. Symptoms appear soon after birth, improve, and then may recur at 2–4 weeks.

Other diagnoses that may be considered in the child with narcotic withdrawal symptoms include hypoglycemia, hypocalcemia, hypomagnesemia, sepsis, meningitis, and infectious diarrhea.

Treatment

The treatment for narcotic withdrawal syndrome attempts to minimize irritability, emesis, and diarrhea and to maximize sleep between feedings. Approximately 40% of infants who have symptoms of narcotic withdrawal syndrome may be treated without medication. Symptomatic care includes holding, rocking, and swaddling the infant and providing the neonate with frequent small feedings of a hypercaloric formula.

Infants of narcotic-abusing mothers should never be given naloxone in the delivery room, because it may precipitate seizures. Narcotic withdrawal symptoms, unresponsive to nonmedicinal care, can be mitigated with tincture of opium, phenobarbital, and paregoric. Paregoric contains 0.4% opium.

◆ KEY POINTS ◆

1. Heroin and methadone are the two narcotics to which fetuses are most commonly exposed.

2. Heroin and methadone are not associated with congenital anomalies, but maternal use does cause intrauterine growth retardation and infant narcotic withdrawal syndrome.

3. Infants of narcotic-abusing mothers should never be given naloxone in the delivery room, because it may precipitate seizures.

4. Narcotic withdrawal symptoms, unresponsive to nonmedicinal care, can be mitigated with tincture of opium, phenobarbital, or paregoric.

Congenital Infections

Toxoplasmosis

Toxoplasmosis is caused by *Toxoplasma gondii*, an intracellular protozoan parasite found in mammals and birds. Members of the cat family are the definitive host. Cats acquire the infection when they are exposed to feces from an infected cat or when they feed on infected animals, such as mice or uncooked household meats. The parasite replicates in the feline small intestine, and 2–4 weeks after primary infection, the cat excretes toxoplasma oocytes in its stool. The feline stool is the vector by which fecal-oral transmission occurs.

There are approximately 3000 cases of congenital infection annually in the United States. Only primary infection of the mother, which is usually asymptomatic, results in congenital infection. Among the women infected with toxoplasmosis, 50% will give birth to an infected neonate. The later in pregnancy the infection occurs, the more likely it is that the fetus will be infected but the less severe the illness.

Clinical Manifestations

Infants infected early in pregnancy suffer from intrauterine meningoencephalitis and present with microcephaly, hydrocephalus, microphthalmia, chorioretinitis, intracranial calcifications, and seizures. These infants may also appear septic and have jaundice, hepatosplenomegaly, purpura, petechiae, a maculopapular rash, and generalized lymphadenopathy. Of infants who are asymptomatic at birth, 70% will suffer long-term sequelae, which may include mental retardation, learning disabilities, and/or chorioretinitis. Ocular disease can become reactivated years after the initial infection, both in healthy and immunocompromised individuals, resulting in impaired vision or blindness.

In toxoplasmosis, serologic tests are the primary means of definitive diagnosis. A fourfold rise in antibody titer or seroconversion from negative to positive indicates the presence of infection. In congenital infection, diagnosis is complicated by the presence of maternally derived transplacental antibody. If the maternal antibody status is negative, the diagnosis of congenital toxoplasmosis is excluded. If maternal and neonate levels are positive, serial studies of antitoxoplasma IgG for several months are necessary to distinguish transplacental antibody from congenital infection. Levels of transplacental antibody fall over the first year of life, whereas antibody levels from congenital infection remain stable or rise. A computed tomography (CT) scan of the head may reveal cerebral calcifications in the central nervous system. The parasite may be visualized in the cerebrospinal fluid by cytocentrifuge preparations or by growth in inoculated infant mice. Typical histopathology or cysts may be identified in biopsy specimens of involved lung, brain, bone marrow, or lymph node.

Treatment

Treatment includes both pyrimethamine and sulfadiazine, which act synergistically against Toxoplasma. These antibiotics inhibit folic acid, so they are used in conjunction with folic acid. Corticosteroids are reserved for infants with severe central nervous system or ocular infection.

Ingestion of well-cooked meat and the avoidance of cats and soil in areas where cats defecate reduce the risk of toxoplasmosis in pregnant or immunocompromised patients. Cat litter should be disposed of daily, because toxoplasma oocytes are not infectious for the first 48 hours after passage.

◆ KEY POINTS ◆

1. Toxoplasmosis is caused by *Toxoplasma gondii*, an intracellular protozoan parasite whose definitive host is the cat family.

2. Only primary infection of the mother, who is usually asymptomatic, results in congenital infection. Among the women infected with toxoplasmosis, 50% give birth to an infected neonate.

3. Infants infected early in pregnancy suffer from intrauterine meningoencephalitis and present with microcephaly, hydrocephalus, microphthalmia, chorioretinitis, intracranial calcifications, and seizures.

4. Of infants who are asymptomatic at birth, 70% suffer from long-term sequelae, which may include mental retardation, learning disabilities, and/or chorioretinitis.

Syphilis

Syphilis results from transplacental transmission of *Treponema pallidum*. Syphilis in the untreated pregnant woman may be transmitted to the fetus at any time, but fetal transfer is most common during the first year of maternal infection.

Clinical Manifestations

Neonates symptomatic at birth exhibit nonimmune hydrops with anemia, thrombocytopenia, leukopenia, pneumonitis, hepatitis, and osteochondritis. Common manifestations described in the first year of life include intermittent fever, osteitis and osteochondritis, hepatosplenomegaly, lymphadenopathy, mucocutaneous lesions (maculopapular rash on the trunk, palms, and soles), persistent rhinitis (snuffles), jaundice, and failure to thrive. Laboratory tests may reveal hyperbilirubinemia, a transaminitis, thrombocytopenia, leukocytosis, and a Coombs'-negative hemolytic anemia.

The late sequelae of congenital syphilis appear many years after birth. They include multiple bone signs (frontal bossing, saber shins), Hutchinson teeth, mulberry molars, a saddle-nose deformity, rhagades, juvenile paresis, juvenile tabes, interstitial keratitis, VIIIth nerve deafness, and Clutton joints (painless joint effusions). These manifestations are rare in the modern era in which penicillin therapy is used to treat congenital syphilis.

Diagnostic Evaluation

Laboratory tests on the mother include rapid plasma reagin (RPR) titers and fluorescent-treponemal antibody absorption test (FTA-ABS) test. These tests are done at the first antenatal visit and during the third trimester. The infant should also have RPR and FTA-ABS titers performed. The IgM-FTA-ABS test is the most specific for fetal infection. Radiographs of the long bones may provide evidence of metaphyseal demineralization or periosteal new bone formation. Dark-field examination of nasal discharge may reveal treponemes. Cerebrospinal fluid should also be sent for RPR and FTA-ABS.

Treatment

Pregnant women with primary, secondary, or latent syphilis are treated with three doses of benzathine penicillin G administered intramuscularly 7 days apart or with procaine penicillin G intramuscularly once each day for 15 days.

If the infant's serologic test results are negative and no symptoms are present, no treatment is necessary. If the serologic test results are positive and the infant is symptomatic, treat the infant. The asymptomatic infant is treated when:

- the infant's titer is three to four times higher than the mother's
- the FTA is 3 to 4+
- the mother has been inadequately treated or untreated
- the mother is unreliable and follow-up is doubtful
- the mother's infection was treated with a drug other than penicillin
- the mother has had a recent sexual exposure to an infected person
- the mother was treated in the last month of pregnancy
- the mother has HIV and has been treated for syphilis with less than a neurosyphilis regimen

If the infant has a positive RPR or FTA, or both, and the history and clinical findings make infection unlikely, it is safe to await the IgM report and repeat the RPR and FTA titers. Any significant rise in titer or any clinical signs require treatment. If the antibodies are transferred maternal antibodies, the infant should have a falling titer and should be negative by 4 months. Treat the infant if the serology is not negative by 6 months of age. For infants with no evidence of central nervous system disease, give penicillin G intravenously for 10–14 days. Infants with central nervous system infection are treated with aqueous crystalline penicillin G or aqueous procaine penicillin for 3 weeks. For infants at low risk for infection for whom follow-up is doubtful, treatment with one intramuscular dose of benzathine penicillin G can be given.

◆ KEY POINTS ◆

1. Syphilis results from transplacental transmission of *T. pallidum*.

2. Common manifestations described in the first year of life include intermittent fever, osteitis and osteochondritis, hepatosplenomegaly, lymphadenopathy, maculopapular rash on the trunk, palms, and soles, persistent rhinitis (snuffles), jaundice, and failure to thrive.

3. Pregnant women with primary, secondary, or latent syphilis are treated with three doses of

benzathine penicillin G intramuscularly 7 days apart or with procaine penicillin G intramuscularly once each day for 15 days.

4. Since the treatment of syphilis is so benign, an infant should be treated if the diagnosis is considered.

Rubella

Rubella virus is an RNA togavirus. Congenital rubella syndrome has become rare, reflecting the success of rubella vaccine.

Clinical Manifestations

Anomalies occur primarily as a result of infection in the first trimester and include heart defects (patent ductus arteriosus, peripheral pulmonic stenosis, ventricular septal defect, atrial septal defects), ophthalmologic defects (cataracts, microphthalmia, glaucoma, and chorioretinitis), auditory deficits (sensorineural deafness), and neurologic malformations (microcephaly, meningoencephalitis, and mental retardation). Sequelae of chronic infection are growth retardation, radiolucent bone disease, hepatosplenomegaly, thrombocytopenia, jaundice, and purple skin lesions ("blueberry muffin spots"). Mild forms of the disease can be associated with few or no obvious clinical manifestations at birth.

Rubella virus is most consistently isolated from nasopharyngeal secretions. Infants with congenital rubella may excrete virus for months to years. Specific rubella IgM antibody or persistence of rubella IgG in the infant is diagnostic.

Treatment

There is no specific antiviral chemotherapy. Appropriate treatment of specific defects is recommended. Infants with congenital rubella are considered contagious until they are 1 year of age, unless they have negative nasopharyngeal and urine cultures after 3 months of age. Rubella vaccination should not be given during pregnancy, but inadvertent administration carries a very low risk of fetal disease.

◆ KEY POINTS ◆

1. Congenital rubella syndrome has become rare, reflecting the success of rubella vaccine.

Anomalies occur primarily as a result of infection in the first trimester and include heart defects, ophthalmologic defects, auditory deficits, and neurologic malformations.

2. Sequelae of chronic infection are growth retardation, radiolucent bone disease, hepatosplenomegaly, thrombocytopenia, jaundice, and purple skin lesions ("blueberry muffin spots").

3. Rubella vaccination should not be given during pregnancy, but inadvertent administration carries a very low risk of fetal disease.

Cytomegalovirus

Neonatal cytomegalovirus (CMV) infection is common, occurring in 2% of all newborns. Higher rates are found in lower socioeconomic populations. Approximately 50% of fetuses become infected during primary maternal CMV infection, and of those infected, only 5% have residual neurologic deficits. Infection occurs in about 10% of pregnancies with recurrent or reactivated maternal infection. Significant neurologic sequelae in offspring have been documented only after primary maternal infection. CMV infection acquired during the birth process, via breast feeding, or from blood or platelet transfusions has not been associated with neurologic deficits.

Clinical Manifestations

Most cases are clinically inapparent. Late sequelae such as nerve deafness and learning disabilities may develop in 10% of clinically inapparent infections. The syndrome of congenital CMV (cytomegalic inclusion disease) is uncommon, occurring in 5% of infants with CMV infection, and includes intrauterine growth retardation, purpura, jaundice, hepatosplenomegaly, microcephaly, intracerebral calcifications, and chorioretinitis. The calcifications tend to be periventricular. A more common symptomatic presentation is intrauterine growth retardation, hepatosplenomegaly, and persistent jaundice. The incubation time for CMV is approximately 3 weeks, after which time the infant may show signs of hepatosplenomegaly, lymphadenopathy, pneumonia, and atypical lymphocytes. Severe interstitial pneumonia in premature infants can be fatal.

Infants with congenital infection excrete CMV in high titers in urine and saliva, making virus detection easy and rapid. Specific CMV IgM may be detected in cord or infant serum. IgG CMV antibody in persistent high titers at 6–12 weeks of age supports diagnosis. Additional diagnostic studies to determine extent of infection include a CT scan of the head for detection of intracranial calcifications, liver function tests, long-bone films, and chest radiograph to detect pneumonitis.

Treatment
No specific, effective antiviral therapy exists. Gancyclovir efficacy in neonatal disease has not yet been demonstrated. Newborn hearing screening by brainstem auditory evoked responses is important. Repeated evaluations are imperative because postnatal development of deafness can occur. Neonates with congenital CMV shed the virus for some time, and pregnant health care workers should not take care of infected infants.

◆ KEY POINTS ◆

1. Cytomegalovirus infection is common in the newborn, occurring in 2% of all neonates.

2. Approximately 50% of fetuses become infected during primary maternal CMV infection, and of those infected, only 5% have residual neurologic deficits.

3. Infection occurs in about 10% of pregnancies with recurrent or reactivated maternal infection.

4. Most cases are clinically inapparent. Late sequelae such as nerve deafness and learning disabilities may develop in 10% of clinically inapparent infections.

5. Cytomegalic inclusion disease occurs in 5% of infants with CMV infection and includes intrauterine growth retardation, purpura, jaundice, hepatosplenomegaly, microcephaly, intracerebral calcifications, and chorioretinitis.

Herpes Simplex Virus
There are two serotypes of herpes simplex virus (HSV), HSV-1 and HSV-2. They both cause severe disease and mortality in the neonate. About 120 cases of neonatal HSV infection occur each year in the United States. HSV-1 usually infects the face and skin above the waist, whereas HSV-2 is generally found on the genitalia and skin below the waist in adults. Most neonatal HSV infection is caused by HSV-2. The child is infected as he or she moves through the vaginal canal. Inoculation occurs at skin trauma sites (fetal scalp monitor). Transplacental infection resulting in spontaneous abortion or congenital malformations is rare.

Clinical Manifestations
Asymptomatic infection is rare. HSV manifests itself in three discrete constellations of symptoms. Infants may have disseminated infection involving the liver and other organs (occasionally including the central nervous system), may have localized central nervous system disease, or may have localized infection of the skin, eye, and mouth (SEM disease). Ocular manifestations include conjunctivitis, keratitis, and chorioretinitis. In about one-third of the patients, SEM involvement is the first indication of the infection. Disseminated disease may present with findings described for sepsis. Localized central nervous system disease may present with fever, lethargy, poor feeding, hypoglycemia, disseminated intravascular coagulation (DIC), and irritability, followed by intractable focal or generalized seizures. Vesicular lesions, when present, are an important clue to the diagnosis. Symptoms can occur shortly after birth or as late as 4–6 weeks after birth. Disseminated disease usually occurs during the first 2 weeks of life, whereas localized central nervous system disease or SEM disease typically occurs during the second or third week.

Neonatal herpetic infections are frequently severe, with a high mortality rate and significant neurologic and/or ocular impairment of survivors, particularly in those not treated with antiviral therapy.

HSV is cultured easily, and viral detection generally takes 1–3 days. Cultures are obtained from skin vesicles, the mouth or nasopharynx, conjunctiva, urine, blood, rectum, and cerebrospinal fluid. Tzanck smear of vesicle scrapings reveals multinucleated giant cells, which are characteristic of herpes viruses. Newer diagnostic techniques, such as direct fluorescent antibody staining of vesicle scrapings or enzyme immunoassay detection of HSV antigens, offer more rapid diagnosis. The most sensitive technique for detecting genital HSV infection in the symptomatic pregnant woman or the symptomatic mother is culture of the labia and cervical lesions or, in the absence of lesions, culture of the cervix and vulva. In infants with suspected HSV encephalitis, a brain biopsy is useful before antiviral therapy is initiated, because it may identify other treatable causes of encephalitis or confirm a diagnosis of HSV infection. Consider diagnosis in the infant who does not respond to antibiotic treatment for sepsis.

Treatment

Antiviral therapy with acyclovir is indicated for all forms of neonatal herpes infection, because even initially localized disease may disseminate with devastating effects.

◆ KEY POINTS ◆

1. Most neonatal herpes simplex virus infection is caused by HSV-2.

2. Asymptomatic infection is rare. HSV manifests itself in three discrete constellations of symptoms. Infants may have disseminated infection involving the liver and other organs (occasionally including the central nervous system), may have localized central nervous system disease, or may have SEM disease.

3. Antiviral therapy with acyclovir is indicated for all forms of neonatal herpes infection, because even initially localized disease may disseminate with devastating effects.

Varicella-Zoster Virus

Of women of childbearing age, 90% are immune to varicella-zoster virus (VZV), and as a result, congenital and neonatal varicella are rare. Only 25% of the infants of infected nonimmune mothers develop congenital or neonatal chickenpox.

Clinical Manifestations

Maternal VZV infection in the first and second trimesters has been associated with cutaneous scars, abnormalities of digits or a limb, defects of the eye, central nervous system anomalies, and low birth weight in newborns. Newborns who acquire VZV infection during the perinatal period have a clinical illness varying from mild to fatal. The acquisition of transplacental antibody determines the outcome in infants.

Diagnosis of congenital varicella is made by specific IgM VZV antibody or the persistence of significant titers of VZV IgG. Neonatal varicella is characterized by diffusely disseminated skin lesions in varying states, from macules, papules, vesicles, and pustules, to crusts. Recovery of varicella-zoster virus by culture, immunofluorescent staining of scrapings, or Tzanck smear of vesicle base scrapings is diagnostic. Tzanck smear shows multinucleated giant cells in both varicella-zoster and herpes simplex infections. Direct immunofluorescence of cells differentiates VZV infection from HSV.

Treatment

Infants with congenital varicella do not require isolation. Infants with neonatal varicella should be placed in strict isolation for at least 7 days after onset of rash. Infants born to mothers with onset of varicella 5 or more days before delivery require no specific treatment other than isolation, if kept in the hospital. Infants whose mothers have onset of varicella within 5 days before delivery, or within 2 days after delivery, should receive varicella-zoster immune globulin (VZIG) preferably at birth or within 96 hours. Infants with acute varicella in the first week of life should receive acyclovir for 10 days. Infants who are exposed to VZV infection as a result of contact with nursery personnel should have their immune status verified and, if susceptible, should receive VZIG within 96 hours of exposure.

◆ KEY POINT ◆

1. Ninety percent of women of childbearing age are immune to varicella-zoster virus, and only 25% of the infants of infected nonimmune mothers develop congenital or neonatal chickenpox.

Human Immunodeficiency Virus

Human immunodeficiency virus (HIV), an RNA retrovirus, causes acquired immunodeficiency syndrome (AIDS). HIV is particularly tropic for CD4 containing cells, which include helper T cells, monocytes, and macrophages. It is the invasion and destruction of these cells that causes immunodeficiency. Vertical transmission from mother to infant accounts for most HIV-infected infants in the world. Eighty percent of pediatric AIDS results from maternal transmission. Most remaining cases are transfusion related. Predisposing factors include mothers with HIV secondary to drug abuse or sexual contact with a male with HIV. Because of the relatively high prevalence of intravenous drug abuse in inner-city areas, it is not surprising that most pediatric AIDS cases occur in racial minority groups. Fifty percent of pediatric AIDS cases due to maternal transmission occur in African American infants and 25% in Hispanics. It is unclear whether fetal infection occurs during the prenatal or perinatal period. Transmission rates of HIV from the mother to the neonate have been estimated at 30–50%. Postnatal transmission of HIV from infected mothers to infants by means of breast milk is well documented.

Clinical Manifestations

Infected infants are generally asymptomatic at birth. Within the first month, they develop persistent thrush, lymphadenopathy, and hepatosplenomegaly. During the first year of life, common symptoms include recurrent refractory infections, severe intractable diarrhea, and failure to thrive. It is estimated that 20% of infants with congenital/perinatal HIV infection die within the first year of life, and 60% of HIV-infected children have severe symptomatic disease by 18 months of age.

Diagnosis of HIV at birth is difficult because of maternal antibodies. If HIV is suspected and the mother is seronegative for HIV, the risk in the child is minimal. The only way a mother could be infected but serologically negative is if she is in her "window period." The diagnosis of HIV infection in children born to mothers who are HIV seropositive can be established before the onset of symptoms in several ways. Methods of HIV diagnosis include p24 viral antigen detection in peripheral blood, polymerase chain reaction to detect viral nucleic acid in peripheral blood, and ELISA for the detection of IgM or IgA antibodies to HIV, demonstrating rising HIV antibody titers. Detection of HIV antigen in an infant's lymphocytes is strongly indicative of disease.

Treatment

Treatment involves nutritional support, *Pneumocystis carinii* prophylaxis, antiviral therapy, and anti-infective agents for specific infections. Studies have shown that maternal azidothymidine (AZT) therapy in the last trimester can dramatically reduce transmission of HIV to the fetus to approximately 10%. Neonates who have HIV-positive mothers or mothers in whom HIV is suspected are treated with AZT to try to eradicate any HIV that may be present in the child's system. Studies are ongoing as to the effectiveness of AZT in the neonate at risk for HIV. The mother with HIV should not breast feed her infant because HIV can be passed through the breast milk.

◆ KEY POINTS ◆

1. Eighty percent of pediatric AIDS results from maternal vertical transmission. Most remaining cases are transfusion related.

2. It is unclear whether fetal infection occurs during the prenatal or perinatal period. Postnatal transmission of HIV from infected mothers to infants by means of breast milk is well documented.

3. Transmission rates of HIV from the mother to the neonate have been estimated at 30%.

4. Studies have shown that maternal AZT therapy in the last trimester can dramatically reduce transmission of HIV to the fetus to approximately 10%.

5. Within the first month, infected infants develop persistent thrush, lymphadenopathy, and hepatosplenomegaly. During the first year of life, common symptoms include recurrent refractory infections, severe intractable diarrhea, and failure to thrive.

6. Treatment involves nutritional support, *P. carinii* prophylaxis, antiviral therapy, and anti-infective agents for specific infections.

7. Table 13–1 provides a summary of congenital infections.

INTRAUTERINE PROBLEMS

Small for Gestational Age

Pathogenesis and Clinical Manifestations

Infants who are small for gestational age have birth weights below the 10th percentile for gestational age. Two broad categories of intrauterine growth retardation have been described: early onset and late onset. One-third of low-birth-weight neonates—infants weighing less than 2500 g—are small for gestational age.

Early onset, or symmetrical, intrauterine growth retardation is thought to result from an insult that begins before 28 weeks' gestation. The early insult results in a neonate whose head circumference and height are proportionately small sized and whose weight-for-height ratio is normal. This pattern is seen in infants whose mothers have severe vascular disease with hypertension and renal disease or in infants with congenital malformations or chromosomal abnormalities.

Late onset, or asymmetrical, intrauterine growth retardation starts after 28 weeks' gestation. In this form, there is sparing of the head circumference. These infants have a normal, or close to normal, head circumference with a reduced height and weight. The weight-for-height

TABLE 13-1

Congenital Infections

Agent	Maternal Epidemiology	Neonatal Features
Toxoplasma gondii	Heterophil-negative mononucleosis Exposure to cats or raw meat or immunosuppression High-risk exposure at 10–24 weeks' gestation	Hydrocephalus, abnormal spinal fluid, intracranial calcifications, chorioretinitis, jaundice, hepatosplenomegaly, fever Many infants asymptomatic at birth Treatment: pyrimethamine plus sulfadiazine
Rubella virus	Unimmunized seronegative mother; fever ± rash Detectable defects with infection: by 8 wks, 85% 9–12 wks, 50% 13–20 wks, 16% Virus may be present in infant throat for 1 yr Prevention: vaccine	Intrauterine growth retardation, microcephaly, microphthalmia, cataracts, glaucoma, "salt and pepper" chorioretinitis, hepatosplenomegaly, jaundice, PDA, deafness, blueberry muffin rash, anemia, thrombocytopenia, leukopenia, metaphyseal lucencies, B- and T-cell deficiency Infant may be asymptomatic at birth
Cytomegalovirus	Sexually transmitted disease: primary genital infection may be asymptomatic Heterophil-negative mononucleosis; infant may have viruria for 1–6 yrs	Sepsis, intrauterine growth retardation, chorioretinitis, microcephaly, periventricular calcifications, blueberry muffin rash, anemia, thrombocytopenia, neutropenia, hepatosplenomegaly, jaundice, deafness, pneumonia Many asymptomatic at birth Prevention: CMV-negative blood products
Herpes simplex type II virus	Sexually transmitted disease (STD): primary genital infection may be asymptomatic; intrauterine infection rare, acquisition at time of birth more common	Intrauterine infection: chorioretinitis, skin lesions, microcephaly Postnatal: encephalitis, localized or disseminated disease, skin vesicles, keratoconjunctivitis Treatment: acyclovir
Varicella-zoster virus	Intrauterine infection with chickenpox during first trimester Infant develops severe neonatal varicella with maternal illness 5 days before or 2 days after delivery	Microphthalmia, cataracts, chorioretinitis, cutaneous and bony aplasia/hypoplasia/atrophy, cutaneous scars Zoster as in older child Prevention of neonatal condition: VZIG Treatment of ill neonate: acyclovir
Treponema pallidum syphilis	Sexually transmitted disease Maternal primary asymptomatic: painless "hidden" chancre Penicillin, not erythromycin, prevents fetal infection	Presentation at birth as nonimmune hydrops, prematurity, anemia, neutropenia, thrombocytopenia, pneumonia, hepatosplenomegaly Late neonatal as snuffles (rhinitis), rash, hepatosplenomegaly, condylomata lata, metaphysitis, cerebrospinal fluid pleocytosis, keratitis, periosteal new bone, lymphocytosis, hepatitis Late onset—teeth, eye, bone, skin, CNS, ear Treatment: penicillin
Human immunodeficiency virus (HIV)	AIDS; most mothers are asymptomatic and HIV positive; high-risk history: prostitute, drug abuse, married to bisexual, or hemophiliac	AIDS symptoms develop between 3 and 6 mo of age in 25–40%; failure to thrive, recurrent infection, hepatosplenomegaly, neurologic abnormalities Management: intravenous immunoglobulin, trimethoprim-sulfamethoxazole, AZT

BCG, bacillus Calmette-Guerin; CNS, central nervous system; HBIG, hepatitis B immune globulin; INH, isoniazid; PPD, purified protein derivative; TB, tuberculosis; VZIG, varicella-zoster immune globulin. Reprinted with permission from Behrman RE, Kliegman RM, eds. Essentials of pediatrics, 2nd ed. Philadelphia: WB Saunders, 1994:207.

ratio is low, and the infant appears long and emaciated. In this type of intrauterine growth retardation, the neonate initially has a normal growth trajectory and follows a normal centile line and then "falls off" the curve late in gestation.

Risk Factors

Growth retardation may result from fetal causes such as multiple gestation, congenital viral infections, chromosomal abnormalities (trisomies or Turner's syndrome), and congenital malformation syndromes, especially of the central nervous system. Placental causes include chorionic villitis, chronic abruptio placentae, twin-twin transfusion, placental tumor, and placental insufficiency secondary to maternal vascular disease. Maternal causes of intrauterine growth retardation include severe peripheral vascular diseases that reduce uterine blood flow, such as chronic hypertension, diabetic vasculopathy, preeclampsia, sickle cell anemia, and cardiac and renal disease. Other maternal causes include reduced nutritional intake, alcohol or drug abuse, cigarette smoking, and uterine anomalies or uterine constraint. Uterine constraint is noted in mothers of small stature and reduced weight gain during pregnancy.

Treatment

Infants who are small for gestational age have a high risk for intrauterine fetal death. Therefore, prenatal management includes identification, evaluation, and monitoring. The standard intrauterine growth retardation workup includes a review of obstetric causes, examination for identifiable syndromes, and laboratory evaluation for congenital infection. Antepartum fetal monitoring with serial ultrasound, biophysical profile, nonstress test, and oxytocin challenge test are often used. Doppler examination of placental flow is used to determine if uteroplacental insufficiency exists. If early delivery is being contemplated, determination of pulmonary maturity is critical. Early delivery is necessary when it is determined that the risk to the fetus of staying in utero is greater than the risk of premature delivery. Fetal lung maturity can be accelerated, if necessary, by steroid administration. If there is placental insufficiency, the fetus may not tolerate labor and may require delivery by cesarean section.

Delivery should take place at a center with a high-risk nursery, because infants who are very small for gestational age are at risk for life-threatening problems at the time of delivery and often require care in a newborn intensive care unit. The delivery team should be prepared for perinatal asphyxia and/or depression, meconium aspiration, and hypothermia. Examination of the placenta after delivery for pathology consistent with congenital infection or infarction may be helpful in determining the cause of the intrauterine growth retardation. The newborn who is small for gestational age should be monitored for hypothermia, hypoglycemia, hypocalcemia, hyponatremia, polycythemia, pulmonary hemorrhage, and persistent pulmonary hypertension. Leukopenia, neutropenia, and thrombocytopenia may be seen in infants born to hypertensive mothers. Commencing feedings as soon as possible minimizes hypoglycemia.

Large for Gestational Age

Infants whose weight is greater than 2 standard deviations above the mean or above the 90th percentile are defined as large for gestational age. Neonates at risk for being large for gestational age are those of diabetic mothers (class A, B, or C); postmature infants; and neonates with transposition of the great vessels, erythroblastosis fetalis, or Beckwith-Wiedemann syndrome. Most infants who are large for gestational age are constitutionally large, from large parents or from a family with a predilection for large infants. After birth, the infant should be evaluated for the disorders described above, as well as birth trauma, which occurs often in large for gestational age neonates. The blood sugar of the large for gestational age infant should be monitored and the child fed early, because large for gestational age infants who have diabetic mothers or who suffer from Beckwith-Wiedemann syndrome or erythroblastosis fetalis are prone to hypoglycemia. Obtaining a hematocrit after birth is advisable, because large for gestational age neonates have an increased incidence of polycythemia.

Macrosomic neonates have birth weights greater than 4000 g. All macrosomic infants are large for gestational age, but not all large for gestational age neonates are macrosomic. Macrosomic infants have an increased risk of shoulder dystocia and other birth trauma. Conditions such as maternal diabetes mellitus and obesity and postmaturity are associated with an increased incidence of macrosomia.

1. Infants who are small for gestational age have birth weights below the 10th percentile for gestational age.

2. Two broad categories of intrauterine growth retardation have been described: early onset and late onset.

3. Intrauterine growth retardation may result from fetal, placental, or maternal causes.

4. Infants who are small for gestational age have a high risk for intrauterine fetal death; therefore, prenatal management includes identification, evaluation, and monitoring.

5. Infants whose weight is greater than 2 standard deviations above the mean or above the 90th percentile are defined as large for gestational age.

6. Neonates at risk for being large for gestational age are those of diabetic mothers (class A, B, or C); postmature infants; and neonates with transposition of the great vessels, erythroblastosis fetalis, or Beckwith-Wiedemann syndrome.

7. Most infants who are large for gestational age are constitutionally large, from large parents or from a family with predilection for large infants.

8. Macrosomic neonates have birth weights greater than 4000 g. All macrosomic infants are large for gestational age, but not all large for gestational age neonates are macrosomic.

9. Birth trauma occurs often in large for gestational age and macrosomic neonates.

Polyhydramnios

Polyhydramnios is defined as an amniotic fluid volume greater than 2 liters and occurs in 1 in 1000 births. Acute polyhydramnios is associated with premature labor, maternal discomfort, and respiratory compromise. More often, polyhydramnios is chronic and is seen with gestational diabetes, immune or nonimmune hydrops fetalis, abdominal wall defects (omphalocele and gastroschisis), multiple gestations, trisomy 18 or 21, neural tube defects, and certain congenital anomalies of the gastrointestinal tract. Anencephaly and meningomyelocele are neural tube defects that impair fetal swallowing, whereas esophageal or duodenal atresia, diaphragmatic hernia, and cleft palate interfere with swallowing and gastrointestinal fluid dynamics.

Oligohydramnios

Oligohydramnios is associated with intrauterine growth retardation, amniotic fluid leak, postmaturity, and congenital anomalies of the fetal kidneys. Bilateral renal agenesis results in a specific deformation syndrome known as Potter's syndrome. The syndrome is characterized by club feet, compressed facies, low-set ears, scaphoid abdomen, and diminished chest wall size that is accompanied by pulmonary hypoplasia and pneumothorax. Uterine compression in the absence of amniotic fluid retards lung growth, and patients with this condition expire of respiratory failure rather than of renal insufficiency. Oligohydramnios increases the risk of fetal distress during labor. This risk may be reduced by normal saline amnioinfusion during labor.

1. Chronic polyhydramnios is seen with gestational diabetes, immune or nonimmune hydrops fetalis, abdominal wall defects (omphalocele and gastroschisis), multiple gestations, trisomy 18 or 21, neural tube defects, and certain congenital anomalies of the gastrointestinal tract.

2. Oligohydramnios is associated with intrauterine growth retardation, amniotic fluid leak, postmaturity, and congenital anomalies of the fetal kidneys.

BIRTH

Apgar Scoring

The Apgar examination, a rapid scoring system based on physiologic responses to the birth process, is an excellent method for assessing the need for neonatal resuscitation. The Apgar scoring system is shown in Table 13–2. At intervals of 1 and 5 minutes after birth, each of the five physiologic parameters is observed or elicited by a qualified examiner. Full-term infants with a normal cardiopulmonary adaptation will score 8–9 at 1 and 5 minutes. By definition, an Apgar score of 0–3 indicates either cardiorespiratory arrest or a condition resulting from

TABLE 13–2

Apgar Score

Signs	Points		
	0	1	2
Heart rate	0	<100/min	>100/min
Respiration	None	Weak cry	Vigorous cry
Muscle tone	None	Some extremity flexion	Arms, legs well flexed
Reflex irritability	None	Some motion	Cry, withdrawal
Color of body	Blue	Pink body, blue extremities	Pink all over

Reprinted with permission from Behrman RE, Kliegman RM, eds. Essentials of pediatrics, 2nd ed. Philadelphia: WB Saunders, 1994:169.

severe bradycardia, hypoventilation, and/or central nervous system depression. Most low Apgar scores are due to difficulty in establishing adequate ventilation and not to primary cardiac pathology.

Birth Trauma

Cephalohematoma

A cephalohematoma is a traumatic subperiosteal hemorrhage usually involving the parietal bone that does not cross suture lines. The scalp hematoma is characteristically firm without discoloration of overlying skin and may not become apparent until hours to days after delivery. Predisposing factors include large head size, prolonged labor, vacuum extraction, and forceps delivery. Underlying linear skull fracture is found in 1–5% of cases, but routine skull radiographs are not indicated. If focal neurologic signs are apparent, a CT scan of the head is the most prudent radiologic examination. Spontaneous resolution occurs over several weeks. Two percent of the hematomas will organize, calcify, and form a central depression in the calvarium. Cephalohematoma in the premature infant results in an indirect hyperbilirubinemia that may require phototherapy.

Caput Succedaneum

A caput succedaneum is a diffuse, edematous, and often dark swelling of the soft tissue of the scalp that extends across the midline and suture lines and is commonly found in infants who are delivered vaginally in the customary occiput-anterior position. Pressure induced from overriding parietal and frontal bones against their respective sutures causes the molding associated with the caput. The soft-tissue edema of the eyelids and face found in infants delivered in the occiput posterior position is an equivalent phenomenon. The caput is commonly seen after prolonged labor in both full-term and premature infants.

Fractured Clavicle

A fractured clavicle is found in 2–3% of vaginal deliveries, and the right clavicle is two times more likely to fracture than the left. This predilection is due to the fact that the right shoulder must move beneath the pubic symphysis during normal delivery and may get entrapped. Predisposing factors include large size, shoulder dystocia, and traumatic delivery. Findings include swelling and fullness over the fracture site, crepitus, and decreased arm movement. Of neonates with clavicular fracture, 80% have no symptoms and only minimal physical findings. It is often diagnosed when a callous is detected at 3–6 weeks. Radiograph is not indicated. No specific treatment is necessary. The parents should be advised to avoid tension on the affected arm.

Erb-Duchenne Palsy

Injury to nerves of the brachial plexus results from excessive traction on the neck, producing paresis. The Erb-Duchenne palsy results from stretching of the fifth and sixth cervical nerves. The infant cannot abduct the arm at the shoulder, externally rotate the arm, or supinate the forearm. When there is an absent morrow reflex in the right arm and the right hand grasp is intact, an Erb-Duchenne palsy should be suspected. Treatment of brachial plexus injuries is supportive and includes positioning to avoid contractures. Active and passive range of motion exercises may be of benefit. If the nerve deficit persists, nerve grafting may be beneficial.

◆ KEY POINTS ◆

1. A cephalohematoma is a traumatic subperiosteal hemorrhage usually involving the parietal bone that does not cross suture lines.

2. A caput succedaneum is a diffuse, edematous, and often dark swelling of the soft tissue of the

scalp that extends across the midline and suture lines.

3. The right clavicle is two times more likely to fracture than the left, because the right shoulder must move beneath the pubic symphysis during normal delivery and may be entrapped. Predisposing factors include large size, shoulder dystocia, and traumatic delivery.

4. Injury to nerves of the brachial plexus results from excessive traction on the neck, producing paresis. The Erb-Duchenne palsy results from stretching of the fifth and sixth cervical nerves and should be suspected when there is an absent morrow reflex of the right arm and an intact right hand grasp.

Neonatal Mortality

The late fetal and early neonatal period is the time of life exhibiting the highest mortality rate of any age interval. The perinatal mortality rate refers to fetal deaths occurring from the 20th week of gestation until the 7th day after birth. Intrauterine fetal death represents 40–50% of the perinatal mortality rate. Such infants, defined as stillborn, are born without a heart rate and are apneic, limp, pale, and cyanotic. Many have evidence of maceration, pale peeling skin, corneal opacification, and very soft cranial contents.

The neonatal mortality rate includes infants dying between birth and 28 days of life. Modern neonatal intensive care has delayed the mortality of many newborn infants who have life-threatening diseases, so that they survive beyond the neonatal period only to die of their original diseases or of complications of therapy sometime after the 28th day of life. This delayed mortality occurs during the postneonatal period, which begins after 28 days of life and extends to the end of the first year of life.

The infant mortality rate includes both the neonatal and the postneonatal periods and is expressed as the number of deaths per 1000 live births. The infant mortality rate in the United States declined in 1990 to 9.1 per 1000 live births. The rate for African American infants in 1990 was a distressing 18.6 per 1000 live births. This mortality rate was one of the highest among Western industrialized nations. The major causes of perinatal and neonatal mortality are shown in Table 13–3.

◆ KEY POINT ◆

1. The 1990 infant mortality rate in the United States was one of the worst among Western industrialized nations, and African American infants were twice as likely to die during the first year of life.

TABLE 13–3

Major Causes of Perinatal and Neonatal Mortality

Fetus	Preterm Infant	Full-term Infant
Placental insufficiency	Respiratory distress syndrome/ bronchopulmonary dysplasia	Congenital anomalies
Intrauterine infection		Birth asphyxia
Severe congenital malformations	Severe immaturity	Infection
Umbilical cord accident	Intraventricular hemorrhage	Meconium aspiration pneumonia
Abruptio placentae	Congenital anomalies	Persistent fetal circulation
Hydrops fetalis	Infection	
	Necrotizing enterocolitis	

Reprinted with permission from Behrman RE, Kliegman RM, eds. Essentials of pediatrics, 2nd ed. Philadelphia: WB Saunders, 1994:158.

PREMATURITY

Low-birth-weight (LBW) infants, defined as those infants having birth weights of less than 2500 g, represent a disproportionately large component of the neonatal and infant mortality rates. Although these infants make up only 7% of all births, they account for two-thirds of all neonatal deaths. Very-low-birth-weight (VLBW) infants, weighing less than 1500 g at birth, represent only about 1% of all births but account for 50% of neonatal deaths. In comparison with infants weighing 2500 g or more, LBW infants are 40 times more likely to die in the neonatal period, and VLBW infants have a 200-fold higher risk of neonatal death.

In contrast to the improvements in the infant mortality rate, there has not been an improvement in the rate of LBW births. This is one reason that the infant mortality rate of the United States is the worst of the large, modern, industrialized countries. If birth-weight mortality rates are calculated, the United States has one of the highest survival rates, but because of the large number of LBW infants, the total infant mortality rate remains high.

LBW is caused by premature birth or intrauterine growth retardation. Maternal factors associated with having an LBW infant include previous LBW birth, low socioeconomic status, low level of educational achievement, lack of prenatal care, maternal age less than 16 years or greater than 35 years, a short time interval between pregnancies, unmarried status, low prepregnancy weight (less than 100 lb) and/or poor weight gain during pregnancy (less than 10 lb), and African American race. Maternal use of cigarettes, alcohol, and/or illicit drug abuse is also associated with having an LBW infant.

In addition to sociodemographic variables associated with LBW, there are specific medical causes of preterm birth, which are listed in Table 13–4. Many of these factors interrelate with poverty and thus may be the final common pathway by which a disadvantaged extrauterine environment becomes expressed as preterm labor.

◆ KEY POINTS ◆

1. Low-birth-weight infants make up 7% of all births but account for two-thirds of all neonatal deaths.
2. Very-low-birth-weight infants represent 1% of all births but account for 50% of neonatal deaths.

TABLE 13–4

Medical Causes of Preterm Birth

Fetal
  Fetal distress
  Multiple gestation
  Erythroblastosis
  Nonimmune hydrops fetalis
  Congenital anomalies
Placental
  Placenta previa
  Abruptio placentae
Uterine
  Bicornuate uterus
  Incompetent cervix (premature dilation)
Maternal
  Pre-eclampsia
  Chronic medical illness (e.g., cyanotic heart disease)
  Infection (e.g., group B streptococcus, herpes simplex, syphilis, chorioamnionitis)
  Drug abuse (e.g., cocaine)
Other
  Premature rupture of membranes
  Hydramnios
  Iatrogenic (e.g., cesarean section)
  Trauma/surgery
  Diethylstilbestrol exposure during mother's gestation

Reprinted with permission from Behrman RE, Kliegman RM, eds. Essentials of pediatrics, 2nd ed. Philadelphia: WB Saunders, 1994:158.

3. In comparison with infants weighing 2500 g or more, LBW infants are 40 times more likely to die in the neonatal period, and VLBW infants have a 200-fold higher risk of neonatal death.

4. One reason that the infant mortality rate of the United States is so high is that the rate of LBW births is high. If birth-weight mortality rates are calculated, the United States has one of the highest survival rates, but because of the large number of LBW infants, the infant mortality rate remains high.

5. LBW is caused by premature birth or intrauterine growth retardation.

POSTMATURITY

Pathogenesis

Infants whose gestation exceeds 42 weeks are considered postmature and are at risk for the syndrome of postmaturity. The cause of prolonged pregnancy is not known in most cases. Known associations include anencephaly, trisomy 18, and Seckel's syndrome (bird-headed dwarfism). Anencephaly results in prolonged gestation because an intact fetal pituitary-adrenal axis is involved in the initiation of labor. There is a correlation between neonatal mortality in the postmature infant and low placental weights.

Clinical Manifestations

The syndrome of postmaturity is characterized by normal length and head circumference but decreased weight. Infants with this syndrome are distinct from small for gestational age infants in that they were doing well until they went beyond 42 weeks' gestation and became nutritionally deprived from placental insufficiency. Common symptoms include dry, cracked, peeling, loose, and wrinkled skin and a malnourished appearance with decreased amounts of subcutaneous tissues. Conditions that occur more frequently in postmature infants include meconium aspiration and perinatal depression at birth, persistent pulmonary hypertension of the newborn (PPHN), hypoglycemia, hypocalcemia, and polycythemia.

Treatment

Prepartum treatment includes estimation of true gestational age using the date from the last menstrual period and ultrasound and monitoring closely the well-being of the fetus by ultrasound, biophysical profile, and nonstress tests. Intrapartum treatment involves preparation for perinatal depression and meconium aspiration. Early feeding to reduce the risk of hypoglycemia and evaluation for the conditions noted above encompass postpartum treatment.

◆ KEY POINTS ◆

1. Infants whose gestation exceeds 42 weeks are considered postmature and are at risk for the syndrome of postmaturity.

2. The syndrome of postmaturity is characterized

by normal length and head circumference but decreased weight. Infants with this syndrome are distinct from small for gestational age infants in that they were doing well until they went beyond 42 weeks' gestation and became nutritionally deprived from placental insufficiency.

3. The cause of prolonged pregnancy is not known in most cases. Known associations include anencephaly, trisomy 18, and Seckel's syndrome (bird-headed dwarfism).

4. Conditions that occur more frequently in postmature infants include meconium aspiration and perinatal depression at birth, persistent pulmonary hypertension of the newborn, hypoglycemia, hypocalcemia, and polycythemia.

NEONATAL DERMATOLOGIC PROBLEMS

Erythema Toxicum Neonatorum

The rash of erythema toxicum consists of evanescent papules, vesicles, and pustules on an erythematous base that usually occurs on the trunk but sometimes appears on the face and extremities. Rash onset usually occurs 24–72 hours after birth but may be seen at birth. Gram stain of vesicular contents reveals sheets of eosinophils. The lesions resolve over 3–5 days without therapy. Fifty percent of full-term babies have erythema toxicum. This figure decreases as the gestational age decreases. Infants less than 1500 g or 30 weeks' gestation rarely exhibit erythema toxicum. The cause of the rash is unknown.

Milia

Milia is characterized by pearly white or pale yellow epidermal cysts found on the nose, chin, and forehead. The benign lesions exfoliate and disappear within the first few weeks of life. No treatment is necessary.

Seborrheic Dermatitis

Seborrhea is characterized by erythematous, dry, scaling, crusty lesions. It occurs in areas rich in sebaceous glands (face, scalp, perineum, postauricular and intertriginous areas). Affected areas are sharply demarcated from uninvolved skin. Seborrhea appears between 2 and 10 weeks and is commonly called "cradle cap" when it appears on the scalp. It may be confused with eczema, although eczema is much more pruritic.

For severe cradle cap, apply baby oil to the scalp for 15 minutes and then wash with a dandruff shampoo. For seborrhea of the diaper area, 1% hydrocortisone cream can be used. If candidal superinfection appears, nystatin ointment is recommended.

Mongolian Spots

Mongolian spots are transient dark blue–black pigmented macules seen over the lower back and buttocks in 90% of African American, Indian, and Asian infants. The spots are never elevated or palpable and result from infiltration of melanocytes deep into the dermis. The hyperpigmented areas fade as the child ages and are probably the result of decreasing transparency of the overlying skin rather than a true disappearance of the lesion. They present no known long-term problems.

◆ KEY POINTS ◆

1. Erythema toxicum neonatorum occurs 24–72 hours after birth and resolves 3–5 days later without therapy. Gram stain of vesicular contents reveals sheets of eosinophils. Fifty percent of full-term babies have erythema toxicum.

2. Milia is epidermal cysts of the nose, chin, and forehead.

3. Seborrheic dermatitis appears between 2 and 10 weeks of life and is commonly called "cradle cap" when it appears on the scalp.

4. Mongolian spots are benign, transient, dark blue–black pigmented macules seen over the lower back and buttocks in 90% of African American, Indian, and Asian infants.

NEONATAL INFECTION

Neonatal Sepsis

Neonatal sepsis is generally divided into early- and late-onset sepsis and nosocomial sepsis. Early-onset sepsis, occurring from birth to 7 days, is an overwhelming multiorgan system disease manifested by respiratory failure, shock, meningitis (30%), DIC, acute tubular necrosis, and symmetric peripheral gangrene. Profound neutropenia, hypoxia, and hypotension may be refractory to treatment with broad-spectrum antibiotics, mechanical ventilation, and vasopressors such as dopamine and dobutamine. Early-onset sepsis is due to infection by the bacteria in the mother's genitourinary tract. These organisms include group B streptococcus, *Escherichia coli*, *Klebsiella*, and *Listeria monocytogenes*. Predisposing factors for early-onset sepsis include vaginal colonization with group B streptococcus, prolonged rupture of the membranes (more than 24 hours), chorioamnionitis, maternal fever or leukocytosis, fetal tachycardia, and preterm birth. African American race and male sex are unexplained additional risk factors for neonatal sepsis.

Late-onset sepsis, occurring between days 7 and 28, usually occurs in the healthy full-term infant who was discharged in good health from the normal newborn nursery. Bacteremia leads to hematogenous seeding that results in focal infections such as meningitis (75%), osteomyelitis (group B streptococcus and *Staphylococcus aureus*), arthritis (*Neisseria gonorrhoeae*, *S. aureus*, *Candida albicans*, gram-negative bacteremia), and urinary tract infection (gram-negative bacteremia).

Nosocomially acquired sepsis (7 days to discharge) occurs predominantly among premature infants in the newborn intensive care unit, because many of these infants have been colonized with the multidrug-resistant bacteria indigenous to the newborn intensive care unit. Frequent treatment with broad-spectrum antibiotics for sepsis and the presence of central venous indwelling catheters, endotracheal tubes, umbilical vessel catheters, and electronic monitoring devices increase the risk for such serious bacterial infection. The most common pathogens are *S. aureus*, *Staphylococcus epidermidis*, gram-negative bacteria, and *Candida albicans*.

Group B streptococcus is the most common cause of neonatal sepsis and classically occurs with a bimodal distribution, early and late. Group B streptococcus is recovered from the vaginal cultures of approximately 25% of American women at the time of delivery. Of their infants, 25% have positive skin or nasopharyngeal cultures, or both. For every 100 colonized infants, one will become ill. Early-onset sepsis with group B streptococcus presents as noted above in the early-onset sepsis discussion and may progress rapidly to shock and death. If the disease presents within a few hours of birth, the mortality is high, irrespective of therapy. Late-onset sepsis with group B streptococcus usually presents as meningitis at 2–4 weeks of age. Diagnosis is confirmed by positive blood or cerebrospinal fluid culture. The latex agglutination test may be helpful in cases in which the mother was treated with antibiotics before delivery so that neonatal cultures are unreliable. Treatment for group B streptococcus sepsis and meningitis was delineated earlier.

Clinical Manifestations

Most infants with early-onset sepsis present with non-specific cardiorespiratory signs such as grunting, tachypnea, and cyanosis at birth. As a result, it is often hard to differentiate sepsis from respiratory distress syndrome (RDS) in the initial stages of early-onset sepsis in the preterm neonate. Because of this difficulty, most premature infants with RDS receive broad-spectrum antibiotics. Common signs and symptoms of early sepsis include poor feeding, emesis, lethargy, apnea, ileus, and abdominal distention. Petechiae and purpura are noted when DIC is present, and seizures often occur with meningitis. Meningitis is present in 25% of neonates with early-onset sepsis.

Infants with suspected early-onset sepsis should have blood and cerebrospinal fluid sent for culture. Cerebrospinal fluid should also be tested for Gram stain, cell count and differential, and protein and glucose levels. Normal newborn infants generally have an elevated cerebrospinal fluid protein content (normal mean 90 mg/dL) and an increased cerebrospinal fluid white blood cell count; a count of up to 25 WBC/mm^3 in the cerebrospinal fluid is considered normal in the newborn infant. Bacterial antigen can be detected by latex agglutination studies on cerebrospinal fluid. Serial complete blood counts are performed to identify neutropenia, an increased number of immature neutrophils (bands), and thrombocytopenia. A white blood cell count less than 5000, a total neutrophil count under 1000, and a ratio of bands to neutrophils of greater than 20% all correlate with an increased risk of bacterial infection. The chest radiograph is used to determine the presence of pneumonia. Arterial blood gases should be monitored to detect hypoxemia and metabolic acidosis that may be due to hypoxia or shock, or both. Blood pressure, urine output, central venous pressure, and peripheral perfusion are monitored to determine the need to treat septic shock with fluids and vasopressor agents.

The clinical manifestations of late-onset sepsis include lethargy, poor feeding, hypotonia, apathy, seizures, bulging fontanelle, fever, and direct hyperbilirubinemia. The evaluation of infants with late-onset sepsis is similar to that for those with early-onset sepsis, with special attention given to the examination of the bones, the laboratory examination, and urine culture obtained by sterile suprapubic aspiration or urethral catheterization. Late-onset sepsis may be due to the same pathogens as early-onset sepsis, but those infants presenting late in the neonatal period also may have infections caused by pathogens usually found in the older infant (*Haemophilus influenzae, Streptococcus pneumoniae, Neisseria meningitidis*).

The initial clinical manifestations of nosocomial infection in the premature neonate may be subtle and include apnea and bradycardia, temperature instability, abdominal distention, and poor feeding as early signs. In the later stages, there may be severe metabolic acidosis, shock, DIC, and respiratory failure.

Treatment

A combination of ampicillin and gentamicin for 10–14 days is effective treatment against most organisms responsible for early sepsis. Once an organism is identified and antibiotic sensitivities are determined, antibiotic therapy may be tailored to treat the infecting organism. If meningitis is present, the treatment is extended to 21 days, or 14 days after a negative cerebrospinal fluid culture. Persistently positive spinal fluid culture is common with neonatal meningitis caused by gram-negative organisms, even with appropriate antibiotic treatment, and may be present for 2–3 days after antibiotic therapy. If gram-negative meningitis is present, treating with an aminoglycoside and a third-generation cephalosporin is recommended, because systemically administered gentamicin has poor penetration into the cerebrospinal fluid, leading to inadequate bactericidal levels. As a result, cefotaxime and amikacin (for synergy) are used to treat *E. coli* or *Klebsiella* meningitis. Sepsis resulting from group B streptococcus meningitis and Listeria are treated with ampicillin and gentamicin (for synergy).

The treatment for late-onset neonatal sepsis and meningitis is the same as that for early-onset sepsis. Because of the increased rate of resistance of *H. influenzae* to ampicillin, some centers recommended that late sepsis be treated with ampicillin and cefotaxime for 10–14 days. Cefotaxime is effective therapy against *H. influenzae*, *S. pneumoniae*, and *N. meningitidis* sepsis and meningitis.

The treatment of nosocomially acquired sepsis depends on the indigenous microbiologic flora of the particular hospital and their antibiotic sensitivities. Because *S. aureus*, which is sometimes methicillin-resistant, and *S. epidermidis*, which is usually methicillin-resistant, and gram-negative pathogens are the most common bacterial nosocomial infections, a combination of vancomycin and gentamicin is used. Persistent signs of infection despite antibacterial treatment suggests candidal sepsis, which is treated with amphotericin B.

◆ KEY POINTS ◆

1. Neonatal sepsis is generally divided into early and late-onset sepsis and nosocomial sepsis.

2. Early-onset sepsis (birth to 7 days of life) is due to infection by the bacteria in the mother's genitourinary tract, which includes group B streptococcus, *E. coli*, Klebsiella, and *Listeria monocytogenes*.

3. Late-onset sepsis (7–28 days of life) may be caused by the same pathogens as early-onset sepsis, but those infants presenting late in the neonatal period also may have infections caused by pathogens usually found in the older infant (*H. influenzae*, *S. pneumoniae*, *N. meningitidis*).

4. Nosocomially acquired sepsis (7 days of life to discharge) occurs predominantly among premature infants in the newborn intensive care unit and is most commonly caused by *S. aureus*, *S. epidermidis*, gram-negative bacteria, and *C. albicans*.

5. Group B streptococcus is the most common cause of neonatal sepsis and classically occurs with a bimodal distribution, early and late.

Chlamydia

Chlamydia trachomatis is transmitted from the genital tract of infected mothers to their newborn infants. Acquisition occurs in about 50% of infants born vaginally to infected mothers. Of the infants who acquire *C. trachomatis*, the risk of conjunctivitis is 25–50%, and the risk of pneumonia is 5–20%. The nasopharynx is the most commonly infected anatomic site. A symptomatic infection of the conjunctiva, pharynx, rectum, or vagina of the infant can persist for more than 2 years. Prevalence among pregnant women varies between 6 and 12% in most populations.

Clinical Manifestations

In neonatal chlamydial conjunctivitis, congestion, edema, and discharge develop a few days to several weeks after birth and last for 1–2 weeks.

Pneumonia in young infants caused by *C. trachomatis* is usually an afebrile illness that presents between 3 and 19 weeks after birth. A repetitive, staccato cough and tachypnea are characteristic but not always present. Rales can be present, whereas wheezing is rare. Hyperinflation on chest radiograph is prominent. Untreated disease can linger or recur.

Treatment

Erythromycin and silver nitrate, the recommended topical antibiotics to prevent gonococcal ophthalmia, will not reliably prevent neonatal chlamydial conjunctivitis or extraocular infection. Chlamydial conjunctivitis and pneumonia in young infants are treated with oral erythromycin for 14 days. Topical treatment of conjunctivitis is ineffective and unnecessary. The efficacy of erythromycin therapy is only 80%, so a second course is sometimes required. A specific diagnosis of *C. trachomatis* infection in the infant should prompt treatment of the mother and evaluation of her sex partner.

◆ KEY POINTS ◆

1. Acquisition occurs in about 50% of infants born vaginally to infected mothers. Of the infants who acquire *C. trachomatis*, the risk of conjunctivitis is 25–50% and the risk of pneumonia is 5–20%.

2. In neonatal chlamydial conjunctivitis, congestion, edema, and discharge develop a few days to several weeks after birth and last for 1–2 weeks.

3. Pneumonia in young infants caused by *C. trachomatis* is usually an afebrile illness that presents between 3 and 19 weeks after birth. A repetitive, staccato cough and tachypnea are characteristic but not always present.

NEONATAL RESPIRATORY DISEASE

Respiratory Distress Syndrome

Pathogenesis

RDS, or hyaline membrane disease, is the most common cause of respiratory failure in newborn infants. It occurs in premature infants who are born with immature lungs. In the average child, lung maturity occurs at 32 weeks' gestation, when surfactant, a phospholipid that lines the alveoli, is produced by the type II pneumocytes. RDS is caused by deficiency of surfactant. The major function of surfactant is to decrease alveolar surface tension and increase lung compliance. Surfactant prevents alveolar collapse at the end of expiration and allows for opening of the alveoli at low intrathoracic pressures. Because of the lack of surfactant, the lungs have poor compliance, which results in progressive atelectasis, intrapulmonary shunting, hypoxemia, and cyanosis. Because of the forces generated by mechanical ventilation, oxygen exposure, and alveolar capillary leak, a hyaline membrane forms. The membrane lines the alveoli and is composed of protein and sloughed alveolar epithelium. The incidence of RDS increases with decreasing gestational age.

The production of surfactant is accelerated by maternal steroid administration, prolonged rupture of fetal membranes, maternal narcotic addiction, pre-eclampsia, chronic fetal stress due to placental insufficiency, maternal hyperthyroidism, and theophylline. The production of surfactant is delayed by combined fetal hyperglycemia and hyperinsulinemia, as occurs in maternal diabetes.

Clinical Manifestations

Affected premature infants characteristically present with tachypnea, grunting, nasal flaring, chest wall retractions, and cyanosis in the first 3 hours of life. There is poor air entry on auscultation. The amniotic fluid lecithin-sphingomyelin ratio is less than 2.0, and phosphatidylglycerol is absent in the amniotic fluid. Diagnosis is confirmed by chest radiograph that reveals a uniform reticulonodular or ground-glass pattern and air bronchograms that are consistent with diffuse atelectasis.

The natural course is a progressive worsening over the first 24–48 hours of life. After the initial insult to the airway lining, the epithelium is repopulated with type II alveolar cells, which produce surfactant. Subsequently, there is increased production and release of surfactant, so that there is a sufficient quantity in the air spaces by 72 hours of life. This results in lung compliance and resolution of respiratory distress. Resolution is frequently preceded by an increase in urine output.

Acute complications associated with RDS include pulmonary interstitial emphysema, pneumothorax, pneumomediastinum, and pneumopericardium. Rupture of the alveolar epithelial lining produces pulmonary interstitial emphysema, as air dissects along the interstitial spaces and the peribronchial lymphatics. Extravasation

of gas into the lung parenchyma reduces lung compliance and worsens respiratory failure.

Treatment

The goal of therapy is to provide respiratory support to the infant until spontaneous resolution occurs. All attempts should be made to minimize barotrauma and damage from high FiO_2.

Conventional therapy for the affected premature infant includes respiratory support with oxygen, continuous positive airway pressure (CPAP), and/or mechanical ventilation. Therapy with artificial surfactant has been shown to improve this condition dramatically and has significantly decreased the rate of neonatal mortality in premature infants. After surfactant administration, the FiO_2 of oxygen should be titrated to keep the PaO_2 greater than 50 mm Hg. If the FiO_2 exceeds 60%, CPAP can be used to decrease the time spent in high oxygen concentrations and to lessen the need for mechanical ventilation. CPAP is also useful to treat apnea that is unresponsive to nasal cannula stimulation and during the weaning process after extubation. Intubation and intermittent positive pressure ventilation are used when CPAP has been optimized and the FiO_2 required to keep the PaO_2 greater than 50 mm Hg exceeds 60%. Other indicators that mechanical ventilation is needed include apnea that is unresponsive to CPAP and/or persistent respiratory acidosis ($PaCO_2$ greater than 60 and pH less than 7.25) on maximum CPAP. In general, CPAP will not be sufficient for neonates with birth weights less than 1000 g. As RDS resolves and surfactant therapy takes affect, the compliance of the lungs increases dramatically and ventilator parameters must be weaned quickly to avoid severe barotrauma. When amniotic fluid assessment of the premature infant reveals fetal lung immaturity and preterm delivery cannot be prevented, administration of corticosteroids to the mother 48 hours before delivery can induce or accelerate the production of fetal surfactant and minimize the incidence of RDS.

Very premature neonates who require mechanical ventilation for long periods of time are at risk for alveolar rupture and the development of pulmonary interstitial emphysema, pneumothorax, pneumomediastinum, and/or pneumopericardium. The risk of barotrauma increases as the duration of mechanical ventilation increases, mean airway pressure escalates, and the intermittent mandatory ventilation rate increases. When RDS is very severe, pulmonary hypertension may occur, causing a right-to-left shunt at the patent foramen ovale and at the ductus arteriosus. Persistent PPHN is mentioned later in the Meconium Aspiration section of this chapter. Infants with respiratory distress deserve evaluation for sepsis and pneumonia, because group B streptococcus infection may mimic RDS clinically and on chest radiograph. Until blood culture results are known, antibiotics are recommended. Because of the periods of hypoxia that accompany RDS, intraventricular hemorrhage and necrotizing enterocolitis are more likely to occur in the neonate with RDS.

Chronic lung disease is the long-term complication of RDS and is due to prolonged mechanical ventilation of the premature infant with high mean airway pressures and high oxygen tensions. Although 15% of premature neonates requiring mechanical ventilation develop some degree of chronic lung disease, 50% of premature infants whose birth weight is less than 1000 g develop the condition. The pathologic changes seen in the lung are termed bronchopulmonary dysplasia (BPD). BPD is a chronic pulmonary disorder characterized by squamous metaplasia and hypertrophy of small airways with subsequent alveolar collapse and air trapping. Infants with chronic lung disease are chronic carbon dioxide retainers. Chest radiograph abnormalities include areas of hyperaeration and atelectasis. These chronic changes make diagnosis of a new infiltrate difficult. Complications include chronic respiratory insufficiency, requiring home use of continuous oxygen therapy; right-sided congestive heart failure secondary to pulmonary hypertension; and pneumothorax. Weaning the infant off oxygen to room air can take up to 6 months. Reactive airway disease is common and can be severe. SIDS is more common in infants with BPD. Lower respiratory infections caused by usually benign viral agents, most notably respiratory syncytial virus, may cause severe respiratory distress. Some infants fully recover, but the healing process takes years.

The use of high oxygen tensions in neonates with RDS results in the development of retinopathy of prematurity in some infants. Retinopathy of prematurity is discussed fully in Chapter 18.

◆ KEY POINTS ◆

1. Respiratory distress syndrome, or hyaline membrane disease, is the most common cause of respiratory failure in newborn infants. It occurs in premature infants who are born at 32 weeks' gestation or less and results from deficiency of surfactant.

2. Conventional therapy for the affected premature infant includes respiratory support with oxygen, continuous positive airway pressure, and/or mechanical ventilation.

3. Therapy with artificial surfactant has been shown to improve RDS dramatically and has significantly decreased the rate of neonatal mortality in premature infants.

4. Chronic lung disease is the long-term complication of RDS and is due to prolonged mechanical ventilation of the premature infant with high mean airway pressures and high oxygen tensions.

5. The pathologic changes seen in chronic lung disease are termed bronchopulmonary dysplasia, which is characterized by squamous metaplasia and hypertrophy of small airways with subsequent alveolar collapse and air trapping.

Meconium Aspiration

Pathogenesis

Meconium aspiration syndrome is a disorder caused by perinatal asphyxia. The fetal hypoxia triggers, by vagal reflex, the passage of meconium into the amniotic fluid. The contaminated amniotic fluid is swallowed into the oropharynx and aspirated at birth with the initiation of breathing. With severe fetal asphyxia and acidosis, the meconium may be aspirated prenatally during fetal gasping. Aspiration of the meconium interferes with gas exchange and obstructs airways by a ball-valve mechanism, resulting in ventilation-perfusion mismatch and pneumothoraces. The resulting hypoxia and acidosis increases pulmonary vascular resistance and causes right-to-left shunting of blood across the patent foramen ovale and/or the ductus arteriosus. This shunting further worsens the hypoxia and acidosis created by aspiration, resulting in a vicious cycle of increasingly severe pulmonary arteriolar hypertension, respiratory distress, and cyanosis.

It is important to note that the same hypoxic insult that caused the meconium to be released puts the infant at risk for persistent PPHN, which is a disorder of intractable pulmonary arteriolar hypertension due to chronic fetal hypoxia. Other organs affected by the prenatal or perinatal hypoxia include the brain, heart, gastrointestinal tract, and kidneys. Hypoxic infants have a higher risk of intracranial hemorrhage, myocardial dysfunction, necrotizing enterocolitis, and renal insufficiency.

Epidemiology

Ten to 15% of newborn infants pass meconium before or at the time of birth, but only a small percentage of these infants aspirate the meconium. Over 50% of infants born with meconium-stained fluid have meconium in the trachea at the time of birth.

Risk Factors

The risk of meconium aspiration is markedly increased in postmature infants (gestational age greater than 42 weeks) and neonates that suffer from intrauterine growth retardation. Both have placental insufficiency as a common pathway for fetal hypoxia. Infants born in the breech position also have an increased risk of meconium in the amniotic fluid.

Clinical Manifestations

Meconium aspiration pneumonitis is characterized by tachypnea, hypoxia, and hypercapnia. Diagnosis is established by the presence of meconium in the tracheal or amniotic fluid, combined with symptoms of respiratory distress and a chest radiograph that reveals a pattern of diffuse infiltrates with hyperinflation. Of infants with meconium aspiration syndrome, 10% develop pneumothoraces.

Treatment

Because most episodes of aspiration occur with the initiation of respiration, the most effective therapy is prevention.

In pregnancies in which uteroplacental insufficiency is either documented or suspected, tests of fetal well-being, such as the nonstress test, biophysical profile, fetal monitoring, and scalp pH sampling, help to identify those infants at high risk for meconium aspiration.

Prevention of meconium aspiration involves removal of meconium before the initiation of ventilation. When meconium is noted, the obstetrician suctions the oropharynx before delivery of the thorax and the pediatrician repeats the procedure when the infant is placed on the warmer bed. The vocal cords are visualized by direct laryngoscopy, and an endotracheal tube is inserted. Approximately 100 mm Hg of suction is applied to the endotracheal tube as it is slowly removed. The procedure is repeated if significant meconium is recovered. The airway should be cleared and ventilation initiated before significant bradycardia results. Only after the trachea is cleared of meconium should artificial ventilation, if necessary, be initiated. Spontaneous respirations may occur before the clinician has the opportunity to insert the endotracheal tube and remove the meconium. If spontaneous respirations occur and thick meconium is noted, the larynx should still be visualized with removal of particulate matter. It is not necessary to suction the trachea of infants born through thin meconium who have effective respirations at the time of delivery.

If aspiration has occurred and the infant is in distress, therapy consists of administration of oxygen and/or mechanical ventilation. The severity of disease is related to the amount of meconium the infant has aspirated and the severity of the pulmonary hypertension present due to the prenatal asphyxia. For persistent hypoxia (PaO_2 less than 50 mm Hg) or severe hypercapnia (PcO_2 greater than 60 mm Hg), intubation and mechanical ventilation are indicated. If severe hypoxia persists with conventional ventilation, it is likely that persistent PPHN is present and high frequency ventilation and/or extracorporeal membrane oxygenation (ECMO) may be beneficial.

◆ KEY POINTS ◆

1. Meconium aspiration syndrome is a disorder caused by perinatal asphyxia. Fetal hypoxia triggers passage of meconium into the amniotic fluid, which is aspirated at birth with the initiation of breathing.

2. Aspiration of the meconium interferes with gas exchange, and obstructs airways by a ball-valve mechanism, resulting in ventilation-perfusion mismatch and pneumothoraces. The resulting hypoxia and acidosis increases pulmonary vascular resistance and causes right-to-left shunting of blood across the patent foramen ovale and/or the ductus arteriosus.

3. The risk of meconium aspiration is markedly increased in postmature infants (gestational age greater than 42 weeks) and neonates that suffer from intrauterine growth retardation.

Persistent Pulmonary Hypertension of the Newborn

Pathogenesis

PPHN, or persistent fetal circulation, is a disorder of term or post-term infants who have experienced acute or chronic hypoxia in utero. The primary abnormality is the failure of the pulmonary vasculature resistance to fall with postnatal lung expansion and oxygenation. Normally, at birth, the systemic vascular resistance rises, as a result of cessation of blood flow through the placenta, and pulmonary vascular resistance decreases after the first few breaths. With persistence of the fetal circulation, the pulmonary vascular resistance continues to be high and may in fact be higher than the systemic resistance. This results in shunting of the deoxygenated blood, which is returning to the right atrium, away from the lungs. The right-to-left shunt can occur at the foramen ovale and/or the ductus arteriosus. Because the lungs are bypassed, the blood is not oxygenated and hypoxemia ensues. The hypoxemia and acidosis caused by the right-to-left shunt only worsens the baseline pulmonary arteriolar hypertension, resulting in a vicious cycle of increasingly severe pulmonary arteriolar hypertension and cyanosis culminating in cardiopulmonary failure. Fetal patients tend to have severe pulmonary arteriolar smooth muscle cell hyperplasia or a marked decrease in the number of pulmonary arterioles, usually from pulmonary hypoplasia.

Risk Factors

PPHN is associated with meconium aspiration, severe RDS, diaphragmatic hernia, pulmonary hypoplasia, and neonatal pneumonia from group B streptococcus or *E. coli*.

Clinical Manifestations

The diagnosis is suggested by a history of perinatal hypoxia and rapidly progressive cyanosis associated with mild to severe respiratory distress. Suspect PPHN when the clinical severity of pulmonary insufficiency is greater than the findings on chest radiograph. The chest radiograph may be normal or abnormal depending on the specific cause of the PPHN. Echocardiography reveals absence of structural heart disease, evidence of increased pulmonary vascular resistance, and the presence of right-to-left shunt at the foramen ovale and/or ductus arteriosus. The severity varies from mild disease, with spontaneous resolution, to death from intractable hypoxemia.

Pulmonary hypertension usually resolves within 5 to 10 days of birth.

Treatment

Treatment focuses on maximizing oxygen delivery and decreasing pulmonary arteriolar hypertension.

Conditions that potentiate PPHN include hypoxia, acidosis, hypoglycemia, hyperviscosity, anemia, and systemic hypotension. Hypoxia and acidosis promote increased pulmonary arteriolar hypertension, whereas systemic hypotension increases right-to-left shunting and tissue hypoxemia. Hypoglycemia results in ketosis, which exacerbates acidosis, and anemia reduces oxygen delivery to the tissues. Hyperviscosity increases pulmonary hypertension by sludging. The therapies used to treat PPHN combat the conditions that worsen pulmonary hypertension and include supplemental oxygen, hyperventilation, administration of sodium bicarbonate, pulmonary vasodilators, and support of systemic blood pressure.

Hyperventilation to a $PaCO_2$ less than 30 mm Hg and a pH greater than 7.5 maximizes pulmonary blood flow without decreasing cerebral blood flow and generally results in improvement in PaO_2. Pulmonary vasodilators include tolazoline and nitric oxide. Tolazoline is a nonspecific alpha-adrenergic blocking agent. Because it may decrease both pulmonary and systemic blood pressures, resulting in systemic hypotension, it has fallen out of favor as a means to treat PPHN. Nitric oxide is a direct relaxant of pulmonary arteriolar smooth muscle cells that has been shown to be effective in PPHN. Sedation facilitates relaxation of the infant and pulmonary vasodilation, whereas muscle paralysis may be needed to assist with hyperventilation. The overall mortality rate associated with PPHN is 25% in term infants. Infants who require very high ventilator settings, marked by an alveolar-to-arterial gradient of greater than 600 mm Hg on room air, have a high mortality rate and may benefit from ECMO. ECMO improves the outcomes in the most severely ill patients.

◆ KEY POINTS ◆

1. PPHN is seen when there is failure of the pulmonary vasculature resistance to fall with postnatal lung expansion and oxygenation. It

occurs in term and post-term infants who have experienced acute or chronic hypoxia in utero.

2. Hypoxemia and acidosis caused by right-to-left shunting worsens baseline pulmonary arteriolar hypertension, resulting in a vicious cycle of increasingly severe pulmonary arteriolar hypertension and cyanosis that culminates in cardiopulmonary failure.

3. The therapies used to treat PPHN include supplemental oxygen, hyperventilation, administration of sodium bicarbonate, pulmonary vasodilators, and support of systemic blood pressure.

NEONATAL GASTROINTESTINAL DISEASE

Hyperbilirubinemia

Hyperbilirubinemia manifests itself as jaundice, which is a yellowing of the skin, mucous membranes, and sclera, and occurs when serum bilirubin levels become greater than 5 mg/dL in neonates and greater than 2 mg/dL in children and adolescents. The two types of hyperbilirubinemia are: unconjugated (indirect), which can be physiologic or pathologic in origin, and conjugated (direct), which is always pathologic. Conjugated hyperbilirubinemia is defined as the direct fraction of bilirubin in the blood exceeding 2 mg/dL or 15% of the total bilirubin. Bilirubin is a bile pigment formed from the degradation of heme that is derived from red blood cell destruction and ineffective erythropoiesis. Figure 13–1 illustrates normal bilirubin metabolism. Depending on its location, overload or impedance of any step in the process may result in unconjugated or conjugated hyperbilirubinemia.

Hyperbilirubinemia is monitored with great care because unconjugated bilirubin at levels greater than 20 in the full-term infant is neurotoxic and causes kernicterus. In premature infants, much lower levels of hyperbilirubinemia result in kernicterus, because the more immature the neonate, the more immature is its blood-brain barrier. Kernicterus is characterized by a yellow staining of the basal ganglia and hippocampus, which results in widespread cerebral dysfunction. Clinical features include lethargy and irritability, hypotonia, opisthotonos, seizures, mental retardation, cerebral palsy, and hearing loss. Unconjugated bilirubin is normally bound tightly to al-

bumin in the blood, but at high levels the unconjugated bilirubin exceeds the binding capacity of albumin and the free bilirubin crosses the blood-brain barrier and damages the cells of the brain.

Most full-term and preterm neonates develop a transient, unconjugated hyperbilirubinemia during the first week of life. This episode of "physiologic jaundice" is due to an elevated bilirubin load (secondary to an increased red blood cell volume, a decreased red blood cell survival, and an increased enterohepatic circulation), defective hepatic uptake of bilirubin, inadequate bilirubin conjugation caused by decreased UDP-glucuronyltransferase activity, and defective bilirubin excretion. Physiologic jaundice begins after 24 hours of life, is associated with a peak of 12–15 mg/dL at 3 days of life, and a return to normal levels by the end of the first week of life. Risk factors for developing more severe physiologic jaundice include prematurity, maternal diabetes, and Asian or Native American ancestry. Infants with these risk factors tend to have higher peaks, and the hyperbilirubinemia is of a longer duration.

The mechanism of breast-milk jaundice, which is also quite common, is not known. Some researchers have theorized that it is due to an increase in enterohepatic circulation from an unknown maternal factor in the breast milk. The infant's peak bilirubin tends to be higher and lasts longer than that found with physiologic jaundice.

Any infant who develops hyperbilirubinemia in the first 24 hours of life, has an increase in serum bilirubin greater than 5 mg/dL/day, is jaundiced and has the risk factors noted above, has prolonged jaundice (more than 1 week in the full-term or more than 2 weeks in the premature neonate), or has conjugated hyperbilirubinemia needs to be evaluated.

Differential Diagnosis
Unconjugated hyperbilirubinemia

- Physiologic jaundice;
- Hemolytic process:

   Immune etiology—ABO/Rh incompatibility, erythroblastosis fetalis, drug reaction (penicillin, sulfonamides, oxytocin);

   Red cell defects—structural (spherocytosis, ellip–tocytosis), hemoglobinopathy (sickle cell, alpha–thalassemia), enzyme deficiency (G6PD or pyruvate kinase deficiency);

   DIC;

- Polycythemia;

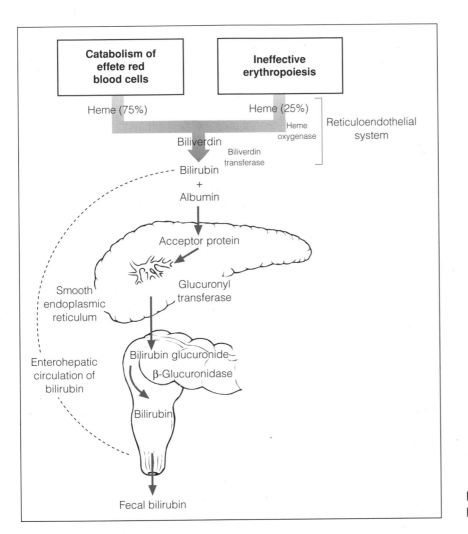

Figure 13–1 Bilirubin metabolism in the neonate.

- Extravascular blood loss—bruising from birth trauma (petechiae, cephalohematoma), hemorrhage (pulmonary, cerebral);
- Swallowed maternal blood;
- Increased enterohepatic circulation—intestinal obstruction (pyloric stenosis, duodenal stenosis or atresia, annular pancreas), Hirschsprung's disease, meconium ileus and/or meconium plug syndrome, drug-induced paralytic ileus (magnesium);
- Breast-milk jaundice;
- Disorders of bilirubin metabolism—Gilbert syndrome, Crigler-Najjar syndrome, and Lucey Driscol syndrome;

- Endocrine disorders—hypothyroidism, infants of diabetic mothers, hypopituitarism;
- Bacterial sepsis.

Conjugated hyperbilirubinemia
- Extrahepatic obstruction—biliary atresia, choledocholithiasis, choledochal cyst, common duct stenosis, inspissated bile syndrome from cystic fibrosis, extrinsic bile duct compression, pancreatitis;
- Persistent intrahepatic cholestasis—paucity of intrahepatic ducts, benign recurrent intrahepatic cholestasis, arteriohepatic dysplasia;
- Acquired intrahepatic cholestasis—neonatal hepatitis (bacterial sepsis; TORCH infections; hepatitis A,

B, and C; varicella; Epstein-Barr virus; echovirus; coxsackie virus; tuberculosis; leptospirosis; amoebiasis), drug-induced cholestasis, total parenteral nutrition cholestasis, cirrhosis, drug or metal toxicity, neoplasms (hepatoblastoma, secondary liver metastases);

- Genetic and metabolic disorders—disorders of bilirubin metabolism (Dubin-Johnson syndrome, Rotor's syndrome), disorders of carbohydrate metabolism (galactosemia, fructosemia), disorders of amino acid metabolism (tyrosinemia, hypermethioninemia), disorders of lipid metabolism (Niemann-Pick disease, Gaucher's disease), chromosomal disorders (trisomy 18 and 21), metabolic liver disease (Wilson's disease, alpha-1-antitrypsin deficiency).

Clinical Manifestations
History
Determine whether the child is breast fed or formula fed. Ascertain if there is a history of red cell structural defects, hemoglobinopathies, or enzyme deficiencies in the family or whether a previous child had an ABO incompatibility. Learn if there is a family history of any genetic or chromosomal disorders. Find out if prenatal screens were negative for TORCH infections. In the child with hyperbilirubinemia, define how long the jaundice has been present, whether it is worsening or improving, if there are associated gastrointestinal or constitutional symptoms, and if there is pruritus. Also, it is important to ask whether the stool color has changed (to a gray color) or the urine has darkened.

Physical Examination
In neonates, the examination should focus on the level of jaundice. In neonates, there is a cephalopedal progression of jaundice. Table 13–5 shows the approximate levels of indirect hyperbilirubin in the full-term infant based on level of jaundice.

Diagnostic Evaluation
Because the most common causes of unconjugated hyperbilirubinemia are physiologic and hemolytic, the initial evaluation should include a complete blood count with peripheral blood smear and reticulocyte count, a determination of maternal and infant blood types, a Coombs' test (direct and indirect), and a determination of the conjugated and unconjugated fractions of the hyperbilirubinemia. Figure 13–2 shows an algorithm for the evaluation of hyperbilirubinemia.

Treatment
The goal in treating unconjugated hyperbilirubinemia is to avoid kernicterus or sublethal bilirubin encephalopathy. The two modalities used to decrease unconjugated bilirubin are phototherapy and exchange transfusion. When to use these treatments depends on the birth weight of the neonate. Given a specific LBW, Table 13–6 shows the indicated treatment at different levels of

TABLE 13–5

The Cephalopedal Progression of Jaundice

Area of the Body	Range of Indirect Bilirubin (mg/100 mL)
Head and neck	4–8
Upper trunk	5–12
Lower trunk and thighs	8–16
Arms and lower legs	11–18
Palms and soles	>15

Reprinted with permission from Markel H, Oski JA, Oski FA, McMillan JA. The portable pediatrician. Philadelphia: Hanley and Belfus, 1992:196.

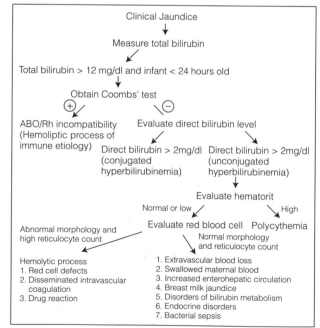

Figure 13–2 Algorithm for the evaluation of hyperbilirubinemia in the neonate.

TABLE 13–6

Management of Indirect Hyperbilirubinemia

Birth weight (g)	Indirect Bilirubin Concentrations					
	5–6 mg/dL	7–9 mg/dL	10–12 mg/dL	12–15 mg/dL	15–20 mg/dL	>20 mg/dL
≤1000	Phototherapy	⟶	Exchange transfusion	⟶		
1000–1500	Observe and repeat BR	Phototherapy	⟶	Exchange transfusion	⟶	
1500–2000	Observe and repeat BR	⟶	Phototherapy	⟶	Exchange transfusion	⟶
>2000	Observe	Observe and repeat BR	Phototherapy (<2500 g)	Phototherapy (>2500 g)	⟶	Exchange transfusion

BR, bilirubin determination.

Reprinted with permission from Graef JW, ed. Manual of pediatric therapeutics, 5th ed. Boston: Little, Brown, 1994:162.

unconjugated hyperbilirubinemia. When to use phototherapy in the full-term neonate is quite controversial. No studies show evidence of encephalopathic damage from unconjugated hyperbilirubinemia peak levels less than 25 mg/dL in the full-term healthy neonate with uncomplicated physiologic jaundice. As a result, there is much debate among pediatricians as to when to begin phototherapy. Phototherapy converts the unconjugated bilirubin into several water-soluble photoisomers that can be excreted without conjugation, whereas exchange transfusion directly removes the bilirubin from the intravascular space. Exchange transfusion is usually reserved for the extremely sick premature neonate with hemolytic disease.

Treatment of conjugated hyperbilirubinemia is directed at the underlying cause of the hyperbilirubinemia. Phototherapy of conjugated bilirubin "bronzes" the skin and takes months to resolve.

◆ KEY POINTS ◆

1. Determine whether hyperbilirubinemia is conjugated or unconjugated. Conjugated hyperbilirubinemia is always pathologic, whereas unconjugated hyperbilirubinemia may or may not be pathologic.

2. The two most common causes of unconjugated hyperbilirubinemia are physiologic jaundice and hemolytic disease.

3. Most neonatal unconjugated hyperbilirubinemia is due to physiologic jaundice, and in the full-term infant, a total bilirubin of up to 20 is tolerated without kernicterus.

Biliary Atresia

Pathogenesis

Biliary atresia is seen in 1:10,000 births and involves the obstruction of the extrahepatic bile ducts. Biliary atresia is more common in females, and the etiology is unknown.

Clinical Manifestations

Children with biliary atresia usually present with jaundice during the second or third week of life. The stools are often acholic, although the shedding of the bilirubin-laden intestinal mucosal cells may color the stool. The liver typically enlarges and becomes hard. Splenomegaly is usually detectable by 8 weeks of age. Other than these physical findings, the infants usually appear healthy. There is an association between biliary atresia and polysplenia syndrome and trisomy 13 and 18.

Diagnostic Evaluation

Laboratory tests demonstrate conjugated hyperbilirubinemia and elevated serum alkaline phosphatase, gamma-glutamyl transferase, and transaminases. Ultrasound examination is helpful in excluding a choledochal cyst or common duct stone. A biliary HIDA scan after 5 days of phenobarbital administration typically demonstrates normal hepatocyte uptake and failure of isotope excretion into the intestine after 24 hours. This test is less reliable in infants with serum bilirubin levels above 10 mg/dL. Percutaneous liver biopsy shows bile duct proliferation and confirms the diagnosis in 95% of patients. The differential diagnosis of direct hyperbilirubinemia is noted earlier.

Treatment

Patients with suspected biliary atresia ultimately require exploratory laparotomy. If biliary atresia is found, a Kasai procedure (hepatoportoenterostomy) is used to connect the bowel lumen and the porta hepatis. Without surgery, patients usually die from cirrhosis before 2 years of age. Surgical success is judged by improvement in bile drainage. The earlier the operation, the greater is the chance of establishing bile flow. Five years after a Kasai procedure 25–50% of patients survive, but complications of the procedure include progressive biliary cirrhosis and ascending cholangitis. Most infants with biliary atresia eventually require liver transplantation, which has an 80–90% survival rate.

◆ KEY POINTS ◆

1. Biliary atresia involves obstruction of the extrahepatic bile ducts.

2. Children with biliary atresia usually present with jaundice, acholic stools, and liver enlargement during the second or third week of life.

3. A biliary HIDA scan after 5 days of phenobarbital administration typically demonstrates normal hepatocyte uptake and failure of isotope excretion into the intestine after 24 hours.

4. The Kasai procedure often fails and liver transplantation is needed to treat biliary atresia.

Necrotizing Enterocolitis

Pathogenesis

Necrotizing enterocolitis refers to a process of acute intestinal necrosis after ischemic injury to the bowel and secondary invasion of the intestinal wall. Bowel ischemia secondary to perinatal asphyxia is regarded as the cause of the bowel injury. The introduction of formula or human milk then provides the substrate for bacterial overgrowth. Bacterial invasion of the bowel wall leads to tissue necrosis and perforation. Pneumatosis intestinalis results from gas production in the bowel wall and is pathognomonic for necrotizing enterocolitis.

Premature infants with birth weights less than 2000 g who have been asphyxiated are the population at risk. Prenatal factors associated with necrotizing enterocolitis include maternal age greater than 35, maternal infection requiring antibiotics, PROM, and cocaine exposure. Perinatal factors include maternal anesthesia, depressed Apgar score at 5 minutes, birth asphyxia, RDS, and hypotension. Postnatal factors include patent ductus arteriosus, congestive heart failure, umbilical vessel catheterization, polycythemia, and exchange transfusion.

Epidemiology

Necrotizing enterocolitis is rarely observed in healthy full-term infants. Approximately 2% of all infants admitted to neonatal intensive care units develop necrotizing enterocolitis. Of infants with necrotizing enterocolitis, 75% are less than 37 weeks' gestation and their birth weight is less than 2000 g.

Clinical Manifestations

The presentation may be mild to fulminant and occurs in the first 6 weeks of life. The earliest signs are feeding intolerance with bilious aspirates and abdominal distention. Infants with medical necrotizing enterocolitis, defined as necrotizing enterocolitis that does not require surgery, follow a course characterized by feeding intolerance, abdominal distention, occult blood in the stool, and dilated bowel loops on abdominal radiograph. These infants improve rapidly with therapy. Surgical necrotizing enterocolitis progresses rapidly with gross blood in the stool, extreme abdominal tenderness with discoloration, hyperglycemia, severe metabolic acidosis, sepsis, shock, DIC, temperature instability, and ineffective respiratory effort requiring mechanical ventilation due to severe abdominal distention. Pneumatosis intestinalis and perforation frequently occur in this setting.

Pneumatosis intestinalis is the hallmark of necrotizing enterocolitis on abdominal radiograph. Dilated thickened bowel loops, portal air, and pneumoperitoneum are also often seen. Long-term complications include intestinal strictures seen by contrast study. Laboratory findings include leukocytosis, neutropenia, and thrombocytopenia.

Treatment

If necrotizing enterocolitis is suspected, feeds should be discontinued immediately and a nasogastric tube should be placed for gastric and intestinal decompression. Systemic antibiotics should be started, and blood cultures should be obtained. Abdominal radiographs should be obtained to monitor for pneumatosis intestinalis, portal air, and free peritoneal air at least every 6 hours. Intravenous fluids are administered to prevent shock. If free air is seen in the peritoneal cavity or intestinal necrosis is suspected, emergent exploratory laparotomy is indicated.

◆ KEY POINTS ◆

1. Necrotizing enterocolitis refers to a process of acute intestinal necrosis after ischemic injury of the bowel and secondary bacterial invasion of the intestinal wall.

2. Infants with medical necrotizing enterocolitis present with feeding intolerance, abdominal distention, occult blood in the stool, and dilated bowel loops on abdominal radiograph.

3. Surgical necrotizing enterocolitis presents acutely with gross blood in the stool, severe metabolic acidosis, shock, sepsis, DIC, temperature instability, and ineffective respiratory effort that requires mechanical ventilation due to severe abdominal distention. Pneumatosis intestinalis and perforation frequently occur in this setting.

NEONATAL HEMATOLOGIC DISORDERS

Polycythemia

Pathogenesis

Polycythemia, or erythrocytosis, is defined as a greater than normal number of red cells in the blood. Erythrocytosis may result from an increase in red blood cell mass (absolute erythrocytosis) or by a decrease in plasma volume (relative erythrocytosis). Neonatal polycythemia is an absolute erythrocytosis and is defined as a hematocrit greater than 55%. Hyperviscosity syndrome, the most severe complication of polycythemia, occurs when the hematocrit exceeds 65%. Although an increase in the hematocrit from 40 to 60% results in only a small increase in blood viscosity, an increase in the hematocrit above 65% increases the blood viscosity markedly, resulting in vascular stasis, microthrombi, hypoperfusion, and tissue ischemia. These derangements result in damage to the cerebral cortex, kidneys, and adrenal glands. Neonatal erythrocytes are less filterable or deformable than adult erythrocytes, further contributing to hyperviscosity. Although a central venous hematocrit of greater than 65% occurs in 3–5% of infants, not all infants have symptoms of hyperviscosity syndrome.

Risk Factors

Infants at risk for polycythemia are post-term and small for gestational age neonates; infants of diabetic mothers; infants with delayed cord clamping (maternal-fetal transfusion); and infants suffering from neonatal hyperthyroidism, adrenogenital syndrome, the trisomies (13, 18, and 21), twin-twin transfusion (recipient), and Beckwith-Wiedemann syndrome. In some infants, polycythemia reflects a compensation for prolonged periods of fetal hypoxia from placental insufficiency; these infants have increased erythropoietin levels at birth.

Clinical Manifestations

Polycythemic infants appear ruddy and plethoric. Symptoms are due to sludging within the vasculature, resulting in tissue ischemia. Irritability, lethargy, poor feeding, emesis, tremulousness, and seizures all reflect abnormalities of the microcirculation of the brain, whereas acute renal failure results from inadequate renal perfusion. Hepatomegaly and hyperbilirubinemia are due to poor hepatic circulation and to the increased amount of hemoglobin that is metabolized into bilirubin. Because of stasis in the pulmonary vessels, pulmonary vascular resistance increases, and persistent PPHN may result. Other complications include necrotizing enterocolitis, due to bowel ischemia, and hypoglycemia, resulting from hypoxia in the adrenal cortex. Vascular impairment in the penis can cause priapism, and the formation of microthrombi may cause thrombocytopenia. If ischemia is severe enough, both electroencephalogram (EEG) and electrocardiogram may be abnormal.

Chest radiograph often reveals cardiomegaly, increased vascular markings, pleural effusions, and interstitial edema.

Long-term complications from neonatal polycythemia are more likely in the symptomatic child, particularly if hypoglycemia is also present. Neurodevelopmental abnormalities include mild deficits in speech, hearing, and coordination. If cerebral infarction occurs, cerebral palsy and mental retardation are likely.

Treatment

Long-term complications may be prevented by treatment of symptomatic infants with partial exchange transfusion after birth. A partial exchange transfusion removes whole blood and replaces it with normal saline or albumin. The equation to calculate the volume exchanged is as follows:

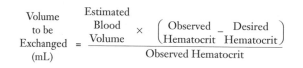

$$\text{Volume to be Exchanged (mL)} = \frac{\text{Estimated Blood Volume} \times \left(\text{Observed Hematocrit} - \text{Desired Hematocrit}\right)}{\text{Observed Hematocrit}}$$

The central venous hematocrit is used as the observed hematocrit, because the peripheral hematocrit may be falsely elevated. The desired hematocrit is 50% and the estimated blood volume is 85 mL/kg. Whether or not to exchange or transfuse the asymptomatic neonate with a hematocrit greater than 70% is controversial.

◆ KEY POINTS ◆

1. Hyperviscosity syndrome, which occurs when the hematocrit exceeds 65%, results in vascular stasis, microthrombi, hypoperfusion, and tissue ischemia. These derangements result in damage to the cerebral cortex, kidneys, and adrenal glands.

2. Polycythemic infants appear ruddy and plethoric.

3. Long-term complications from neonatal polycythemia are more likely in the symptomatic child, particularly if hypoglycemia is also present, and include mild deficits in speech, hearing, and coordination.

4. Long-term complications may be prevented by treatment of symptomatic infants with partial exchange transfusion after birth.

Anemia

Anemia in the neonate can result from blood loss, hemolysis, decreased red blood cell production, or physiologic decreased erythropoiesis. Blood loss is manifested by a decreased or normal hematocrit, an increased or normal reticulocyte count, and a normal bilirubin (unless the hemorrhage is retained). If blood loss is acute, the hematocrit and reticulocyte count may be normal and yet the infant may be in shock. The hematocrit will fall later due to hemodilution. If the bleeding is chronic, the hematocrit will be low, the reticulocyte count up, and the infant normovolemic. Blood loss may result from obstetric causes, occult blood loss, or iatrogenic causes and may occur during the prenatal, perinatal, or neonatal period.

Obstetric causes of blood loss include abruptio placenta, placenta previa, incision of the placenta during cesarean section, rupture of anomalous vessels (vasa previa, velamentous insertion of the cord, or rupture of communicating vessels in a multilobed placenta), hematoma of the cord caused by varices or aneurysm, or rupture of the cord (more common in short cords and dysmature cords).

Occult blood loss may result from fetomaternal bleeding, fetoplacental bleeding, or twin-to-twin transfusion. Fetomaternal bleeding may be chronic or acute. It occurs in 8% of all pregnancies. The diagnosis of this problem is by Kleihauer-Betke stain of maternal smear for fetal cells. Conditions that predispose to fetomaternal transfusion include placental malformations such as chorioangioma or choriocarcinoma, obstetric procedures such as traumatic amniocentesis, external cephalic version, internal cephalic version, and breech delivery. Fetoplacental bleeding results from chorioangioma or choriocarcinoma with placental hematoma, cesarean section, with infant held above the placenta, and tight nuchal cord or occult cord prolapse.

Bleeding in the neonatal period may be due to intracranial bleeding, massive cephalohematoma, retroperitoneal bleeding, ruptured liver or spleen, adrenal or renal hemorrhage, gastrointestinal bleeding, or bleeding from the umbilicus. Excessive blood loss may result from blood sampling with inadequate replacement.

Hemolysis is manifested by a decreased hematocrit, increased reticulocyte count, and an increased bilirubin level. Hemolysis may result from immune mechanisms, hereditary red cell disorders, or acquired hemolysis. Immune mediated hemolysis results from Rh incompatibility, ABO incompatibility, minor blood group incompatibility (c, E, Kell, Duffy), and maternal hemolytic anemia from systemic lupus erythematosus. Hereditary red cell disorders that result in hemolysis include red blood cell membrane defects (spherocytosis, elliptocytosis, stomatocytosis), enzymopathies (G6PD deficiency, pyruvate kinase deficiency), and hemoglobinopathies (alpha and beta thalassemias). Causes of acquired hemolysis include bacterial or viral infection, DIC, vitamin E deficiency, or microangiopathichemolytic anemia (giant hemangioma, renal artery stenosis, severe coarctation of the aorta).

Diminished red blood cell production is manifested by a decreased hematocrit, decreased reticulocyte count, and normal bilirubin level. Etiologies include Diamond-Blackfan syndrome, Fanconi's anemia, congenital leukemia, infections (especially rubella and parvovirus), osteopetrosis leading to inadequate erythropoiesis, drug-induced red blood cell suppression, physiologic anemia, or anemia of prematurity.

Physiologic anemia of the full-term or premature neonate is due to physiologically decreased erythropoiesis. Full-term infants have a nadir of the hemoglobin level at 6–12 weeks, premature infants (1200–2400 g) have a nadir at 5–10 weeks, and very LBW neonates (birth weight less than 1200 g) have a nadir at 4–8 weeks. The laboratory manifestations of physiologic anemia are a decreased hematocrit and a low reticulocyte count. When the infant's oxygen demand increases, erythropoietin will increase; if iron stores are adequate, the reticulocyte count will increase and the hemoglobin level will rise.

Clinical Manifestations

A complete family history including inquiring about anemia, jaundice, cholestatic disease, and splenectomy may define important clues to newborn disease. The obstetric history may identify blood loss as the cause of the anemia. The physical examination can usually differentiate acute blood loss, chronic blood loss, and chronic hemolytic disease. Manifestations of acute blood loss include shock, tachypnea, tachycardia, low venous pressure, weak pulses, and pallor. Chronic blood loss is manifested by extreme pallor and a low hematocrit, with less distress than one would expect given the level of hematocrit. These infants are typically normovolemic and may have congestive heart failure or hydrops fetalis. Chronic hemolysis is associated with pallor, jaundice, and hepatosplenomegaly.

Neonatal anemia may be classified by evaluation of the reticulocyte count, bilirubin level, Coombs' test, and red blood cell morphology (Table 13–7). The Apt test helps to identify maternal blood that has been swallowed by the neonate, and the Kleihauer-Betke preparation determines if fetomaternal transfusion has occurred. Ultrasound of the head is used to define an intracranial bleed. Laboratory tests on the parents help to determine the likelihood of a hemolytic process. If a TORCH infection is suspected as the cause of the anemia, the appropriate studies may be done. Bone marrow aspiration is performed in rare cases in which bone marrow failure is suggested.

Treatment

Healthy, term, asymptomatic newborns self-correct a mild anemia, provided that iron intake is adequate. Although nonbreast-feeding infants are sent home on iron-fortified formulas, iron supplementation is not required until 2 months of age, when reticulocytosis resumes.

If the neonate has acute blood loss at birth, immediate access should be obtained, and blood may be sent for typing and cross matching. If hypovolemic shock is present (decreased venous pressure, pallor, tachycardia), 20 mL/kg of volume expander is recommended. Unmatched O blood should be available for transfusion if needed. Albumin and normal saline are also useful to replete the intravascular volume. Chronic blood loss and the anemia from hemolysis is generally well tolerated. Only if the neonate is symptomatic with congestive heart failure should he or she be transfused. It is recommended that the hematocrit in the child with cardiac or respiratory diseases be kept above 35–40.

Anemia of prematurity is prevented by vitamin E and iron administration in premature formulas. Premature infants tolerate hemoglobins of 6.5–8.0 g/dL. The level itself is not an indication for transfusion. Transfusion should occur if another condition exists that requires an increased oxygen-carrying capacity, such as sepsis, necrotizing enterocolitis, pneumonia, chronic lung disease, and apnea.

◆ KEY POINTS ◆

1. Anemia in the neonate can result from blood loss, hemolysis, decreased red blood cell production, or physiologically decreased erythropoiesis.

2. Neonatal anemia may be classified by evaluation of the reticulocyte count, bilirubin level, Coombs' test, and red blood cell morphology (see Table 13–7).

TABLE 13–7

Classification of Anemia in the Newborn

Reticulocytes	Bilirubin	Coombs' Test	RBC Morphology	Diagnostic Possibilities
Normal or ↓	Normal	Negative	Normal	Physiologic anemia of infancy or prematurity; congenital hypoplastic anemia; other causes of decreased production
Normal or ↑	Normal	Negative	Normal	Acute hemorrhage (fetomaternal, placental, umbilical cord, or internal hemorrhage)
↑	↑	Positive	Hypochromic microcytes	Chronic fetomaternal hemorrhage
			Spherocytes	Immune hemolysis (blood group incompatibility or maternal autoantibody)
Normal or ↑	↑	Negative	Spherocytes	Hereditary spherocytosis
			Elliptocytes	Hereditary elliptocytosis
			Hypochromic microcytes	Alpha- or gamma-thalassemia syndrome
			Spiculated RBCs	Pyruvate-kinase deficiency
			Schistocytes and RBC fragments	Disseminated intravascular coagulation; other microangiopathic processes
			Bite cells (Heinz bodies with supravital stain)	Glucose 6-phosphate dehydrogenase deficiency
			Normal	Infections; enclosed hemorrhage (cephalohematoma)

RBC, red blood cell; ↓, decreased; ↑, increased.

Adapted with permission from Cloherty JP, Stark AR, eds. Manual of neonatal care, 3rd ed. Boston: Little, Brown, 1991:339.

NEONATAL CENTRAL NERVOUS SYSTEM DISORDERS

Apnea of Prematurity

Pathogenesis

Apnea in the premature infant is defined as a cessation of breathing for longer than 20 seconds or a shorter pause associated with cyanosis, pallor, hypotonia, or bradycardia with a heart rate of less than 100 beats/min. Apnea in the full-term neonate is defined as absent breathing for longer than 16 seconds. In the premature infant, apneic episodes may be due to a central, obstructive, or mixed mechanism. In central apnea, there is a complete cessation of air flow and respiratory effort with no chest wall movement, whereas in obstructive apnea, there is respiratory effort and chest wall movement but no air flow. Apnea of prematurity, which results from a central mechanism, reflects immaturity of the respiratory control center in the brain stem. Periodic breathing, which must be differentiated from apnea, is defined as pauses in breathing of 5–10 seconds with normal respirations between episodes.

Epidemiology

Apnea occurs in most infants less than 28 weeks' gestation, approximately 50% of infants 30–32 weeks, and in less than 7% of infants 34–35 weeks' gestation.

Clinical Manifestations

Apnea of prematurity is associated with bradycardia, which is a heart rate less than 80 beats/min. Bradycardia and cyanosis are usually present after 20 seconds of apnea but may occur more rapidly in the small premature infant. After 30–40 seconds, pallor and hypotonia are also seen, and the infant may be unresponsive to tactile stimulation. The three types of bradycardias are self-stimulation bradycardia, tactile stimulation bradycardia, and bradycardia requiring intervention. In a self-stimulation bradycardia, the neonate rouses itself and stops the apneic spell, whereas with a tactile stimulation bradycardia, a caregiver must touch the infant to discontinue the apnea. When an infant has a bradycardia requiring intervention, the infant is generally hypotonic with pallor, and bag mask ventilation is required to return the child to a normal breathing pattern.

A diagnosis of apnea of prematurity is made after excluding other causes of apnea, which can be grouped into the broad categories: hypoxemia, diaphragmatic fatigue, respiratory center depression, infection, vagal stimulation, airway obstruction, and inappropriate environmental temperature. Hypoxemia may result from anemia, hypovolemia, and congenital heart disease, whereas RDS and pneumonia can cause diaphragmatic fatigue. Respiratory center depression can occur with metabolic abnormalities (hypoglycemia, hypocalcemia, hyponatremia), drugs, seizures, or intraventricular hemorrhage (IVH). Infectious processes such as sepsis, necrotizing enterocolitis, and meningitis can all cause apnea, whereas gastroesophageal reflux, suction in the oropharynx, and nasogastric tube passage can cause vagally mediated depression of the respiratory center. Excessive oral secretions, anatomic obstruction, or malposition may result in obstructive apnea. Apnea is more frequent in the absence of a skin-core temperature gradient, and sudden increases in incubator temperature increase the frequency of apneic spells.

Treatment

Treatment for apnea of prematurity includes maintenance of a skin-core gradient in the incubator, supplemental oxygen, tactile stimulation, and administration of respiratory stimulants (caffeine, aminophylline, doxapram). Doxapram is used when methylxanthines fail and is given by continuous intravenous infusion. Apnea of prematurity may also be managed by increasing the mean airway pressure through the use of CPAP or intermittent assisted ventilation. For the other causes of apnea, treatment of the underlying disorder usually leads to cessation of the apneic episodes.

When an infant reaches 34–35 weeks' postconception age, is tolerating feeds orally, and has not had an apneic or bradycardiac episode for 7 days, the infant is ready to be discharged to home. The use of an apnea monitor sent home with an infant can be discontinued when the infant has been apnea free for 2 months.

◆ KEY POINTS ◆

1. Apnea in the premature infant is defined as a cessation of breathing for longer than 20 seconds or a shorter pause associated with cyanosis, pallor, hypotonia, or bradycardia with a heart rate of less than 100 beats/min.

2. In the premature infant, apneic episodes may be due to a central, obstructive, or mixed mechanism.

3. A diagnosis of apnea of prematurity is made after excluding other causes of apnea, which can be grouped into the broad categories: hypoxemia, diaphragmatic fatigue, respiratory center depression, infection, vagal stimulation, airway obstruction, and inappropriate environmental temperature.

4. The treatment for apnea of prematurity includes maintenance of a skin-core gradient in the incubator, supplemental oxygen, tactile stimulation, administration of respiratory stimulants, and in the most severe cases CPAP or intermittent assisted ventilation.

Intraventricular Hemorrhage

Pathogenesis

IVH is seen almost exclusively in preterm infants and results from bleeding of the germinal matrix, which result from surges of cerebral inflow on the arterial side or compromise of cerebral outflow on the venous side of the matrix circulation. Surges of cerebral arterial flow may occur with seizures, episodes of hypoxia, apnea, respiratory distress, rapid infusion of colloid, patent ductus arteriosus, ECMO, and possibly with certain caretaking procedures such as tracheal suctioning. Increased venous pressure may be associated with RDS, pneumothorax, congestive heart failure, ventilator parameters such as CPAP, and hyperviscosity. IVH is very common among VLBW infants, and the risk decreases as gestational age increases. Approximately 50% of infants under 1500 g have evidence of intracranial bleeding. Small intraventricular hemorrhages that are confined to the germinal matrix (grade I) or are associated with a small amount of blood in the ventricle (grade II) often resolve without sequelae. Large IVHs that are associated with ventricular dilatation (grade III) or with extension into the brain parenchyma (grade IV) are associated with permanent functional impairment and hydrocephalus.

Hydrocephalus refers to an excessive collection of cerebrospinal fluid within the ventricular system due to imbalanced production and absorption of cerebrospinal fluid. High-pressure, or obstructive, hydrocephalus results when normal drainage or reabsorption of cerebrospinal fluid does not occur. It is seen in congenital aqueductal stenosis, Dandy-Walker malformation, myelomeningocele with Arnold-Chiari malformation, meningitis, and after IVH. Low pressure, or communicating, hydrocephalus is seen after intracranial hemorrhage and in some rare malformations. Communicating hydrocephalus does not require therapeutic intervention.

Clinical Manifestations

Approximately 50% of hemorrhages occur in the first day of life, and approximately 90% occur within the first 3 days of life. Most hemorrhages are asymptomatic. If a severe hemorrhage occurs, the neonate may develop anemia, pallor, hypotension, focal neurologic signs, seizures, an acute increase in the level of ventilatory assistance, apnea, and/or bradycardia.

Ultrasonography through the anterior fontanelle is the method of choice to screen for, grade, and follow IVHs. All premature infants with birth weights less than 1500 g should have diagnostic ultrasound within the first week of life.

Treatment

The risk of IVH is minimized by preventing premature delivery if possible, through the use of appropriate neonatal resuscitation measures to minimize hypoxemia by stabilizing the arterial blood pressure, intravascular volume, hematocrit, and oxygenation. The goal in acute management of IVH is to maintain adequate cerebral perfusion and to control intracerebral pressure. Normal arterial blood pressure is preserved by volume replacement with packed red blood cells and/or inotropic support. Intracerebral pressure is managed by repeated lumbar puncture or ventriculostomy. Hemorrhage is followed

by serial ultrasound evaluation, because ventriculomegaly occurs before there is an increase in head circumference. Posthemorrhagic hydrocephalus is treated by serial lumbar punctures, external ventriculotomy, or permanent ventricular-peritoneal shunt. Ventricular-peritoneal shunt placement is delayed until the high protein content of the hemorrhagic fluid subsides.

Outcome is dependent on the severity of the hemorrhage and the success in maintaining cerebral perfusion after IVH. Grades I and II hemorrhages result in no long-term morbidity. Of infants with grade III IVH, 30–45% will have motor and intellectual impairment, and 60 to 80% of neonates with grade IV IVH develop motor and intellectual disabilities.

◆ KEY POINTS ◆

1. Intraventricular hemorrhage is seen almost exclusively in preterm infants and results from bleeding of the germinal matrix, which results from surges of cerebral inflow on the arterial side or compromise of cerebral outflow on the venous side of the matrix circulation.

2. Approximately 50% of hemorrhages occur in the first day of life, and approximately 90% occur within the first 3 days of life.

3. The risk of IVH is minimized by preventing premature delivery if possible, through the use of appropriate neonatal resuscitation measures to minimize hypoxemia and rapid cerebral flow changes by stabilizing the arterial blood pressure, intravascular volume, hematocrit, and oxygenation.

4. Grades I and II hemorrhages result in no long-term morbidity. Of infants with grade III IVH, 30–45% have motor and intellectual impairment, and 60–80% of neonates with grade IV IVH develop motor and intellectual disabilities.

Neonatal Seizures

The causes of neonatal seizures are categorized below, and neonatal seizures are classified in Table 13–8:

- Metabolic: hypoglycemia, electrolyte abnormalities (hypocalcemia, hypomagnesemia, hyponatremia), inborn errors of metabolism (organic acidemias, error of amino acid metabolism, pyridoxine deficiency);

TABLE 13–8

Classification of Neonatal Seizures

Type	Manifestations
Subtle	Eye deviation, blinking, mouth movements, apnea, fluctuation of vital signs
Focal clonic	Localized jerking movement
Multifocal clonic	Multiple random clonic movements
Tonic	Extensor posturing with tonic eye deviation
Myoclonic	Synchronized single or multifocal rapid jerks
	Hypsarrhythmia on EEG possible
Tonic-clonic	Less common than in older children

Reprinted with permission from Behrman RE, Kliegman RM, eds. Essentials of pediatrics, 2nd ed. Philadelphia: WB Saunders, 1994:209

- Toxic: maternal drug ingestion, neonatal drug withdrawal, inadvertent local anesthetic poisoning, bilirubin;

- Hemorrhagic: intraventricular, subdural, subarachnoid hemorrhage;

- Infectious: bacterial meningitis, viral (TORCH) encephalitis;

- Asphyxia: neonatal encephalopathy;

- Genetic/dysmorphic syndromes: cerebral dysgenesis, chromosomal abnormalities, phakomatoses (tuberous sclerosis).

Seizures are difficult to differentiate from benign jitters or clonus in neonates with hypoglycemia or hypocalcemia, in infants of diabetic mothers, in newborns with narcotic withdrawal syndrome, and in infants after an episode of asphyxia. In contrast to seizures, jitters and tremors are sensory dependent, elicited by stimuli, and may be interrupted by holding the extremity. Seizure activity is coarse, with fast and slow clonic activity, whereas jitters are characterized by fine, very rapid movement. It is often difficult to identify seizures in the newborn period because the infant, especially the LBW infant, usually does not demonstrate the tonic-clonic major motor activity typical of the older child.

Subtle seizures constitute 50% of seizures in newborns (both term and preterm). Subtle seizure activity may include rhythmic fluctuations in vital signs, apnea, eye deviation, nystagmus, tongue thrusting, eye blinking, staring, and "bicycling" and "swimming" movements. Continuous bedside EEG monitoring can help identify subtle seizures.

The movements in **focal clonic seizures** involve well-localized clonic jerking. These types of seizures are not associated with loss of consciousness and are most often provoked by metabolic disturbances. Subarachnoid hemorrhage and focal infarct may also promote this type of seizure. The EEG is unifocally abnormal, but the prognosis is generally good.

Multifocal clonic seizures are characterized by random clonic movements of the limbs. Multifocal anomalies are seen on the EEG and the prognosis is poor.

Tonic seizures manifest as extensor posturing with tonic eye deviation and are most often seen in premature neonates with diffuse central nervous system disease or IVH. The EEG has multifocal abnormalities and has a mixed prognosis that is generally poor.

Synchronized single or multiple slow jerks of the upper or lower limbs (or both) characterize **myoclonic seizures**. These seizures are noted when there is diffuse central nervous system pathology, and the prognosis is poor. The EEG shows a burst suppression pattern.

Seizures noted in the delivery room may be due to direct injection of local anesthetic into the fetal scalp, severe anoxia, or congenital brain malformation. Seizures due to hypoxic-ischemic encephalopathy (postasphyxial seizures), a common cause of seizures in the full-term neonate, usually occur 12–24 hours after a history of birth asphyxia and are often refractory to conventional doses of anticonvulsant medications. Postasphyxial seizures may also result from metabolic disorders such as hypoglycemia and hypocalcemia. IVH is a common cause of seizures in premature infants and often occurs from the first to third days of life. Seizures with IVH may be associated with a bulging fontanelle, hemorrhagic spinal fluid, anemia, lethargy, and coma. Seizures after the first 5 days of life may be due to infection or drug withdrawal. Seizures associated with lethargy, acidosis, ketonuria, respiratory alkalosis, and a family history of infantile death may be due to an inborn error of metabolism.

Clinical Manifestations

A careful prenatal and perinatal history may shed light on the seizure etiology. The diagnostic evaluation of infants with seizures should include a determination of blood levels of glucose, sodium, calcium, magnesium, and ammonia. In the jaundiced neonate, measurement of bilirubin level is indicated. When infection is suspected, a blood culture and lumbar puncture to obtain cerebrospinal fluid are indicated. If an inborn error of metabolism is suspected, urine organic acids and serum amino acids may be examined. Further evaluation may include an ultrasound or CT scan of the head. If physical examination or head imaging suggest a TORCH infection, titers should be done. Continuous bedside video and EEG monitoring provides the best information in defining the type of seizure present. Continuous EEG with pyridoxine infusion helps establish a diagnosis of pyridoxine deficiency. If seizures result from narcotic withdrawal syndrome, paregoric is indicated.

Treatment

If possible, the primary cause of the seizure should be identified and treated. Correcting any metabolic disturbances is advised. If a toxin (hyperammonemia, hyperbilirubinemia) is isolated as the etiology of the seizure, exchange transfusion may be used to remove it. Meningitis is treated with the appropriate antibiotic agent. In the absence of an identifiable cause, anticonvulsant therapy is used. Agents include phenobarbital, phenytoin (Dilantin), lorazepam (Ativan), diazepam (Valium), and paraldehyde. Phenobarbital is standard primary therapy. Phenytoin is used when seizures persist with a phenobarbital level greater than 50 mg/L. Lorazepam, diazepam, and paraldehyde are used primarily for status epilepticus. Paraldehyde may be given per rectum, which may be helpful in the child in whom intravenous access is problematic. The long-term outcome of neonatal seizures is determined by the type of seizure and its etiology.

◆ KEY POINTS ◆

1. Seizures may result from metabolic disturbances, inborn errors of metabolism, toxic exposures, hemorrhagic brain insult, infectious etiologies, asphyxia, and genetic defects.

2. Neonatal seizures are divided into subtle, focal clonic, multifocal clonic, tonic, myoclonic, and tonic-clonic seizures.

3. Continuous bedside video EEG monitoring provides the best information in defining the type of seizure present.

4. Phenobarbital is the primary anticonvulsant used to manage neonatal seizures.

NEONATAL DISORDERS OF THE ENDOCRINE SYSTEM

Hypothyroidism

The physical stigmata of congenital hypothyroidism in the newborn are often too subtle for physical diagnosis in many cases; however, the incidence of 1 in 4000 live births and the development of mental retardation make diagnostic screening cost effective. All states currently require newborn screening for hypothyroidism, in addition to galactosemia and phenylketonuria. The sooner treatment is initiated, the better will be the prognosis for intellectual development of the child. Most programs can diagnose an infant and initiate therapy within 4 weeks.

The etiology is usually sporadic athyreosis or thyroid ectopy. Less common is familial goitrous hypothyroidism. Children of mothers with Graves' disease on propylthiouracil have transient hypothyroidism.

Clinical Manifestations

Primary hypothyroidism is indicated by a low T_4 and an elevated thyroid-stimulating hormone (TSH) level. A serum T_4 and TSH should be drawn to confirm abnormal screening results.

A low T_4 level accompanied by a low TSH value may indicate a physiologically normal thyroid status due to a low concentration of thyroid-binding globulin (TBG). This is frequently seen in premature infants or may be seen on a hereditary basis. Alternatively, a low T_4 and low TSH, with a normal TBG level, may indicate hypopituitarism or hypothalamic deficiency. Hypothalamic deficiency usually is accompanied by growth hormone or corticotropin deficiency, which may cause acute hypoglycemia. An algorithm for the diagnosis of hypothyroidism is delineated in Figure 13–3.

Treatment

If the screening results indicate primary hypothyroidism, repeat the T_4 and TSH studies and start therapy. If the definitive serum tests reveal a normal T_4 and TSH, reevaluate the case. Serum T_4 is measured after 5 days of therapy, and the thyroxine dosage is adjusted to keep the T_4 level in the upper half of the normal range for age. The TSH concentration may remain elevated for months in some patients because of immaturity of the feedback mechanism. Levothyroxine is administered at an initial dose of 10 mcg/kg. Tablets are crushed and given orally.

Before therapy commences, a bone scan, to obtain a

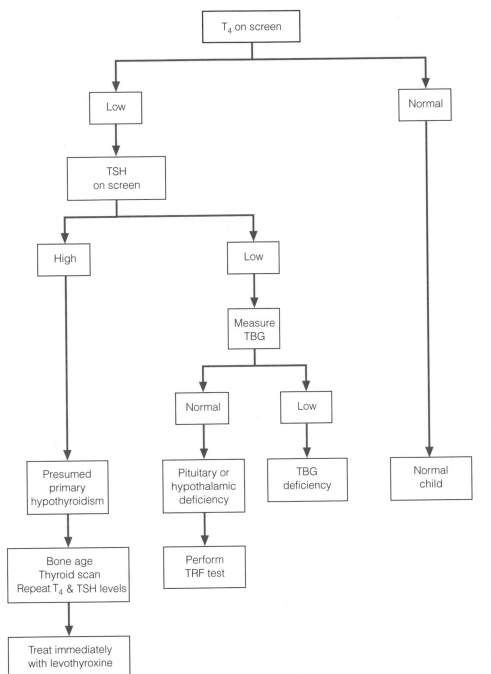

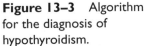

Figure 13–3 Algorithm for the diagnosis of hypothyroidism.

baseline bone age, and a thyroid scan should be done. An iodinated ^{123}I or technetium scan of the thyroid gland evaluates the presence of a rudimentary or ectopic thyroid gland. Scans must be performed before therapy commences and the TSH decreases. Maternal antibodies can suppress the newborn thyroid gland function temporarily so that there is no uptake by the thyroid gland on scan. Thus, even if there is no indication of thyroid gland on scan, there remains the rare possibility that thyroid function will recover later in infancy.

If therapy is started within the first month after birth, the prognosis is excellent. The thyroxine dose must be carefully adjusted, because too little thyroxine results in persistent hypothyroidism, whereas too much thyroxine may result in advanced bone age and craniosynostosis.

◆ **KEY POINTS** ◆

1. All states currently require newborn screening for hypothyroidism, in addition to galactosemia and phenylketonuria.

2. If therapy is started within the first month after birth, the prognosis for intellectual development of the child is excellent.

Neonatal Hypoglycemia

Pathogenesis

Infants with hypoglycemia may be divided into those with hyperinsulinism and those without hyperinsulinism. Infants with transient hyperinsulinism include infants of diabetic mothers and infants with Rh hemolytic disease. Infants with protracted hyperinsulinism include those who have Beckwith-Wiedemann syndrome, islet cell adenomas, and functional hyperinsulinism. Infants who do not have hyperinsulinism and have transient hypoglycemia include those with intrauterine growth retardation, birth asphyxia, polycythemia, cardiac disease, central nervous system disease, sepsis, maternal use of propranolol, oral hypoglycemic agents, or narcotic addiction. Infants who do not have hyperinsulinism and have protracted hypoglycemia include those with neonatal hypopituitarism and defects in carbohydrate metabolism and in amino acid metabolism. Deficiencies of growth hormone and/or corticotropin cause hypoglycemia in neonatal hypopituitarism. Defects in carbohydrate metabolism that result in hypoglycemia include glycogen storage disease type I, glycogen synthetase deficiency, fructose 1,6-diphosphatase deficiency, fructose intolerance, galactosemia, and pyruvate carboxylase deficiency. Disorders of amino acid metabolism that result in hypoglycemia include methylmalonic acidemia, tyrosinosis, proprionic acidemia, and maple syrup urine disease.

Clinical Manifestations

Onset of hypoglycemia may occur anywhere from a few hours after birth to several days of age. Subtle symptoms such as poor feeding, apathy, lethargy, and hypotonia are most common, but life-threatening manifestations such as seizures, apnea, and cyanosis may also occur.

A blood sugar level less than 30 mg/dL in a full-term or less than 20 mg/dL in a premature infant is diagnostic of hypoglycemia. In persistent or recurrent hypoglycemia, consider inborn errors of metabolism and, when the infant is hypoglycemic, obtain serum for glucose, insulin, cortisol, growth hormone, lactate, and pyruvate levels. Serum amino acid screening is indicated if no definitive diagnosis is made. The infant need not be hypoglycemic at the time of the sample collection.

Treatment

In asymptomatic infants, oral feedings can be tried with infant formula. If oral feedings are not accepted, start an intravenous infusion of maintenance dextrose at 5–7 mg/kg/min.

In symptomatic infants, give an intravenous push of 1 mL/kg of 25% dextrose and infuse intravenous dextrose at a rate of 5–7 mg/kg/min. Adjust the rate upward or downward to keep the blood sugar between 45 and 120 mg/dL. Do not abruptly decrease dextrose infusion because rebound hypoglycemia may occur. Monitor blood sugar frequently using Dextrostix, and confirm abnormal values with a true blood sugar. When the infant is stabilized, slowly decrease the dextrose infusion rate with careful monitoring of blood glucose. After dextrose infusion is discontinued, monitor the blood sugar for 24 hours.

Glucagon in doses of 300 µg/kg up to 1 mg/kg can be used in conditions with adequate glycogen stores, such as hyperinsulinism. Glucocorticoids are used as replacement therapy in infants with hypoadrenalism. Growth hormone is used in those infants with growth hormone deficiency. Diazoxide can be used in hyperinsulinemic states and may serve as a diagnostic technique, because insulinomas are far less likely to respond to diazoxide than are functional hyperinsulinemic patients. Pancreatectomy is reserved for intractable hypoglycemia due to hyperinsulinism. If an isolated tumor is found, it must be removed.

◆ **KEY POINTS** ◆

1. Infants with hypoglycemia may be divided into those with hyperinsulinism and those without hyperinsulinism.

2. Infants who do not have hyperinsulinism and have transient hypoglycemia include those with

intrauterine growth retardation, birth asphyxia, polycythemia, cardiac disease, central nervous system disease, and sepsis and whose mothers have used propranolol, oral hypoglycemic agents, and narcotics.

3. Infants who do not have hyperinsulinism and have protracted hypoglycemia include those with neonatal hypopituitarism and defects in carbohydrate metabolism and in amino acid metabolism.

4. In asymptomatic infants, oral feedings can be tried with infant formula. If oral feedings are not accepted, start an intravenous infusion of maintenance dextrose at 5–7 mg/kg/min. In symptomatic infants, give an intravenous push of 1 mL/kg of 25% dextrose and infuse intravenous dextrose at a rate of 5–7 mg/kg/min.

CONGENITAL ANOMALIES

Tracheoesophageal Fistula

The lower section of the esophagus develops as an elongation of the superior portion of the primitive foregut. When there is abnormal anastomosis of superior and inferior portions of the esophagus, esophageal atresia results. Of neonates with esophageal atresia, 85% have tracheoesophageal fistula (TEF). The four types of tracheoesophageal atresia are shown in Figure 13–4. Esophageal atresia with distal TEF accounts for 85% of the cases of TEF. Forty percent of patients with TEF have other defects. Associated cardiovascular anomalies include patent ductus arteriosus, vascular ring, and coarctation of the aorta. The incidence of imperforate anus, malrotation, and duodenal anomalies also are increased. VACTERL syndrome describes the association of *V*ertebral, *A*nal, *C*ardiac, *T*racheal, *E*sophageal, *R*enal, and *L*imb anomalies.

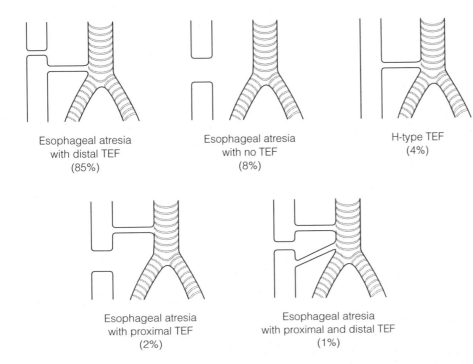

Esophageal atresia
with distal TEF
(85%)

Esophageal atresia
with no TEF
(8%)

H-type TEF
(4%)

Esophageal atresia
with proximal TEF
(2%)

Esophageal atresia
with proximal and distal TEF
(1%)

Figure 13–4 Types of tracheoesophageal fistulas with relative frequencies.

Clinical Manifestations

Neonates with TEF have excessive oral secretions, inability to feed, gagging, and respiratory distress. Polyhydramnios is often noted on ultrasound while the child is in utero. Lateral and anteroposterior chest radiograph of the thoracocervical region and abdomen with a Replogle tube in the proximal esophageal pouch reveals a blind pouch with air in the gastrointestinal tract. In esophageal atresia without TEF, gas is absent from the gastrointestinal tract, whereas in TEF without esophageal atresia (H type), infants may have nonspecific symptoms for several months and then exhibit chronic cough with feeding and recurrent pneumonia. Abnormal lower esophageal sphincter function results in gastroesophageal reflux, which may lead to esophagitis, stricture formation, wheezing, and recurrent pneumonia.

Treatment

Placing the infant in a 60-degree head-up prone position and minimizing disturbance of the infant is recommended to prevent reflux and aspiration of gastric contents. To remove swallowed oral secretions from the proximal esophageal pouch, a Replogle tube may be placed to suction. The usual corrective procedure is division and closure of the TEF and end-to-end anastomosis of the proximal and distal esophagus. If the distance between esophageal segments is too long for primary anastomosis, delayed anastomosis follows stretching of the upper segment. Strictures at the anastomosis site require periodic dilation.

◆ **KEY POINT** ◆

1. When there is abnormal anastomosis of superior and inferior portions of the esophagus, esophageal atresia results. Of neonates with esophageal atresia, 85% have tracheoesophageal fistula.

Duodenal Atresia

Duodenal obstruction may be complete (atresia) or partial (stenosis), owing to a web, band, or annular pancreas. Duodenal atresia results from a failure of the lumen to recanalize during the eighth to tenth weeks of gestation. Seventy percent of the cases of duodenal atresia are associated with other malformations including cardiac anomalies, and gastrointestinal defects such as annular pancreas, malrotation of the intestines, and imperforate

anus. Twenty-five percent of infants with duodenal atresia are premature. Duodenal atresia is often associated with trisomy 21.

Clinical Manifestations

With complete obstruction, in utero polyhydramnios may be present. After birth, bilious emesis begins within a few hours after the first feeding. Abdominal radiographs usually show gastric and duodenal gaseous distention. This finding is known as the "double bubble" sign, proximal to the atretic site. The presence of gas in the distal bowel suggests partial obstruction, and a contrast radiographic study of the abdomen should be performed.

Treatment

Treatment is surgical. Mortality is related to prematurity and other associated anomalies.

◆ **KEY POINTS** ◆

1. Duodenal atresia results from a failure of the lumen to recanalize during the eighth to tenth weeks of gestation.

2. Seventy percent of the cases of duodenal atresia are associated with other malformations including cardiac anomalies, and gastrointestinal defects such as annular pancreas, malrotation of the intestines, and imperforate anus.

Congenital Diaphragmatic Hernia

Congenital diaphragmatic hernia results from a defect in the posterolateral diaphragm that allows abdominal contents to enter the thorax and compromise lung development. This defect is commonly referred to as a Bochdalek hernia. Ninety percent of congenital diaphragmatic hernias occur on the left side of the diaphragm. The combination of pulmonary hypoplasia and pulmonary arteriolar hypertension makes this congenital defect lethal in many cases.

Clinical Manifestations

Early symptoms include respiratory distress with decreased breath sounds on the affected side and shift of heart sounds to the opposite side with a scaphoid abdomen. Diagnosis is sometimes made via ultrasound while the fetus is in utero. If the diagnosis is not known at birth, a simple chest radiograph will make the diagnosis.

Treatment

Because of pulmonary hypoplasia and pulmonary hypertension, the child must be intubated and ventilated. Sometimes conventional ventilation is not sufficient to provide adequate oxygen delivery and carbon dioxide excretion; in such cases, high-frequency ventilation or ECMO may be needed to manage the child's pulmonary hypertension. A Replogle tube is placed to minimize gastrointestinal distention that would further diminish effective lung volume. Muscle relaxants are given, and the patient is mildly hyperventilated to create a respiratory alkalosis to minimize pulmonary arteriolar hypertension. Sodium bicarbonate is also given to increase the pH and minimize pulmonary hypertension. Operative repair with balanced chest drainage is needed to avoid excessive transalveolar pressure gradients.

◆ **KEY POINTS** ◆

1. Congenital diaphragmatic hernia results from a defect in the left posterolateral diaphragm that allows abdominal contents to enter the thorax and compromise lung development.

2. The combination of pulmonary hypoplasia and pulmonary arteriolar hypertension makes this congenital defect lethal in many cases.

3. Sometimes conventional ventilation is not sufficient to provide adequate oxygen delivery and carbon dioxide excretion; in such cases, high-frequency ventilation or ECMO may be needed to treat pulmonary hypertension.

Omphalocele

Omphalocele results when the abdominal viscera herniate through the umbilical and supraumbilical portions of the abdominal wall into a sac covered by peritoneum and amniotic membrane. The defect results from a failure of migration of the bowel from the umbilical coelom. Large defects may contain the entire gastrointestinal tract and the liver and spleen. The sac covering the defect is thin and may rupture in utero or during delivery. The incidence of omphalocele is 1:6000 births.

Clinical Manifestations

Polyhydramnios is noted in utero, and 10% of infants with omphaloceles are born prematurely. Diagnosis is often made by prenatal ultrasound. Thirty-five percent of afflicted infants have other gastrointestinal defects, and 20% have congenital heart defects. Ten percent of children with omphalocele have Beckwith-Wiedemann syndrome (exophthalmos, macroglossia, gigantism, hyperinsulinemia, and hypoglycemia).

Treatment

Cesarean section may prevent rupture of the sac. Small defects may sometimes be closed primarily, whereas larger defects often require a staged repair that involves covering the sac with prosthetic material.

Treatment of the intact omphalocele sac includes low-pressure intermittent nasogastric tube suction to minimize gastrointestinal distention, covering the sac with petrolatum-impregnated gauze, wrapping the infant in a dry sterile towel to minimize heat loss, and wrapping the sac on the abdomen with Kling gauze to support the viscera on the abdominal wall. There should be no attempt to reduce the sac, because this may cause rupture of the sac, interfere with venous return from the sac, and cause respiratory distress. Broad-spectrum antibiotics should be given. Surgical consultation should be arranged, and definitive surgery should be delayed until the infant is thoroughly resuscitated. Definitive care can be postponed as long as the sac remains intact.

Treatment of the ruptured sac is similar to that of the intact sac, except that saline-soaked gauze is placed over the exposed intestine, and emergent surgical intervention is needed to cover the intestine.

◆ **KEY POINTS** ◆

1. Omphalocele results when the abdominal viscera herniate through the umbilical and supraumbilical portions of the abdominal wall into a sac covered by peritoneum and amniotic membrane. The defect results from a failure of migration of the bowel from the umbilical coelom.

2. Treatment of the intact omphalocele sac includes nasogastric sump suction to minimize gastrointestinal distention, covering the sac with petrolatum-impregnated gauze, wrapping the infant in a dry sterile towel to minimize heat loss, and wrapping the sac on the abdomen with Kling gauze to support the viscera on the abdominal wall.

3. Treatment of the ruptured sac is similar to that of the intact sac, except that saline-soaked gauze is placed over the exposed intestine, and emergent surgical intervention is needed to cover the intestine.

Gastroschisis

Gastroschisis, by definition, contains no sac and the intestine is herniated through the abdominal wall 2 cm lateral to the umbilicus. The eviscerated uncovered mass is adherent, edematous, dark in color, and covered by a gelatinous matrix of greenish material.

Clinical Manifestations

Polyhydramnios is noted in utero. Sixty percent of these infants are born prematurely, and 15% have associated jejunoileal stenoses or atresias.

Treatment

Treatment of gastroschisis involves placement of a nasogastric tube to suction, covering the exposed intestine with saline-soaked gauze, wrapping the infant in a dry, sterile towel to minimize heat loss, and starting antibiotics to cover for bowel flora. Gastroschisis is a surgical emergency, and single-stage primary closure is possible in only 10% of infants.

◆ KEY POINTS ◆

1. Gastroschisis, by definition, contains no sac and the intestine is herniated through the abdominal wall 2 cm lateral to the umbilicus.

2. Gastroschisis is a surgical emergency, and single-stage primary closure is possible in only 10% of infants.

Cleft Lip and/or Palate

Pathogenesis

Cleft lip with or without cleft palate occurs in 1:1000 births and is more common in males. Unilateral cleft lip is the result of failure of the ipsilateral maxillary prominence to fuse with the medial nasal prominence. This process produces a persistent labial groove. Failure of bilateral fusion produces bilateral cleft lip.

Cleft palate occurs in 1:2500 births. Development of the palate proper, which includes the hard palate, soft palate, uvula, and maxillary teeth, is completed by the ninth week of gestation. This region develops from the maxillary bone plates that are initially separated by the tongue. As the tongue descends in the floor of the mouth and moves forward, the two plates fuse. Failure of the tongue to descend produces the midline palatal clefts.

Epidemiology

Multiple genetic and environmental factors play a role in the etiology of the cleft lip. The recurrence risk in siblings is 3–4%. The risk of a child with a mother with cleft lip is 14%. Genetic factors are important in cleft palate and recurrence risk is the same as that for cleft lip. Cleft palates are common in patients with chromosomal abnormalities.

Clinical Manifestations

Malformations associated with cleft lip include hypertelorism, hand defects, and cardiac anomalies. In general, feeding difficulties are not seen in isolated cleft lip.

Treatment

Most cleft lips are repaired shortly after birth or once the infant demonstrates steady weight gain. Cleft palate repair is usually undertaken at 12–24 months of age. In the newborn period, respiratory and feeding problems may occur. Repositioning the tongue and feeding the baby on his or her side should resolve respiratory difficulties. Most patients do well with a long, soft nipple that has a hole that is longer than usual. Complications after cleft palate repair include speech difficulties, dental disturbances, and recurrent otitis media. Although two-thirds of children demonstrate acceptable speech, it may have a nasal quality or a muffled tone.

◆ KEY POINTS ◆

1. Most cleft lips are repaired shortly after birth or once the infant demonstrates steady weight gain.

2. Cleft palate repair is usually undertaken at 12–24 months of age.

3. In the newborn period, respiratory and feeding problems may occur with cleft lip and/or palate.

Neural Tube Defects

Neural tube defects are discussed in detail in Chapter 15.

Nephrology and Urology

The renal system is the primary regulator of body fluid volume, osmolarity, composition, and pH. The kidneys collect and excrete many waste products of metabolism, such as urea and creatinine, and preserve the ionic equilibrium by conserving or secreting specific electrolytes as needed. Abnormalities may result in growth failure, hypertension, acidosis, or end-stage renal disease.

Infants, in particular, are susceptible to renal challenges. Their kidneys are relatively less effective in filtering plasma, regulating electrolytes, and concentrating urine. Dosing of medications that undergo renal clearance should be adjusted to avoid toxicity in neonates.

RENAL DYSPLASIA

The most common renal dysplasia is multicystic kidney, in which the organ consists of multiple fluid-filled cysts that do not communicate with one another. Affected kidneys are nonfunctional, but the condition is virtually always unilateral. Multicystic kidney is one of the two most common causes of renal masses in the newborn (the other is hydronephrosis resulting from ureteropelvic junction obstruction). The diagnosis is confirmed by ultrasound. Many cases eventually undergo involution; nephrectomy is appropriate for those that do not. Long-term complications, such as hypertension and malignancy, are rare.

Polycystic kidney disease is an inherited disorder that occurs in two forms: the infantile autosomal-recessive type and the adult autosomal-dominant type. In the former, the kidneys appear grossly normal but the renal collecting tubules are dilated, producing small cysts. Unaffected segments are interspersed, but in general the kidneys function poorly. The condition is usually discovered as a result of workup for a palpable renal mass. Similar dilation is found in the hepatic bile ducts, with varying degrees of periportal fibrosis. Most patients die before reaching adulthood.

URETEROPELVIC JUNCTION OBSTRUCTION

Ureteropelvic junction obstruction (UPJ) is the most common cause of hydronephrosis in childhood. Possible causes include intrinsic fibrosis at the junction of the renal pelvis and ureter, kinking of the ureter, or a crossing renal vessel.

Clinical Manifestations

The obstruction leads to increased intrapelvic pressure, dilation of the pelvis and calyces, urinary stasis, infection, hematuria, pain, and gradual destruction of the renal parenchyma. Occasionally, the condition is suggested by prenatal ultrasound; in the infant, both intravenous pyelography and ultrasound are sensitive diagnostic tests for UPJ.

Treatment

Pyeloplasty, which provides an alternative route of transport from the pelvis to the ureter, is the surgical repair of choice.

VESICOURETERAL REFLUX

Vesicoureteral reflux is the retrograde projection of urine from the bladder up through the ureters toward the kidneys. The reflux may be mild or severe, producing large, tortuous, dilated ureters and gross pyelocaliectasis. In children, the condition is usually bilateral and most commonly results from insufficient tunneling of the ureters into the submucosal bladder tissue. When bladder pressure increases during voiding, the one-way valve mechanism needed to shut off retrograde flow is ineffective.

Clinical Manifestations

The most frequent presentation is recurrent urinary tract infections (UTIs). A voiding cystourethrogram detects abnormalities at ureteral insertion sites and allows classification of the grade of reflux (Fig. 14–1). The test should include urethral images to rule out posterior urethral valves as an etiology in males. Low grades of reflux often resolve spontaneously, although prophylactic antibiotic treatment may be required. Severe grades produce progressive renal injury and scarring.

Treatment

Ureteral reimplantation is highly successful in preventing reflux; the ureters are surgically tunneled through

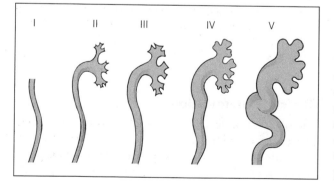

Figure14–1 International classification of vesicoureteral reflux.

larger segments of submucosa at a more physiologic, advantageous angle.

POSTERIOR URETHRAL VALVES

Occurring only in males, posterior urethral valves consist of posteriorly situated leaflets within the prostatic urethra, which result in partial bladder outlet obstruction. The increased pressure upstream causes urethral dilation, bladder neck hypertrophy, mucosal trabeculation, and, not infrequently, vesicoureteral reflux and renal dysgenesis.

Clinical Manifestations

The disorder may be detected by prenatal ultrasound or during the newborn examination (distended bladder or renal mass). In older infants, parents often comment that their boys have weak or dribbling streams. Occasionally, the condition is diagnosed in young children during workup for a UTI.

Treatment

Transurethral ablation of the obstructing tissue is the treatment of choice. In neonates who are too small for the procedure, temporary supravesical diversion is appropriate until ablation can be performed. Prognosis depends on the degree of renal and bladder impairment at the time of repair.

HYPOSPADIAS

Hypospadias is the most common congenital anomaly of the penis, resulting from incomplete development of the distal urethra. The urethral meatus is malpositioned along any point of the ventral shaft of the penis, midline of the scrotum, or perineum. Proximal hypospadias may cause curving of the penis, termed chordee. Associated anomalies include hernias and undescended testes. Circumcision is contraindicated because surgical repair requires preputial tissue. The aims of therapy are to extend the urethral meatus to the tip of the glans penis and produce the appearance of a normal circumcised phallus. Prognosis is excellent for distal lesions; proximal lesions may require multiple revisions before an acceptable result is achieved.

CRYPTORCHIDISM

Cryptorchidism is defined as testes that have not fully descended into the scrotum and, unlike retracted testes, cannot be manipulated into the scrotum with gentle pressure. Testes that remain outside the scrotum are more vulnerable to trauma and testicular cancer. Bilateral cryptorchidism results in oligospermia and infertility. Term infants have a 3–4% incidence at birth; the rate is much higher in premature infants.

Clinical Manifestations

One or both testes may be positioned in the abdomen or anywhere along the inguinal canal. Most are palpable on examination.

Treatment

By age 1 year, all but 1% of males have bilateral descended testicles. Descent after 12 months is unlikely. Surgical repair has a much higher success rate (90–95%) than hormone therapy (30%). It is unclear whether testes that are surgically relocated within the first year have a lower incidence of later malignant degeneration.

TESTICULAR TORSION

Torsion is a true surgical emergency, requiring prompt diagnosis to prevent loss of the testicle. Most patients with testicular torsion lack the posterior attachment to the tunica vaginalis that keeps the testis from rotating around the spermatic cord.

Clinical Manifestations

Clinical manifestations include the acute onset of unilateral scrotal pain; nausea; vomiting; a swollen, exquisitely tender testis; and scrotal edema. Epididymitis, which is more common during puberty and adolescence, presents with a similar clinical picture. Doppler ultrasound is only marginally helpful in differentiating between the two conditions and may delay appropriate treatment. Occasionally, the torsion is limited to testicular or epididymal appendices; localized tenderness and the "**blue dot**" sign suggest limited involvement.

Treatment

Early surgical intervention is critical; irreversible changes occur as soon as 2 hours after onset. Necrotic testes must be removed. The contralateral testis is fixed to the posterior scrotal envelope during surgery to avoid subsequent torsion.

HYDROCELES AND VARICOCELES

Hydroceles are fluid-filled sacs in the scrotal cavity consisting of remnants of the processus vaginalis. Hydroceles that communicate with the peritoneal cavity may develop into hernias when a piece of bowel descends along the path into the scrotum. Communicating hydroceles and scrotal hernias should be repaired as soon as possible to prevent the development of an incarcerated hernia. Most noncommunicating hydroceles involute by 12 months of age.

A **varicocele** is defined as a dilated testicular vein and enlarged pampiniform plexus resulting from the absence of the venous valves responsible for advancing the blood toward the heart. They generally occur in adolescent males and are more common on the left. Varicoceles that are large and painful, interfere with testicular hormone function, or cause ipsilateral testicular atrophy should be surgically repaired. Unrepaired varicoceles place the patient at an increased risk of infertility.

ENURESIS

Successful bladder control is usually achieved between the ages of 24 and 36 months, although many developmentally normal children take significantly longer. Enuresis is the involuntary loss of urine in a child older than age 5 years. It may be nocturnal or daytime, primary or secondary. **Primary** enuretics are patients who have never successfully maintained a dry period, whereas **secondary** enuretics are usually dry for several months before regular wetting recurs.

Clinical Manifestations

A careful history and physical examination may suggest secondary causes for enuresis such as UTI, developmental delay, obstruction, emotional strain, or inappropriate parental toilet training expectations. Primary nocturnal enuresis, which is far more common, is thought to be due to delayed maturational control or inadequate levels of antidiuretic hormone secretion during sleep.

Treatment

The most popular method of treatment is a nighttime audio alarm that sounds as soon as the child starts to urinate, eventually conditioning controlled bladder emptying before enuresis. Intranasal **desmopressin acetate** (analogous to endogenous vasopressin) acts to concentrate the urine. If given in the evening, less urine is produced overnight, decreasing the likelihood of wetting.

NEPHROTIC SYNDROME

Pathogenesis

Nephrotic syndrome (NS) is a noninflammatory disorder of glomerular function characterized by extreme proteinuria, hypoalbuminemia, hyperlipidemia, and edema.

Epidemiology

NS may be idiopathic (90%) or secondary in nature (Table 14–1). Minimal change disease (MCD) is by far the most common cause of primary NS in the pediatric population. Most patients present between the ages of 2 and 6 years, and boys outnumber girls. Focal segmental glomerulosclerosis (FSGS) and diffuse mesangial proliferative glomerulonephritis (DMPG) account for the remainder of idiopathic NS in children.

Clinical Manifestations

History and Physical Examination

Patients with early NS appear quite well. Periorbital edema is commonly the first abnormality noted. This is followed by lower extremity and then generalized edema and ascites. Anorexia and diarrhea are variably present.

Differential Diagnosis

The differential diagnosis of edema, the most frequent presenting complaint in NS, is discussed in Chapter 7. Other conditions associated with proteinuria include exercise, trauma, UTI, dehydration, and acute tubular necrosis; however, none of these causes the degree of protein loss seen in NS. Of note, glomerular filtration rate (GFR) and blood pressure are less likely to be affected in NS than in the nephritic syndromes (Table 14–2).

Diagnostic Evaluation

The hallmark of NS is severe proteinuria. Affected individuals lose more than **40 mg protein/m^2/hr** in their urine when averaged over a 24-hour period, a large proportion of which is albumin. As the liver rapidly manufactures replacement proteins, large amounts of lipids are created as well.

Renal biopsy is indicated for patients outside the typical age range for MCD and those who do not respond to steroids. True to the disease's name, gross sections and light microscopy in MCD show few if any abnormali-

---

TABLE 14–1

Conditions Associated with Secondary NS

Postinfectious glomerulonephritis
Acute viral illnesses
Hemolytic-uremic syndrome
Congestive heart failure
Constrictive pericarditis
Bacterial endocarditis
Alport syndrome
Renal vein thrombosis
Systemic lupus erythematosus
Medications
Malignant hypertension
Pre-eclampsia

TABLE 14–2

Glomerulonephritic Syndromes versus Nephrotic Syndromes

Nephritic Syndromes	Primary Nephrotic Syndromes
IgA nephropathy	Minimal change disease
Acute poststreptococcal GN	Focal segmental glomerulosclerosis
GN of systemic lupus erythematosus	Membranoproliferative GN
GN of Henoch-Schönlein purpura	Membranous GN
Rapidly progressive GN	

GN, glomerulonephritis.

ties; the only consistent finding is effacement of epithelial cell foot processes demonstrated by electron microscopy. FSGS is characterized by focal sections of distorted glomeruli, with mesangial hypertrophy and segmental capillary loop destruction. Increased mesangial cellularity and glomerular basement membrane (GBM) thickening are found in DMPG.

Treatment

If the clinical presentation is consistent with uncomplicated primary NS, strict dietary salt restriction and oral steroid therapy are appropriate. If symptoms do not resolve within 8–12 weeks or if the patient experiences frequent or severe relapses, renal biopsy is indicated to confirm the diagnosis.

Steroids result in prompt remission in most cases of MCD. NS that does not respond to oral steroids may require treatment with stronger immune suppressants such as cyclophosphamide.

Bacterial infections, particularly **spontaneous peritonitis**, are the most frequent complications of NS and usually occur while the patient is on immunosuppressant therapy. The prognosis of MCD is excellent; although up to 80% of patients relapse at least once, very few develop any long-standing renal insufficiency. Unfortunately, patients with FSGS and DMGN do not respond well to steroid therapy, and end-stage renal disease is common. Renal transplant is not a cure, because both diseases recur in the transplanted kidney.

◆ KEY POINTS ◆

1. Nephrotic syndrome is characterized by proteinuria, hypoalbuminemia, hyperlipidemia, and edema.

2. Minimal change disease is the most common type of idiopathic NS.

3. Most cases respond to oral steroid therapy; renal biopsy is recommended for those that do not.

GLOMERULONEPHRITIS

The term glomerulonephritis implies **inflammation** of the GBM. Antigen-antibody complexes are formed or deposited in the subepithelial or subendothelial areas; immune mediators follow, resulting in inflammatory injury. **Hematuria**, overt or microscopic, is the hallmark of the disease. Distinguishing characteristics of the major glomerulonephritic syndromes of childhood are discussed next.

Acute poststreptococcal glomerulonephritis (APGN) is by far the most common glomerulonephritis in childhood. It occurs sporadically in older children and is twice as common in males. Streptococcal infections involving either the throat or the skin precede the clinical syndrome by an average of 8–12 days. Antibody titers indicative of a recent streptococcal infection must be elevated to make the diagnosis and are often accompanied by depressed C3 levels. The histology is characterized by mesangial and capillary cell proliferation, inflammatory cell infiltration, and granular "humps" of IgG and C3 below the GBM.

IgA nephropathy, once thought to be a benign condition, is now known to slowly progress to renal failure in almost half of cases. Renal biopsy alone makes the diagnosis, demonstrating mesangial deposits of IgA in the glomeruli. Henoch-Schönlein purpura, a systemic vasculitis characterized by purpura, crampy abdominal pain, and arthritis, may progress to a glomerulonephritis-type syndrome that is indistinguishable from IgA nephropathy.

The multiple forms of progressive hereditary nephritis are collectively known as **Alport syndrome**. Inheritance may be either X-linked or autosomal dominant. The defective GBM is fragile and ruptures easily, healing into thickened bands. Most forms are associated with bilateral cochlear hearing loss, which roughly parallels renal involvement in severity.

Rapidly progressive glomerulonephritis (RPGN) is the description given to a number of glomerulopathies that, for unknown reasons, deteriorate over a few weeks or months to renal failure, uremia, encephalopathy, and even death. All forms demonstrate generalized crescent formation in the glomeruli thought to represent cellular destruction by macrophages with subsequent necrosis and fibrin deposition. Fortunately, RPGN is rare in children.

Glomerulonephritis associated with systemic lupus erythematosus is discussed in Chapter 11.

Differential Diagnosis

The differential diagnosis of hematuria, the most prominent manifestation of glomerulonephritis, includes other renal conditions (infection, trauma, malignancy, stones, cystic disease) and hematologic disorders. Hematuria can be entirely benign or occur normally after strenuous exercise. Vaginal bleeding produces false-positive results if the specimen is collected incorrectly. Both hemoglobin and myoglobin test positive for blood on urine dipstick; however, the urinalysis will be negative.

Clinical Manifestations

The initial presentation includes hematuria, azotemia, oliguria, malaise, edema, and **hypertension**. Red cell casts are invariably present; in fact, the urine is often described as "**tea-colored**" by parents. Proteinuria occurs as well but is less prominent than in NS. The GFR is compromised, leading to salt and water retention and circulatory overload. Azotemia is marked by increasing serum blood urea nitrogen and creatinine levels. Sodium and potassium regulation may be temporarily disrupted. Important laboratory studies include urinalysis, urine culture, hematocrit and platelet counts, coagulation studies, serum electrolytes, blood urea nitrogen and creatinine, streptococcal antibody titers, and complement levels.

Treatment

Positive streptococcal cultures are treated with appropriate antibiotic therapy. Hypertension, when present, can be severe, requiring vasodilators, diuretics, and fluid restriction. Steroids and immunosuppressants have not been shown to affect the progression or ultimate outcome.

Although the clinical manifestations of APGN may take a few months to resolve, the overall prognosis for return to normal function is excellent. Patients with other types of glomerulonephritis fare less well. Virtually all males and 20% of females with Alport syndrome progress to end-stage renal disease (ESRD) by middle adulthood. The course of RPGN is particularly devastating, with most patients becoming dialysis dependent within a few years. Most syndromes eventually recur in a transplanted kidney (APGN is a notable exception).

◆ KEY POINTS ◆

1. Glomerulonephritic syndromes are inflammatory and characterized by hematuria, azotemia, oliguria, edema, and hypertension.

2. Specific syndromes include acute poststreptococcal glomerulonephritis, IgA nephropathy,

hereditary nephritis, rapidly progressive glomerulonephritis, and systemic lupus erythematosus–associated glomerulonephritis.

3. Treatment is generally supportive; steroids have no proven benefit.

4. Most syndromes recur in a transplanted kidney.

RENAL TUBULAR ACIDOSIS

All classifications of renal tubular acidosis (RTA) are characterized by **hyperchloremic metabolic acidosis** resulting from insufficient renal transport of bicarbonate or acids. The nephron tubules are the site of reabsorption and secretion. Most of the bicarbonate filtered from the plasma is reabsorbed in the proximal tubule, along with amino acids, glucose, sodium, potassium, calcium, phosphate, and water. In the distal tubule, the remainder of the bicarbonate is reabsorbed and hydrogen ions are secreted into the tubules from the peritubular capillaries. Defects in either transport site compromise the kidney's ability to maintain pH homeostasis.

Differential Diagnosis

In **proximal** RTA (type 2), the proximal tubule fails to reabsorb bicarbonate from the ultrafiltrate. **Distal** RTA may result from either deficient hydrogen secretion into the filtrate (type 1) or impaired ammonia production in the face of hyperkalemia from hypoaldosteronism or pseudohypoaldosteronism (type 4). Distal type 4 is the most common RTA in both children and adults. Most types of RTA can be either hereditary or sporadic, acute or chronic, occurring alone or as part of a disease complex. For example, most patients exhibit proximal RTA (type 2) in conjunction with **Fanconi syndrome**, a generalized disorder of proximal tubule transport resulting in excessive urinary losses of bicarbonate, amino acids, small proteins, glucose, electrolytes, and water.

Clinical Manifestations

History and Physical Examination

Most patients who manifest proximal RTA (type 2) as part of Fanconi syndrome present with failure to thrive; associated signs and symptoms include chronic acidosis, hypokalemia, vomiting, anorexia, polydipsia and polyuria, volume contraction, and impaired vitamin D metabolism (rickets).

Distal RTA (type 1) also presents with metabolic acidosis and failure to thrive. Hypokalemia, hypercalciuria, and kidney stones are common. In contrast, the acidosis in distal RTA (type 4) occurs in the presence of hyperkalemia in conjunction with primary or secondary hypoaldosteronism or end-organ resistance.

Diagnostic Evaluation

Any patient with hyperchloremic metabolic acidosis of unclear etiology warrants further workup to rule out RTA (Fig. 14–2).

Treatment

Treatment consists of providing children with sufficient amounts of an **alkalinizing agent** (either bicarbonate or citrate) to completely correct the acidosis and restore normal growth. Thiazide diuretics are administered in proximal RTA to increase proximal tubular reabsorption of bicarbonate. Hypokalemia is treated concurrently when the alkali is coupled with potassium as a salt. Hyperkalemia is usually more difficult to correct; furosemide is prescribed unless the defect results in salt wasting. If RTA is associated with an underlying condition, the primary disorder must be treated.

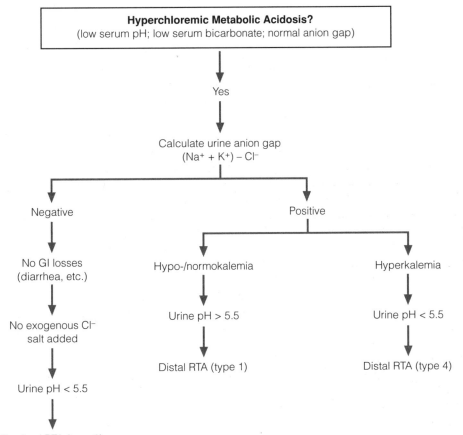

Figure 14–2 Diagnostic workup of hyperchloremic metabolic acidosis of unknown etiology.

◆ KEY POINTS ◆

1. All classifications of renal tubular acidosis are characterized by hyperchloremic metabolic acidosis.

2. The most common type in children is distal RTA type 4, resulting from hyperkalemia that interferes with ammonia production.

3. Fanconi syndrome is a generalized disorder of proximal tubule transport with excessive urinary losses of bicarbonate, proteins, glucose, electrolytes, and water.

4. Alkalizing agents correct the acidosis.

NEPHROGENIC DIABETES INSIPIDUS

Pathogenesis

Diabetes insipidus (DI) involves a disorder in renal concentrating ability. Patients produce up to 400 mL/kg/day of very dilute urine regardless of hydration status. DI may be central or nephrogenic in origin. In **central DI**, the production or release of antidiuretic hormone is insufficient (see Chapter 6). **Nephrogenic DI** results when either the nephron tubules are unresponsive to antidiuretic hormone or the concentration gradient pulling fluid from the tubule into the medullary interstitium is somehow disrupted.

Epidemiology

Nephrogenic DI may be hereditary or acquired and ranges in severity from mild to severe. It usually presents within the first several years of life. Acquired nephrogenic DI has been associated with polycystic kidney disease, chronic pyelonephritis, lithium toxicity, and sickle cell disease.

Clinical Manifestations

History and Physical Examination

All patients present with polyuria, resulting polydipsia, and thirst. Other features may include intermittent fever, irritability, vomiting, developmental delay, and growth retardation. Most affected children also have a history of chronic or recurrent hypernatremic dehydration. Some patients manifest no symptoms until they are stressed with illness. Others remain completely unable to keep themselves in fluid balance without continual therapy.

Differential Diagnosis

Other conditions that may present in a similar manner include diabetes mellitus and RTA. Differentiating central DI from nephrogenic DI is not possible based on symptomatology alone, although the former is more likely to follow head trauma or complicate meningitis.

Diagnostic Evaluation

Patients with nephrogenic DI are unable to concentrate their urine. Even in the face of significant dehydration, their urine specific gravity and osmolarity measurements remain inappropriately low. The workup presented in Figure 14–3 is recommended when the diagnosis is in question.

Treatment

Acute treatment consists of rehydrating the child, replacing ongoing urinary losses, and correcting electrolyte abnormalities.

Thiazide diuretics and aggressive oral fluid intake are helpful in the long-term management of this disease, but specific therapy is lacking.

Children with nephrogenic DI are at risk for poor growth and mental retardation. The disease is lifelong but carries a good prognosis provided that episodes of hypernatremic dehydration remain limited.

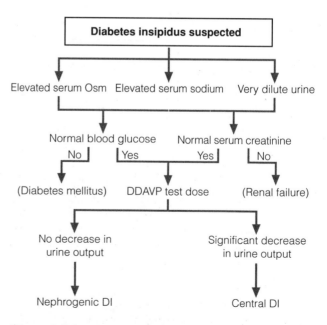

Figure14–3   Diagnosing nephrogenic DI.

1. Diabetes insipidus is a disorder of urine concentration.
2. Clinical manifestations include polyuria, polydipsia, and growth retardation.
3. There is no specific therapy for nephrogenic DI.
4. Repeated episodes of hypernatremic dehydration predispose to developmental delay.

HYPERTENSION

Blood pressure rises as a child grows, reaching adult values during adolescence. Hypertension in the pediatric population is defined as blood pressure greater than 95th percentile for age on three separate occasions.

Differential Diagnosis

Essential (primary) hypertension is the most common form in adults. Children are more likely to manifest **secondary hypertension**, usually related to renal disease. Endocrine, vascular, and neurologic conditions have also been associated with increased blood pressure (Table 14–3).

Clinical Manifestations

History

Hypertension that is stable or slowly progressive is unlikely to cause symptoms. The family history is often positive for hypertension, stroke, or premature heart attack. Patients with secondary hypertension often come to medical attention for complaints related to their underlying disease (i.e., growth failure, edema). The child's past medical history, state of health, recent medications, and review of systems for urinary tract symptoms provide pertinent information.

Severe hypertension or hypertension that has developed over a short period of time can cause headache, dizziness, and vision changes. Hypertensive encephalopathy is characterized by vomiting, ataxia, mental status changes, and seizures.

Physical Examination

The most important part of the examination is obtaining an accurate blood pressure reading. The air bladder portion of the cuff should encircle the patient's arm and

TABLE 14–3

Differential Diagnosis of Hypertension

Pain, anxiety	Endocrine
Inappropriate cuff size	Congenital adrenal
Essential hypertension	hyperplasia
Renal	Cushing syndrome
Glomerulonephritis	Hyperthyroidism
Pyelonephritis	Pheochromocytoma
Parenchymal (i.e.,	Hyperparathyroidism
cystic) disease	Hyperaldosteronism
Obstructive uropathy	SIADH
Nephrotic syndrome	Vascular
Renal tumor	Coarctation of the aorta
Renal failure	Renal vein thrombosis
Renal trauma	Renal artery stenosis
Neurologic	Large arteriovenous
Increased intracranial	fistula
pressure	Infective endocarditis
Hemorrhage	Vasculitis
Brain injury	Other
Familial	Chronic upper airway
dysautonomia	obstruction
Drugs and toxins	Pre-eclampsia
Oral contraceptives	Neurofibromatosis
Corticosteroids	Hypercalcemia
Cyclosporin	Malignant hyperthermia
Cocaine	Hypernatremia
	Acute intermittent
	porphyria

SIADH, syndrome of inappropriate antidiuretic hormone secretion.

be wide enough to cover 75% of the upper limb. A cuff that is too small will give a falsely elevated reading. At least once, the blood pressure should be taken in all four extremities to rule out **aortic coarctation**. Particular attention should be given to the heart sounds and peripheral pulses. Poor growth, flank pain, a retroperitoneal mass, large bladder, or abdominal bruit suggest a renal or renal vascular etiology. Obesity contributes to hypertension in a genetically predisposed patient.

Diagnostic Evaluation

The initial laboratory workup should include a complete blood count, serum electrolytes, blood urea nitrogen, and creatinine, urinalysis, and renin level. Renal ultrasound is the preferred study for looking at kidney size and anatomy; if Doppler is added, the renal vasculature can be examined as well. The chest radiograph, electrocardiogram, and echocardiogram allow assessment of heart function, whether cardiac deficits are the cause or the effect of the hypertension.

Treatment

The best treatment of essential hypertension is preventive health care. High-salt diet, sedentary lifestyle, cigarette use, alcohol abuse, high serum cholesterol levels, and obesity compound the disorder and increase the morbidity and mortality. Secondary hypertension responds to treatment of the underlying disorder when possible.

Pharmacologic therapy is indicated in patients with persistent or refractory hypertension. Diuretics and beta-blockers are used in younger children; calcium channel blockers and angiotensin-converting enzyme inhibitors are second-line treatment in this age group but are effective first-line agents in adolescents and adults due to fewer side effects.

In patients with severe hypertension, rapid decreases in blood pressure compromise organ perfusion. Hypertensive crisis is treated with intravenous nitroprusside or labetalol, which blocks both α_1 and beta receptors. Hydralazine and diazoxide are also effective; however, they are reserved for unresponsive hypertension due to their tendency to drop the blood pressure too quickly.

Stroke, heart attack, and renal disease are the most devastating complications of hypertension. Prognosis depends on the underlying disorder and degree of control.

◆ **KEY POINTS** ◆

1. Blood pressure norms are related to age and gender.

2. Three blood pressure readings on separate occasions that are greater than the 95th percentile for age and gender constitute hypertension.

3. Symptoms of hypertension range in severity depending on absolute value and rapidity of onset.

4. Children with hypertension should have screening tests to evaluate renal and cardiac function.

---

5. The first line of therapy is diet control, weight loss, and exercise.

6. Rapid drops in blood pressure, even if maintained in the normal range, may compromise cerebral perfusion in a patient with a history of sustained high blood pressure.

ACUTE RENAL FAILURE

Renal failure is an uncommon but potentially life-threatening condition in children. Acute renal failure (ARF) consists of an abrupt reduction in renal function, occurring over several hours to days, with retention of nitrogenous waste products (azotemia) and fluid and electrolyte imbalances.

Differential Diagnosis

The mechanism of ARF may be prerenal, intrarenal, or postrenal in nature (Table 14–4). **Prerenal** failure is the most common form of ARF in the pediatric population and results when a normal kidney experiences significant hypoperfusion, through the reduction of plasma volume, hypotension, or hypoxia. The decreasing GFR produces oliguria or anuria. Most patients completely recover from prerenal failure unless it is prolonged, unrecognized, or inappropriately treated.

By contrast, **intrarenal** failure results from an abnormality of the kidney itself, such as glomerulonephritis,

---

TABLE 14–4

Conditions Associated with Acute Renal Failure

Prerenal	Renal	Postrenal
Hypovolemia	Glomerulonephritis	Obstructive
Hypotension	Henoch-Schönlein	uropathy
Hypoxia	purpura	Vesicoureteral
	Pyelonephritis	reflux
	Aminoglycoside	Kidney stones
	toxicity	
	Acute tubular	
	necrosis	
	Interstitial nephritis	
	Renal vein	
	thrombosis	

interstitial nephritis, renal vasculitis, or acute tubular necrosis, a poorly understood condition in which damaged tubules become obstructed with cellular debris. Intrarenal conditions usually present with oliguria or anuria, although the urine output may be quantitatively normal in some cases. In **postrenal failure**, obstructive lesions at or below the collecting ducts produce increased intrarenal pressure and result in a rapidly declining GFR and hydronephrosis. The lesions may be congenital, structural, acquired, or functional. Patients with complete obstruction will be anuric. However, partial obstructions may present with normal or increased urine output.

Clinical Manifestations

History and Physical Examination

A medical history of recent dehydration, shock, cardiac surgery, aminoglycoside administration, streptococcal infection, or posterior urethral valves may help clarify the etiology. Reports of growth failure, bony abnormalities, anemia, deafness, and previous renal conditions suggest acute deterioration superimposed on chronic renal failure. On physical examination, particular attention is paid to hydration and cardiovascular status, abdominal tenderness, and abdominal or suprapubic masses. Edema, oliguria, and hypertension are usually evident.

Any finding consistent with congestive heart failure (hepatomegaly, diffuse crackles on lung examination) should be noted.

Diagnostic Evaluation

ARF is characterized by hyperkalemia, azotemia, and metabolic acidosis. Increased blood urea nitrogen and creatinine levels signal diminished renal function and should be followed closely. Anemia is variably present. Urinalysis and dipstick for hematuria, proteinuria, leukocytes, and casts also provide useful information. Spot checks of urine and plasma urea nitrogen, creatinine, osmolarity, and sodium can be used to differentiate between prerenal and intrinsic failure (Table 14–5).

Renal ultrasonography is the single best noninvasive radiographic test for determining the site of obstruction in postrenal failure, as well as kidney size and shape and renal blood flow. **Renal nuclear** scans delineate renal perfusion and functional differences. Intravenous pyelography, voiding cystourethrogram, and computed tomography may also be helpful depending on the results of preliminary studies. A **renal biopsy** is indicated when the diagnosis remains unclear or the extent of involvement is unknown.

TABLE 14–5

Acute Renal Failure: Urinary Indices

| Indices | Acute Renal Failure | |
	Prerenal	Intrinsic*
Older children and adults		
U/P urea nitrogen	>8	<3
U/P creatinine	>40	<20
U/P osmolality	>500 mOsm/kg H$_2$O; >1.5	<350 mOsm/kg H$_2$O; <1.5
FE$_{Na}$(%)†	<1.0	>1.0
Neonates and infants		
U/P urea nitrogen	Variable	Variable
U/P creatinine	Variable	Variable
U/PO osmolality	>1.0	<1.0
FE$_{Na}$(%)†	>2.5	<2.5

*Refers to classic acute tubular necrosis from various causes.

†Fractional excretion or filtered sodium = (U/P)Na (U/P) creatinine × 100.

Reproduced with permission from Cronan KM, Norman ME. Renal and electrolyte emergencies. In: Fleisher GR, Ludwig S, eds. Textbook of pediatric emergency medicine. 3rd ed. Baltimore, MD: Williams and Wilkins, 1993:704.

Treatment

Treatment consists of appropriate fluid management, correction of electrolyte abnormalities and pH, protein restriction, and, occasionally, short-term hemodialysis. The underlying abnormality must be corrected to achieve total resolution and prevent recurrence. The prognosis of ARF depends on the underlying etiology, the length of impairment, and the severity of functional disturbance.

◆ KEY POINTS ◆

1. ARF may be prerenal, intrarenal, or postrenal. Prerenal, due to hypovolemia, is the most common in children.

2. Laboratory findings include azotemia, hyperkalemia, and metabolic acidosis.

3. Treatment consists of resolution of the inciting condition, appropriate fluid management, correction of electrolyte abnormalities and pH, protein restriction, and, occasionally, short-term hemodialysis.

CHRONIC RENAL FAILURE

Chronic renal failure (CRF) implies that renal function has dropped below 30% of normal; function at 10% or less defines end-stage renal disease (ESRD). The most common cause of CRF in the pediatric population is obstructive uropathy, followed by renal dysplasia, glomerulonephropathies (particularly focal glomerulosclerosis), and hereditary renal conditions.

Clinical Manifestations

History and Physical Examination
Growth failure is the most frequent sign prompting a renal screening workup in the primary setting. Subjective complaints range from none to polyuria, episodic unexplained dehydration, salt craving, anorexia, nausea, malaise, lethargy, and decreased exercise tolerance. Hypertension and pallor are noted on examination. Longstanding CRF produces rickets.

Diagnostic Evaluation

Patients with CRF demonstrate many of the same laboratory abnormalities seen in ARF, including azotemia,

acidosis, sodium imbalance, and hyperkalemia. Anemia is more pronounced in CRF.

Treatment

Treatment for CRF includes nutritional, pharmacologic, and dialysis therapy. Children should receive at least 100% of the recommended daily allowance of calories, although dietary protein and sodium must be restricted. Growth failure is particularly difficult to treat; normalization of all metabolic parameters is virtually impossible short of renal transplant, and even then, catch-up growth is unlikely.

Renal transplantation is the ultimate therapy for all children with ESRD, and there are very few absolute contraindications. The donated organ may come from a living related donor or a cadaver; living related donor transplants have a better host and graft survival rate.

Calcium carbonate and activated vitamin D help to combat renal osteodystrophy. Recombinant erythropoietin is available in an intramuscular form and, together with oral iron, decreases the incidence of anemia.

Renal replacement therapy is indicated for children with renal function less than 10% of normal or children who can no longer fully participate in life. Aggressive hemodialysis can provide close to 10% of normal renal function but is very time-consuming. Peritoneal dialysis is becoming increasingly popular due to its portability and lower cost.

The indwelling vascular hemodialysis catheters may lead to complications such as bleeding, thrombosis, and infection. A life-threatening complication, termed disequilibrium syndrome, occurs when the serum urea nitrogen level drops too rapidly, resulting in brain edema evidenced by headache, nausea, vomiting, abdominal pain, and muscle cramps. Convulsions and coma may ensue. Hemodialysis in pediatric centers today is associated with a very low mortality rate. The most frequent complication of peritoneal dialysis is peritonitis, usually due to coagulase negative staphylococci.

Because of the need for complex and time-consuming treatment, children with CRF often experience a decrease in their quality of life and are predisposed to developmental and social delays.

◆ KEY POINTS ◆

1. The most common cause of chronic renal failure in children is obstructive uropathy.

---

2. Children with growth failure should be screened for renal disease.

3. Both hemodialysis and peritoneal dialysis are available but cannot achieve the equivalent of normal renal function.

4. Dysequilibrium syndrome is a life-threatening but uncommon complication of hemodialysis. Peritonitis may complicate peritoneal dialysis.

URINARY TRACT INFECTIONS

Pathogenesis

Bacterial UTIs are a frequent cause of morbidity in the pediatric population. An infection may be limited to the bladder (**cystitis**) or, less commonly, may involve the kidney as well (**pyelonephritis**). Most UTIs result from exterior fecal flora ascending the urinary tract.

Epidemiology

Female children have almost a tenfold risk over males. Although uncircumcised male neonates are more prone to UTIs, this susceptibility alone is not a sufficient indication for universal routine circumcision.

Risk Factors

The most significant risk factor is the presence of a urinary tract abnormality that causes urinary stasis, obstruction, or reflux.

Clinical Manifestations

History and Physical Examination

In older children, the signs and symptoms of cystitis are similar to those in adults and include low-grade fever, frequency, urgency, dysuria, incontinence, and hematuria. The picture in neonates is less clear; irritability, weight loss, cyanosis, and lethargy have all been reported. In contrast, pyelonephritis often presents with high fever and shaking chills, nausea and vomiting, and flank pain.

Differential Diagnosis

The differential diagnosis includes external genital inflammation and infections and vaginosis. **Pinworm infestation** may be mistaken for a UTI. Adenovirus can cause a hemorrhagic cystitis, which is self-limited and does not respond to antibiotics. Lower lobe pneumonia often presents with flank pain, fever, and chills.

Diagnostic Evaluation

Although pyuria, hematuria, and bacteriuria on urinalysis suggest a UTI, a positive urine culture is the gold standard for diagnosis. Sensitivity testing should also be done to ensure that an appropriate antibiotic is chosen for treatment. Current guidelines recommend that all children under the age of 24 months, all males, and nonadolescent females with UTIs undergo some imaging study to rule out vesicoureteral reflux, posterior urethral valves, and other anatomic defects that predispose to infection. Renal ultrasound, voiding cystourethrogram study, and nuclear medicine scanning are all appropriate for this purpose.

Treatment

Nontoxic-appearing children with a urinalysis suggestive of a UTI should be treated with ampicillin or cotrimazole until culture results are available. If the culture is negative, antibiotics may be discontinued. Positive urine culture results require a 10- to 14-day course with an appropriate oral antibiotic. Patients who are toxic appearing or patients with vomiting who cannot take oral antibiotics must be admitted to the hospital for intravenous antibiotics and observation. Usually, an aminoglycoside is added at this time. With improvement, these patients may be discharged home on an appropriate oral antibiotic to finish the course.

Most complications of UTIs are associated with pyelonephritis, including renal scarring, loss of function, and occasionally abscess formation. The prognosis for patients with isolated cases of cystitis is excellent; morbidity increases with recurrent infection.

◆ KEY POINTS ◆

1. Most urinary tract infections result from contamination of the urinary tract with exterior fecal flora.

2. Children with high-grade fevers, shaking chills, vomiting, and flank pain usually have infection involving the kidney and the lower tract.

3. Children less than 2 years of age, males, and nonadolescent females should undergo an imaging study to rule out anatomic abnormalities.

4. Pyelonephritis causes renal scarring and, with repeated infections, decreasing renal function.

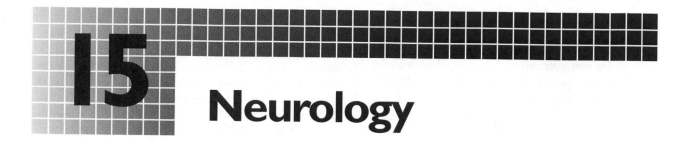

15 Neurology

The nervous system is the command-control station of the body, continually initiating, modulating, regulating, and reacting. It affords us our senses and sensations, movements and memory, emotions and equilibrium. Neurologic disorders range from those that are easily managed to others that are devastatingly cruel. Unfortunately, the phenomenal diagnostic advances over the past two decades have steadily outpaced progress in curative treatments.

NEURAL TUBE DEFECTS

Closure of the neural tube occurs during the third and fourth weeks of gestation. Maternal malnutrition, drug exposure, positive family history, low socioeconomic group, and older maternal age have all been associated with an increased risk of neural tube defects. Because failure of closure results in persistent leakage of alpha-fetoprotein into the amniotic fluid, the maternal serum **alpha-fetoprotein** level at 16–18 weeks is an excellent screening tool for identifying high-risk pregnancies. The incidence of neural tube defects is decreased in infants whose mothers receive folic acid supplementation during pregnancy.

Clinical Manifestations

Abnormalities may occur anywhere along the central nervous system; the higher the lesion, the more devas-

tating the sequelae. Neonates with **anencephaly** are born with large skull defects and virtually no cortex. Brainstem function is marginally intact. Many are stillborn; others die within days of birth. **Encephaloceles** are projections of cranial contents through a bony skull defect, usually in the occipital region. Such patients manifest severe mental retardation, seizures, and movement disorders. Hydrocephaly is a frequent complication.

Myelomeningocele, meningocele, and **spina bifida occulta** are neural tube defects in the spinal region associated with bony abnormalities. Myelomeningoceles are protruding sacs of neural and meningeal tissue, whereas meningoceles contain meninges only. Both are most common in the lumbosacral region. Bowel and bladder sphincter dysfunction are the rule, and sensorimotor loss occurs below the lesion. In spina bifida occulta, the bony vertebral lesion occurs without herniation of any spinal contents. Birthmarks, dimples, or hairy tufts at the base of the back suggest an underlying defect. Although the infant may initially appear neurologically normal, the caudal end of the cord is affixed or "tethered" to the distal spine. As the cord grows throughout childhood, it is unable to ascend into the adult position, resulting in scoliosis, sphincter dysfunction, lower extremity deformities, and increasing motor deficits. Twisting, stretching, or kinking of the upper cord results in the so-called **Arnold-Chiari malformation** and hydrocephalus.

1. The maternal serum alpha-fetoprotein level at 16–18 weeks of gestation is an excellent screen for neural tube defects.

2. The incidence of neural tube defects is decreased in infants whose mothers receive folic acid supplementation during pregnancy.

HYDROCEPHALUS

Pathogenesis

Hydrocephalus results when cerebrospinal fluid (CSF) production outpaces absorption, usually secondary to outflow obstruction. In **noncommunicating** hydrocephalus, the block exists somewhere within the ventricular system, and the ventricles above the obstruction are selectively enlarged. In contrast, all ventricles are proportionately enlarged in **communicating** hydrocephalus, which occurs when the subarachnoid villi are dysfunctional or obliterated. Hydrocephalus may result from a congenital malformation or be acquired later in life.

Risk Factors

Intrauterine infections, bacterial meningitis, intraventricular hemorrhaging, and subarachnoid bleeds all interfere with the absorption of CSF at the arachnoid villi. The process may be permanent if inflammation and scarring occur.

Clinical Manifestations

History and Physical Examination

The clinical manifestations of hydrocephalus depend on the rate of onset and the patency of the fontanelles. An inappropriate increase in head circumference or bulging anterior fontanelle may be the only indication in infants; poor feeding, irritability, lethargy, apnea, and bradycardia often provide additional clues. Clonus, a positive Babinski sign, and excessively brisk deep tendon reflexes are consistent with hydrocephalus. In older patients with acute courses, the signs are relatively clear and include headaches, nausea, vomiting, irritability, lethargy, papilledema, upward gaze paralysis, and diplopia (third and/or sixth cranial nerve palsies). **Cushing's triad**, consisting of bradycardia, hypertension, and changes in respiratory rate, is a late and ominous development.

Differential Diagnosis

Conditions that lead to increased intracranial pressure without hydrocephalus include intraventricular bleed, diffuse brain edema, abscesses, and tumors, all of which are easily differentiated by computed tomography (CT) or magnetic resonance imaging (MRI).

Diagnostic Evaluation

The CT scan is an important adjunct in the evaluation of hydrocephalus. Anatomic malformations, ventricular size, and source of obstruction are clearly delineated. An ultrasound scan may be sufficient in the young infant. A lumbar puncture is rarely indicated and should not be attempted if there is any danger of herniation.

Treatment

If the underlying etiology cannot be corrected, surgical diversion with a ventriculoperitoneal shunt decreases intracranial pressure and relieves the symptoms. Acetazolamide decreases CSF production and may be effective in the short term if the hydrocephalus is not severe.

Indwelling shunts are fraught with complications, most commonly obstruction and infection. *Staphylococcus epidermidis* is the most frequently isolated pathogen. Infected and nonfunctioning shunts must be replaced. Patients with hydrocephalus are at risk for developmental delay, visual impairment, and motor disturbances.

1. Clinical manifestations of hydrocephalus include inappropriately large head circumference, bulging fontanelle, poor feeding, irritability, and lethargy.

2. Cushing's triad is a late indicator of hydrocephalus.

3. A lumbar puncture is contraindicated if herniation is a concern.

CEREBRAL PALSY

Cerebral palsy (CP) is a nonprogressive disorder of movement and posture that results from a lesion of the immature brain. It is the most common movement disorder in children. Most cases occur in the absence of identifiable risk factors (i.e., prematurity, birth asphyxia, intrauterine growth retardation, early infection, or trauma). Contrary to earlier speculation, isolated obstetric complications are not associated with an increased risk of CP.

Clinical Manifestations

The presentation of CP varies widely. Infants with CP are initially hypotonic. In older patients, CP can be divided into two separate categories depending on physiologic characteristics. **Spastic** (pyramidal) CP is the most common and is further classified according to pattern of limb involvement (Table 15–1). **Extrapyramidal** CP may be broken down into **ataxic**, **choreoathetoid**, and **dystonic** forms. Patients with ataxic CP have pronounced difficulty coordinating purposeful movements; those with choreoathetoid or dystonic CP have uncontrollable abnormal jerking, writhing, or posturing movements. Differential characteristics on examination are summarized in Table 15–2.

Treatment

A multidisciplinary approach, developed by a physiatrist, general pediatrician, physical and occupational therapist, nutritionist, language therapist, and social support services, results in optimal therapy. Therapeutic goals include minimizing impairment, maximizing function, and preserving general health.

Associated neurologic deficits are common in patients with CP. Over half are mentally retarded. A third develop seizure disorders. Many have hearing and vision impairments. Other frequently encountered conditions include oral-motor dysfunction, language disorders, learning disabilities, and behavior problems.

◆ KEY POINT ◆

1. CP is a static disorder of movement and posture, which may be spastic, ataxic, choreoathetoid, and dystonic.

SEIZURE DISORDERS

Pathogenesis

Seizure disorders, collectively referred to as **epilepsy**, represent the clinical consequences of abnormal, excessive cerebral neuron discharge. There are many diseases, derangements, and disorders that cause seizures. In about 50% of patients, the etiology remains undetermined.

Epidemiology

In neonates, trauma, hypoxia, and infection are the primary causes of seizures. Infections and febrile seizures rank high in infancy and young childhood. Idiopathic epilepsy is the most common form diagnosed in older children and adolescents. Systemic disease, hypoglycemia, electrolyte and metabolic abnormalities, ingestions, and congenital or developmental defects can also result in seizure activity.

Risk Factors

Children with a history of febrile seizures are at a minimally increased risk of epilepsy later in life.

TABLE 15–1

Topographic Classification of Spastic (Pyramidal) Cerebral Palsy

Diplegia—bilateral lower extremity spasticity

Quadriplegia—all limbs severely involved, lower extremities more than upper

Hemiplegia—one side involved, upper extremity more than lower

Bilateral hemiplegia—all limbs severely involved, upper extremities more than lower

---

TABLE 15–2

Clinical Manifestations, Pyramidal versus Extrapyramidal CP

Pyramidal (Spastic) CP	Extrapyramidal CP
Tone remains relatively constant regardless of activity, level of arousal	Tone is variable depending on level of arousal
"Claps knife" resistance to applied force (sudden give alternating with increased resistance)	"Candle wax" (or "lead pipe") sustained, consistent resistance (no sudden give)
Primitive and pathologic reflexes	Primitive (but not pathologic) reflexes
Significant hyperreflexia	± hyperreflexia

Clinical Manifestations

History, Physical Examination, and Diagnostic Evaluation

The diagnosis of a seizure disorder is primarily based on the historical account of the episode and the physical examination. Electroencephalogram (EEG) studies are complementary and particularly useful in confirming the diagnosis, documenting baseline activity, and selecting effective treatment. Table 15–3 delineates the current international classification of epileptic seizures.

In **partial** seizures, only a small focus in one hemisphere is involved. The child remains conscious, and there is no postictal phase. Partial seizures involve very specific movements or sensations that remain stable with recurrent episodes. The symptoms are specific to the area of the brain involved and may be motor, cognitive, affective, or somatosensory. **Jacksonian** seizures are partial motor seizures in which a rhythmic twitching begins in one extremity and "marches" proximally until the entire limb is involved. Other partial seizures are more complex; semipurposeful movement continues without direction, or the child may begin lip-pursing or picking

---

TABLE 15–3

International Classification of Epileptic Seizures

Partial seizures

    Simple partial (intact consciousness)

        Motor

        Sensory

        Autonomic

        Psychic

    Complex partial (impaired consciousness)

    Partial seizures with secondary generalization

Generalized seizures

    Absence (typical, atypical)

    Tonic

    Clonic

    Tonic-clonic

    Myoclonic

    Atonic

    Infantile spasms

---

at his clothes. Occasionally, partial seizures progress to generalized convulsions.

Generalized seizure disorders produce a clinical syndrome indicative of bilateral hemispheric involvement, such as impaired consciousness, symmetric bilateral activity, and a postictal phase of confusion and lethargy. Tonic-clonic seizures are what most people think of as typical seizures. The tonic phase is characterized by sustained flexor or extensor contraction; these episodes are interspersed with clonic activity, consisting of rhythmic, symmetric, generalized contractions of the trunk and extremity muscle groups. Breathing may be irregular, although most episodes do not progress to cyanosis. Bowel or bladder incompetence is not uncommon. Seizures may also be solely tonic or solely clonic.

Absence, or **petit mal** seizures occur only in children. They are brief, staring episodes associated with alterations in consciousness. The child is unaware and immediately returns to the task at hand with no postictal phase. Although very brief, petit mal seizures can occur hundreds of times a day and may interfere with learning and socialization. An EEG demonstrates the characteristic generalized, symmetric 3-per-second spike and wave pattern.

Ataxic seizures consist of abrupt, total loss of postural tone lasting several minutes. **Myoclonic** seizures are simple, short jerks, similar to those occasionally experienced by normal subjects while in light sleep. Consciousness is minimally impaired, and there is no postictal phase. Myoclonic seizures are common in patients with cerebral palsy and degenerative disorders. **Akinetic** seizures are a subclass of myoclonic seizures; they resemble ataxic seizures but are extremely brief.

Two particularly devastating generalized seizures syndromes are **infantile spasms** and **Lennox-Gastaut syndrome**. Infantile spasms, which usually present between 2 and 7 months of age, are recurrent mixed flexor-extensor spasms that last only a few seconds but may repeat more than 100 times in a row. These seizures may be manifestations of a long list of neurodevelopmental and infectious nervous system diseases. The diagnosis is confirmed by a typical EEG pattern known as **hypsarrhythmia.** Corticotropin and corticosteroid administration has been shown to control the seizures in many patients but does not prevent developmental delay. Infantile spasms may evolve into Lennox-Gastaut syndrome, characterized by the frequent occurrence of mixed, generalized seizures that are notoriously refractory to pharmacologic treatment.

Differential Diagnosis

Febrile seizures do not represent true epilepsy. They typically occur in children 6 months to 5 years with fevers greater than 39°C. The rapid rise in temperature, rather than the height of the fever, is the important determinant. Most febrile seizures are simple; that is, they last less than 10 minutes, are generalized rather than focal, and do not recur within 24 hours. Complex febrile seizures last longer than 15 minutes, recur within 24 hours, or show signs of focalization. Such children should receive additional studies and close follow-up or hospitalization for observation. Simple febrile seizures do not require evaluation beyond determining the source of the fever. Caretakers should be counseled concerning fever avoidance and seizure precautions. Children who are toxic appearing, have meningeal signs, present with abnormal neurologic examinations, or have an underlying brain abnormality should not be presumed to have had a febrile seizure without ruling out more serious etiologies. Significant neurologic deficits resulting from febrile seizures are exceedingly rare. In most cases, the seizures do not recur with subsequent febrile episodes.

Essential tremor, spasmus nutans, tics, Tourette's syndrome, and myoclonus are various movement disorders that originate in the basal ganglia and may mimic seizures. Essential tremor begins in infancy or childhood and may involve the chin, head, neck, and hands; it usually does not interfere with normal functions. Spasmus nutans includes head nodding and rapid, small-amplitude nystagmus as well. Tourette's syndrome consists of motor and vocal tics, obsessive-compulsive tendencies, and attention-deficit hyperactivity disorder. Myoclonic movements are sudden involuntary jerk-like motions, similar to startle responses. Myoclonus is occasionally experienced by normal subjects during light sleep.

Other conditions that may be confused with seizures include breath-holding spells, syncope, benign paroxysmal vertigo, and temper tantrums. Pseudoseizures should be suspected in the patient with implausible findings (i.e., alert and responsive during generalized tonic-clonic movements).

Treatment

Effective treatment combines education and medication. Both the child and the parents should become knowledgeable about acute care and local emergency medical services.

The antiepileptic medications available today allow most patients to lead normal lives. These drugs have potentially dangerous side effects; there is little room for error between therapeutic and toxic dosing. Their names, indications, and side effects are listed in Table 15–4. Regular monitoring of serum concentration is recommended for all anticonvulsants.

Inducing ketosis through a high-fat "ketogenic" diet may control symptoms in some children with severe, unresponsive seizure disorders.

Emergency Management of Status Epilepticus

Status epilepticus is defined as a prolonged episode of seizure activity (greater than 15–30 minutes) or an ex-

TABLE 15–4

Indications and Side Effects of Anticonvulsants

Medication	Indications	Side Effects/Toxicity
Carbamazepine (Tegretol)	Partial, tonic-clonic	Diplopia, nausea and vomiting, ataxia, leukopenia, thrombocytopenia
Ethosuximide (Zarontin)	Absence	Rash, anorexia, leukopenia, aplastic anemia
Phenobarbital (Luminal)	Tonic-clonic, partial	Hyperactivity, sedation, nystagmus, ataxia
Phenytoin (Dilantin)	Tonic-clonic, partial	Rash, nystagmus, ataxia, drug-induced lupus, gum hyperplasia, anemia, leukopenia, polyneuropathy
Valproic acid (Depakene, Depakote)	Tonic-clonic, absence, partial	Hepatotoxicity, nausea and vomiting, abdominal pain, weight loss, weight gain, anemia, leukopenia, thrombocytopenia

tended period of recurrent seizures between which the patient does not return to consciousness. Status is dangerous, leading to hypoxia, brain damage, and death. Airway, breathing, and circulation should be evaluated and addressed as necessary. Intravenous or rectal short-acting benzodiazepines often break the seizure. Usually, a phenytoin loading dose is administered as well to prevent recurrence; phenobarbital is preferred in newborns and young infants.

Most children with seizure disorder undergo remission, after which the medication can be tapered. Unfortunately, this is not true for children who have seizure disorders as a result of congenital or acquired brain damage.

◆ KEY POINTS ◆

1. Generalized seizures are always associated with impairment of consciousness.

2. Petit mal seizures show a characteristic 3-per-second spike and wave pattern on EEG; infantile spasms show hypsarrhythmia on EEG.

3. Febrile seizures are complex if they last more than 15 minutes, recur within 24 hours, or show signs of focalization.

4. Regular serum drug level monitoring is recommended for all anticonvulsants.

HEAD TRAUMA

Acute head trauma is a significant, often preventable cause of morbidity and mortality. Head injuries in children most often result from motor vehicle accidents, bicycle mishaps, falls, or child abuse. Males are twice as likely as females to sustain significant head trauma. The primary determinant of neurologic outcome is the length of coma; patients who remain unconscious for more than 14 days are at high risk for major cognitive and motor deficits. Severe injury is often associated with behavioral changes and memory problems. About 10% of children who are hospitalized after head trauma experience at least one seizure episode; 35% of these have recurrent, recalcitrant seizures termed post-traumatic epilepsy.

A concussion is defined as a brief loss of consciousness after head injury associated with retrograde and anterograde amnesia. Brain injury is undetectable, and the neurologic examination returns to normal within hours. In contrast, cerebral contusions represent direct bruise injury to the brain parenchyma. Tears within the brain tissue are referred to as cerebral lacerations.

Brain hemorrhages that occur after trauma are usually subdural or epidural rather than intraparenchymal (Table 15–5; Fig. 15–1).

TABLE 15–5

Differentiating Acute Subdural and Epidural Bleeds

	Subdural	Epidural
Location	Between the dura and arachnoid layers	Between the skull and the dura
Symmetry	Usually bilateral	Usually unilateral
Etiology	Rupture of bridging cortical veins	Rupture of middle meningeal artery or dural veins
Typical injury	Direct trauma or shaking	Direct trauma in the temporal area
Consciousness	Intact but altered	Impaired-lucid-impaired
Common associated findings	Seizures, retinal hemorrhages	Ipsilateral pupillary dilatation, papilledema, contralateral hemiparesis
Appearance on CT with contrast	Crescentic	Biconcave
Prognosis	High morbidity; low mortality	High mortality; low morbidity
Complications	Herniation	Skull fracture; uncal herniation

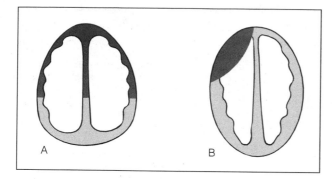

Figure 15–1 A. Subdural bleed. B. Epidural hematoma.

Clinical Manifestations

History

The source of injury should be described by the child and caretaker separately whenever possible. A history that is not consistent with a given injury is suspicious for child abuse. Reports of vomiting, severe headache, and mental status changes strongly suggest increased intracranial pressure. Confusion, loss of consciousness, amnesia, seizures, and visual impairment may also be present after significant injury.

Physical Examination

Bradycardia, hypertension, and changes in respiration form **Cushing's triad**, the hallmark of increased intracranial pressure. Palpation of the head may reveal step-off skull fractures or a bulging fontanelle. Basilar skull fractures are characterized by periorbital (**"raccoon eyes"**) or postauricular (**"Battle's sign"**) bruising, hemotympanum, or CSF rhinorrhea or otorrhea. Serial neurologic examinations track evolving lesions. Cranial nerve function, especially pupillary size and reactivity, may help localize the injury. Sensory and motor function are difficult to assess in the patient with impaired mental status, who may respond minimally even to noxious stimuli. Deep tendon and pathologic reflexes should be assessed in all patients.

The Glasgow Coma Score (Table 15–6) provides a rapid, widely used, easily reproducible method of quantifying and following neurologic ability.

Diagnostic Evaluation

Cervical spine films should be performed in all children with head trauma to rule out cervical injury or compression. Skull radiographs detect depressed fractures and some foreign bodies in penetrating injuries. Patients with loss of consciousness, persistent altered mental status, focal signs on neurologic examination, signs and symptoms of increased intracranial pressure, or a history of significant injury should have a CT with contrast.

Treatment

Treatment depends on the severity of the injury. Patients should be strapped to a board with a cervical collar in place upon initial evaluation in the field. Those with a Glasgow Coma Score less than 8 generally require intubation. Hypotension is uncommon in isolated head trauma, but associated injuries may lead to substantial hemorrhage and shock. Cerebral edema is the most important complication in the acute period. Oxygenation, fluid restriction, and elevation of the head of the bed may

TABLE 15–6

Glasgow Coma Scale

Activity	Score	Activity*
Eye opening		
Spontaneous	4	Spontaneous
To speech	3	To speech
To pain	2	To pain
None	1	None
Verbal		
Oriented	5	Coos, babbles
Confused	4	Irritable
Inappropriate words	3	Cries to pain
Nonspecific sounds	2	Moans to pain
None	1	None
Motor		
Follows commands	6	Normal, spontaneous movements
Localizes pain	5	Withdraws to touch
Withdraws to pain	4	Withdraws to pain
Abnormal flexion	3	Abnormal flexion
Abnormal extension	2	Abnormal extension
None	1	None

*Modified for infants.

be sufficient therapy to reduce increased intracranial pressure. However, patients with evidence of significant edema require intracranial pressure monitoring, hyperventilation, and mannitol administration.

Children with a history of loss of consciousness or abnormal neurologic findings should be hospitalized for observation. Patients who remain asymptomatic for 4–6 hours may be safely observed at home if caretakers are deemed reliable.

◆ KEY POINTS ◆

1. Length of unconsciousness correlates with degree of subsequent neurologic deficiency.

2. Subdural and epidural hemorrhaging is more common than intraparenchymal bleeding when the injury is trauma related.

3. "Racoon eyes" and Battle's sign suggest a basilar skull fracture.

ARTERIOVENOUS MALFORMATIONS

Strokes are relatively rare in children but may be caused by sickle-cell hemoglobinopathy, vasculitis, emboli, trauma, hypercoagulable states, and abnormalities of lipid metabolism. Congenital vascular abnormalities, including arteriovenous malformations (AVMs), are the most common cause of intracranial hemorrhaging in the pediatric population. An AVM is an abnormal collection of arteries and veins. It may present with physical findings consistent with seizures, acute hemorrhaging, or a focal mass. Occasionally, a cranial bruit is present on physical examination. Arteriography allows determination of the site of the abnormality and feeding vessels. Surgery is appropriate in some cases; however, extensive lesions are usually treated by selective embolization.

MIGRAINES

Migraines remain an underdiagnosed condition in the pediatric population. These severe, recurrent, pounding, often focal headaches may be precipitated by stress or specific food ingestions (i.e., chocolate). Nausea may accompany the pain. Migraines are typically preceded by an aura, a specific visual experience such as a receding

tunnel or flashing lights. Most patients give a positive family history. Occasionally, migraines are associated with transient neurologic deficits such as aphasia or hemiparesis. **Ergotamine**, a frequently prescribed vasoconstrictor, relieves or obviates the headache if administered early in its course. AVMs, meningitis, and space-occupying lesions should also be considered in every child with severe headaches.

ENCEPHALOPATHY

To function normally, the brain needs adequate blood flow, oxygen, energy substrates, removal of metabolic waste, and appropriate electrolyte balance. Disruption of any of these will lead to generalized cerebral dysfunction termed encephalopathy.

Differential Diagnosis

Conditions that may lead to encephalitis are listed in Table 15–7. Recent or concurrent febrile illness is consistent with encephalitis. Focal findings on examination and seizures are more common with herpes simplex virus than other viral etiologies. **Reye syndrome** tends to follow an acute viral illness, especially when aspirin has been administered to the child. Severe headache, vomiting, papilledema, and alteration in vital signs are characteristic of the increased intracranial pressure that always accompanies this disease. Metabolic disorders typically present with recurrent episodes of mental status changes that clear when the acute process is corrected. A careful history may suggest environmental exposures or drug use.

Clinical Manifestations

History and Physical Examination
Encephalopathy is characterized by mental status changes, confusion, odd or inappropriate behavior, disorientation, a shortened attention span, cognitive deficits, hyporesponsiveness, lethargy, stupor, or coma. The onset may be rapid or insidious.

Diagnostic Evaluation

Electrolyte abnormalities, uremia, hypoglycemia, acidemia, and hyperammonemia (as in Reye syndrome) can be ruled out with simple blood tests. The white blood cell count is elevated in the presence of infection. Urine and blood should be sent for toxicologic screening. Emergency CT scanning is indicated in patients with

TABLE 15–7

Causes of Encephalopathy in Children

Burns	Infection
Electrolyte disorders	AIDS encephalopathy
Hyponatremia	Encephalitis
Hypernatremia	Varicella
Hypocalcemia	Mumps
Hypercalcemia	Measles
Hypomagnesemia	Enterovirus
Hypermagnesemia	Cytomegalovirus
Factitious fever	Herpes simplex encephalitis
Hypertension	Lyme disease
Hypoxia/ischemia	Tuberculosis
Hysteria	Reye syndrome
Toxins	Metabolic disorders
Lead	Uremia
Illicit drugs	Hypoglycemia
Carbon monoxide	Ketoacidosis
Sedatives	Environmental toxins
Anticholinergics	Parainfectious syndromes
Salicylates	

evidence of increased intracranial pressure or focal neurologic signs. A lumbar puncture is appropriate when meningitis or encephalitis is suspected and increased intracranial pressure has been ruled out. Herpes simplex virus encephalitis is characterized by focal slowing or local wave pattern changes in temporal lobe activity on EEG and temporal lobe abnormalities on CT.

Treatment

The therapy for Reye syndrome involves close monitoring of serum glucose, electrolytes, transaminases, and ammonia. Patients with severe disease require intubation and close intracranial pressure monitoring in an intensive care unit. Treatment of infectious meningitis consists of appropriate antibiotic therapy. Metabolic disorders are discussed in Chapter 9. Ingestions are discussed in Chapter 2.

◆   **KEY POINT**   ◆

1. Reye syndrome is an encephalopathy associated with liver dysfunction that has been observed occasionally in children with viral illnesses treated with aspirin.

WEAKNESS OR PARALYSIS

Abnormalities leading to weakness and/or paralysis may occur at any level of the neuromotor axis, from the motor cortex and pyramidal tracts to the anterior horn cell, peripheral nerve, neuromuscular junction, and muscle.

Differential Diagnosis

Conditions causing muscular weakness in the pediatric population include the following.

Guillain-Barré syndrome (GBS) is an acute onset, progressive, ascending weakness caused by peripheral nerve demyelination that typically develops 7–21 days after an acute viral illness. Sensory and autonomic impairment is present but not prominent. Initial symptoms include symmetrical paresthesias of the distal extremities and proximal weakness. Deep tendon reflexes wane and disappear. Severity varies from mild weakness to progressive involvement of the trunk, respiratory muscles, and cranial nerves; respiratory muscle involvement may necessitate mechanical ventilation. Symptomatology peaks at 1 week; recovery takes weeks to months, and some patients experience permanent lingering disability. Plasmapheresis or intravenous immune globulin may hasten resolution.

Tick paralysis resembles GBS. Certain ticks in the Appalachian and Rocky Mountains are capable of producing a neurotoxin that blocks acetylcholine release. The patient recovers completely when the tick is removed from the skin.

Myasthenia gravis (MG) is an autoimmune disorder of the neuromuscular junction. The principal symptoms are easy fatigability and weakness that is exacerbated by sustained activity and improves with rest. MG typically presents in late childhood or adolescence; the onset may be rapid or insidious, and symptoms wax and wane over time. Almost half of patients experience ocular muscle involvement, resulting in ptosis and/or diplopia. Bulbar weakness leads to dysarthria and difficulty swallowing. MG may go into complete or partial remission after several years; however, most patients continue to experience periodic exacerbations throughout adulthood. Anticholinesterase therapy may relieve all or most of the symptoms in patients with mild involvement. Corticosteroids and other immune suppressants help curb the autoimmune response. Finally, thymectomy has been recognized as a potential method of treatment, presumably because the thymus is thought to sensitize the lymphocytes producing the offending antibodies.

Duchenne type muscular dystrophy (DMD), an X-linked recessive disease of muscle tissue, is the classic myopathy. Although present at birth, the disease presents in early childhood with motor delay. Weakness is greatest in the proximal muscle groups, so the patient must rise from sitting on the floor in two steps: first leaning on the hypertrophied calves and then pushing the trunk up with the arms (**Gower's sign**). Eventually, ambulation is lost, the muscles atrophy, and contractures develop. Cardiac and cognitive abnormalities are often present but seldom severe. Treatment is supportive. Most children become wheelchair bound early in the second decade with death before age 30.

Werdnig-Hoffmann disease is an inherited disorder involving degeneration of the anterior horn cells and cranial nerve motor nuclei. The more severe form becomes evident in utero or early infancy with generalized hypotonia, weakness, and decreased movement. Chronic, or type 2, Werdnig-Hoffmann disease presents between 6 and 12 months of age and is usually less severe. Cognitive abilities remain unaffected in both forms of the illness. No specific therapy is available; death occurs from repeated aspiration or lung infections.

Poliomyelitis is a viral illness affecting primarily the anterior horn cells of the spine. The incidence of paralytic poliomyelitis has been drastically reduced by the oral polio vaccine. **Tumors** that compress the spinal cord result in weakness and paralysis below the lesion and constitute a surgical emergency. **Cervical spinal cord injuries** produce sudden-onset paresthesias and paralysis. **Environmental toxin** exposure may induce acquired neuropathies or myopathies. For example, infants fed honey in their formula may develop infantile botulism.

Clinical Manifestations

Diagnostic workup is tailored by findings on history and physical examination. Patients with asymmetric weakness or signs of increased intracranial pressure should receive neuroimaging to rule out mass or hemorrhage. Findings that stop above a certain level of the spinal cord require evaluation for cord compression or injury. A lumbar puncture is helpful when infection is suspected. A significantly increased CSF protein level is consistent with Guillain-Barré syndrome. Administration of an anticholinesterase results in a transient increase in muscle strength in MG by blocking the breakdown of acetylcholine in the synaptic cleft. Repetitive electrical nerve stimulation studies demonstrate a significant fall in response strength over several rapid-fire trials. Werdnig-Hoffmann and DMD are confirmed by characteristic changes on EMG and muscle biopsy.

◆ KEY POINTS ◆

1. GBS is an acute, ascending, progressive weakness caused by peripheral nerve demyelination.
2. Myasthenia gravis is an autoimmune disorder of the neuromuscular junction characterized by easy fatigability and weakness.
3. Gower's sign is classically observed with DMD.

NEURODEGENERATIVE DISORDERS

Neural tissue degeneration can occur at any level of the nervous system from the brain cell bodies to the peripheral nerves. Many of the diseases are inherited; most are progressive and debilitating.

Clinical Manifestations and Treatment

Gray Matter Degeneration

Tay-Sachs, Gaucher's, and Niemann-Pick diseases all result from lipid buildup in neuronal cell bodies (see Chapter 10). Hypotonia, mental retardation, and seizures are common.

White Matter Degeneration (Leukodystrophies)

Leukodystrophies are inherited progressive degenerative diseases resulting from abnormal myelin formation and conduction. They present in younger patients with spasticity and developmental milestone loss; older children and adolescents experience visual disturbances, changes in personality, and dropping school grades.

Adrenoleukodystrophy, so named because of its frequent association with adrenal insufficiency, is characterized by areas of demyelination coupled with an intense perivascular inflammatory reaction. Psychomotor retardation progresses to spasticity, extensor posturing, and death within 12 years. Dietary therapy is controversial; no curative treatment is available.

◆ KEY POINT ◆

1. Adrenoleukodystrophy is the classic white matter degenerative disease.

ATAXIA

Ataxia is the inability to coordinate purposeful movement. Conditions that affect the cerebellum or inner ear are likely to cause ataxia in children.

Differential Diagnosis

Viral infections have been known to cause ataxia during attacks of acute labyrinthitis. Acute cerebellar ataxia may follow some viral infections by 2–3 weeks and is thought to be autoimmune in origin. These children present with horizontal nystagmus, postural ataxia, vomiting, and occasionally dysarthria. Headache and nuchal rigidity are absent, and examination of the CSF is negative.

Ataxia-telangiectasia is an autosomal-recessive neurodegenerative disorder that presents in toddlers and progresses to wheelchair dependence. The ataxia is associated with extensive telangiectasis and immunodeficiency (see Chapter 11).

Friedreich ataxia presents later in childhood with progressive ataxia, weakness, and muscle wasting. Skeletal deformities invariably follow. Most patients die of cardiomyopathy-related heart disease before the age of 30.

Intoxications, metabolic derangements, cerebellar hemorrhages, and tumors may also cause ataxia. Otitis media is a frequent cause of ataxia in young children.

Clinical Manifestations

Neuroimaging rules out hydrocephalus, mass lesions, and cerebellar hemorrhages. An MRI is preferable to CT, given its superior detail of posterior fossa structures. Patients with a fever should receive a lumbar puncture to evaluate for infection. Toxicologic screens of blood and urine should be obtained in all cases of acute ataxia. Chronic or recurrent ataxia warrants metabolic and genetic workup.

◆ KEY POINT ◆

1. The differential diagnosis for ataxia (incoordination) includes labyrinthitis, acute cerebellar ataxia, ataxia-telangiectasia, and Friedreich ataxia.

PHAKOMATOSES

Phakomatoses are neurocutaneous diseases characterized by lesions in the nervous system, skin, and eyes. Three autosomal-dominant conditions are described: neurofibromatosis, tuberous sclerosis, and von Hippel-Lindau disease. Sturge-Weber disease, a sporadic disorder, is traditionally included as well.

Clinical Manifestations and Treatment

Neurofibromatosis

Of the several variants of neurofibromatosis, types 1 (**von Recklinghausen's disease**) and 2 (bilateral acoustic neurofibromatosis) are the most common in children. Von Recklinghausen's disease is characterized by multiple café au lait spots; neurofibromas in the skin, major nerves, and CNS; Lisch nodules (iris lesions); optic gliomas; axillary freckling; and specific bony dysplasias. The diagnosis is clinically based (Table 15–8). Treatment is available for the associated seizures, learning disorders, renovascular hypertension, and scoliosis. Neurofibromas that cause impairment may be surgically removed; however, most will recur.

TABLE 15–8

Diagnosis of Neurofibromatosis Type 1 (von Recklinghausen's Disease)

For a patient to be diagnosed with von Recklinghausen's disease, two of the following must be present:

1. Affected first-degree relative;
2. ≥ 6 café au lait spots (≥ 5 mm in diameter in children; ≥ 15 mm diameter in adolescents/adults);
3. ≥ 2 neurofibromas, or 1 plexiform (involving proximal nerve roots or major nerves) neurofibroma;
4. Axillary or inguinal freckling;
5. ≥ 2 Lisch nodules;
6. Optic glioma;
7. A distinctive osseous lesion (most often sphenoid wing dysplasia or long-bone cortex thinning, ± bowing of the tibia [pseudoarthrosis])

From a 1987 National Institutes of Health Consensus Development Conference on NF.

Bilateral acoustic neuromas are the hallmark of type 2 neurofibromatosis. Complications include hearing loss and vestibular disorientation. MRI demonstrates bilateral eighth cranial nerve masses. Neurofibromas, meningiomas, schwannomas, and astrocytomas are also associated with type 2 neurofibromatosis. Cataracts and retinal hamartomas are not uncommon. Surgical debulking is appropriate when hearing impairment becomes pronounced.

Tuberous Sclerosis

Tuberous sclerosis, like neurofibromatosis, is a progressive autosomal-dominant neurocutaneous disorder. Typical skin lesions include **ash-leaf spots** (flat, hypopigmented macules), **shagreen patches** (areas of abnormal skin thickening), sebaceous adenomas, and hyperpigmented macular forehead lesions. Neuroimaging demonstrates the distinctive periventricular knob-like areas of localized swelling, or "tubers." Mental retardation and seizures are common. Tumors of the kidney and heart, particularly cardiac rhabdomyomas, are not uncommon. Treatment consists of antiepileptic therapy and surgical removal of related tumors when indicated.

Von Hippel-Lindau Disease

Von Hippel-Lindau disease is characterized by retinal vascular hamartomas (usually unilateral), similar vascular lesions in the central nervous system, and associated neoplasms including renal cell carcinomas and pheochromocytomas. Ocular lesions respond to laser therapy; no specific treatment exists for the CNS growths.

Sturge-Weber Disease

Sturge-Weber is a progressive neurologic disorder associated with a port-wine stain (nevus flammeus) over the area innervated by the **first division** of the trigeminal nerve. Affected children manifest mental retardation, seizures, and visual impairment; about a third develop glaucoma. Laser therapy may "fade" the port-wine stain but does not address the neurologic dysfunction.

◆ **KEY POINTS** ◆

1. Von Recklinghausen's disease is characterized by multiple café au lait spots on examination.

2. In contrast, the typical skin lesions of tuberous sclerosis include ash-leaf spots and shagreen patches.

3. Sturge-Weber disease is associated with a port-wine stain over the area innervated by cranial nerve V, 1st division (CNV_1).

SKULL ABNORMALITIES

Microcephaly describes a head circumference that is greater than 2 standard deviations below mean head size for age. It often results from genetic abnormalities (i.e., trisomy 21, Prader-Willi syndrome) or congenital insults (maternal drug ingestions, congenital infections, or insufficient placental blood flow). Microcephaly accompanies an abnormally small brain, which is usually abnormal in appearance and function as well. Affected children demonstrate both cognitive and motor delay; associated seizure disorders are not uncommon.

Macrocephaly, in contrast, refers to a head circumference greater than 2 standard deviations above the mean. Macrocephaly may be the result of a large brain; however, cranioskeletal dysplasias, storage diseases, and hydrocephalus should be explored as possible causes.

Craniosynostosis is the premature fusion of one or more cranial sutures. It may be idiopathic or occur as part of a syndrome. Bony growth continues along the open sutures, resulting in an abnormally shaped head. If early obliteration of the sagittal suture occurs, the child will have a long head and a narrow face (dolichocephaly). In contrast, premature closure of the coronal sutures results in a very wide face with a short, almost box-like, skull. The need for and timing of surgical intervention, which consists of reopening the sutures and retarding their subsequent fusion, is controversial. Most defects are repaired before age 2 years for cosmetic reasons; those threatening normal brain growth and development are addressed sooner.

16 Nutrition

Good nutrition is necessary for optimal physical growth and intellectual development. A healthy diet protects against disease, provides reserve in times of stress, and contains adequate amounts of protein, carbohydrates, fats, vitamins, and minerals. Children with vegetarian diets are at risk for vitamin B_{12} and trace mineral deficiencies. Failure to thrive, obesity, and infant feeding intolerance are the most common pediatric conditions associated with malnutrition.

FAILURE TO THRIVE

Failure to thrive (FTT) is defined here as persistent weight below the third percentile or falling off the growth curve. Risk factors include low birth weight, lower socioeconomic status, physical or mental disability, and caretaker neglect.

Differential Diagnosis

Most cases of FTT in developed countries are "non-organic" or **psychosocial** in origin; that is, there is no coexistent medical disorder. The list of "organic" diagnoses predisposing to FTT is extensive, and virtually all organ systems are represented (Table 16–1).

Clinical Manifestations

History

The caretaker must be questioned in detail about the child's diet, including how often the child eats, how much at each feeding, what the child is fed, how the formula is prepared, and who feeds the child. Information regarding diarrhea, fatty stools, irritability, vomiting, food refusal, and polyuria should be documented. Recurrent infections suggest congenital or acquired immunodeficiency. Constitutional growth delay can usually be diagnosed by family history alone. Foreign and domestic travel, source of water, and developmental delay are occasionally overlooked topics. The psychosocial history includes questions concerning the caretaker's expectations of the child, parental and sibling health, financial security, recent major life events, and chronic stressors.

Physical Examination

Weight, height, and head circumference should be plotted out on an appropriate **growth chart**. Relatively recent growth failure is usually limited to weight alone, whereas height and head circumference are affected as well in chronic deficiency. Severely deprived children may present with lethargy, edema, scant subcutaneous fat, atrophic muscle tissue, decreased skin turgor, coarsened hair, dermatitis, and distended abdomen.

Observation of caretaker–child interaction and feeding behavior is critical. Children who are listless, minimally responsive to the examiner and/or caretaker, withdrawn, or excessively fearful often have contributing psychosocial issues. Findings suspicious for physical abuse or neglect (see Chapter 2) should be sought and documented.

A complete physical examination, with careful atten-

TABLE 16–1

Differential Diagnosis of Failure to Thrive

Cardiac
  Congenital heart
    malformations
Endocrine
  Diabetes mellitus
  Hypothyroidism
  Hyperaldosteronism
Gastrointestinal
  Malabsorption
  Milk protein intolerance/
    allergy
  Gastroesophageal reflux
  Pyloric stenosis
  Celiac disease
Infectious
  HIV
  Chronic gastroenteritis
  Intestinal parasites
  Urinary tract infection
Neonatal
  Prematurity
  Low birth weight
  Congenital or perinatal
    infection
Neurologic
  Cerebral palsy
  Mental retardation
  Degenerative disorders

Pulmonary
  Cystic fibrosis
  Bronchopulmonary
    dysplasia
  Chronic aspiration
  Respiratory
    insufficiency
Renal
  Renal tubular acidosis
  Chronic renal
    insufficiency
Nonorganic
  Neglect
Psychosocial
  Abuse
  Inadequate amount fed
  Incorrect preparation
    of formula
Other
  Inborn errors of
    metabolism
  Malignancy
  Cleft palate
  Congenital
    immunodeficiency
    syndromes

♦ KEY POINTS ♦

1. Consistent weight below the third percentile and falling off the growth curve are both evidence of failure to thrive.
2. Most cases of FTT are nonorganic.
3. Any organ system may be implicated in organic FTT; screening tests should help focus the search.

OBESITY

Obesity, defined as actual weight at least 120% of ideal body weight, is a growing problem among all age groups. The cause is simply caloric intake in excess of expenditure. The social and psychological consequences of being a "fat" child may be particularly damaging to self-esteem at a critical age. Obesity is treated by altering dietary habits (limiting intake of high-calorie, high-fat foods) and developing a regular exercise program. Rather than losing weight (which may compromise growth), the goal for overweight children is slowing weight gain until back within the normal growth curve. Patients who are morbidly obese, obese adolescents, and children of obese parents are more likely to become obese adults. Obesity increases the risks of diabetes, cardiovascular disease, and hypertension. **Sleep apnea** and **slipped capital femoral epiphysis** are the more likely childhood complications.

INFANT FEEDING INTOLERANCE

tion for dysmorphism, pallor, bruising, cleft palate, rales or crackles, heart murmurs, and muscle tone, may suggest the etiology in nonorganic cases.

Diagnostic Evaluation

Information obtained from the history and physical determine the direction of further diagnostic workup. Any child with FTT should receive a complete blood count, serum electrolytes, blood urea nitrogen and creatinine, and protein and albumin measurements. Severely malnourished children and patients with suspected nonorganic FTT should be admitted to the hospital. Adequate catch-up growth during hospitalization on a regular diet is virtually diagnostic of psychosocial FTT.

Infant feeding addresses physical and emotional needs of both mother and child. Babies triple in weight during the first year. Although breast feeding is strongly recommended, many commercially prepared iron-fortified formulas provide appropriate calories and nutrients. Newborns feed on demand, usually every 1–2 hours. Neonates normally lose up to 10% of their birth weight over the first several days; formula-fed babies regain their birth weight by the second week of life, whereas breast-fed babies usually take about a week longer. Healthy infants automatically regulate intake to meet caloric demand. Feeding intolerance may lead to food aversion and FTT; the most significant cause is cow milk protein intolerance or allergy.

Clinical Manifestations

History and Physical Examination

Feeding intolerance may present with any number of clinical manifestations. **Malabsorption** is characterized by poor growth and chronic diarrhea. **Colitis**, indicated by anemia or obvious blood in the stools, can occur. **Allergy** may be accompanied by eczema or wheezing. Other possible symptoms include vomiting, irritability, and abdominal distention.

Differential Diagnosis

Infectious gastroenteritis, necrotizing enterocolitis, intussusception, intermittent volvulus, celiac disease, cystic fibrosis, chronic protein malnutrition, aspiration, and eosinophilic enteritis should be considered. The most common condition mistaken for milk protein intolerance is colic, which is generally limited to infants less than 3 months of age. Colic is a syndrome of recurrent abdominal pain that persists for several hours, usually in the late afternoon or evening. During the attacks, the child draws the knees to the abdomen and cries inconsolably. The pain resolves as suddenly and spontaneously as it begins.

Treatment

Exclusive breast feeding during the first year of life eliminates the problem posed by milk protein intolerance except in severely allergic infants. If there is no evidence of any underlying disease, many pediatricians recommend a trial of soy protein formula. Unfortunately, 25% of patients with milk protein allergy are also intolerant of soy. Casein hydrolysate formulas (i.e., Nutramigen or Progestimil) are generally effective; poor taste and high price make them a less practical alternative.

◆ KEY POINTS ◆

1. Newborns initially lose weight but should regain to birth weight by the third week of life.

2. Cow milk protein intolerance can lead to feeding intolerance and aversion.

3. The sporadic nature and sudden onset of colic usually distinguishes this condition from feeding intolerance.

Oncology

LEUKEMIA

The leukemias account for the greatest percentage of cases of childhood malignancies: 31% of neoplastic disease in white children and 24% in African American children. There are 2500 new cases of leukemia each year in the United States, and approximately 40 children per million are affected under the age of 15 years. Table 17–1 lists each type of childhood cancer and the fraction of the total childhood malignancies that each accounts for annually.

Leukemias are classified on the basis of leukemic cell morphology into lymphocytic leukemias, which are proliferations of cells of lymphoid lineage, and nonlymphocytic leukemias, which are proliferations of cells of granulocyte, monocyte, erythrocyte, or platelet lineage. **Acute leukemias** constitute 97% of all childhood leukemias and are subdivided into acute lymphocytic leukemia and acute nonlymphocytic leukemia. If untreated, they are rapidly fatal within weeks to a few months of diagnosis, but with treatment they are often curable. **Chronic leukemias** make up 3% of childhood leukemias and are further delineated into adult chronic myelogenous leukemia and juvenile chronic myelogenous leukemia. Unlike those with acute leukemias, these patients may survive without treatment for many months to years. Unfortunately, the chronic leukemias evolve into forms of acute leukemia that cannot be cured by available chemotherapy. All chronic leukemias in children are of nonlymphocytic lineage. Because they are so rare, a

TABLE 17–1

Types of Childhood Cancer

Cancer	Percentage of Total Pediatric Malignancies Annually	
	White Children (%)	African American Children (%)
Leukemia	30.9	24.3
Central nervous system	18.3	21.6
Lymphoma, including Hodgkin's	13.8	11.3
Neuroblastoma	6.8	5.4
Soft-tissue sarcoma	6.2	8.6
Wilms' tumor	5.7	8.1
Bone	4.7	3.6
Eye	2.5	4.1
Germ cell	2.4	4.1
Liver	1.3	—
Other	7.4	8.9

From Dworkin PH, ed. Pediatrics, 2nd ed. Philadelphia: Harwal Publishing, 1992.

discussion of the chronic leukemias goes beyond the scope of this review text. The following discussion focuses on acute lymphocytic and acute nonlymphocytic leukemia.

Pathogenesis

The acute leukemias result from the malignant transformation and clonal expansion of hematopoietic cells that have stopped at a particular stage of differentiation and are unable to progress to more mature forms. The distinguishing characteristic of acute lymphocytic leukemia (ALL) is the presence of large numbers of lymphoblasts in the bone marrow, whereas acute nonlymphocytic leukemia, which is also termed acute myelogenous leukemia (AML), displays large numbers of nonlymphoid precursors in the bone marrow.

ALL is classified by both morphologic and immunologic methods. **Morphologic classification** is based on the appearance of the lymphoblasts. The L1 type lymphoblast is the most common (85% of cases) and has a favorable prognosis. The L2 type lymphoblast (14% of cases) and the L3 type lymphoblast (1% of cases) have unfavorable prognoses. **Immunologic classification** is based on immunophenotype. Non-T, non-B cell ALL accounts for 80% of cases and has a good prognosis. T-cell ALL, which is responsible for 19% of cases, has a variable prognosis, and B-cell ALL, which accounts for 1% of cases, has a very poor prognosis.

The French-American-British (FAB) classification system uses morphologic and histochemical information to subdivide AML into seven subtypes: M1 is myeloblastic leukemia without differentiation; M2 is myeloblastic leukemia with differentiation; M3 is promyelocytic leukemia; M4 is myelomonocytic leukemia; M5 is monoblastic leukemia; M6 is erythroleukemia; and M7 is megakaryoblastic leukemia.

Epidemiology

ALL is the most common pediatric neoplasm and accounts for 80% of all childhood acute leukemia. ALL is more common in white children than in African American children and 1.3 times more common in males than in females. The peak incidence of ALL is in the 3- to 5-year-old age group.

AML accounts for 20% of all childhood acute leukemias. It is more common in males than females and more common in African American children than in white children. The incidence of AML, in contrast to ALL, has a fairly constant incidence without a distinct peak.

Risk Factors

Syndromes with an increased risk for leukemia include trisomy 21, Fanconi's anemia, Bloom syndrome, ataxia-telangiectasia, and severe combined immunodeficiency. Identical twins have a 20% risk of leukemia if one twin develops it during the first 5 years of life. Children with solid tumors, especially Hodgkin's disease and Wilms' tumor, who have undergone intense radiation and/or chemotherapy with alkylating agents may develop leukemia as a secondary malignancy. Children with congenital marrow failure states, such as Shwachman-Diamond syndrome (exocrine pancreatic insufficiency and neutropenia) and Diamond-Blackfan syndrome (congenital red cell aplasia), have an increased risk of leukemia.

The risk factors for AML are the same as those for ALL. The presence of Fanconi's anemia results in a higher risk for AML than for ALL.

Clinical Manifestations

History and Physical Examination

Common presenting symptoms include fever, pallor, lethargy, malaise, anorexia, and extremity or joint pain. Signs commonly noted on presentation are petechiae or ecchymoses and hepatosplenomegaly. At the time of diagnosis, extramedullary involvement may be seen in the central nervous system, skin, or testicles. Central nervous system infiltration may manifest itself as diffuse or focal neurologic signs and symptoms, including headache, emesis, papilledema, and sixth nerve palsy. In patients with AML, a soft-tissue tumor called a chloroma may be found in the spinal cord or on the skin. The lesions have a greenish hue due to the presence of myeloperoxidase in the tumors. Of note, promyelocytic leukemia (M3 type AML) is associated with disseminated intravascular coagulation, and monoblastic leukemia (M5 type AML) is associated with central nervous system involvement and gingival hyperplasia.

Leukemic dissemination results in bone marrow failure, reticuloendothelial system infiltration, bony involvement, and penetration of sanctuary sites. Bone marrow failure results from myelophthisis, which is the replacement of the normal hematopoietic elements in the marrow by the leukemic cell population. This causes a decrease in the normal population of red blood cells, white cells, and platelets. Signs and symptoms of marrow failure include anemia, bleeding, and infection. The anemia accompanying marrow failure is well tolerated, despite its severity, because it progresses slowly, allowing the compensatory mechanisms of the cardiovascular system to minimize its effects. Bleeding due to thrombocytopenia appears as mucosal bleeding, epistaxis or melena, or petechiae and ecchymoses of the skin. Infection from bacterial and nonbacterial pathogens is often present because of the paucity of functional white blood cells. Granulocytopenia dramatically increases the risk of bacterial infection. Neutropenic children cannot mount an effective inflammatory response, and as a result, many of the common symptoms found with bacterial infection cannot arise; examples include rales in pneumonia or pus in an abscess. Fever is the most common sign of infection in the neutropenic child. It is important to note that localized infection often disseminates, producing bacteremia and sepsis.

Reticuloendothelial system infiltration manifests itself as lymphadenopathy. In ALL, this lymph node enlargement may be so massive that lymphoma is sometimes suspected initially. Hepatosplenomegaly is often present and may be mild to massive. Bone pain is due to expansion of the marrow cavity, destruction of cortical bone by leukemic cells, or by a metastatic tumor. If the long bones of the lower extremities are involved, a limp may develop. If the skull is involved, proptosis or palpable nodules may develop.

Sanctuary sites, which include the central nervous system and the testes, are rarely involved at diagnosis but may be involved with the recurrence of disease. The sites are known as sanctuary sites because they are relatively impermeable to treatment with chemotherapeutic agents. Leukemic penetration of the central nervous system generally occurs through the meninges. Testicular infiltration produces enlargement of the testes that is out of proportion to the child's sexual development.

Differential Diagnosis

The differential diagnosis includes aplastic anemia, idiopathic thrombocytopenic purpura, Epstein-Barr virus infection, other malignancies, and virus-induced or familial hemophagocytic syndromes. Rarely, a collagen vascular disease or rheumatologic disorder mimics the presenting symptoms of leukemia.

Diagnostic Evaluation

The complete blood count often reveals anemia, thrombocytopenia, and neutropenia. Anemia and thrombocytopenia are present in 90% of cases at presentation. The anemia is normochromic and normocytic and a low reticulocyte count is seen from decreased marrow production of red blood cells. The white blood cell count is low (less than 5000/mm^3) in one-third of patients, normal 5000 to 20,000/mm^3) in one-third of patients, and high (greater than 20,000/mm^3) in one-third of patients. Blast cells are frequently seen on peripheral smear, especially if the white blood cell count is normal or high. Even if there are blasts in the peripheral blood, it is critical to examine the bone marrow, because the morphology of the peripheral blasts may not reflect the true bone marrow morphology, which is diagnostic. It is possible to identify human lymphocytes and granulocytes at different stages of development by using specific monoclonal antibodies to define cell surface antigens. When this application is combined with cytochemical histology, molecular probes, and cellular morphology, the diagnostic classification, treatment, and prognosis become more specific.

Treatment

The treatment strategy in leukemia is to treat the complications of the leukemia at presentation, to treat the leukemia, and to deal effectively with the metabolic derangements brought about by therapy.

Managing leukemic complications at presentation involves blood product transfusions and the treatment of metabolic abnormalities, infection, hyperviscosity, and compressive symptoms. All blood products transfused into the immunocompromised leukemic host must be irradiated before infusion to remove any donor lymphocytes that might mount a graft-versus-host response. Packed red blood cells are transfused for a hematocrit less than 20, and platelet concentrates are used for thrombocytopenia less than 20,000. Granulocyte infusion is controversial and rarely used. Neutropenia or granulocytopenia is defined as an absolute neutrophil count less than 500/mm^3. In the presence of granulocytopenia, treatment of suspected infection is of critical importance because the risk of bacteremia and dissemination is so high. When the neutropenic leukemic patient becomes febrile, blood, throat, stool, and urine cultures and a chest radiograph should be obtained promptly, and broad-spectrum antibiotics should be started soon thereafter. A white blood cell count greater than 100,000/mm^3 can cause significant hyperviscosity. This is often seen in patients with AML. The cell count may be lowered by exchange transfusion or leukophoresis. Without therapy, hyperviscosity may result in stroke or cause hypoxemia from sludging in the lungs. Large collections of malignant cells in the mediastinum, common in T-cell leukemia, may produce an obstructing mass that results in tracheal de-

Tumor lysis Triad
- hyperuricemia
- hyperkalemia
- hyperphosphatemia

viation and superior vena cava syndrome. Superior vena cava syndrome manifests itself as facial plethora, venous distention, and increased intracranial pressure. The mass and the compressive symptoms it creates usually resolve with chemotherapy and radiation.

Antileukemic therapy varies somewhat among institutions and depends most on the type of leukemia that is present and whether the leukemia is deemed high risk or standard risk. Given these facts, it is impossible to address all the specific nuances of antileukemic therapy. In general, antileukemic therapy is instituted in three distinct phases with specific objectives. **Remission induction** generally lasts 4 weeks, during which maximum log kill is achieved. If remission is achieved, all blasts will disappear from the bone marrow and the complete blood count values will return to normal. The goals of **consolidation** are to kill additional leukemic cells with further systemic therapy and to prevent leukemic relapse within the central nervous system by giving intrathecal chemotherapy. The objectives of **maintenance therapy** are to continue the remission achieved in the previous two phases and to provide additional cytoreduction to cure the leukemia. Discontinuation of chemotherapy occurs when the patient has remained in remission throughout the prescribed course of maintenance therapy. At the conclusion of maintenance therapy, a relapse-free patient is considered cured. A few patients who have successfully completed the maintenance phase have a recurrence of leukemia, or relapse, in the bone marrow, central nervous system, or testes. If chemotherapy fails to produce remission or there is relapse, then multiple-drug intensive reinduction and central nervous system irradiation or bone marrow transplantation may be considered. More than half of AML cases end up with attempted bone marrow transplantation because of the low cure rate with conventional chemotherapy.

ALL induction chemotherapy is successful in 95% of children. Prednisone, vincristine, and L-asparaginase are generally used, and depending on whether the leukemia in question is of standard or high risk, other agents may be used. Consolidation includes intrathecal methotrexate and, in high-risk patients, cranial irradiation. Cranial irradiation causes learning disabilities, especially in young children; transient somnolence syndrome; and brain tumors in rare instances. Maintenance therapy involves oral 6-mercaptopurine and intramuscular methotrexate and usually lasts 2 years. Local tissue relapse of ALL in the central nervous system or testes is treated with local irradiation and reinduction chemotherapy.

AML chemotherapy is more intensive than that used for ALL, and remission induction regimens tend to include an anthracycline-like drug and cytosine arabinoside. Myelosuppression is severe, and good supportive care is essential. Eighty percent of patients with AML achieve initial remission after induction chemotherapy, but most patients will relapse within a year.

Both before and especially after the start of chemotherapy, metabolic support for hyperuricemia, hyperkalemia, and hyperphosphatemia is essential. This triad of metabolic derangements is known as tumor lysis syndrome. A large malignant cell burden, which is common in leukemia, is present when there is a high white count or when significant organ infiltration is noted. When the malignant cells are killed by chemotherapy, large amounts of potassium, phosphate, and purines are released from within the cells. Hyperkalemia, if not corrected, can cause cardiac arrhythmias. Phosphate, especially at high serum levels, binds to calcium, resulting in precipitation of calcium phosphate in renal tubules, hypocalcemia, and tetany. When the calcium phosphate product rises to greater than 60, precipitation of calcium phosphate and renal tubular damage begins to occur. Purines released by the dying leukemic cells are processed to uric acid. Hyperuricemia, if untreated, can result in precipitation of uric acid in renal tubules and renal failure. To treat hyperuricemia, vigorous hydration is used to promote uric acid excretion, the urine is alkalinized to improve uric acid solubility, and allopurinol is administered to minimize the uric acid burden. Allopurinol blocks the enzyme xanthine oxidase, which helps convert purines to uric acid.

Prognostic factors have been identified that place children with ALL into either the high-risk or the standard-risk category. These variables are shown in Table 17–2. Children who fall into the standard risk category have a more favorable prognosis and require less intensive therapy. Overall, the initial white blood count and the age of the patient are the most significant variables. L2 or L3 FAB classification and the presence of massive organomegaly, T-cell leukemia, and central nervous system disease all indicate poor prognosis.

In general, the prognosis for AML is worse than that for ALL. Prognoses vary between subtypes. The best chemotherapeutic regimens are curative for less than one-half of the patients with AML. Bone marrow transplantation is curative in up to two-thirds of patients with AML.

TABLE 17–2

Prognostic Factors in Acute Lymphoblastic Leukemia of Childhood

Factor	Favorable (Standard Risk)	Unfavorable (High Risk)
Demographic		
Age (yr)	2–9	<2, >10
Race	White	African American
Sex	Female	Male
Leukemic burden		
Initial WBC count ($\times 10^9$L)	<10	>50
Adenopathy	Absent	Present
Hepatosplenomegaly	Absent to mild (<3 cm)	Marked (>3 cm)
CNS disease at diagnosis	Absent	Present
Hemoglobin (g/dL)	<7	>10
Platelet count ($\times 10^9$L)	>100	<100
Mediastinal mass	Absent	Present
LDH	Not high	High
Morphology, histochemistry, cytogenetics, and biochemistry		
Lymphoblasts*	L1*	L2* or L3*
Periodic acid–Schiff stain	Positive	Negative
Cytogenetics†	Modal number: 50	t(1;19) or t(8;14), 22q–, 9q+
Mitotic and labeling index	Low	High
Immunologic factors		
Immunoglobulins	Normal IgG, IgA, IgM	Decreased IgG, IgA, IgM
Surface markers	Non-T, non-B cell ALL, CALLA+	T or B-cell ALL or pre-B
Glucocorticoid receptors	High number	Lower number
Response to induction therapy	M2 marrow (5% blasts) on day 14	M3 marrow (25% blasts) on day 14

*FAB classification: L1 typical (85%), small cells, little cytoplasm; L2 undifferentiated (15%), large cells, large cytoplasm; L3 Burkitt type (1%), cytoplasmic vacuoles.

†Cytogenetics refers to chromosome changes; t is transposition. LDH, lactic dehydrogenase; WBC, white blood cell; CNS, central nervous system; CALLA, common acute lymphoblastic antigen.

From Behrman RE, Kliegman RM, eds. Essentials of pediatrics, 2nd ed. Philadelphia: WB Saunders, 1994.

◆ KEY POINTS ◆

1. The leukemias account for the greatest percentage of cases of childhood malignancies: 31% of neoplastic disease in white children and 24% in African American children.

2. Leukemias are classified on the basis of leukemic cell morphology into lymphocytic leukemias, which are proliferations of cells of lymphoid lineage, and nonlymphocytic leukemias, which are proliferations of cells of granulocyte, monocyte, erythrocyte, or platelet lineage.

3. Acute leukemias constitute 97% of all childhood leukemias and are subdivided into acute lymphocytic leukemia and acute nonlymphocytic leukemia.

4. ALL is the most common pediatric neoplasm and accounts for 80% of all childhood acute leukemia.

5. Anemia and thrombocytopenia are present in 90% of leukemic patients at presentation.

6. The management strategy in leukemia is to manage leukemic complications at presentation, to treat the leukemia, and to deal effectively with the metabolic derangements brought about by therapy.

7. Antileukemic therapy is instituted in three distinct phases: induction, consolidation, and maintenance.

8. In general, the prognosis for AML is worse than that for ALL. Standard-risk ALL has a 80% cure rate, whereas the prognoses for AML varies widely among subtypes.

BRAIN TUMORS

Central nervous system tumors are the most common solid tumors in children and are second to leukemia in overall incidence of malignant diseases. In contrast to adults, in whom supratentorial brain tumors are more common, brain tumors in children are predominantly infratentorial tumors (posterior fossae) involving the cerebellum, midbrain, and brainstem.

Table 17–3 denotes the location, incidence, and prognosis of central nervous system tumors in children. Childhood brain tumors are differentiated further from those in adults in that they are usually low-grade astrocytomas or embryonic neoplasms (medulloblastomas, ependymomas, or germ cell tumors), whereas most central nervous system tumors in adults are malignant astrocytomas and metastatic carcinomas.

TABLE 17–3

Location, Incidence, and Prognosis of CNS Tumors in Children

Location	% of Pediatric Brain Tumors	5-Yr Survival (%)
Infratentorial (posterior fossa)	60	
Astrocytoma (cerebellum)		90
Medulloblastoma		44–55
Glioma (brainstem)	0–5 (high grade)	30 (low grade)
Ependymoma		50–60
Supratentorial (cerebral hemispheres)	25	
Astrocytoma		10–50
Glioblastoma multiforme		0–5
Ependymoma		50–60
Choroid plexus papilloma		60–80
Midline	15	
Craniopharyngioma		70–90
Pineal (germinoma)		65–75
Optic nerve glioma		50–90

From Behrman RE, Kliegman RM, eds. Essentials of pediatrics, 2nd ed. Philadelphia: WB Saunders, 1994.

Clinical Manifestations and Treatment

Common presenting signs and symptoms of central nervous system tumors in childhood often are dismissed initially as intercurrent viral or nonspecific illnesses but usually represent increased intracranial pressure or a focal neurologic deficit. Headache is suggestive of increased intracranial pressure if it is present at night or at awakening, worsens with cough or straining, or is intermittent but recurs with increasing frequency and intensity. Emesis without nausea, another nonspecific sign of increased intracranial pressure, usually is intermittent and occurs on arising in the morning. Obstructive hydrocephalus may produce a large cranium if it occurs before the sutures have fused, and papilledema may be a late but specific sign of increased intracranial pressure. Strabismus with diplopia can result from a sixth nerve palsy induced by increased intracranial pressure.

Because it can result from increased intracranial pressure, a sixth nerve palsy is not considered a localizing focal neurologic deficit, whereas other cranial nerve deficits, by definition, localize the lesion to the brain stem. Head tilt, as a compensation for loss of binocular vision, is noted with focal deficits of cranial nerve III, IV, or VI, which causes extraocular muscle weakness. Nystagmus usually is due to cerebellovestibular pathway lesions, but nystagmus may also be seen with a marked visual deficit (peripheral or cortical blindness).

Personality changes, poor school performance, and change in hand preference should suggest a cortical lesion, whereas ataxia suggests a cerebellar or brainstem lesion. Babinski reflex, hyperreflexia, spasticity, and loss of dexterity are suggestive of brainstem or cortical tumors, whereas seizures are noted with just cortical lesions. Endocrine abnormalities are noted with pituitary, hypothalamic, or pineal tumors.

Differential diagnosis includes arteriovenous malformation, aneurysm, brain abscess, parasitic infestation, herpes simplex encephalitis, granulomatous disease (tuberculosis, cryptococcal, sarcoid), intracranial hemorrhage, pseudotumor cerebri, primary cerebral lymphoma, vasculitis, and rarely, metastatic tumors.

Computed tomography (CT) and magnetic resonance imaging (MRI) scans of the head have revolutionized the field of neurodiagnosis and are the procedures of choice for diagnosing and localizing tumors and other intracranial masses. MRI is especially helpful in diagnosing tumors of the posterior fossae and spinal cord. CTs are less effective because the surrounding bone often limits resolution. Examination of cerebrospinal fluid by cytocentrifuge histology is essential to determine the presence of metastasis in medulloblastoma and pinealoma.

Table 17–4 shows the manifestations and treatment of primary central nervous system tumors.

◆ KEY POINTS ◆

1. Central nervous system tumors are the most common solid tumors in children and are second to leukemia in overall incidence of malignant diseases.

2. In contrast to those in adults, in whom supratentorial brain tumors are more common, brain tumors in children are predominantly infratentorial tumors (posterior fossae) involving the cerebellum, midbrain, and brainstem.

NON-HODGKIN'S LYMPHOMA

Pathogenesis

Non-Hodgkin's lymphomas (NHLs) are a heterogeneous group of diseases characterized by neoplastic proliferation of immature lymphoid cells, which, unlike the malignant lymphoid cells of ALL, accumulate outside the bone marrow. Histopathologic subtypes in childhood non-Hodgkin's disease include lymphoblastic (T cell), 50%; histiocytic large cell (B cell, non-T/non-B), 20%; and undifferentiated small cell (B cell), 30%. Small cell undifferentiated NHL can be subdivided into Burkitt's and pleomorphic types.

NHL in children differs from that in adults in several important ways. Most cases of NHL in children are diffuse, highly malignant, extremely aggressive, and show little differentiation beyond primitive cells. Adult NHL is usually highly differentiated and nodular. Distant noncontiguous metastases are common in childhood NHL, making adult staging systems that depend primarily on nodal involvement of little relevance and mandating that systemic therapy should be given to all patients. NHL in childhood resembles ALL more than it does adult-onset NHL or Hodgkin's lymphoma. Almost half the cases of NHL in childhood are of T-cell origin, compared with approximately 5% of those in adults.

TABLE 17–4

Manifestations and Treatment of Primary CNS Tumors

Tumor/Site	Manifestations	Treatment	Comments
Cerebellar astrocytoma	Onset between 5 and 8 yr of age; ↑ ICP, ataxia, nystagmus, head tilt, intention tremor	Surgical excision plus adjuvant radiotherapy if a solid tumor; corticosteroids to ↓ tumor edema	Symptoms present for 2–7 mo; cystic tumors have favorable outcome
Medulloblastoma Cerebellar vermis and floor of 4th ventricle	Onset between 3 and 5 yr of age; ↑ ICP, obstructive hydrocephalus, ataxia, cerebrospinal fluid metastasis, and spinal cord compression	Surgical excision and radiotherapy plus adjuvant chemotherapy*; corticosteroids to ↓ tumor edema	Acute onset of symptoms; tumor is radiosensitive; CSF checked for metastatic cells
Ependymoma Floor of 4th ventricle	↑ ICP, obstructive hydrocephalus; rarely seeds spinal fluid	Surgical excision, radiotherapy, chemotherapy*; corticosteroids to ↓ tumor edema	Onset intermediate between astrocytoma and medulloblastoma
Brainstem glioma	Onset between 5 and 7 yr of age; triad of multiple cranial nerve deficit (VII, IX, X, V, VI) pyramidal tract, and cerebellar signs; skip lesions common; ↑ ICP is late	Excision impossible; radiotherapy is palliative; corticosteroids to ↓ tumor edema; experimental chemotherapy*	Small size but critical location makes this tumor highly lethal
Pinealoma	Paralysis of upward gaze (Parinaud syndrome); lid retraction (Collier sign); hearing loss; precocious puberty; ↑ ICP; may seed spinal fluid	Radiotherapy, chemotherapy; shunting of CSF	Germ cell line; germinoma — dermoid, teratoma, mixed lesions may calcify or secrete hCG or alpha-fetoprotein
Diencephalic glioma Hypothalamus	Onset between 2 and 5 mo of age; alert, euphoric but emaciated appearance; emesis, optic atrophy, nystagmus	Radiotherapy	Patient may become obese after treatment
Astrocytoma/glioma Cerebral cortex	Onset between 5 and 10 yr of age; personality changes; headache, motor weakness, seizures, ↑ ICP later	Location determines surgery or radiotherapy; anticonvulsant and corticosteroids; chemotherapy*	*Differential diagnosis:* Abscess, hydatid or porencephalic cyst; herpes simplex encephalitis, granuloma (TB, cryptococcus); arteriovenous malformation; hematoma; lymphoma
Optic glioma	Onset before 2 yr of age; poor visual acuity, exophthalmos, nystagmus; ↑ ICP; optic atrophy, strabismus	Surgical resection or radiotherapy; chemotherapy*	Neurofibromatosis in 25% of patients
Craniopharyngioma Pituitary fossa	Onset between 7 and 12 yr of age; ↑ ICP, bitemporal hemianopia, sexual and growth retardation; growth hormone and gonadotropic deficiency	Begin cortisol replacement prior to surgery; total excision, adjuvant radiotherapy if extensive	Calcification above sella turcica; diabetes insipidus common postoperatively

CSF, cerebrospinal fluid; hCG, human chorionic gonadotropin; ↑ ICP, increased intracranial pressure: headache, vomiting (papilledema, third and sixth nerve palsies, wide sutures); TB, tuberculosis.

*Chemotherapy may delay need for radiotherapy, thus avoiding treatment-related neurotoxicity. Chemotherapy includes alternating cycles of cyclophosphamide plus vincristine with cisplatin plus etoposide.

From Behrman RE, Kliegman RM, eds. Essentials of pediatrics, 2nd ed. Philadelphia: WB Saunders, 1994.

Epidemiology

Lymphomas are the third most common malignancy in childhood. Two-thirds of lymphomas are the non-Hodgkin's type. NHL occurs at least three times more frequently in boys than in girls and has a peak incidence between the ages of 7 and 11 years.

Risk Factors

NHLs have been described in association with congenital or acquired immunodeficiency states, chronic immune stimulation, autoimmune disease, and Epstein-Barr virus–induced lymphoproliferation. Congenital or acquired immunodeficiencies linked with NHL include Wiskott-Aldrich syndrome, X-linked immunodeficiency, and severe combined immunodeficiency. Acquired immunodeficiency syndrome may be associated with T-cell NHL. Patients with Bloom syndrome and ataxia-telangiectasia also have had a higher incidence than expected for lymphoma.

Clinical Manifestations

All childhood NHLs grow rapidly, and as a result, symptom duration is short. The abdomen is the most common site of initial manifestation of B-cell NHL, whereas the anterior mediastinum is the primary site for T-cell NHL. Abdominal involvement can result in rapid abdominal enlargement, pain, ascites, urinary tract obstruction, and gastrointestinal obstruction by serving as the lead point for an intussusception. Anterior mediastinal masses are associated with pleural effusions, respiratory distress from airway compromise, and superior vena cava syndrome. Superior vena cava syndrome, which results from a superior-anterior mediastinal mass, is characterized by distended neck veins, plethora, edema of the head and neck, cyanosis, proptosis, and Horner's syndrome. Childhood NHL has a high frequency of dissemination to extranodal sites, such as the central nervous system or bone marrow. Peripheral lymph node enlargement can be seen with any type of childhood NHL, and fever and weight loss may be present. Less common presentations include an obstructing nasopharyngeal tumor or primary bone, skin, or central nervous system tumor. The progression of disease in childhood NHL does not follow an orderly anatomic sequence of spread as seen with Hodgkin's disease.

The evaluation before therapy should include a complete blood count to look for leukocytosis and thrombocytopenia and/or anemia if marrow infiltration is present. Marrow aspiration, chest radiograph, lumbar puncture with cerebrospinal fluid cytology, and radionuclide bone scan are used to look for disseminated disease. Evaluation of renal and hepatic function can be undertaken if disseminated disease is found. Chest and/or abdominal CT and ultrasound studies may be used to determine the extent of disease. Staging laparotomy with splenectomy and liver biopsy is not indicated in childhood NHL.

Treatment

No generally agreed-on staging classification for childhood NHL is available. It is essential to ascertain whether a patient has local disease (nodal or extranodal) in one site, which has an excellent prognosis, or disseminated disease, which has a less favorable prognosis.

Systemic disease, occult or overt, is present in about 80% of children with NHL. Aggressive multidrug chemotherapy with the agents known to be effective in childhood ALL are the mainstay of therapy. Induction produces remission in 90% of affected children, and maintenance chemotherapy reduces the incidence of relapse. With radiotherapy alone, 30% of patients develop leukemic transformation and bone marrow relapse. Central nervous system prophylaxis is essential.

Patients with localized disease have a significantly better survival rate than that of patients with disseminated disease. Patients with hyperuricemia or an elevated serum lactic dehydrogenase level are considered to have a high tumor load, are at risk for tumor lysis syndrome, and have a worse prognosis than those that do not. The long-term survival of all children with NHL is 50–75%.

◆ KEY POINTS ◆

1. Non-Hodgkin's lymphomas are a heterogeneous group of diseases characterized by neoplastic proliferation of immature lymphoid cells, which, unlike the malignant lymphoid cells of ALL, accumulate outside the bone marrow.

2. NHL in children differs from that in adults in several important ways. In contrast to NHL in adults, most cases of NHL in children are diffuse, highly malignant, and extremely aggressive and show little differentiation beyond primitive cells.

3. Lymphomas (NHL and Hodgkin's lymphoma) are the third most common malignancy in childhood. Two-thirds of lymphomas are the non-Hodgkin's type.

4. Patients with localized disease have a significantly better survival rate than that of patients with disseminated disease.

HODGKIN'S LYMPHOMA

Pathogenesis

The cause of Hodgkin's disease is unknown, but some indirect evidence suggests an infectious agent. Histopathologic subtypes in childhood Hodgkin's disease are similar to those in adults: 40–60% nodular sclerosis, 10–20% lymphocytic predominance, 20–40% mixed cellularity, and 10% lymphocyte depletion.

Epidemiology

Hodgkin's disease accounts for 4% of all childhood cancer. It occurs in older children and teenagers and has a slight female predominance. Its peak incidence has a bimodal distribution at 15–30 years of age and after the age of 50. It rarely occurs in children less than 10 years of age. There is a 3:1 male predominance in early childhood Hodgkin's disease. Hodgkin's disease occurs in clusters within families.

Clinical Manifestations

History and Physical Examination

The most common presentation is painless, firm lymphadenopathy that is confined to one to two lymph node areas, usually involving the supraclavicular and cervical nodes. Mediastinal lymphadenopathy is another frequent initial presentation. Fever, night sweats, weight loss, and occasionally pruritus are noted in 30% of children. Right-sided cervical lymph nodal involvement is associated with mediastinal disease, and bilateral or left-sided cervical nodes are associated with splenic disease.

Differential Diagnosis

The differential diagnosis for Hodgkin's and NHL includes lymphadenitis, infectious mononucleosis, tuberculosis, atypical mycobacteria, cat scratch disease, human immunodeficiency virus infection, and toxoplasmosis.

Diagnostic Evaluation

Elevation of the erythrocyte sedimentation rate and serum copper level is nonspecific but may correlate with disease activity. The hallmark of diagnosis is the identification of Reed-Sternberg cells in tumor tissue. Autoimmune hemolytic anemia and thrombocytopenia are unusual findings, but leukocytosis with eosinophilia is often seen. Cutaneous antigen testing reveals anergy and a diminished cellular immunity that predisposes the patient to opportunistic infections. Initial chest radiograph for evaluation of mediastinal, hilar, or pulmonary parenchymal involvement and CT of the retroperitoneal nodes are recommended. If disseminated disease is suspected, tests of hepatic and renal function and a bone marrow biopsy should be performed.

Treatment

The approximate stage can be assigned by a combination of clinical information and laboratory tests, but definitive staging often requires exploratory laparotomy with splenectomy. Surgical staging is not indicated unless therapy will be influenced by the findings. If the patient clearly has disseminated disease (stage III or IV), surgical staging is unnecessary. With surgical staging, as many as 30% of patients with stages I and II are reclassified to higher stages. Four stages are described, and for any given stage, patients are further subdivided into "A" or "B" subgroups depending on the absence (A) or presence (B) of systemic symptoms. Systemic symptoms are defined as unexplained weight loss greater than 10% of body weight in the preceding 6 months, fever higher than 38°C, and night sweats. Approximately 60% of children with Hodgkin's disease have stage I or II disease:

- Stage I: Involvement of a single lymph node region or a single extralymphatic organ.

- Stage II: Involvement of two or more lymph node regions on the same side of the diaphragm, or localized involvement of an extralymphatic organ, and one or more lymph node regions on the same side of the diaphragm.

- Stage III: Involvement of lymph node regions on both sides of the diaphragm. This may be accompanied by localized involvement of an extralymphatic organ or site, involvement of the spleen, or both.

- Stage IV: Disseminated involvement of the liver, bone marrow, lungs, or other non-nodal sites.

Radiotherapy to involved nodes and the confluent node group to which spread could occur is often used for localized disease. For patients treated with radiotherapy alone who have relapsed, chemotherapy is used successfully to place the patient back in remission.

Combination chemotherapy is indicated for all stage IV and many stage III patients and for patients with localized but bulky disease, such as a large mediastinal mass. Chemotherapy is given in conjunction with radiotherapy. Nitrogen mustard, vincristine, prednisone, and procarbazine have been the most commonly used combination of chemotherapeutic agents, but other four-drug combinations may be as effective and may have fewer side effects.

Late effects of therapy include secondary malignancies (AML, NHL) from combined radiotherapy and procarbazine-containing chemotherapy regimens, thyroid gland dysfunction, growth retardation, and sterility.

Splenectomy in young children leaves them susceptible to bacterial sepsis, and as a result, splenectomy is not done routinely. If splenectomy is anticipated, immunization with pneumococcal, meningococcal, and Hib vaccine is imperative before the operation.

Prognosis is good and varies from a 90% cure of stage I disease to a 50% cure of stage IV disease. As in adults, lymphocyte predominance is most favorable and lymphocyte depletion least favorable.

◆ KEY POINTS ◆

1. The peak incidence of Hodgkin's disease has a bimodal distribution at 15–30 years of age and after the age of 50.

2. A diminished cellular immunity that predisposes the patient to opportunistic infections is common in Hodgkin's lymphoma. Hodgkin's lymphoma must be considered in an otherwise healthy adolescent with an opportunistic infection.

NEUROBLASTOMA

Pathogenesis

Neuroblastoma is a malignancy of the primitive neural crest cells that form the adrenal medulla and the paraspinal sympathetic ganglia. Tumors may manifest themselves in the abdomen, the thoracic cavity, or the head and neck. Abdominal tumors account for 70% of tumors, one-third of which arise from the retroperitoneal sympathetic ganglia and two-thirds from the adrenal medulla itself. Thoracic masses, accounting for 20% of the tumors, tend to arise from paraspinal ganglia in the posterior mediastinum. Neuroblastoma of the neck, 5% of the tumors, often involves the cervical sympathetic ganglion of the neck, resulting in Horner's syndrome.

Epidemiology

Its 7% incidence makes neuroblastoma the second most common solid tumor of childhood in white children; only brain tumors are more common. Neuroblastoma is the most common malignant tumor in infancy, with a median age of onset of 20 months. Greater than half of patients are less than 2 years of age and one-third are less than 1 year. There is a slight male predominance. Although its incidence is 7%, neuroblastoma accounts for 15% of the cancer deaths each year.

Risk Factors

The incidence of neuroblastoma is 1:100,000 infants, and it is associated with Hirschsprung's disease, fetal hydantoin syndrome, and von Recklinghausen's disease.

Clinical Manifestations

The clinical manifestations are extremely variable because of the widespread distribution of neural crest tissue and the length of the sympathetic chain.

History and Physical Examination

Abdominal tumors are hard, smooth, nontender, abdominal masses, which are most often palpated in the flank and displace the kidney anterolaterally and inferiorly. Abdominal pain and systemic hypertension may occur if the mass compresses the renal vasculature. Respiratory distress is the primary symptom seen in thoracic neuroblastoma tumors. Sometimes the thoracic variant is asymptomatic, and the tumor is discovered as an incidental finding on chest radiograph obtained for an unrelated reason. Neuroblastoma of the neck presents as palpable tumors that can sometimes cause ipsilateral miosis, ptosis, enophthalmos, anhidrosis, and heterochromia of the iris on the affected side (i.e., Horner's syndrome). Sometimes thoracic or abdominal tumors can invade the epidural space posteriorly in a dumbbell fashion, compromising the spinal cord and resulting in back pain and symptoms of cord compression.

Metastases are common at diagnosis and often cause the sequelae that lead to tumor diagnosis. Nonspecific symptoms of metastatic disease include weight loss and fever. Specific metastatic sequelae include bone marrow failure, resulting in pancytopenia; cortical bone pain, causing a limp; liver infiltration, resulting in hepatomegaly; periorbital infiltration manifested as proptosis and periorbital ecchymoses; distant lymph node enlargement; and skin infiltration, causing palpable subcutaneous nodules. Remote effects such as watery diarrhea in patients with differentiated tumors that secrete vasoactive intestinal peptide and acute myoclonic encephalopathy (opsoclonus, myoclonus, truncal ataxia) have been noted.

Differential Diagnosis

The differential diagnosis of abdominal neuroblastoma includes benign lesions such as hydronephrosis, polycystic kidney disease, and splenomegaly and malignant tumors such as renal cell carcinoma, Wilms' tumor, lymphoma, retroperitoneal rhabdomyosarcoma, and ovarian tumors.

Diagnostic Evaluation

For abdominal tumors that arise from the adrenal medulla, the intravenous pyelogram shows displacement of the kidney with minimal distortion of the calyceal system. Conversely, Wilms' tumor generally results in distortion of the calyceal system. Catecholamines are produced by most neuroblastoma tumors, and the urinary excretion of vanillylmandelic acid and homovanillic acid, which are the breakdown products of epinephrine and norepinephrine, is useful for diagnosis, for following response to therapy, and for detection of recurrence.

Treatment

Treatment involves surgery and chemotherapy, because 70% of patients at diagnosis have distant metastases. After surgical resection of the primary tumor and any lymph nodes or selected metastases, surgical and radiologic data are gathered to stage the tumor, as follows:

- Stage I: Tumor limited to the area of origin, complete gross excision, with or without microscopic residual disease, and negative lymph nodes.
- Stage IIa: Unilateral tumor with incomplete gross resection, with negative lymph nodes.
- Stage IIb: Unilateral tumor with complete or incomplete gross excision, with positive ipsilateral and negative contralateral lymph nodes.
- Stage III: Tumor infiltrating across the midline, with

or without regional lymph node involvement, or midline tumor with bilateral regional lymph node involvement.

- Stage IV: Dissemination of tumor to distant lymph nodes, bone, bone marrow, liver, and/or other organs (except as defined in stage IVS).
- Stage IVS: Localized primary tumor as defined for stage I or II with dissemination limited to liver, skin, and/or bone marrow.

Postsurgical radiation is used to treat residual local disease and selected metastatic foci, whereas chemotherapy varies in duration and intensity depending on the stage and histology. Regimens usually include vincristine, cyclophosphamide, adriamycin, and cisplatin. Spontaneous regression is common in stage IVS infants. In stage IVS, surgical removal of the small primary tumor is indicated to prevent late local recurrence. Bone marrow transplantation is often the best therapy for extensive stage III and IV disease.

Infants less than 1 year old have the best prognosis. Stages I, II, and IVS have a good prognosis, whereas stages III and IV have a poor prognosis. Serum markers associated with a poor prognosis include elevated neuron-specific enolase, ferritin, and lactic dehydrogenase. N-myc oncogene amplification within the tumor cells is associated with a poor prognosis. Each stage's percentage of new cases annually and its respective 5-year survival rate is as follows:

- Stage I: 5% of cases at diagnosis and greater than 90% survival.
- Stage II: 10% of cases at diagnosis and 75% survival.
- Stage III: 25% of cases at diagnosis and 40–70% survival, depending on the success of surgical resection.
- Stage IV: 60% incidence and 60% survival if age at diagnosis is less than 1 year, 20% if age at diagnosis is older than 1 year and less than 2 years, and 10% if age at diagnosis is greater than 2 years.
- Stage IVS: 5% of cases at diagnosis and greater than 80% survival.

◆ KEY POINTS ◆

1. Neuroblastoma may manifest itself in the abdomen, the thoracic cavity, or the head and neck; 70% of cases have abdominal tumors.

2. The fact that neuroblastoma accounts for 7% of the new cases of malignancy in children each year makes neuroblastoma the second most common solid tumor in white children; only brain tumors are more common.

3. Neuroblastoma is the most common malignant tumor in infancy, with a median age of onset of 20 months.

4. For abdominal tumors that arise from the adrenal medulla, the intravenous pyelogram often shows displacement of the kidney with minimal distortion of the calyceal system. Conversely, Wilms' tumor generally results in distortion of the calyceal system.

5. Treatment involves surgery and chemotherapy, because 70% of patients at diagnosis have distant metastases.

6. Infants less than 1 year old have the best prognosis. Stages I, II, and IVS have a good prognosis, whereas stages III and IV have a poor prognosis.

WILMS' TUMOR

Pathogenesis

Wilms' tumor results from neoplastic embryonal renal cells of the metanephros. Both Wilms' tumor and retinoblastoma are postulated to evolve through two distinct hits to the host genome. Usually, there is prezygotic (germline) inheritance of the first hit. Postzygotic (somatic) mutation, the second hit, induces malignancy in the tissue rendered susceptible by the first hit. The most often cited genetic anomaly in Wilms' tumor is a deletion of part of chromosome 11-[del(11p13)].

Epidemiology

This tumor accounts for 6% of all childhood cancers. It is predominantly found in the first 5 years of life, with a mean age of recognition of 3–3.5 years of age, and has equal occurrence in both males and females.

Risk Factors

Children with sporadic aniridia (1:100 in patients with Wilms' tumor versus 1:50,000 in the general population), hemihypertrophy (2:100 in patients with Wilms' tumor versus 3:100,000 in the general population), and genitourinary anomalies (5:100 in patients with Wilms' tumor) are all at risk for Wilms' tumor.

Clinical Manifestations

History and Physical Examination

Abdominal mass, seen in 85% of cases, is by far the most common presenting symptom. It is usually discovered incidentally by the child's parents while bathing or dressing the child or by the pediatrician during a routine well child care physical examination. Abdominal pain, after hemorrhage into the tumor, is characteristic. Other associated symptoms include fever, hypertension, and microscopic or gross hematuria. Hypertension occurs in 25% of afflicted patients due to either renin secretion by tumor cells or compression of the renal vasculature by the tumor. Hematuria is not common and, when present, is more often microscopic than gross.

Other associated findings include complete or partial sporadic aniridia, hemihypertrophy, and genitourinary anomalies including hypospadias, cryptorchidism, horseshoe or fused kidneys, ureteral duplication, polycystic kidneys, and ambiguous genitalia.

Differential Diagnosis

The differential diagnosis of Wilms' tumor includes benign lesions such as hydronephrosis, polycystic kidney disease, and splenomegaly, as well as malignant tumors such as renal cell carcinoma, neuroblastoma, lymphoma, retroperitoneal rhabdomyosarcoma, and ovarian tumors.

Wilms' tumor accounts for one-third of malignant intra-abdominal tumors in childhood.

Diagnostic Evaluation

Screening tests include a complete blood count, urinalysis, liver function tests, and renal function tests. Radiologic studies include abdominal ultrasound to define the site of origin within the kidney and to distinguish Wilms' from polycystic kidney disease, hydronephrosis, and neuroblastoma. An abdominal CT scan is useful to assess the degree of local extension and involvement of the inferior vena cava. Also, a liver scan, bone scan, and CT scan of the chest are required to search for distant metastases. In children with unfavorable histology, a CT scan of the head is needed to rule out central nervous system metastases.

Treatment

Treatment involves surgery, radiotherapy, and chemotherapy. Often there is presurgical treatment with chemotherapy and/or radiation to shrink the tumor to attempt to salvage some renal function in the affected kidney. After surgical resection of the primary tumor and any lymph nodes or selected metastases, the surgical and radiologic data are gathered to stage the tumor, as follows:

- Stage I: Tumor limited to the kidney and completely excised.
- Stage II: Tumor extends beyond the kidney but is completely excised.
- Stage III: Residual nonhematogenous tumor confined to the abdomen.
- Stage IV: Hematogenous metastases to lung, liver, bone, and/or brain.
- Stage V: Bilateral renal involvement at diagnosis.

Based on the staging of the tumor, chemotherapy and/or radiation is used to eradicate any tumor remaining.

Postsurgical radiation is used to treat residual local disease and selected metastatic foci. Chemotherapy varies in duration and intensity depending on the stage and histology, but regimens usually include actinomycin D and vincristine.

Prognostic factors include tumor stage and tumor histology. Classic nephroblastoma, a favorable histology, has an 88% overall survival rate, whereas anaplastic or sarcomatous variant, an unfavorable histology, has a 12% cumulative survival rate. The 4-year relapse-free survival of patients with favorable histology is directly related to stage and with treatment can be expected to be 97% for stage I, 92% for stage II, 87% for stage III, and 73% for stage IV.

◆ KEY POINTS ◆

1. Wilms' tumor and retinoblastoma are postulated to evolve through two distinct hits to the host genome. Usually, there is prezygotic (germline) inheritance of the first hit; then postzygotic (somatic) mutation, the second hit, induces malignancy in the tissue rendered susceptible by the first hit.

2. Wilms' tumor accounts for one-third of malignant abdominal masses in children.

3. Staging is done after exploratory laparotomy.

4. The tumor's histology rather than its stage is more important to prognosis. With favorable histology, taking into account all stages, the aggregate survival is 88%.

BONE TUMORS

Primary malignant bone tumors account for 4% of childhood cancer. Two forms predominate, Ewing's sarcoma and osteogenic sarcoma.

Ewing's Sarcoma

Pathogenesis

Ewing's sarcoma is an undifferentiated sarcoma that arises primarily in bone. The clonal nature of the disease is revealed by the consistent translocation from chromosome 11 to chromosome 22. A possible neurogenic origin has been suggested for highly undifferentiated Ewing's sarcoma because it has the same translocation that is found in the cells from primitive neuroectodermal tumors of the peripheral nervous system; these tumors are often referred to as primitive neuroectodermal tumors.

Epidemiology

Ewing's sarcoma is seen primarily in adolescents and is 1.5 times more common in males than females. It is an extremely rare occurrence in African Americans. Unlike osteogenic sarcoma, it occurs in young children and adolescents.

Clinical Manifestations

Pain and localized swelling are the most common presenting complaints. Systemic manifestations include fever, weight loss, and fatigue. The tumor most often involves the diaphyseal portion of the long bones, but the most likely sites include the midproximal femur and the bones of the pelvis. Other sites include the tibia, fibula, ribs, humerus, clavicle, and scapulae. Leukocytosis and an elevated erythrocyte sedimentation rate are often seen. Radiographs characteristically reveal a lytic bone lesion with calcified periosteal elevation (onion skin) and/or a soft tissue mass.

Differential Diagnosis

The differential diagnosis includes osteomyelitis, eosinophilic granuloma, and osteosarcoma. Metastasis to the bone by neuroblastoma or rhabdomyosarcoma should be considered in younger children with a solitary bone lesion.

Treatment

Radiation, chemotherapy, and surgery provide local control of the primary tumor. If the tumor affects an expendable bone (fibula, rib, or clavicle), complete surgical excision may be warranted. Most patients with Ewing's sarcoma have micrometastatic disease at the time of diagnosis, and as a result, chemotherapy is a critical component of therapy. Chemotherapy is used to reduce the size of the primary tumor, to treat metastases seen at diagnosis, and to prevent potential future metastases. Specific agents used include vincristine, cyclophosphamide, dactinomycin, and doxorubicin.

The prognosis is excellent for patients with distal extremity nonmetastatic tumors treated with chemotherapy and radiation. Children with metastatic disease at diagnosis or tumors of the pelvic bones or proximal femur have less favorable outcomes. Other less favorable features include soft-tissue extension, a low lymphocyte count, and an elevated serum lactic dehydrogenase. Without metastatic disease, greater than 50% of patients will have long-term survival.

◆ KEY POINTS ◆

1. Ewing's sarcoma is an undifferentiated sarcoma that arises primarily in bone.

2. It is seen primarily in adolescents and is extremely rare in African Americans.

3. Pain and localized swelling are the most common presenting complaints.

4. The most common sites for Ewing's sarcoma are the midproximal femur and the bones of the pelvis, which have the least favorable prognosis.

Osteogenic Sarcoma

Pathogenesis

Osteogenic sarcoma is a malignant tumor of the bone-producing osteoblasts. Osteosarcoma arises in either the medullary cavity or the periosteum. The primary tumor is located most often at the epiphysis or metaphysis of anatomic sites that are associated with maximum growth velocity, which include the distal femur, proximal tibia, and proximal humerus.

Epidemiology

Osteosarcoma is seen mainly in adolescence and is two times more common in males than females. Peak incidence occurs during the maximum growth velocity period.

Clinical Manifestations

There is often a history of trauma at the primary tumor site, but this is an incidental finding.

Similar to Ewing's sarcoma, pain and localized swelling are the most common presenting complaints, but in contrast to Ewing's sarcoma, systemic manifestations are rare. The most common tumor sites in decreasing order of frequency are distal femur (40%), proximal tibia (20%), and proximal humerus (10%). Metastases occur primarily to the lung and occur in 10–15% of cases. Gait disturbance and pathologic fractures also may be present. The erythrocyte sedimentation rate is generally normal, whereas the serum alkaline phosphatase level is usually elevated at diagnosis and can be used as a marker of treatment response.

Lytic bone lesion with periosteal reaction is characteristic on radiograph. The periosteal inflammation has the appearance of a radial "sunburst" that results as the tumor breaks through the cortex and new bone spicules are produced. A CT scan of the chest is essential to detect pulmonary metastases, which appear as calcified nodules.

Differential Diagnosis

The differential diagnosis for osteosarcoma includes Ewing's sarcoma, benign bone tumors, and chronic osteomyelitis.

Treatment

Various limb salvage surgical procedures that limit resection to the tumor-bearing portion of the bone are often used. Chemotherapy dramatically increases disease-free survival. Particular chemotherapeutic agents include high-dose methotrexate, doxorubicin, and cisplatin. The tumor is not radiosensitive at conventional doses.

Before adjuvant chemotherapy, survival from osteosarcoma was only 20%. Currently, with aggressive chemotherapy before and after surgical resection, long-term relapse-free survival is greater than 50%. Aggressive treatment of metastatic disease is indicated, because some patients can be salvaged with high-dose chemotherapy and surgical resection of pulmonary metastases. Poor prognostic findings include age less than 10 years, large tumor (greater than 15 cm), osteoblastic cell type, involvement of the axial skeleton or humerus, elevated serum lactic dehydrogenase, presence of symptoms less than 2 months, and metastases.

◆ KEY POINTS ◆

1. Osteogenic sarcoma is a malignant tumor of the bone-producing osteoblasts.

2. Osteosarcoma arises most often during maximum growth velocity in the distal femur, proximal tibia, or proximal humerus.

3. Similar to Ewing's sarcoma, pain and localized swelling are the most common presenting complaints, but in contrast to Ewing's sarcoma, systemic manifestations are rare.

4. Various limb salvage surgical procedures that limit resection to the tumor-bearing portion of the bone are often used.

18 Ophthalmology

VISION SCREENING

Visual screening in children is critical because the young eye is part of a dynamic system that may be quickly damaged by visual deprivation. The recommendations of the American Academy of Ophthalmology concerning visual examinations in children are found in Table 18–1. Children older than 8 years can be screened according to adult guidelines. Children with a history of prematurity, maternal intrauterine infection, disease of the central nervous system, or a family history of ocular disease are considered to be at high risk for eye pathology and require more extensive follow-up by an ophthalmologist.

STRABISMUS

Strabismus is a condition in which the eyes are misaligned. It is a common condition, occurring in approximately 4% of children in the United States. Certain neurologic diseases are associated with an especially high incidence of strabismus, including cerebral palsy, Down syndrome, hydrocephalus, and brain tumors. Unilateral visual deprivation may also lead to strabismus.

Clinical Manifestations

The deviating eye of a patient with strabismus may turn inward (esodeviation), outward (exodeviation), upward (hyperdeviation), or downward (hypodeviation). Diagno-

sis is made by means of the corneal light reflection and cover tests.

Treatment

The most important consequences of untreated strabismus, aside from the cosmetic deformity, are amblyopia (see later) and reduced stereopsis. Treatment is aimed at correction of the underlying cause, elimination of amblyopia, and medical and/or surgical realignment of the eyes.

◆ KEY POINTS ◆

1. Screening for strabismus by means of cover testing should be included in every pediatric examination.
2. Early recognition and treatment offer the best means of obtaining permanent realignment and avoiding amblyopia.

AMBLYOPIA

Amblyopia, literally meaning "dull sight," refers to reduced vision developing in early childhood in an otherwise normal eye. The condition is common, with an

TABLE 18–1

Pediatric Vision Screening Recommendations of the American Academy of Ophthalmology

Age	Examination	Referral
Newborn	Corneal light reflex test	Abnormal red reflexes
	Red reflexes	Any other ocular abnormality
By age 6 months	Fixation to light or small toys	Aversion to occlusion
	Monocular occlusion	Strabismus
	Corneal light reflex test	Nystagmus
	Cover/uncover test	Abnormal red reflexes
	Red reflexes	Any other ocular abnormality
Age 3.5 yr	Visual acuity	Visual acuity of 20/50 or less
	Corneal light reflex test	in one or both eyes
	Cover/uncover test	Strabismus
	Fundus examination	Any other ocular abnormality
Age 5 or older	Visual acuity	Visual acuity of 20/40 or less
	Corneal light reflex test	in one or both eyes
	Cover/uncover test	Strabismus
	Fundus examination	Any other ocular abnormality

Source: Communication of the American Academy of Ophthalmology, San Francisco, 1988.

incidence of 2–5% in the adult population. Strabismus is the most common cause of amblyopia and is due to the suppression of retinal images from a misaligned eye. Visual deprivation due to opacities of the optical axis (ptosis, corneal opacity, cataract) or to unequal refractive errors in the two eyes (anisometropia) also results in amblyopia. Low birth weight and a family history of amblyopia or strabismus are other risk factors for the development of amblyopia.

Clinical Manifestations

Subnormal vision is the only sign of amblyopia, and amblyopia remains a diagnosis of exclusion. If not treated, amblyopia results in permanent vision loss and diminished stereopsis.

Treatment

The cornerstone of therapy involves occlusion of the better-seeing eye. The vulnerable period for the development of amblyopia is up to approximately age 8. Beyond that period, amblyopia is unlikely to develop, and, conversely, treatment is unlikely to be successful.

♦ **KEY POINTS** ♦

1. Amblyopia represents a common and potentially reversible cause of vision loss in children.

2. Successful treatment depends on early recognition and referral for elimination of predisposing conditions and occlusion therapy.

NASOLACRIMAL DUCT

Obstruction

Obstruction of the nasolacrimal duct is a common cause of overflow tearing (epiphora) in neonates. The most common cause of obstruction is a persistent membrane that blocks the distal end of the nasolacrimal duct where it empties into the nose.

Clinical Manifestations

Chronic tearing in a quiet eye is the hallmark of nasolacrimal duct obstruction. The presence of a mucopurulent discharge and tenderness over the medial aspect of the lower lid should suggest superimposed dacryocystitis. Other causes of excess tearing include chronic irritation from allergens, smoke, wind, or congenital glaucoma.

Treatment

In most cases, nasolacrimal duct obstruction resolves spontaneously. Referral to an ophthalmologist is indicated if symptoms persist beyond the age of 9 months so that probing of the tear duct system may be performed before the age of 1 year. Rarely, surgery is required to create a patent tear drainage system. Superimposed dacryocystitis may be treated with hot compresses, nasolacrimal massage, and topical antibiotics, with the addition of systemic antibiotics in select cases.

◆ KEY POINTS ◆

1. Nasolacrimal duct obstruction is a common cause of tearing in infants and neonates and typically resolves spontaneously.

2. Referral is indicated if symptoms persist beyond 9 months of age and for infants with recurrent dacryocystitis.

LEUKOCORIA

Leukocoria, or a white pupil, in an infant or child may be caused by a number of entities ranging from isolated ocular abnormalities to life-threatening systemic disease. Only the more common etiologies are discussed here. All cases of leukocoria require prompt ophthalmologic referral.

Differential Diagnosis

Retinoblastoma is the most common intraocular malignancy of childhood and is the most life-threatening cause of leukocoria. The disease occurs in approximately 1 in 20,000 live births, resulting in 250 to 500 new cases in the United States each year. Untreated retinoblastoma leads to death from brain and visceral metastasis in almost all cases. Cataracts (opacities of the crystalline lens) occur with an incidence of roughly 1 in 250 live births, making them the most common cause of leukocoria. They may be congenital or acquired and may be unilat-

eral or bilateral. Cataracts are often genetically determined but may result from metabolic or infectious diseases. Retinopathy of prematurity (ROP) is a retinal vascular disease of premature infants. As many as 65% of neonates weighing less than 1000 g at birth may be affected. Risk factors include birth weight less than 1250 g, gestational age less than 32 weeks, mechanical ventilation, and need for supplemental oxygen. Other, less common causes of leukocoria include congenital glaucoma and ocular toxocariasis.

Clinical Manifestations

Leukocoria may be detected by routine screening of the red reflex in all neonates and, if found, requires prompt referral to an ophthalmologist. Infants at high risk for the development of ROP should be seen by an ophthalmologist when discharged from the nursery and again at 3–6 months of age.

Treatment

Successful therapy in all cases must combine treatment of the underlying condition with attention to associated amblyopia. Treatment options for retinoblastoma include enucleation (removal of the eye), radiation therapy, chemotherapy, and cryotherapy. Prognosis is directly related to the size of the tumor at diagnosis, and cure rates today approach 90%. Unilateral or bilateral congenital cataracts may be surgically removed. The visual prognosis for children requiring cataract extraction is not as good as that seen in adults, because amblyopia or associated ocular abnormalities may limit the ultimate level of visual acuity. Most cases of ROP regress spontaneously; however, cryotherapy performed at an intermediate stage of ROP reduces progression to the vision-threatening stages of the disease. Eyes with treated or regressed ROP remain at increased risk for the development of amblyopia, strabismus, myopia, and glaucoma.

◆ KEY POINTS ◆

1. The most common cause of leukocoria is congenital cataract.

2. All cases of leukocoria require prompt ophthalmologic referral.

3. All children at high risk for ROP should be seen by an ophthalmologist before discharge from the nursery.

RED EYE IN THE INFANT

Ophthalmia neonatorum refers to a red eye that occurs within the first 21 days of life. Although most cases are due to mild chemical irritation from ophthalmia prophylaxis, bacterial conjunctivitis, if left untreated, may cause permanent blindness. Any ocular discharge in the neonate should be regarded as suspicious, because tears are generally absent before the age of 3 weeks.

Differential Diagnosis

Roughly 80% of red eyes in neonates is due to chemical irritation after silver nitrate prophylaxis (ophthalmia medicamentosa). Tearing and mild conjunctival hyperemia typically resolve within 24 hours. *Chlamydia trachomatis* accounts for most infectious red eyes in infants, presenting with a mucopurulent discharge and conjunctival hyperemia 2 days to 8 weeks after delivery. Of infants infected with chlamydia, 25–50% develop conjunctivitis. The most damaging infectious agent is *Neisseria gonorrhoeae*, which causes a hyperacute purulent conjunctivitis 2–5 days after delivery that may progress to corneal perforation and blindness if left untreated. Other causes of neonatal conjunctivitis (nongonococcal bacteria and herpes simplex virus) are uncommon and generally present more than 5 days after delivery

Clinical Manifestations

All red eyes in infants require urgent evaluation. The onset, duration, and severity of symptoms should be recorded. If chlamydia is suspected, both a nasopharyngeal and conjunctival eye culture should be sent. If gonorrhea is considered, a conjunctival eye culture will suffice.

Treatment

No treatment is required for irritation due to chemical prophylaxis. Chlamydial conjunctivitis is treated with tetracycline ointment and oral erythromycin. Parents should be treated systemically as well. Suspected gonococcal infection should be referred to an ophthalmologist and treated emergently with topical and intravenous penicillin. Treatment of nongonococcal bacterial infection consists of topical antibiotics with close and regular follow-up. All patients should be referred urgently if signs worsen after 3 days of treatment or if symptoms persist longer than 7 days.

◆ KEY POINTS ◆

1. A red eye in an infant may represent chemical irritation or acquired infection.

2. Chlamydia and gonorrhea are the most common infectious agents.

3. Suspected gonococcal infection requires emergent treatment to prevent blindness.

CHILD ABUSE

Suspected child abuse warrants special mention, given its delicate social and medicolegal implications. Retinal and vitreous hemorrhages may indicate shaken-baby syndrome and may be the only verifiable sign of child abuse. Permanent vision loss may result if these hemorrhages are left untreated. Suspected abuse mandates urgent systemic evaluation for other evidence of trauma and referral to Children's Protective Services to ensure the child's safety. A full discussion of child abuse is found in Chapter 2.

◆ KEY POINT ◆

1. Retinal and vitreous hemorrhages may indicate shaken-baby syndrome and may be the only verifiable sign of child abuse.

19 Orthopedics

Pediatricians and family practitioners require a basic knowledge of orthopedic principles to treat injuries, facilitate rehabilitation, and recognize the musculoskeletal manifestations of many systemic illnesses. The timely diagnosis and management of genetic, congenital, developmental, and infectious bone and joint conditions in children can minimize potential deformities and loss of function.

ACHONDROPLASIA

Achondroplasia is a disorder of cartilage calcification and remodeling. Inheritance is **autosomal dominant**. The physical appearance is strikingly characteristic; these patients are very short with proportionally large heads. Long bones tend to be wide, short, and curved, and digits are short and stubby. Kyphoscoliosis and lumbar lordosis may be quite pronounced. Heterozygotes have fairly normal intelligence, sexual function, and life expectancy. Homozygotes fare less well, given their increased susceptibility to pulmonary complications and an abnormally small foramen magnum that predisposes to brainstem compression.

OSTEOGENESIS IMPERFECTA

Osteogenesis imperfecta (OI) describes a group of closely related genetic disorders resulting in fragile, brittle bones.

The common denominator in all variants is the abnormal synthesis of type I collagen, which normally comprises about 90% of the bone matrix but is also dispersed in the teeth, ligaments, skin, ears, and sclerae. The most severe form is type II, or fetal OI, which results in multiple intrauterine and birth fractures and is uniformly fatal in the perinatal period. Inheritance is autosomal dominant in most cases.

Clinical Manifestations

Clinical severity depends on the subclass of OI (Table 19–1). Some variants cause death early in life; others present with only moderately increased susceptibility to fractures. Blue sclerae are a characteristic feature in some forms of the disease. Short stature is not uncommon due to frequent recurrent fractures. Fractures associated with OI occasionally raise the suspicion of child abuse.

Treatment

Treatment involves standard fracture care, pneumatic bracing, and careful avoidance of even minor trauma.

◆ KEY POINTS ◆

1. Type II OI is the most severe form, resulting in intrauterine or perinatal death.

2. Patients with OI types I, III, or IV may have blue sclerae.

TABLE 19-1

Classification of Osteogenesis Imperfecta

Syndrome	Orthopedic Manifestations	Nonorthopedic Manifestations	Life Expectancy
Type I	Neonatal fractures; bow legs; kyphoscoliosis; joint laxity; mild short stature	Blue sclerae; conductive hearing loss	Generally shortened
Type II	Short, deformed limbs; severe bone fragility	Intrauterine growth retardation; stillbirth	Days
Type III	Neonatal fractures; severe bone fragility; lower limb deformities; short stature	Blue sclerae	Infancy/childhood
Type IV	Increased susceptibility to fractures	Blue sclerae	Near normal

DEVELOPMENTAL HIP DYSPLASIA

Pathogenesis

Developmental dysplasia of the hip (DDH) results when contact between the acetabulum and the head of the femur is lost during intrauterine development, most likely due to positioning of the fetus.

Epidemiology

DDH is more common in females, first-born children, and breech presentations. Severity of dysplasia ranges from "subluxatable" (partial dislocation induced on examination) to "dislocatable" (full dislocation induced on examination) to "dislocated" (abnormally positioned most of the time).

Clinical Manifestations

A careful physical examination is the key to diagnosis. Performed with the examiner's fingers on the greater and lesser trochanters, both Barlow's test (posterosuperior dislocation of the hip with adduction and posterior pressure) and the Ortolani maneuver (abduction with a resulting "click" as the head relocates into the joint) are essential parts of every newborn evaluation (Fig. 19–1). Older infants may present with limited hip abduction and apparent shortening of the thigh. A "false" acetabulum is noted in the lateral ileum on hip radiographs, whereas the true acetabulum is distorted and shallow.

Treatment

Most subluxatable and dislocatable hips stabilize without intervention within the first 4 weeks of life. If treatment is indicated in children under 6 months of age, a Pavlik harness (which keeps the hip abducted and flexed) may be prescribed. Traction is used in older patients. Patients who do not respond to conservative measures require open reduction.

Avascular necrosis of the femoral head is the most serious complication and is more likely to occur when the child has been left untreated for longer than 6 months.

◆ KEY POINT ◆

1. DDH may be demonstrated on physical examination using Barlow's test and the Ortolani maneuver.

FOOT DEFORMITIES

Foot deformities predispose children to difficulty walking, poor shoe fit, and pain. Some disorders correct themselves as the child begins to ambulate; others require bracing or surgical correction. In general, any congeni-

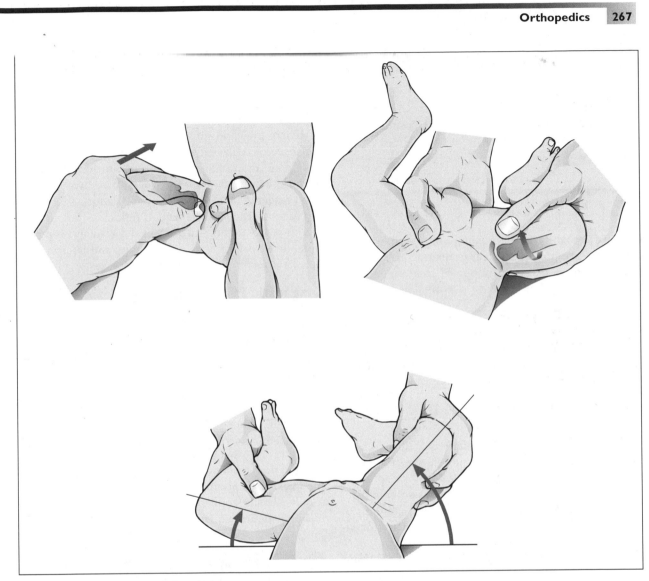

Figure 19–1   Barlow and Ortolani maneuvers.

tal orthopedic condition of the foot that can be molded by the examiner's hands to its anatomically correct position requires minimal intervention.

Clinical Manifestations and Treatment

Metatarsus Adductus

Metatarsus adductus (in-toeing of the forefoot without hindfoot abnormalities) is a common, relatively benign condition due to intrauterine positioning. As opposed to clubfoot, dorsiflexion and plantar flexion at the ankle joint are unrestricted. Eighty-five percent correct spontaneously once the infant begins ambulating. Mild passive stretching may also be beneficial. More severe or persistent cases are treated with serial splinting or casting. Surgery is rarely indicated.

Talipes Equinovarus

Talipes equinovarus, or clubfoot, is a rarer but more debilitating deformity that includes medial rotation of the tibia, flexion at the ankle, and inversion of the foot and forefoot adduction. Without treatment, the foot becomes progressively more deformed, and ulcerations develop when the child is old enough to limp. Early intervention is essential for subsequent normal function and development. Initial treatment consists of serial casting; most patients require surgical repair, preferably before 1 year of age.

LIMP

Limp is probably the most common musculoskeletal complaint prompting medical evaluation in children. Pain, weakness, decreased range of motion, and leg-length discrepancy all disrupt the normal gait.

Differential Diagnosis

The list of conditions that present with limp is extensive (Table 19–2); some are benign and self-limited, whereas others result in significant morbidity.

Clinical Manifestations

History
The patient's age affects the differential. Infection is a common etiology in younger children, whereas Legg-Calve-Perthes disease, slipped capital femoral epiphysis (SCFE), and juvenile rheumatoid arthritis occur in older patients. **Trauma** is the most common cause of limp at any age. The absence of pain suggests weakness or instability. Pain may be severe (fracture, infection), constant, associated with activity (injury), acute, or chronic. Swelling and stiffness are common in rheumatologic

TABLE 19–2

Differential Diagnosis of Limp

Injury	Legg-Calve-Perthes
Fracture	disease
Growing pains	Slipped capital femoral
Leg-length discrepancy	epiphysis
Shin splints	Cerebral palsy
Toxic synovitis	Foot deformity
Osteomyelitis	Neuromuscular disease
Bursitis	Malignancy
Arthritis (rheumatologic, reactive)	

disease. Toxic synovitis may follow a recent viral illness. Any history of bowel or bladder incontinence suggests spinal cord compression.

Physical Examination
Watching the child walk is particularly important; certain gaits are associated with specific disorders. Each joint should be examined for range of motion, swelling, warmth, erythema, and tenderness. Fractures produce point tenderness and occasionally angulation. Neurologic evaluation includes deep tendon reflexes, strength, and sensation. Extremities are assessed for adequate perfusion and deformities. Muscle atrophy and fasciculation may be present in neuromuscular disease.

Diagnostic Evaluation

All patients with significant limp should have plain films. An elevated white blood count may indicate infection; if greater than 30,000/μL, malignant marrow invasion should be considered. The erythrocyte sedimentation rate is increased in both infection and rheumatologic disease. A bone scan reveals areas of increased blood flow consistent with inflammation. Patients with weakness should have electrolytes, calcium, serum creatinine kinase, and urine myoglobin studies done; electromyography and nerve conduction studies may also be helpful. If the weakness is progressive and limited to the lower extremities, spinal cord compression must be ruled out with imaging studies (i.e., magnetic resonance imaging).

SLIPPED CAPITAL FEMORAL EPIPHYSIS

Pathogenesis
SCFE is the gradual or acute separation of the proximal femoral growth plate, with the femur rotating externally under the capital epiphysis. The cause is unknown but

may be immunologic or hormonal in origin. Antecedent trauma is not a contributing factor.

Epidemiology and Risk Factors

SCFE typically occurs during the adolescent growth spurt. The incidence is highest in patients who are male and obese. Although usually asymmetric at presentation, 25% of cases will eventually progress to bilateral involvement.

Clinical Manifestations

History and Physical Examination

The typical patient presents with a limp and pain, which may be centered in the hip or groin but often is referred to the knee. Limited internal rotation and limb shortening are present on examination.

Differential Diagnosis

The differential includes trauma, Legg-Calve-Perthes disease, toxic synovitis of the hip, and avascular necrosis.

Diagnostic Evaluation

Radiographs with the child's hips in the **frog-leg lateral position** are the study of choice for epiphyseal displacement (Fig. 19–2).

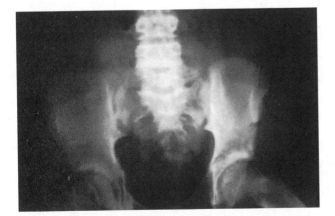

Figure 19–2 Radiograph of a slipped capital femoral epiphysis. Frog-leg view in this 13-year-old boy demonstrates increased radiolucency of the left femoral epiphysis with medial and perhaps posterior angulation of the femoral head on the neck.

Treatment

The primary goal of treatment is prevention of further misalignment. Pin fixation is effective in the acute setting. Chronic cases generally require osteotomy.

Long-term complications include avascular necrosis and late degenerative changes similar to those seen with osteoarthritis.

◆ KEY POINTS ◆

1. Trauma is not a cause of SCFE.
2. The typical SCFE patient is an obese adolescent male.

LEGG-CALVE-PERTHES DISEASE

Legg-Calve-Perthes disease is defined as avascular necrosis (ischemic compromise) of the femoral epiphysis. The etiology is unknown. Eventually, the ischemic bone is resorbed and reossification occurs, with continued (but not necessarily normal) growth. Legg-Calve-Perthes disease occurs more often in males and younger children (ages 4–8). Occasionally, it is bilateral.

Clinical Manifestations

A limp is the most common presenting complaint. If pain is present, it is often referred to the knee, clouding the diagnostic picture. Range of motion is limited upon abduction, flexion, and internal rotation. The differential diagnosis is similar to that for slipped capital femoral epiphysis. Initial radiographic studies may appear normal; subsequent films demonstrate epiphyseal radiolucency.

Treatment

Treatment involves containing the fragile femoral head within the acetabulum, preserving its spherical contour, and maintaining normal range of motion. Younger children with minimal involvement and full range of motion may be observed. Orthotic bracing or surgery is necessary in older patients with significant changes in the femoral head. The amount and area of ischemic damage affect the prognosis. Collapse of the femoral head is the most serious acute complication; long-term disability is related to abnormal or asymmetric growth.

OSGOOD-SCHLATTER DISEASE

Osgood-Schlatter disease involves the **tibial tuberosity**, an extension of the proximal tibial epiphysis. Inflammation results in tenderness and swelling over the anterior tubercle. It typically occurs between the ages of 10 and 17. Repetitive stress and trauma may be contributing factors. Radiographs reveal irregularities of the tubercle contour and possibly haziness of the adjacent metaphyseal border. Most cases are mild and are treated with activity restriction. More severe cases may require casting for up to 6 weeks. Long-term morbidity is quite low.

IDIOPATHIC SCOLIOSIS

Pathogenesis

One in 20 children displays some degree of spinal deformity. **Scoliosis**, or lateral curvature, is the most common. Idiopathic scoliosis is found in otherwise healthy children with normal bones, muscles, and vertebral discs. The cause is unknown, but familial factors definitely play a role.

Epidemiology

Severe scoliosis requiring intervention occurs more often in females. Progression of the curve is most rapid during the adolescent growth spurt.

Clinical Manifestations

History and Physical Examination
Idiopathic scoliosis is not associated with back pain or fatigue; such symptoms warrant further investigation. The physical examination consists of two parts. First, the child is examined from the rear while standing up. Shoulder girdle and iliac crest areas are noted for symmetry and height. Then the child bends forward from the waist, a test maneuver that is very sensitive for discerning lateral thoracic and lumbar curvature.

Differential Diagnosis

Occasionally, scoliosis may be due to neuromuscular abnormalities or congenital deformities. Scoliosis should not be confused with **kyphosis**, an increase in the **posterior** convexity of the thoracic spine. Kyphosis is usually postural and responds well to specific daily exercises.

Treatment

Curvatures less than 25° need only be followed. More pronounced deformity in a child who is still growing should be treated with external bracing until the growth spurt is completed. Bracing does not reduce the curve, but it does halt progression and is 85% effective if used correctly. Unfortunately, compliance tends to be low. Curvature that is greater than 40–50° after the growth spurt will continue to progress; such patients require spinal fusion to reduce the curve and stabilize the spine. Curves of 50° or greater are associated with decreased vital capacity and low functional pulmonary reserve.

COMMON FRACTURES IN CHILDREN

Fractures in children deserve special attention because their bones are characteristically different from those of adults. For one, they are more porous, which limits fracture propagation. Ligaments and tendons are relatively stronger than bones; injuries that would cause sprains or tears in adults can fracture bones in children. Fractures through the epiphyseal growth plate require particular care, because they may result in deformity or limb-length discrepancy.

Clinical Manifestations

History and Physical Examination
The history is positive for trauma in virtually all cases of nonpathologic fractures; caretakers who have abused a child may not offer this information. Isolated point tenderness occurs over the site of the fracture. Angulation is variably present and may be quite subtle.

Differential Diagnosis

Greenstick fractures occur when the force applied breaks one side of a bone and bends the other. A fracture is complete if the bone is broken through both sides. **Spiral fractures** are often the result of child abuse. When a spiral fracture is diagnosed, obtaining a careful history of the event is warranted. **Epiphyseal fractures** disrupt the growth plate, the weakest portion of the child's skeletal system. Epiphyseal fractures are categorized according to the Salter-Harris classification (Fig. 19–3). **Stress fractures** are hairline cracks related to repetitive activity and are usually seen in athletes. **Pathologic fractures** result when underlying disease weakens the bone, as may occur in osteogenesis imperfecta, malignancies, long-term steroid use, infection, endocrine disorders, and some inborn errors of metabolism.

Treatment

Most fractures can be adequately treated with external stabilization. Fractures that are unstable, misaligned, or through the growth plate require operative reduction. In younger children, bony overgrowth at the site of the fracture may produce limb angulation or asymmetric length if not correctly set.

◆ **KEY POINTS** ◆

1. Fractures through the growth plate may result in deformity or leg-length discrepancy.
2. Spiral fractures suggest child abuse.

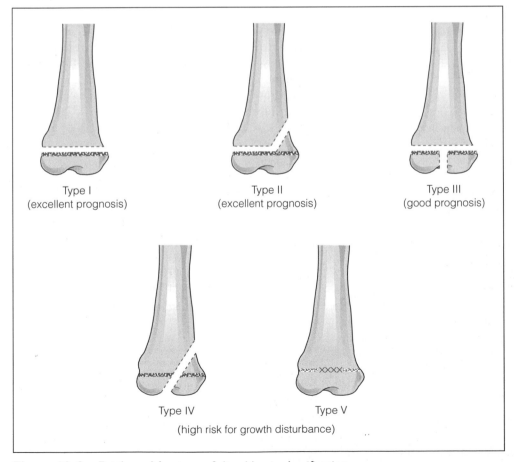

Type I
(excellent prognosis)

Type II
(excellent prognosis)

Type III
(good prognosis)

Type IV

Type V

(high risk for growth disturbance)

Figure 19–3 Epiphyseal fractures: Salter-Harris classification.

SUBLUXATION OF THE RADIAL HEAD

Subluxation of the radial head, or nursemaid's elbow, is one of the most common injuries seen in young children. The history is often remarkable for a sudden strong jerking of the child's pronated hand resulting in rapid extension at the elbow. The patient holds the arm slightly flexed with the hand pronated. Motion at the elbow is limited. Treatment consists of holding the patient's elbow at 90° flexion and firmly manipulating the forearm into supination.

OSTEOMYELITIS

Pathogenesis

Bone infections require early recognition and aggressive treatment to effect a favorable outcome. Hematogenous seeding is the usual source of origin; trauma seems to increase susceptibility. The femur and tibia account for two-thirds of cases. Infection usually begins in the metaphysis, an area of relative blood stasis and few phagocytes.

Epidemiology and Risk Factors

Incidence peaks in the neonatal period and again in older children (ages 9–11), when it becomes more common in males. The predominant organism in all age groups is *Staphylococcus aureus*. Osteomyelitis due to group A streptococcus and *Haemophilus influenzae* occurs in children as well. Group B streptococci and *Escherichia coli* are important pathogens in the neonate. Although patients with sickle cell disease are particularly susceptible to Salmonella osteomyelitis, *S. aureus* is still the most common pathogen in this population.

Clinical Manifestations

History and Physical Examination

Infants present with a history of fever and refusal to move the involved limb. Older patients also complain of localized bone pain. The physical examination may reveal soft-tissue swelling, limited range of motion, and erythema. Occasionally, sinus tracts will drain purulent fluid onto the skin surface.

Differential Diagnosis

Traumatic injury and malignant invasion of the bone may also present with similar symptoms. Range of motion

generally remains intact in patients with osteomyelitis, as opposed to septic arthritis and epiphyseal disorders.

Diagnostic Evaluation

White blood count is often within the normal range, although the sedimentation rate tends to be significantly elevated. Only 50–60% of blood cultures are positive. Aspiration of the involved bone is imperative for recovery, identification, and sensitivity testing of the causative organism, especially if initial blood cultures are negative. Radiographs are initially normal but demonstrate periosteal elevation or radiolucent necrotic areas in 2–3 weeks. Bone scans are positive within 24–48 hours.

Treatment

Treatment consists of intravenous or high-dose oral antibiotics for 4–6 weeks.

Initially, broad-spectrum antistaphylococcal agents, such as oxacillin, are appropriate. Cefuroxime may be chosen if immunization status is deficient. Treatment of neonates requires coverage for group B streptococci and gram-negative bacilli. When the organism has been recovered and sensitivities are available, therapy may be narrowed. Most patients do not require surgery.

Abscess formation within the metaphyseal shaft is not uncommon. If the infection extends to the epiphyseal plate, growth deformities may occur. Septic arthritis is also a known complication.

◆ KEY POINTS ◆

1. Peak incidence is bimodal (neonatal period and ages 9–11).

2. Only about half of blood cultures are positive, so aspiration of the bone yields invaluable information.

3. The bone scan is more sensitive than plain films early in the disease process.

4. *S. aureus* is the most common pathogen in all age groups.

SEPTIC ARTHRITIS

Pathogenesis

Septic arthritis (purulent infection of the joint space) is more common and potentially more debilitating than osteomyelitis.

Epidemiology

The incidence is highest in infants and young children. In infants, the hip is the most common site, and *S. aureus* is the most likely pathogen. The knee is more often involved in older children; *S. aureus* is still the primary organism, although streptococci and gram-negative bacteria are not uncommon. *Neisseria gonorrhoeae* must be considered in the sexually active adolescent, especially if multiple joints are involved. Recently, the gram-negative rod *Kingella kingae* has emerged as an important cause of septic arthritis.

Clinical Manifestations

History and Physical Examination

Septic arthritis presents as a painful joint, often accompanied by fever, irritability, and refusal to bear weight. On examination, range of motion is clearly limited; swelling, erythema, warmth, and tenderness are also present to varying degrees.

Differential Diagnosis

Osteomyelitis and arthritis should be considered in the differential diagnosis. Toxic synovitis is a frequent cause of joint pain in children. It has not been definitively proven to be an infectious condition, although it often follows viral illnesses. The hip is most commonly involved. In contrast to septic arthritis, range of motion is minimally limited, and the white blood cell count, sedimentation rate, and fever curve are usually normal to slightly elevated.

Diagnostic Evaluation

Aspiration of the synovial fluid usually yields a white blood cell count in excess of 25,000 and a pathologic organism. The exception is *N. gonorrhoeae*, which is difficult to recover; blood, cervical, rectal, and nasopharyngeal cultures may be more helpful.

Treatment

Delay in treatment may result in permanent destructive changes and functional impairment. Intravenous antibiotic therapy remains the treatment of choice; conversion to oral therapy is appropriate when sensitivities are known and symptoms substantially improve. Surgery is rarely indicated unless the infection is overwhelming, resistant, or advanced.

◆ KEY POINTS ◆

1. The most common cause of septic arthritis in infants and children is *S. aureus*.
2. *N. gonorrhoeae* must be considered in the sexually active adolescent.

20 Pulmonology

Respiratory diseases are among the leading causes of mortality in the Western world. In children younger than 4 years, only accidents result in more deaths. More children visit pediatricians for respiratory symptoms than for any other complaint. Children have smaller and more collapsible airways, decreased lung recoil, relatively more mucous glands, and lower antibody levels than adults, all of which increase their susceptibility to pulmonary disease.

REACTIVE AIRWAY DISEASE

Pathogenesis

Reactive airway disease (RAD; commonly termed asthma) is a chronic disease of reversible airway obstruction characterized by bronchial hyperreactivity, inflammation, and mucous secretion. Bronchospasm, which results from smooth muscle constriction, may occur after allergic, environmental, infectious, or emotional stimuli. Common precipitants include cigarette smoke, upper respiratory infections, pet dander, dust mites, weather changes, exercise, and seasonal or food allergens. Exacerbations can last minutes to hours; some resolve spontaneously, whereas others require aggressive medical therapy.

Epidemiology

RAD is the most frequently encountered pulmonary disease in children, and its prevalence is on the rise despite advances in therapy. It is the most common reason for hospitalization in pediatric practice. Ninety percent of patients present before the age of 6 years. Boys are affected twice as often as girls before adolescence, at which time the numbers become equal.

Risk Factors

Risk factors include genetic predisposition, atopy, cigarette smoke exposure, living in urban areas, poverty, and being of the black race. Respiratory syncytial virus (RSV) infection necessitating hospitalization has also been associated with a higher incidence of subsequent asthma.

Clinical Manifestations

History and Physical Examination

The presentation of asthma is varied. The history may be positive for wheezing with colds, decreased exercise tolerance, or persistent nighttime coughing. Children with acute attacks present in respiratory distress with dyspnea, wheezing, subcostal retractions, nasal flaring, tracheal tugging, and a prolonged expiratory phase due to obstruction of airflow. Cyanosis is uncommon. The absence of wheezing with poorly heard breath sounds is an ominous sign, indicating that the child's respiratory system is too obstructed to move air. Mental status changes suggest advanced hypercarbia and impending respiratory arrest.

Differential Diagnosis

When an infant presents with wheezing and respiratory distress, the differential diagnosis includes bronchiolitis, foreign body aspiration, gastroesophageal reflux with aspiration, tracheoesophageal fistula, and vascular sling. Anaphylaxis and angioneurotic edema may cause wheezing at any age. Cough-variant asthma produces a chronic nighttime cough similar to that accompanying postnasal drip, bronchitis, or cystic fibrosis.

Diagnostic Evaluation

The chest radiograph demonstrates significant hyperinflation and occasionally atelectasis (Fig. 20–1). CO_2 retention occurs early and may be quite dramatic; hypoxemia is usually less pronounced.

Treatment

With appropriate therapy and compliance, most patients can remain symptom free with few exacerbations. The most effective form of treatment consists of removing inciting agents from the child's environment. Cigarette smoke should be strictly avoided. Limiting dust mite, mold, and pet exposure is beneficial to patients with an allergic component to their RAD.

The mainstays of medical maintenance therapy are bronchodilators, cromolyn, and steroids. Beta$_2$-agonists such as albuterol reduce smooth muscle constriction and may be administered via nebulization or metered-dose inhalation or orally. Longer-acting preparations (salbutamol) are currently marketed for overnight use. Beta$_2$-agonists are effective in preventing exercise-induced asthma if used 30 minutes before vigorous activity. The abuse of bronchodilators may result in tolerance to their effects.

Cromolyn works by stabilizing the mast cell membrane, preventing release of inflammatory mediators. It is available in nebulized and metered-dose inhaler forms and is well tolerated, with no known adverse effects. It is not helpful during an acute attack but is an excellent form of prevention.

The advent of inhaled corticosteroid therapy has had a remarkable impact on the treatment of RAD. Aerosolized formulas are breathed directly into the lungs with a substantial decrease in systemic side effects, and their use as a daily medication in moderate to severe asthma

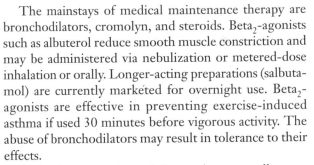

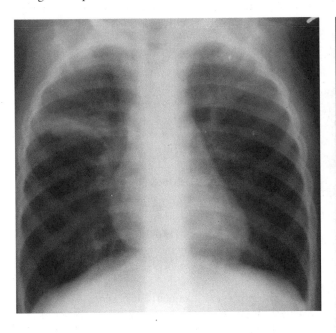

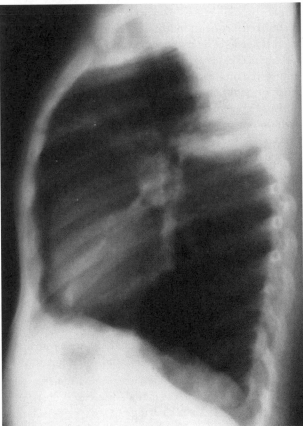

Figure 20–1 Chest radiograph of a 3-year-old taken during a RAD exacerbation shows severe hyperinflation, increased anteroposterior diameter of the chest, a depressed diaphragm, and several areas of atelectasis.

has increased. Five-day oral pulse steroid treatment is recommended during an acute exacerbation.

The use of theophylline, once a commonly prescribed oral bronchodilator, has fallen out of favor as a first-line treatment option. It has virtually no anti-inflammatory properties, is often poorly tolerated, and requires frequent drug-level monitoring.

Recently, a new class of drugs called leukotriene receptor antagonists has been developed. These oral medications are recommended for the treatment of chronic moderate to severe asthma and may allow some patients to reduce their dependence on as-needed beta$_2$-agonist and daily inhaled steroid use.

Children who present to the emergency department in an acute asthma attack are initially assessed for airway patency and ability to aerate. Pulse oximetry measurement is a simple, rapid screen for hypoxemia. Patients in severe respiratory distress require arterial blood gas measurements to assess the need for supplemental oxygen and recognize increasing PaCO_2, a sign of impending respiratory failure. (Note: a normal PaCO_2 in the face of tachypnea is an equally ominous sign, because the PaCO_2 should be well below 40 with a rapid respiratory rate.) Nebulized bronchodilators are administered continuously if needed. Subcutaneous epinephrine or terbutaline rapidly decreases airway reactivity. Corticosteroids, administered orally or intravenously, require 4–6 hours for a response but are indicated for treatment of inflammation and prevention of the late-phase response. Children who do not respond with complete resolution of symptoms after several hours (i.e., children in status asthmaticus) or those who require ongoing oxygen therapy should be hospitalized for continued treatment and close observation.

Despite advances in therapy, the mortality of RAD in children has continued to rise over the past 2 decades. Factors that increase the risk of death include noncompliance, delay in treatment, history of intubation, black race, and steroid dependence.

◆ KEY POINTS ◆

1. The three components of RAD are bronchospasm, mucous secretion, and inflammation.

2. The disappearance of wheezing with increased respiratory distress signals increased obstruction rather than clearing.

3. Bronchodilators are the treatment of choice in an acute attack; cromolyn is not effective under these circumstances.

4. The effectiveness of corticosteroids is delayed 4–6 hours after administration.

CYSTIC FIBROSIS

Pathogenesis

Cystic fibrosis (CF) is a multisystem inherited disease characterized by disordered exocrine gland function. The product of the CF gene is a cell membrane protein that functions as a cAMP-activated chloride channel on the epithelial cells of the respiratory tract, pancreas, sweat and salivary glands, intestines, and reproductive system. This channel is nonfunctional in patients with CF, so chloride remains sequestered inside the cell. Sodium and water are drawn into the cell to maintain ionic osmotic balance, resulting in relative dehydration at the cell surface and abnormally viscid secretions.

Epidemiology

CF is acquired through autosomal-recessive inheritance, with a disease frequency of 1 in 2500 live white births. The gene occurs with lower frequency in other populations. Over 200 distinct gene mutations have been described, so the disease spectrum is widely variable and prenatal diagnosis is difficult.

Clinical Manifestations

History and Physical Examination

The most common presenting signs and symptoms of CF are listed in Table 20–1. All levels of the respiratory tract may be affected, including the nasal passages, sinuses, and lower airways. Nasal polyps in any pediatric patient should prompt further testing for CF. Opacification of the sinuses and sinusitis are extremely common. Mucus stasis and ineffective clearance potentiate repeated bacterial pneumonias. Frequent pathogens include *Staphylococcus aureus*, *Haemophilus influenzae*, and, most important, *Pseudomonas aeruginosa*; 90% of patients acquire *P. aeruginosa* and it is seldom eradicated. Colonization with *Burkholderia* (Pseudomonas) *cepacia* is particularly ominous and is associated with accelerated pulmonary deterioration and death. Digital clubbing is almost universal.

TABLE 20–1

Clinical Manifestations of Cystic Fibrosis

Respiratory
   Nasal polyps
   Sinusitis
   Cough
   Bronchiectasis
   Clubbing/cyanosis
   Recurrent pneumonia
   Reactive airway
      disease
   Hemoptysis
   Pneumothorax
   Cor pulmonale
Hepatobiliary
   Obstructive neonatal
      jaundice
   Portal hypertension
   Cirrhosis

Gastrointestinal
   Meconium ileus
   Distal intestinal
      obstruction
      syndrome
   Pancreatic insufficiency
   Malabsorption
   Failure to thrive
   Pancreatitis
   Diabetes
   Rectal prolapse
   Duodenal ulcers
Other
   Hyponatremic
      dehydration
   Metabolic alkalosis
   Impaired fertility
      (males)

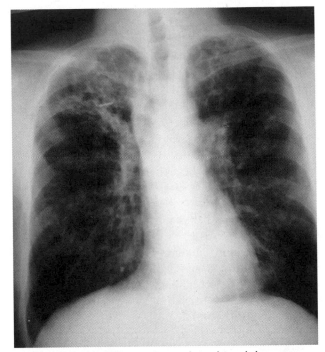

Figure 20–2 Chest radiograph in this adolescent male with cystic fibrosis demonstrates marked chronic disease and bleb formation.

Gastrointestinal manifestations include pancreatic insufficiency, bowel obstruction and rectal prolapse, diabetes, and hepatic cirrhosis. Interference with normal pancreatic enzyme secretion leads to decreased fat absorption; parents may notice that the child's stools are large and bulky. Failure to thrive is the most common manifestation of CF in infants and children. In the neonate, meconium ileus is pathognomonic for CF.

Diagnostic Evaluation

Recurrent lower airway infection results in bronchiectasis, fibrosis, parenchymal loss, and the characteristic "bleb" formation found on chest radiographs (Fig. 20–2). Pulmonary function tests demonstrate both obstructive and restrictive changes. The sweat chloride level remains the diagnostic test of choice; a level greater than 60 mEq/L is considered abnormal. Genetic testing is available for the 14 most common gene mutations, accounting for 85% of cases.

Treatment

Chest physical therapy, exercise, and frequent coughing are helpful in mobilizing secretions. Bronchodilators and anti-inflammatory medications relax smooth muscle walls, decrease airway reactivity, and curb tissue destruction. Dornase (Pulmozyme), administered via nebulization, breaks down thick DNA complexes present in mucus due to cell destruction and bacterial infection. Normal growth can often be achieved with pancreatic enzyme replacement, fat-soluble vitamin supplements, and high-calorie, high-protein diets. Nasogastric or gastrostomy tube feedings may be instituted if oral intake is inadequate.

Frequent disease exacerbations may be triggered by viral or bacterial infections and are treated by aggressive chest physical therapy, postural drainage, and antibiotics, which may be given orally if the exacerbation is mild and the organisms are not resistant. Usually, however, bacterial infections must be treated with an aminoglycoside (e.g., tobramycin) and a semisynthetic penicillin or cephalosporin, depending on organism sensitivities. Research aimed at providing gene replacement therapy is currently under way.

Prognosis continues to improve with aggressive treatment of pulmonary exacerbations and optimal nutritional support. Respiratory complications remain the major contributors to morbidity and mortality in CF.

Hemoptysis is an alarming development that may occur during pulmonary exacerbations in long-standing disease. Frequent coughing and inflammation lead to erosion of the walls of bronchial arteries in areas of bronchiectasis, and expectorated sputum becomes streaked with blood. Blood loss of more than 300 mL/day or 100 mL/day for 3 consecutive days is considered an emergency, often treated by arterial embolization.

Pneumothorax is another potentially life-threatening complication that may occur in CF. It is characterized by the sudden onset of severe chest pain and difficulty breathing. Placement of a chest tube results in rapid re-expansion, but over half of pneumothoraces recur unless sclerosis or surgery is used.

Progressive obstruction and hypoxia in advanced disease can lead to chronic pulmonary hypertension and right heart failure (cor pulmonale). For CF patients with a life expectancy of 1–2 years, lung transplantation is a potentially viable option.

◆ KEY POINTS ◆

1. Cystic fibrosis is a disorder of exocrine gland function, affecting the lungs, sinuses, pancreas, sweat and salivary glands, intestines, and reproductive system.

2. Inheritance is autosomal recessive.

3. The disease is far more prevalent in whites than in other races.

4. Failure to thrive is the most common presentation of CF in children.

5. Meconium ileus in the neonate is pathognomonic for CF.

6. An elevated sweat chloride level is diagnostic.

7. Therapy involves aggressive nutritional support, infection control, chest physical therapy, and DNase.

APNEA

Apnea is defined as the cessation of breathing for longer than 20 seconds or pauses of any duration associated with color changes (cyanosis, pallor), hypotonia, decreased responsiveness, or bradycardia. It may be central (neurally mediated), obstructive, or mixed. Apnea is not a diagnosis but a potentially dangerous symptom, requiring aggressive workup to determine and treat the underlying cause.

The three most frequently encountered apnea syndromes in the pediatric population are apnea of prematurity, apnea of infancy (apparent life-threatening events), and obstructive sleep apnea. Apnea of prematurity is discussed further in Chapter 13.

Clinical Manifestations and Treatment

Apparent Life-Threatening Events

In contrast to apnea of prematurity, apnea of infancy occurs in full-term infants. Often, the disorder comes to medical attention after an apparent life-threatening event (ALTE). ALTEs are very frightening to the caretaker; the infant either stops breathing or is found apneic and may be cyanotic or pale, hypotonic, difficult to rouse, or choking and gagging. The observer often believes that the child would have died without intervention (vigorous stimulation, cardiopulmonary resuscitation). Infantile apnea can result from many causes (Table 20–2).

Management involves treating the underlying disorder. When no treatable cause can be found, the infant may be placed on a home monitor that senses chest movement (breathing) and heart rate and alarms when the child becomes apneic or bradycardic; however, home monitors have never been proved to decrease the likelihood of sudden infant death syndrome (SIDS). In about half the cases of apnea of infancy, no predisposing condition is ever found.

Obstructive Sleep Apnea

Obstructive sleep apnea is an important and treatable cause of apnea in children. Symptoms include restless

---

TABLE 20–2

Causes of Apnea of Infancy

Sepsis	Metabolic disorders
Meningitis	Electrolyte disorders
Pneumonia	Arrhythmias
Bronchiolitis (RSV)	Aspiration
Seizures	Gastroesophageal reflux
Airway obstruction	Idiopathic

sleep, snoring or gasping, altered personality, morning headache, and excessive daytime sleepiness. In older children and adults, obstructive sleep apnea may be associated with obesity and chronic hypercarbia, termed the Pickwickian syndrome. Much more common in children, however, is obstruction due to anatomic abnormalities (large tonsils and adenoids, macroglossia) or insufficient airway tone (tracheomalacia or laryngeomalacia). Polysomnography, which measures respiratory effort, air flow, oxygenation, and heart rate, can be helpful in determining the type and severity of the apneic events.

Some children's symptoms are relieved with removal of the adenoids and/or tonsils. Otherwise, treatment involves overnight continuous positive airway pressure (CPAP) or, in very severe cases, tracheostomy.

◆ KEY POINTS ◆

1. Apnea is a symptom, not a diagnosis.
2. Home apnea monitors do not decrease the risk of SIDS.
3. Obstructive sleep apnea is diagnosed by polysomnography and treated with CPAP.

LYMPHOCYTIC INTERSTITIAL PNEUMONITIS

Lymphocytic interstitial pneumonitis (LIP) consists of infiltration of mature lymphocytes into the lung tissue with resultant interstitial inflammation. Dyspnea is the most consistent presenting complaint. The chest radiograph reveals patchy or diffuse fluffy infiltrates, representing epithelial cell hyperplasia. LIP is an acquired immunodeficiency syndrome–defining illness; almost a fourth of human immunodeficiency virus patients acquire it. Occasionally, it occurs in conjunction with other immunologic or rheumatologic diseases. LIP is treated with corticosteroids regardless of the etiology. The disease course may be indolent or rapidly progressive, resulting in pulmonary fibrosis.

PULMONARY HEMOSIDEROSIS

Pulmonary hemosiderosis involves an abnormal accumulation of hemosiderin in the lungs as a result of diffuse alveolar hemorrhage. It may be associated with cow milk allergy in infants or Goodpasture's syndrome in older children. Clinical manifestations include hemoptysis/hematemesis, productive cough, dyspnea, and a microcytic hypochromic anemia. Diagnosis is based on the presence of hemosiderin-laden macrophages (siderophages) in bronchial washings or gastric aspirates.

Bibliography

Avery GB, Fletcher MA, MacDonald MG, eds. Neonatology: Pathophysiology and management of the newborn, 5th ed. Philadelphia: Lippincott Williams & Wilkins, 1999.

Baldwin G, ed. Handbook of pediatric emergencies, 2nd ed. Boston: Little, Brown, 1994.

Behrman RE, Kliegman RM, eds. Essentials of pediatrics, 2nd ed. Philadelphia: WB Saunders, 1994.

Cloherty JP, Stark AR, eds. Manual of neonatal care, 4th ed. Philadelphia: Lippincott-Raven, 1998.

Dixon SD, Stein MT. Encounters with children: Pediatric labor and development, 2nd ed. St. Louis: Mosby Yearbook, 1992.

Dworkin PH, ed. Pediatrics, 2nd ed. Philadelphia: Harwal Publishing, 1992.

Goetzman BW, Wennberg RP, eds. Neonatal intensive care handbook, 2nd ed. St. Louis: Mosby Yearbook, 1991.

Graef JW, ed. Manual of pediatric therapeutics, 5th ed. Boston: Little, Brown, 1994.

Guyton AC. Textbook of medical physiology, 8th ed. Philadelphia: WB Saunders, 1991.

Jandl JH. Blood pathophysiology. Boston: Blackwell Science, 1991.

Kott PB, Eitzman D, Neu J. Neonatal and pediatric respiratory care, 2nd ed. St. Louis: Mosby Yearbook, 1993.

Macklis RM, Mendelsohn ME, Mudge GH. Introduction to clinical medicine, 3rd ed. Boston: Little, Brown, 1994.

Markel H, Oski JA, Oski FA, McMillan JA. The portable pediatrician. Philadelphia: Hanley and Belfus, 1992.

McMillan JA, De Angelis CD, Feigin RD, Warshaw JB, eds. Oski's Pediatrics: Principles and practice, 3rd ed. Philadelphia: Lippincott Williams & Wilkins, 1999.

Nelson LB, Calhoun JH, Harley RD. Pediatric ophthalmology, 3rd ed. Philadelphia: WB Saunders, 1991.

Nichols DG, Yaster M, Lappe DG, Buck JR, eds. Golden hour: The handbook of advanced pediatric life support. St. Louis: Mosby Yearbook, 1991.

Pickering LK, ed. 2000 Red book: Report of the Committee on Infectious Diseases, 25th ed. Elk Grove Village, IL: American Academy of Pediatrics, 2000.

Rogers MC, Helfaer MA, eds. Handbook of pediatric intensive care, 2nd ed. Baltimore: Williams & Wilkins, 1995.

Rosenstein BJ, Fosarelli PD. Pediatric pearls: The handbook of practical pediatrics, 2nd ed. St. Louis: Mosby Yearbook, 1993.

Siberry GK, Iannone R, eds. The Harriet Lane handbook, 15th ed. St. Louis: Mosby, 2000.

Shulman ST, Phair JP, Sommers HM. The biologic and clinical basis of infectious diseases, 4th ed. Philadelphia: WB Saunders, 1992.

Trobe JD. The physician's guide to eye care. San Francisco: American Academy of Ophthalmology, 1993.

Wallach J, ed. Interpretation of diagnostic tests: A synopsis of laboratory medicine, 5th ed. Boston: Little, Brown, 1992.

Zitelli BJ, Davis HW, eds. Atlas of pediatric physical diagnosis, 2nd ed. London: Wolfe Publishing, 1993.

Sources of Redrawn Figures

Behrman RE, Kliegman RM, eds. Essentials of pediatrics, 2nd ed. Philadelphia: WB Saunders, 1994.

Cloherty JP, Stark AR, eds. Manual of neonatal care, 3rd ed. Boston: Little, Brown, 1991.

Dworkin PH, ed. Pediatrics, 2nd ed. Philadelphia: Harwal Publishing, 1992.

Graef JW, ed. Manual of pediatric therapeutics, 5th ed. Boston: Little, Brown, 1994.

Johnson KB, ed. The Harriet Lane handbook, 13th ed. St. Louis: Mosby Yearbook, 1994.

Markel H, Oski JA, Oski FA, McMillan JA. The portable pediatrician. Philadelphia: Hanley and Belfus, 1992.

Nichols DG, Yaster M, Lappe DG, Buck JR, eds. Golden hour: The handbook of advanced pediatric life support. St. Louis: Mosby Yearbook, 1991.

Shulman ST, Phair JP, Sommers HM. The biologic and clinical basis of infectious diseases, 4th ed. Philadelphia: WB Saunders, 1992.

Trobe JD. The physician's guide to eye care. San Francisco: American Academy of Ophthalmology, 1993.

Questions

A 12-year-old male adolescent presents with a one-month history of fever, weight loss, fatigue, and pain and localized swelling of the mid-proximal femur.

1. What is the *most* likely diagnosis?

   a. Ewing's sarcoma

   b. osteosarcoma

   c. chronic osteomyelitis

   d. benign bone tumor

   e. eosinophilic granuloma

An obese adolescent male presents to your urgent care facility with a chief complaint of intermittent knee pain for 2 weeks. He has no known history of trauma but does play soccer twice a week. He has had no fever or upper respiratory symptoms. The knee exam is normal; however, the hip exam demonstrates limited internal rotation and mild tenderness.

2. What is the most likely cause of this patient's limp based on the history and exam?

   a. Legg-Calve-Perthes disease

   b. osteomyelitis

   c. septic arthritis

   d. Osgood-Schlatter disease

   e. slipped capital femoral epiphysis

3. What is the most appropriate initial diagnostic test?

   a. anterior-posterior hip films

   b. frog-leg hip films

   c. "setting sun" knee films

   d. aspiration of the affected joint

   e. magnetic nuclear resonanace

4. The study indicates severe involvement of the affected joint. What is the treatment of choice?

   a. none; the condition resolves spontaneously.

   b. casting

   c. arthroscopic surgery

   d. pin fixation

   e. chemotherapy

A 1-month-old infant female, born at full term, is noted to have a harsh holosystolic 3/6 heart murmur heard best at the left lower sternal border. The child is acyanotic and does not have hepatomegaly or tachypnea at rest. The child feeds without tachypnea or diaphoresis, and weight gain is appropriate. There is no cardiomegaly on chest radiograph.

5. What is the *most* likely diagnosis?

   a. ventricular septal defect

   b. atrial septal defect

c. patent ductus arteriosus

d. pulmonary stenosis

e. aortic stenosis

6. What is the *most* appropriate therapy?

a. surgical intervention

b. anticongestive medical therapy

c. evaluation and follow-up by a pediatric cardiologist with subacute bacterial endocarditis prophylaxis

d. no evaluation needed by pediatric cardiologist

e. evaluation and follow-up by a pediatric cardiologist without subacute bacterial endocarditis prophylaxis

A 5-year-old African American female with sickle cell disease presents with a vaso-occlusive pain crisis.

7. All of the following phenomena are also complications of sickle cell disease, *except*:

a. cholecystitis

b. hyperhemolytic crisis

c. sepsis

d. acute chest syndrome

e. pancreatitis

A 4-month-old infant presents at your office with complaints of fever, poor feeding, and fussiness. The physical exam is normal except for moderate dehydration, poor perfusion, and irritability. The white blood count is elevated with a left shift. The cerebrospinal fluid is unremarkable. Urinalysis of a catheterized specimen reveals red blood cells, white blood cells, and scant bacteria.

8. What is the most appropriate course of treatment?

a. empiric intravenous antibiotic therapy

b. empiric oral antibiotic therapy

c. aggressive fluid restriction

d. surgical intervention

e. delayed antibiotic therapy based on culture results

9. Which imaging study is most likely to demonstrate vesicoureteral reflux?

a. renal ultrasound

b. voiding cystourethrogram

c. nuclear medicine scan

d. intravenous pyelography

e. abdominal CAT scan

10. The above test demonstrates grade 5 reflux on the right side. What is the most appropriate therapeutic intervention?

a. ureteral reimplantation surgery

b. renal resection

c. pyeloplasty

d. transurethral ablation

e. prophylactic antibiotic therapy

A 15-year-old known asthmatic presents to the emergency room with shortness of breath. He has used his inhaler three times in the past hour. His respiratory rate is 34 with a pulse oxygenation measurement of 92%. However, no wheezing is heard on exam.

11. What is the most appropriate initial pharmacologic intervention?

a. oral bronchodilators

b. nebulized bronchodilators

c. nebulized cromolyn

d. intravenous steroids

e. intravenous theophylline

12. Given what you know about the pathophysiology of asthma, what medicine is most likely to address the underlying inflammation and prevent the "late-phase" response?

a. methylprednisolone

b. theophylline

c. albuterol

d. cromolyn

e. terbutaline

A 3-month-old female infant presents to your emergency room unresponsive and with fever, tachypnea, bradycardia, and hypotension.

13. What order do you follow in your initial assessment:

   a. airway, breathing, circulation, disability, exposure

   b. breathing, airway, circulation, disability, exposure

   c. circulation, airway, breathing, exposure, disability

   d. exposure, breathing, airway, circulation, disability

   e. exposure, airway, breathing, circulation, disability

14. How would you assess and establish an airway in this infant?

   a. sweep oropharynx for foreign body, jaw thrust, hyperextend the neck, 100% oxygen via facemask

   b. clear airway with suction catheter, chin lift, place head in midline "sniffing position," 100% oxygen via facemask

   c. clear airway with suction catheter, sweep oropharynx for foreign body, jaw thrust, place head in midline "sniffing position," 100% oxygen via facemask

   d. clear airway with suction catheter, chin lift, hyperextend neck, 2 liters O_2 via nasal cannula

   e. clear airway with suction catheter, sweep oropharynx for foreign body, chin lift, place head in midline "sniffing position," 2 liters O_2 via nasal cannula

15. Which of the statements regarding the assessment or treatment of circulation in the primary survey is *true*?

   a. Blood pressure is the most sensitive indicator of intravascular volume status.

   b. In the infant and child, hypotension is an early finding when hypovolemia exists.

   c. Chest compressions should be done with two fingers on the sternum, at the xiphoid process, to a depth of 2 inches, at a rate of 60 compressions/minute.

   d. Chest compressions should be done with two fingers on the sternum, 1 fingerbreadth below

the intermammary line, to a depth of 0.5–1.0 inch, at a rate of 60 compressions/minute.

   e. Capillary refill is the most sensitive measure of adequate circulation.

Match the following resuscitation drugs with the appropriate indication:

16. atropine

17. bicarbonate

18. epinephrine (1:10,000)

19. lidocaine

   a. ventricular ectopy

   b. asystole, bradycardia, ventricular fibrillation

   c. severe refractory metabolic acidosis and/or hyperkalemia

   d. bradycardia and atrioventricular block

Preventive counseling should be an important part of every well-child visit.

20. Which of the following statements is true?

   a. Infants who are 20 pounds or heavier may ride in forward-facing car seats regardless of age.

   b. Infants should be placed in the supine position for sleeping.

   c. When poisoning is suspected, parents should always give syrup of ipecac, regardless of the ingested substance.

   d. The most effective method of removing lead poisoning risk is to paint over lead-containing paint with paint manufactured after 1977.

   e. Driver education programs substantially reduce the risk of accidents involving adolescents.

A 2-year-old male presents to your office with a fever of 103°F that has lasted for the past 5 days.

21. Which of the following signs and symptoms is not consistent with a diagnosis of Kawasaki disease?

   a. bilateral conjunctivitis

   b. dry, red, fissured lips

   c. cervical lymphadenopathy

   d.   a maculopapular rash over the buttocks and extremities

   e.   indurative edema of the hands and feet

22. The child meets the diagnostic criteria for Kawasaki disease. What is the most appropriate initial therapy?

   a.   corticosteroids

   b.   antibiotics

   c.   cautious electrolyte replacement

   d.   dialysis

   e.   aspirin and intravenous immunoglobulin (IVIG)

23. 'What is the most significant serious complication arising from Kawasaki disease?

   a.   coronary aneurysms

   b.   kidney failure

   c.   arthritis

   d.   gastrointestinal bleeding

   e.   hypertension

A child presents to your office with a complaint of frequent short staring spells. These spells have been noticed by both the parents and the child's preschool teacher. The spells last only a few seconds each; however, the child is not responsive during the spells, and they are increasing in frequency. The parents are concerned.

24. Which of the following diagnostic procedures is most likely to yield a definitive diagnosis?

   a.   cerebrospinal fluid analysis

   b.   electroencephalogram

   c.   head CAT scan

   d.   muscle biopsy

   e.   magnetic resonance imaging

25. What is the above study likely to demonstrate?

   a.   increased levels of protein and myelin in the cerebrospinal fluid

   b.   an asymmetric mass lesion

   c.   hypsarrythmia

   d.   a generalized, symmetric 3-per-second spike and wave pattern

   e.   generalized brain edema

26. What is the most appropriate initial trial medication following diagnosis?

   a.   ethosuximide

   b.   phenytoin

   c.   phenobarbital

   d.   valproic acid

   e.   carbamazepine

A full-term 4000 g male infant is noted to be cyanotic 6 hours after birth. He has increased pulmonary vascular markings on chest radiograph without cardiomegaly. He is tachypneic with good pulses and perfusion. There is no heart murmur, but there is a loud single S2. The electrocardiogram is normal for a newborn. The preductal and postductal oxygen saturation levels are 65%. A hyperoxia test revealed a preductal right radial ABG on 100% O_2 of 7.33/35/35/21/−1.5.

27. All of the following statements concerning cyanosis are true, *except*:

   a.   Cyanosis is the physical sign characterized by blue mucous membranes, nail beds, and skin.

   b.   Cyanosis appears when the absolute concentration of unsaturated hemoglobin is greater than or equal to 3.5 g/dL.

   c.   Neonates with acrocyanosis have blue mucous membranes.

   d.   Factors that influence whether cyanosis will appear include the hematocrit, which determines the absolute amount of hemoglobin, and those factors that affect the oxygen dissociation curve.

   e.   Cyanosis in the newborn may result from cardiac, pulmonary, neurologic, or hematologic causes.

28. Which of the following congenital heart defects is *most* likely?

   a.   transposition of the great arteries with intact ventricular septum

   b.   Ebstein's anomaly

c. total anomalous pulmonary venous return with obstruction

d. tricuspid atresia with normally related great arteries

e. tetralogy of Fallot

Match the congenital infections with the clinical manifestation:

29. toxoplasmosis *B*

30. syphilis *A*

31. rubella *D*

32. cytomegalovirus *C*

33. herpes simplex virus-2 *F*

34. HIV *E*

a. nonimmune hydrops, thrombocytopenia, osteitis and osteochondritis, persistent rhinitis (snuffles), hepatosplenomegaly, jaundice

b. intrauterine meningoencephalitis, microcephaly, hydrocephalus, choreoretinitis, intracerebral calcifications, and seizures

c. intracerebral calcifications, chorioretinitis, microcephaly, jaundice, hepatosplenomegaly

d. peripheral pulmonic stenosis, atrial septal defect, ventricular septal defect, chorioretinitis, hepatosplenomegaly, jaundice, "blueberry muffin spots"

e. thrush, lymphadenopathy, hepatosplenomegaly

f. localized infection of skin, eye, mouth, or disseminated infection or localized central nervous system infection

You are called to evaluate a newborn in the nursery. The parents are very concerned because the child's right foot points inward. You note that the foot is easily molded into the correct anatomic position; moreover, range of motion at the ankle is normal.

35. What is the most likely deformity?

a. there is no deformity

b. developmental hip dysplasia

c. metatarsus adductus

d. talipes equinovarus

e. genu varum

36. What is the child's most likely prognosis for normal gait?

a. The deformity will correct spontaneously when the child begins to walk.

b. Serial casting will be required.

c. Surgical treatment will provide normal gait.

d. Surgical treatment will correct the deformity but not result in normal gait.

e. The child will have a permanent limp.

A newborn infant with suspected congenital heart disease is noted to have no thymic shadow on chest radiograph.

37. What is the most likely electrolyte abnormality?

a. hypocalcemia

b. hypercalcemia

c. hypokalemia

d. hyperkalemia

e. hypophosphatemia

DiGeorge prone to opportunistic - PCP, fungi

38. This patient is at greatest risk for infections with which of the following organisms?

a. encapsulated bacteria

b. catalase (+) bacteria

c. rickettsial diseases

d. opportunistic infections

T-cell defect

A 3-year-old female is diagnosed with new onset insulin dependent diabetes mellitus.

39. All the following symptoms are consistent with a diagnosis of new onset diabetes mellitus *except*:

    a. polydipsia

    b. polyphagia

    c. polyuria

    d. new onset weight loss

    e. diarrhea

40. All of the following symptoms are consistent with a diagnosis of diabetic ketoacidosis *except*:

    a. confusion

    b. polyuria

    c. fruity breath odor

    d. hyperpnea

    e. paresthesias

41. Which of the following laboratory data is consistent with diabetic ketoacidosis?

    a. hypoglycemia

    b. hypercarbia

    c. ketones in urine

    d. high venous blood pH

    e. normal blood urea nitrogen

42. All of the following are appropriate therapeutic maneuvers for diabetic ketoacidosis *except*:

    a. normal saline or lactated ringer's solution 20 mL/kg intravenous bolus

    b. intravenous bolus of 0.1unit/kg of regular insulin

    c. intravenous insulin drip at 0.1 unit/kg/hour of regular insulin

    d. total fluid deficit is calculated, and one-half is given over the first 8 hours and the other half is given over the next 16 hours

    e. potassium infusion during the initial fluid bolus

43. Which of the following is *not* a possible etiology of diabetes insipidus?

    a. head trauma

    b. brain tumor

    c. central nervous system infection

    d. post-craniopharyngioma

    e. pseudotumor cerebri

A 7-year-old boy presents to your office with a chief complaint of severe headache and photophobia. His temperature on arrival is 104.5°F. You notice several large annular erythematous lesions with central clearing on his trunk and legs, consistent with erythema migrans. There is no known history of a tick bite.

44. What is the most likely diagnosis?

    a. Lyme disease

    b. Rocky Mountain spotted fever

    c. ehrlichiosis

    d. leptospirosis

    e. bacterial meningitis

45. Following appropriate initial tests, the child is admitted to the hospital. The cerebrospinal fluid is positive for numerous white blood cells. What is the most appropriate course of therapy?

    a. intravenous tetracycline

    b. intravenous cefotaxime

    c. oral doxycycline

    d. oral penicillin

    e. oral amoxicillin-clavulanic acid

Match the following disorders with their most likely electrolyte imbalances:

46. congenital adrenal hyperplasia   a. Na 134, K 4.8, Cl 114, bicarb 9, glucose 101

47. diabetic ketoacidosis   b. Na 135, K 3.5, Cl 86, bicarb 37, glucose 69

48. pyloric stenosis   c. Na 130, K 5.0, Cl 102, bicarb 14, glucose 400

49. diarrheal dehydration   d. Na 128, K 6.0, Cl 95, bicarb 21, glucose 59

A 3-year-old female presents at your office with a history of rash on the extensor surfaces as an infant. She now has a rash on the flexor surfaces of her body.

50. Which of the following signs and symptoms is *not* consistent with a diagnosis of eczema (atopic dermatitis)?

    a. nonpruritic rash on the knees, elbows, scalp, and genital area

    b. bacterial superinfection

    c. lichenification

    d. rash is characterized by remissions and exacerbations

    e. "itch-scratch-itch cycle"

51. Which of the following diagnostic criteria is *not* consistent with atopic dermatitis?

    a. elevated serum IgE

    b. elevated eosinophil count

    c. skin biopsy reveals hyperplasia of the epidermis

A 5-year-old male presents to the pediatrician with fever and new 3/6 systolic ejection murmur heard best at the right upper sternal border. On extremity examination, splinter hemorrhages and petechiae are noted.

52. What is the most likely diagnosis based on the clinical description?

    a. endocarditis

    b. rheumatic heart disease

    c. Kawasaki's disease

    d. pericardial effusion

    e. dilated cardiomyopathy

An infant presents at the emergency room following a seizure that resolved without intervention. She has a history of a fever and two days of diarrhea. Her white blood count is elevated, and a stool sample is full of mucus and streaked with blood, but she appears nontoxic and is well-hydrated.

53. Which of the following pathogens is most likely?

    a. *Shigella dysentariae*

    b. *Vibrio cholerae*

    c. *Giardia lamblia*

    d. *Yersinia enterolytica*

    e. *Salmonella typhae*

54. The decision is made to institute therapy for bacterial diarrhea. Which of the following treatments is most appropriate for this patient?

    a. oral trimethoprim-sulfamethoxazole

    b. intravenous cefotaxime

    c. oral mebendazole

    d. ciprofloxacin

    e. intravenous hydration only; antibiotic therapy is contraindicated

55. The most likely pathogen responsible for this child's disease is also associated with which of the following complications?

    a. pseudo-appendicitis

    b. erythema nodosum

    c. failure to thrive

    d. cholera

    e. hemolytic uremic syndrome

A 7-year-old child is referred to your office because of declining school performance. There is no known change in the child's life stressors. The teacher reports that he has been falling asleep in his classes. The grandmother notes that she has begun sleeping in the same room with him because he snores so badly that he frequently stops breathing in his sleep and begins to gasp. The tonsils appear quite large but not erythematous on exam, and the child does not complain of throat pain.

56. What test is indicated to rule out obstructive sleep apnea?

    a. chest radiographs

    b. polysomnography

    c. complete blood count

    d. blood gas analysis

    e. brain CAT scan

57. Obstructive sleep apnea is confirmed. What treatment is most likely to be effective in this patient?

    a. continuous positive airway pressure

    b. oxygen therapy

    c. prophylactic antibiotic therapy

    d. removal of the tonsils and adenoids

    e. stimulants

A woman who has received no prenatal care presents in active labor and shortly delivers a small-for-gestational-age infant. She admits to frequent cocaine use and unprotected sexual intercourse before and during her pregnancy. On physical exam, the newborn is noted to have a large liver and spleen, marked lymphadenopathy, and nasal discharge that your attending physician labels "the snuffles."

58. Which test on the infant is most likely to reveal the diagnosis?

    a. blood culture

    b. complete blood count

    c. hepatitis B antigen

    d. urine for cytomegalovirus

    e. FTA-ABS

59. Following an appropriate workup, what is the therapy of choice?

    a. ampicillin

    b. penicillin

    c. ceftriaxone

    d. amphotericin

    e. No therapy is known to be beneficial.

A 6-month-old male presents to the pediatrician with a resting heart rate of 50. Physical examination reveals no rash, and there is no history of rash. On chest radiograph, there is no cardiomegaly. Electrocardiogram revealed d-looped ventricles. The family history reveals maternal systemic lupus erythematosis.

60. Which of the following diagnoses is the *most* likely cause for the bradycardia?

    a. Lyme disease

    b. congenital complete heart block

    c. sinus node dysfunction

    d. cardiomyopathy

    e. corrected transposition of the great arteries

Match the signs and symptoms with the corresponding disease:

61. Koplik's spots

62. generalized lymphadenopathy, especially of the posterior auricular, cervical, and suboccipital nodes

63. high fever followed by maculopapular rash that starts on the trunk and spreads to the periphery

64. marked erythema of cheeks, "slapped-cheek appearance"

65. ulcers on the tongue and oral mucosa; maculopapular vesicular rash on hands and feet

66. crops of papular, vesicular, pustular lesions starting on the trunk and spreading to the extremities

67. crops of vesicular lesions along a dermatomal distribution in an individual with previous varicella zoster infection

    a. measles

    b. erythema infectiosum (Fifth disease)

    c. roseola infantum

    d. herpes zoster (shingles)

    e. rubella

    f. hand-foot-mouth disease

    g. chickenpox

A 4-year-old who has recently been started on potassium-sparing diuretics develops muscle weakness and tetany. His STAT serum potassium level is 7.7, with no hemolysis noted.

68. Which of the following EKG changes is *not* consistent with hyperkalemia?

    a. T-wave elevation

    b. loss of P waves

    c. wide QRS complexes

    d. ST segment depression

    e. notched PR segment

69. What is the most appropriate initial treatment?

    a. intravenous glucose

    b. intravenous calcium gluconate

    c. intravenous 3% NaCl solution

    d. hemodialysis

An afebrile 5-year-old female presents with tachycardia at 220 beats per minute. On electrocardiogram, a regular narrow-complex tachycardia is seen. The rhythm converts with one dose of adenosine intravenously to normal sinus rhythm with pre-excitation (delta waves) noted throughout the precordial leads. There is no cardiomegaly on chest radiograph.

70. The narrow-complex tachycardia is *most* likely consistent with which of the following?

    a. Wolff-Parkinson-White syndrome

    b. idiopathic concealed bypass tract

    c. sinus tachycardia

    d. atrial flutter

    e. atrial fibrillation

Match the following diagnoses with the appropriate description.

71. Strabismus   a. misaligned eye

72. Amblyopia   b. "Dull sight"

→ from untreated strabismus

A 15-year-old female presents to your emergency room with a history of recent acetaminophen ingestion.

73. What is the most common significant morbidity associated with this ingestion?

    a. cardiac arrhythmias

    b. malignant hypertension

    c. seizures

    d. hepatotoxicity

    e. ineffective hemostasis

74. Which of the following is most predictive of a good outcome?

    a. a low blood acetaminophen level at 1 hour after ingestion

    b. a low blood acetaminophen level at 4 hours after ingestion

    c. a supportive, intact family

    d. presentation within 2 hours of ingestion

    e. the absence of other substances on the urine drug screen

75. What is the most appropriate sequence of treatment if the ingestion has occurred less than 2 hours before presentation?

    a. assessment of airway, breathing, and circulation; gastric emptying; activated charcoal; N-acetylcysteine if indicated

    b. emesis induction and gastric emptying only

    c. immediate naloxone; airway stabilization; observation for 24 hours

    d. electrocardiogram and intravenous atropine if indicated

    e. No treatment is needed.

76. Which of the following statements concerning neural tube defects is true?

    a. A low maternal serum alpha-fetoprotein level is associated with an increased risk of a neural tube defect in the fetus.

    b. There is no increased risk of a neural tube defect in a second child when the first child is born with an encephalocele.

    c. Maternal folic acid supplementation decreases the incidence of neural tube defects.

    d. Children with spina bifida are invariably paralyzed in their lower extremities.

You are called to the neonatal intensive care unit to evaluate a small newborn who has not passed meconium in the first 72 hours of life. There is no evidence of heart or lung disease, and the infant is feeding appropriately. The surgeon called to consult notes that the anus appears patent. You suspect meconium ileus.

77. What genetic disorder is most consistent with this child's presentation?

    a. cystic fibrosis

    b. phenylketonuria

    c. Tay-Sachs disease

    d. galactosemia

    e. Wilson's disease

78. Which of the following medical conditions is a known complication of this child's most likely illness?

    a. failure to thrive

    b. chronic sinusitis

    c. recurrent pneumonia

    d. pneumothorax

    e. all of the above

Match the enzyme deficiency with the disease:

79. phenylalanine hydroxylase   a. homocystinuria

80. cystathionine synthetase   b. PKU
    deficiency

81. galactose-1-phosphate   c. galactosemia
    uridyl transferase

82. ornithine transcarbamylase   d. OTCD
    deficiency

A 12-month-old male infant presents with a hemoglobin of 7.5 and a hematocrit of 22%. The MCV is 65 and the adjusted reticulocyte count is 1.0.

83. All of the following statements about anemia are true, except:

    a. Anemia may result from increased destruction of red blood cells.

    b. Anemia may result from decreased production of red blood cells.

    c. Anemia may result from blood loss.

    d. Anemia is not a disease but rather a symptom of another disorder.

    e. The adjusted reticulocyte count is utilized to determine whether an anemia is microcytic, macrocytic, or normocytic.

84. What is the *most* likely cause of anemia in the child?

    a. iron deficiency anemia

    b. anemia of chronic disease

    c. transient erythrocytopenia of childhood

    d. thalassemia syndromes

    e. parvovirus B-19 aplastic crisis

A 2-month-old female infant presents for a well child care visit and leukocoria is noted.

85. All of the following diagnoses may result in leukocoria, *except?*

    a. retinal hemorrhages

    b. congenital cataract

    c. retinopathy of prematurity

    d. retinoblastoma

    e. congenital glaucoma

86. Which of the following statements regarding childhood nutrition is false?

    a. The majority of cases of failure to thrive in developed countries are nonorganic in origin.

    b. Children with exclusively vegetarian diets are at risk for vitamin B$_{12}$ and trace mineral deficiencies.

    c. Newborns should regain their birth weight by 3 weeks of age.

    d. Low-iron formulas provide sufficient iron for most infants' needs.

    e. Rather than losing weight, overweight children should be encouraged not to gain weight until they reach an appropriate height for their weight.

An 18-month-old female child presents with blood-streaked stool. The stool is grossly hemocult positive.

87. Which of the following diagnoses is *most* likely?

    a. anal fissure

    b. peptic ulcer disease

    c. Mallory-Weiss tear

    d. inflammatory bowel disease

    e. necrotizing enterocolitis

A 5-year-old boy presents to your office with a chief complaint of swollen face. On exam, you notice that heart, lung, and abdominal findings are normal. However, his hands and feet are quite edematous. You check a urine dipstick, which is markedly positive for protein but demonstrates no blood.

88. What is the most likely etiology of this child's edema?

    a. urinary tract infection

    b. renal mass

    c. undiagnosed heart disease

    d. minimal change nephropathy

    e. focal segmental glomerulosclerosis

89. What is the most effective therapy?

    a. salt restriction and corticosteroids

    b. chemotherapy

    c. antibiotics

    d. diuretics

    e. No treatment is necessary.

90. If a biopsy is done, what is the most likely finding?

    a. normal heart tissue

    b. bladder trabeculations

    c. glomerular basement membrane thickening

    d. inflammatory cell infiltration

    e. no abnormality expected on biopsy

Match the following developmental milestones and the age at which each occurs:

91. babbles

92. walks alone

93. walks up and down steps without help

94. uses three-word sentences

95. knows colors

    a. 12 months

    b. 6 months

    c. 36 months

    d. 24 months

    e. 48 months

A 5-year-old male presents pulseless, with ventricular tachycardia at 280 beats per minute on electrocardiogram. The child is intubated, ventilated, and successfully defibrillated. After defibrillation, an electrocardiogram revealed a corrected QT interval of 500 msec.

96. Which of the following therapies is the *most* appropriate chronic therapy for long QT syndrome?

    a. nadolol

    b. digoxin

    c. verapamil

    d. lidocaine

    e. lasix

A 3-year-old male presents with an elbow hemarthrosis after falling on his elbow. There is no history of spontaneous bleeding. There is no history of epistaxis, gingival bleeding, or cutaneous bruising. The child's maternal grandfather had frequent spontaneous bleeding and hemarthroses after trauma on multiple occasions. Laboratory data revealed a prolonged PTT, normal PT, and a platelet count of 150,000. The factor VIII coagulant activity (VIIIC) is low and the factor IX level is normal.

97. What is the *most* likely diagnosis?

    a. idiopathic thrombocytopenic purpura

    b. Von Willebrand's disease

    c. vitamin K deficiency

    d. hemophilia A

    e. liver disease

98. What is the *most* appropriate therapy?

    a. factor VIII concentrate

    b. observation

    c. surgical decompression

    d. aminocaproic acid

    e. factor IX concentrate

A 3-year-old male presents to the pediatrician with fever, pallor, anorexia, joint pain, petechiae, and hepatosplenomegaly.

99. Which of the following is the *most* likely diagnosis?

    a. acute lymphoblastic leukemia

    b. acute myelogenous leukemia

    c. juvenile chronic myelogenous leukemia

    d. aplastic anemia

100. Which of the following is *not* standard therapy for newly diagnosed leukemia?

    a. In general, chemotherapy involves remission induction, consolidation, and maintenance therapy.

    b. Packed red cells should be transfused for a hematotcrit less than 20.

    c. If the child is febrile and neutropenic, appropriate cultures should be obtained and broad spectrum antibiotics should be started because the risk of bacteremia and disseminated infection is high.

    d. Platelets should be given for a platelet count less than 20,000.

    e. Regardless of white blood cell count, exchange transfusion should be performed to decrease the load of leukemic cells.

101. All of the following statements concerning brain tumors are true, *except*:

    a. Central nervous system tumors are the most common solid tumors in children.

    b. Central nervous system tumors are second to leukemia in overall incidence of malignant disease.

    c. In contrast to those in adults, brain tumors in children are predominantly supratentorial.

    d. The most common presenting symptoms of brain tumors are due to increased intracranial pressure and focal neurologic deficit.

    e. Personality changes suggest a cortical brain tumor, whereas ataxia suggests a cerebellar or brainstem lesion.

102. Which of the following statements about neuroblastoma is *true*?

    a. Neuroblastoma is a benign tumor of the neural crest cells that form the adrenal cortex and the paraspinal parasympathetic ganglion.

    b. The majority of neuroblastoma tumors occur in the thoracic cavity.

    c. Neuroblastoma is the most common malignant tumor in infancy.

    d. In neuroblastoma of the abdomen, displacement of the kidney and distortion of the calyceal system often occurs.

    e. Most patients are treated with surgery alone, since distant metastases are rare.

103. A 6-week-old breast-fed infant presents to your office one morning appearing quite well. The mother states that, for the last week, the infant has had numerous periods of inconsolable crying lasting several hours each. Nothing seems to help. You find that most of the spells occur in the late afternoon and evening; between the episodes, the baby looks and feeds quite well. What is the most likely diagnosis?

    a. otitis media

    b. intussusception

    c. milk protein intolerance

    d. colic

    e. malabsorption

A 1500g 29-week-old Asian male neonate was born prematurely to a 28-year-old G2P1001, serology-negative female by normal spontaneous vaginal delivery. APGAR scores were 5 and 7 at 1 and 5 minutes, respectively. The neonate is in significant respiratory distress, with poor air movement. The neonate is intubated, given surfactant, and taken to the newborn intensive care unit (NICU) for further management.

104. All of the following statements concerning prematurity are true, *except*:

    a. Low-birth-weight infants make up 7% of all births but account for two-thirds of all neonatal deaths.

    b. Very-low-birth-weight infants represent 1% of all births but account for 50% of all neonatal deaths.

    c. Low birth weight is caused by premature birth or intrauterine growth retardation.

    d. Maternal age is not associated with low birth weight.

    e. Multiple gestation may cause preterm birth.

A blood culture is sent soon after arrival in the NICU. Ampicillin and gentamicin are started empirically until the blood culture result is known. Over the next 12 hours, the child is noted to have poor perfusion, hypotension, decreased urine output, coagulation tests consistent with disseminated intravascular coagulation, and bilateral pulmonary infiltrates. The group B streptococcus status of the neonate's mother is unknown.

105. Which of the following bacteria is *not* likely to be responsible for the child's sepsis?

    a. group B streptococcus

    b. *Listeria monocytogenes*

    c. *Escherichia coli*

    d. *Klebsiella pneumoniae*

    e. *Staphylococcus aureus*

The child is stabilized with fluid, dopamine, and blood products. The child receives total parenteral nutrition. The mother's blood type is A–, and the child's blood type is A+. The mother's previous child also had an A+ blood type. Indirect hyperbilirubinemia is noted.

106. All of the following factors in the neonate described increase the risk of indirect hyperbilirubinemia, *except*:

    a. Asian neonate

    b. disseminated intravascular coagulation

    c. Rh incompatibility

    d. sepsis

    e. total parenteral nutrition

When the neonate is two weeks of age, nasogastric feeds are started. Forty-eight hours after starting feeds, the neonate develops a distended abdomen, bloody stool, pneumatosis intestinalis, and free air on abdominal radiograph. The child becomes persistently hypotensive despite maximal medical therapy. Exploratory laparotomy reveals necrotic gut from the duodenum to the descending colon. The child's abdomen is closed, and the child is brought back to the NICU. The child expires. Necrotizing enterocolitis is noted as the primary cause of death. Autopsy reveals a large patent ductus arteriosus.

107. All of the following are risk factors for necrotizing enterocolitis, *except*:

    a. premature infants with birth weight less than 2000g

    b. hypotension

    c. total parenteral nutrition

    d. patent ductus arteriosus

    e. birth asphyxia

108. Which of the following is the proper initiation sequence of sexual development in the male?

    a. testicular enlargement, penile enlargement, height growth spurt, and pubic hair

    b. pubic hair, testicular enlargement, penile enlargement, height growth spurt

    c. testicular enlargement, penile enlargement, pubic hair, height growth spurt

    d. penile enlargement, height growth spurt, testicular enlargement, pubic hair

Match the following diseases and syndromes with their endocrinologic defect:

109. Cushing's syndrome   a. hypoaldosteronism and hypercortisolism

110. Addison's disease   b. hypercortisolism

111. Graves' disease   c. hypothyroidism

112. Hashimoto thyroiditis   d. hyperthyroidism

113. congenital adrenal hyperplasia   e. hypocortisolism

114. Modes of inheritance in single gene defects include all of the following, *except*:

 a. autosomal dominant

 b. autosomal recessive

 c. X-linked disorders

 d. incomplete penetrance

115. All of the following statements are true, *except*:

 a. Genes defective in autosomal dominant disorders typically code for structural proteins, whereas those in autosomal recessive disorders code for enzymes.

 b. Ornithine transcarbamylase deficiency is not an autosomal recessive disorder.

 c. Fragile X syndrome or inborn error of metabolism should be considered in a child with progressive developmental delay and/or mental retardation without a known etiology.

 d. Following up on the neonatal screen is not important because the majority of inborn errors of metabolism present right after birth.

A 6-year-old male who received Bactrim for otitis media presents to the emergency department with high fever; target lesions on the palms and soles, trunk, and the extensor surfaces of the extremities; and inflammatory bullae on his mucosal membranes.

116. What type of hypersensitivity rash does this child have?

 a. eczema

 b. urticaria

 c. erythema multiforme

 d. Stevens-Johnson syndrome

 e. toxic epidermal necrolysis

A newborn male child has a flat facial profile, upslanted palpebral fissures, epicanthal folds, a small mouth with a protruding tongue, small genitalia, and simian creases on his hands.

117. What chomosomal disorder does this child have?

 a. trisomy 21

 b. trisomy 18

 c. trisomy 13

 d. Klinefelter's syndrome

 e. Turner's syndrome

118. All of the following are structural and functional abnormalities associated with Trisomy 21, *except*:

 a. duodenal atresia

 b. endocardial cushion defect

 c. atlantoaxial instability

 d. hypothyroidism

 e. tracheoesophageal fistula with esophageal atresia

A 4-year-old male child presents with abrupt onset petechiae and ecchymoses. Other than the skin findings, the child appears well and is hemodynamically stable. No splenomegaly is noted. A complete blood count reveals a normal white blood cell count, a normal hematocrit, and a platelet count of 30,000. Large platelets are seen on the peripheral smear. No premature white cell forms are seen on peripheral smear. The parent reports that the child had a viral illness 2 weeks before presentation.

119. Which of the following is the *most* likely diagnosis?

 a. isoimmune thrombocytopenia

 b. leukemia

 c. sepsis

 d. immune thrombocytopenic purpura

 e. hypersplenism

A 4-year-old child presents to the emergency room with stupor and posturing. His mother reports that he has been acting disoriented for the past 24 hours. She was not initially concerned because the child had similar episodes of confusion with the high fevers he had a week ago with his chickenpox, which she treated successfully with aspirin. You suspect possible Reye syndrome.

120. Which of the following lab results is most supportive of your diagnosis?

   a. hyperammonemia
   b. hypernatremia
   c. hypercalcemia
   d. hyperkalemia
   e. hyperglycemia

121. The diagnosis is confirmed. What is the most appropriate course of action?

   a. involvement of neurosurgery and admission to the intensive care unit
   b. twice-daily dialysis
   c. phenobarbital coma
   d. intravenous vancomycin
   e. intravenous calcium gluconate

122. Which of the following statements about polyhydramnios is *true*.

   a. Potter's syndrome is associated with polyhydramnios.
   b. Acute polyhydramnios is more common than chronic polyhydramnios.
   c. Lesions that impair fetal swallowing are associated with polyhydramnios.
   d. Polyhydramnios may result in postmaturity.
   e. Polyhydramnios is associated with fetal lung hypoplasia.

An 8-year-old male presents with a 1-day history of emesis and periumbilical pain that has moved to the right lower quadrant. There is no history of diarrhea. Abdominal examination reveals guarding and rebound tenderness. The white blood cell count is elevated, at 20,000 with a left shift.

123. What is the *most* likely diagnosis?

   a. appendicitis

   b. pancreatitis
   c. viral gastroenteritis
   d. urinary tract infection
   e. diabetes mellitus

A 3-year-old male presents with violent episodes of intermittent colicky pain, emesis, and blood per rectum. A tubular mass is palpated in the right lower quadrant. The abdominal radiograph reveals a dearth of air in the right lower quadrant and air fluid levels consistent with ileus.

124. Which of the following procedures will *best* assist in diagnosis *and* treatment?

   a. esophagogastroduodenoscopy
   b. rectal biopsy
   c. air contrast or barium enema
   d. stool culture
   e. colonoscopy

A 4-week-old male infant born at full term presents with emesis, dehydration, and poor weight gain. The pediatrician evaluating the child palpates an olive in the child's epigastrium. She believes the neonate may have pyloric stenosis.

125. Which of the following clinical presentations is *most* consistent with pyloric stenosis?

   a. projectile non-bilious emesis
   b. bilious emesis
   c. bloody diarrhea
   d. violent episodes of intermittent colicky pain and emesis
   e. right lower quadrant abdominal pain

126. Which of the following statements is *true*?

   a. Ulcerative colitis typically is characterized by rectal sparing.
   b. Ulcerative colitis typically is characterized by skip lesions.
   c. Crohn's disease typically is characterized by transmural disease.
   d. Crohn's disease typically is characterized by crypt abscesses.
   e. Having Crohn's disease dramatically increases the risk of carcinoma of the colon.

Answers

1. a (chapter 17)

The clinical description is most consistent with Ewing's sarcoma. Unlike osteosarcoma, Ewing's sarcoma tends to have systemic symptoms, such as fever, weight loss, and fatigue. Ewing's sarcoma tumor usually involves the diaphyseal portion of the long bones. The most common sites for Ewing's sarcoma are the midproximal femur and the bones of the pelvis. The most common sites of osteosarcoma tumor are the distal femur, proximal tibia, and proximal humerus. Benign bone tumors and eosinophilic granuloma are generally not painful. Chronic osteomyelitis may present with fever, pain, and localized swelling, but weight loss is unlikely.

2. e (chapter 19)

Slipped capital femoral epiphysis (SCFE) is the gradual or acute separation of the proximal femoral growth plate. The cause is unknown, but trauma is not thought to play a factor in development of the condition. It typically occurs in obese adolescent males during the growth spurt. Legg-Calve-Perthes disease also presents with a limp, but these patients are typically younger (age 4–8 years). Osteomyelitis and septic arthritis are unlikely in the nonfebrile patient with this duration of symptoms. Osgood-Schlatter disease presents with pain and swelling over the tibial tuberosity and does not involve the hip.

3. b (chapter 19)

Radiographs of the patient's hips in the frog-leg lateral position are the study of choice to rule out epiphyseal displacement. Anterior-posterior hip films often are false negative. "Setting sun" knee films are indicated to rule out abnormalities of the patella. Patients with suspected septic arthritis require joint aspiration. Magnetic nuclear resonance scanning is reserved mostly for delineating subtle soft-tissue lesions.

4. d (chapter 19)

The primary goal of treatment is prevention of further misalignment with pin fixation. Chronic cases may require osteotomy. Casting is not effective. Arthroscopic surgery is more commonly used to diagnose and repair injuries to the soft-tissue structures in and around injured joints. Chemotherapy is inappropriate. "Watchful waiting" usually results in progressive deformity.

5. a (chapter 3)

A harsh holosystolic murmur heard best at the left lower sternal border is most consistent with a ventricular septal defect. The child does not have symptoms of congestive heart failure (no cardiomegaly on chest radiograph, tachypnea or diaphoresis with feeds, or hepatomegaly); therefore, the defect is likely restrictive. A systolic ejection murmur at the left upper sternal border is consistent with either an atrial septal defect or pulmonic stenosis. A systolic ejection murmur at the right upper sternal border is consistent with aortic stenosis. A continuous "machinery-type" murmur heard best at the left upper sternal border radiating to the left axilla is consistent with a left patent ductus arteriosus.

---

6. c (chapter 3)

The loud, harsh murmur requires evaluation and follow-up by a pediatric cardiologist. A restrictive ventricular septal defect generally does not require surgical intervention. In this case there is no evidence of congestive heart failure and anticongestive medical therapy (digoxin and lasix) is not required. Due to the turbulent nature of the congenital heart defect, subacute bacterial endocarditis is required.

---

7. e (chapter 10)

Sickle cell disease is a normocytic hemolytic anemia caused by an intracorpuscular hemoglobinopathy that is inherited in an autosomal recessive manner. Although almost every body system is affected by the disease, pancreatitis is not associated with sickle cell disease. The clinical manifestations of sickle cell disease result from anemia, infection, and vaso-occlusion. At baseline, patients with sickle cell disease have a depressed but stable hemoglobin. Hyperhemolytic crisis occurs when a sickle cell patient with G6PD deficiency is exposed to an oxidative stress, resulting in an acute hemolysis superimposed on a chronic hemolytic anemia. Over time, most sickle cell patients have autoinfarction of the spleen. This makes the child susceptible to overwhelming sepsis from encapsulated bacterial organisms (*Streptococcus pneumoniae* and *Haemophilus influenzae* type B). Acute chest syndrome is a vaso-occlusive crisis within the lung parenchyma and is associated with infection and/or infarction. There is a higher incidence of bilirubin stones and cholecystitis in sickle cell patients because of the high red cell turnover from the hemolytic anemia.

---

8. a (chapter 14)

The patient discussed in this question has signs and symptoms of significant illness and probably will require

parenteral antibiotics, ideally in a hospital setting, without delay. Oral antibiotic therapy would be ineffective and inadvisable. Since the patient is not taking fluids well, aggressive intravenous fluid therapy (rather than fluid restriction) may be necessary. A surgical lesion is very unlikely, given the presentation, although if the patient has a urinary tract infection secondary to an anatomic lesion, delayed surgery may not be unreasonable.

---

9. b (chapter 14)

A voiding cystourethrogram will demonstrate vesicoureteral reflux if any is present. Renal ultrasound and intravenous pyelography are beneficial for ruling out a renal mass, whereas the nuclear medicine scan may show areas of renal scarring demonstrating previous episodes of pyelonephritis. CAT scans are not generally part of the workup for uncomplicated urinary tract infections in this age group.

---

10. a (chapter 14)

Ureteral reimplantation surgery is the most appropriate option, given the severe nature of the reflux; milder grades of reflux are best treated with prophylactic antibiotic therapy and repeat studies at a later date. Renal resection is not indicated in the case of a healthy kidney. Transurethral ablation is indicated for cases of posterior urethral valves. Pyeloplasty should be used when ureteropelvic junction obstruction is present.

---

11. b (chapter 20)

Nebulized bronchodilators, most appropriately albuterol, are the intervention of choice in this situation. Beta-2 agonists, such as albuterol, reduce smooth muscle constriction and can be invaluable for asthmatics in acute distress. This asthmatic is in severe distress; he is moving so little air that no breath sounds can be appreciated. Oral bronchodilators would take too long to take effect in this situation. Cromolyn is an excellent form of prevention but is not helpful during an acute attack. Intravenous steroids may be appropriate in this case but would not be the initial therapy as they take 4–6 hours to be effective. Theophylline has fallen out of favor for use in emergent situations but may be employed later if the disease does not respond to first-line therapies.

12.   a (chapter 20)

Corticosteroids, such as prednisone and methyprednisolone, require 4–6 hours to take effect. However, they are very important in the treatment of an acute attack because they address the underlying inflammation and prevent the "late-phase" response. Theophylline, albuterol, and terbutaline are bronchodilators that have virtually no anti-inflammatory properties. Cromolyn is a mast cell stabilizer that is not effective in acute attacks.

13.   a (chapter 1)

The primary survey is the initial evaluation of the critically ill or injured child when life-threatening problems are identified and prioritized. The proper order of the primary survey or initial assessment is *airway*, *breathing*, *circulation*, *disability*, and *exposure*. After the primary survey is complete, resuscitation should occur if the condition is life-threatening. If the injury or illness is not immediately life-threatening the secondary survey should be performed.

14.   b (chapter 1)

The goals of airway management are to recognize and relieve obstruction, prevent aspiration of gastric contents, and promote adequate gas exchange. The airway should be cleared with a suction catheter, and the airway should be opened with either the jaw-thrust or chin-lift maneuver. The head is placed in the midline "sniffing position" to optimize airway positioning. When establishing an airway, avoid the blind finger sweep of the oropharynx, because this may force a foreign body down the oropharynx. Hyperextension of the neck may result in obstruction of the airway in the pediatric patient. The proper position to optimize the airway is the midline "sniffing position." After the airway has been assessed and established, starting 100% oxygen via facemask will likely improve oxygenation more effectively than 2 liters of O_2 via nasal cannula.

15.   e (chapter 1)

In children, heart rate is the most sensitive measure of intravascular volume status and capillary refill is the most sensitive measure of adequate circulation. Blood pressure fluctuations are an insensitive indicator, as hypotension is a late finding in hypovolemia. Chest compressions in the infant should be performed with two fingers on the sternum, one fingerbreadth below the intermammary line, to a depth of 0.5–1.0 inch at a rate of 100 compressions/min.

16.   d (chapter 1)

Atropine is given for bradycardia and atrioventricular block. Atropine increases heart rate and conduction through the atrioventricular node by decreasing vagal tone.

17.   c (chapter 1)

Bicarbonate is utilized when there is severe refractory metabolic acidosis and/or hyperkalemia. Bicarbonate increases the blood pH, thereby correcting acidosis. By increasing the blood pH, potassium is moved intracellularly and protons are moved extracellularly, thereby helping to correct hyperkalemia.

18.   b (chapter 1)

Epinephrine is used for asystole, bradycardia, and/or ventricular fibrillation. Low-dose epinephrine increases systemic vascular resistance, chronotropy, and inotropy, thereby increasing cardiac output and systolic and diastolic blood pressure. By increasing systolic blood pressure cerebral blood flow is increased, and by increasing diastolic blood pressure coronary perfusion is increased. Low-dose epinephrine may change fine ventricular fibrillation to coarse ventricular fibrillation and promote successful defibrillation.

19.   a (chapter 1)

Lidocaine is indicated when there is significant ectopy. Lidocaine helps to make refractory ventricular tachyarrhythmias and ventricular fibrillation more susceptible to cardioversion and decreases the likelihood of recurrence of ventricular ectopy.

20. b (chapter 2)

Barring unusual medical conditions, infants should be placed on their backs to sleep rather than on their stomachs; this significantly decreases the risk of SIDS. In most states, infants must be *both* 20 pounds and 1 year of age to ride in forward-facing car seats. In certain ingestions, particularly those involving strong bases or hydrocarbons, syrup of ipecac is contraindicated. Lead-containing paint should be removed, rather than painted over, because of the continued risk of ingestion of chipped paint. While entertaining and instructive, driver education courses do not appear to decrease the risk of vehicle accidents involving adolescents.

21. d (chapter 11)

There is no definitive lab test for Kawasaki disease, so it remains a clinical diagnosis. The patient must have at least five of the following six findings on physical exam:

1. fever lasting ≥5 days
2. bilateral conjunctivities
3. specific changes of the lips and/or oral cavity
4. changes of the peripheral extremities (including possible indurative edema of the hands and feet)
5. acute cervical lymph node swelling
6. polymorphous rash, primarily seen on the trunk

The rash described in the answer section is more consistent with Henoch-Schönlein purpura.

22. e (chapter 11)

Kawasaki disease is one of the few diseases of childhood in which aspirin therapy is appropriate. IVIG helps decrease the incidence of coronary artery aneurysms. Corticosteroids are contraindicated in Kawasaki disease, because they actually increase the incidence of aneurysms. Electrolyte abnormalities are not typical of Kawasaki disease, so dialysis is not an option. Although the etiology of Kawasaki disease is not known, antibiotics have not been found to alter the course or outcome of the illness.

23. a (chapter 11)

The primary serious complications of Kawasaki disease are cardiac, including coronary vasculitis and aneurysm formation. Prognosis is tied to cardiac involvement; cardiac instability can produce arrhythmias, infarction, or congestive heart failure within days of presentation. Aneurysms and coronary artery disease persist and may result in death months to years later. Patients with Kawasaki disease may manifest sterile pyuria; however, they are not at risk for kidney failure. Arthritis, gastrointestinal bleeding, and hypertension are also neither early nor late complications of Kawasaki disease.

24. b (chapter 15)

The spells described are most consistent with petit mal seizures. An electroencephalogram would demonstrate the characteristic generalized, symmetric 3-per-second spike and wave pattern. Cerebrospinal fluid analysis, CAT scan, muscle biopsy, and magnetic resonance imaging would all show a normal result in a patient with petit mal seizures as his or her only diagnosis.

25. d (chapter 15)

A characteristic generalized, symmetric 3-per-second spike and wave pattern would be expected in a patient with petit mal seizures. Increased levels of protein and myelin can be seen in multiple sclerosis. A mass lesion is not expected in cases of petit mal seizures. Hypsarrythmia is the pattern seen on electroencephalogram in patients with infantile spasms. Generalized brain edema would not be present with seizures alone; some level of generalized neurologic depression would also be present.

26. a (chapter 15)

Ethosuximide is the most appropriate initial therapy for patients with petit mal seizures. Phenytoin and phenobarbital are indicated for tonic-clonic and partial seizures. Valproic acid is useful in the management of tonic-clonic, absence, and partial seizures. Carbamazepine is most effective when used to prevent partial seizures.

27. c (chapter 3)

Acrocyanosis is blueness of the extremities due to peripheral vasoconstriction noted in the first 24–48 hours of life. Neonates with acrocyanosis have pink mucosal membranes.

28. a (chapter 3)

The most likely congenital heart defect is d-transposition of the great arteries with intact ventricular septum. Typically there is increased pulmonary vascularity on chest radiograph, a single S2, and no heart murmur. To differentiate among cyanotic congenital heart defects that present with a Pao_2 less than 50 mm Hg on the hyperoxia test, the clinician should first examine the chest radiograph. If massive cardiomegaly is noted, Ebstein's anomaly is the most likely diagnosis. If massive cardiomegaly is ruled out, the pulmonary vascularity should be evaluated. Increased pulmonary blood flow suggests the presence of d-transposition of the great arteries with intact ventricular septum, whereas pulmonary edema may indicate the presence of total anomalous pulmonary venous return with obstruction. The remaining possible diagnoses (tetralogy of Fallot, tetralogy of Fallot with pulmonary atresia, pulmonary atresia with intact ventricular septum, critical pulmonary stenosis, tricuspid atresia with normally related great arteries) all have decreased pulmonary vascularity and normal or slightly enlarged cardiac silhouette on chest radiograph. These defects are differentiated by their axis of ventricular depolarization and the presence or absence of a heart murmur. Tricuspid atresia with normally related great arteries has a superior axis, lying in the 270- to 0-degree quadrant. Critical pulmonic stenosis and pulmonary atresia with intact ventricular septum both have axes in the 0- to 90-degree quadrant. They are differentiated by the presence of the loud pulmonary ejection murmur heard in critical pulmonic stenosis. Similarly, tetralogy of Fallot and tetralogy of Fallot with pulmonic atresia both have axes in the 90- to 180-degree quadrant, and they are distinguished from each other by the pulmonic stenosis murmur noted in tetralogy of Fallot.

29. b (chapter 13)

Toxoplasmosis is caused by *Toxoplasma gondii*, an intracellular protozoan parasite found in mammals and birds. Members of the cat family are the definitive host. Feline stool is the vector by which fecal oral transmission occurs. Infection in humans may also be acquired through ingestion of undercooked infected meat. Infected infants suffer from intrauterine meningoencephalitis and present with microcephaly, hydrocephalus, microphthalmia, choreoretinitis, intracerebral calcifications, and seizures.

30. a (chapter 13)

Congenital syphilis results from *Treponema pallidum*. Syphilis in the untreated pregnant woman may be transmitted to the fetus at any time, but fetal transfer is most common during the first year of maternal infection. Neonates symptomatic at birth exhibit nonimmune hydrops, thrombocytopenia, leukopenia, pneumonitis, hepatitis, and osteochondritis. Infants diagnosed in the first year of life have intermittent fever, osteochondritis, persistent rhinitis (snuffles), hepatosplenomegaly, lymphadenopathy, jaundice, and failure to thrive.

31. d (chapter 13)

Congenital rubella is caused by rubella virus. Thanks to rubella vaccine, congenital rubella has become extremely rare. Clinical manifestations of congenital rubella include peripheral pulmonic stenosis, atrial septal defect, ventricular septal defect, ophthalmologic defects (cataracts, microphthalmia, glaucoma, chorioretinitis), hepatosplenomegaly, jaundice, "blueberry muffin spots," and failure to thrive.

32. c (chapter 13)

Congenital cytomegalovirus (CMV) infection is the most common congenital infection in the newborn in developed countries. Approximately 50% of fetuses become infected during primary maternal CMV infection, and of those infected only 5% have residual neurologic deficits. Most cases are clinically inapparent. Late sequelae such as nerve deafness and learning disabilities may develop in 10% of clinically inapparent infections. The syndrome of congenital CMV (cytomegalic inclusion disease) is uncommon, occuring in 5% of infants with CMV infection. Clinical manifestations include intrauterine growth retardation, intracerebral calcifications (usually periventricular), chorioretinitis, microcephaly, jaundice, hepatosplenomegaly, and purpura.

33. f (chapter 13)

Most neonatal HSV infection is caused by herpes simplex virus 2. Neonatal infection generally occurs during the infant's transit through the vaginal canal. Asymptomatic infection is rare. HSV virus manifests itself in three distinct constellations of symptoms. Infants may have localized infection of skin, eye, mouth (SEM disease); disseminated infection; or localized central nervous system infection.

34. e (chapter 13)

Infants infected with HIV are, in the vast majority of cases, infected via vertical transmission. Infected infants are generally asymptomatic at birth. During the first few months, infants develop thrush, lymphadenopathy, and hepatosplenomegaly. During the first year of life, common symptoms include recurrent refractory infection, severe intractable diarrhea, and failure to thrive.

35. c (chapter 19)

Metatarsus adductus (in-toeing of the forefoot without hindfoot abnormalities) is a common, relatively benign condition due to intrauterine positioning. As opposed to talipes equinovarus, range of motion at the ankle is unrestricted. Developmental hip dysplasia is most common in firstborn girls and may not be evident to the casual observer; Ortalani and Barlow maneuvers demonstrate this lesion. Genu varum is a knee deformity and does not involve the ankle or foot.

36. a (chapter 19)

Eighty-five percent of cases of metatarsus adductus correct spontaneously once the infant begins ambulating. More severe or persistent cases may need serial casting or surgical repair. Regardless, the prognosis for normal gait is excellent.

37. a (chapter 11)

A newborn infant with suspected congenital heart disease and no thymic shadow on chest radiograph should be suspected of having DiGeorge syndrome. DiGeorge syndrome is a congenital T-cell deficiency resulting in increased susceptibility to opportunistic infections such as fungi and *Pneumocystis carinii*. It typically presents early in infancy with congenital heart disease, hypocalcemic tetany, and the absence of a thymic shadow on chest radiograph. None of the other electrolyte abnormalities that are listed are associated with DiGeorge syndrome.

38. d (chapter 11)

As previously noted, a patient with DiGeorge syndrome has a primary T-cell immunodeficiency. These children are at increased risk for frequent, recurrent infections with opportunistic or low-grade organisms such as Candida, mycobacteria, and protozoa, as well as viruses. The immunodeficiency of DiGeorge syndrome has been successfully treated with both thymic and bone marrow transplantation. Patients with primary humoral or complement immunodeficiencies are more susceptible to encapsulated bacterial infections. Catalase (+) bacteria have the advantage in patients with phagocytic disorders. Increased risk of rickettsial disease is not specifically associated with any of the immune deficiencies and may cause severe disease in immunocompetent individuals as well.

39. e (chapter 6)

New onset insulin dependent diabetes mellitus presents with a history of polydipsia, polyphagia, polyuria, and weight loss. Diarrhea is not typically seen. A lack of insulin results in hyperglycemia, which causes an osmotic diuresis (polyuria). The loss of intravascular volume results in polydipsia, and is partly responsible for weight loss. The catabolic state that arises from insulin deficiency results in polyphagia and weight loss.

40. e (chapter 6)

The child with diabetic ketoacidosis (DKA) usually reports polyuria, polydipsia, fatigue, headache, nausea, emesis, and abdominal pain. On physical examination, the child may have a fruity breath odor due to ketosis, as well as tachycardia and hyperpnea (Kussmaul's respirations). The tachycardia is the result of dehydration and the hyperpnea is caused by metabolic acidosis. Intravascular volume depletion may be so marked that hypotension is detected. Cerebral edema may occur during DKA resuscitation in rare patients, due to fluid shifts. Cerebral edema may manifest itself as confusion, changing mental status, unequal pupils, decorticate or decerebrate posturing, and/or seizures. Early identification and aggressive management of increased intracranial pressure are pivotal to improve outcome. Paresthesias is not a typical presenting symptom in DKA.

---

41. c (chapter 6)

When diabetic ketoacidosis occurs, ketones are formed in the blood and cleared in the urine. Hyperglycemia, and not hypoglycemia, is typical. Primary metabolic acidosis with secondary respiratory alkalosis is noted (decreased venous blood pH and hypocarbia). Dehydration results in an elevated blood urea nitrogen.

---

42. e (chapter 6)

When DKA is present, the patient is total body potassium depleted from significant potassium loss in the osmotic diuresis. Metabolic acidosis results in the movement of potassium extracellularly and protons intracellularly. Patients with DKA may be hyperkalemic, normokalemic, or hypokalemic at presentation. The initial fluid bolus should be given without any potassium. As resuscitation occurs with insulin and fluid, the metabolic acidosis due to ketosis will slowly resolve and the serum potassium will fall. When the potassium falls below 3.0 mEq/L, potassium should be infused with the deficit and maintenance intravenous fluid.

---

43. e (chapter 6)

In diabetes insipidus, there is a loss of antidiuretic hormone secretion from the posterior pituitary gland and an inability to concentrate the urine. Pseudotumor cerebri is a benign increase in intracranial pressure that is not associated with diabetes insipidus. Head trauma, brain tumor, central nervous system infection, and craniopharyngioma may be associated with diabetes insipidus.

---

44. a (chapter 12)

Many patients with Lyme disease do not give a history of a tick bite, presumably because they are unaware of it. Cases of Lyme disease are clustered around the North-

east, Midwest, and West Coast and peak during the summer and early fall. The patient described is obviously quite ill and has meningeal symptoms; however, the characteristic rash is the giveaway. Erythema migrans consists of erythematous macules progressing to annular lesions with central clearing that develop both at the innoculation site and secondary areas. The rash may be fleeting or last for several weeks. All of the other pathogens listed can cause severe illness and meningitis. Rocky Mountain spotted fever produces a maculopapular rash that begins at the wrists and ankles and spreads proximally; the lesions progress to a petechiael stage. Ehrlichiosis and leptospirosis do not typically cause rashes. Meningococcemia may cause a petechiael rash that is quite dissimilar from erythema migrans.

---

45. b (chapter 12)

Patients with severe or persistent arthritis, cardiac involvement, or CNS disease warrant parenteral therapy with high-dose penicillin G or a third-generation cephalosporin such as cefotaxime. Children with uncomplicated disease may receive oral doxycycline if they are older than 8 years or oral amoxicillin if they are younger. Tetracycline is appropriate for patients with Rocky Mountain spotted fever. Oral penicillin and amoxicillin-clavulanic acid are not indicated for Lyme disease.

---

46. d (chapter 7)

The majority of children with congenital adrenal hyperplasia have 21-hydroxylase deficiency, and are salt-wasters. Those who present in shock (usually in the first several weeks of life) generally are deficient in sodium and chloride. Additionally, potassium is usually elevated. The patient is usually quite acidotic and may be hypoglycemic as well.

---

47. c (chapter 7)

Patients in diabetic ketoacidosis have markedly elevated glucose measurements, which result in fictitious hyponatremia. Potassium levels may be normal or slightly elevated, but in truth the body overall is potassium depleted. Hydrogen ions are driven intracellularly in exchange for potassium; however, ketones result in severe acidosis.

18. b (chapter 7)

Patients with pyloric stenosis vomit primarily hydrochloric acid, the primary fluid in the stomach. There are no small intestinal losses because the pylorus is too small to allow retrograde propulsion. Thus, the bicarbonate level tends to be high, with a decrease in the chloride measurement. Sodium and potassium measurements are usually not affected until late in the presentation.

49. a (chapter 7)

Diarrheal illness is one of the most common causes of dehydration in pediatric medicine. Patients with diarrheal dehydration usually experience normonatremic (or isotonic) dehydration with a slightly increased anion gap due to bicarbonate loss from the small bowels.

50. a (chapter 5)

Atopic dermatitis or eczema is characterized by paroxysms of severe pruritis with remissions and exacerbations. The itching is a constant feature that creates an "itch-scratch-itch" cycle. The rash is erythematous, edematous, and papular and weeps in the active phase. During infancy, the rash is predominantly found on the face, neck, scalp, trunk, and extensor surfaces of the extremities. Childhood eczema appears on the flexor surfaces predominantly. Over time, scaling and lichenification may occur on the extensor surfaces. Bacterial superinfection of the eczematous base is not uncommon. Psoriasis is a non-pruritic rash on the knees, elbows, scalp, and genital area that is also characterized by remissions and exacerbations. Psoriasis usually occurs at sites of physical, thermal, or mechanical trauma.

51. c (chapter 5)

The eosinophil count and serum IgE are often elevated in patients with eczema and tend to vary with the activity of the disease. In psoriasis, there is hyperproliferation of the epidermis that results from an accelerated turnover time and may be seen on skin biopsy. Epidermal hyperplasia is not seen on skin biopsy in patients with atopic dermatitis.

52. a (chapter 3)

Fever and new murmur may be consistent with rheumatic heart disease or endocarditis. The splinter hemorrhages and petechiae make endocarditis highly likely and rheumatic heart disease unlikely. Dilated cardiomyopathy may present with new murmur, but the murmur is generally due to atrioventricular valve regurgitation, which has a blowing quality and is heard best at the left lower sternal border or apex. If ventricular thrombus is associated with the dilated cardiomyopathy, splinter hemorrhages and petechiae may be noted. Kawasaki's disease patients present with high fever, but murmur and splinter hemorrhages are not commonly noted.

53. a (chapter 12)

Of the options listed, Shigella is the most likely, given the history of a seizure. Children with shigellosis can present with neurologic manifestations, including lethargy, seizures, and mental status changes possibly due to a neurotoxin elaborated by the organism. Cholera causes "rice-water" stools and leads quickly to hypovolemic shock but does not cause neurologic complications. Giardiasis, the most common parasitic disease in the United States, typically causes only mild disease. Yersinia can cause a "pseudo-appendicitis" picture. Salmonella can invade the bloodstream and cause extraintestinal disease, including meningitis, arthritis, and osteomyelitis; it is no more likely to cause seizures than any other bacteria.

54. a (chapter 12)

Regardless of the etiology, any child with suspected diarrhea and significant systemic symptoms (including seizures) should receive antibiotic therapy. Given that the patient appears essentially nontoxic, outpatient therapy with oral trimethoprim-sulfamethathoxazole is most appropriate. If the patient appeared quite ill and required hospitalization, intravenous cefotaxime would be the drug of choice. Mebendazole is reserved for the treatment of pinworms. Ciprofloxacin is not approved for use in young children secondary to concerns about cartilage development. Although antibiotic treatment prolongs the shedding of Salmonella, the benefit of empiric treatment outweighs the risk in a patient with systemic manifestations.

55. e (chapter 12)

Both *Shigella dysenteriae* and *E. coli* 0157H7 produce an enterotoxin ("Shiga" or Shiga-like toxin) associated with hemolytic uremic syndrome, a serious complication consisting of microangiopathic hemolytic anemia, nephropathy, and thrombocytopenia. Pseudo-appendicitis and erythema nodosum are associated with Yersinia infections. Failure to thrive can occur in small children with chronic giardiasis. Cholera is a separate cause of infectious diarrhea.

56. b (chapter 20)

This child has obstructive sleep apnea, most likely from enlarged tonsils and/or adenoids. This is easily diagnosed with a sleep study, which can also differentiate central from obstructive sleep apnea. Chest radiographs have a very low yield for significant pathology in sleep apnea. A complete blood count may show a slightly increased hematocrit, but this is hardly diagnostic. Blood gas analysis should be normal in the awake state. A brain CAT scan also has a very low yield for pathology in sleep apnea and would certainly be normal in obstructive sleep apnea.

57. d (chapter 20)

Removal of the obstructing tissue is the treatment of choice in obstructive sleep apnea. Continuous positive airway pressure is more appropriate in cases of central sleep apnea. Oxygen therapy will not help if the patient is not breathing well to begin with. Antibiotic therapy is not indicated because there is no infection to treat. Stimulants have not been proven to be effective.

58. e (chapter 12)

The newborn described in this scenario demonstrates signs and symptoms of congenital syphilis, characterized by hepatomegaly, splenomegaly, mucocutaneous lesions, jaundice, lymphadenopathy, and the characteristic "snuffles," a clear, copious nasal discharge. The mother's high-risk behaviors suggest that multiple sexually transmitted diseases may be present. Both RPR and VDRL tests are very likely to be positive, but the fluorescent treponemal antibody absorption (FTA-ABS) is a true treponemal test and is less likely to result in a false-positive result. A complete blood count may suggest infection but will not give the specific diagnosis. A blood culture will be negative in this case. Newborns infected with hepatitis B have a high likelihood of developing chronic disease but generally appear unaffected at birth. Most cases of congenital cytomegalovirus are also clinically inapparent; however, 5% of those infected present with some constellation of intrauterine growth retardation, purpura, jaundice, hepatosplenomegaly, microcephaly, intracerebral calcifications, and chorioretinitis.

59. b (chapter 12)

For infants with no evidence of central nervous system disease (e.g., a negative spinal tap), 10–14 days of intravenous penicillin G is appropriate. If the cerebrospinal fluid is RPR or FTA-ABS positive, the infant should receive aqueous crystalline penicillin G or aqueous procaine penicillin for 3 weeks. None of the other therapies is appropriate for newborns with suspected or known syphilis infection.

60. b (chapter 3)

Congenital complete heart block is most likely given the maternal history of systemic lupus erythematosis. Since there is no history of rash, Lyme disease causing complete heart block is unlikely. Tick exposure at this age is also unlikely. Cardiomyopathy is an unlikely cause of the complete heart block, given the lack of cardiomegaly on chest radiograph. Sinus node dysfunction usually occurs secondary to atrial suture lines or atrial dilation. This child has no history of surgery, and there is no evidence of atrial dilation on chest radiograph or electrocardiogram. The d-loop noted on electrocardiogram rules out corrected transposition of the great arteries (L-transposition of the great arteries).

61. a (chapter 5)

Measles is caused by a paramyxovirus and is characterized by malaise, high fever, cough, coryza, conjunctivitis, Koplik's spots, and an erythematous maculopapular rash. Koplik's spots are small, irregular red spots with central gray or bluish-white specks that appear on the buccal mucosa.

62. e (chapter 5)

Rubella is caused by rubella virus and is characterized by mild fever, erythematous maculopapular rash, with generalized lymphadenopathy, especially of the posterior auricular, cervical, and suboccipital nodes.

63. c (chapter 5)

Roseola infantum is caused by herpes virus 6 and is characterized by high fever followed by maculopapular rash that starts on the trunk and spreads to the periphery. The fever typically resolves as the rash appears.

64. b (chapter 5)

Erythema infectiosum is caused by parvovirus B-19 and is characterized by marked erythema of the cheeks "slapped cheek appearance," and an erythematous, pruritic, maculopapular rash starting on the arms and spreading to trunk and legs.

65. f (chapter 5)

Hand-foot-mouth disease is caused by coxsackie A virus and is characterized by ulcers on the tongue and oral mucosa and a maculopapular vesicular rash on the hands and feet.

66. g (chapter 5)

Chickenpox is caused by varicella zoster virus and is characterized by fever and a pruritic papular, vesicular, pustular rash starting on the trunk and spreading to the extremities. The infected child is infectious until the last lesion is crusted over.

67. d (chapter 5)

Herpes zoster or shingles is caused by reactivation of varicella zoster virus from the dorsal root ganglion and is characterized by fever, painful pruritic crops of vesicles along dermatomal distribution in an individual with previous varicella zoster infection

68. e (chapter 7)

EKG changes associated with significant hyperkalemia include loss of P waves, "peaked" T waves, wide QRS complexes, and ST segment depression. A notched PR segment is not consistent with hyperkalemia. These changes may be seen at potassium levels of 7.0 or greater.

69. b (chapter 7)

Calcium gluconate does not rid the body of potassium; however, it does stabilize the cardiac cell membranes so that electrical activity is less likely to be disrupted. In emergent situations, intravenous calcium gluconate is the best initial management of hyperkalemia. Dialysis is a wonderful option for decreasing total body potassium; however, it takes time to set up, so it is not a reasonable option in emergent situations. Neither intravenous glucose nor hypertonic NaCl solution is appropriate in the management of this patient.

70. a (chapter 3)

The regular narrow-complex rhythm during tachycardia excludes atrial fibrillation, which is an irregularly irregular narrow-complex rhythm. Flutter waves were not noted when adenosine was given, making a diagnosis of atrial flutter unlikely. The pre-excitation noted after conversion with adenosine is consistent with Wolff-Parkinson-White (WPW) syndrome. The fact that the tachycardia was narrow complex makes the tachycardia "orthodromic," re-entract tachycardia that travels down the atrioventricular node and up the bypass tract. If no pre-excitation was noted after conversion with adenosine, then an idiopathic bypass tract would be more likely. Sinus tachycardia is unlikely given that the child is afebrile and there is no evidence of cardiomyopathy.

71. a (chapter 18)

Strabismus is a condition in which there is misalignment of the eyes. The misalignment may be upward, downward, inward or outward. Management of the misalignment may be medical or surgical. Failure to treat strabismus may result in amblyopia.

72. b (chapter 18)

Amblyopia or "dull sight" refers to reduced vision in early childhood in an eye that has anatomic abnormalities that cause abnormal retinal imagery. Strabismus is the most common cause of amblyopia. Amblyopia caused by strabismus results from suppression of retinal images from a misaligned eye. Other causes of amblyopia include retinal deprivation from opacities of the optical axis (ptosis, corneal opacities, cataracts) or from unequal refractive errors in the two eyes (anisometropia).

73. d (chapter 2)

Hepatotoxicity, manifested initially by elevated liver enzymes and jaundice, may progress over several days to liver failure in people who have ingested large amounts of acetaminophen when appropriate treatment is not sought. Cardiac arrhythmias can occur with anticholinergic ingestions. Acute iron overdose and other specific ingestions can cause seizures. Malignant hypertension and ineffective hemostasis are not associated with acetaminophen ingestion.

74. b (chapter 2)

The blood acetaminophen level at 1 hour is *not* predictive of outcome because timely intervention, even more than an hour after ingestion, can prevent or ameliorate complications. However, the blood acetaminophen level at 4 hours after ingestion is *very* predictive of outcome, because by then the drug has been absorbed and is passing through the liver, its primary organ of toxicity. Although a supportive social system and a single drug ingestion may be desirable, neither is particularly predictive of a good medical outcome. Finally, presentation within the first 2 hours after ingestion is helpful, but would not really affect the outcome if the 4-hour acetaminophen blood level were low.

75. a (chapter 2)

All patients who come in with a chief complaint of ingestion, whether voluntary or accidental, must initially be evaluated for respiratory and cardiac stability. Gastric emptying may be effective up to 2 hours after ingestion if the substance ingested happens to delay gastric empty-

ing. Activated charcoal certainly is effective at this time range. N-acetylcysteine is the antidote for acetaminophen ingestion and can prevent hepatotoxicity if given in a timely fashion. Naloxone is the antidote for narcotic ingestions. Acetaminophen does not affect the electrical activity of the heart. Any patient who has seriously attempted suicide via ingestion should receive intervention, whether the substance they ingested is truly harmful or not.

76. c (chapter 15)

Maternal folic acid supplementation decreases the incidence of neural tube defects. A family history of neural tube defects increases the risk slightly in subsequent children. A high maternal serum alpha-fetoprotein level is associated with an increased risk of neural tube defect in the fetus; low levels are more predictive of Down syndrome. Children with spina bifida have wide variation in the level of lower extremity involvement.

77. a (chapter 20)

Meconium ileus is virtually pathognomonic for cystic fibrosis, an autosomal-recessive disease with a frequency of about 1 in 2500 births. Infants with phenylketonuria are usually caught on state newborn screening tests; those who are not generally are diagnosed much later with mental retardation and behavioral problems. Tay-Sachs disease is a lipidosis, whereas galactosemia is a disorder of carbohydrate metabolism; neither presents with meconium ileus. Tay-Sachs disease presents with developmental delay and seizures in the first year of life. Galactosemia becomes evident soon after feedings start, manifesting as vomiting, growth failure, and hepatomegaly. Wilson's disease presents with hepatitis, usually after the age of 5 years.

78. e (chapter 20)

Failure to thrive, chronic sinusitis, recurrent pneumonia, and pneumothorax are all possible complications of cystic fibrosis. Additional complications include nasal polyps, pancreatitis, diabetes, and impaired fertility in males.

79. b (chapter 9)

PKU is the most common amino acid metabolism disorder and results from a deficiency in the enzyme phenylalanine hydroxylase. Lack of the phenylalanine hydroxylase results in an inability to convert phenylalanine to tyrosine and the creation of the toxic metabolites phenylacetic acid and phenyllactic acid. Unlike most amino acid disorders, symptoms of PKU are not seen in early infancy, but rather in childhood if the disorder is untreated. Neurologic manifestations include moderate to severe mental retardation, hypertonicity, tremors, and behavioral problems. Tyrosine is needed for the production of melanin. Due to the block in the conversion of phenylalanine to tyrosine, there is hypopigmentation in most cases. Prevention of mental retardation in PKU is achieved by early detection and dietary restriction of phenylalanine.

80. a (chapter 9)

Homocystinuria is caused by a cystathionine synthetase deficiency. Cystathionine synthetase converts methionine to cysteine and serine. If homocystinuria is present, methionine levels are increased in the blood. There are no symptoms in infancy. Clinical manifestations observed during childhood include a Marfan's body habitus (long thin limbs and digits, scoliosis, sternal deformities, and osteoporosis), dislocated eye lenses, mild to moderate mental retardation, and vascular thromboses that result in childhood stroke or myocardial infarction. Dietary management is extremely difficult because restriction of sulfhydryl groups leads to a very-low-protein, foul-tasting diet.

81. c (chapter 9)

Galactosemia is the most common error of carbohydrate metabolism and is caused by deficiency of the enzyme galactose-1-phosphate uridyl transferase. Deficiency of galactose-1-phosphate uridyl transferase results in impaired conversion of galactose-1-phosphate to glucose-1-phosphate, which may then undergo glycolysis. Unlike PKU and homocystinuria, clinical manifestations are noted within a few days to weeks after initiation of feedings with formula or breast milk. Initial symptoms include evidence of liver failure (hepatomegaly, direct hyperbilirubinemia, disorders of coagulation), abnormal renal function (acidosis, glycosuria, aminoaciduria), emesis, anorexia, and poor

growth. Galactosemic infants are at increased risk for *E. coli* sepsis. Diagnosis is made by demonstrating an extreme reduction in the level of erythrocyte galactose-1-phosphate uridyl transferase. Galactose in the urine is detected by a positive reaction for reducing substances and no reaction with glucose oxidase on urine strip tests. Treatment centers around eliminating all formulas and foods containing galactose.

82. d (chapter 9)

OTCD is a urea cycle defect and is one of the few inborn errors of metabolism that is inherited in an X-linked manner. In the urea cycle, ornithine joins with carbamylphosphate through the action of ornithine transcarbamylase (OTC) to form citrulline within the mitochondria. When OTC is not present or exists at levels less than 20% of normal, ornithine and carbamylphosphate build up. Because of OTC deficiency, the nitrogen-containing moiety in ornithine cannot be converted to urea and excreted and, instead, ammonia is formed, resulting in severe hyperammonemia when a protein challenge is given. Within 24-48 hours after the initiation of protein-containing feedings, the newborn becomes progressively lethargic and may develop seizures as the serum ammonia becomes greater than 500 mg/dL. Diagnosis is made by measuring the level of orotic acid in the urine, which is the by-product of carbamylphosphate metabolism. Treatment centers on an extremely-low-fat diet and the exploitation of alternative pathways for nitrogen excretion using benzoic acid and phenylacetate. Early intervention may minimize deleterious effects from the defect, but management is complex and extremely difficult for parents to maintain.

83. e (chapter 10)

The adjusted reticulocyte count (ARC) = [(measured hematocrit)/(normal hematocrit for age)] × reticulocyte count. An ARC less than 2.0 suggests ineffective erythropoiesis, whereas an ARC greater than 2.0 signifies effective erythropoiesis. Anemia caused by a lack of production of red blood cells will, therefore, have an ARC less than 2.0, whereas anemias resulting from hemolysis or chronic blood loss will have an ARC greater than 2.0. The mean corpuscular volume (MCV) is used to describe the anemia as microcytic, macrocytic, or normocytic.

84. a (chapter 10)

All of the anemias noted in the question result from decreased red cell production and have an inadequate reticulocytosis (ARC <2). Decreased red cell production is due to either deficiency of hematopoietic precursors or bone marrow failure. The microcytic anemia described above is most likely due to iron deficiency, which is not only the most common microcytic anemia, but also the most common cause of anemia during childhood. It is most often seen between 6 and 24 months of age. Thalassemia syndromes are also microcytic anemias but are less common than iron deficiency anemia. Anemia of chronic disease may be microcytic or normocytic. Transient erythrocytopenia of childhood is a normocytic anemia that is an acquired red cell aplasia. Parvovirus B-19 aplastic crisis is a normocytic anemia that results from parvovirus B-19 marrow suppression of erythropoietic precursors.

85. a (chapter 18)

Leukocoria, or a white pupil, is detected by routine screening of the red reflex in all neonates. The most common cause of leukocoria is congenital cataract. Other causes of leukocoria include retinoblastoma, retinopathy of prematurity, congenital glaucoma, and ocular toxocariasis. All cases of leukocoria require prompt ophthalmologic referral. Retinal hemmorhages may indicate child abuse. If retinal or vitreous hemorrhages are seen, a systematic workup for child abuse must be undertaken.

86. d (chapter 16)

Low-iron formulas do not provide sufficient iron to prevent anemia in infants. Breast milk has iron in low amounts, but it is very well absorbed, as opposed to the iron in formula. Only fully fortified formulas should be used for non–breast-fed infants in the first year of life. Introducing whole milk prior to a year of age also places a child at risk for iron-deficiency. The other statements listed in the answer section are all true. Most cases of failure to thrive in developed countries are psychosocial in origin. Children on exclusively vegetarian diets may require B_{12} and trace mineral supplements. Both breast- and formula-fed infants should regain their birth weight by age three weeks. Obese children who are still gaining in height should be encouraged to maintain their present weight until their height catches up with their weight. Placing obese children on restrictive diets could lead to deficiencies in their intakes of essential vitamins and nutrients.

87. a (chapter 8)

The most common cause of rectal bleeding in toddlers is an anal fissure. If there were significant upper gastrointestinal tract bleeding from peptic ulcer disease or Mallory-Weiss tear, the child would have melena instead of blood-streaked stool. Inflammatory bowel disease and necrotizing enterocolitis could both cause lower gastrointestinal tract bleeding (hematochezia or blood-streaked stool) but are unlikely in an 18-month-old.

88. d (chapter 14)

Edema can be caused by protein losses from the GI tract, vasculature, or kidneys. Congestive heart failure will also result in edema, but this etiology is rare in children. Nephrotic syndrome is characterized by proteinuria, hypoalbuminemia, hyperlipidemia, and edema. Marked hematuria is more common with the glomerulonephritis syndromes. The most common cause of nephrotic syndrome in children, and fortunately the most benign, is minimal change disease. Focal segmental glomerulosclerosis is much less common, but the prognosis is worse. Urinary tract infections do not cause edema, although mild proteinuria is possible. Most causes of renal masses also do not cause edema or proteinuria; hematuria and hypertension are more typical.

89. a (chapter 14)

The most common cause of nephrotic syndrome in children is minimal change disease. Although minimal change disease has a wonderful prognosis generally, it does need to be treated, most effectively with salt restriction and corticosteroids. In severe cases, diuretics may be necessary as well, although this is the exception rather than the rule. Since nephrotic syndrome is not an infection, it does not respond to antibiotics. Chemotherapy is also inappropriate as an initial therapy.

90. c (chapter 14)

Once nephrotic syndrome is diagnosed, any biopsy would obviously be done on the kidneys, although kidney biopsies are not indicated in uncomplicated, initial episodes of childhood nephrotic syndrome. Glomerular basement membrane thickening is more consistent with diffuse mesangial proliferative glomerulonephritis. Inflammatory cell infiltrate is seen in the various nephritic syndromes, most commonly acute poststreptococcal glomerulonephritis. In terms of minimal change disease, gross sections and light microscopy show few if any abnormalities; the only consistent finding is effacement of epithelial cell foot processes demonstrated by electron microscopy.

91. b (chapter 4)

At 6 months, an infant is expected to reach the following milestones

Gross motor	Sits well unsupported, puts feet in mouth in supine position
Visual motor	Reaches with either hand, transfers, uses raking grasp
Language	Babbles
Social	Recognizes strangers

92. a (chapter 4)

At 12 months, an infant is expected to reach the following milestones

Gross motor	Walks alone
Visual motor	Throws objects, lets go of toys, uses mature pincer grasp
Language	Uses two words other than "dada/mama," immature jargoning
Social	Imitates actions, comes when called, cooperates with dressing

93. d (chapter 4)

At 24 months a child is expected to reach the following milestones

Gross motor	Walks up and down steps without help
Visual motor	Removes pants and shoes, turns pages one at a time
Language	Uses pronouns (I, you, me) inappropriately, understands two-step commands
Social	Parallel play

94. c (chapter 4)

At 36 months, a child is expected to reach the following milestones

Gross motor	Pedals tricycle, alternates feet when going up steps
Visual motor	Dresses and undresses partially, draws a circle
Language	Uses three-word sentences/plurals/past tense, knows all pronouns, >250 words
Social	Group play, shares toys, takes turns, knows full name/age/sex

95. e (chapter 4)

At 48 months, a child is expected to reach the following milestones

Gross motor	Hops, skips, alternates feet going downstairs
Visual motor	Ties shoes, spreads with knife
Language	Knows colors, asks questions, says song or poem from memory
Social	Tells "tall tales," plays cooperatively with group of children

96. a (chapter 3)

Beta-blocker therapy is the most appropriate chronic therapy for long QT syndrome. Nadolol minimizes the number of premature ventricular contractions (PVCs). Fewer PVCs decreases the risk of PVC R-wave depolarization on the vulnerable part of the T wave, thereby decreasing the risk of ventricular tachycardia and ventricular fibrillation seen in long QT syndrome. Lidocaine would be an appropriate acute therapy at the time of the ventricular tachycardia to stabilize the myocardium.

97. d (chapter 10)

The most likely diagnosis is hemophilia A. Hemophilia A is an X-linked disorder that is caused by deficiency of factor VIII. Hemophilia B is also an X-linked disorder and is caused by factor IX deficiency. Hemophilia A and B are characterized by spontaneous or traumatic hemorrhages, which can be subcutaneous, intramuscular, or within joints (hemarthroses). Life-threatening internal hemorrhages may follow trauma or surgery. The PTT is prolonged, the PT is normal, and in hemophilia A the factor VIII coagulant activity (VIIIC) is decreased. Other than their factor replacement regimens, there is no distinguishable difference between hemophilia A and B. Idiopathic thrombocytopenic purpura is unlikely, given that the platelet count is normal at 150,000. With no history of epistaxis, gingival bleeding, or cutaneous bruising, von Willebrand's disease is unlikely. Hemarthroses are not typical for von Willebrand's disease. Vitamin K deficiency occurs in the neonate who is exclusively breast-fed and has not received prophylactic vitamin K injection after birth or in the child with significant fat malabsorption. In vitamin K deficiency and in liver disease, there is a prolonged PT and normal factor VIII coagulant activity.

98. a (chapter 10)

The most appropriate therapy for complications of hemophilia A is to infuse factor VIII concentrate. The goal of therapy for hemophilia A is to prevent long-term crippling orthopedic complications due to hemarthroses. Surgical decompression is rarely necessary to relieve intra-articular hemorrhage. Observation will not decrease the bleeding, only factor infusion will diminish further bleeding. Factor IX concentrate is infused for bleeding complications associated with hemophilia B. Aminocaproic acid is a fibrinolysis inhibitor that may help minimize oral bleeding in hemophiliacs who undergo dental procedures.

99. a (chapter 17)

The leukemias account for the greatest percentage of childhood malignancies. Acute leukemias constitute 97% of all childhood leukemias and are divided into acute lymphocytic leukemia (ALL) and acute myelogenous leukemia (AML). ALL accounts for 80% of all childhood acute leukemias. A history of fever, pallor, anorexia, bone pain, lymphadenopathy, petechiae, and hepatosplenomegaly is consistent with ALL. Leukemic cell dissemination results in bone marrow failure, reticuloendothelial system infiltration, and penetration of sanctuary sites (central nervous system and testicles). Marrow infiltration results in crowding out of normal marrow blood cell precursors, which then results in anemia (pallor) and thrombocytopenia (petechiae). Infiltration of the reticuloendothelial system results in lymphadenopathy and hepatosplenomegaly. Bone pain is due to expansion of the marrow cavity, destruction of cortical bone by leukemic cells, or metastatic tumor. Although fever and petechiae are consistent with aplastic anemia, bone pain, lymphadenopathy, and hepatosplenomegaly are not.

100. e (chapter 17)

Therapy for leukemia involves managing leukemic complications at presentation, chemotherapeutic treatment, and management of the metabolic and blood product complications associated with chemotherapy. Blood products may be needed for severe anemia or thrombocytopenia. Chemotherapy is generally divided into three stages: remission induction, consolidation, and maintenance therapy. When the leukemic child presents with fever and neutropenia, a thorough evaluation (blood culture, urine culture, stool culture, throat culture, and chest radiograph) should be undertaken and broad-spectrum antibiotics should be started, because the risk of bacteremia and disseminated infection is high. Although hyperviscosity, due to white blood cell counts of greater than 100,000, may be seen in patients with acute myelogenous leukemia, exchange transfusion is needed infrequently.

101. c (chapter 17)

In contrast to those in adults, brain tumors in children are predominantly infratentorial, involving the posterior fossae (cerebellum, midbrain, and brainstem). Childhood brain tumors are further differentiated from those in adults in that they are usually low-grade astrocytomas or embryonic neoplasms (medulloblastomas, ependymomas, or germ cell tumors), whereas most central nervous system tumors in the adult are mature astrocytomas or metastatic carcinomas.

102. c (chapter 17)

Neuroblastoma is the most common malignant tumor in infancy. Neuroblastoma is a malignant tumor of the neural crest cells that form the adrenal medulla and the paraspinal sympathetic ganglion. Abdominal tumors account for 75% of the neuroblastoma tumors (two-thirds adrenal medulla, one-third retroperitoneal sympathetic ganglion). Thoracic tumors account for 20% of neuroblastoma tumors and tend to arise from paraspinal ganglion in the posterior mediastinum. Neuroblastoma of the neck, 5% of neuroblastoma tumors, involves the cervical sympathetic ganglion. In neuroblastoma of the abdomen, there is often displacement of the kidney and minimal distortion of the calyceal system. This is in contrast to Wilm's tumor, in which there is significant distortion of the calyceal system. Since 70% of children with neuroblastoma have distant metastases, treatment generally involves surgery, for tumor debulking, and chemotherapy.

103. d (chapter 16)

The infant in this question most likely has colic, although significant disease should be ruled out with a good history and physical exam. Colic begins around age 3 weeks and can last up to age 3 months. It is characterized by an infant who seems generally well during most of the day but develops crying spells that last several hours at a time up to three times a week. These tend to be in the evening hours. The infant is generally inconsolable during these spells. Formula changes have not been found to ameliorate true colic. A 6-week-old breast-fed infant is a little young for both otitis media and intussusception; no fever is present, and the symptoms have been going on for too long to be either of the above. Malabsorption presents with diarrhea and often failure to thrive, neither of which is present here. Milk protein intolerance is extremely unlikely in a breast-fed infant.

104. d (chapter 13)

Maternal age less than 16 years or greater than 35 years of age is associated with low birth weight. Other maternal factors associated with having a low-birth-weight neonate include maternal smoking, previous low-birth-weight infant, low socioeconomic status, lack of prenatal care, unmarried status, low pre-pregnancy weight and/or poor weight gain during pregnancy, and African American race. Medical causes of preterm birth include multiple gestation, non-immune hydrops fetalis, erythroblastosis fetalis, congenital anomalies, placental abnormalities (placenta previa, abruptio placentae), bicornuate uterus, incompetent cervix, pre-eclampsia, infection (syphilis, herpes simplex virus, chorioamnionitis, group B streptococcus), cocaine abuse, and premature rupture of membranes.

105. e (chapter 13)

Neonatal sepsis is generally divided into early-onset sepsis, late-onset sepsis, and nosocomial sepsis. *Staphylococcus aureus* is typically a nosocomial infection found in preterm infants in the NICU from 7 days of life to discharge. It is not a typical pathogen of early-onset sepsis. The neonate described has early-onset sepsis (birth to 7 days of life), which is caused by bacteria from the mother's genitourinary tract. The bacteria responsible for early-onset sepsis include group B streptococcus, *Escherichia coli*, *Klebsiella pneumoniae*, and *Listeria monocytogenes*. Group B streptococcus is the most common cause of neonatal sepsis and classically occurs with a bimodal distribution, early and late.

106. e (chapter 13)

Total parenteral nutrition does not increase the risk for indirect hyperbilirubinemia acutely, but given chronically may induce a direct hyperbilirubinemia. Asian ancestry increases the risk of hyperbilirubinemia due to genetic differences between Asian and non-Asian populations in the conjugating enzyme in the hepatocytes. The child and mother are Rh incompatible. Rh incompatibility and disseminated intravascular coagulation result in increased turnover of red blood cells and may increase the load of bilirubin that needs to be excreted. Sepsis may result in hypotension, decreased liver perfusion, and a diminished ability to conjugate bilirubin.

107. c (chapter 13)

Total parenteral nurtrition is not associated with necrotizing enterocolitis. Necrotizing enterocolitis refers to a process of acute intestinal necrosis after ischemic injury to the bowel and secondary bacterial invasion of the intestinal wall. Bowel ischemia secondary to perinatal asphyxia is regarded as the cause of the bowel injury. The introduction of formula or human milk then provides the substrate for bacterial overgrowth. Bacterial invasion of the bowel wall leads to tissue necrosis and perforation. Pneumatosis intestinalis results from gas production in the bowel wall and is pathognomonic for necrotizing enterocolitis. Premature infants with birth weights less than 2000 g who have been asphyxiated are the population at risk. Prenatal factors associated with necrotizing enterocolitis include maternal age greater than 35, maternal infection requiring antibiotics, premature rupture of membranes, and cocaine exposure. Perinatal factors include maternal anesthesia, depressed Apgar score at 5 minutes, birth asphyxia, respiratory distress syndrome, and hypotension. Postnatal factors include patent ductus arteriosus, congestive heart failure, umbilical vessel catheterization, polycythemia, and exchange transfusion.

108. a (chapter 4)

The initiation sequence of sexual development in males is testicular enlargement, penile enlargement, height growth spurt, and pubic hair, whereas the sequence for females is thelarche, height growth spurt, pubic hair, and menarche. Although the events of puberty occur in a predictable sequence, the timing of the initiation and velocity of the changes are highly variable among individuals.

109. b (chapter 6)

Cushing's syndrome is a constellation of symptoms and signs that result from hypercortisolism and is due to either endogenous overproduction of cortisol or excessive exogenous treatment with pharmacologic doses of cortisol. Endogenous causes include Cushing's disease and adrenal tumors. Cushing's disease, also known as bilateral adrenal hyperplasia, is the most common etiology of Cushing's syndrome in children older than 7 years. In most instances, it is caused by a microadenoma of the pituitary resulting in ACTH oversecretion.

110. e (chapter 6)

Addison's disease is due to hypocortisolism. Primary adrenal insufficiency may be congenital or acquired and results in decreased cortisol secretion. Depending on the disease process, there may be a concomitant decrease in aldosterone release. In the newborn, primary adrenal insufficiency may be due to adrenal hypoplasia, ACTH unresponsiveness, adrenal hemorrhage, or ischemic infarction with sepsis (Waterhouse-Friderichsen syndrome). In older children and adolescents, autoimmune adrenal insufficiency is most common. It may occur alone or in association with another autoimmune endocrinopathy, such as thyroiditis or IDDM. In contrast to primary adrenal insufficiency, secondary adrenal insufficiency is due to ACTH deficiency. The most common cause of ACTH deficiency is chronic steroid therapy that results in suppression of pituitary ACTH. Pituitary tumors and craniopharyngiomas also result in depressed pituitary ACTH secretion from either destruction of the pituitary gland or pituitary compression.

111. d (chapter 6)

Most cases of hyperthyroidism in children are caused by Graves' disease. Other causes include a hyperfunctioning, "hot" thyroid nodule or acute suppurative thyroiditis. Graves' disease results from autoimmune-induced thyroid hyperplasia. Thyrotoxicosis is caused by circulating thyroid-stimulating immunoglobulins binding to thyrotropin receptors on thyroid cells, resulting in diffuse hyperplasia and increased levels of free T_4. Neonatal Graves' disease results from transplacental passage of maternal thyroid-stimulating immunoglobulins.

112. c (chapter 6)

Acquired hypothyroidism during childhood or adolescence is known as juvenile hypothyroidism. The most common cause of juvenile hypothyroidism is Hashimoto's thyroiditis, which is a chronic lymphocytic thyroiditis that results in autoimmune destruction of the thyroid gland. Other causes of hypothyroidism include panhypopituitarism, ectopic thyroid dysgenesis, administration of antithyroid medications, and surgical or radioactive iodine ablation for treatment of hyperthyroidism. Most children present at adolescence; it is unusual to develop thyroiditis before 5 years of age.

---

113. a (chapter 6)

21-Hydroxylase deficiency accounts for 90% of the cases of congenital adrenal hyperplasia. The disease is inherited as an autosomal recessive trait and tends to occur as either classic salt-wasting 21-hydroxylase deficiency or as virilizing 21-hydroxylase deficiency. 21-Hydroxylase is needed to produce aldosterone and cortisol. 21-Hydroxylase deficiency results in a buildup of the precursors of aldosterone and cortisol synthesis, which are then metabolized to androgens. Both forms of 21-hydroxylase deficiency result in decreased cortisol and aldosterone secretion, increased corticotropin (ACTH), and increased 17-hydroxyprogesterone. 11-Hydroxylase deficiency accounts for 5% of the cases of congenital adrenal hyperplasia and is also inherited as an autosomal recessive trait. Similar to 21-hydroxylase deficiency, 11-hydroxylase deficiency impairs the production of aldosterone and cortisol. With reduction of or absence in 11-hydroxylase, cortisol and aldosterone precursors build up and are shunted to androgen synthesis.

---

114. d (chapter 9)

Single gene defects may be inherited in an autosomal dominant, autosomal recessive, or X-linked pattern. Incomplete penetrance is not a mode of inheritance, but a description of the variable expressivity of autosomal dominant single-gene defects in affected individuals.

---

115. d (chapter 9)

Following up on neonatal screens is critically important, because phenylketonuria (PKU) and homocystinuria do not manifest themselves in infancy. They manifest themselves in childhood after irreversible damage to the central nervous system has already been done. Prevention of central nervous system damage from PKU is achieved by early detection and dietary restriction of phenylalanine.

---

116. d (chapter 5)

Erythema multiforme is an acute, self-limited, uncommon hypersensitivity reaction that may be secondary to sulfa drugs. Erythema multiforme is characterized by symmetric lesions evolving through multiple morphologic stages: erythematous macules, papules, plaques, vesicles, and target lesions, with sparing of the mucosal surfaces. Stevens-Johnson syndrome is the most severe form of erythema multiforme. Stevens-Johnson syndrome is characterized by fever, erythema multiforme rash, and inflammatory bullae of two or more mucous membranes (oral mucosa, lips, bulbar conjunctiva, anogenital area). Toxic epidermal necrolysis is the most severe form of cutaneous hypersensitivity and is characterized by widespread skin erythema, tenderness, mucosal involvement, and sloughing of the epidermis. Eczema is not usually exacerbated by medication exposure. Urticaria is the most common hypersensitivity reaction in the skin, is characterized by hives, and may result from medication exposure.

---

117. a (chapter 9)

The clinical description is that of a patient with trisomy 21 or Down syndrome. Common dysmorphic facial features include flat facial profile, upslanted palpebral fissures, a flat nasal bridge with epicanthal folds, a small mouth with a protruding tongue, micrognathia, and short ears with downfolding ear lobes. Other dysmorphic features are excess skin on the back of the neck, microcephaly, a flat occiput (brachycephaly), short stature, a short sternum, small genitalia, and a gap between the first and second toes ("sandal gap toe"). Anomalies of the hand include single palmar creases (simian creases) and short, broad hands (brachydactyly) with fingers marked by an incurved fifth finger and a hypoplastic middle phalanx (clinodactyly).

---

118. e (chapter 9)

Tracheoesophageal fistula with esophageal atresia is not associated with trisomy 21. Functional and structural abnormalities include generalized hypotonia (obstructive sleep apnea), cardiac defects (endocardial cushion defects and septal defects are seen in 50% of cases), gastrointestinal anomalies (duodenal atresia and Hirschsprung's disease), atlanto-axial instability, developmental delay, moderate mental retardation, and hypothyroidism. There is a higher frequency of leukemia in children with trisomy 21 than in the general population.

---

119. d (chapter 10)

The most likely diagnosis is immune thrombocytopenia purpura. Isoimmune thrombocytopenia is noted in newborns, not in children. Isoimmune IgG antibodies are produced against the fetal platelet, when the fetal platelet crosses the placenta and has antigens that are not found on the maternal platelet. The maternal antibodies cross the placenta and attack the fetal platelets. Leukemia, sepsis, and hypersplenism may all cause thrombocytopenia in the child age group, but are unlikely in this case. The white blood cell count is normal and no immature white cells are seen on the peripheral smear. Sepsis is unlikely, given that the child appears well and is hemodynamically stable. Hypersplenism is unlikely when the spleen is normal on palpation.

---

120. a (chapter 15)

Reye syndrome is much less common now that parents are instructed to avoid aspirin in children. The most consistent laboratory abnormality in Reye syndrome is hyperammonemia, although glucose, electrolytes, and transaminases may be abnormal as well. Hypercalcemia is not typical of Reye syndrome.

---

121. a (chapter 15)

Early involvement of neurosurgery and monitoring in an intensive care unit are the most appropriate therapies for patients with suspected Reye syndrome, especially when the disease is severe. Calcium gluconate is useful in severe cases of hyperkalemia. Reye syndrome is not thought to be infectious, so antibiotics are not helpful. Dialysis may be indicated if electrolyte abnormalities and hyperammonemia cannot be controlled in more conservative ways. Phenobarbital coma is indicated for intractable status epilepticus (that is, seizures that are prolonged and unresponsive to other emergency pharmacologic measures).

122. c (chapter 13)

Polyhydramnios is defined as an amniotic fluid volume greater than 2 liters. Chronic polyhydramnios is more common than acute polyhydramnios. Polyhydramnios may result in prematurity. Polyhydramnios is associated with lesions that impair fetal swallowing, such as neural tube defects (anencephaly and myelomeningocele), abdominal wall defects (omphalocele and gastroschisis), esophageal or duodenal atresia, and cleft palate, as well as gestational diabetes, immune or nonimmune hydrops fetalis, multiple gestations, and trisomy 18 or 21. Oligohydramnios is a decreased amount of amniotic fluid and is associated with postmaturity, amniotic fluid leak, intrauterine growth retardation, and congenital anomalies of the fetal kidneys. Bilateral renal agenesis results in Potter's syndrome. Due to renal anomalies, there are oligohydramnios and pulmonary hypoplasia.

---

123. a (chapter 8)

The abdominal examination reveals peritoneal signs (rebound tenderness and guarding) that are consistent with appendicitis or pancreatitis, but not viral gastroenteritis, urinary tract infection, or diabetes mellitus. In the latter three diagnoses, there may be some diffuse nonspecific abdominal pain, but peritoneal signs are unlikely. The description of the movement of the pain from periumbilical to the right lower quadrant is typical for appendicitis. Pain from pancreatitis is generally noted in the epigastric area.

---

124. c (chapter 8)

The history, physical examination, and abdominal radiograph are classic for a diagnosis of intussusception. In cases of intussusception, barium enema demonstrates a "coiled spring" appearance to the bowel in the right lower quadrant. The barium or air enema results in hydrostatic reduction of the intussusception in 75% of cases.

125. a (chapter 8)

Projectile nonbilious vomiting is the cardinal feature seen in virtually all patients with pyloric stenosis. Physical findings vary with the severity of the obstruction. The classic finding of an olive-sized, muscular, mobile, nontender mass in the epigastric area occurs in most cases. Dehydration and poor weight gain are common when the diagnosis is delayed. Hypokalemic, hypochloremic, metabolic alkalosis with dehydration is seen secondary to persistent emesis in the most severe cases.

126. e (chapter 8)

Crohn's disease typically is associated with ileal and/or colonic involvement with skip lesions, rectal sparing, segmental narrowing of the ileum (string sign), granuloma, intestinal fistula, and transmural disease. The presence of Crohn's disease increases the risk of colon cancer only slightly. Ulcerative colitis typically is characterized by rectal involvement, rectal bleeding, crypt abscesses, and diffuse superficial mucosal ulceration, and its presence significantly increases the risk of colon cancer.

Appendix A: Normal Lab Values

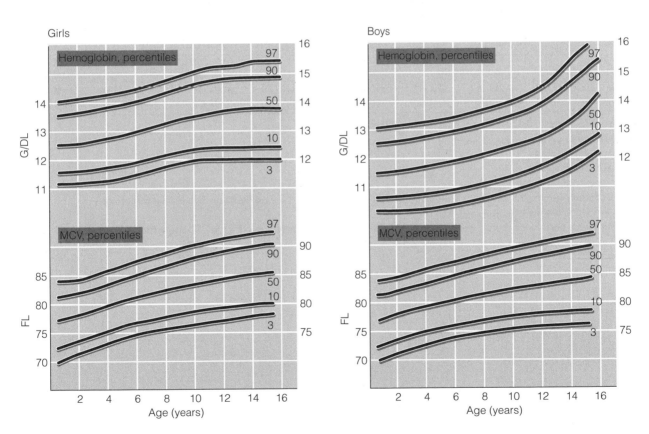

Table A–1

Reprinted with permission from Siberry G., et al., eds. The Harriet Lane handbook, 15th ed. St. Louis: Mosby Yearbook, 1999.

TABLE A–2

Age-Specific Blood Cell Indices

Age	Hb (g%)[a]	HCT (%)[a]	MCV (fL)[a]	MCHC (g/% RBC)[a]	Reticulocytes	WBCs (×10³/mm³)[b]	Platelets (10³/mm³)[b]
26–30wk gestation[c]	13.4 (11)	41.5 (34.9)	118.2 (106.7)	37.9 (30.6)	—	4.4 (2.7)	254 (180–327)
28wk	14.5	45	120	31.0	(5–10)	—	275
32wk	15.0	47	118	32.0	(3–10)	—	290
Term[d] (cord)	16.5 (13.5)	51 (42)	108 (98)	33.0 (30.0)	(3–7)	18.1 (9–30)[e]	290
1-3dy	18.5 (14.5)	56 (45)	108 (95)	33.0 (29.0)	(1.8–4.6)	18.9 (9.4–34)	192
2wk	16.6 (13.4)	53 (41)	105 (88)	31.4 (28.1)		11.4 (5–20)	252
1mo	13.9 (10.7)	44 (33)	101 (91)	31.8 (28.1)	(0.1–1.7)	10.8 (4–19.5)	
2mo	11.2 (9.4)	35 (28)	95 (84)	31.8 (28.3)			
6mo	12.6 (11.1)	36 (31)	76 (68)	35.0 (32.7)	(0.7–2.3)	11.9 (6–17.5)	
6mo–2yr	12.0 (10.5)	36 (33)	78 (70)	33.0 (30.0)		10.6 (6–17)	(150–350)
2–6yr	12.5 (11.5)	37 (34)	81 (75)	34.0 (31.0)	(0.5–1.0)	8.5 (5–15.5)	(150–350)
6–12yr	13.5 (11.5)	40 (35)	86 (77)	34.0 (31.0)	(0.5–1.0)	8.1 (4.5–13.5)	(150–350)
12–18yr							
Male	14.5 (13)	43 (36)	88 (78)	34.0 (31.0)	(0.5–1.0)	7.8 (4.5–13.5)	(150–350)
Female	14.0 (12)	41 (37)	90 (78)	34.0 (31.0)	(0.5–1.0)	7.8 (4.5–13.5)	(150–350)
Adult							
Male	15.5 (13.5)	47 (41)	90 (80)	34.0 (31.0)	(0.8–2.5)	7.4 (4.5–11)	(150–350)
Female	14.0 (12)	41 (36)	90 (80)	34.0 (31.0)	(0.8–4.1)	7.4 (4.5–11)	(150–350)

Data from Forestler[1]; Oski[2]; Nathan[3]; Metoth[4]; and Wintrobe[5].

Hb, hemoglobin.

[a]Data are mean (-2SD)

[b]Data are mean (+2SD)

[c]Values are from fetal samplings.

[d]<1mo, capillary hemoglobin exceeds venous: 1hr = 3.6g difference; 5dy = 2.2g difference; 3wk = 1.1g difference.

[e]Mean (95% confidence limits)

Reprinted with permission from Siberry G, et al., eds. The Harriet Lane handbook, 15th ed. St. Louis: Mosby Yearbook, 1999:325.

TABLE A–3

Age-Specific Leukocyte Differential

Age	Total Leukocytes[a] Mean (range)	Neutrophils[b] Mean (range)	%	Lymphocytes Mean (range)	%	Monocytes Mean	%	Eosinophils Mean	%
Birth	18.1 (9–30)	11 (6–26)	61	5.5 (2–11)	31	1.1	6	0.4	2
12hr	22.8 (13–38)	15.5 (6–28)	68	5.5 (2–11)	24	1.2	5	0.5	2
24hr	18.9 (9.4–34)	11.5 (5–21)	61	5.8 (2–11.5)	31	1.1	6	0.5	2
1wk	12.2 (5–21)	5.5 (1.5–10)	45	5.0 (2–17)	41	1.1	9	0.5	4
2wk	11.4 (5–20)	4.5 (1–9.5)	40	5.5 (2–17)	48	1.0	9	0.4	3
1mo	10.8 (5–19.5)	3.8 (1–8.5)	35	6.0 (2.5–16.5)	56	0.7	7	0.3	3
6mo	11.9 (6–17.5)	3.8 (1–8.5)	32	7.3 (4–13.5)	61	0.6	5	0.3	3
1yr	11.4 (6–17.5)	3.5 (1.5–8.5)	31	7.0 (4–10.5)	61	0.6	5	0.3	3
2yr	10.6 (6–17)	3.5 (1.5–8.5)	33	6.3 (3–9.5)	59	0.5	5	0.3	3
4yr	9.1 (5.5–15.5)	3.8 (1.5–8.5)	42	4.5 (2–8)	50	0.5	5	0.3	3
6yr	8.5 (5–14.5)	4.3 (1.5–8)	51	3.5 (1.5–7)	42	0.4	5	0.2	3
8yr	8.3 (4.5–13.5)	4.4 (1.5–8)	53	3.3 (1.5–6.8)	39	0.4	4	0.2	2
10yr	8.1 (4.5–13.5)	4.4 (1.5–8.5)	54	3.1 (1.5–6.5)	38	0.4	4	0.2	2
16yr	7.8 (4.5–13.0)	4.4 (1.8–8)	57	2.8 (1.2–5.2)	35	0.4	5	0.2	3
21yr	7.4 (4.5–11.0)	4.4 (1.8–7.7)	59	2.5 (1–4.8)	34	0.3	4	0.2	3

From Dallman[6].

[a]Numbers of leukocytes are $\times 10^3/mm^3$; ranges are estimates of 95% confidence limits; percents refer to differential counts.

[b]Neutrophils include band cells at all ages and a small number of metamyelocytes and myelocytes in the first few days of life.

Reprinted with permission from Siberry G, et al., eds. The Harriet Lane handbook, 15th ed. St. Louis: Mosby Yearbook, 1999:327.

TABLE A–4

Age-Specific Coagulation Values

Coagulation tests	Preterm Infant 30–36wk, day of life #1	Term infant, day of life #1	1–5yr	6–10yr	11–16yr	Adult
PT (sec)	15.4 (14.6–16.9)	13.0 (10.1–15.9)	11 (10.6–11.4)	11.1 (10.1–12.1)	11.2 (10.2–12.0)	12 (11.0–14.0)
INR	—	—	1.0 (0.96–1.04)	1.0 (0.91–1.11)	1.02 (0.93–1.10)	1.10 (1.0–1.3)
aPTT (sec)	108 (80–168)	42.9 (31.3–54.3)	30 (24–36)	31 (26–36)	32 (26–37)	33 (27–40)
Fibrinogen (g/L)	2.43 (1.50–3.73)	2.83 (1.67–3.09)	2.76 (1.70–4.05)	2.79 (1.57–4.0)	3.0 (1.54–4.48)	2.78 (1.56–4.0)
Bleeding time (min)	—	—	6 (2.5–10)	7 (2.5–13)	5 (3–8)	4 (1–7)
Thrombin time (sec)	14 (11–17)	12 (10–16)	—	—	—	10
II (U/mL)	0.45 (0.20–0.77)	0.48 (0.26–0.70)	0.94 (0.71–1.16)	0.88 (0.67–1.07)	0.83 (0.61–1.04)	1.08 (0.70–1.46)
V (U/mL)	0.88 (0.41–1.44)	0.72 (0.43–1.08)	1.03 (0.79–1.27)	0.90 (0.63–1.16)	0.77 (0.55–0.99)	1.06 (0.62–1.50)
VII (U/mL)	0.67 (0.21–1.13)	0.66 (0.28–1.04)	0.82 (0.55–1.16)	0.85 (0.52–1.20)	0.83 (0.58–1.15)	1.05 (0.67–1.43)
VIII (U/mL)	1.11 (0.50–2.13)	1.00 (0.50–1.78)	0.90 (0.59–1.42)	0.95 (0.58–1.32)	0.92 (0.53–1.31)	0.99 (0.50–1.49)
vWF (U/mL)	1.36 (0.78–2.10)	1.53 (0.50–2.87)	0.82 (0.47–1.04)	0.95 (0.44–1.44)	1.00 (0.46–1.53)	0.92 (0.50–1.58)
IX (U/mL)	0.35 (0.19–0.65)	0.53 (0.15–0.91)	0.73 (0.47–1.04)	0.75 (0.63–0.89)	0.87 (0.59–1.22)	1.09 (0.55–1.63)
X (U/mL)	0.41 (0.11–0.71)	0.40 (0.12–0.68)	0.88 (0.58–1.16)	0.75 (0.55–1.01)	0.79 (0.50–1.17)	1.06 (0.70–1.52)
XI (U/mL)	0.30 (0.08–0.52)	0.38 (0.10–0.66)	0.97 (0.56–1.50)	0.86 (0.52–1.20)	0.74 (0.50–0.97)	0.97 (0.67–1.27)
XII (U/mL)	0.38 (0.10–0.66)	0.53 (0.13–0.93)	0.93 (0.64–1.29)	0.92 (0.60–1.40)	0.81 (0.34–1.37)	1.08 (0.52–1.64)
PK (U/mL)	0.33 (0.09–0.57)	0.37 (0.18–0.69)	0.95 (0.65–1.30)	0.99 (0.66–1.31)	0.99 (0.53–1.45)	1.12 (0.62–1.62)
HMWK (U/mL)	0.49 (0.09–0.89)	0.54 (0.06–1.02)	0.98 (0.64–1.32)	0.93 (0.60–1.30)	0.91 (0.63–1.19)	0.92 (0.50–1.36)
XIIIa (U/mL)	0.70 (0.32–1.08)	0.79 (0.27–1.31)	1.08 (0.72–1.43)	1.09 (0.65–1.51)	0.99 (0.57–1.40)	1.05 (0.55–1.55)
XIIIs (U/mL)	0.81 (0.35–1.27)	0.76 (0.30–1.22)	1.13 (0.69–1.56)	1.16 (0.77–1.54)	1.02 (0.60–1.43)	0.97 (0.57–1.37)
D-Dimer	—	—	—	—	—	Positive titer = 1:8
FDPs	—	—	—	—	—	Borderline titer = 1:25 / Positive titer = 1:50

Coagulation inhibitors

Coagulation tests	Preterm Infant 30–36wk, day of life #1	Term infant, day of life #1	1–5yr	6–10yr	11–16yr	Adult
ATIII (U/mL)	0.38 (0.14–0.62)	0.63 (0.39–0.97)	1.11 (0.82–1.39)	1.11 (0.90–1.31)	1.05 (0.77–1.32)	1.0 (0.74–1.26)
α_2-M (U/mL)	1.10 (0.56–1.82)	1.39 (0.95–1.83)	1.69 (1.14–2.23)	1.69 (1.28–2.09)	1.56 (0.98–2.12)	0.86 (0.52–1.20)
C_1-Inh (U/mL)	0.65 (0.31–0.99)	0.72 (0.36–1.08)	1.35 (0.85–1.83)	1.14 (0.88–1.54)	1.03 (0.68–1.50)	1.0 (0.71–1.31)
α_2-AT (U/mL)	0.90 (0.36–1.44)	0.93 (0.49–1.37)	0.93 (0.39–1.47)	1.00 (0.69–1.30)	1.01 (0.65–1.37)	0.93 (0.55–1.30)
Protein C (U/mL)	0.28 (0.12–0.44)	0.35 (0.17–0.53)	0.66 (0.40–0.92)	0.69 (0.45–0.93)	0.83 (0.55–1.11)	0.96 (0.64–1.28)
Protein S total (U/mL)	0.26 (0.14–0.38)	0.36 (0.12–0.60)	0.86 (0.54–1.18)	0.78 (0.41–1.14)	0.72 (0.52–0.92)	0.81 (0.60–1.13)

Fibrinolytic system

Coagulation tests	Preterm Infant 30–36wk, day of life #1	Term infant, day of life #1	1–5yr	6–10yr	11–16yr	Adult
Plasminogen (U/mL)	1.70 (1.12–2.48)	1.95 (+/- 0.35)	0.98 (0.78–1.18)	0.92 (0.75–1.08)	0.86 (0.68–1.03)	0.99 (0.7–1.22)
TPA (ng/mL)	—	—	2.15 (1.0–4.5)	2.42 (1.0–5.0)	2.16 (1.0–4.0)	4.90 (1.40–8.40)
α_2-AP (U/mL)	0.78 (0.4–1.16)	0.85 (+/- 0.15)	1.05 (0.93–1.17)	0.99 (0.89–1.10)	0.98 (0.78–1.18)	1.02 (0.68–1.36)
PAI (U/mL)	—	—	5.42 (1.0–10.0)	6.79 (2.0–12.0)	6.07 (2.0–10.0)	3.60 (0–11.0)

Data from Andrew[9,11].

HMWK, high-molecular-weight kininogen; PK, prekallikrein; VIII, factor VIII procoagulant.

α_2-AP, α_2-antiplasmin; α_2-AT, α_2-antitrypsin; α_2-M, α_2-macroglobulin; ATIII, antithrombin III; PAI, plasminogen activator inhibitor; TPA, total plasminogen activator.

Reprinted with permission from Siberry G, et al., eds. The Harriet Lane handbook, 15th ed. St. Louis: Mosby Yearbook, 1999:327.

TABLE A–5

Age-Specific RBC/Iron Indicators

RCB Iron indicator	Term neonate	Infant (1–12mo)	Child	Adolescent	Adult
Erythrocyte sedimentation rate (ESR)	0–4mm/hr	—	4–20mm/hr	—	0–20mm/hr female 0–10mm/hr male
Ferritin (ng/mL)	25–200	200–600 (1mo) 50–200 (2–5mo)	7–140 (6mo–15yr)	7–140 (6mo–15yr)	10–120 female 20–250 male
Folate (serum) (ng/mL)	5–65	15–55	5–21	5–21	5–21
Folate (RBC) (ng/mL)	150–200	75–1000	>160	>160	140–628
Free erythrocyte protoporphyrin FEP)	30–70μmol/mol heme; <30μg/dL whole blood	30–70μmol/mol heme; <30μg/dL whole blood	30–70μmol/mol heme; <30μg/dL whole blood	30–70μmol/mol heme; <30μg/dL whole blood	30–70μmol/mol heme <30μg/dL whole blood
Haptoglobin (mg/dL)	5–50	25–185	25–185	25–185	25–185
Hemoglobin A₁C (%Hb)	5–7.5%	5–7.5%	5–7.5%	5–7.5%	5–7.5%
Hemoglobin F (fetal) (%Hb)	77 +/- 7% (1day) 77 +/- 6% (5day) 70 +/- 7% (3wk)	53 +/- 11% (6–9wk) 23 +/- 16% (3–4mo) 5 +/- 2% (6mo) 1.6 +/- 1% (8–11mo)	<2%	<2%	<2%
Hemopexin (mg/dL)	18% of maternal concentration	—	—	—	50–115 >75 pregnant women
Iron (mg/dL)	100–250	40–100	50–120	—	50–170 female 65–175 male
Methemoglobin (%Hb)	0–1.5%	0–1.5%	0–1.5%	0–1.5%	0–1.5%
TIBC (μg/dL)	150–250	200–400	250–500	300–600	250–425
Transferrin (mg/dL)	130–275	200–360	200–360	220–400	220–400
Vitamin B₁₂ (pg/mL)	160–1300	200–900	200–900	130–800	200–835

From Painter[14], Saarinen[15], and Lockitch[16].
Reprinted with permission from Siberry G, et al., eds. The Harriet Lane handbook, 15th ed. St. Louis: Mosby Yearbook, 1999:329.

These values are compiled from the published literature[1-5] and from the Johns Hopkins Hospital Department of Laboratory Medicine. Normal values vary with the analytic method used. If any doubt exists, consult your laboratory for its analytic method and range of normal values.

TABLE A–6

Reference Values

	Conventional Units	SI Units
Acid Phosphatase		
(Major sources: prostate and erythrocytes[10])		
Newborn	7.4–19.4U/L	7.4–19.4U/L
2–13yr	6.4–15.2U/L	6.4–15.2U/L
Adult male	0.5–11.0U/L	0.5–11.0U/L
Adult female	0.2–9.5U/L	0.2–9.5U/L
Alanine Aminotransferase (ALT)		
(Major sources: liver, skeletal muscle, and myocardium[10])		
Infant	<54U/L	<54U/L
Child/adult	1–30U/L	1–30U/L
Aldolase		
(Major sources: skeletal muscle and myocardium[10])		
Newborn	<32U/L	<32U/L
Child	<16U/L	<8U/L
Adult	<8U/L	<8U/L
Alkaline Phosphatase		
(Major sources: liver, bone, intestinal mucosa, placenta, and kidney[10])		
Infant	150–420U/L	150–420U/L
2–10yr	100–320U/L	100–320U/L
11–18-yr-old boy	100–390U/L	100–390U/L
11–18-yr-old girl	100–320U/L	100–320U/L
Adult	30–120U/L	30–100U/L
α₁-Antitrypsin	93–224mg/dL	0.93–2.24g/L
α-Fetoprotein		
>1yr–adult	<30ng/mL	<30mcg/L
Tumor marker	0–10mg/mL	
Ammonia (heparinized venous specimen on ice analyzed within 30min)		
Newborn	90–150mcg/dL	64–107mcmol/L
0–2wk	79–129mcg/dL	56–92mcmol/L
>1mo	29–70mcg/dL	21–50mcmol/L
Adult	0–50mcg/dL	0–35.7mcmol/L
Amylase		
(Major sources: pancreas, salivary glands, and ovaries[10])		
Newborn	0–44U/L	5–65U/L
Adult	0–88U/L	0–130U/L
Antihyaluronidase Antibody		
	<1:256	

	Conventional Units	SI Units
Antinuclear Antibody (ANA)		
Not significant	<1:80	
Likely significant	>1:320	
Patterns with clinical correlation		
Centromere—CREST		
Nucleolar—Scleroderma		
Homogeneous—nDNA, antihistone Ab		
Antistreptolysin O Titer (4x rise in paired serial specimens is significant)		
Preschool	<1:85	
School age	<1:170	
Older adult	<1:85	
Note: Alternatively, values up to 200 Todd units are normal.		
Arsenic		
Normal	<3mcg/dL	<0.39mcmol/L
Acute poisoning	60–930mcg/dL	7.98–124mcmol/L
Chronic poisoning	10–50mcg/dL	1.33–6.65mcmol/L
Aspartate Aminotransferase (AST)		
(Major sources: liver, skeletal muscle, kidney, myocardium, and erythrocytes[10])		
Newborn/infant	20–65U/L	20–65U/L
Child/adult	0–35U/L	0–4350U/L
Bicarbonate		
Preterm	18–26mEq/L	18–26mmol/L
Full term	20–25mEq/L	20–25mmol/L
>2yr	22–26mEq/L	22–26mmol/L

Bilirubin (total)

		Conventional Units	SI Units
Zero	Preterm	<2mg/dL	<34mcmol/L
	Term	<2mg/dL	<34mcmol/L
0–1dy	Preterm	<8mg/dL	<137mcmol/L
	Term	<6mg/dL	<103mcmol/L
1–2dy	Preterm	<12mg/dL	<205mcmol/L
	Term	<8mg/dL	<137mcmol/L
3–5dy	Preterm	<16mg/dL	<274mcmol/L
	Term	<12mg/dL	<205mcmol/L
Thereafter	Preterm	<2mg/dL	<34mcmol/L
	Term	<1mg/dL	<17mcmol/L
Adult		0.1–1.2mg/dL	1.7–20.5mcmol/L
Bilirubin (conjugated)		0–0.4mg/dL	0–8mcmol/L

TABLE A–6 (continued)

Reference Values

	Conventional Units	SI Units
Calcium (total)		
Preterm <1wk	6–10mg/dL	1.5–2.5mmol/L
Full term <1wk	7.0–12.0mg/dL	1.75–3.0mmol/L
Child	8.0–10.5mg/dL	2–2.6mmol/L
Adult	8.5–10.5mg/dL	2.1–2.6mmol/L
Calcium (ionized)		
Newborn <48hr	4.0–4.7mg/dL	1.00–1.18mmol/L
Adult	4.52–5.28mg/dL	1.13–1.32mmol/L
Carbon Dioxide (CO$_2$ content)		
Cord blood	14–22mEq/L	14–22mmol/L
Infant/child	20–24mEq/L	20–24mmol/L
Adult	24–30mEq/L	24–30mmol/L
Carbon Monoxide (carboxyhemoglobin)		
Nonsmoker	0–2% of total hemoglobin	
Smoker	2–10% of total hemoglobin	
Toxic	20–60% of total hemoglobin	
Lethal	>60% of total hemoglobin	
Carotenoids (carotenes)		
Infant	20–70mcg/dL	0.37–1.30mcmol/L
Child	40–130mcg/dL	0.74–2.42mcmol/L
Adult	50–250mcg/dL	0.95–4.69mcmol/L
Ceruloplasmin	21–53mg/dL	210–530mg/L
Chloride (serum)		
Pediatric	99–111mEq/L	99–111mmol/L
Adult	96–109mEq/L	96–109mmol/L
Cholesterol (see Lipids)		
Copper		
0–6mo	20–70mcg/dL	3.1–11mcmol/L
6yr	90–190mcg/dL	14–30mcmol/L
12yr	80–160mcg/dL	12.6–25mcmol/L
Adult male	70–140mcg/dL	11–22mcmol/L
Adult female	80–155mcg/dL	12.6–24.3mcmol/L
C-Reactive Protein	0–0.5mg/dL	

(Other laboratories may have different reference values)

Creatine Kinase (creatine phosphokinase)
(Major sources: myocardium, skeletal muscle, smooth muscle, and brain[10])

	Conventional Units	SI Units
Newborn	10–200U/L	10–200U/L
Man	12–80U/L	12–80U/L
Woman	10–55U/L	10–55U/L

	Conventional Units	SI Units
Creatinine (serum)		
Cord	0.6–1.2mg/dL	53–106mcmol/L
Newborn	0.3–1.0mg/dL	27–88mcmol/L
Infant	0.2–0.4mg/dL	18–35mcmol/L
Child	0.3–0.7mg/dL	27–62mcmol/L
Adolescent	0.5–1.0mg/dL	44–88mcmol/L
Man	0.6–1.3mg/dL	53–115mcmol/L
Woman	0.5–1.2mg/dL	44–106mcmol/L
ESR (refer to ch. 15)		
Ferritin		
Newborn	25–200ng/mL	25–200mcg/L
1mo	200–600ng/mL	200–600mcg/L
6mo	50–200ng/mL	50–200mcg/L
6mo–15yr	7–140ng/mL	7–140mcg/L
Adult male	15–200ng/mL	15–200mcg/L
Adult female	12–150ng/mL	12–150mcg/L
Fibrinogen	200–400mg/dL	2–4g/L
Folic Acid (folate)	3–17.5ng/mL	4.0–20.0nmol/L
Folic Acid (RBCs)	153–605mcg/mL RBCs	
Galactose		
Newborn	0–20mg/dL	0–1.11mmol/L
Thereafter	<5mg/dL	<0.28mmol/L

γ-Glutamyl Transferase (GGT)
(Major sources: liver [biliary tree] and kidney[10])

	Conventional Units	SI Units
Cord	19–270U/L	19–270U/L
Preterm	56–233U/L	56–233U/L
0–3wk	0–130U/L	0–130U/L
3wk–3mo	4–120U/L	4–120U/L
>3mo boy	5–65U/L	5–65U/L
>3mo girl	5–35U/L	5–35U/L
1–15yr	0–23U/L	0–23U/L
Adult male	11–50U/L	11–50U/L
Adult female	7–32U/L	7–32U/L
Gastrin	<100 pg/mL	<100ng/L
Glucose (serum)		
Preterm	45–100mg/dL	1.1–3.6mmol/L
Full term	45–120mg/dL	1.1–6.4mmol/L
1wk–16yr	60–105mg/dL	3.3–5.8mmol/L
>16yr	70–115mg/dL	3.9–6.4mmol/L

TABLE A–6 (continued)

Reference Values

	Conventional Units	SI Units
Iron		
Newborn	100–250mcg/dL	18–45mcmol/L
Infant	40–100mcg/dL	7–18mcmol/L
Child	50–120mcg/dL	9–22mcmol/L
Adult male	65–170mcg/dL	12–30mcmol/L
Adult female	50–170mcg/dL	9–30mcmol/L
Ketones (serum)		
Qualitative	Negative	
Quantitative	0.5–3.0mg/dL	5–30mg/L
Lactate		
Capillary blood		
Newborn	<27mg/dL	0.0–3.0mmol/L
Child	5–20mg/dL	0.56–2.25mmol/L
Venous	5–20mg/dL	0.5–2.2mmol/L
Arterial	5–14mg/dL	0.5–1.6mmol/L

Lactate Dehydrogenase (at 37°C)

(*Major sources: myocardium, liver, skeletal muscle, erythrocytes, platelets, and lymph nodes[10]*)

	Conventional Units	SI Units
Neonate	160–1500U/L	160–1500U/L
Infant	150–360U/L	150–360U/L
Child	150–300U/L	150–300U/L
Adult	0–220U/L	0–220U/L

Lactate Dehydrogenase Isoenzymes (% total)

LD_1 heart	24–34%
LD_2 heart, erythrocytes	35–45%
LD_3 muscle	15–25%
LD_4 liver, trace muscle	4–10%
LD_5 liver, muscle	1–9%

Lead		
Child	<10mcg/dL	<48mcmol/L
Lipase	4–24U/dL	

Lipids[6]

	Cholesterol (mg/dL)		
	Desirable	Borderline	High
Child/adolescent	<170	170–199	≥200
Adult	<200	200–239	≥240
HDL	>45		

	LDL (mg/dL)		
	Desirable	Borderline	High
	<110	110–129	≥130
	<130	130–159	≥160

	Conventional Units	SI Units
Magnesium	1.3–2.0mEq/L	0.65–1.0mmol/L
Manganese (blood)		
Newborn	2.4–9.6mcg/dL	0.44–1.75mcmol/L
2–18yr	0.8–2.1mcg/dL	0.15–0.38mcmol/L
Methemoglobin	0–1.3% total Hgb	
Osmolality	285–295mOsmol/kg	285–295mmol/kg
Phenylalanine		
Preterm	2.0–7.5mg/dL	0.12–0.45mmol/L
Newborn	1.2–3.4mg/dL	0.07–0.21mmol/L
Adult	0.8–1.8mg/dL	0.05–0.11mmol/L
Phosphorus		
Newborn	4.2–9.0mg/dL	1.36–2.91mmol/L
0–15yr	3.2–6.3mg/dL	1.03–2.1mmol/L
Adult	2.7–4.5mg/dL	0.87–1.45mmol/L
Potassium		
<10dy of age	4.0–6.0mEq/L	4.0–6.0mmol/L
>10dy of age	3.5–5.0mEq/L	3.5–5.0mmol/L
Prealbumin		
Newborn–6wk	4–36mg/dL	
6wk–16yr	13–27mg/dL	
Adult	18–45mg/dL	

TABLE A–6 (continued)

Reference Values

Proteins

Protein electrophoresis (g/dL)

Age	TP	Albumin	α-1	α-2	β	γ
Cord	4.8–8.0	2.2–4.0	0.3–0.7	04.–0.9	0.4–1.6	0.8–1.6
Newborn	4.4–7.6	3.2–4.8	0.1–0.3	0.2–0.3	0.3–0.6	0.6–1.2
1dy–1mo	4.4–7.6	2.5–5.5	0.1–0.3	0.3–1.0	0.2–1.1	0.4–1.3
1–3mo	3.6–7.4	2.1–4.8	0.1–0.4	0.3–1.1	0.3–1.1	0.2–1.1
4–6mo	4.2–7.4	2.8–5.0	0.1–0.4	0.3–0.8	0.3–0.8	0.1–0.9
7–12mo	5.1–7.5	3.2–5.7	0.1–0.6	0.3–1.5	0.4–1.0	0.2–1.2
13–24mo	3.7–7.5	1.9–5.0	0.1–0.6	0.4–1.4	0.4–1.4	0.4–1.6
25–36mo	5.3–8.1	3.3–5.8	0.1–0.3	0.4–1.1	0.3–1.2	0.4–1.5
3–5yr	4.9–8.1	2.9–5.8	0.1–0.4	0.4–1.0	0.5–1.0	0.4–1.7
6–8yr	6.0–7.9	3.3–5.0	0.1–0.5	0.5–0.8	0.5–0.9	0.7–2.0
9–11yr	6.0–7.9	3.2–5.0	0.1–0.4	0.7–0.9	0.6–1.0	0.8–2.0
12–16yr	6.0–7.9	3.2–5.1	0.1–0.4	0.5–1.1	0.5–1.1	0.6–2.0
Adult	6.0–8.0	3.1–5.4	0.1–0.4	0.4–1.1	0.5–1.2	0.7–1.7

	Conventional Units	SI Units		Conventional Units	SI Units
Pyruvate	0.3–0.9mg/dL	0.03–0.10mmol/L	**Troponin**	0.03–0.15ng/mL	
Rheumatoid factor	<20		**Urea Nitrogen**	7–22mg/dL	2.5–7.9mmol/L

Rheumaton Titer (modified Waaler-Rose slide test)
<10

Uric Acid

	Conventional Units	SI Units
0–2yr	2.4–6.4mg/dL	0.14–0.38mmol/L
2–12yr	2.4–5.9mg/dL	0.14–0.35mmol/L
12–14yr	2.4–6.4mg/dL	0.14–0.38mmol/L
Adult male	3.5–7.2mg/dL	0.20–0.43mmol/L
Adult female	2.4–6.4mg/dL	0.14–0.38mmol/L

Sodium

	Conventional Units	SI Units
Preterm	130–140mEq/L	130–140mmol/L
Older	135–148mEq/L	135–148mmol/L

Transaminase (SGOT) (see Aspartate aminotransferase [AST])

Transaminase (SGPT) (see Alanine aminotransferase [ALT])

Vitamin A (retinol)

	Conventional Units	SI Units
Newborn	35–75mcg/dL	1.22–2.62mcmol/L
Child	30–80mcg/dL	1.05–2.79mcmol/L
Adult	39–65mcg/dL	1.05–2.27mcmol/L

Transferrin

	Conventional Units	SI Units
Newborn	130–275mg/dL	1.3–2.75g/L
Adult	200–400mg/dL	2.0–4.0g/L

Triglycerides (fasting)[11]

	Male (mg/dL)	Female (mg/dL)	Male (g/L)	Female (g/L)
Cord blood	10–98	10–98	0.10–0.98	0.10–0.98
0–5yr	30–86	32–99	0.30–0.86	0.32–0.99
6–11yr	31–108	35–114	0.31–1.08	0.35–1.14
12–15yr	36–138	41–138	0.36–1.38	0.41–1.38
16–19yr	40–163	40–128	0.40–1.63	0.40–1.28
20–29yr	44–185	40–128	0.44–1.85	0.40–1.28
Adults	40–160	35–135	0.40–1.60	0.35–1.35

TABLE A–6 *(continued)*

Reference Values

	Conventional Units	SI Units
VitaminB$_1$ (thiamine)	5.3–7.9mcg/dL	0.16–0.23mcmol/L
Vitamin B$_2$ (riboflavin)	3.7–13.7mcg/dL	98–363mcmol/L
Vitamin B$_{12}$ (cobalamin)	130–785pg/mL	96–579pmol/L
Vitamin C (ascorbic acid)	0.2–2.0mg/dL	11.4–113.6mcmol/L
Vitamin D$_3$ (1,25-dihydroxy-vitamin D)	25–45pg/mL	60–108pmol/L
Vitamin E	5–20mg/dL	11.6–46.4mcmol/L
Zinc	70–150mcg/dL	10.7–22.9mcmol/L

Reprinted with permission from Siberry G, et al., eds. The Harriet Lane handbook, 15th ed. St. Louis: Mosby Yearbook, 1999:119.

Index

FIGURE CREDITS

The following figures were modified with permission from the publisher.

Figures 1–1 and 1–2: Modified from Nichols DG, Yaster M, Lappe DG, et al. Golden Hour: The Handbook of Advanced Pediatric Life Support. St. Louis: Mosby Yearbook, 1991: 2, 128

Figure 1–4: Modified from Baldwin G. Handbook of Pediatric Emergencies. Boston: Little, Brown. 1994:29

Figures 3–1 to 3–13: Cloherty JP, Stark AR. Manual of Neonatal Care, 4th ed. Philadelphia: Lippincott-Raven, 1998: 426.

Figures 3–14 to 3–18: Modified from Nichols DG, Yaster M, Lappe DG, et al. Golden Hour: The Handbook of Advanced Pediatric Life Support. St. Louis: Mosby Yearbook, 1996: 164, 165, 172, 173, 176.

Figures 4–1, 4–2, and 13–4: Modified from Behrman RE, Kliegman RM, eds. Essentials of Pediatrics, 2nd ed. Philadelphia: W.B. Saunders, 1994: 217, 413.

Figures 6–1 and 13–1: Modified from Dworkin P, Paul H, eds. Pediatrics, 2nd ed. Philadelphia: Harwal, 1992: 441, 119.

Figure 8–1: Modified from Johnson KB, ed. The Harriet Lane Handbook, 13th ed. St. Louis: Mosby Yearbook, 1994: 182–183.

Figures 12–4 and 12–5: Modified from Shulman ST, Phair JP, Sommers HM. The Biologic and Clinical Basis of Infectious Diseases, 4th ed. Philadelphia: W.B. Saunders, 1992: 315, 319.

Figure 13–2: Modified from Cloherty JP, Stark AR, eds. Manual of Neonatal Care, 3rd ed. Boston: Little, Brown, 1991: 301.

Figure 14–1: Modified from International Reflux Committee. Medical versus surgical treatment of primary vesicouretal reflux. Pediatrics 1981; 67:392.

Figure 19–1: Modified from Oski FA, DeAngelis CD, et al., eds. Principles and Practices of Pediatrics. Philadelphia: Lippincott, 1994:1091.

Figure 19–3: Modified from Salter RB, Harris WR. Injuries involving the epiphyseal plate. J. Bone J Surg [Am] 1963; 45A:587.